INFORMATION SYSTEMS
A Management Approach

Second Edition

THE DRYDEN PRESS

Harcourt Brace College Publishers

Fort Worth Philadelphia San Diego New York Orlando Austin San Antonio
Toronto Montreal London Sydney Tokyo

INFORMATION SYSTEMS
A Management Approach

Second Edition

Judith R. Gordon
Boston College

Steven R. Gordon
Babson College

Publisher	**George Provol**
Executive Editor	**Christina Martin**
Market Strategist	**Debbie K. Anderson**
Associate Editor	**Elizabeth Hayes**
Project Editor	**Kathryn M. Stewart**
Art Director	**Candice Johnson Clifford**
Production Manager	**Eddie Dawson**
Electronic Publishing Coordinator	**Cathy Spitzenberger**

Cover credit: Piet Mondrian, *Trafalgar Square*. 1939–43. The Museum of Modern Art, New York. Gift of Mr. and Mrs. William A.M. Burden. Photograph © 1998, The Museum of Modern Art, New York.

ISBN: 0-03-022469-1
Library of Congress Catalog Card Number: 98-87395

Address for Orders
The Dryden Press, 6277 Sea Harbor Drive, Orlando, FL 32887-6777
1-800-782-4479

Address for Editorial Correspondence
The Dryden Press, 301 Commerce Street, Suite 3700, Fort Worth, TX 76102

Web-site Address
http://www.hbcollege.com

THE DRYDEN PRESS, DRYDEN, and the DP LOGO are registered trademarks of Harcourt Brace & Company.

Printed in the United States of America

9 0 1 2 3 4 5 6 7   0 4 8   9 8 7 6 5 4 3 2

The Dryden Press
Harcourt Brace College Publishers

To Our Children

Brian, Laurie, and Michael

with Much Love

THE DRYDEN PRESS SERIES IN INFORMATION SYSTEMS

All people need and use information in their personal and professional lives, but most do not appreciate that they must *manage* information to maximize its usefulness. Although they are bombarded with information from an array of media, individuals generally feel able to select with ease the most important information to retain. They may use a relatively simple noncomputerized information system, such as a date book, checkbook, or address book, or a simple computer-based system, such as an electronic calendar or personal financial manager, to assist them in dealing with the information. At the organizational level, however, and sometimes even at the personal level, the volume or complexity of information being processed, its importance to the organization or individual, and the difficulty of sorting and interpreting the information require careful control, systematic processing, and refined analyses. Increasing the rigor of information management normally involves the development of more complex formal, typically computerized systems that collect, organize, retrieve, and communicate information.

The second edition of *Information Systems: A Management Approach* focuses on the manager's use of information technology to support the management of information. Specifically, it addresses the use of computer-based systems for the following: (1) determining the type of information that is needed for the effective performance of organizational activities; (2) collecting, accessing, and organizing this information; (3) retrieving, handling, and processing the information once it is available; and (4) interpreting and communicating information to diverse constituencies both inside and outside the organization. Although the book looks at information and information management primarily from a manager's perspective, it also considers the perspectives of knowledge workers and other job holders in diverse functions, such as marketing, manufacturing, human resources management, engineering, and finance, in organizations of all sizes.

As with the first edition, the second edition of the book takes the viewpoint of the manager as the user of information technology within an organizational context. The two authors bring complementary strengths in understanding both the technical requirements and the organizational implications of using computer-based information systems to manage information in contemporary organizations. This book considers the management of information from the individual, team, and organizational perspectives.

This book is intended for use in a management information systems course in either undergraduate or graduate programs of business or management. Its goal is to prepare future managers to use information systems to meet their information needs. It includes extensive examples of real-world situations in which managers successfully and unsuccessfully use information systems and technologies.

THE MANAGEMENT APPROACH

Information Systems: A Management Approach, Second Edition presents a framework for thinking about and improving the management of information by using high-quality information systems. It offers a unique four-step approach to the process of managing information. This approach is integrated throughout the text; the chapters are organized around it (see next section below), and minicases and activities are structured around it as well.

First, managers begin with a diagnosis of information needs. This diagnosis requires a description of the existing problem, the context in which it occurs, the type of information available, the type of information required to solve it, and the possible ways of securing the needed information. Next, managers evaluate the options to meet these needs. Managers assess the hardware, software, database, data communication, and internal and external networks required to meet their information needs. Then they move to the design or selection of appropriate systems. Design involves correcting deficiencies in existing systems and integrating state-of-the-art practices and technology into them. Finally the managers implement these changes. They must identify each party's responsibility for implementation, including the roles individual managers, information systems staff, or specialists from outside the organization will play, as well as the implementation budget and timetable.

ORGANIZATION OF THE TEXT

The four-step approach described above is carried throughout the organization of the text (see figure). Part I, "Diagnosing Information Needs for Management," focuses on the way managers, groups, and organizations use information. Chapter 1 sets the stage by describing the nature of information management, the role of the

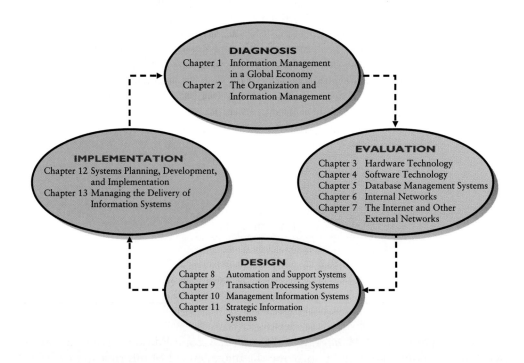

manager, and the four-step management approach. Chapter 2 looks at the organizational context of information management, focusing on the changing nature of organizations, new organizational structures and their information requirements, the use of information technology to support team-based management, and the role of information in setting and implementing organizational strategy.

Part II, "Evaluating Information Technologies," illustrates how managers evaluate the technologies available to meet their information needs. Chapter 3 discusses hardware for data input, processing, storage, and output. Chapter 4 examines computer software, including vertical and horizontal application software, computer languages, and systems software. Chapter 5 investigates database management systems, including their use, their development through data design, their technical underpinnings, and their contribution to the effective use of data. Chapter 6 discusses internal networks, including their types and uses, the infrastructure of the communication industry, and network management. Chapter 7 looks at the Internet and other external networks, including the use, development, and design of Web sites.

Part III, "Designing Information Systems," presents the types of information systems that organizations use to manage information. Chapter 8 looks at automation systems, including office, workflow, sales force, design, and factory automation, as well as automation for education and training and expert systems. Chapter 9 discusses transaction processing systems, including the reasons for recording transactions, examples and characteristics of transaction processing systems, and ways of developing, updating, and ensuring their effectiveness. Chapter 10 investigates management information systems, including management reporting systems, decision support systems, groupware, and executive information systems. Chapter 11 concludes this part with a discussion of strategic information systems used for low-cost leadership, for differentiation, to create focus, to support linkages, and to develop information leadership.

Part IV, "Implementing Information Systems and Managing the Information Resource," investigates issues associated with developing and managing the information resource. Chapter 12 looks at the systems development process, including assessing requirements; analyzing alternatives; designing, developing, and implementing new systems; and maintaining and reviewing systems. Chapter 13 looks at ways of structuring and managing the information systems function and managing change.

TEXT FEATURES

Information Systems: A Management Approach provides an integrated presentation of each topic using text, cases, exercises, and special Web activities and links. It is designed to be versatile in its use, offering flexibility in the sequencing of chapter coverage and the selection of instructional materials. The major features include the following:

- *Current, real-world examples* integrated throughout the text illustrate key concepts in action.
- Extensive integration of *Web-based references and material* ensures that the second edition remains current.

- *The four-step management approach* helps develop critical thinking skills. Students learn to analyze a situation, evaluate existing systems for managing information, design the features of new systems, and consider the issues associated with implementing them.
- A *new chapter on the Internet* (Chapter 7, "The Internet and Other External Networks") discusses the ways managers use the Internet. The technological underpinnings of the Internet are discussed in light of business applications such as electronic commerce, and ways to develop and manage Web sites.
- Issues associated with the *globalization of business* are highlighted throughout the text. Students consider the implications of managing information in transnational organizations with diverse cultures, skills, languages, and legal systems.
- A *strong ethical focus* permeates each chapter, with a boxed feature and activity in each chapter encouraging students to consider the ethical implications of various managerial choices.
- A *strong focus on current and future technologies* ensures that students know about an array of technological possibilities. Updates on the book's Web site ensure that the discussion of technologies remains current.
- A *short case* introduces each chapter. Key concepts throughout the chapter are applied to the opening case where appropriate.
- An *integrated and comprehensive pedagogy* supports student learning. The pedagogical elements include a chapter outline, learning objectives, chapter summary, key terms, review questions, minicases, activities, notes, and recommended readings.
- *Special boxed features* highlight the manager in action, information technology and global business, ethical use of information technology, and new or future advances in technology.
- *Minicases* allow students to experience real-life situations without leaving the classroom.
- *Activities* at the end of each chapter provide students the opportunity to understand information needs, assess the effectiveness of information management strategies, and apply course concepts to developing aspects of information systems.
- *IS on the Web Exercises.* New to the second edition, these exercises at the end of each chapter make use of the Internet as a tool for further exploring chapter concepts.

SUPPLEMENTARY MATERIALS

INSTRUCTOR'S MANUAL

The detailed instructor's manual, written by M. Lisa Miller, includes chapter summaries, teaching tips, lecture outlines with key terms and transparency masters referenced, and answers to review questions for each chapter of the book. Each end-of-chapter activity is given a full discussion in the instructor's manual. Also included is a set of supplementary hands-on spreadsheet and database problems for each chapter.

TEST BANK

The test bank, by Ellen Hoadley, is available in both printed and computerized forms. It includes over 1300 items including true/false, multiple choice, fill-in-the-blank, and short essay questions for each chapter. Questions are keyed to learning objectives as well as level of difficulty.

The computerized test bank, available for IBM PC-compatible and Apple Macintosh computers, contains all the questions found in the printed test bank. It allows you to preview, add, delete, or edit test questions, as well as to output questions in any order and to print answer keys.

INSTRUCTOR'S RESOURCE CD-ROM

This CD-ROM contains a set of PowerPoint presentations for each chapter in the text. In addition, for those who want to create their own presentations, there is a set of figures from the text (Electronic Transparencies) in pcx format for incorporating into presentations. The electronic version of the Instructor's Manual and the Test Bank are also on the CD.

THE GORDON WEB SITE

Located at

http://www.dryden.com/infosys/gordon2/

this Web site contains a wealth of information and activities for both instructor and student. At the Instructor's Home, instructors can access an electronic version of the Instructor's Manual, view and download illustrations (electronic transparencies) from the text for use in presentations, or download a set of PowerPoint presentations to correspond with each chapter in the text. Instructors can also sign up for a mailing list to communicate with others teaching in the discipline.

For students, the Web site contains a number of learning resources. Here they can test themselves on chapter topics by taking an online review for each chapter. Links from the text's "IS on the Web" activities can be found here as well as a variety of additional activities not found in the text. Students can also access an interactive glossary of key terms from the text. For further practice in spreadsheet and database problems, a set of activities is provided to give students hands-on experience. A set of longer case studies can also be accessed from the site as well as a student mail list.

The Dryden Press will provide complimentary supplements or supplement packages to those adopters qualified under our adoption policy. Please contact your sales representative to learn how you may qualify. If as an adopter or potential user you receive supplements you do not need, please return them to your sales representative or send them to:

ATTN: Returns Department
Troy Warehouse
465 South Lincoln Drive
Troy, MO 63379

ACKNOWLEDGMENTS

The development of both the first and second editions of this book has been influenced by the contributions of many individuals. We would first like to thank the reviewers of the current and past edition, who made important contributions that significantly influenced its development and quality:

Second Edition

Mark Dishaw, University of Wisconsin—Oshkosh
William Harrison, Oregon State University
Ellen Hoadley, Loyola College in Maryland
Jane MacKay, Texas Christian University
Lisa Miller, University of Central Oklahoma
Connie L. Washburn, DeKalb College, North
Robert T. Watts, Idaho State University
Michael E. Whitman, University of Nevada—Las Vegas

First Edition

Warren Boe, University of Iowa
Kent R. Burnham, Eastern Washington University
William R. Cornette, Southwest Missouri State University
Richard Fenzl, Syracuse University
Ellen D. Hoadley, Loyola College
John Landry, Metropolitan State University
M. Khris McAlister, University of Alabama—Birmingham
Ralph McCrae, University of Texas at El Paso
M. Lisa Miller, University of Central Oklahoma
Thomas C. Richards, University of North Texas
James B. Shannon, New Mexico State University
David C. Whitney, San Francisco State University

We would also like to thank the editorial and production team from The Dryden Press for their editorial and technical support. We would like to especially thank Wesley Lawton, executive editor; Elizabeth Hayes, associate editor; Kathryn Stewart, senior project editor; Eddie Dawson, production manager; Candice Clifford, art director; Cathy Spitzenberger, electronic publishing coordinator; Adele Krause, permissions editor; and the rest of the team for all their hard work on the second edition.

We also wish to thank our colleagues at Babson College and Boston College for their support of the project. Finally, we thank our family whose interest, encouragement, and patience we greatly appreciate.

The approach to information systems in *Information Systems: A Management Approach,* Second Edition is strengthened by the unique pairing of real world expertise in information systems and organizational behavior.

Judith R. Gordon is an Associate Professor of Management at the Carroll School of Management of Boston College. She received an A.B. in Psychology from Brandeis University, an M.Ed. in Educational Research and Measurement from Boston University, and a Ph.D. in Organization Studies from the Sloan School of Management at the Massachusetts Institute of Technology. Dr. Gordon recently completed her second term as chairperson of the Organizational Studies Department. Dr. Gordon now teaches in the areas of organizational behavior, human resources management, organizational change, and quality in organizations. She has extensive training and consulting experience in organizational behavior, human resources management, and career development. Dr. Gordon's research interests focus on organizational design, career development of professional women, organization structure and information technology, and women in management. She is also the author of a successful textbook in organizational behavior.

Steven R. Gordon is an Associate Professor of Information Systems and holder of the James Perry Term Chair at Babson College. He received a B.S. in mathematics and electrical engineering, and an M.S. and Ph.D. in Transportation Systems from the Massachusetts Institute of Technology. Dr. Gordon was the founder of Beta Principles, Inc., a software manufacturer and computer reseller, and a consultant to the airline industry for Simat, Helliesen & Eichner. Dr. Gordon now teaches in the areas of information systems and quantitative methods. His current research interests focus on organizational issues surrounding information systems, including the effectiveness of different organizational structures for delivery of information technology (IT), identification of factors affecting adoption of new technology, and procedures for setting technology standards within organizations. He is the moderator of the Information Technology Focus Group, an industry roundtable for discussing long-range IT planning.

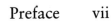

CONTENTS IN BRIEF

CONTENTS

II   EVALUATING INFORMATION TECHNOLOGIES   83

III

DESIGNING INFORMATION SYSTEM   313

Chapter 8   Automation and Support Systems   314

IV IMPLEMENTING INFORMATION SYSTEMS AND MANAGING THE INFORMATION   479

Piet Mondrian, *Composition with Yellow, Blue, Black, Red, and Gray*, 1921. Private collection. Stephen Mazoh, Rhinebeck, New York.

Chapter 1

Information Management in a Global Economy

LEARNING OBJECTIVES

After completing Chapter 1, you will be able to

1. Define information and discuss its role in organizations.
2. Identify the role of information technology in organizations.
3. Identify the key issues in managing information in today's organizations.
4. Describe the manager's use of information on the job.
5. Identify the information requirements for effective management.
6. Offer an approach to addressing ethical issues in information management.
7. Identify the four steps in the effective management of information.

I

DIAGNOSING INFORMATION NEEDS FOR MANAGEMENT

Managers today face the challenge of managing information effectively. Information technology can support information management and help organizations compete successfully in a global environment. This part introduces the management of information at the managerial, team, and organizational levels. Chapter 1 presents the basic issues related to information and its management. It defines information and information management, identifies key issues for information management, and discusses information's role in managerial jobs. The chapter concludes with the four-step management approach. Chapter 2 continues the introduction to information management by examining how organizations use information to address the information requirements of new organizational structures, the role of information management in supporting team-based management, and the relationship between information and organizational strategy.

MANAGING INFORMATION AT GULF INDUSTRIES, RITZ-CARLTON HOTELS, AND FARR, BURKE, GAMBACORTA & WRIGHT

Michael Hays, a regional sales manager for Gulf Industries, a sign-making company based in Torrance, Calif., remembers the old days of selling signs. He'd spend nearly an hour with a potential customer trying to come up with a design the customer couldn't resist. After cutting and pasting various pictures and shapes from color printouts and having the customer imagine a range of typefaces and logos, he'd sometimes get an enthusiastic response. But it wouldn't last long. As soon as Hays said he'd have to run the artwork by Gulf's designers and engineers to make sure it was executable, he could feel the room go cold. But recently, when Hays visited a car dealership, he sailed through the entire call. After about 10 minutes of asking the owner questions about his business—How many customers were from out of town? How busy was the location?—Hays whipped out his laptop. To the owner's amazement, in less than 15 minutes Hays had designed the perfect sign, down to the squiggly border and the red Mustang the owner had said was his favorite car. Hays quoted the owner a price of $5,000—the computer did all the calculations—and [gave him] a contract.... Because Gulf's designers and engineers had already OK'd the design combinations stored in the laptop, Hays knew there would be no problem transforming the digital sign into a real one. The delighted dealer couldn't sign fast enough.[1]

The Ritz Carlton Hotel chain relies on information technology to help it manage information about its guests and meet their needs. The company uses computerized information systems to maintain a database about guests' rooms, food, arrival, and other preferences so hotel staff know and can satisfy their guests' requirements.

Clients at Ritz-Carlton Hotels expect top-notch, personal service. Staff members of the Ritz-Carlton Hotels, in turn, want to delight their guests. The more information employees have about the guests, the more they can ensure that the Ritz meets or exceeds the guests' expectations. Does a guest want her bed turned down at 9 P.M.? Does a guest want a city view or garden view? Does a guest want a chocolate on his pillow in the evening? Hotel employees collect anecdotal information about guest preferences and record them on cards that the clerical staff keys into an international guest preferences database. Employees use this information to provide a more personal level of service.[2]

What attorney Bill Wright was facing was a failure to communicate. First, one of his three partners suddenly up and left, taking 17 employees of the Bellmawr, N.J., law firm and lots of clients with him. Then, within days of his departure, the prodigal lawyer sued his former partners. Of course, Wright's firm turned around and filed a countersuit. What with impromptu hallway discussions, emergency meetings, news flashes, urgent requests for background, and the rest of their caseload, the remaining staff at Farr, Burke, Gambacorta & Wright barely had time to breathe. "We had to find a way to help us handle the flood of information," says Wright. "And we had to find it fast."[3]

How do managers in these companies ensure that their employees have the information they need? Once they get the required information, how do managers guarantee that their employees can use it to do their jobs well? How do managers and their employees handle the daily challenge of managing information effectively?

In this chapter we first explore the role of information in organizations and its management. Then we investigate the issues involved in the management of information in today's organizations. We next examine how managers use and manage information in their job. We conclude by examining the four-step management approach to information management used throughout this book.

WHAT IS INFORMATION MANAGEMENT? ✗

Managers deal with information in all aspects of their lives. Managers at Gulf Industries use information about customer preferences, feasible designs, and pricing to prepare customer contracts. Managers at Ritz-Carlton use information about customer expectations to develop procedures, train staff, and respond to customer requests. Partners at the law firm of Farr, Burke, Gambacorta & Wright use information to identify key issues in pending lawsuits and handle their cases.

WHAT IS INFORMATION?

We define **data** as fundamental facts, figures, observations, and measurement, without context or organization. A weather station, for example, might report the following data: 2597, 1400, 35, 30.2R, 10NW, 28. We define **information** as processed data—data that have been organized, interpreted, and possibly formatted, filtered, analyzed, and summarized. The weather station data might provide the following information, for example. Weather station 2597 reported at 14:00 (2:00 P.M.), a temperature of 35 degrees Fahrenheit, a rising barometric pressure of 30.2, a wind velocity of 10 mph from the northwest, and a humidity of 28 percent. A map, summarizing the data from many stations, provides information about the location and movement of fronts and storms. We present and use information today in many media, including sound, graphics, and video.

Managers can use information to obtain knowledge. **Knowledge** is an understanding, or model, about people, objects, or events derived from information about them. Knowledge provides a structure for interpreting information, usually by assimilating and explaining variations over time or space. For example, managers at the Ritz-Carlton obtain knowledge about customers' preferences from the information obtained as a result of accumulating data about specific customer requests, as Figure 1.1 illustrates. **Wisdom** is the ability to use knowledge for a purpose. Computer systems collect data, produce and present information, and sometimes create knowledge. We trust people to apply their wisdom to such output to create effective information systems.

FIGURE 1.1	Managers obtain information from data and use it to obtain knowledge.

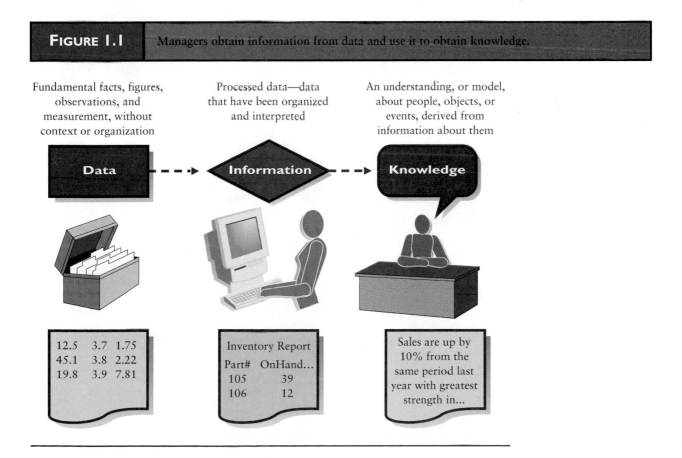

Fundamental facts, figures, observations, and measurement, without context or organization

Processed data—data that have been organized and interpreted

An understanding, or model, about people, objects, or events, derived from information about them

Data Information Knowledge

12.5	3.7	1.75
45.1	3.8	2.22
19.8	3.9	7.81

Inventory Report

Part#　OnHand...
105　　39
106　　12

Sales are up by 10% from the same period last year with greatest strength in...

THE ROLE OF INFORMATION IN ORGANIZATIONS

Managers use information as a resource, an asset, or a commodity, as Figure 1.2 illustrates.

- *Information as a Resource.* Like money, people, raw materials, machinery, or time, information can serve as a **resource,** an input to the production of outputs. Sign designers, hotel workers, and attorneys use information to serve their customers better. Managers can use information to replace capital and

| FIGURE I.2 | Managers use information as a resource, asset, or commodity. |

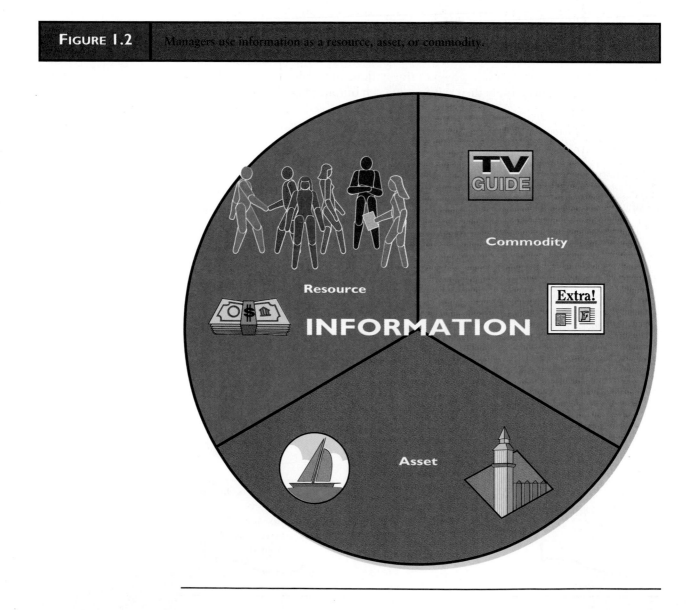

labor, often reducing costs at the same time. For example, managers with good information about the demand and customer inventories for a product can schedule production to reduce or eliminate unsold items and to keep inventory levels low.

- *Information as an Asset.* Information can serve as an asset, which is the property of a person or an organization that contributes to a company's output. In this way, information resembles plant, equipment, goodwill, and other corporate assets. Managers need to view information as an investment that they can use strategically to give the company an advantage over its competitors.
- *Information as a Commodity.* Companies can also sell information, making it a commodity similar to corn, automobiles, or washing machines. In our service-oriented economy, an increasing number of companies view information in this way. For example, publishers of directories, television guides, and airline guides make a profit from selling information.

THE ROLE OF INFORMATION TECHNOLOGY

Information technology allows individuals, groups, and organizations to manage information effectively and efficiently. Think about the information available through the Internet and on internal company networks. Information technology eases communication among people within and between organizations. Consider the ability of a company to track thousands of products in its warehouses and sales of the products in hundreds of retail outlets. Significant advances in information technology have made it possible to acquire, manage, and use large quantities of information at a relatively low cost.

The widespread availability of affordable computer technology has dramatically changed the way people acquire, process, store, retrieve, transmit, communicate, and use information. The Westinghouse Savannah River Company, for example, plans to use information technology to track millions of paper documents and images about nuclear waste management and environmental recovery. The company is building a document management system to replace its paper-based systems for tracking the company's engineering drawings, technical documents, and written policies and procedures.[4] The New York City district attorney's office uses videoconferencing for interviewing police officers about cases to reduce the time and cost of transporting the officers.[5] This book explores how information technology affects how we work.

Information technology (IT) includes computer hardware, software, database management systems, and data communication technologies.

Computer hardware refers to the equipment used in electronic information processing. Today affordable desktop and portable computers can outperform the room-sized, million-dollar computers of ten years ago.

- Input hardware captures raw data and information from interactive uses.
- Processing hardware converts or transforms data.
- Storage hardware includes removable and fixed media that allow rapid access to information.
- Output hardware provides copies of data on paper, microform, and video screens.

THE MANAGER in ACTION

Doug Meredith first arrived in Sturgeon Bay, Wisconsin, on a raw March day in 1974, wind and rain lashing out from a dark sky. "It was an ugly, ungodly day," Meredith recalls. "Everything about it said, 'Don't come.'"

But Meredith, intent on owning a business, was out to defy the gods. He set his sights on a local pharmacy whose owner wanted to retire. Meredith and a coworker bought the pharmacy. Today Bay Pharmacies encompasses two locations, 38 employees, and enough sales per square foot to put the business in the top 5% of all U.S. pharmacies. Others—competitors, partners, neighboring merchants—have quit along the way. Partnerships have blown up in Doug Meredith's face. Employees have stolen from him—and have been stolen away by competitors. The local economy, supported by an old-line industry, nearly collapsed. Wal-Mart came to town, as did Kmart. The nature of competition changed with the arrival of these stores. The types of information Meredith needed also changed.

"Brutal" is how Meredith describes the past five years of intensifying competition and eroding profitability in his industry.

Bill Divine, his current partner, thinks Doug Meredith is a top-notch retailer. "He knows the front end of these stores better than anybody I've ever seen." Divine says Meredith rarely gets stuck with inventory that will not move. He knows his audience.

Perhaps that's because Meredith is a bulldog, never one to sit back and let things just be. He remodels one of his stores every year. He has to keep things looking fresh. In the midst of such an effort, his workweek lengthens from 65 hours to 80. He and Pat [his wife] are believers in the faith of hard work. For them, the ability to outwork the competition provides a necessary edge. Bay Pharmacies has 24-hour emergency service every day of the year. It delivers prescriptions; Wal-Mart will not.... Meredith intends to survive by hammering service. He will wade into the labor-intensive niches where the big discounters would never go.

Doug Meredith uses many types of information to perform his job and keep his company profitable. How have his information needs changed over time? Why must he repeatedly diagnose the information he requires, evaluate the information technology he uses to meet these needs, and design or redesign and implement responsive information systems?

SOURCE: Edward O. Welles, The Years of Living Dangerously, *Inc. The State of Small Business 1997*, pp. 88–98.

Computer software provides the instructions, in the form of computer code and its accompanying documentation, for processing data electronically.

- Systems software directs the functioning of the hardware.
- Applications software assists in the acquisition, processing, storage, retrieval, and communication of information.
- Software development tools also facilitate modifying software to respond better to an organization's information needs.

Database management systems offer a vehicle for storing and supporting the processing of large quantities of business information, such as data on employees, products, customers, and suppliers. San Francisco's Bay Area Rapid Transit (BART) uses a database management system to help run the company. For example, BART has an automatic fare collection system that lets passengers buy and redeem their tickets every day using debit/credit ticket purchasing.[6] Database management technology allows managers to easily access, sort, and analyze databases of information along a variety of dimensions.

Data communication technologies, specifically company networks and the Internet, a worldwide network of networks, have dramatically improved the communication of information across small and large distances. Managers and other employees can easily send data from one plant location to another or access data located halfway around the world using dial-in options, computer networks, videoconferencing, and other electronic media. Advances in communication technology occur frequently, reducing the cost and increasing the accuracy and speed of data transmission. Companies use the Internet for communication and for electronic commerce.

AT&T eliminated the paper trail for its 15,000 customer-service agents. They now access data on products, services, and procedures by using the company's computer network. The systems provide instant information from databases that the company updates five times each day. The agents have desktop software that gives them access to data they previously obtained from 25 different systems. The company also offers intelligent call processing, which routes customers to the right agents. For example, the system will automatically connect a customer who prefers to speak Spanish to a Spanish-speaking agent.[7]

MANAGING INFORMATION WITH INFORMATION SYSTEMS

An **information system (IS)** combines information technology with data, procedures for processing data, and people who collect and use the data, as shown in Figure 1.3. A human resources department might have an information system that tracks

| FIGURE 1.3 | Information systems include information technology, data, data processing procedures, and people who use the data. |

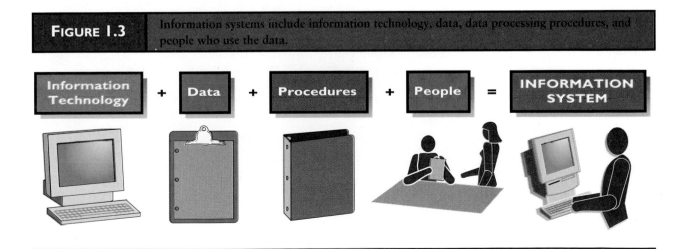

all current and potential employees' work and salary history, training experiences, and performance evaluations and regularly provides reports summarizing the data to their managers. Optima Health uses a human resources information system to consolidate the 12 payroll systems from the hospitals that merged to form this health care organization.[8] An operations department might have an information system that incorporates data about equipment, staff, and product or service requirements.

Organizations and their employees use a variety of computerized systems to help manage information. Managers may use computerized systems to maintain information about employee performance, customer preferences, and industry trends, as well as to motivate and develop employees, communicate with other managers, make decisions, negotiate agreements, and manage resources. As managers become more sophisticated in performing their tasks, they require increasingly sophisticated systems to help them meet their information needs.

Organizations that lack quality information systems may experience problems in accessing the data they need for executive decision making. They may lose important data during a relocation or power failure. They may also perform the wrong activities in dealing with customers or suppliers or fail to respond quickly to changes in the marketplace or industry.

Although you can classify information systems in several ways, in this book we place them into four categories, loosely based on the way information is used, as shown in Figure 1.4. **Automation and support systems** use information technology to perform tasks that were formerly done manually.

FIGURE 1.4 Information systems can be categorized into four types.

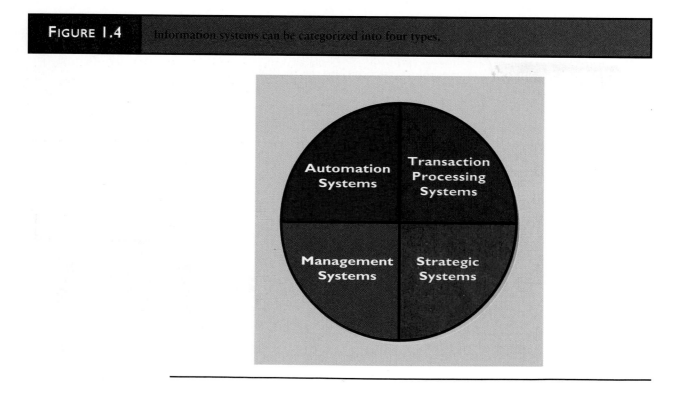

- Office automation systems speed the processing of information and aid in time management, communication, document preparation, and filing.
- Workflow systems coordinate the movement of documents and other data among various groups in the organization. Chase Manhattan Bank uses high-speed imaging to process more than 15 million checks each night. Using the new systems, not more than 3 people handle each check, rather than the 12 to 15 people who did so previously.[9]
- The automation of manufacturing and design through computer-aided design and computer-aided manufacturing systems often improves product quality, worker efficiency, and organizational performance.
- The automation of education and training through the use of computer-aided instruction can make large amounts of diverse information available to students inexpensively and easily.
- Expert systems automate functions that require highly specialized knowledge, such as product design, medical diagnosis, or equipment repair.

Transaction processing systems (TPSs) process and record an organization's transactions. A transaction is a unit of business activity, such as purchasing a product, making a banking deposit, or reserving an airline seat. Transaction processing includes activities such as recording, filing, retrieving records, and filling out forms, such as order forms and checks. Transaction processing systems support low-level employees in performing routine business functions by providing data to answer questions, such as those shown in Figure 1.5. Components of TPSs include systems for payroll, accounts payable, accounts receivable, general ledger, inventory control, fixed asset accounting, reservations, and billing, among others.

| FIGURE 1.5 | Transaction processing systems help managers answer numerous questions that keep their businesses running smoothly and profitably. |

- ◆ From whom do we buy our copier paper?
- ◆ How many envelopes did we purchase in the last order?
- ◆ Which sweaters were delivered last week?
- ◆ Where has the inventory of lug nuts been stored?
- ◆ How much does the company owe its chemicals supplier?
- ◆ How much of the money owed to company X has been paid?
- ◆ How many hours have employees worked?
- ◆ How much is the total payroll this week?
- ◆ How much should be deducted from each paycheck for taxes and benefits?
- ◆ What is the customer's account balance?
- ◆ Has the shipment arrived at the customer's site or is it in route?
- ◆ Has the customer paid yet?

INFORMATION TECHNOLOGY AND GLOBAL BUSINESS

EAST AFRICA

- There are 500,000 computers in East Africa. Sixty-five percent are in Kenya; the rest are spread equally between Tanzania and Uganda.
- The annual growth rate of the IT market is 75%. The highest growth is in Uganda.
- There are 6,000 active Internet users in Kenya, 2,000 in Uganda, and 1,200 in Tanzania. The annual growth rate of Internet usage in the region is 100%.

THE RUSSIA FEDERATION

- Continued growth of Western companies leaves less space for Russian software in local and export software markets. While Russian companies exported about $30 million worth of packaged software a few years ago, that has shrunk to less than $15 million today.
- Five years ago, there were more than 200,000 programmers in Russia. Today there are 50,000 to 60,000.
- Only 10 to 20 Russian software companies produce shrink-wrapped software. There are also about 100 to 120 small and midsize companies that produce custom software and 50 to 70 systems integration companies.
- Software piracy is in the 90% range.
- About 4,000 to 5,000 students graduate with university degrees in computer science annually. Only 10% find work specializing in computers.

Transaction processing systems have transformed the work done by clerical and other low-level employees. Now they input data directly into electronic forms, which allows them, for example, to modify an airline reservation or automobile registration online. Ryder Trucks's sophisticated transaction processing systems help the firm track and manage its fleet of 200,000 vehicles.[10]

Management systems supply the information managers need to perform their jobs better and communicate more effectively.

- **Management reporting systems** provide summary information about business operations, such as which customers do not pay their bills on time.
- **Decision support systems (DSSs)** assist managers in evaluating the impact of alternative decisions and in making the best possible choice. Shopko uses a DSS to analyze merchandising trends and marketing opportunities.[11]
- **Groupware,** which includes electronic mail, electronic notes, bulletin board systems, and electronic meeting systems, eases the sharing of information and helps reach a consensus among group members. Reebok International uses a Web-based groupware system to encourage interaction between customers and the company. The company offers microsites devoted to particular fitness categories where customers can get training tips from coaches and athletes' profiles.[12]
- **Executive information systems (EISs)** allow executives easy access to their favorite reports, let them focus on interesting items in more detail, and scan news-wire and other information services for items of greatest interest to the executive.

Strategic systems extend information systems beyond organizational borders, seeking to make customers, suppliers, and distributors that are strategic partners part of the information system. They support the implementation of an organizational

- A good salary for a Russian programmer is about $12,000 per year but can vary from $4,000 to $24,000 per year.

ASIA-PACIFIC REGION

- The Asia-Pacific PC market, excluding Japan, reached more than 7.4M units in 1996, up from more than 5.4M units in 1995. This represents a 36.5% compound annual growth rate (CAGR). Dataquest expects this market to hit more than 9M units and grow by only 22% in '97.
- Korea, Australia, Taiwan, and Hong Kong account for more than half of total regional unit sales annually in the Asia-Pacific region.

- China was the hottest market in the region, growing by 53% CAGR in '96. It outpaced Australia to become the second-largest market in the region.
- The Australian PC market slowed, growing only 10% in '96. Taiwan also suffered low growth of 14%.

Reprinted with permission from *Wired* world; Notes from around the globe, *Computerworld Global Innovators* (June 9, 1997): 7.

strategy by creating a competitive advantage through the provision of unique information or control over other firms. The Vanguard Group uses the **World Wide Web (the Web)**, an interconnected store of documents on the Internet, to help clients research investments and access their accounts more easily. The company updates data about mutual funds and individual accounts in real-time, which allows its agents to provide high-quality information to customers.[13]

Not INFORMATION MANAGEMENT IN THE TWENTY-FIRST CENTURY

Diagnosing needs for information, evaluating information technology to meet these needs, and designing responsive information systems form the backbone of effective performance in today's environment. Even well-managed companies can fail as a result of unexpected events or a few bad decisions. Good managers can increase the likelihood of their company's success by using information to make good decisions, motivate employees, and initiate necessary changes.

SUCCEEDING IN A GLOBAL ENVIRONMENT

Managers function in a global marketplace, where organizations deal within and across national boundaries. Understanding this global context and sharing information worldwide have become challenges that managers face. Differences of time, culture, and language create barriers to effective communication that information systems can reduce. Managers at different Ritz-Carlton Hotels, for example, want to share information about guests so the hotel chain can meet those individual needs at any location. Information systems can support such sharing by making information about a specific customer available instantly at any location in the world.

THE FOCUS ON QUALITY AND PERFORMANCE

Increased competition from abroad has required U.S. companies to reexamine the quality of their goods and services. Large numbers of defects, complaints from customers about outdated products, and declining productivity caused U.S. manufacturers to introduce **total quality management (TQM)** as a solution to these problems. Companies such as Xerox, Motorola, Teradyne, Texas Instruments, and others introduced broad-based, systemwide programs to address these concerns. TQM programs emphasize responding to customers' needs as a top priority. By giving workers more responsibility for making decisions, these programs change the way employees perform work. TQM programs foster continuous improvement in both an organization's product and the processes for creating it. Statistical control techniques use extensive information collected about the organization's functioning to improve its product and processes. Managers also collect information about other companies' best practices as a way of establishing a standard of high-level performance for their own company.

Xerox's assembly operation incorporates total quality management principles to support the continuous improvement of its operations. Xerox uses information systems to implement statistical control techniques that improve both products and processes.

BUSINESS PROCESS REDESIGN

Incorporating the best principles of total quality management and reengineering, business process design focuses on improving an organization's processes. **Reengineering** refers to rethinking, reinventing, and redesigning one or more of an organization's business systems—such as accounts receivable, purchasing, or product development—and its related jobs.[14] **Business process redesign** identifies core processes and looks for better ways to do them. Often companies use automation extensively to improve these processes.

American Standard, the world's largest plumbing supplier, undertook a major redesign by implementing more than 75 reengineering projects. The company redesigned manufacturing processes and office functions. It replaced traditional departments in the three main business units with five processes: business strategy, product development, order acquisition, order fulfillment, and customer service. American Standard retooled the information systems group and outsourced some mainframe information systems processing until it could switch to client/server systems. The company eliminated nearly $35 million in yearly debt payments and significantly reduced manufacturing cycle time.[15]

BUILDING INDIVIDUAL CAPABILITIES AND PRODUCTIVITY

High-performing organizations emphasize the employment of **knowledge workers**—employees, such as engineers, accountants, lawyers, and technical specialists, who have specialized skills and knowledge that allow them to function effectively in today's organizations. These knowledge workers rely on information to help them perform well. Ernst & Young will use IntelliServ to provide 75,000 employees with indexing, searching, and analysis capabilities on the firm's database of information. The company will combine this with 400 Lotus Notes databases that hold information about best practices and news articles.[16]

Through extensive training and development, companies build individual capabilities and productivity. Information systems contribute directly by helping people process the large quantities of information available. Pacific Northwest National Laboratory developed a Web-based system for processing financial statistics about ongoing laboratory projects. The lab employees can now "subscribe" to one of seven preformatted reports that capture the most commonly requested information. They can also perform ad hoc queries on the financial database, getting immediate information about the status of current projects.[17]

THE MANAGER AND INFORMATION MANAGEMENT

Management refers to the process of achieving organizational goals by planning, organizing, leading, and controlling organizational resources. Managers face an array of challenges in performing their work in a global environment. They must deal with increasing competition, decreasing resources, and rapidly changing technology. They must understand and respond to dramatic cultural differences, imposing legal constraints, and dynamic customer requirements.

THE MANAGER'S JOB

Managers at all levels cope with less than perfect information in an uncontrollable environment. They perform a great quantity of work at an unrelenting pace.[18] This level of activity requires a manager to seek continually and then quickly process large amounts of information, generally without time for leisurely reflection. Managers also participate in a variety of brief activities that significantly fragment their time. They become accustomed to a rapid exchange of information with others and hence must have the needed information readily available. Recall Michael Hays's job at Gulf Industries. He needs to agree to a feasible design with a customer, quote a reasonable price, and then present a signed contract almost instantly. He needs to know that his staff can deliver what he promised in a timely, cost-effective fashion. Because time is precious and managers tend to deal with issues that are current and specific, they seek ways to secure information as efficiently as possible.

Managers also spend extensive amounts of time communicating with other managers both inside and outside the organization. As more information becomes available to them, managers seem to want and need even more information to perform effectively. Managers spend increasing amounts of time interpreting historical data, anticipating future trends, setting accurate goals, measuring performance against goals, identifying variances quickly, allocating resources dynamically, and adapting to unanticipated events.[19]

Managers at different hierarchical levels in the organization have special concerns, as shown in Figure 1.6.

The Strategic Focus of Top Management Teams.

Top-level managers establish the overall, long-term direction of an organization by setting its strategy and policies. They develop programs and activities in line with stated profit or service objectives. Top executives typically have both an internal and an external orientation. They must ensure that work gets done within their particular subsidiary or division while they interact with executives in other organizations and the general public. Increasingly, such interactions span regional and national boundaries, requiring executives to have large repositories of information about an array of global issues. Robert Iger, president of ABC, Inc., for example, oversees ABC TV, as well as a media empire that includes television and radio stations, cable, magazines, newspapers, and the Internet in the United States and abroad. He needs strong management skills and quality information to succeed.[20]

Top executives often need performance-related information about the results of various divisions or product groups. They may require summary data about sales, production levels, or costs to assess the organization's performance. Top executives also use information about new technology, customers, suppliers, and others in the industry to gain a competitive advantage over other firms. They may want detailed information about particular aspects of their organization, such as the total number of employees or sales at any particular time. They may also want general information that focuses on a division's profitability, market share, return on

FIGURE 1.6	Managers at different levels in the organization have different information needs.

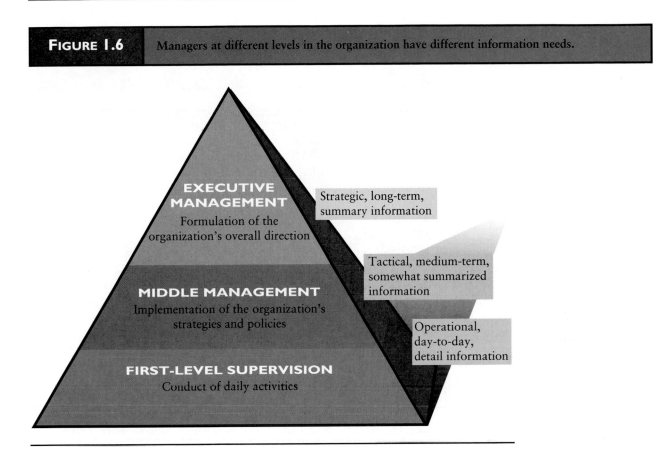

investment, or trouble spots. As you can see, the information needs of top executives vary considerably.

Consider the job of a senior marketing manager in a hair-care products division of a large company. She must determine the best mix of products for the company, authorize advertising and marketing research expenditures, and supervise a staff of managers responsible for accomplishing the department's goals. What types of information might she require? Now compare her information needs to those of a senior financial manager or even to those of a senior marketing manager in a computer software firm. Clearly these managers have some needs in common, but each also has needs unique to that manager's job, organization, and industry. Diagnosing the particular information needs of a senior executive requires tracking the executive's organizational and job goals and then assessing the information that helps accomplish them.

Planning and Implementation Needs of Middle Managers. Middle managers primarily focus on implementing the policies and strategies set by top management. They translate the long-term direction set by top management into medium-term decisions and activities that affect the way the organization does business. Plant managers, regional sales managers, directors of staffing, and other middle managers almost always deal with internal organizational issues, such as finding ways to increase

ETHICAL ISSUES IN IT

PC Corp. (not its real name) had a problem with anonymity that was driving top managers crazy. Unauthorized software appeared on the network that let employees send anonymous E-mail messages. There was a rash of sexually suggestive—and even obscene—E-mail sent to female employees.

Unpopular managers received insulting E-mail appraisals of their personal style and professional performance.

More ominously, several messages detailed serious problems with PC Corp.'s key projects. Like kerosene poured on a smoldering fire, these anonymous acts ignited once-covert resentments and turned them into openly burning issues. While half the company was thrilled that anonymity raised these problems for corporate-wide discussion, the other half was furious that the leakers couldn't be found and punished.

Ultimately, PC Corp.'s top managers pulled the plug on its global E-mail system, rewrote its network software to assure that all messages could be tracked, and issued edicts that forbade

anonymity on the company's network. The traffic that now flows on PC Corp.'s net is quite polite.

This example is hardly fictitious; it's an unhappy composite of real-world confrontations that have occurred at several Fortune 1,000 companies.

More than any other E-mail issue, anonymity provokes heated debate. The "right" to E-mail anonymity strikes at the very heart of values that organizations either cherish or try to suppress. Some organizations see anonymity as a healthy, essential part of their internal dialogue, a mechanism that promises free and unfettered comment. Others see it as a sleazy software mask that lets mischief-makers and malcontents get away with taking cheap shots at people who have the guts to sign their names to their messages.

At a giant aerospace manufacturer in the Northwest, for example, managers are grateful that their brainstorming software encourages anonymous contribution. "If we had to attach our names to our suggestions, I think

productivity, profitability, and service. Middle managers must meet production schedules and budgetary constraints while acting independently. They participate actively in an array of personnel decisions, including the hiring, transfer, promoting, or firing of employees. Middle managers pass top management's directives to lower levels of the organization and communicate problems or exceptional circumstances up the hierarchy. Working in the United States or abroad, they directly manage one or more work teams, coordinate interdependent groups, or supervise support personnel.

Middle managers require more detailed information than executives do about the functioning of the groups or workers they supervise; generally, however, they don't require as detailed information as first-level supervisors do. Often middle managers need detailed budget data; extensive information about workers' performance, schedules, and skills; and data about their group's products or services in order to perform their jobs well and to ensure their work group focuses on organizational goals. Often they cannot obtain perfect information and must use the best information they can secure.

Middle managers who act as **project managers** might be responsible for one or more unique projects, such as the development of new spreadsheet software or a new computer chip, or ongoing projects, such as the provision of accounting services to

people would be less forthcoming," insists one engineer there who, yes, asked not to be identified. The culture of the company, he argues, makes it difficult for younger engineers to publicly make comments critical of senior engineering decisions. The fact that anonymity effectively subsidizes the existing culture rather than encouraging a more open and honest exchange of ideas is dismissed as politically unrealistic.

The issue becomes more intense when one considers the speed at which organizations are linking their E-mail networks in hopes of accelerating the flow of vital data among corporate partners. Some companies are linking E-mail networks with those of key customers and suppliers. Suppose one business partner permits and even encourages anonymous messages, while another forbids them. When these two companies collaborate on a project, whose E-mail protocol should win?

Ironically, the ability to E-mail may lead more to a hostile clash of values than to the desired goal of better communications. Privacy is relative; anonymity is an absolute.

Market forces have created innovations for anonymity. Remailers can "launder" messages in ways that completely obliterate their origins. Although companies can use remailers to send anonymous messages, there are no known Fortune 500 companies that provide such remailers internally.

1. What would improve open and honest communications in your organization? Anonymity or attribution? How do you know?
2. How would you decide whether or not to permit anonymous messages in your organization?
3. How would you deal with offensive or insulting anonymous messages?
4. How would you deal with them if they were not anonymous?

SOURCE: Reprinted with permission from Michael Schrager, Anonymous E-Mail Fans Flames of Corporate Conflict, *Computerworld*, June 9, 1997, 33.

a small business. Project managers typically supervise teams of workers who together must accomplish a specific goal. The manager must ensure that the project team works together effectively toward its common goal. She must have information about the project's goal, task, timetable, and team members. Middle managers might also serve as links between their own work groups and others in the organization.

Operational Needs of First-Line Supervisors.
First-level managers are most directly responsible for ensuring the effective conduct of the daily activities in the organization. The supervisor of long-distance telephone operators handles any problems that arise in servicing customers. The customer services manager in an insurance company oversees the interactions between customer service representatives and policyholders. Such supervisors might plan work schedules, modify subordinates' job duties, train new workers, or generally handle problems employees encounter. They ensure that their subordinates accomplish their daily, weekly, and monthly goals and regularly provide workers with feedback about their performance. They screen problems and may pass particularly significant, unusual, or difficult problems to middle managers for handling.

First-line supervisors also spend large amounts of time in disturbance-handling roles, such as replacing absent workers, handling customer complaints, or securing repairs for equipment. They too may receive imperfect information; they must recognize these deficiencies and respond accordingly. Diagnosis of information needs must be ongoing and responsive to the particular situations these managers face.

THE ROLES OF THE MANAGER

Managers assume a variety of roles on the job, as shown in Table 1.1.[21] The information needs of plant managers differ from the needs of corporate controllers. The vice president of human resources has different information needs than the chief financial officer. Managers perform roles such as the following, each with their own information needs:

TABLE 1.1   The use of information technology can make performing managerial roles easier.

Role	Examples of Information
Gathering information and monitoring the environment	Company and industry information
	Minutes of task force and committee meetings
	Competitor information
Sharing information	Industry trends
	Technological developments
	Market requirements
	Organizational information
Leading, motivating, and coaching employees	Performance management
	Training opportunities
	Job descriptions
Making decisions and plans	Problem situations
	Operational and strategic plans
	Company goals
Distributing and negotiating about resources	Employee assignments and scheduling
	Budget
	Available equipment
Resolving problems and developing strategic responses	Problems and possible solutions
	Attitudes toward change
	Local political and economic conditions
Monitoring the impact of managerial actions	Performance standards
	Corporate goals
	Performance measurements

ADVANCED TECHNOLOGY

This is as good as it gets, Dick Tracy fans.

Imagine a digital watch with a pager built in. Then, envision one that will beep when you have voice-mail messages. Now, suppose it can also display weather forecasts, stock market information, lottery picks, sports scores, and ski conditions.

No, you can't call home from it yet. But hey, that's why you have a cell phone, right?

Seiko Corp. may be on to something here. Just ask Andrew Krasny, 30, a producer of NBC's Leeza Gibbons Show who has been wearing the new Seiko MessageWatch for less than a month. He already swears he'll never go back to his 10-year-old Rolex, except maybe when he's wearing a tux. Every night, he checks the winning lottery numbers and has become a fanatic about the weather forecasts on his MessageWatch. "Who would have thought you'd wake up and look at your watch to decide what to wear every day?" he says.

SOURCE: Excerpted with permission from Larry Armstrong, It's 10 P.M. Do You Know What Your Bank Balance Is? *Business Week* (November 1994).

- *Gathering Information and Monitoring the Environment.* Managers gather information from the environment inside or outside the organization. They review written information about the company and its industry, attend meetings that present information about the organization, or participate in task forces or committees that provide additional information about organizational functioning. They scan worldwide for large amounts of diverse information to assist them. Information systems can help managers both to collect and to process this information.
- *Sharing Information.* Having collected information about the organization's functioning, managers then share it with subordinates, peers, supervisors, or people outside the organization. Managers share information about the environment in which the organization functions, including industry trends, technological developments, and market requirements. Managers also share their knowledge of the organization—its structure, goals, resources, and culture. They share information in face-to-face meetings or by using electronic systems.
- *Leading, Motivating, and Coaching Employees.* Managers establish a formal reporting structure and a system of accountability among workers. They attempt to build effective work teams by encouraging cooperation and handling conflict that arises. Managers direct and motivate employees to accomplish personal and organizational goals. They train, coach, and evaluate their employees and help them develop the skills, knowledge, materials, equipment, and time to perform their jobs.
- *Making Decisions and Plans.* All managers act as decision makers. Top managers determine their company's goals and the strategy for accomplishing them. Lower-level managers decide the number and type of employees necessary to accomplish the organization's goals. Managers require information about individuals, groups, and organizations involved in or affected by the problem

situation. They need information about the alternatives available and the costs and benefits associated with each one. Managers often incorporate their decisions into long-term and short-term plans for the organization. They should diagnose each decision situation to identify its unique information needs.

- *Distributing and Negotiating about Resources.* Managers determine the assignment of people to tasks; the allocation of money and materials to individuals, departments, and other work groups; and the scheduling of the time of various employees. To allocate resources effectively, managers need information about enterprise goals and resource availability as well as employees' existing work assignments, capabilities, and vacation schedules. They also should know the costs of various projects or products. They need to understand the trade-offs between various scheduling or budgeting alternatives. Managers frequently negotiate with their subordinates or other managers about how to best allocate resources to accomplish various group or organizational goals. Information systems can provide managers with the information they need to improve the allocation of resources.

- *Resolving Problems and Developing Strategic Responses.* In conjunction with resource allocation and negotiation, managers define problems in a situation, analyze them, and then propose solutions. Managers can act as change agents in dealing with problems. As change agents they need data about workers' and management's attitudes toward change, the resources available for the change, and the consequences of similar changes in other situations. Developing strategic responses in organizations that function globally may pose special challenges. Managers may need to account for significant currency fluctuations, unpredictable local political conditions, or an unknown labor pool. They may need to consider variations in national customs, worker expectations, and product acceptance.

- *Monitoring the Impact of Managerial Actions.* Control means ensuring that performance meets established standards, workers' activities occur as planned, and the organization proceeds toward its established goals. In the control process, as shown in Figure 1.7, managers establish standards and methods for measuring performance, assess performance, and then compare performance to the standards. They require information about how the organization functions to help them anticipate and handle organizational problems and challenges. Managers commonly use information provided in budgets and financial controls to guide and constrain organizational activities.

THE CHALLENGES FOR EFFECTIVE INFORMATION MANAGEMENT

Managers need to collect, process, and disseminate information quickly and accurately to help their organizations compete effectively in today's global marketplace.

Using Technology Appropriately to Meet Information Needs.

Although computers can make large quantities of information available, such information may not address managers' or employees' needs. Managers continually need to reassess whether they have the information they need for performing their various roles.

| FIGURE 1.7 | Managers implement the control process to ensure that actual performance meets expected standards. |

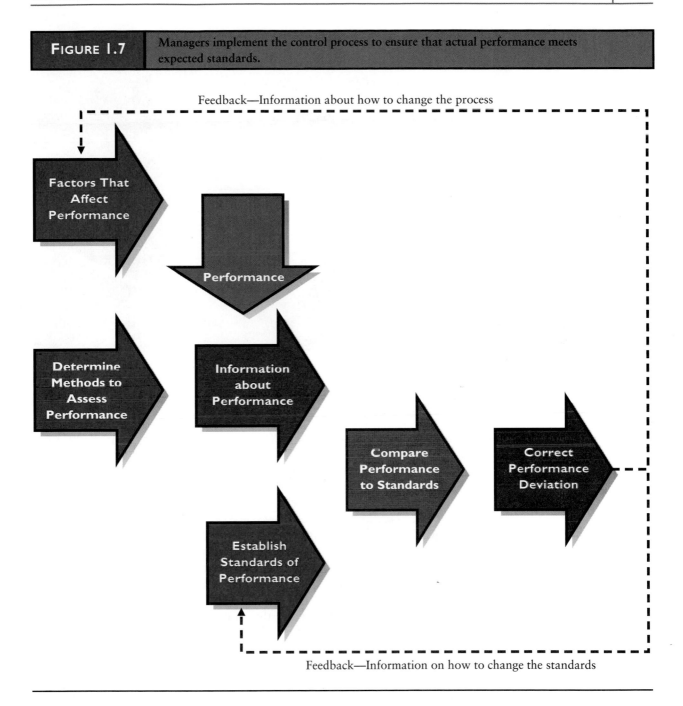

Feedback—Information about how to change the process

Factors That Affect Performance

Performance

Determine Methods to Assess Performance

Information about Performance

Compare Performance to Standards

Correct Performance Deviation

Establish Standards of Performance

Feedback—Information on how to change the standards

Using information technology effectively means ensuring that the technology chosen best meets these information needs. Companies must frequently make trade-offs between securing the best technology and making cost-effective choices. The rapid pace of new technology introductions challenges managers to assess on a continuous basis how well existing technologies meet information needs.

Using technology effectively also requires that the technical skills of personnel are continuously updated. Although many companies provide training to their

Grocery stores, pharmacies, and other retail outlets scan the universal products codes on items. This scanning allows the companies to collect extensive information about product sales, inventory, and even customer preferences.

employees, others do not. Ensuring that employees have the appropriate skills has both financial and time-cost implications. Without on-the-job training, employees may find their mobility and productivity limited by the extent to which they can learn new technical skills independently of their employers.

Dealing with Too Little, Too Much, or Conflicting Information.
The gap between the amount of information an organization can collect and the ability of its employees to make sense of the information has widened rather than narrowed. Often employees face an **information glut,** an overload of information. For example, universal product code scanners provide 100 to 1,000 times as much information about product sales as was available before their use. According to an international survey of 1,300 managers, almost one-half believed that the Internet will be a primary cause of information glut over the next two years.[22] As managers move higher in the organization and assume more responsibilities, information overload becomes a more significant challenge.

To avoid such overload, people must carefully assess their information needs and then find effective ways of managing the information. Because computers process input from diverse sources, users may also obtain conflicting information if one source updates information more frequently than another does. Companies such as Sherwin Williams has its IS staff talk with managers and identify the information they need. After selecting a number of sources, they meet again and check whether the managers have too much, too little, or the right information.[23]

Responding in a Timely Fashion.
Manual filing systems satisfy many personal needs for organizing and retrieving information, but they make it difficult

for managers to retrieve large quantities of information easily. They also make it impossible to collect information from different sites worldwide. Not only do computerized systems ease access to material in a single location, but they allow managers to retrieve information from multiple locations, often instantly. In addition, they can support quick, repeated searches of data. For example, people who require patent information for scientific inventions can use software to perform sophisticated and rapid patent searches.[24]

A variety of information industries, such as newspaper, magazine, radio, television, and advertising industries, assist people in acquiring timely information for use at work. The World Wide Web, in particular, makes information readily available through the Internet. For example, not only does the Official Airline Guide, available in hard-copy and electronic form, provide complete airline schedules, but consumers can make reservations online at airline and travel Web sites.

Ensuring Cost-Effectiveness.

Although information can be valuable, it is costly to use. Acquiring, processing, storing, retrieving, transmitting, communicating, and using information each have costs. Generally, acquiring information through informal sources, such as conversations with customers or suppliers, costs less than through formal ones, such as electronic forms or monitoring equipment, but the information acquired may be harder to organize and use effectively. Experts estimate that electronic forms for capturing data cost at least 70 percent less to design, purchase, use, carry, and revise than the equivalent paper forms.[25] Electronic processing, such as with electronic scanners, can significantly reduce the costs of handling information. Saint Alphonsus Hospital in Boise, Idaho, uses a network of personal computers and servers to simplify its billing cycle and save $140,000 in lost payments each year.[26]

The primary cost of storing information is the expense of the storage medium and space. The cost of media, physical facilities, and staff for backup systems also contributes to the storage costs. Storing large amounts of data calls for simultaneously developing and storing an index or map that assists in locating the data. Electronic systems provide rapid and inexpensive retrieval of electronically stored information. Transmitting information long distance or exchanging large volumes of data can occur more effectively by electronic communication.

Ensuring Security.

Users of computer systems must pay special attention to securing their information. Particularly with the widespread use of the Internet, security issues have become more common. Computer files are highly susceptible to theft and sabotage, particularly because these security breaches are not easily noticeable. The threat to computer files has increased as many people have unprecedented access to them through the Internet. Levels of security can be placed on information systems so that only specified information can be shared with others.

Using Information Systems Ethically.

Ethics regarding the use of information technology involves making a principled choice between right and wrong.[27] Ethical issues relate to security, privacy, use of company resources, computer viruses, and unprofessional behavior, among others. They can involve any type of information technology and any type of information system. The ethical use of information systems has become a major concern for managers and IS professionals.

Controls over access to information, particularly on the World Wide Web, have raised ethical concerns related to censorship. Most of the limitations have focused on

The widespread use of the World Wide Web and easy accessibility to it by users of all ages has raised concerns about its content. A fine line exists between censorship and ensuring free speech on the Web and preventing children from having access to pornographic and other inappropriate material.

preventing children from reading pornographic material. In a business-related instance, however, the Singapore Broadcast Authority requires all computers with Net access to link through a proxy server. This allows the government agency to block "dangerous" Web sites that discuss pornography, politics, and religion.[28]

Protecting personal privacy has also become a key issue as computer information systems can maintain large amounts of data about individuals without their knowledge.[29] Privacy advocates call for policies and procedures to protect individuals' privacy, such as ensuring the legal collection of correct and up-to-date data relevant to the organization's goals.[30]

People often face options regarding the use of information that they cannot label clearly as right or wrong, ethical or unethical. For example, what should you do if, after promising your employees that their data are private, you learn that one employee has stolen company information? What if you learn that one employee has plans to harm another? Should you examine their data files? People can apply a variety of ethical principles to determine what is or is not ethical in cases such as these:[31]

- *The Principle of Harm Minimization.* Make the decision that minimizes harm. To apply this principle, you must look at how the decision affects all parties, not only you and your company. You will probably have to weigh the harm done to one person against the harm done to another.

- *The Principle of Consistency.* Assume that everyone who faces a similar decision makes the same choice as you. Would you approve of the consequences? For example, if you believe that copying software rather than purchasing it is ethical, examine the implication of everyone copying software.
- *The Principle of Respect.* Make the decision that treats people with the greatest respect. This implies that you act toward them in the same way that you hope they would act toward you.

If these principles conflict, are too difficult to apply, or provide no clear solution, you can also use a variety of practical approaches for making ethical decisions.[32]

- *Use the Law to Guide Your Ethical Choice.* For example, apply existing copyright protection laws to determine whether permission or payment is necessary to use a software product for a specific application.
- *Apply the Formal Guidelines of Your Company or an Appropriate Professional Organization.* These guidelines might help you decide among legal choices. For example, the Code of Ethics and Professional Conduct of the Association for Computing Machinery includes provisions, which you could legally ignore, for respecting the privacy of others and honoring confidentiality.
- *Use One of the Following Informal Guidelines.* What would your mother (or father) say if you acted in that way? How would you feel if you saw your situation described in the newspaper? Does the situation "smell bad"? How would you feel if the roles were reversed and the act were done to you? Would you use your behavior as a marketing tool?
- *Avoid Decisions That Answer the Following Questions with "No."* Does the action cause unnecessary social harm or fail to serve the public interest? Does the action violate any basic human rights? Does the action abridge any commonly accepted duties?

Texas Instruments offers the Quick Ethics Test shown in Figure 1.8.

FIGURE 1.8	Managers and employees can use this quick test to determine whether an action is ethical.

**Texas Instruments
Quick Ethics Test**

- Is the action legal?
- Does it comply with company values?
- If you do it, will you feel bad?
- How will it look in the newspaper?
- If you know it is wrong, don't do it!
- If you are not sure, ask.
- Keep asking until you get an answer.

SOURCE: Texas Instruments Inc., Reprinted in Diane Trommer, Lead us not into temptation—Supply chain model poses new ethical challenge, *Electronic Buyers' News* (August 4, 1997), http://www.techweb.com/se/directlink.cgi?EBN1997090450005.

THE FOUR-STEP MANAGEMENT APPROACH

How can managers meet the challenges of managing information efficiently and effectively? We propose that a systematic approach to diagnosing needs, evaluating information technology, designing information systems, and then implementing them will improve information management. This model involves four steps, as shown in Figure 1.9: diagnosis, evaluation, design, and implementation. Although this model has some of the same characteristics as the systems development life cycle (see Chapter 12), unlike the systems development life cycle the four-step management approach helps managers and other employees, not information systems professionals, improve their information management.

DIAGNOSING INFORMATION NEEDS

Managers, employees, and other individuals must first assess their needs for information according to a particular situation facing them. **Diagnosis** requires a description of the existing problem, the context in which it occurs, the type of information available, the type of information required to solve it, and the possible ways of securing the needed information. Mike Hays, for example, must determine the types of

FIGURE 1.9	Managers should use the four-step approach to managing information.

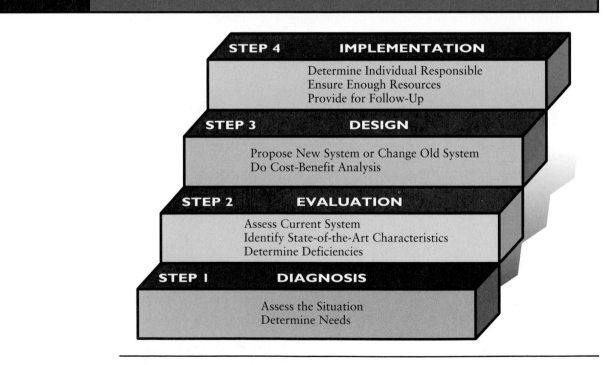

STEP 4   IMPLEMENTATION
Determine Individual Responsible
Ensure Enough Resources
Provide for Follow-Up

STEP 3   DESIGN
Propose New System or Change Old System
Do Cost-Benefit Analysis

STEP 2   EVALUATION
Assess Current System
Identify State-of-the-Art Characteristics
Determine Deficiencies

STEP 1   DIAGNOSIS
Assess the Situation
Determine Needs

information he needs for making a good customer presentation. Executives at Gulf Industries must determine the particular information they need for making such organizational decisions as the company's strategic direction, general marketing policies, or human resources practices. Bill Wright at Farr, Burke, Gambacorta & Wright needs to figure out how to handle the flood of information at the law firm. What information does each attorney need? How can they effectively get and process the information?

The diagnosis of information needs can occur at the individual, managerial, organizational, or societal levels. Employees must assess the information they need to do their jobs effectively. Managers often have needs for transaction processing, financial control, project management, and communication, among others. Organizations use information to increase their competitive advantage or implement their strategy, such as by improving customer service, cost control, or quality monitoring.

Society too uses information for communication, economic development, and generally improving the quality of life. The city of Cambridge, Massachusetts, has a Web site that makes it easier for residents to deal with city hall. It reduces the number of phone calls city employees have to handle by including information on every department, maps about department locations, a bulletin board of events, and an electronic-mail facility.[33] Specifying in detail the information needs at each of these levels is the first step in the effective management of information.

EVALUATING INFORMATION TECHNOLOGY AND SYSTEMS

Evaluation of the hardware, software, database, and data communication used to handle information follows the diagnosis of needs. Evaluation has several steps, as Figure 1.10 shows:

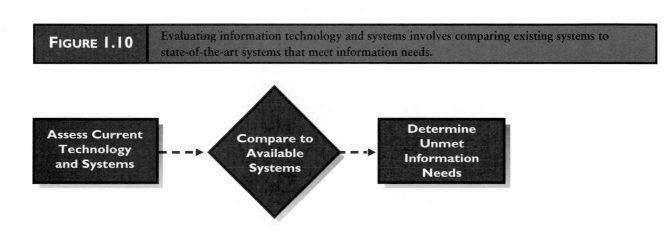

FIGURE 1.10 Evaluating information technology and systems involves comparing existing systems to state-of-the-art systems that meet information needs.

Assess Current Technology and Systems → Compare to Available Systems → Determine Unmet Information Needs

1. *Assess the Current Technology and Systems for Handling Information.* A manager, for example, might first describe the components of the information technology and systems used to acquire, process, store, retrieve, or communicate information.

2. *Compare These Components to Available Systems.* Ask the following questions: How well do the current technology and systems respond to the information needs? Are technologies and systems available that would significantly improve the handling of information? What consequences will result from changing the handling of information?

3. *Determine What Information Needs Are Not or Cannot Be Handled.*

Figure 1.11 offers a list of questions the manager might ask as part of the evaluation step.

DESIGNING RESPONSIVE SYSTEMS

After evaluating how well existing technology and systems meet information needs, managers, staff specialists, or information systems professionals design coherent systems for information management. **Design** involves correcting deficiencies in existing systems and integrating state-of-the-art practices and technology into them. Another law firm, Brooks, Pierce, McLendon, Humphrey & Leonard, for example, decided to implement a groupware system to let its lawyers share case files and communicate electronically.[34]

The design phase involves making decisions about specific information technology and their integration into information systems. It involves a cost-benefit

| **FIGURE 1.11** | Answer these questions to evaluate your company's information systems and technology. |

◆ What are the current systems for handling information?

◆ Are they manual or computerized?

◆ What are the components of the information systems and technology?

◆ How do these components compare to available state-of-the-art systems?

◆ How well does the current system respond to the information needs?

◆ Would other systems respond better to the information needs?

◆ Would state-of-the-art systems significantly improve the handling of information?

◆ What consequences will result from a change in the way information is handled?

◆ What information needs are not handled and cannot be handled, regardless of the information technology or information systems used?

analysis to ensure that the new design provides a sufficient return for the additional costs incurred. System users and skilled professionals often collaborate to ensure the best design.

IMPLEMENTING INFORMATION SYSTEMS

The final step focuses on issues associated with **implementation** of the new or altered systems. Who will be responsible for overseeing the implementation? How will it occur? What additional resources will be required for implementation? What types of follow-up will occur? How will the change affect other aspects of an individual's or organization's functioning? Identifying each party's responsibility for implementation involves determining the roles individual managers, information systems staff, or specialists from outside the organization will play. Specifying the timetable for implementation typically follows.

Top management must ensure that sufficient resources are available for the implementation as well as for dealing with changes that occur as a result of the implementation. They must also assess whether the information systems professionals function effectively throughout the four phases. Recognizing that the new system and technology likely will have unanticipated consequences should be a key aspect of planning; monitoring such effects and providing solutions for problems that arise should be part of the implementation. Implementation also includes ensuring that the new systems perform as expected and result in the predicted costs and savings.

ORGANIZATION OF THIS BOOK

This book applies the four-step approach to examining the management of information, as shown in Figure 1.12. Part I, composed of Chapters 1 and 2, diagnoses information needs by focusing on the way managers, groups, and organizations use information. Part II, which includes Chapters 3 through 7, evaluates the information technologies available to meet these needs. Part III, Chapters 8 through 11, examines four types of information systems that organizations use to manage information. Part IV, Chapters 12 and 13, investigates implementation issues and managing the information resource.

SUMMARY

This book investigates the management of information. We define information as processed data. Information can be used as a resource, asset, or commodity. Information technology, in the form of computer hardware, software, database

FIGURE 1.12   This book follows the four-step approach of information management.

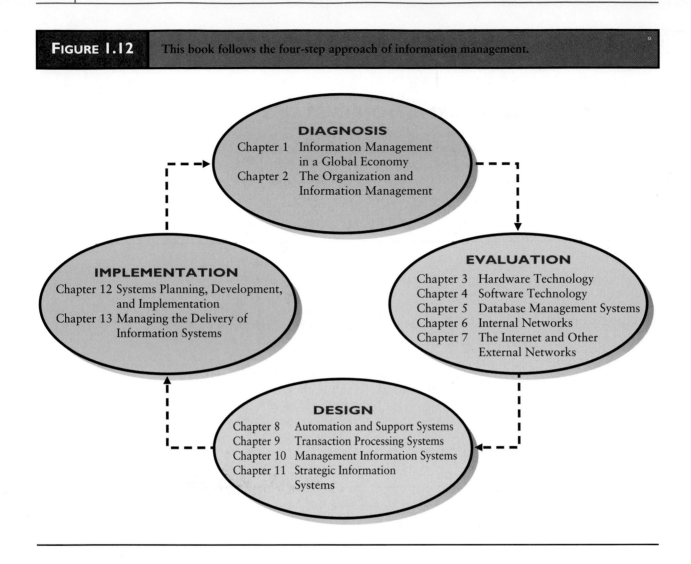

management systems, and data communication technology, helps meet the information needs of managers and employees. We can combine information technologies into automation, transaction processing, management, and strategic information systems.

Information management poses unique challenges to managers. They must succeed in a global environment. Companies focus on quality and performance and increasingly use business process redesign to improve their functioning. They build individual capabilities and productivity by creating a knowledge-based workforce.

Managers in the global marketplace face a dynamic and unpredictable environment. They perform a great quantity of work at an unrelenting pace. Differences exist in the types of information needed by managers at different levels. All managers perform a variety of roles that require different types of information. They also face a variety of challenges in managing information.

Managers can use a four-step analytical model to improve their management of information. They first assess their situation and their information needs. Next they evaluate the quality of their existing information systems for meeting their information needs. Third they propose modifications in the systems to better meet the needs. Fourth and finally they deal with issues of implementation and follow-up.

KEY TERMS

automation system
business process redesign
computer hardware
computer software
data
data communication technology
database management system
decision support system (DSS)
design
diagnosis
evaluation
executive information system (EIS)
groupware
implementation
information
information glut
information system (IS)

information technology (IT)
Internet
knowledge
knowledge worker
management
management reporting system
management system
project manager
reengineering
resource
strategic system
support system
total quality management (TQM)
transaction
transaction processing system (TPS)
wisdom
World Wide Web (the Web)

DISCUSSION AND REVIEW QUESTIONS

1. What is information management?
2. What is information?
3. How do data, information, knowledge, and wisdom differ?
4. What three ways can managers use information?
5. What is information technology?
6. What are four major types of information technology?
7. What four types of information systems do managers use?
8. What are the major issues managers face in managing information today?
9. What aspects of a manager's job influence his management of information?
10. How does the global marketplace affect information management?
11. What roles does a manager perform?
12. How do managers use information to improve the quality of their products and services?
13. How does a manager use information and information systems in performing each of her roles?
14. What challenges do managers face in ensuring effective information management?

15. What ethical issues do managers face?
16. What steps comprise the four-step management approach?
17. Why should managers diagnose their information needs?
18. What steps should they take in evaluating information technology and systems?
19. What issues should they consider in designing responsive systems?
20. What issues must they resolve as part of implementation?

IS ON THE WEB

Exercise 1. Visit one of the sites on the Web page for Chapter 1 in the section called "Cyberethics." Summarize the ethical issues involved in writing laws to control the electronic dissemination of documents, software, and other intellectual property.

Exercise 2. Visit one of the sites on the Web page for Chapter 1 in the section called "Information Management Research." Identify an issue of controversy in current information systems practice, and summarize the viewpoints of the opposing sides.

MINICASE

SHIPPER AUTOMATES THE SALES FORCE

Several months ago, employees selling cargo space for Maersk, Inc., one of the world's largest shipping companies, still stuffed customer account information into file cabinets.

Some sales managers—who are making multimillion-dollar deals—connected to the office mainframe using old laptops from home; others printed information from computers at a branch office. Little valuable information was shared among the sales force, and when employees left, client histories often went with them.

"It was, 'Whatever you want to do,'" said Lee Johnson, a regional sales manager in Los Angeles who has worked at Maersk for seven years. "We didn't have [a system]. We had a primitive database that covered about 25% of our customers."

SOURCE: Case reprinted with permission from Kim Girard, Shipper automates sales force, *Computerworld*, August 18, 1997, 59–60.

Chris Ruhalter, sales automation manager at the Madison, N.J.-based company, last year aimed to save the sales force time and the company money by changing the customer management application from mainframe to an easy-to-use client/server platform.

Maersk looked at software from Saratoga Systems in Campbell, Calif.; Maximizer Technologies, Inc. in Vancouver, British Columbia; Aurum Software, Inc. in Santa Clara, Calif.; and other companies before choosing upstart Borealis Technology Corp. in Carson City, Nev. Borealis' software was the easiest to adapt to meet the needs of the sales department, Ruhalter said.

"A lot of the [other sales] systems are overbuilt, and some systems have a built-in methodology applied to them that doesn't apply to the way we sell," he said.

Johnson said he soon will be able to filter—assign categories to 22,000 accounts based on a customer's financial history—and query for reports that will help him determine customer buying patterns. He will also be able to separate customers into groups—for instance, all customers in the Los Angeles area or all import accounts from Hong Kong—so he can target sales pitches or send faxes more quickly and easily.

Maersk began to install Arsenal 3.0, Borealis' sales force automation software, in late May and finished the job last month—much quicker than the expected six to 12 months.

Borealis' challenge—in a market where projects often fail—is to deliver on its promise of a shorter installation time and provide a system that is easy to use, said Chris Pavlic, an analyst at Aberdeen Group, Inc. in Boston. "If it's not easy to use, the laptop will stay in the car trunk under the old golf clubs." Pavlic. said.

Maersk's 200 sales representatives and telemarketers use IBM ThinkPad 760 PC notebooks that run Windows 95 and are equipped with remote access software from XcelleNet, Inc. in Atlanta. Users dial in to a Hewlett-Packard Co. 9000 server. The company created a virtual private network using IBM 8235 routers.

"Once we get this up and running, we'll have 80% of customers covered," Johnson said. "It enables you to manage your time better, track customer contacts much better, and plan and organize sales calls on a much higher level."

Case Questions

Diagnosis

1. What information needs did Maersk have?

Evaluation

2. What types of information systems did the company have?
3. How well did these systems meet the company's needs?

Design

4. What changes in information systems did the company make?
5. Did these changes better meet Maersk's needs?

Implementation

6. What implementation issues did Maersk face?
7. How will Maersk know whether or not the new systems are effective?

ACTIVITY 1.1   MANAGERIAL ACTIVITIES ANALYSIS

Step 1: Review the excerpt of the daily work diary shown in Figure 1.13 of Joseph Michaelson's morning. Michaelson is the plant manager for one of five plants of a large manufacturer that produces and sells components for computers. The plant operates 24 hours a day, seven days a week.

FIGURE 1.13	Joseph Michaelson holds numerous meetings and performs a variety of activities as part of his job.

8:00   Joseph meets the night supervisor for their daily meeting. They discuss the production runs during the previous night, problems with staffing, and plans for tonight's runs.

8:30   Joseph runs into the plant's human resource representative at the coffee machine. They discuss some new federal regulations that affect their plans for hiring temporary workers.

8:40   Joseph receives a telephone call from the corporate accounting department. He has been meeting regularly with a representative from accounting to discuss new ways of accounting for unused inventory. They chat for 20 minutes about the project as well as exchange some corporate gossip.

9:00   Joseph meets with the five people who report directly to him to review their plans for the week. They spend much of the meeting discussing their plans for increasing the number of self-managing work teams on the plant floor. They also spend some time talking about problems they are having with machining several key parts.

10:00   Joseph participates in a conference call with the four other plant managers to discuss the installation of some new assembly-line technology on the plant floor.

10:30   Joseph completes the paperwork for the performance evaluations of his subordinates that he performed over the past two weeks.

11:00   Joseph meets with two newly hired team leaders to welcome them to the plant.

11:15   Joseph speaks at length with a vendor who has been providing problem parts for use in one of the computer components. Together they discuss ways of solving the problem and schedule another telephone conversation for the next day.

11:30   Joseph takes his daily walk about the plant, speaking with about 30 workers on the floor.

Step 2: For each activity performed, record the information the manager used during that activity as follows:

ACTIVITY	INFORMATION USED

Step 3: Now select a manager to interview. Ask him or her to describe in detail two or three activities he or she performed during the previous workday. Then ask the manager to tell you what information was required to perform these activities. Ask the manager what additional information he or she needed to perform the activities more effectively.

Step 4: Answer the following questions in small groups or with the entire class:

1. Which activities did the managers perform?
2. What information did the managers use during those activities?
3. How did the managers secure the needed information?
4. What additional information did the managers require to perform the activities more effectively?

FINE LEATHER STORES   ACTIVITY 1.2

Step 1: Read the following scenario:

The owner of a chain of five leather goods stores has decided to install a computerized information system to support the accounting, sales, operations, and human resource functions for the stores. Located in small suburban shopping centers, these stores carry an assortment of luggage, briefcases, wallets, and other leather products as well as travel accessories and small electronic products. So far, each store in the chain has operated independently, with a single personal computer to support store functions at the manager's discretion. Some stores use it to record transactions; others maintain inventory records on it; still others use it for primitive payroll systems.

Step 2: Individually or in small groups, diagnose the situation. List the types of information each store manager requires.

Step 3: In small groups or with the entire class, share the lists you have developed. Then prepare a comprehensive list of information after answering the following questions:

1. What elements do these lists have in common?
2. What information has been omitted from the lists?
3. Which information can be part of a computerized information system?

ACTIVITY 1.3   WHAT INFORMATION IS NEEDED?

Step 1: Read each of the following managerial problems. For each situation, decide what information the manager needs to solve the problem.

Problem 1: The manager of benefits in a moderate-size manufacturing company has just received four complaints from employees who state that their retirement accounts have not been properly credited for the third quarter in a row. What information does the manager need to ensure the correct assignment of money?

Problem 2: The owner of a chain of five ice cream stores has just spoken with one of his managers about an ongoing supply problem. The manager noted that a large number of comments in his customer suggestion box were complaints that the store was out of the flavor of ice cream the customer wanted to purchase. Although such complaints do not seem to have affected sales yet, the manager is afraid that he will soon lose valuable customers to a competing chain. What information do the manager and the owner need to ensure that each store has the correct supply of ice cream?

Problem 3: As the project manager of a major audit, you are responsible for allocating the work to the various associates working on the project. You have heard one of the associates complaining that you play favorites in assigning tasks. She insisted that the male associates get the more visible tasks that require fewer hours to complete. You do not believe that you discriminate in this way. What information do you need to refute this charge?

Step 2: For each situation, describe two ways the manager could secure the information he or she requires.

Step 3: Individually, in small groups, or with the entire class, answer the following questions:

1. What types of information needs do managers have?
2. How can they secure the information they require?
3. What role can information systems play in providing the needed information?

ACTIVITY 1.4   THE MANAGER'S DILEMMA

Step 1: Read the following scenario:

John Estes, the CEO of a small start-up biotechnology firm, returned to his office after a brief walk around the company's plant and offices. In general, he was satisfied with the way the company was growing and how well the employees did their jobs. But something about this latest tour of the plant nagged at John. It seemed to him that several times employees quickly changed the computer application on their computer screens when John approached. He saw more screen-saving software than he expected.

John had instituted a clear policy that all software used in the company must have appropriate licenses. His sister was the head of a software company and often complained about the high costs of pirated software. John thought he had made it clear to his employees that pirating software was unacceptable. He also knew that the software budget was inadequate for ensuring that employees had the best software available. John had heard rumors that company employees had secured illegal versions of software. He knew that if he discovered the illegal versions he might have to take the unpopular action of firing some employees to make his point. What should John do?

Step 2: Individually or in small groups, outline John's alternatives. Then evaluate each alternative using the basic ethical criteria.

Step 3: Based on your analysis, develop an action plan. Share the action plan with the rest of the class.

PLANNING FOR "GOING GLOBAL"   ACTIVITY 1.5

Step 1: You have recently assumed the position of chief information officer of a medium-sized company that manufactures and sells professional-sports-related products in the United States. The company's market research shows that a demand exists for similar products in Europe, and the executive team has decided to open outlets in three major European cities. If these outlets are successful, top management plans to open ten more within a year, move at least one manufacturing plant to Europe, and continue this rate of expansion over the next three to five years.

You have been assigned to prepare recommendations for updating the company's information systems to meet the needs of a global company. As a first step in this planning, you have decided that you need to develop a comprehensive checklist of the issues you and your staff need to consider about the move to a global company. You know that at a minimum you must consider the tax implications of purchasing hardware and the availability of telecommunications services into each location. What else will influence your plan?

Step 2: Individually or in small groups, develop a checklist of issues that you should consider when making your recommendations about information systems in this company.

Step 3: Share the checklist with the rest of the class and together develop a comprehensive checklist of issues for global companies. For each issue included on the checklist, answer the following two questions:

1. What implications does this issue have for the company's information systems?
2. What would happen if you ignored this issue?

RECOMMENDED READINGS

Beneviste, G. *The Twenty-First Century Organization*. San Francisco: Jossey-Bass, 1994.

Grochow, Jerrold M. *Information Overload*. Englewood Cliffs, NJ: Prentice Hall, 1997

Hammer, Michael. *Beyond Reengineering: How the Process Centered Organization Is Changing Our Work and Our Lives*. New York: Harper Business, 1996.

Rao, Ashok (ed.) *Total Quality Management: A Cross Functional Perspective*. New York: Wiley, 1996.

Shenk, David, *Data Smog*. New York: Harper Collins, 1997.

NOTES

1. Sarah Schafer, Supercharged sell, *Inc. Technology, 1997,* No. 2 (1997): 42–51.

2. James Cash, Gaining customer loyalty, *InformationWeek* (April 10, 1995): 88; Laura Struebing, Measuring for excellence, *Quality Progress* 29 (12) (1996): 25–28.

3. Anne Field, Groupthink, *Inc. Technology, 1996,* No. 3 (1996): 38–44.

4. Stephanie Stahl, Make documents, not war, *InformationWeek* (May 20, 1996): 46–47.

5. Tamara Ford and Brad Kayton, New York City DA uses desktop conferencing to speed up the legal process, *Virtual Workgroups* (March–April 1996): 15–18.

6. Mark Smith, Database technology moves Bay area, *American City & County* 113(2) (February 1998): 8.

7. Bob Violino, The billion, *InformationWeek* (November 25, 1996): 34–44; Harry M. Lasker and David P. Norton, The new CIO/CEO partnership, *Computerworld Leadership Series* (January 22, 1996): 1–7.

8. Maintaining a healthy position in managed care, *Systems Management* 24(10) (1996): 58.

9. Violino, The billion.

10. Candee Wilde, Trains, trucks & bucks, *Computerworld Client/Server Journal* (February 1996): 38–40.

11. Michael Goldberg, Extra room on the shelf, *Computerworld* (October 7, 1996): 79, 84.

12. Barb Cole-Gomolski, Groupware gives lift to Reebok site, *Computerworld* (January 19, 1998): 49–50.

13. Candee Wilde, The fab four: The Vanguard Group, *Computerworld Client/Server Journal,* Special Issue (August 1996): 14–15.

14. M. Hammer and J. Champy, *Reengineering the Corporation: A Manifesto for Business Revolution* (New York: Harper Business, 1993); Michael Hammer, *Beyond Reeingineering: How the Process Centered Organization Is Changing Our Work and Our Lives* (New York: Harper Business, 1996).

15. Joseph Maglitta, Flushed with success, *Computerworld* (August 7, 1995): 1, 79–80.

16. Justin Hibbard, Ernst & Young deploys app for knowledge management—IntelliServ to offer one-query searches, *InformationWeek* (July 28, 1997), http://www.techweb.com/se/directlink.cgi?IWK19970728S0031.

17. Alice LaPlante, Web-enabling an app saves $350K, *Computerworld* (February 24, 1997): 27.

18. H. Mintzberg, *The Nature of Managerial Work*, 2d ed. (Englewood Cliffs, NJ: Prentice-Hall, 1979).

19. Howard Dresner, For the data-hungry, *Computerworld* (July 26, 1993): 73–74.

20. Marc Gunther, Can he save ABC? *Fortune* (June 23, 1997): 91–100.

21. The roles presented here are drawn in large part from Mintzberg, *The Nature of Managerial Work*.

22. Julie King, Information overload threatens managers' health, *Computerworld* (October 17, 1996), http://www.computerworld.com.

23. King, Information overload.

24. Lynda Radosevich, Patent searching gets faster, *Computerworld* (November 8, 1993): 61.

25. M. Bragen, Form fitting, *Computerworld* (September 14, 1992): 105–107.

26. Tom Dellecave, Jr., Hospitals plan their own Rx, *InformationWeek* (July 31, 1995): 62–68,

27. This discussion is based on Ernest A. Kallman and John P. Grillo, *Ethical Decision Making and Information Technology: An Introduction with Cases* (New York: McGraw-Hill, 1993).

28. R. J. Thompson, Singapore's single point of censorship, *InformationWeek* (September 9, 1996): 10.

29. Louise Benjamin, Privacy, computers, and personal information: Toward equality and equity in the information age, *Communications & the Law* 13(2) (June 1991): 3–16.

30. Michael H. Agranoff, Protecting personal privacy exposed in corporate data bases, *Information Strategy: The Executive's Journal* 7(4) (Summer 1991): 27–32.

31. Kallman and Grillo, *Ethical Decision Making and Information Technology*.

32. Kallman and Grillo, *Ethical Decision Making and Information Technology*.

33. Steve Alexander, Expect the unexpected: Mission municipal, *Computerworld Premier 100* (February 24, 1997): 40–41.

34. A law firm uses Lotus Domino on the AS/400 to tie offices together, provide remote communications, *I/S Analyzer* 37(1) (January 1998): 13–15.

Chapter 2

The Organization and Information Management

LEARNING OBJECTIVES

After completing Chapter 2, you will be able to

1. Describe the key characteristics of today's organizations.
2. Discuss the four information requirements of today's organizations.
3. Describe the new organizational forms that have arisen and their information requirements.
4. Identify the information needs of team-based management.
5. Illustrate the types of information required to make and implement strategic decisions in an organization.
6. Relate information to the design and implementation of organizational structures.
7. Offer ways of using information for achieving a competitive advantage.

CHRYSLER FACES THE CHALLENGES AND SUCCEEDS

Robert Eaton, who became chairman and CEO of Chrysler in 1993, led the rescue of the troubled automobile manufacturer. Chrysler began to net increased sales, record revenues, and record earnings as a result of its new blueprint for growth, focus on stability, and new corporate culture.

Eaton first charted a new vision for Chrysler. "We started working on what kind of company we want to be: what's our purpose in life, our mission, our key success factors, and how are we going to focus from a strategic standpoint." Eaton created a management team with a shared vision of the future for Chrysler. He decided to sell Chrysler's nonautomotive assets quickly and focus on its core business. He helped managers focus on bottom-line results.

Eaton reengineered the entire product line, clearly responding to Chrysler's customer. Chrysler changed every product and plans to introduce a new model on the average of every three months through the year 2000. The company correctly expected and took advantage of a shift in customer demand from cars to trucks and sport-utility vehicles.

Eaton changed the corporate culture. Chrysler uses interdisciplinary teams to develop new products. These "platform teams" decide with upper management the type of product they want. Then the team has all the resources to make the vehicle. Eaton commented, "They have a one-page contract with us, and we don't make any decisions for them." This approach has cut development time in half and made Chrysler the lowest-cost U.S. automobile manufacturer. Eaton encourages individual managers to continually think of ways to improve the process. By empowering them in this way, he has increased both individual and corporate performance.[1]

Chrysler has succeeded because its leadership has focused on the company's core business, increased new product introduction, and changed the corporate culture. Its merger with Daimler-Benz AG, the manufacturer of the high-end Mercedes automobile, will pose additional challenges for Chrysler.

What characteristics make Chrysler and other organizations successful in today's environment? What information requirements do these companies have? In this chapter we answer these questions by first looking at the changing nature of organizations and their information requirements. Next we examine a number of new organizational structures and consider the information required to support them. We then investigate the trend toward using teams in the workplace and review the information team-based management requires. Finally, we explore the use of information in determining and implementing an organization's strategy, as well as achieving a competitive advantage.

THE CHANGING ORGANIZATION

Organizations today function in a global marketplace, which has created numerous challenges and opportunities. They must bring high-quality products to market quickly, and at a competitive price, while meeting customer needs. Chrysler has faced these challenges in the automotive industry.

THE BUSINESS CONTEXT

The following characteristics provide the backdrop for organizational functioning:

- *The Globalization of Management.* **Globalization** calls for managers who have strong leadership skills in cross-cultural situations. They must respond to continuous and unpredictable economic changes, rapidly accelerating technological advances, and dramatic political upheavals. They need to think creatively about the best locations for operations to take advantage of low labor costs around the world.
- *Organizational Flexibility, Adaptability, and Collaboration.* Companies need the capability to reorganize quickly to respond to changing market conditions. They need to put resources where they achieve the greatest payback. Today's organizations often create partnerships with other companies, even competitors, to meet customer demands and create new product niches. Extensive, rapid communication has become a key to effective organizational functioning. Companies have introduced flexible organizational structures to ease communication within and between organizations. The CEO of Merix Corporation, an Oregon electronics supplier, for example, sees people who work for Merix's suppliers every day.[2]
- *Work Teams and Empowered Workers.* Empowering the workforce helps meet the need for greater flexibility, adaptability, and collaboration. Companies use cross-functional teams to bring products to the market faster and less expensively. They give workers new responsibilities in decision making

so that employees with the best knowledge can quickly respond to changing conditions. By putting more decision-making power lower in the organization, Hewlett-Packard, for example, uses employee expertise and local knowledge to provide a better product.[3]

- *The Changing Workforce.* Diversity among employees has caused companies to consider the value of the special perspectives and knowledge women and minorities bring to organizations. Combined with white male workers who made up the traditional workforce, the more diverse workforce creates a powerful mechanism for understanding the marketplace and improving organizational performance. Companies also grapple with the benefits and challenges created by the growing contingent labor market, where workers move among companies on a contract basis. Some companies staff as many as half of their information systems jobs with contractors.[4]

- *Knowledge Management.* Knowledge workers actively manage the vast stores of knowledge and information in a company. Northeast Utilities, for example, created a cross-functional central information group that identifies, categorizes, and shares knowledge across the organization.[5]

Knowledge workers have become key players in organizations as they prepare for the next century. These workers know how to access and use vast stores of information, often relying on sophisticated computerized information systems to support their job performance.

Chrysler has created a new mission, a new management style, and new ways of doing business to compete effectively. It has created interdisciplinary teams, revamped its organization, and introduced a new strategy. Significant requirements for information accompany these changes.

INFORMATION REQUIREMENTS FOR ORGANIZATIONS

Today's organizations have special and increased requirements for information to support their new way of doing business. They must ensure the accessibility, reliability, accuracy, and security of information at a reasonable cost.

- *Making Information Accessible.* Companies need the appropriate information available to users at the right time, the right place, and in the right format. Increasingly, organizations use computerized systems to improve information accessibility. They may rely on information systems professionals to design these systems and meet users needs. More often, collaboration between design professionals and information users ensures the right availability of information. Chrysler has seven major corporate computer networks. One serves engineers, and another serves financial users. A third provides public relations information for journalists. Computer systems, however, can also make data inaccessible when they break down or when managers design them to withhold information from employees.
- *Ensuring the Reliability and Accuracy of Information.* The proper design and use of information systems ensures the availability of accurate and reliable data. Managers need consistent and correct information to make good decisions. Corrupted or unavailable data can significantly and negatively affect organizational performance. The Massachusetts Registry of Vehicles' new system, specially designed as a fault-tolerant system that couldn't fail, crashed and left the agency and its customers without data for 15 hours.[6]
- *Creating Secure Information.* Security means protection against theft, manipulation, and loss of data. Companies protect their information to preserve their competitive advantage and to guarantee the integrity of their operations. Without security, competitors or disgruntled employees could steal or modify key information, including proprietary technology, production methodologies, product data, and research and development breakthroughs. Foreign intelligence agencies have used sophisticated technology to intercept data transmissions.
- *Making Information Available at an Appropriate Cost.* Because the cost of acquiring, manipulating, and maintaining information can be high, reducing it by a small percentage can greatly increase profitability. Information systems specialists need to focus on the cost of collecting and maintaining information as well as on the value of the outputs of an information system when justifying its cost.

Hale and Dorr, a major Boston law firm, requires accessibility, reliability, and security in the technology it uses to gain an edge in delivering legal services. The attorneys pack laptops wherever they go, so they can take their documents with them. They can prepare documents at remote locations and then use an automatic file exchange program to update the main computer and send the files to the appropriate agency. They also use computerized equipment to present information in the courtroom for the judge and jury to see. They regularly use a voice recognition telephone system, videoconferencing, and online scheduling.[7]

NEW ORGANIZATIONAL STRUCTURES AND INFORMATION REQUIREMENTS

Organization structure refers to the division of labor, coordination of positions, and formal reporting relationships that exist in the organization. This structure may promote specific information needs for the organization.

The traditional hierarchical structure of organizations supports a control and command mode of operation. Information moves from low levels of the hierarchy up to decision-making managers. Managerial decisions filter down to lower levels where they are executed. The more important the decision, the higher up and down the hierarchy the information flows, taking time in the process and increasing the likelihood that information and decisions are misinterpreted.

Today's changing organizations have two important characteristics. First, managers give more responsibility for decision making to employees rather than retaining control themselves. Systems that make information readily available to workers at all levels in the organization can replace managers, service staffs (such as legal or public relations), and central management. As Figure 2.1 illustrates, this flatter structure increases each manager's span of control and reduces the need to move information up the corporate hierarchy for decision making. The company can respond faster to changes in the marketplace because decision makers are closer to the source of information.

Second, organizations more often have an organic structure. This structure emphasizes lateral communication and involves more flexible interactions among parts of the organization. A bank manager might serve on a task force to develop new products for the bank at the beginning of the year and several months later participate in a reorganization of the sales functions in the bank. Organizations might institute project and product management structures that group workers according to the project or product on which they work. The matrix form and other integrated structures simultaneously group employees on multiple dimensions, such as functional area, project, client, and geographical location, as illustrated in Figure 2.2. These structures create intense information needs for workers throughout the organization to ensure the coordination of activities.

ALLIANCES AND JOINT VENTURES

Organizations do not always need to acquire and develop their own resources to compete. Sometimes it is faster and cheaper to form a mutually beneficial **alliance**, an official working partnership, with another organization. Companies may license

FIGURE 2.1 Flattening the organizational structure increases managers' span of control and moves decision making closer to the source of information.

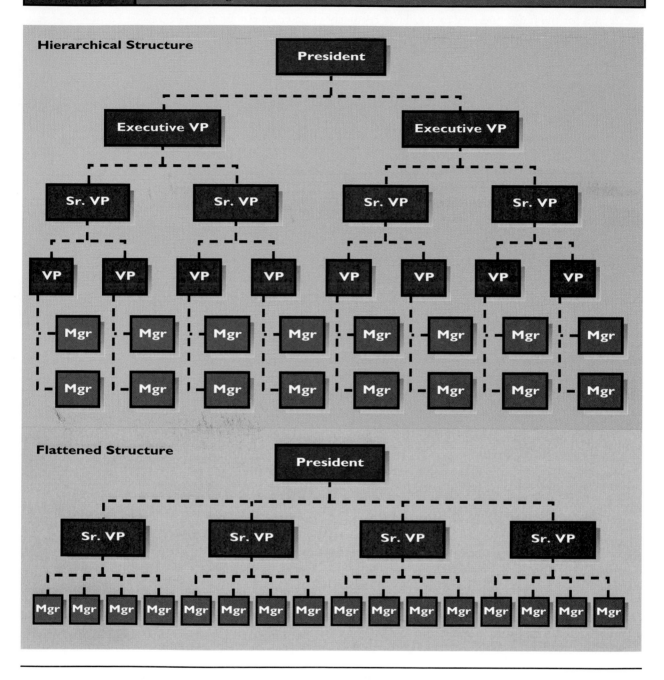

technologies to other companies. They may form **joint ventures,** where together they develop or market specific products or services, with partners here and abroad. Such alliances help organizations compete successfully because they bring additional

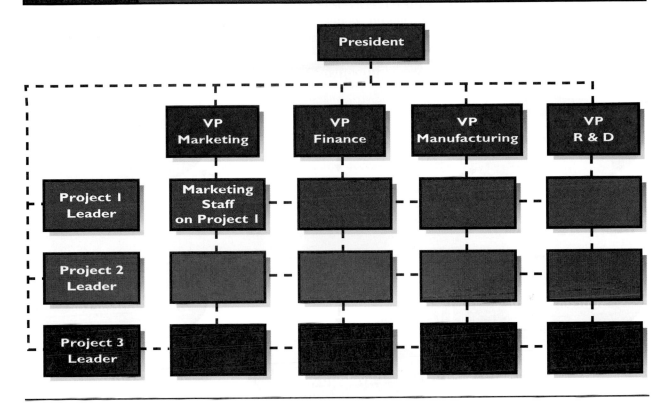

FIGURE 2.2 A matrix organizational structure such as the one shown here and other organic structures create intense information needs to coordinate activities and planning.

resources to solving organizational problems. Roadway Logistics, Inc., Nippon Express USA Inc., and Royal Frans Maas Group formed an information-based alliance to manage the global distribution network for Sun Microsystems. Each partner picks, packs, distributes, transports, and otherwise manages distribution in its geographical area. On-time delivery runs between 99.3 and 99.7 percent.[8] The companies involved must find ways to share key information effectively.

The health care industry has experienced widespread consolidation through the formation of joint ventures, umbrella organizations, and alliances. Tenet Healthcare, a group of 75 acute-care hospitals with $5.5 billion in revenue, is among the many health care organizations that build their own provider networks of hospitals, clinics, physicians, and alternative health care providers. These organizations use information technology to coordinate their services and help provide cost-effective health care. Tenet is trying to create and implement at each health care provider's office a portfolio of applications that work together, including administration, billing, and insurance claim processing.[9]

Managers in these situations need to blend different cultures and management styles, reconcile variations in job design, and develop compatible human resources systems. Information systems support these and other tasks. The managers require compatible information systems to ease the sharing of relevant information on a timely basis.

participating organization contributes only its core competencies. The ability to easily regroup companies into virtual corporations creates the flexibility required to seize new opportunities and remain competitive.

Virtual companies have five major characteristics:[15]

- *Absence of Borders.* The virtual corporation lacks the traditional corporate borders because the extent of cooperation among competitors, suppliers, and customers spans normal borders.
- *Technology.* Computer networks link distant companies, and they use electronic contracts to form partnerships.
- *Excellence.* Each partner brings its core competencies to the corporation, allowing the creation of a "best-of-everything" company.
- *Opportunism.* Partnerships are relatively impermanent, informal, and more opportunistic because companies join to meet a specific market opportunity and then disband after meeting it.
- *Trust.* The relationships in a virtual corporation require mutual trust because of their great interdependency.

A virtual company has intensive information needs because it exists essentially as a function of shared information. Sophisticated computer systems must link the various members of the network, providing current, complete, and compatible information. The Independent Grocers Alliance (IGA), a group of 3,600 independent supermarkets, links its stores with computer systems to reduce costs so they can match the margins of their larger competitors. IGA coordinates marketing programs for national brands and gets members bulk rates on supermarket equipment. New software lets IGA bill its members for equipment, packaging, and supplies while paying the vendors' bills.[16]

SUPPORTING TEAM-BASED MANAGEMENT

Companies in the United States and abroad have altered their cultures to encourage teamwork and collaboration. Just as Chrysler did, they empower individual managers and workers to make decisions. After a major product failed to get significant market share and a competitor significantly cut prices, Charles Strauss, the CEO of Lever Brothers, decided to introduce a team-based, customer-focused company organized along business process lines. This restructuring resulted in new products, improved customer service, increased market share, and doubling of profits.[17]

TEAMS IN THE WORKPLACE

Teams can vary in their leadership, longevity, and composition, as illustrated in Figure 2.5.

FIGURE 2.5	Team types differ along three dimensions. The box in the lower left-hand corner represents the traditionally managed, permanent, single-discipline team.

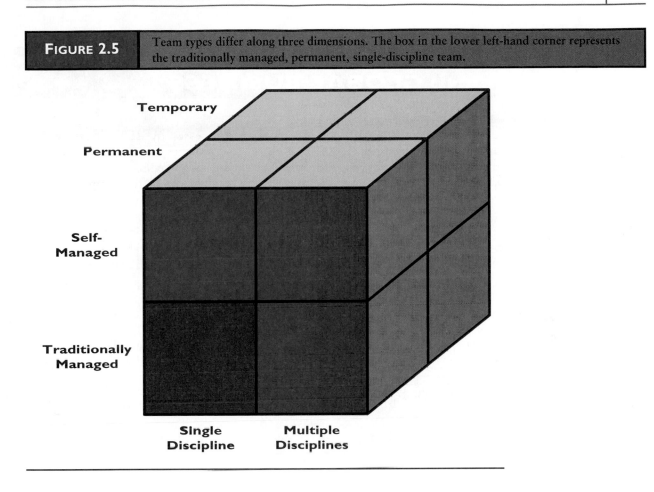

Traditionally Managed versus Self-Managed.

Traditionally managed teams have a designated individual who serves as the official leader or manager. This person oversees the daily activities of the team, as well as sets its direction, evaluates its employees, and ensures that it accomplishes its goals. **Self-managed teams** have members who share the responsibility for managing the work group without an officially appointed leader. Such teams have full responsibility for completing a well-defined part of the work process, generally the finished product or service or a significant component of it, and have discretion over decisions. Managers do not oversee the daily activities of a self-managed team, but they may coach it, develop an overall strategy for the teams in their area, champion innovation, and provide resources for the team.

The manager may also serve as a liaison to other parts of the organization, suppliers, and customers. About 67 percent of the production workforce at Xel Communications participates in self-directed work teams. The company eliminated three management levels when it changed to this team structure. The executive team remains committed to self-directed work teams because these executives believe that only the employees can create success for Xel.[18]

INFORMATION TECHNOLOGY AND GLOBAL BUSINESS

What do you do if your Manhattan model can't fit into a factory sample garment that just came in from Hong Kong? If you are Liz Claiborne, Inc., a $2 billion apparel and accessories giant based in the U.S., information technology has a lot to do with the answer.

Three years ago, North Bergen, N.J.-based Liz Claiborne faced a problem similar to that confronting other U.S. garment makers. Designs originate in the U.S., but production is often farmed out overseas. Keeping tabs on product timing and quality is a challenge when contract mills and factories are a dozen or so time zones away. And trimming cycle times is a must, both to cut down excess inventory and to have more time to concentrate on new fashions.

Liz Claiborne was also facing declining profits. According to company officials, the company had stagnated, both in design work and business practices. Inventories were high, and the time was ripe for a top-down change. The result: LizFirst, a project intended to transform the company into one that is first in responsiveness, service, and total value. A critical piece of that project was an investment in IT, according to John Thompson, Liz Claiborne's chief information officer.

The major goals of LizFirst were to reduce excess inventory by 50%, reduce cycle time in major business processes by 25%, increase responsiveness to customers, and improve timeliness and accuracy in shipments.

Two years into the project, the company is about 70% of the way toward its goal of saving $100 million in operating costs. It is also meeting cycle time reductions in most of its business processes, Thompson said. The savings have come primarily from payroll management, renegotiated freight agreements, facilities management, and licensed divisions.

Today, a global network knits together designers on the East Coast with manufacturing representatives in the Far East. For textile design, Liz Claiborne standardized on U4ia from Computer Design, Inc. in Grand Rapids, Mich., as its computer-aided design (CAD) package. The software was installed in all its divisions last year.

CAD images are shipped to manufacturing offices in Asia through a pilot project with DuPont ESnet, a subsidiary of DuPont Co. For the pilot, local Liz Claiborne staffers bring tape copies of the CAD files to factories that use CAD or print them out for factories that don't. Ultimately, Liz Claiborne would like to see the images delivered to the mills electronically, said Kathryn Shipman, director of corporate computer-aided design.

Permanent versus Temporary. Permanent teams work together for long periods of time, generally at least one year, on a repetitive set of tasks. Chrysler organizes numerous permanent teams to work on new products. Temporary teams form for short, prespecified amounts of time to complete a unique set of tasks or projects. For example, a mutual fund company may form a temporary team to develop a special promotion for a new type of fund the company introduces.

Single Discipline versus Multiple Disciplines. Companies can form teams that include workers from a single functional area, such as research and development, manufacturing, or marketing. Increasingly, companies form interdisciplinary

MAKING IT FIT

Liz Claiborne also uses the DuPont ESnet service to facilitate "fit sessions," during which a live model tries on a factory garment. Before, if a sample from Hong Kong was too big on a model in Manhattan, designers had to write out detailed instructions describing which alterations to make. Now, Shipman said, designers can snap a digital photo of the garment, annotate it in U4ia and then, using DuPont ESnet's Image Link software, send the image to the manufacturing office. They can also shoot a video clip to show a tricky alteration.

To standardize pattern specs, Liz Claiborne has begun rolling out Style Manager by Animated Images, Inc. in Camden, Maine. This software combines a vector-based drawing package with an Oracle Corp. database for storing pattern designs and specifications. All information needed to produce a particular style, such as color and fabric, starts in Style Manager.

Now, under a pilot that began early last year in two of the nine apparel divisions, manufacturing reps, design liaisons, and the mills in Asia can access the files stored on a Hewlett-Packard Co. HP 9000 server in New Jersey via their desktop PCs, using a frame-relay service offered by Infonet Services Corp. These staffers work with manufacturing and product development staffers in the U.S. to ensure Liz Claiborne gets the quality it needs from its contracted factories in the region.

"As we implement Style Manager, they will have access to that data any time they need it," said Tim Loftus, data communications manager at Liz Claiborne. "They won't have to wait for an E-mail, which can take a long time, especially with the time difference."

Liz Claiborne also uses Infonet's frame-relay service, a recent major upgrade of its connectivity in the region, for applications such as electronic mail and taxing, Loftus said. . . .

Over the next year or two, Liz Claiborne hopes to use the frame-relay service to give its 250 workers in the Asia-Pacific region access to electronic data interchange data and other core business systems, Loftus said. . . .

Liz Claiborne's efforts seem to be paying off. "They've cut cycle time, they've lowered costs, they've gotten more efficient," said Laurence Leeds, managing director at the Buckingham Research Group in New York.

SOURCE: Excerpted with permission from Sari Kalin, Global Net Knits East to West at Liz Claiborne, *Computerworld Global Innovators*, June 9, 1997, 4–6.

or **cross-functional teams** that include employees from several functional areas. Chrysler, for example, combines employees from engineering, manufacturing, marketing, and finance on its platform teams that develop new models. Sharing information effectively becomes critical to the functioning of these teams.

INFORMATION NEEDS OF TEAMS

Empowered workers need access to diverse types of information throughout the organization. Because teams often assume managerial functions, they have information needs similar to those of managers discussed in Chapter 1. They require information to perform the following functions:

- Monitoring the environment
- Updating employees and other managers about team activities
- Leading, motivating, and coaching team members
- Planning
- Making decisions
- Allocating resources
- Resolving problems
- Monitoring quality and performance

Team members need to communicate information quickly as a way of coordinating their actions. Because teams often function at dispersed locations, even at sites in different time zones, they need access to current information and should have the ability to update it in real time. For example, teams need to schedule, track, and ensure the timely completion of team activities. They need information about individual performance and task accomplishment to coordinate the team's attainment of its goals.

Team members also require task-related information so that they can perform their jobs as effectively as possible. Because teams often function as part of a total quality management effort or business process redesign, they require information to support continuous improvement and customer focus. The Cheshire Medical Center in New Hampshire has had a six-year history of continuous quality improvement, and its focus has moved from quality assurance to customer needs. The center carefully defines the team members' roles and makes sure the teams perform effectively.[19]

USING INFORMATION SYSTEMS FOR TEAM ACTIVITIES

Computerized systems can more easily provide teams with the types of information they require. Teams use automation systems to improve work flow, design, and manufacturing. They use transaction processing systems to track orders, shipments, and accounts payable and receivable. They use management information systems for forecasting and analyses. They even use strategic information systems for developing marketing and sales plans.

Groupware, computer software that particularly supports the coordination of team activities, has seen explosive growth. Groupware supports electronic messaging, schedules meetings, facilitates conferencing, and performs other functions, as shown in Table 2.1. Although groupware supports team operations, it can be used for additional functions that include but are not restricted to team operation, as shown in Table 2.2. For example, project team members around the world can update specifications of a new product in real time so that the team continues to make progress in developing its product.

These systems allow teams to process information more quickly and accurately. They can obtain the information they need to help their organization sustain its competitive advantage. National Semiconductor's Phillip Gibson, director of interactive

TABLE 2.1	Groupware can be classified according to the application's functionality.

Electronic mail and messaging
Group calendaring and scheduling
Electronic meeting systems
Desktop video and real-time data conferencing
Non-real-time data conferencing
Workflow management
Group document handling
Work-group utilities and development tools
Groupware services
Groupware applications
Collaborative Internet-based applications and products

SOURCE: Based on David Coleman, Groupware for collaboration, *Virtual Workgroups* (July/August 1996):28–32.

TABLE 2.2	The top three most popular business applications for groupware are office automation and productivity, business process reengineering, and group project management.

Rank	Most Important Applications
1	Office productivity
2	Business process redesign
3	Group project management
4	Publications coordinating routing
5	Customer service
6	Electronic meeting facilitation
7	Integrating compound documents and multimedia
8	Change management
9	Distribution/restructuring organization
10	Sales force automation
11	Downsizing report
12	Moving from mainframe to local area networks

SOURCE: Adapted from Table 1 in David Coleman, Groupware for collaboration, *Virtual Workgroups* (July/August 1996):28–32.

Managers can use videoconferencing to coordinate projects with employees or coworkers at distant locations. Computers that support videoconferencing allow the managers to see as well as hear their employees or coworkers.

marketing, credits Lotus' Notes groupware for increasing communication among the company's departments and improving decision making.[20]

INFORMATION AND ORGANIZATIONAL STRATEGY

Regardless of its structure, each organization must develop a **strategy**—a long-term direction or intended set of activities for attaining its goals. Strategic-level decisions include plans for accomplishing long-term goals concerning market share, profitability, return on investment, service, and performance. Managers who make strategic decisions need to determine their organization's distinctive competence by answering questions such as those shown in Figure 2.6. Answering these questions requires the manager to obtain information from both outside and inside the organization.

What strategy did Chrysler decide to pursue? More importantly for purposes of this book, what information does Chrysler's top management need to determine its strategy? In the past, Chrysler acquired an array of nonautomotive businesses. Now Eaton has decided to sell all nonautomotive assets and focus on the core business. The

FIGURE 2.6	Managers can assess the distinctive competencies of their organization by answering these questions.

◆ What kind of business should we be in?

◆ What should be the organization's markets?

◆ What market niches exist in which the organization can compete?

◆ What products or services should the organization offer?

◆ What technological investment is required?

◆ What human resources are available and required?

◆ What financial, time, material, or other resources are available and required?

information Eaton needs to make such decisions differs from the information needed for the day-to-day running of the company. He must obtain significant environmental, industry, and marketplace information to make such decisions effectively.

LEVELS OF STRATEGY

Companies can develop strategy at three levels, as shown in Figure 2.7. **Corporate-level strategy** addresses which lines of business a company should pursue. It views an organization as a portfolio, agglomeration, federation, or amalgam of businesses or subunits. Strategic management at the corporate level focuses on decisions about acquiring new businesses, divesting old businesses, establishing joint ventures, and creating alliances with other organizations.

To determine its corporate-level strategy top management needs to obtain information about the speed of industry growth and the portion of the industry market captured by the business unit, among other information. Information on industry growth and market share is often public, at least in the United States, due to the disclosures required of companies issuing stocks and bonds. Industry lobbyists, stock market researchers, trade magazine journalists, and other researchers also act as sources of this information. Information systems can regularly provide organizations with such information by tapping into commercially sold databases or Web-based information resources that offer extensive economic, technological, demographic, and even legal information. This ongoing availability of information allows organizations to determine their strategic position, as well as the appropriate actions to maintain or change this position.

Information systems can provide the information for making resource allocation and other investment decisions. Information about market share, profit margins, ownership of patents, technical capability, customer requirements, and competitive strengths and weaknesses helps management determine its investment strategy.

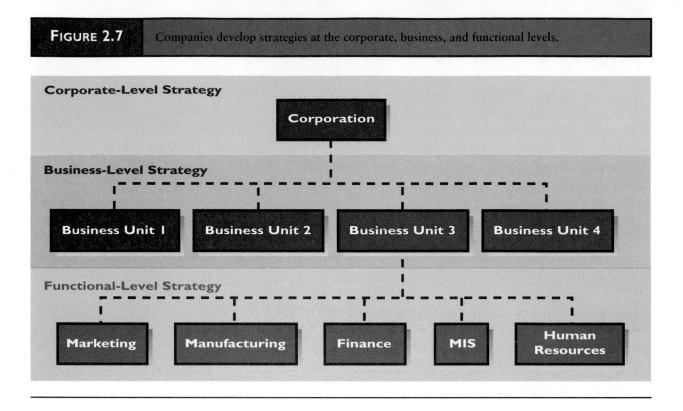

FIGURE 2.7 Companies develop strategies at the corporate, business, and functional levels.

Business-level strategy matches the strengths and weaknesses of each business unit or product line to the external environment to determine how each unit can best compete for customers. Strategic decisions include what products or services the company should offer, what customers it should service, and how it will deploy resources of advertising, research and development, customer service, equipment, and staffing. G.E. Capital has launched an average of one **electronic commerce** project, where they market products ands services using the World Wide Web, every six weeks as part of its strategic plan to increase its customer base.[21] For example, it has Web pages particularly designed for its metalworking customers. The pages present best practices, product information, and other bidding information.

Strategic management also addresses how functions such as finance, marketing, research and development, operations, and human resource management can best support the organization's strategies. **Functional-level strategies** direct the way individual departments perform their tasks to accomplish organizational objectives.[22] Marketing strategies focus on product development, promotion, sales, and pricing. Finance strategies focus on the acquisition, allocation, and management of capital. Operations strategies include decisions about plant size, plant location, equipment, inventory, and wages. Research and development strategies emphasize basic, applied, or developmental research. Human resource strategies revolve around the deployment of employees and the relations between labor and management. Managers need information about state-of-the-art practice and competitors' activities in each functional area to help develop their companies' strategies.

THE MANAGER IN ACTION

Michael A. Azarian, managing director at J.P. Morgan, led efforts to outsource (contract out) one-third of Morgan's global information systems and telecommunications operations to four vendors: AT&T Solutions, Computer Sciences Corp., Andersen Consulting, and Bell Atlantic Network Integration. The $2 billion deal, which involved 369 performance targets, shared the risks and rewards of outsourcing among the five companies, known as the Pinnacle Alliance.

The Alliance runs the bank's IS and telecommunications operations in New York and London, but not in Tokyo. Coordinating information technology projects between the separate geographies and partners poses significant challenges.

Azarian found that he had to counsel many employees and longtime contractors who were being transferred to the new Pinnacle Alliance during the first months of the outsourcing. "Things came out of the woodwork that just amazed me," Azarian said. Contractors complained about the alliance signing their paychecks, for example.

The partnership remains on target to reduce J.P. Morgan's costs by 15 percent during the next seven years. It has also freed Azarian to spend more time on long-range planning.

SOURCE: Based on Thomas Hoffman, Pinnacle alliance hits highs, lows in first year of J.P. Morgan deal, *Computerworld* (June 26, 1997), http://cwlive.cw.com:8080/home/online9697.nsf/All/970626pinnacle; Thomas Hoffman, J.P. Morgan alliance meets most targets in first year, *Computerworld* (June 30, 1997), http://cwlive.cw.com:8080/home/print9497. nsf/All/SL26pin.

DETERMINING THE ORGANIZATION'S STRATEGY

Managers often use a **situational analysis**—the process of collecting and analyzing information about a company's strengths, weaknesses, opportunities, and threats—to help determine a company strategy. The acronym **SWOT** is often used for these four components of situational analysis. **Strengths** and **weaknesses** are internal characteristics of the organization that enhance and impede its ability to compete. A reputation for quality exemplifies a strength, whereas having costs above the industry average typifies a weakness. **Opportunities** and **threats** are external or environmental factors that might help an organization to meet or hinder it from meeting its strategic goals. Weak competitors illustrate an opportunity, whereas adverse regulatory rulings represent a threat. Table 2.3 displays some major issues to consider in situational analysis.

Situational analysis requires extensive internal and external data. To evaluate internal strengths and weaknesses, such as a reputation for quality or above average costs, a company must compare data on its internal condition with industry and competitor averages. Quality information systems can assist organizations in securing comprehensive information for the SWOT analysis. Organizations can use these systems to maintain, update, or access environmental and organizational data, such as demographic trends, potential customer lists, financial data, or staffing patterns. Strategic management involves matching the strengths and weaknesses of each

ETHICAL ISSUES IN IT

When it became obvious a few years ago that the relationship between a decision-maker at Texas Instruments Inc. and a TI supplier had become too close, the TI ethics office went into action.

After evaluating the situation and determining that the supplier was clear on the company's stance on personal relationships between employees and suppliers but did not respect these guidelines, TI terminated its business with the supplier.

That action might seem a bit drastic, especially considering how much time, energy, and even money electronics companies put into nurturing business relationships with suppliers these days. But consider, too, that today's electronics companies outlay million and even billions of dollars annually to their suppliers. There can be no doubt that decisions are made for business reasons, not personal ones....

Since most suppliers recognize that today's purchasers are professionals who cannot be swayed by traditional gratuities, some have resorted to more inventive tactics in an effort to get around corporate gift policies. The problem is, purchasers often do not recognize these nontraditional gifts as "gifts."...

"Our suppliers can be very creative," Coleman [TI's manager of ethics, communication, and education] said. "So we offer ourselves in the ethics office as a source of opinion where procurement people can call to determine if a gift is acceptable or not."...

"International gifts are a difficult issue," Skooglund said. "You will find in different parts of the world really different guidelines as far as what are acceptable and unacceptable levels of gifts and entertainment. Because of the customs and practices in those cultures, there may be gifts of value that may be accepted, for example, in Japan that we would find unacceptable in the U.S."...

"We try to head off any potential problems down the line by telling suppliers up front how we expect to do business and what our guidelines are," said Leon Barbee, an instructional designer in professional development in corporate services with TI.

"At TI, we view our reputation as an asset as vital as the technologies that we develop and bring to the marketplace," said Carl Skooglund, vice president and director of the ethics office at TI, Dallas.

1. Why does TI have ethical guidelines regarding the acceptance of gifts?
2. Why are these guidelines flexible in their treatment of international gifts?
3. What are the ethical issues in accepting gifts from suppliers?

SOURCE: Excerpted with permission from Diane Trommer, Lead Us Not into Temptation—Supply Chain Model Poses New Ethical Challenges, *Electronic Buyers' News* (August 4, 1997).

A company uses internal corporate information to reduce costs by achieving efficiencies in production, distribution, and sales.

- **Focus** achieves competitive advantage by concentrating on a single market segment. A company following the focus strategy concentrates its resources to become a big player in a small market rather than a small player in a larger market. Tiffany, for example, focuses on the high-end jewelry market. Bread and Circus, a Boston grocer, focuses on the market for natural and organically grown foods. These companies require information about the nature of available markets and the characteristics of the players in them.

- **Linkage** obtains a competitive advantage by establishing special, exclusive relationships with customers, suppliers, and even competitors. These organizations require detailed information about customers' needs, special arrangements with suppliers, and potential synergies with competitors. Hazelden Foundation, a nonprofit organization that helps people with chemical dependencies, has a Web site that offers self-help to recovering alcoholics and drug users. The site functions both as an outreach site and a revenue vehicle. It includes chat rooms, an online bookstore, and a biweekly newsletter for registered subscribers. It also provides referrals to its treatment services.[25]
- **Information leadership** increases the value of a product or service by infusing it with expertise and information. Managers can supplement products with summary and activity reports for an account or customer, product and market information relevant to the customer, or information about related products and services. DHL, Federal Express, and UPS treat the Web as critical parts of their enterprises. They have infused their sites with general information, package tracking, downloadable software, Web shipping, drop box/office locators, and current events.[26]

USING INFORMATION TO ACHIEVE A COMPETITIVE ADVANTAGE

In many organizations, information management is a backroom operation intended to support the other functions of the business. Information systems can also be used proactively and strategically as a competitive weapon, as shown in Table 2.4. Colorado's Boulder Community Hospital, for example, leveraged its information technology knowledge by providing it for others. The hospital created a management services subsidiary that supplies and manages staff, leases space, schedules and bills patients, and provides general management assistance to individual physicians. This new subsidiary generated $10 million in revenue in its first year.[27]

Reacting to Market Conditions.   A firm that can respond quickly to market conditions has an advantage over its slower competitors in a number of ways. It can keep its costs lower by reducing excess inventory and eliminating mistakes in purchasing or manufacturing products that will not sell. It can tailor its prices more accurately to what the market will bear. It can react more quickly to lagging sales by adjusting advertising and price promotions. It can leverage its cash better, taking long or short positions and moving money quickly to where the opportunity for profit is the greatest. It can more quickly introduce products that the consumer wants. Being first in the market gives a company the opportunity to be a market share leader, with resulting scale efficiencies in manufacturing and marketing.

Companies can also use competitive pricing to give them a strategic advantage.[28] Information from computer systems can assist. Restaurants can assess the impact of various pricing and promotion strategies on their profit margins. A resort hotel can evaluate the success of special promotional packages by tracking an individual guest's expenditures by revenue center (for example, its golf course, restaurant, and health club) and can then adjust the promotions offered to increase their effectiveness.

TABLE 2.4	Managers can use information systems to help their companies achieve a competitive advantage.

Company Gains a Competitive Advantage By	Information System Helps Company Gain Advantage By
Reacting to market conditions	Reducing excess inventory Tailoring prices to the market Reacting quickly to lagging sales Leveraging cash Introducing new products Setting prices
Improving customer services	Maintaining appropriate inventory Responding to customer needs Monitoring customer service
Controlling costs	Classifying expenditures Monitoring spending Controlling budgets
Improving quality	Providing feedback Giving production workers immediate access to analyses
Expanding globally	Easing communication Supporting coordination
Creating strategic alliances	Sharing information with suppliers, customers, and competitors Providing information links Creating electronic markets

The ability to react rapidly to the market depends on a firm's ability to monitor external conditions. The government, news providers, and many private enterprises collect leading indicators of economic and market trends that organizations can use to monitor external conditions. *Nation's Restaurant News* provides such information on the World Wide Web. It targets 120,000 food service operators with Internet access. This online publication, which aspires to be the "CNN of restaurant trade," updates news and financial information twice daily for its subscribers.[29]

Most companies also collect information about external conditions in the normal course of business. For example, the record of customers' purchases can also become a weather vane of consumer opinion and product evaluation. Companies need to view such data not only from the context of operations management but also from the context of planning for competitive advantage. Information systems help companies organize and use such data. Organizations with information systems that facilitate the collection and processing of such data have a competitive advantage over those that do not.

Improving Customer Service.   Chrysler knows that its customers want a reliable automobile that requires minimal servicing. To meet these expectations and to diagnose and correct any failures, Chrysler needs to collect and monitor information about how well it succeeds in meeting the customer's objectives. For example,

Chrysler keeps a database of repairs so that it can target specific systems for improvement in future vehicles.

Making product and service innovations tends to increase an organization's competitive advantage.[30] For example, Chrysler introduced infant seats into its minivans to meet a consumer need. Such a competitive advantage, however, can be short-lived if other automobile manufacturers introduce the same feature.

DuPont contends that "a sale is not a sale until we get paid." The company believes that all activities, including selling, manufacturing, delivery, and getting paid, should focus on pleasing the customer. For example, DuPont is standardizing the process of shipping products from the United States to Asia in an effort to speed product shipments. DuPont found that simplifying the order-fulfillment process had extremely positive results, including a reduction in the number of steps in the process, significant reduction in working capital, and improved cycle times.[31]

Controlling Costs. Organizations can create a competitive advantage by becoming a low-cost producer. But how does a firm keep costs below its industry's average? Organizations can do so by achieving economies of scale in production, distribution, and sales. However, as volume increases, keeping track of and rationalizing business activities becomes more complex. The ability to handle, process, and summarize large amounts of information is, therefore, a prerequisite to achieving cost reduction through volume growth. Information systems can easily serve this function.

Systems that classify, monitor, and limit spending also ease cost control. To set budgets, managers need information about previous spending and about new plans and objectives. Budgetary information, in turn, permits managers to optimize their resources within prescribed limits.

First Union Bank of Asheville has completely changed the way it delivers services to its customers as a way of controlling costs.

> Customers entering the branch in Arden, a blue-collar suburb of Asheville, are greeted by a new look. The space has been redesigned, walls knocked out to create open areas, and desks repositioned to seem less intimidating. Telephones link to First Union's service center outside Charlotte, the bank's base. The branch's automated teller machines (ATMs) have been enhanced to offer such services as instant check-cashing, mini-statements of recent transactions, split deposits (the ability to send, say $100 to one account and $50 to another while making a single deposit) and coin facilities. Customers get another dose of novelty when they are approached by a "customer relationship manager" (CRM), who asks what they want to do. If the transaction can be done electronically or remotely, the CRM politely shows the customer a faster alternative to standing in a queue for a human teller.[32]

Improving Quality. Having a reputation for quality offers a strategic advantage for any organization. Consumers will usually pay more for a product or service that they know always meets their expectations than one whose quality varies. Improving quality also decreases costs by reducing waste, eliminating rework, and permitting more orderly processing.

Achieving quality requires production workers to have constant feedback about the production process so that they can spot problems immediately and correct them. In the past, systems were built so that production workers collected and entered data about production but did not have immediate access to analyses performed on the

In turn, Wackenhut uses those statistics when bidding on new contracts. This helps demonstrate its fulfillment of regulatory responsibilities and dramatize the superior quality of the inmate services it can provide.

Case Questions

Diagnosis

1. What information needs does a prison have?
2. How have these needs changed over time?

Evaluation

3. What types of information systems do prisons use?
4. How well do these systems meet their needs?

Design

5. What changes in information systems would benefit prisons?
6. How would these changes better meet their needs?

Implementation

7. What implementation issues do prisons face?
8. What factors affect the cost-effectiveness of information systems in prisons?

ACTIVITY 2.1 RECRUITING AT COMMUNITY UNIVERSITY

Step 1: Read the following scenario:

The graduate business school at Community University recently experienced significant declines in the number of inquiries and applicants for both its full-time and part-time M.B.A. programs. The recently hired director of admissions, Susan Sellers, believed that the decline resulted in part from the decreasing interest in management education. Sellers also believed that the decline could be attributed to a lack of a clear strategy for selling the program. She intended to change the recruiting focus from students with business undergraduate degrees to recent graduates with a liberal arts background and significant work experience.

Sellers planned to use a large part of her budget to improve the information systems in the admissions office. Her initial step was to identify the particular information needs of the new strategic direction of the admissions process.

Step 2: Individually or in small groups, develop a list of information Susan Sellers needs to support the new recruiting strategy.

Step 3: In small groups or with the entire class, share the list you have developed. Then answer the following questions:

1. What are the information needs of the new recruiting strategy?
2. How can the organization satisfy these needs?

SAVING JOBS AT MANSFIELD UNIVERSITY   ACTIVITY 2.2

Step 1:   Mansfield University has decided to redesign all of its business processes over the next three years, automating as many as possible by using advanced technologies. The university's goals in the redesign, known as Project Millennium, include improving service to students and their families and reducing costs.

You are the vice president for human resources at Mansfield. You have just returned from a meeting at which you were asked to lead an effort to reduce the number of employees by 20 percent as part of Project Millennium. Although you know that the redesign will improve the university and help guarantee its success over the next decades, you feel that cutting jobs in this way is not ethical. What should you do?

Step 2:   Individually or in small groups, analyze the situation using the basic ethical criteria.

Step 3:   Based on your analysis, develop an action plan. Share the action plan with the rest of the class.

INCREASING THE COMPETITIVE ADVANTAGE   ACTIVITY 2.3

Step 1:   Read the descriptions of the situations that follow. For each situation, offer two strategies for increasing the organization's competitive advantage over others in its industry. Then list three types of information required to implement each strategy.

Problem 1:   Stable pricing is difficult for restaurants like Red Lobster that specialize in such foods as crabmeat or shrimp, where costs are volatile. Customers react unfavorably to frequent changes in menu prices; therefore, the restaurant must protect itself against overpricing and losing customers or underpricing and losing margins. How can Red Lobster use information to maintain a competitive advantage?

Problem 2:   The owner of a small manufacturer of digital scales has recently exhibited his product at a trade show in Germany. He has also begun to speak with representatives of the Chamber of Commerce in several small towns in Ireland about the issues associated with opening a manufacturing plant in their town. How can the company use information to increase its competitive advantage?

Problem 3:   A small real estate office that had specialized in residential properties recently began to list a small number of commercial properties. It also began a trial membership in a national network of real estate offices. The consortium provides national advertising and referrals as well as assists in human resource functions such as payroll, training, and recruiting. How can the small real estate office use information to further develop a competitive advantage over other real estate offices?

Step 2: In small groups, compile the strategies that organizations can use to attain a competitive advantage. Then list the types of information required to implement these strategies.

Step 3: Individually, in small groups, or with the entire class, answer the following questions:

1. In what ways can an organization increase its competitive advantage?
2. What types of information are required to do this?
3. How can the organizations secure this information?
4. What role can information systems play in providing the needed information?

ACTIVITY 2.4   ASSESSING THE QUALITY OF INFORMATION

Step 1: Individually or in small groups, design a questionnaire to assess how well an organization's information meets the criteria of low cost, accessibility, reliability, and security.

Step 2: Select a department in your college or university or in an organization of your choice, and administer the questionnaire to two or three members of that organization.

Step 3: Tabulate the results.

Step 4: Individually, in small groups, or with the entire class, share your results. Next, list the conclusions you can draw from the data. Then answer the following questions:

1. How well does organizational information meet the criteria of low cost, accessibility, reliability, and security?
2. What two recommendations would you offer for improving the quality of the organization's information?

ACTIVITY 2.5   SWOT ANALYSIS AND INFORMATION

Step 1: Individually, in twos, or in threes, choose a local business to analyze.

Step 2: Locate four sources of information about the company.

Step 3: Using the information, list three of each of the following:

Strengths: _____

Weaknesses: _____

Threats: _____

Opportunities: _____

Step 4: In small groups, list the types and sources of data you used to perform the SWOT analysis.

Step 5: With the entire class, formulate a comprehensive list of the sources and types of data used to perform a SWOT analysis. Then answer the following questions:

1. Which sources provided the most useful data? The least useful data?
2. What other information would be helpful in doing the SWOT analysis?
3. How could computerized information systems assist with the SWOT analysis?

RECOMMENDED READINGS

Granrose, Cherlyn S., and Oskamp, Stuart (eds.). *Cross-Cultural Work Groups.* Thousand Oaks, CA: Sage, 1997.

Mankin, Donald A., Cohen, Susan G., and Bikson, Tora K. *Fulfilling the Promise of the New Organization.* Boston: Harvard Business School Press, 1996.

Miles, Raymond, and Snow, Charles C. *Fit, Failure, and the Hall of Fame: How Companies Succeed or Fail.* New York: The Free Press, 1995.

NOTES

1. John Bell, Building the new Chrysler, *Industry Week* (September 16, 1996): 10–15; Joseph Maglitta, Infrastructure: Project: Chrysler Corp., *Computerworld* (October 28, 1996): B6.
2. Polly LaBarre, The seamless enterprise, *Industry Week* (June 19, 1995): 22–34.
3. Stratford Sherman, Secrets of HP's 'muddled team,' *Fortune* (March 18, 1996): 116–120.
4. Marianne Kolbasuk McGee, Staffing—Just don't call them TEMPS—Record numbers of IS managers, tired of searching for experienced workers, are turning to temporary staffing agencies, *InformationWeek* (May 12, 1997) http://www.techweb.com/se/directlink.cgi?IWK19970512S0051.
5. Joseph Maglita, Smarten up!, *Computerworld* (June 5, 1995): 84–86; Alice LaPlante, Sharing the wisdom, *Computerworld* (June 2, 1997): 73–74.
6. Michael Goldberg, Iceberg meltdown slips up Registry, *Computerworld* (May 20, 1996): 1, 16.
7. Neal Weinberg, Law firm thrives on bleeding edge, *Computerworld* (September 25, 1995): 73, 80.
8. Tony Dollar, An alliance eclipses competition, *Distribution* 94 (November 1995): 52–58.
9. Barbara DePompa, Sharing the cost of recovery, *InformationWeek* (September 9, 1996): 146–150.
10. J. Y. Bakos, Information links and electronic marketplaces: The role of interorganizational information systems in vertical markets, *Journal of Management Information Systems* 8(2) (Fall 1991): 31–52.

Piet Mondrian, *Tableau No. IV: Lozenge Composition with Red, Gray, Blue, Yellow, and Black*. 1924–25. Gift of Herbert and Nannette Rothschild. Photograph © 1998 Board of Trustees, National Gallery of Art, Washington.

II

EVALUATING INFORMATION TECHNOLOGIES

Managers use information technology—computer hardware, software, and telecommunications networks—to meet their information needs. Although managers can no longer expect to have the technical expertise required to design, select, or install information technology, they should have enough knowledge to ask specialists key questions and provide relevant information for selecting the best information technology to meet their information needs. Part II provides such an overview of information technology. Chapter 3 examines computer hardware—the physical equipment used for data input, processing data, storing data, and output. Chapter 4 investigates computer software—the instructions that command a computer to perform a desired task. It discusses horizontal and vertical business application software, computer languages, and systems software. Chapter 5 considers database management systems. Specifically it looks at the uses, development, and technological underpinnings of database management systems, as well as ways of using data effectively. Chapter 6 explores internal computer networks. It describes the uses and types of networks, the communication infrastructure, network management, and international data communication. Chapter 7 considers the Internet and other external networks. It discusses the use and technological underpinnings of the Internet and ways of using, developing, and managing Web sites.

Chapter 3

Hardware Technology

CHAPTER OUTLINE

LEARNING OBJECTIVES

After completing Chapter 3, you will be able to

1. Identify the major types of hardware.
2. Describe how manufacturers package hardware by size and function.
3. Contrast active and passive data entry.
4. Describe how a processor performs its work.
5. Describe six ways of comparing a computer's processing power.
6. Describe Moore's law and discuss its implications.
7. Compare and contrast the uses and characteristics of primary and secondary storage devices.
8. Describe the types of primary and secondary storage devices.
9. Discuss ways of measuring the quality of graphics output.
10. Describe three soft-copy and five hard-copy devices.

REENGINEERING THE METROPOLITAN DOVAY POLICE DEPARTMENT

Two years ago, while running for mayor of Dovay, a metropolis of four million people, June Allain pledged to reengineer city services. She claimed that Dovay's government was bloated and inefficient. On winning the election, Allain reaffirmed her commitment to reengineering. She immediately demanded a review of her executive office procedures, and then she began implementing change. Soon, other city departments began to follow her lead.

Albert Duval, director of operations of the Metropolitan Dovay Police Department, was not surprised when the police commissioner asked him to review the department's systems and practices. "We need to trim $20 to $25 million a year from the police budget while improving services," the commissioner had said. Duval felt that these goals could be achieved, but not without investing substantially in new equipment. The commissioner indicated that he could find funding for capital improvement if "it would make us lean and efficient."

Duval felt that much of the inefficiency in the department's current practices resulted from bad systems for maintaining records. The police collected the same data over and over again, wasting time and often obtaining conflicting information. He knew that there were times when the police could not find records rapidly enough, if at all. It would certainly help, Duval thought, if he could propose changes to reduce the administrative burden and get the police back to doing police work.

The department maintained its information on a Unisys Corporation A16 dual-processor mainframe, and 715 dumb terminals provided access. The computer

Police departments increasingly rely on information technology to support their work activities. They use computerized systems to maintain up-to-date records, such as outstanding warrants, traffic violations, fingerprint information, and crime scene information.

seemed to be powerful enough for most of the department's needs, however it was not able to accommodate some of the improvements that Duval had suggested in the past, such as equipping detectives and beat officers with mobile terminals.

Duval also thought that the use of graphics could make a big difference. Current emergency dispatch systems identify only the address of incoming calls. Dispatchers were trained to know the city well, but none could precisely locate every address in the city. Furthermore, dispatchers had only a vague knowledge of where patrol cars were located at any point in time. Systems showing a map and the precise location of cars would greatly reduce response time and would also likely reduce the number of cars needed for patrol. Processing mug shots, fingerprints, and other graphic input would be useful if it could be kept in a database accessible by police personnel.[1]

Duval will work with computer professionals to determine whether the department can modify its computer systems to meet the new demands. Duval needs a basic understanding of hardware so he can effectively work with these professionals to evaluate existing and alternative systems. In this chapter we first define hardware by discussing the types of hardware and ways of packaging it. In the rest of the chapter we explore the hardware used for data input, processing, storage, and output.

WHAT IS HARDWARE?

Computer **hardware** is the physical equipment used to process information. It includes all the components inside the box that we call a computer. It also includes **peripheral devices**—those devices attached to a computer, such as keyboards, video units, printers, and scanners—that collect, display, communicate, and store data.

Not all computer hardware actually processes information. For example, a **power supply** regulates the voltage and amperage supplied to other components within the computer. A box called a cabinet holds the computer devices. In this chapter, however, we focus only on hardware that is directly related to processing information.

TYPES OF HARDWARE

Figure 3.1 provides a conceptual illustration of a computer and its peripheral devices. Managers often make choices about purchasing or upgrading each of these components after diagnosing their needs and evaluating available computer hardware.

- **Processing hardware** controls the peripheral devices, as directed by computer software (see Chapter 4).
- The **data bus,** the electrical connection between various parts of the computer, manages the flow of data between the processing hardware and the rest of the

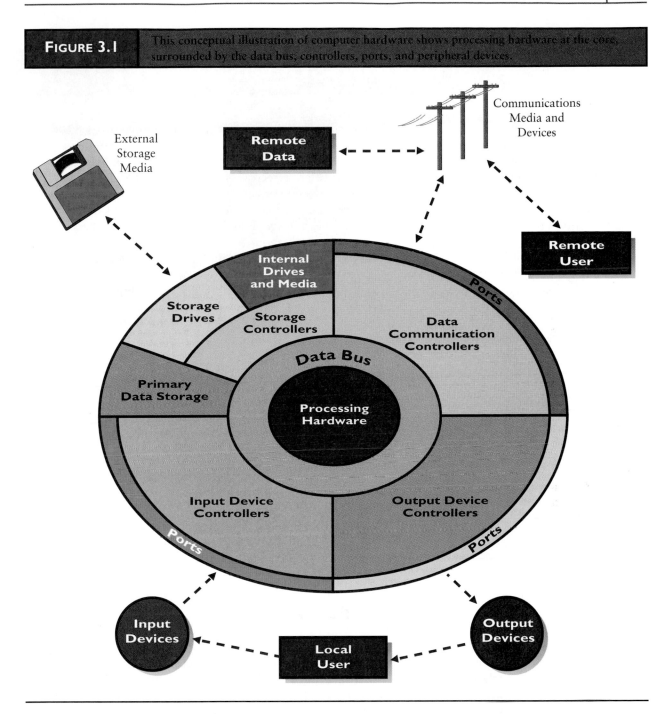

FIGURE 3.1 This conceptual illustration of computer hardware shows processing hardware at the core, surrounded by the data bus, controllers, ports, and peripheral devices.

computer. The processing hardware puts information in the form of electrical signals on the bus to direct the other devices and accepts information from the bus to determine the state of the devices and to acquire information that may come as input from them. Some computers have additional specialized buses to provide faster connections to certain devices.

ETHICAL ISSUES IN IT

Think of computer security threats, and things such as Internet hacking and password cracking likely come to mind. But at Levi Strauss & Co., sensitive data apparently fell victim to a screwdriver. A hard disk containing the names, birth dates, and Social Security numbers of thousands of employees was stolen from the apparel maker's San Francisco headquarters.

Company officials, who don't know if the disk was swiped for its information or simply for the hardware, had to warn 20,000 of its U.S. employees that thieves might have their personal data. They could use that information to apply for fraudulent credit cards in the employees' names or gain access to other information about them. And the stolen hard disk contained bank account numbers for retired workers who opted for direct-deposit pension checks.

"If you have a stupid criminal, it's a $200 theft. If you have a smart criminal, you have a [potential] $200 million crime," said Ira Winkler, director of technology at the National Computer Security Association in Carlisle, Pa., and author of the recently published *Corporate Espionage*. Fraudulent credit-card numbers are worth about $5,000 on the street, and a criminal gang could apply for two illegal cards in each name.

Theft of computers and components has always been a problem, but experts say companies need to pay more attention to physically safeguarding valuable data residing on their hardware and not just the equipment. Levi Strauss could quickly restore the data and buy a new hard disk. But notifying thousands of workers, sending out special information packets, and

- **Controllers** or **adaptors** reside inside the computer and convert commands and data from the data bus into signals that peripheral devices can use.
- A **port,** an opening in the computer that accepts a specially configured connector, and a cable connect a device outside a computer to its controller. Some devices, such as computer screens on portable computers, connect directly to their controllers without a port or cable.

PACKAGING HARDWARE

Computer systems differ in the power and features of the hardware they contain. Computer manufacturers package various input, processing, storage, output, and telecommunications hardware into a single computer model to sell to a particular market segment. We can classify these models and the market segments they represent along the dimensions of size and function.

Size. We categorize computer systems as mainframe, midrange, and microcomputers, as shown in Figure 3.2. Although the placement of a particular computer into one of these categories is somewhat arbitrary, they differ in the amount of data they can readily process, their power, and their cost.

Mainframe systems handle the massive data processing needs of the largest organizations. They can handle hundreds of transactions per second as well as the data

setting up a toll-free hot line for concerned employees cost considerably more.

"This is one of the things we've been trying to tell people for years," said James Wade, director of fraud management at Airtouch Cellular Corp. in Columbus, Ohio, and past president of the Information Systems and Security Association. If a company has strong network security and password protection, "people will eventually figure out it's easier to pick up a screwdriver," he said. "They will find those things you're not looking for."

Data on a machine can be worth substantially more than the hardware itself—if the thief knows about it. A laptop stolen from the British Defense Ministry in the early 1990s had the entire Desert Storm war plan on it. The theft caused a furor among NATO allies, Wade said.

But it is believed that data was never used and the computer was stolen simply as hardware.

"[Data theft from stolen hardware] happens a lot more frequently than companies report," Winkler said. "Every security manager I have ever spoken to tells me how they lose PCs on a regular basis."

1. What responsibility do companies have to safeguard data?
2. Did Levi Strauss & Company act ethically?
3. What ethical issues does hardware theft create?

SOURCE: Extracted from: Sharon Machlis, Levi Strauss caught with its pants down, *Computerworld* (May 5, 1997): 1.

analysis and word processing needs of thousands of employees. They have extremely quick and powerful processors and can store massive amounts of data. They often use dedicated subcomputers to handle their input and output.

Midrange computers meet the needs of smaller companies or departments in larger companies. They have less power, less data processing capability, and a lower cost than mainframes.

Microcomputers, the small computers at the other end of the scale, include **personal computers (PCs)** as well as small processors specialized for other tasks. They have the lowest cost and easily fit on a desktop. Although their power does not approximate that of midrange or mainframe computers, they have more than adequate power to perform the work activities of most office staff. They can also support some manufacturing and design functions as well as provide easy access to the Internet. The Unisys computer in Dovay's police department is considered a small mainframe even though it serves only a department. Dovay's police department is as large as many midsized companies, and 715 terminals is a lot for one computer to handle.

Function.   Computer systems perform a range of applications, and managers help choose hardware that best fits their specific application. Desktop computers designed for personal and office computing can run office automation applications and the user-interface side of most business applications. Typically, microcomputers fill these roles adequately.

Microcomputers used for mobile computing are packaged to be more rugged, to be lighter, and to use less power. They may also have different communication

FIGURE 3.2 Computer systems vary in size, from mainframe to midrange to microcomputers.

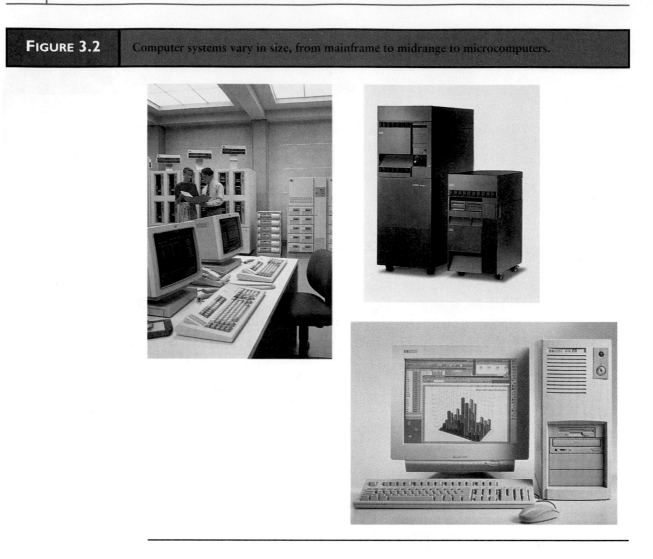

hardware, including equipment that enables communication over cellular telephone connections. A rechargeable battery provides their power. Mobile computers, shown in Figure 3.3, vary in weight and size.

- **Laptop computers** weigh under ten pounds and fold into a unit the size of a small briefcase or smaller. The Dovay's police officers could use laptop computers in their cars but would find them too cumbersome to carry and use if they had to leave the car. Although you can operate a laptop computer in your lap (as its name implies), most people find it easier to use on a desk or table.
- **Notebook computers** are thin, lightweight laptops that fold into a unit the size of a notebook and generally weigh less than seven pounds.
- **Subnotebook computers** are ultralight, typically weighing between two and four pounds. The market, which changes constantly as technology improves, defines the difference between a notebook and a subnotebook.
- **Handheld** or **palmtop computers** typically weigh about a pound but may be as small as a credit card. They generally have less storage and so have less

FIGURE 3.3   Mobile computers vary in weight and size, from laptops to palmtops. Police departments increasingly rely on information technology to support their work activities.

functionality. Dovay police officers would be able to carry palmtops in their pockets and would use a pen to enter data. They could use the computers' cellular communication features to relay data to the home office. They could also plug the computers into **docking stations** in their offices. These special ports on desktop computers can transfer data between mobile and desktop units.

A **workstation**, which sometimes refers to any desktop computer, more commonly describes a powerful single-user computer used for engineering and for executive support. These systems typically incorporate high-end microprocessors and 19-inch or 20-inch screens with very high resolution. Some may have two screens—one for selecting and showing commands and another for viewing the output. Some workstations have no permanent or removable storage, relying instead on a data communication network for their programs and data files. Duval and the computer professionals must determine the type of workstations needed by the police department staff. The Dovay dispatchers likely will need workstations that can simultaneously show the location of police cars on a detailed map, look up the addresses of incoming calls based on their phone numbers, and enter data from the caller into the database.

Scientific computers help scientists to build and run complicated mathematical models. These computers come in a variety of models depending on the power they provide. Typically the most powerful scientific computers can outperform even the largest business mainframes. However, scientific computers cannot easily support the high level of input and output that business mainframes support nor do they have the large amounts of storage that business mainframes need.

Computers of varying sizes also act as **servers**. Companies use file servers to store the files for their network, print servers to control their network's printers, and database servers to meet their database needs. Microcomputer manufacturers have adapted their personal computer designs to include more storage and more powerful controllers for input and output. Mainframe manufacturers have entered the server market, particularly the database server market, by carefully packaging their hardware. Executives in the Dovay Police Department must decide whether to retain their existing Unisys mainframe as the department's main file and database server or to substitute or add smaller servers. The department likely will base its decision on the cost of replacement and continued operation as well as the availability of software to meet its needs.

HARDWARE FOR DATA INPUT

Input hardware consists of devices that send signals to a computer. These devices allow people to communicate with computers and allow computers to sense their environment. In this section, we examine the uses and types of input devices that managers might choose as they design computer systems to meet their needs.

USES OF INPUT HARDWARE

Input hardware gets information into the computer. It performs three types of tasks, which can occur on mainframe, midrange, or microcomputers: interactive dialogue, active data entry, and passive data entry.

Interactive Dialogue. An employee is engaging in **interactive dialogue** when she uses an input device to send messages to the computer about actions she would like to take. For example, the computer presents the employee with a menu of choices and she selects a word-processing program. Many desktops have icons that represent applications. The user directs the computer by selecting the appropriate icon.

Active Data Entry. With **active data entry,** the employee enters data, often from written records, directly into a computer. Metropolitan Dovay police inspectors might use a keyboard to enter data collected at the scene of a crime, such as the names, phone numbers, and statements of witnesses and descriptions and inventory of evidence.

Passive Data Entry. With **passive data entry,** the computer obtains information without the active participation of a user. For example, as a car passes through an automatic toll booth without paying, a video device could read its license plate and record it electronically. A computer system could then read such data, identify repeat offenders, and fine them.

TYPES OF INPUT HARDWARE

Input hardware devices use the following technologies to recognize data: keyboards, pointing devices, readers of formatted input, graphic scanners, video input devices, microphones, and sensors. Often a number of different technologies can accomplish similar input objectives. Managers select a device for an application based on its performance rather than its technological design.

Keyboards.   A **keyboard** consists of a plastic or metal housing containing keys that when pressed send a signal to the computer. Every key sends a different signal. People use keyboards for both interactive dialogue and active data entry.

Figure 3.4 illustrates two common types of keyboards: data processing keyboards and point-of-sale keyboards. General-purpose computing requires data processing keyboards. You'll find this type on most personal computers. Computers dedicated to sales order processing and some other single applications might use point-of-sale keyboards. These keyboards usually have two areas, one for numeric data entry and one for registering sales of different products. At Burger King or McDonald's, for example, one key may represent the sale of a chicken sandwich whereas another key may represent the sale of a fish sandwich.

Data processing keyboards differ in the arrangement of their keys and the design of their surface.

- *QWERTY Keyboards.* Named for the arrangement of letters on their second row, QWERTY keyboards are the most popular. Also used for typewriters, they were designed to slow down a typist so that the mechanical devices on the typewriter would not become entangled.

- *Dvorak Keyboards.* Designed by August Dvorak in 1930, Dvorak keyboards are arranged so that the most commonly used letters are on the middle row of keys. Figure 3.5 compares Dvorak and QWERTY keyboards. The Dvorak keyboard increases speed and reduces fatigue and hand stress. Experts have estimated that the fingers on a typist's hands travel an average of 16 miles a day on a QWERTY keyboard but only 1 mile on a Dvorak keyboard.[2]

FIGURE 3.4   People use data processing keyboards for most computer work. Sales people use point of sale terminals for registering customer sales.

FIGURE 3.5 Most people learn to type on QWERTY keyboards, but Dvorak keyboards increase typing speed by placing the most commonly used letters in the home hand position.

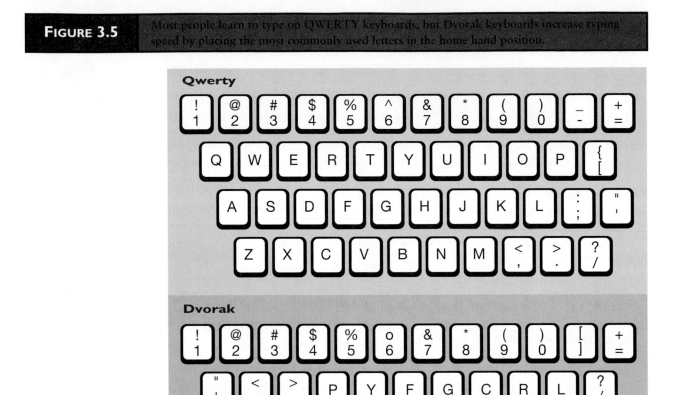

- *Ergonomic Keyboards.* To reduce stress, ergonomic keyboards are designed so that users can rest their hands more comfortably and strike keys without twisting their wrists (see Figure 3.6).

Pointing Devices. A variety of devices exist that allow users to enter data or control the movement of a **cursor,** or pointer, on the screen by moving, touching, or positioning a pointing device.

- *Mouse.* A user operates a mouse (see Figure 3.7), the most popular pointing device for desktop computers, by placing his hand on it and rolling it across a tabletop or other surface. As the mouse moves, it sends a signal about its direction and amount of movement to the computer. The computer processes this signal and moves an arrow or some other pointing symbol in parallel on the screen. A mouse also has two or three buttons that a user can "click" to send additional signals to the computer.

FIGURE 3.6	Ergonomic keyboards reduce the incidence of carpal tunnel syndrome by reducing stress on the wrists.

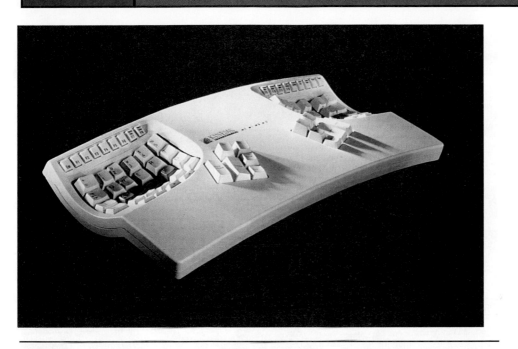

FIGURE 3.7	Most desktop computers are equipped with a mouse, a popular, easy-to-use pointing device. Some mouses, called bats, don't have tails.

- *Trackball.* A **trackball** (see Figure 3.8), popular for mobile computing, differs from a mouse in that the user rotates rather than moves it. A user can operate a trackball with a single finger, making it possible to use a trackball without lifting one's hand from the computer.

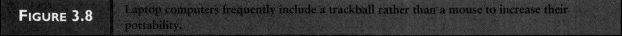

FIGURE 3.8 Laptop computers frequently include a trackball rather than a mouse to increase their portability.

- *Joystick.* A **joystick** (see Figure 3.9) acts as a steering device. The user pushes the stick in the direction of the desired movement and releases the stick to stop movement. Often, the speed of movement depends on the pressure placed on the stick. Joysticks are popular for computer games, but they are also used on mobile computers because the user can move the cursor with a single finger while keeping the hands on the keyboard.

- *Light Pen.* A **light pen** (see Figure 3.10) consists of a stylus that transmits a narrow light beam to a transparent sensor overlaying the surface of a computer screen. The device transmits a signal to the computer indicating where the light beam touches the screen. Compared to a mouse, trackball, and joystick, a light pen has the advantage of directly identifying a point on the screen without having to move and stop a cursor. But, like a mouse, the user needs to lift her hand off the keyboard to operate it, and when used on an upright screen, this causes arm fatigue. The light pen works well for capturing handwriting on handheld computers.

- *Touch Screen.* A **touch screen** (see Figure 3.11) is a transparent surface overlaying a computer screen. When someone touches it with a finger or a stylus, it sends a signal to the computer indicating the point of contact. Finger-based systems work well for public-access systems because they have no moving parts

FIGURE 3.9 People use a joystick as a steering device when they play computer games or use some types of mobile computers.

 **FIGURE 3.10** An employee uses a light pen to write on a computer screen.

FIGURE 3.11   A mechanic uses a touch screen to simplify data entry in tight spaces. A UPS signature recorder is a touch screen that responds to a pen-shaped stylus.

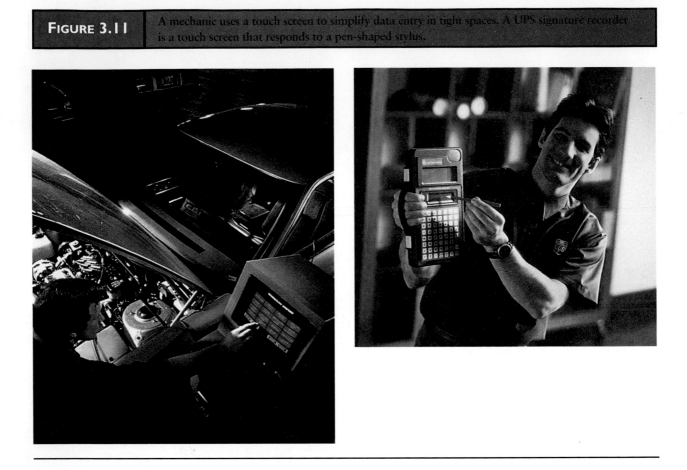

and novice users can easily operate them. Stylus-based systems work better where more accuracy is desired, such as for handwriting and drawing. United Parcel Service uses stylus-based touch screens to record the signatures of its parcel recipients. Long Beach Memorial Medical Center in Long Beach, California, mounted touch-screen displays with virtual keyboards on the walls of hallways, patient rooms, and operating rooms. [3]

- *Touch pad.* A **touch pad** (see Figure 3.12), popular for mobile computers, is a pressure-sensitive input device placed on a keyboard. The user controls a cursor on the screen by moving his thumb along the touch pad. A touch pad is small, has no moving parts, and allows the user to control the position of the cursor without lifting his fingers from the keyboard.

Readers of Formatted Input.   **Readers of formatted input** read text specially formatted for the device in use, as shown in Figure 3.13. They include bar-code readers, mark sense readers, and magnetic ink character readers. Most of these devices support passive input, and managers such as Albert Duval need to explore possible uses for them. These devices can capture lots of data quickly, but they can only read appropriately formatted text or data.

FIGURE 3.12 Touch pads simplify pointing control on mobile computers. The user positions the cursor with her thumbs without lifting her hands from the keyboard.

FIGURE 3.12 Touch pads simplify pointing control on mobile computers. The user positions the cursor with her thumbs without lifting her hands from the keyboard.

Bar-code readers have the broadest market acceptance of the readers of formatted input. The bar code in Figure 3.14 represents a UPC (Universal Product Code), a standard adopted by retailers worldwide. Bar-code readers capture data quickly, cheaply, easily, and relatively accurately. Prices depend on a variety of factors such as size, reading speed, portability, how close the device has to be to a bar code to read it, and its sensitivity to low light. Upcoming two-dimensional bar codes will significantly increase the amount of information that a bar code contains.[4]

The Dovay police might use bar codes to tag their evidence. They might also code the shelves in their evidence room. The officer placing evidence into the evidence room would then use a bar-code scanner to associate the evidence tag with the shelf tag. The police would use a similar procedure when removing evidence from the evidence room to reduce the amount of lost evidence. The crime record would include the location of all evidence associated with any crime file.

Graphics Scanners. **Graphics scanners** input pictures and other graphics into a computer after first converting them into a numeric format that the computer can process. Scanners differ in their ability to capture detail, the number of colors or scales of gray they support, and the number of pages they can scan in a minute. Low-end scanners produce only black and white input and require the user to manually move the device over a page. More expensive scanners have a sheet feeder, read at least six pages per minute, and provide a resolution of over 600 dots per inch. Flat-bed scanners scan books, magazines, and other media that cannot be fed through a sheet feeder (see Figure 3.15).

The inability of software to mimic human abilities in processing graphical images limits the effectiveness of graphics scanners. To use scanners as an input

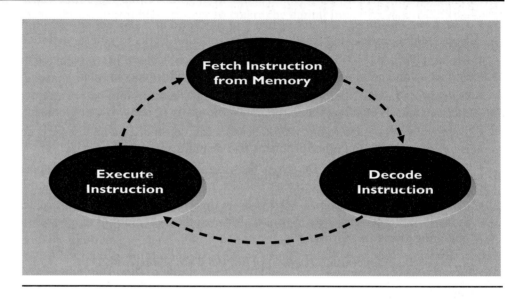

what the instruction tells it to do. Finally, it executes the instruction. The processor repeats the three steps of fetch, decode, and execute until someone turns off the power.

MEASURING PROCESSING POWER

A manager who purchases a computer needs to understand how computer professionals talk about computer processing power so that he can evaluate and trade-off price against performance. Duval will tell the Dovay Police Department's computer professionals what response time his employees want. Because a variety of processors might achieve the desired performance, Duval must understand the alternatives to make sensible decisions.

Managers and computer professionals can't evaluate a processor on its specifications alone for several reasons. First, no single measure of processor power exists; rather several characteristics determine a processor's effective power. Second, processors differ in speed and capability depending on the task they perform. Finally, the input, storage, and output devices that surround a processor will influence its power. You can best evaluate a computer by using it for a sample of tasks similar to those that it will perform. You can also use the six characteristics shown in Table 3.2 to assess a computer's processing power.

CHOOSING PARALLEL PROCESSING

Managers who work with employees who solve complex problems may choose hardware with parallel processing. **Parallel processing** uses two or more processors in a single computer. These processors either share a common bus and devices or

TABLE 3.2 Six different measures reflect the processing power of a computer.

Clock Speed	Speed of Arithmetic
• The number of pulses (Hertz) per second measure clock speed; most computers operate at more than 150 megahertz. An electronic circuit called a "clock" emits a regular or electronic beat or pulse that synchronizes the operation of the processor. With each pulse the processor performs one operation, such as fetching or decoding. Some operations, particularly the execution of complex instructions, may take several pulses.	• The megaflop (millions of floating point operations per second) measures arithmetic prowess. Computers use more than a single clock cycle to perform an arithmetic operation. Floating point arithmetic—calculations with numbers having a decimal point and stored in exponential format—consume the most time.
Instruction Speed	**Instruction Set**
• MIPS (millions of instructions per second) measures instruction speed for a given processor type. Instruction speed usually varies directly with the clock speed. A 200 megahertz Pentium will have twice the MIPS of a 100 megahertz Pentium. You can therefore use MIPS and clock speed interchangeably when comparing similar processors. To compare different processors, you should use MIPS rather than clock speed because one type of processor may average one instruction every 1.5 cycles while another averages one instruction every 2 cycles.	• The number of instructions a processor can decode and execute. Until the late 1980s, experts believed that the more instructions a processor could decode and execute, the greater its power. Complex instructions, however, require that many more cycles be performed than are required for simple instructions, so they reduce a computer's effective speed relative to its clock speed. Reduced instruction set computing (RISC) processors understand only a few instructions but execute them faster than traditional complex instruction set computing (CISC) processors. For example, a 200 MIPS RISC processor may perform tasks no faster than a 150 MIPS CISC processor.
Word Length and Bus Width	**Pipelining**
• The word length, or the number of bits a computer can process at one time, is usually at least 32 for personal computers and 64 for mainframes. Its bus width refers to the number of bits a computer can move at one time from one area of memory to another and is generally less than word length. Doubling the word length will more than double the speed of certain arithmetic operations, such as multiplying large numbers. It will also increase the amount of memory that the processor can address directly. Doubling the bus width will double the speed of moving characters from one area of memory to another.	• A processor's ability to overlap the fetching, decoding, and executing of different instructions. A processor with pipelining will operate faster that one without it. While a pipelined processor decodes one instruction, it simultaneously fetches a second instruction. Then, while it executes the first instruction, it decodes the second and fetches a third.

operate more independently. A parallel processing computer overcomes limits in the speed of any one processor by dividing the work among its processors.

Symmetric multiprocessing (SMP) systems combine multiple processors in a computer with a common bus and common input, output, and storage devices. In massively parallel processor (MPP) computers, which connect tens or hundreds of processors, each processor or SMP-processor group has its own bus, memory, and

ADVANCED TECHNOLOGY

We can build computers powerful enough to simulate a nuclear explosion, but even our most whizbang machines still can't calculate fast enough to predict tomorrow's weather.

Here's the problem: Today's computers still do their calculating sequentially, counting on their digital fingers and chewing on one bit of information before moving at light speed to the next one. Even "massively parallel" supercomputers—machines built with myriad processors to strip apart a problem and mull it over in chunks—can't hack through science's most cosmic problems fast enough to be useful. Why bother asking the fastest supercomputer a question if it's still going to take centuries to spit out a response?

But a quantum computer—an entirely different animal altogether, one that does its figuring in the subatomic world—now that would be fast. A quantum computer could take a question and examine all possible answers—the right ones and the wrong ones—virtually at

once. In theory anyway, the right answers would rise to the top like cream on milk, ready for the skimming.

If only researchers could figure out how to build one.

They're working on it. While quantum computers once were a philosophical conundrum mulled over by theoretical physicists over a round of beers after work, they recently have come under increasingly intense professional attention. One proposal even theorizes that such a computer could do its calculating inside a mug of coffee.

No one laughs anymore at the idea that researchers here and elsewhere may one day build this fanciful machine.

SOURCE: Extracted from Janet Rae Dupree, A quantum leap: Computer researchers really think about getting small, *Mercury News* (March 4, 1997). http://www.sjmercury. com/ news/scitech/quantum/quantum.htm.

copy of the operating system. MPP systems connect tens or even hundreds of processors in this fashion.

Although MPP manufacturers originally targeted scientists, many business applications can take advantage of the MPP's parallel construction. Manufacturers have shown that MPP computers make excellent managers of data warehouses.[8] Charles Schwab & Company, Inc., the first major financial services firm to offer trading on the Internet, used IBM's MPP RS/6000 SP computer to handle the high volume of electronic-trade transactions at its Web site.[9] United Airlines uses the same computer with 30 to 64 processors operating in parallel to perform calculations and analyses to determine how many seats United should make available for special fares. United estimates that it can generate $50 million more in revenue per year by using this computer.[10]

SPECIALIZED PROCESSORS

Specialized processors respond to a limited set of commands to perform highly specialized tasks. They lack the capacity to accept a programmer's directions on how to manipulate data. Because their instructions have been "hard wired" into their chips, and their chips have been optimized for their designed tasks, specialized processors can perform these tasks more quickly than general-purpose processors.

- An **image compressor** recognizes similarities among parts of a digitized image and among sequential frames of a moving image. It helps to process, store, and transmit images more quickly by reducing the amount of data needed to represent an image to between 1/50th and 1/200th of the amount needed without compression.[11] Inexpensive boards combining digitizers and image compressors, for example, can capture video in 320-by-240 dot resolution at 30 frames per second.[12] A variety of compression exist, such as MPEG, which is used for moving pictures.

- **Graphics processors** rapidly manipulate images—rotate them, zoom in and out, present appropriate views of three-dimensional objects, color regions, and detect and draw edges.

- **Voice processors** can translate sound-wave inputs into sound-groups called phonemes and then into written words. They can increase the intelligibility and amplification of voice communications. They can also digitize and reproduce audio stored in computer files.

- A **digital signal processor** or **DSP** (see Figure 3.18) converts an electronic wave signal, such as one arising from sound or other sensory inputs, into a stream of digital bits and vice versa. DSP applications include digitally encoding cellular telephone transmissions to prevent eavesdropping and increase clarity, modifying recorded music to sound as if it were recorded in a specific concert hall, suppressing noise from vehicles and appliances by generating sounds that will cancel the offending sounds, recognizing phone numbers spoken aloud and automatically dialing them, recognizing military objects from their radar signals, and avoiding aircraft collisions by responding to radar and visual signals.[13]

FIGURE 3.18 Digital signal processors, such as this one, provide processing power for applications such as computer graphics, image processing, modems, and cellular telephones standard.

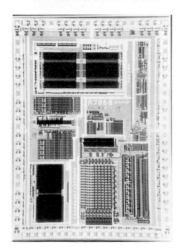

Main processors can off-load work onto a variety of specialized processors, such as a graphics processor, to increase their efficiency. Some specialized processors, such as those that handle input or output, can achieve further efficiencies by performing tasks while the main processor independently acts on the next set of instructions. Modern processors now perform many of the tasks previously relegated to specialized processors. For example, the Pentium MMX and Pentium Pro processors provide functions that previously required special floating-point and graphics processors.

PROCESSING TRENDS

Computer processing power, as measured by MIPS (millions of instructions per second) for newly introduced processors has increased at a rate of about 20 percent a year for mainframes and 25 percent a year for microcomputers and minicomputers. At this rate, processing power doubles every three or four years and increases by a factor of ten every ten to twelve years. Because the price of state-of-the-art processors has not changed much within each category, the price of an MIP has dropped about 20 percent per year. This exponential increase in processing power reflects Moore's Law, a 1965 prediction by Gordon Moore, a cofounder of Intel, that the amount of information storable in a square inch of silicon would double about every 18 months, as illustrated in Figure 3.19.

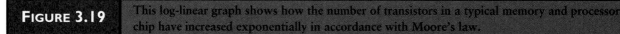

FIGURE 3.19   This log-linear graph shows how the number of transistors in a typical memory and processor chip have increased exponentially in accordance with Moore's law.

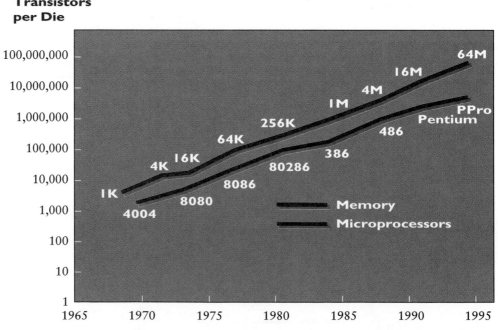

HARDWARE FOR STORING DATA

Managers and other computer users rarely discard data immediately after collecting, processing, and printing them. The Dovay Police Department stores some data, such as the locations of its patrol cars, for only short periods. It keeps other data, such as criminal case files, indefinitely. Managers need to know the options for storing data. Then they can evaluate their current systems and design revisions after diagnosing their storage needs. In this section we first answer the question they ask most often: "How much storage do I need?" Then we investigate available primary and secondary storage devices.

MEASURING STORAGE

Sequences of **bits**, the smallest amount of data that can be stored, can represent all information. For example, newspapers and magazines print a black and white picture as a series of inked dots separated by white space. If you lay a 1,000-by-1,000 line grid over a picture, you can observe the color, black or white, at each of the million points lying at the grid intersections. You can then represent the picture by one million bits set to one for black or zero for white. If you require a finer resolution, you can increase the number of lines in the grid and the number of bits used to represent the picture.

Bits can represent letters, numbers, and other characters in this fashion. But a coding scheme, such as the Morse Code with bits set to one for a dot and zero for a dash, can represent a character with many fewer bits. Codes that use only seven bits, for example, can represent as many as 128 different characters. Two coding schemes that use eight bits have become industry standards. Most microcomputers use a code called **ASCII** to represent characters. IBM uses a code called **EBCDIC** for its mainframes and minicomputers; some other mainframe manufacturers also use EBCDIC.

Because of the use of standard eight-bit coding schemes, most manufacturers measure storage capacity in **bytes**, where one byte equals eight bits. Greek prefaces attached to the word "byte" indicate orders of magnitude, as shown in Table 3.3.

PRIMARY STORAGE DEVICES

Primary storage is electrical, resides on the bus, and is directly accessible to the processor. Because processors access primary storage directly, a computer equipped with

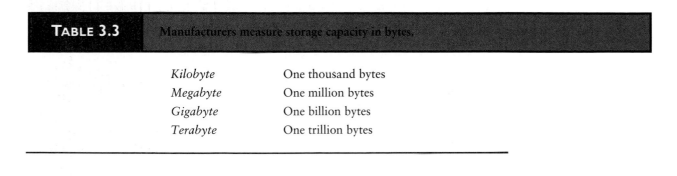

TABLE 3.3	Manufacturers measure storage capacity in bytes.
Kilobyte	One thousand bytes
Megabyte	One million bytes
Gigabyte	One billion bytes
Terabyte	One trillion bytes

THE MANAGER IN ACTION

Wal-Mart is the world's largest retailer, with more than 2,900 stores, 3,500 independent suppliers, and 700,000 employees. Its annual revenues exceeded $104 billion for the year ended January 31, 1997.

According to Wal-Mart's chief information officer, Randy Mott, "[Wal-Mart's] business strategy depends on detailed data at every level. Every cost, every line item is carefully analyzed, enabling better merchandising decisions to be made on a daily basis. It is the foundation for maintaining Wal-Mart's competitive edge and its continuing success in providing everyday low prices and superior customer satisfaction."

Wal-Mart keeps the information its managers need in a "data warehouse," a computerized repository of its transaction and pricing information containing 65 weeks of data kept by item, by store, by day. Managers analyze information in the data warehouse to examine buying trends by location and by season. This helps them make decisions about when to mark down the price of items or when to move inventory geographically. It also enables them to make rational decisions on whether and when to replenish inventory on an item-by-item basis. The warehouse receives as many as 50,000 queries in one week.

primary storage that runs slower than its processor will operate more slowly than it should. Remember that a processor in a single machine cycle will want to retrieve its next instruction from memory. Because processors operate at millions of cycles per second, primary access devices must be able to retrieve and store whatever data the processor wants within a millionth of a second or less. This requirement precludes the use of mechanical devices for primary storage and suggests the use of chips that store electrical signals. Today's primary storage devices pack millions of transistors, each able to represent a single bit of data, into a chip (see Figure 3.20). Tomorrow's primary storage devices may be opto-electrical, operating at or near the speed of light.

Cache memory describes a small amount of primary storage that is faster than the rest of the primary storage in a computer. In recent years, computer processor speeds have increased rapidly, and memory speeds have not kept pace, at least not inexpensively. To compensate for this problem and to keep processors from having to wait while retrieving data and instructions from memory, computer designers equip their fastest computers with a small amount of fast, expensive cache memory. When the processor requests data or instructions from an address not in cache memory, the computer moves that data along with a block of nearby addresses into the high speed cache. Then, if the computer requests the instruction or data from nearby addresses, as it usually does, it can find the data rapidly in cache memory.

Volatile versus Nonvolatile Devices. Most chips cannot store data without power. This volatile storage, known as **random access memory (RAM)**, loses whatever data it has if someone turns off the computer. Without any data or programs in its memory, the computer could not do anything when turned on. Some portion of the computer's memory must retain instructions that the

How can Randy Mott ensure that the information needs of Wal-Mart's managers will be met? Mott needs to be sure that Wal-Mart has sufficient processing power and a vast amount of storage. The storage and processing need to be scalable, so that when new applications arise, Wal-Mart's systems can respond.

In March 1996, Wal-Mart purchased a 32-node massively parallel WorldMark 5100M computer from NCR. Each node is an SMP with eight Pentium Pro 200 processors The system provided Wal-Mart with access to 7.5 terabytes of data and the power to run 30 applications. By mid-1997, Wal-Mart was ready for an upgrade in order to add customer preference data to its warehouse. The 32-node system was upgraded to a 96-node system containing 768 Pentium Pro 200 processors and 16 terabytes of data storage.

SOURCES: http://www.ncr.com/press_release/pr021097a. html, June 27, 1997; Barbara DePompa, Wal-Mart orders a super warehouse, *Information Week* (March 11, 1996): 22; and http://www.ncr.com/product/retail/stories/wal-mart/ index.shtml, June 27, 1997.

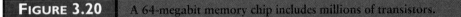

FIGURE 3.20   A 64-megabit memory chip includes millions of transistors.

computer needs to start functioning and to copy or load the operating system software from secondary storage into primary storage. Computer designers use a type of electronic storage device known as **read-only memory (ROM)** that retains its state in the absence of electrical power to hold the computer's initial instructions. The state of these (nonvolatile) ROM devices does not change in response to an electronic signal; data must be burned into ROM memory using special equipment. Because of the expense of ROM and because data on ROM cannot be changed, computers contain only a few kilobytes of ROM compared to a few megabytes of RAM.

Trends.   As shown in Figure 3.21 the price, size, and power consumption of primary storage devices has declined rapidly. Between 1987 and 1997, the cost of a megabyte of RAM dropped from about $120 to about $5, and the amount of RAM in most computers increased from less than 1 MB to 16 MB. At the same time, Parkinson's Law of Data, which states that "data expands to fill the space available for storage," appears to have held. With each reduction in storage costs and increase in storage availability, users demanded more sophisticated software, which required more storage. Duval wants to be sure that the Dovay Police Department can easily add RAM to the computers it buys.

| **FIGURE 3.21** | This log-linear graph shows that the price of memory has declined exponentially, while its use in a typical system has increased exponentially |

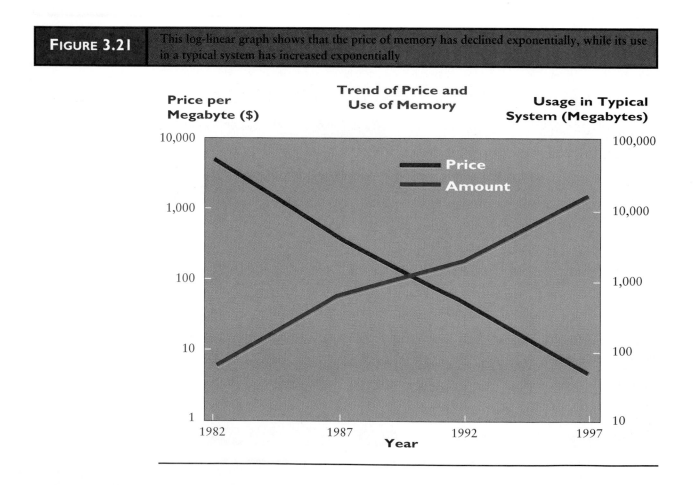

Trend of Price and Use of Memory

SECONDARY STORAGE DEVICES

The processor cannot directly access **secondary storage.** When the processor needs data, it commands the controller to obtain the data from the storage device and place it on the bus. The processor then uses the data immediately or keeps it in primary storage.

Primary and secondary storage differ in how fast they retrieve and store data, their capacity, their durability, and their cost. Although secondary storage retrieves and stores data more slowly than primary storage, it costs much less. As a result, computers tend to have ten to one-hundred times as much secondary storage as primary storage, and the ratio between primary and secondary storage may exceed one thousand to one.

A computer needs only enough primary memory to support one task or the tasks its user plans to perform simultaneously. The computer should have enough secondary storage to maintain all data and programs its user will collect. Duval will spend a great deal of time forecasting his need for secondary storage. Although he can add secondary storage to his systems if his original estimates are incorrect, adding it then can be costly and disruptive.

Computer users employ secondary storage devices, such as hard disks, diskettes, tapes, and compact disks, to retain data temporarily and permanently. Access to data in secondary storage occurs at speeds of 8 to 75 thousandths of a second, approximately a million times slower than access to data in primary storage. Still, secondary storage offers three advantages over primary storage. First, it is much less expensive. Second, it retains data without electrical power. Third, it can be removed from its computer, allowing data to be transferred between computers or shipped as products.

Unlike primary storage devices, secondary storage devices typically save data on a variety of nonelectrical media, such as magnetic or optical films covering tapes or disks. To retrieve data stored this way, electromechanical and other mechanical devices position the desired data under a sensing device that detects a magnetic flux or an optical property and interprets it as data. This mechanical positioning process makes retrieval of data from secondary storage so much slower than retrieval of data from primary storage.

Fixed Media.   A fixed media storage device cannot be removed from its computer. The most common type, a **hard disk,** consists of metal platters with a magnetized coating arranged on a spindle, encased in a vacuum chamber, and packaged with a motor, electronics, and magnetic sensors. A hard disk stores a single bit of data by orienting the magnetic field at a disk location in one direction to indicate a zero and in another direction to indicate a one. Because it rotates rapidly, a hard disk provides quick access to any randomly selected bit of information.

Because of the small size and low power needs of microcomputers, vendors usually package hard disks inside the cabinet housing of the microcomputers. People unfamiliar with computer technology often confuse hard disk storage with RAM primary storage.

The price per megabyte of hard disk storage has declined rapidly in recent years, while disk speed has increased. In 1987, the cost of hard disk storage with an average access time of 35 milliseconds was greater than $10 per megabyte. By 1997, a megabyte of disk storage cost less than 15 cents. This decline in cost has helped fuel a growth in types of software that demand more disk storage. For example, in 1987, microcomputer users typically found that 20 MB of hard disk was sufficient for their text-based programs and data. Now users of Windows need at least 500 MB because the graphics images and their processing programs require more capacity.

The rapid decline in hard disk prices has increased the use of **file servers**—computers that provide programs and data to other computers through a network. They generally need capacities of several tens of gigabytes because a single file server must satisfy the storage needs of many computer users. File servers allow organizations to centralize storage of data and take advantage of economies of scale in the price of disk capacity.

Declining hard disk prices have also resulted in the increased use of **redundant arrays of inexpensive disks (RAID)**. RAID storage devices (see Figure 3.22) use a large number of relatively small hard disks to create what appears to be a single storage device. If errors arise in any of the hard disks, the device can be disabled and replaced without a loss of data because of the redundancies in the system. British Airways switched to a RAID storage system for its reservations because the airline incurs huge financial loses for even a few seconds of downtime.[14]

RAID reduces the time required to read or write data because the computer can simultaneously read or write to each of the disks in the RAID array. Such parallelism can dramatically reduce the time required to access secondary storage. RAID storage

| **FIGURE 3.22** | RAID provides high-volume, reliable storage by using many hard disks in a single device. |

also takes significantly less room than conventional large disks. Certain levels of RAID, however, can cost more. North Pacific Insurance Company (NPIC) found that switching to a RAID storage system reduced the average time for underwriters to gain access to a document from 18 seconds to less than a second. NPIC also gained back 50 percent of its floor space dedicated to storage, enabling it to upgrade its systems without expanding its computer center, saving a significant amount of money.[15]

Removable Media. Removable storage media include diskettes, laser-servo diskettes, cartridge disks, tape, CD-ROM, other optical storage, and flash memory.

- A **diskette** is a random access magnetic medium consisting of a circle of mylar or similar material coated with a magnetic film and protected with a cardboard or hard plastic cover. Although diskettes are inexpensive, costing less than one dollar each, they hold relatively small amounts of data, typically 1.44 MB. This low capacity makes them ineffective for backing up an entire computer system. They can effectively and quickly store copies of small office files such as spreadsheets or word processing documents that do not contain too many graphics.
- A **laser-servo diskette** looks and operates like a 1.44 MB diskette, except the tracks separating the locations on the drive are much closer to one another and are tracked by a laser, allowing capacities greater than 100 MB.
- **Cartridge disks** are similar to removable hard disks. The disk is sealed in a cartridge reducing the possibility of contamination due to dust and allowing the read/write head to approach the disk surface more closely. Disk cartridge capacities can easily reach or exceed a gigabyte (see Figure 3.23).
- **Tape** storage devices use a thin mylar tape covered with a magnetic coating. Cartridge tapes resemble those used to record music, and reel tapes look like reels of movie film. Tape offers a low cost per unit of storage capacity. A tape capable of archiving 1 gigabyte can be purchased for less than $20. Tape lacks random access, so it may take several seconds or even minutes to retrieve a desired item of data. Therefore, tape offers an ideal medium for archiving files.

FIGURE 3.23 Cartridge disks and their drives provide hard-disk-like capacity and speed for removable media.

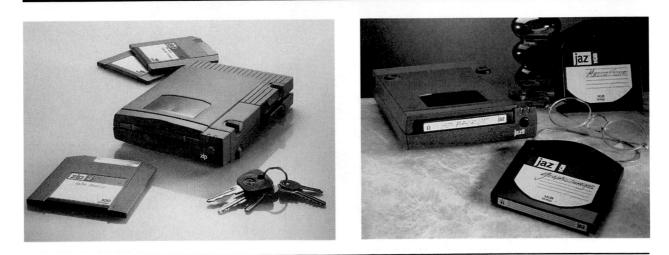

- A **CD-ROM,** standard in most personal computers, is an optical disk that resembles a music CD. CD-ROMs are read-only optical disks that can be written to once. The storage capacity of a CD-ROM ranges from 580 to 777 MB, depending on its format, which makes it capable of holding more information than 400 diskettes. Software vendors and vendors of publications, abstracts, and indices for libraries commonly distribute their products on CD-ROM media.
- Other optical media are also available. Standards have emerged for CD-R, an affordable, recordable optical disk; CD-RW, an erasable, re-recordable optical disk; and DVD, a CD-ROM-like optical disk that holds 4.7 gigabytes of information on 5-inch (diameter) media. Shipments of rewritable 3.5-inch optical drives reportedly exceeded 1 million units in 1996.[16] Mainframe systems typically use 14-inch media, which provide about 16 times the capacity of 3.5-inch media, and drives that make several optical disks available simultaneously. The Dovay Police Department will likely use optical disks for archiving its files.
- **Flash memory** is an electromagnetic storage device that stores data onto computer chips in a nonvolatile fashion. Although expensive, flash memory requires no moving parts, low power, and is more rugged than a diskette. For this reason, it is popular as a storage medium for mobile computers.

Switching devices speed the use of removable media. They automate the insertion and removal of storage media into a computer. For example, Digital Equipment Corporation's TL822 automated mass-storage library (see Figure 3.24) stores more than 10 terabytes of data on up to 264 tape cartridges. Such libraries are ideal

| **FIGURE 3.24** | IBM's Model 3495 tape library provides automated and rapid access to an extensive data archive. |

for archiving a mainframe's data. Anthem Blue Cross and Blue Shield, serving Ohio, Indiana, and Kentucky, uses an NCR 6400 Robotic Tape Library to back up its 1.3 terabytes of storage.[17]

Jukeboxes automate the switching of optical disks into and out of a single drive in 10 seconds or less. Digital's RW557 jukebox (see Figure 3.25), for example, provides access to 618 gigabytes of information on 238 optical drives, any six of which can be accessed simultaneously. Because the Dovay Police Department rarely accesses its archives, Duval should not consider purchasing jukeboxes for its optical storage.

HARDWARE FOR OUTPUT

Computer systems use output devices to transfer information from computer storage into a form that individuals can see, hear, or feel. Managers need to decide what type of output they need:

- **Softcopy output** describes information presented on an unmovable medium, such as a computer screen.

| **FIGURE 3.25** | Digital Equipment Corporation's RW557 optical jukebox holds 238 optical disks. It automatically selects from among these disks and inserts them into one of its six optical drives. |

- **Hardcopy output** describes information presented on a medium such as paper that can be removed from the computer.
- **Robotic output** describes output that controls the movement of a target device.

Text devices produce letters and numbers such as those you would see on a typewritten page. Graphics devices generate pictures and diagrams. Graphics devices can also draw text by producing small dots in the design of characters, as shown in Figure 3.26. You might have trouble reading the text produced in this way if the output device can't provide enough dot density and resolution in dot placement.

Density refers to the number of dots a device produces per inch horizontally and vertically. The use of a single dot-per-inch (dpi) statistic in its specifications means that the vertical and horizontal directions have the same density (for example, 300 dpi or 1,000 dpi). When horizontal and vertical dpi differ, manufacturers usually quote both numbers. Most users cannot tell the difference between output produced by text printers, graphics printers at 300 dpi, and professional typesetters at 1200 dpi. Computer screen manufacturers often specify density by the total number of dots in each direction, such as 640 × 480. Alternatively, they might specify the space between adjacent dots, known as the **dot pitch**. Experts recommend dot pitch of not more than .35 millimeters to minimize eye strain. **Resolution** describes the quality of output: a printer has a resolution of 300 dpi.

SOFTCOPY DEVICES

The three most commonly used softcopy output devices are video monitors, video terminals, and speakers. Video monitors and video terminals are both called computer screens. Each of these devices consists of electronics that reside on a circuit board inside the computer and a physical device, such as a cathode-ray tube or a speaker, that produces the output.

Video Monitors. Monitors are graphical devices. Each dot or **pixel** on the screen corresponds to a location or locations (for color monitors) in the computer's primary

---

FIGURE 3.26   A graphics output device produces characters such as this from closely spaced ink dots.

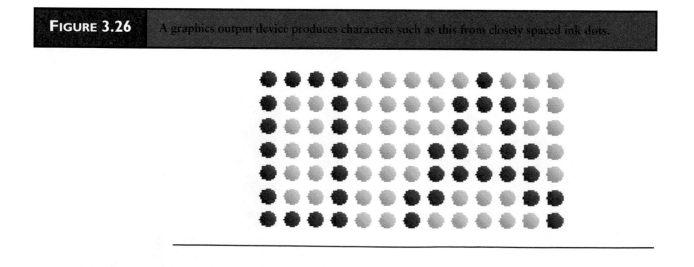

memory or in the memory on the **video adaptor**—a circuit board inside the computer that supports the monitor. A monitor receives an analog electrical signal from the video adaptor, a signal similar to that received by a television set, and shows a display of text or graphics. Video monitors are the primary display screens for most microcomputers.

The video monitors used with most desktop terminals are built with cathode-ray tubes (CRTs), the same heavy and deep tubes that are used for television sets. Mobile computers use flat-screen technologies. Flat-screen monitors (see Figure 3.27) weigh less and use less power than CRT monitors, but they cost more and produce dimmer pictures. The most popular technologies, active matrix and passive matrix (or dual scan), use liquid crystals. Liquid crystals do not change state rapidly, producing ghost images behind a moving cursor or multimedia movie. Active matrix costs more than passive matrix. It produces a brighter picture with fewer ghosts and can be viewed at a wider angle. Emerging technologies include enhanced passive matrix, which produces quality similar to active matrix at a much lower cost, and plasma discharge, which does not suffer the disadvantages of liquid crystals but costs much more.

Video adapter manufacturers have agreed on a small set of standards that specify how software should address video memory, how many pixels compose a video display, and how many colors each pixel may assume. Usually two or three standards

FIGURE 3.27   IBM's 9516-A23 is a TFT LCD flat panel color monitor that sports a 16.1-inch screen. Its compact size and thin design takes minimal space when used with a desktop computer.

INFORMATION TECHNOLOGY AND GLOBAL BUSINESS

Nissan, Europe's leading Japanese car manufacturer, firmly established its European presence when it opened a car manufacturing plant in Sunderland, England, in 1984. Since then the company has become one of the greatest success stories for inward investment in the United Kingdom. From a base of producing its first car in the U.K. in 1986, then employing a staff of 470, the company has grown in ten years; it now has a head office in Amsterdam with manufacturing bases in the U.K., Spain, and Germany and it employs more than 16,000 people. Nissan has achieved this success by massive investment, $2 billion in its Sunderland plant alone. In 1996, Nissan's European operations produced more than 215,000 cars and accounted for 3.1 percent of the European passenger car market.

The rapid growth in the company led to the establishment of a wide range of IT systems within Nissan's operations throughout the world. In 1995, the company decided to consolidate its entire computer operations in three major data centers: Atsugi near Tokyo for the Pacific Rim; Denver in Colorado for North America; and Sunderland for its European operations.

Neil Melville, the manager of the Nissan European Data Center (NEDC) in Sunderland, explains, "The consolidation offered a number of key benefits. There were obvious cost savings to be made by benefiting from the economies of scale by centralizing operations. In addition, as each country operation had developed its own IT system, communication and data sharing between offices became increasingly difficult. Consolidation would overcome this by creating

are available in the market simultaneously, giving buyers a range of image qualities at a range of prices.

Video Terminals. Terminals differ from monitors in that the terminal, rather than an adaptor board inside the computer, holds most of their intelligence. Video terminals receive a digital signal that consists of a series of codes. Some codes represent characters that the terminal displays upon receipt at the next position on its screen. Some codes position the cursor so that new characters will appear in a different place. Other codes may generate graphics, perhaps specifying the drawing of a line between two locations on the screen. Because minicomputers and mainframes that support hundreds of users would require a tremendous amount of memory to store the screen pattern of each of its users, most multiuser computers employ terminals rather than monitors. Some companies, such as Gambro Healthcare, Inc., the Lakewood, Colorado, manufacturer of kidney dialysis machines, have replaced their PCs with terminals connected to a small number of servers in order to reduce costs. They can manage the servers more easily than the PCs.[18]

Sending a scanned picture to a video terminal is more cumbersome than sending a picture to a monitor. After scanning a picture, the computer stores the picture in its memory as a series of bits. The computer then sends these bits to a video monitor to output the picture. Sending the same picture to a terminal requires software that sends codes to sequentially position a pointer at each pixel and then turn that pixel on

a central data repository that all of the European users would access."

To achieve this objective meant overcoming a number of major issues in the computing migration. Says Melville, "We were accepting all Europe's computing capabilities—all the major systems needed for the business to function—accounting for 500 gigabytes of data. We had to find a way of storing the data so that everyone who needed to could access it from wherever in Europe. The users needed the same or better performance and reliability as they had from their previous computing arrangements. In physical terms alone, this level of storage could have necessitated us building an entirely new data center just to house it. This would have cost as much as $22 million. We needed to find an innovative solution."

Melville turned to a RAID storage system from EMC Corporation. When the new system went live in January 1996, it halved the response times for online transactions from one second to half a second and reduced processing time for overnight batch jobs by one hour. These improvements saved Nissan from having to upgrade its computer processor. The European data center now handles more than 600,000 transactions daily from across Europe.

SOURCE: http://www.emc.com/customers/cvs/nissan/nisancvs. htm, June 27, 1997.

or off. A monitor paints a picture to the screen almost instantaneously; a terminal may take several minutes to laboriously draw the picture.

Speakers. A sound controller, also called a **sound card,** produces an electrical signal that drives one or more speakers. This signal can produce music, special effects such as the sound of a passing train, or the sound of a voice. Manufacturers now include the circuitry for a sound controller and a CD controller on the same board, which they sell as a multimedia board.

Recent advances in DSP processors (see the section on specialized processors) have made voice output relatively inexpensive to produce. As a result, a number of new products take advantage of this technology. Consider voice mail. When a person leaves a message on a voice-mail system, a DSP digitizes the message and sends it to a computer. The computer saves the data on a hard disk. When the message recipient signals the computer to play the message, the computer outputs the message to a device containing a DSP that reverses the digitizing process, converting the data back into a signal that sounds just like the person who left the message.

Researchers are developing software that will produce the digital equivalent of voice from the digital representation of text.[19] When this technology becomes widely available commercially, programmers will be able to write programs that can give voice messages rather than display messages on the screen. Also, blind people will be able to order books in electronic form and then play them on their computers.

HARDCOPY DEVICES

Hardcopy devices produce output on media that can be removed from a computer and hence can be retained for a long time. The most common hardcopy medium for computer output is paper, and a large variety of output devices produce paper output. In selecting a hardcopy device, the user must consider whether he requires character or graphics output, as well as the density and resolution of output desired.

Printers. Printers, used by most individuals and businesses for the bulk of their output, produce text and graphics on paper without using a pen. Printers include laser, ink jet, matrix, and character impact, as described in Table 3.4.

Plotters. Plotters operate by moving a pen or pens over paper, much the way a person writes (see Figure 3.28). Architectural and engineering firms often use plotters

TABLE 3.4	Although companies can choose among four types of printers, most use ink jet and laser printers.

Type	Quality	Speed	Cost	Process
Laser	Produces high-quality text and graphics; 300 to 600 dpi	Can print four pages per minute for personal versions; high-end systems can print up to 464 pages per minute	$600 to $1,000 for personal systems; more for high-end systems	Uses an internal laser to place dots of selected charge on a heated cylinder, called a drum or platen; the charges attract particles of a dark powder called a toner; as paper rolls over the drum, the drum transfers the toner to the paper and the heat fuses the toner permanently, fixing the image.
Ink Jet	Similar to laser printer quality; copies can smudge when wet	Can print three to five pages per minute	Less than $700	Sprays streams of ink at the paper, producing dots
Matrix	Poorer resolution than ink jet or laser printers; relatively noisy; useful for printing multipart forms	Some print 700 characters per second; 1,400 lines per minute	Less than $200	Uses a print head that contains pins that can be fired individually at a print ribbon; each pint hits the ribbon and leaves a dot on the paper.
Character Input	Used by midrange and mainframe computers; called band printers or chain printers	Can print 2,200 lines per minute	More costly than ink jet and laser printers	Presses a metal or hard plastic image of a character into a ribbon, which leaves an ink impresion on the paper.

| FIGURE 3.28 | Architects and designers often use plotters rather than printers to draw output. A plotter uses a pen or group of pens to create line drawings. A flat-bed plotter can produce large blueprints. |

rather than printers to produce drawings. The plotters produce high-resolution graphical output. They work on oversized paper and on long rolls of paper.

Other Hardcopy Output Media. Devices exist to produce output directly onto transparencies, microfilm, microfiche, CD-ROM, and slides. These devices generally cost more than devices that produce output of similar quality on paper. For example, most laser and ink jet printers can print overhead transparencies. Special equipment, not necessarily found in every office, is needed to produce output onto microfilm, microfiche, and CD-ROM. Increasingly, people create slides in their computer programs and show them directly from the computer.

ROBOTIC DEVICES

Robotic output devices physically move in response to signals from a computer. Usually a robotic device interprets a digital code output by the computer as a signal to turn on, turn off, speed up, or slow down a motor. In more complicated devices, the output signal addresses one of several motors. Advances in robotics depend less on the sophistication of such output devices than on the software needed to direct the output and processors that can rapidly run software to interpret input video and pressure signals. Only recently have scientists programmed computers to control a robot so that it avoids bumping into objects as it proceeds toward its goal. Such software must first synthesize the two-dimensional signals produced by each of the robot's eyes into a three-dimensional representation of its world. Then the software must logically plan and execute a route that safely negotiates this three-dimensional world.

SUMMARY

Computer hardware is the physical equipment used to process information. It includes processing hardware, the data bus, controllers, and devices for input, output, data communication, and data storage. Managers should diagnose their needs and work with information professionals in evaluating, designing, and implementing solutions to meet these needs.

Computer hardware varies by size and function. On the size dimension, systems are designated as mainframes, midrange, or microcomputers. On the functional dimension, systems may be designed as desktop systems, mobile systems, workstations, scientific systems, or servers.

Input hardware captures raw data and eases the interaction between the user and the computer. Most people are familiar with the keyboard, mouse, trackball, joystick, light pen, touch screen, bar-code readers, and scanners. Other output devices include other readers of formatted text and sensors that acquire data using the senses of sight, sound, and touch. Managers should try to simplify input and reduce human intervention in acquiring data.

Processing hardware implements the instructions encoded into software. After an individual turns on the computer, the processor retrieves the instructions stored at the location indicated by the instruction register, decodes the instruction, and then executes it. Measures of the processor's power help managers assess the trade-off between price and performance. Parallel processing combines the power of several processors in one computer. Specialized processors do specific jobs. Over time, processing power has increased dramatically whereas costs have dropped significantly.

Managers store data for both the short and long run. Bits and bytes measure the quantity of storage. Primary storage occurs on circuit boards. Volatile primary storage (RAM) loses data when the computer is turned off; nonvolatile storage (ROM) does not change its state in response to electronic signals. Secondary storage devices include removable media, such as tapes, diskettes, and optical disks, and fixed media, such as hard disks and RAID storage devices. Primary and secondary storage differ in their retrieval and storage speed, capacity, and cost.

Output devices transfer information from computer storage into softcopy, hardcopy, or robots. Softcopy devices, such as video terminals, video monitors, and speakers, produce output that cannot be removed from the computer. Hardcopy devices, such as printers and plotters, produce output that can be removed from the computer. Robotic devices move in response to signals from a computer.

KEY TERMS

active data entry
adaptor
ASCII
bar-code reader
bit
byte
cache memory
cartridge disk
CD-ROM
controller
cursor
data bus
density
digital signal processor (DSP)
digital video camera
diskette
docking station
dot pitch
EBCDIC
file server
flash memory
graphics processor
graphics scanner
handheld computer
hard disk
hardcopy output
hardware
image compressor
input hardware
instruction counter
instruction register
interactive dialogue
joystick
jukebox
keyboard
laptop computer
laser-servo diskette

light pen
mainframe
microcomputer
mouse
notebook computer
palmtop computer
parallel processing
passive data entry
peripheral devices
personal computer (PC)
pixel
plotter
port
power supply
primary storage
printer
processing hardware
random access memory (RAM)
read-only memory (ROM)
reader of formatted input
redundant arrays of inexpensive disks
    (RAID)
resolution
robotic output
secondary storage
server
softcopy output
sound card
subnotebook computer
tape
touch pad
touch screen
trackball
video adaptor
voice processor
workstation

DISCUSSION AND REVIEW QUESTIONS

1. What is "hardware"?
2. How does processing hardware communicate with peripheral devices?
3. What is the difference between mainframe, midrange, and small computer systems?
4. Identify and contrast different types of mobile computers.
5. What is "active data entry" and what is an example? How does it differ from passive data entry and interactive dialogue?

6. How do point-of-sale keyboards differ from generic data processing keyboards?
7. How do the QWERTY and Dvorak keyboards differ?
8. What are the advantages and disadvantages of readers of formatted input as input devices?
9. Describe four input devices other than a keyboard and a mouse.
10. What steps does a computer processor go through to perform its work?
11. What is a digital signal processor (DSP) and what are some of its applications?
12. Why do computers typically have more secondary than primary storage?
13. What is ROM? Why do computers need ROM?
14. Describe and contrast two types of parallel processing. For what type of applications are parallel processors used?
15. What are three types of removable storage?
16. What is RAID? For what applications is it most desirable?
17. What is the difference between hardcopy and softcopy output?
18. What is the difference between a video monitor and a video terminal? Why is one more often used with mainframe and midrange computers whereas the other is more often used with microcomputers?
19. What is the difference between a printer and a plotter?
20. What are four different types of printers and how are they used?

IS ON THE WEB

Exercise 1: You have a friend who recently started a small interior design business. Your friend has told you that she wishes to purchase a personal computer to help keep track of her accounts payable, accounts receivable, orders, and customers. Your friend knows that you are taking a course in information systems and wants your advice about which computer she should buy. Before offering your recommendations, you want to learn more about the available hardware. Visit the Web sites of three personal computer vendors. Compare and contrast them on their relative speed, features and options, price, and any other relevant issues. Then write a brief review of your findings for your friend so that she can understand the pros and cons of each option.

Exercise 2: Visit IBM's Web site. Describe the array of products offered. How does IBM differentiate the computers it manufactures? Briefly summarize your conclusions.

A MODEL PAPERLESS LIBRARY

In 1994, New York publishing giant Simon & Schuster was racing headlong into the digital future when it discovered a major technology gap. Clearly, books would continue to be the mainstay of the business. But Chairman Jonathan Newcomb had set an ambitious goal: to generate half of Simon & Schuster's revenues from electronic publishing—via CD-ROMS, videodisks, and the World Wide Web—by 2000, versus 25 percent today. Plus, he saw big opportunities in custom publishing—quickly creating textbook-CD-ROM packages customized for one professors course, say.

But how to cope with this digital deluge? There would be thousands upon thousands of graphics, video chips, and audio files to manage as well as millions of pages of text. Each year, the $2.2 billion company's Higher Education Division alone uses 85,000 photos and illustrations in textbooks and CD-ROMs.

To hit the CEO's target, the company would have to be a lot better at locating, acquiring, recombining, editing, preparing, and accounting for those and other "intellectual properties." But if the company could improve these processes, it would produce not only growth but greater profitability. As Chunka Mui, partner at Chicago consulting firm Diamond Technology Partners Inc., puts it, "If you can customize new publications without raising your costs, the new revenue drops directly to the bottom line."

So Newcomb ordered a reengineering of Simon & Schuster's editing, production, and even certain accounting processes. It's all built around a powerful new Corporate Digital Archive (CDA) designed by SRA International Inc., a supplier of information systems for government agencies and corporations. The $750,000 computer system, says Newcomb, "will become the centerpiece of how we develop and produce everything as we move forward. It will give us the ability to reuse information over and over again."

Indeed, such digital archives are fast becoming a must for publishers and other media companies as they career down the Information Superhighway. These "content providers" won't be able to compete effectively if they continue to spend the time and money to handle information stored on paper and film. With a digital archive, it's possible to organize everything in databases, recall material as needed, and combine it instantly in new ways—pulling biographical data to help promote a movie on a Web site, say.

Simon & Schuster isn't the only digital archive under construction. Time Warner Inc. is digitizing its magazines photo collection, and Conde Nast Publications Inc. is

SOURCE: Case extracted from John W. Verity, A model paperless library, *Business Week* (December 23, 1996): 80, 82.

doing the same with 350,000 fashion shots. Corporations such as General Motors, Amway, and John Deere have set up digital archives of their promotional materials, to help in-house and outside designers. The McGraw-Hill Companies, Simon & Schuster's main rival in textbooks, is setting up specialized archives in each of its business units, too. On paper, at least, Simon & Schuster's plans are the most ambitious yet, with one archive to serve all 30 of its business units.

Consider what it's already doing for the $400 million Higher Education Division, the first unit on-line. Researchers there used to spend weeks finding photos for a new textbook, sifting through disjointed files and searching stock-photo agencies. Then, photos would be sent out to be separated and proofed at a cost of $75 each. The separations were sized for a specific book, usually making them unusable for other publications. "We always had to start from scratch," says Henry Hirschberg, the unit's president.

All that has changed. Now there's one place to start looking for photos—the CDA, which has 40,000 of S&S's photos and will soon include more than 40,000 diagrams, charts, and other line art. And the company is working with stock agencies such as Photo Researchers Inc. and Tom Stack & Associates to get tens of thousands of their photos stored there, too—an easy way to win more of Simon & Schuster's business, says George F. Werner, executive vice-president.

Crucial to an archive's effectiveness is its ability to locate any item. Cataloging images and other nontextual items presents a huge software challenge. Simon & Schuster turned to SRA International Inc. for technology it developed for intelligence agencies. SRA's PhotoFile software accepts natural language queries, not rigid computer codes, so it can even understand captions written years ago. "We're capturing the past and building the foundation for our future," says Richard Walkus, an assistant vice-president who runs the archives.

But that's just the beginning. Once a photo has been chosen, the archive tells another set of in-house systems to create a print-ready copy in just the right size and image resolution—high for books, low for the Web, for instance. And the cost is now just $6 or $7 per item, which will produce savings of $3 million this year, says Werner. Plus, the system automatically routes images and related electronic business forms—rights contracts, for instance—from desk to desk. And it tracks each use of an image, automatically calculates royalties, and adds invisible "digital watermarks" that can identify illegal electronic copies taken from a CD-ROM or Web page.

Simon & Schuster is now scrambling to expand its archive—and open it to more people. It's indexing reams of text, videotape and audiotape. The system will become accessible for browsing by editors anywhere on the company's intranet. Now, Newcomb has his I-way vehicle.

Case Questions

Diagnosis

1. What are the information needs of Simon & Schuster's editors and authors?

Evaluation

2. Prior to the development of the CDA, how were these needs met?
3. What were the problems associated with the pre-CDA approach?

Design

4. What input devices are needed to implement the CDA?
5. What output devices are needed to use the CDA effectively?
6. Assuming a typical digital image requires 50 MB of storage, how much storage is required for the CDA (excluding videotape and audiotape images)?
7. What type of storage devices will Simon & Schuster need to implement the CDA?

Implementation

8. What processes will Simon & Schuster have to put into place for its authors and editors to identify and index appropriate images for its CDA?
9. How would you plan to overcome the work habits of existing employees to be sure that they took full advantage of the CDA?

CHILDLIFE CENTERS INC.'S PURCHASING PROBLEM   ACTIVITY 3.1

Step 1:   Read the following scenario:

You have just been hired as the first business manager for Childlife Centers, a chain of ten day care centers for infants, toddlers, and preschool-age children. Jane Stewart began the company ten years ago when she expanded a small preschool in her home into Childlife's first full-service center. Since that time Stewart has added nine additional centers to the company. During the next five years she expects to double the size of the company by opening ten additional centers. Each center services approximately 60 children and has 12–15 staff members. Until recently Stewart used a combination of part-time clerical employees and outside services to meet the administrative needs of the company. Stewart's secretary has the only computer owned by the company; she uses it solely for preparing correspondence.

You have been given a budget of $25,000 during this fiscal year to begin computerizing the company's administration. You and your small staff will eventually be responsible for handling personnel data, student information, accounts payable, accounts receivable, payroll, and purchasing. You have hired a consultant to assist you in making the final decisions about appropriate computer hardware and software, but you want to use her time as effectively as possible. Therefore, you want to list the general types of hardware you expect to purchase.

Step 2:   Prepare the case for class discussion.

Step 3:   Answer each of the following questions, individually or in small groups, as directed by your instructor.

Diagnosis

1. What are the information needs at Childlife Centers Inc. in the areas for which you are responsible?

Evaluation

2. What problems are likely to exist with the manual systems that are currently in place?
3. Which of these problems are most critical to the survival of the company?

Design

4. In broad terms, what is your solution to the information needs at Childlife Centers?
5. What input and output devices would you recommend? Be as specific as possible.
6. What type of processing and storage would you recommend?

Implementation

7. How should you plan to use the consultant you have hired?
8. What issues should you expect to address when implementing the new system?

Step 4: In small groups, with the entire class, or in written form, share your answers to the previous questions. Then answer the following questions:

1. What are the information needs at Childlife Centers?
2. What are the similarities and differences among the hardware options proposed?
3. What types of hardware would most effectively meet the needs of Childlife Centers?

ACTIVITY 3.2   SELECT THE INPUT TECHNOLOGY

Step 1: Read the following scenarios. Each describes the data needs of one area of operations in a company or professional organization.

1. In a law office, lawyers need to keep track of how much time they spend on each activity for every one of their cases. They also need to identify and access any documents relevant to the case as quickly as possible when clients call. Some of these documents may be kept electronically, whereas others need to be kept in paper form (the office may keep electronic copies). Some cases are assigned to a single lawyer in the firm, and others may be assigned to several lawyers.
2. In a hospital while visiting a patient, doctors need to access the patient's chart. This chart contains records of the patient's critical signs, the results of tests performed, and medications administered. The doctor also needs to be able to give orders to the nurses attending the patient and prescribe medications. Nurses need to access the doctor's orders, to enter critical signs, and to update the record of medication. The pharmacy needs access to the prescriptions the doctor has ordered. The lab needs access to the patient's records in order to update the results of tests performed. Some of the tests, such as cardiograms and X-rays, produce graphical results.
3. In a warehouse, *receivers* unload materials from a truck or train car and compare them to the order placed with the supplier. They will note all discrepancies. *Stockers* move the material to the shelves or bins where they should be stored. At that point, they update the inventory count so that it is available to sales people, assemblers, and others who need to access inventory amounts. *Pickers* remove inventory from the shelves and place them in a bin for shipment. They respond to a pick list that is generated in response to orders from customers, stores, or assemblers. Picked items should be removed from the inventory count.

Step 2: For each scenario identify what data are required, who requires the data, and who generates and inputs the data.

Step 3: Individually, or in small groups, as directed by your instructor, identify the best two input technologies for each scenario and each type of data. Consider keyboard, voice, bar-coding, scanning, and other technologies covered in this chapter. Identify the pros and cons of each technology and select the one that you think is best.

Step 4: In small groups, with the entire class, or in written form, share your answers to the previous questions.

BAKER & YOUNG ACTIVITY 3.3

Step 1: Read the following scenario:

Baker & Young is a national distributor of industrial machinery and accessories. The firm carries a range of manufacturing equipment and supplies including drill presses, electric motors, workbenches, precision measuring equipment, and fasteners.

Twice each year Baker & Young mails 5,000 catalogs to its customers. The current catalog is over 300 pages long and includes some 20,000 items.

THE ORDER-ENTRY PROCESS

Orders are placed in one of three ways. Most customers place orders by calling an 800 number; others send orders through the mail; and some place orders through independent sales reps that carry the line.

When an order is received, it is written on an order entry form and sent to central data processing, where data entry clerks enter the data using machines that transfer what was typed at the keyboard directly onto computer diskettes. After the data are entered and verified they are later used to update the central order file.

Although this order-entry system has proven satisfactory in the past, Peter Barbera, vice president of marketing, feels that technological developments in the computer industry offer the firm the opportunity to upgrade its order-entry process and obtain several benefits. These would include a strategic edge over its competitors, lower error rates in the order-entry process, a reduction in the cost to process an order, and quicker shipments of customer orders.

At the present time it takes about four working days for an order to get through the system. Since shipping by UPS—the carrier used to ship most small orders—takes on the average another three days, customers must wait at least a week for a shipment to arrive. In many situations this is simply too long.

Errors in the data entry process have always been a problem. In the worst case a customer places an order with a rep, the rep calls the order into headquarters, the order taker writes the order on an order form, and the order is entered by data entry clerks in the data entry department. With four people involved, there are many opportunities for order numbers, quantities, and shipping instructions to be relayed incorrectly.

Step 2: Prepare the case for class discussion.

SOURCE: Activity 3.3 scenario taken from B. Shore and J. Ralya, *Cases in Computer Information Systems* (New York: Holt, Rinehart and Winston, 1988).

Step 3: Answer each of the following questions, individually or in small groups, as directed by your instructor.

Diagnosis

1. What are the information needs of Baker & Young regarding customer orders?
2. How is the information currently entered?

Evaluation

3. How well are Baker & Young's information needs currently being met?
4. What are the shortcomings of the current system?

Design

5. How would you recommend that the order entry process be redesigned?
6. What computer hardware would you recommend for input and output?
7. What computer hardware would you recommend for data storage and processing?

Implementation

8. What issues might arise in implementing a new system?
9. How would you address these issues?

Step 4: In small groups, with the entire class, or in written form, share your answers to the previous questions. Then answer the following questions:

1. What are Baker & Young's information needs regarding customer orders?
2. What problems exist with the current order-entry process?
3. What recommendations did you offer for improving the process?
4. How effective are these recommendations likely to be?

ACTIVITY 3.4   DISASSEMBLING A MICROCOMPUTER

Under the supervision of your instructor, follow these steps to disassemble a microcomputer. When you are done, reverse the steps to reassemble the computer.

1. Turn off the computer, unplug it, and remove the plug from the back of the computer.
2. Identify the cables connecting to the back of the computer. Notice the different type of ports they connect to. Using tape, label each port with the type of peripheral device it serves. Then remove the cables.
3. Open the case. Your instructor will show you which screws need to be removed before the case will open.
4. Identify the power supply. Number the cables as they connect to devices from the left to the right of the computer and from the front to back. Then disconnect these cables from the devices they are attached to.
5. Identify the disk drives. Follow the cables from any disk drive to the disk controller board. Remove the cables connecting the drives to the controller. Remove the screw that connects the disk controller to the case. Remove the disk controller board from the motherboard by rocking it gently while lifting it.

6. Identify the CD-ROM drive. Follow the cables from the CD-ROM drive to the multimedia board. Remove the cable connecting the drive to the board. Remove the screw that connects the multimedia board to the case. Remove the multimedia board from the motherboard by rocking it gently while lifting it.

7. Locate the diskette, hard disk, and CD-ROM drives. Remove the screws that hold them to the structure that is mounted in the case. Slide them out and inspect them individually.

8. Locate the processor chips and the memory chips on the motherboard. If your computer has additional SIM or DIP memory boards, your instructor will point them out to you and show you how they can be removed from the motherboard.

9. If your computer has a modem or network connection, you can identify the modem or network card by following the port that resembles a telephone jack through the computer case.

10. Identify the video adaptor by following the port that connects to your monitor.

LACCARIA AND EAGLE ACTIVITY 3.5

Step 1: Read the following scenario:

Laccaria is a large South American country located between Brazil and Argentina. Its new military government understands the strategic importance of a strong information technology industry. Government officials feel that to encourage technological growth they must impose strict protectionist measures. These will help ensure that emerging Laccarian firms will be able to take full advantage of the domestic market, the ninth largest in the world. The trade barriers and high tariffs are not imposed on larger-scale computers, arbitrarily classified as mainframes by Laccarian officials.

The imposition of these protectionist measures has resulted in the formation of many small and medium-sized high-tech firms. They either assemble components imported from abroad or they manufacture Laccarian clones of equipment made by large USA vendors such as Epsilon. In many cases, the locally produced equipment is copied exactly from U.S. equipment—often without licensing agreements.

Laccaria has many software houses to support this manufacturing effort. Although the government of Laccaria has international copyright agreements with the United States, Laccarian officials often look the other way, allowing local software houses to make and market unauthorized copies of U.S. software.

Multinational corporations that operate branches or subsidiaries in Laccaria have felt the effect of the protectionist measures. It is difficult to get the right hardware configurations to run the software specifically designed for use at overseas sites. Sometimes a planned system cannot be implemented because some critical part, such as a router, is not available in Laccaria.

Eagle Bank is a large holding company headquartered in the United States. It has a network of international offices in nearly 40 countries. At most of these international sites, Eagle Bank has installed Epsilon System 45s from Epsilon Corporation of Syracuse, New York. The hardware uses Eagle's Corporate Core Software Package. However, all seven of the Eagle-Laccaria sites are operating in batch mode with punched

SOURCE: Activity 3.5 scenario taken from E. A. Kallman and J. P. Grillo, *Ethical Decision Making and Information Technology: An Introduction with Cases* (Watsonville, CA: Mitchell McGraw-Hill, 1993).

cards and tape drives. The systems have not been upgraded because the Laccarian government's Informatics Bureau lists the System 45 as a minicomputer, so it cannot be imported from the United States or neighboring countries.

The manager of Eagle-Laccaria's head office asked Carlo, his DP manager, to contact Orista, the Laccarian vendor that makes a system similar to the System 45. The Laccarian system is called the Orista 45K. Carlo discovered that using these clones would force major changes to the Corporate Core Software Package, and that the hardware price was $270,000—almost three times the price of the same configuration in the United States. Carlo also found that the Orista 45K hardware was unreliable and subject to frequent breakdowns, that Orista lacked what he called "a properly trained maintenance staff," and that the firm offered poor support.

Carlo's next step was to talk to his contact at the Informatics Bureau. When Carlo asked what could be done, his bureau contact suggested that Eagle-Laccaria purchase an Epsilon mainframe, the 4311, a machine manufactured by Epsilon in Laccaria. Unfortunately, it costs $380,000—$30,000 higher than its U.S. price.

During the discussion, Colonel Cuervo of the Informatics Bureau warned Carlo not to get into difficulty by purchasing a "parallel market" System 45. These are Epsilon System 45s that have been brought into the country illegally. These may look tempting, he said, because they cost only $120,000 and are made in the United States. However, these "unofficial import channels" are not recognized by the government, which considers them detrimental to the economy of Laccaria. Carlo knows, though, that many firms in Laccaria, some competing directly with Eagle, have these illegal machines. The government rarely prosecutes violators of its protectionist policy.

The manager must make his decision. Carlo has supplied him with this simple summary table:

MACHINE	SOURCE	COST	NOTES
Orista 45K	Orista	$270,000	Unreliable Poor service Software changes necessary Good for local economy, in the government's opinion
Epsilon 4311	Epsilon-Laccaria	$380,000	Too much machine Software conversions needed
Epsilon 45	Parallel market	$120,000	No changes to software Known entity Bad for local economy, in the government's opinion

The manager studies the table and tells Carlo, "It's obvious, isn't it?"

Step 2: Prepare the case for class discussion.

Step 3: Answer each of the following questions, individually or in small groups, as directed by your instructor.

1. For each alternative, who benefits and who is harmed?
2. Using relevant ethical principles, how would you evaluate each alternative?
3. What course of action would you take? Why?

RECOMMENDED READINGS

The following publications provide regular features about computer hardware:

Byte   *InfoWorld*
Computer Equipment Review   *Mac World*
Computerworld   *PC Week*

NOTES

1. This vignette is based on Peter Wolchak, Public sector stars: Metropolitan Toronto Police, *Computerworld: The Global 100* (May 1, 1995): 22.
2. http://www.sandybay.com/pc-web/Dvorak_keyboard.htm, June 11, 1997.
3. Rich Levin, The chameleon PC, *InformationWeek* (September 23, 1996): 48–58.
4. Jack Robertson, Chip to drive Apple camera—Motorola IC also geared to 2-D bar-code market, *Electronic News* (September 23, 1996) http://www.techweb.com/se/directlink.cgi?EBN19960923S0121.
5. April Jacobs, Mass. tax returns are only a scan or phone call away, *Computerworld* (July 15, 1996): 76.
6. Mary E. Thyfault, Just say it and pay it—Visa adopts voice recognition for bill payment system, *InformationWeek* (December 16, 1996), http://www.techweb.com/se/directlink.cgi?IWK19961216S0052.
7. Jerry Zeidenberg, Multimedia computing: A virtual reality by 2001, *Computing Canada* (November 9, 1992): 17.
8. Kevin Burden, Servers on steroids, *Computerworld* (March 10, 1977): 77, 78.
9. http://www.chess.ibm.com/learn/html/e.5.html, June 13, 1997.
10. Tim Ouellette, United parallel system flied through data, *Computerworld* (May 19, 1997): 37, 38.
11. Nick Lippis, Putting the squeeze on video data, *Data Communications* 22 (February 1993): 67.
12. Kelley Damore, "Captain Crunch" plays back video at 30 frames per second, *InfoWorld* (April 5, 1993): 29.
13. Ibid.; Alicia Hills Moore, A U.S. comeback in electronics, *Fortune* (April 20, 1992): 77–86; Stephan Ohr, Hot DSP market tantalizes analog and digital IC makers, *Electronic Business* (July 1992): 106–109.
14. http://www.emc.com/customers/cvs/british/britishcvs.htm, June 11, 1997.
15. http://www.emc.com/customers/cvs/npac/npaccvs.htm, June 11, 1997.
16. Attributed to Freeman Reports by http://www2.osta.org/osta/html/ostaoptical.nclk, June 11, 1997.
17. Joe Bruscato, Data warehousing for health at Anthem, *Teradata Review* (Spring 1998): 42–45.
18. Laura Didio, X terminals try for another go-round, *Computerworld Client/Server Journal* (June 1996): 10.
19. Mark Fischetti, Pursuing the universal translator, *Technology Review* 95, 8 (November/December, 1992): 16–17; Ned Snell, Making IS accessible, *Datamation* 38, 11 (May 15, 1992): 79–82.

Chapter 4

Software Technology

LEARNING OBJECTIVES

After completing Chapter 4, you will be able to

1. Define software.
2. Describe the difference between the two-tiered, three-tiered, and multitiered client/server models.
3. Compare and contrast the functions of business application software, software-development software, and systems software.
4. Compare and contrast vertical and horizontal software.
5. Cite the relative advantages of packaged, customized, and custom vertical applications software.
6. Identify types of office automation software and describe why people would use it.
7. Describe how computer languages differ from one another.
8. Explain the role of the operating system kernel.
9. Describe how people use utility software to manage the resources of their personal computers.
10. Illustrate the way a particular type of software meets a manager's information needs.

ANTICIPATING THE YEAR 2000

Alan Conder first noticed the problem in 1993. Suddenly, insurance policies dating from 1892 started showing up in his new business report. Ellen Harris, his technical liaison, told him that this problem was caused by software that recognized only the last two digits of the year. The computer could not distinguish between policies originating in 1892 and those originating in 1992. Harris solved the problem by archiving and removing the historical records from the computer system. Lately, the problem resurfaced in a different way. Conder's report of policies sorted by renewal date listed those due to be renewed in the year 2000 before those due in 1998 or 1999. Conder once again notified Harris. This time Harris had no quick work-around. She told him that the Information Technology Group (ITG) was working on this problem company-wide.

Mutual's CNS system includes more than 1,500 modules, each addressing different information needs. In total, the CNS system consists of more than 2 million lines of computer instructions, many of which utilize two-digit dates. Somehow, Mutual's ITG will have to find and fix all of these problems. In addition, the group will need to change data in more than 3 million records relating to policies, payables, personnel, and other entities.[1]

Conder hoped that Mutual would decide to replace its computer systems entirely. He had been unhappy for many years with how they worked. They seemed old and inflexible. Many of the reports he received on a daily or weekly basis came only on paper and could not be viewed on the screen. He could not analyze the information without reentering data into his PC. Entering data into the system

Many computer systems cannot accurately move from the year 1999 to the year 2000. The "Y2K" problem is receiving a great deal of attention.

was cumbersome. He had to tab frequently through the data entry fields. He could not use his mouse. Most importantly, he did not receive all the information he or his people needed to do their jobs effectively. Yet, whenever he asked for changes to the system, the cost that ITG quoted him was so high that he could not justify it even if he had the funds in his budget.

A couple of days later, Harris called to invite Conder to join the management team for the Year-2000 project. "The committee consists of our key business managers and our top technical people," she told him. Conder gladly accepted. Having been with the company for ten years, two in his present position, he understood his information needs and the information needs of others throughout the company extremely well. Diagnosis would not be a problem. But he wondered whether or not he knew enough about software to evaluate the alternatives. What types of software exist? How are they acquired? How might they be combined to best satisfy his needs? Would Mutual have to change the way it does business if it simply bought software to replace CNS rather than rebuilding it from scratch? Conder realized that he had a lot to learn before he could be an effective member of the project team.

WHAT IS SOFTWARE?

Software refers to the instructions that command a computer to perform a desired task. Sometimes people use the terms **program, package,** and **application** to refer to software products, although each has a slightly different connotation.

Computers require software to perform every task they do. For example, computer software allows a user to type, edit, and print a document; to calculate and project financial ratios; or to schedule equipment usage. Conder uses CNS software to track and evaluate the sales performance of Mutual's insurance products. Order takers at Silicon Graphics Inc. (SGI) use Salesbuilder software from Trilogy Development Group to configure SGI's workstations properly, to help salespeople tailor custom orders, and to schedule shipping dates while the customer is on the phone.[2] Dispatchers at Burlington Northern's Fort Worth operations center use software developed by Union Switch & Signal Company to control signals and switches for the entire railway.[3]

A LAYERED VIEW OF SOFTWARE

As Figure 4.1 illustrates, at least two layers of software usually exist between the computer and the user.

- The **operating system kernel,** discussed in more detail later in this chapter, performs the most basic tasks required to keep a computer running. These tasks include organizing computer files, allocating computer memory, managing the interface between the computer and the network, and scheduling the computer to run other software. The kernel also interfaces with the user, as

FIGURE 4.1

FIGURE 4.1   Layers of software exist between a computer and its users.

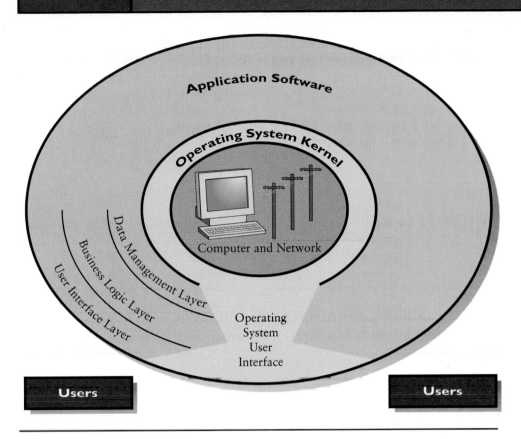

shown in Figure 4.1, so that the user can control some of these activities directly.

- **Application software** satisfies specific user needs, including data management, business functions, and the interface between the user and the software. When you use a word processor to create a document or a spreadsheet to help analyze data, for example, you use application software. Conder uses application software to list policies due for renewal. Application software contains the instructions to perform tasks that the user wants to accomplish.

When application software needs computer or network resources to perform its work, it calls on the operating system kernel to provide them. This division of labor lets application software developers create software that runs on different types of computer systems. An application can run on computers with different designs and configurations because the operating system kernel handles the interface between the application and the hardware.

Separating the functions of the kernel and application software, however, can slow down the application because the processor must do extra work to pass tasks from the application to the kernel and back again. Also, because the application software does not control how the kernel executes its tasks, it cannot fully optimize its performance. As a result, some performance-critical software products, such as some database management systems, bypass the kernel to speed processing.

THE CLIENT/SERVER MODEL

Managers such as Alan Conder first must decide whether a client/server or a centralized approach to software best meets their information needs. The client/server model divides an application into at least two separate but interdependent parts called the **client** and the **server**. The client software occasionally passes a request to the server software, such as to retrieve data from a database. The server software tries to satisfy each request. Although the client and server might operate on the same computer, generally they run on different computers in a networked environment.

Two-Tier Model.   The **two-tier client/server model** assigns the responsibility for handling all data storage and management requests to the server. The client handles the interface with the user and the processing of business functions. For example, to add a new insurance policy, client software presents the data entry screen, processes the data entered by the user, calculates a rate class and a premium amount, and performs other functions, such as generating letters to lien holders. The server stores the policy data in a central database, retrieves rate tables so that the client software can calculate premiums, and perhaps even retrieves information, such as a customer address, from other policies held by the same customer to simplify data entry.

The two-tier client/server approach centralizes data storage on one computer, making shared data storage easier. It allows the user interface and business processing to take place on each user's personal computer. This separation of functions reduces the processing load on the data storage computer. The server software can handle requests from copies of the client software running simultaneously on different computers. For example, a single server can store new policy information and process requests from ten agents, each with their own PC and client software.

Three-Tier Model.   The **three-tier client/server model** divides an application into user interface, business logic, and data management components (see Figure 4.1). It produces two pairs of client/servers, as shown in Figure 4.2. The user interface is the primary client, obtaining data from the user and issuing a request to the business logic server to process these data. The business logic server becomes a client to the data manager, issuing requests as needed to perform its processing. When done, the business logic server sends its results to the user interface client, which in turn presents them to the user.

The three-tier model reduces the resources required at the desktop. Business programs tend to be large and complex, requiring a great deal of storage even when not in use and demanding significant amounts of computer memory when in use. Separating the business logic from the user interface allows the business logic software to run on a centralized computer, reducing the demands on the desktop computer. As a result, employees can use less powerful and less costly desktop computers, known as thin clients, which include little software and storage. For companies that support thousands of desktop computers, using thin clients can result in

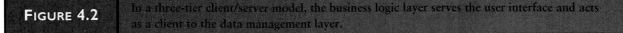

FIGURE 4.2   In a three-tier client/server model, the business logic layer serves the user interface and acts as a client to the data management layer.

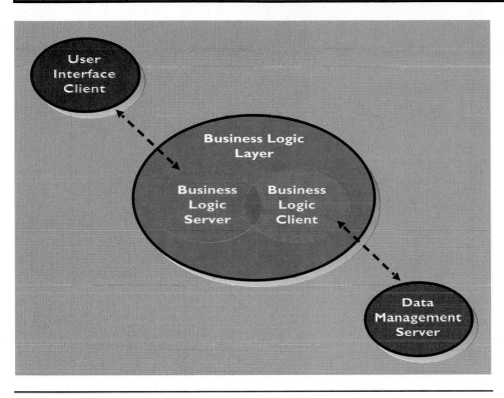

major cost savings. Two-tier models, in contrast, result in clients with a lot of software and storage, called fat clients.

The three-tier model also eases the task of upgrading software. When business rules change, computer professionals can modify the server software without upgrading the software on each desktop computer. For this reason, the three-tier model is particularly popular in organizations that use mobile computers because mobile computers are often off-site and unavailable for upgrade.

Multitier Model.   The **multitier client/server model** or **n-tier client/server model** divides application software into multiple components, each of which can call on the others to perform services for it. Consider, for example, order-entry software. This software might pass a variety of related tasks to inventory management, sales scheduling, and accounting systems. These systems might run on the same or a different computer as the order-entry system. Splitting the application allows these systems to change without affecting the order-entry system. This approach also splits the processing load among different computers, but it increases processing and network overhead by sending messages and requests back and forth among the interrelated systems.

The CNS system at Mutual is not a client/server system. It runs on a single large centralized computer that serves the entire company. Conder expects to evaluate many client/server alternatives. The new software will use a graphical interface on his personal computer and will be modular and flexible so that it can be modified cheaply and frequently as needs change. Erie Family Life Insurance recently reached an agreement with Cybertek to provide this type of client/server software.[4] Some insurance industry watchers have estimated that spending for client/server systems consumed about one-third of the industry's investment in information technology in 1997.[5]

A SOFTWARE CLASSIFICATION MODEL

In this chapter we classify software according to its users and the types of tasks it performs, as shown in Figure 4.3. Understanding these distinctions can help managers select the right software for their needs. Businesspeople use **business application software** to perform business functions. Managers must decide whether to use vertical or horizontal business application software, as illustrated in Figure 4.4:

- **Vertical application software** performs tasks common to a specific industry and often has some or extensive options for customization. Programs to manage dog kennels, support hospital billing, or create architectural drawings illustrate vertical application software. Conder, for example, will require vertical application software for the insurance industry to monitor the sales of Mutual's insurance products.
- **Horizontal application software** performs generic tasks common to many types of business problems across and within industries and usually discourages customization. These tasks include office automation activities, such as the creation and filing of documents and presentations, communication by electronic mail, and frequent calculations. Many tasks in business functions, such as accounting, human resource management, and inventory management, are also similar across industries. Software manufacturers have created horizontal software to support such functions.

FIGURE 4.3	Business application software, software development software, and systems software perform different tasks for different types of users.

Types	Business Application Software		Software-Development Software		Systems Software		
Task	Meet Business Needs		Develop Software		Manage Computer Environment		
Sub-Types	Vertical Software	Horizontal Software	Computer Languages	CASE Tools	Systems Utilities	Network and Systems Management	Operating System Kernel
Users	Businesspeople		Computer Professionals		Business-people	Computer Professionals	

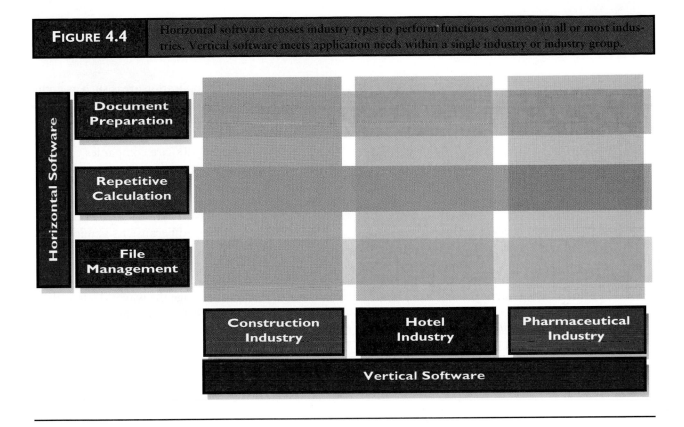

FIGURE 4.4 Horizontal software crosses industry types to perform functions common in all or most industries. Vertical software meets application needs within a single industry or industry group.

Software-development software helps people create new software. It includes computer programming languages and computer-aided software engineering (CASE) tools that automate and provide ongoing technical support for software development (see Chapter 12). **Systems software** manages the computer and its network and includes systems utilities, network and systems software, and the operating system kernel.

VERTICAL APPLICATION SOFTWARE

Managers choose vertical application software because it meets the needs of their industry, such as real estate development, or a function within their industry, such as government contracting for defense contractors and accounting for advertising agencies. Managers of continuous manufacturing processes, such as chemical production or oil refining, for example, have different information needs and so require different software than managers of discrete manufacturing processes, such as the assembly of automobiles or consumer goods. A generic manufacturing package will not likely satisfy either group. Airline and railroad managers, although both are in the transportation industry, have unique information needs and require different software for tracking baggage or ticketing passengers.

Vertical software cannot capture a mass market because it addresses specialty needs. Its manufacturers generally distribute it through nonretail channels such as the following:

- *Consulting Firms.* Firms that have expertise in application areas such as architectural planning or government contracting may distribute vertical software.
- *Integrators.* **Integrators** are companies that package hardware and software to meet a customer's specification; and
- *Value-added resellers.* **Value-added resellers (VARs)** are companies that represent the manufacturer and whom the manufacturer has trained and authorized to customize the software.

Vertical software costs more than mass-marketed software because its developers need to recover their investment over fewer sales and because its vendors have higher selling costs.

In evaluating vertical software, managers should focus on whether the software supports the way their company conducts its business. Conder, for example, will strongly oppose new software that forces Mutual to change the way it deals with its customers and agents. Those managers at Mutual who believe that the company does not operate as efficiently or effectively as it could might choose to change the way it does business and select software that supports these changes. Companies that lack resources to purchase or develop customized software sometimes change their business practices to fit with available software.

Managers who buy vertical software must also consider the quality and availability of support and customization. They must believe that the software vendor can respond to their unique needs and that the vendor has enough installations to guarantee its existence for many years. Because businesses rely on vertical software in their daily operations, vendors must respond rapidly to emergencies and to requests for changes in the software's design. Failure of the software or of its vendors can have disastrous consequences for these businesses.

THE MAKE VERSUS BUY DECISION

A company can acquire vertical software in three ways: (1) purchase packaged software from a software manufacturer and use it without modification; (2) purchase software that can be customized; and (3) develop the software from scratch, creating custom software. Business managers and information technology specialists need to decide which acquisition or development alternative makes the most sense for each application. Figure 4.5 illustrates the relative advantages of packaged, customized, and custom vertical application software.

Packaged Software. Managers and other users can purchase a large variety of uncustomized vertical software products for all types of computers through retail outlets or directly from software developers. Known as **packaged** or **off-the-shelf software,** these uncustomized software packages exist for a wide range of applications and industries. The software that Erie Family Life Insurance purchased from Cybertek is just one such example. Table 4.1 offers other examples of vertical software for selected industries. Although a number of printed directories list vertical

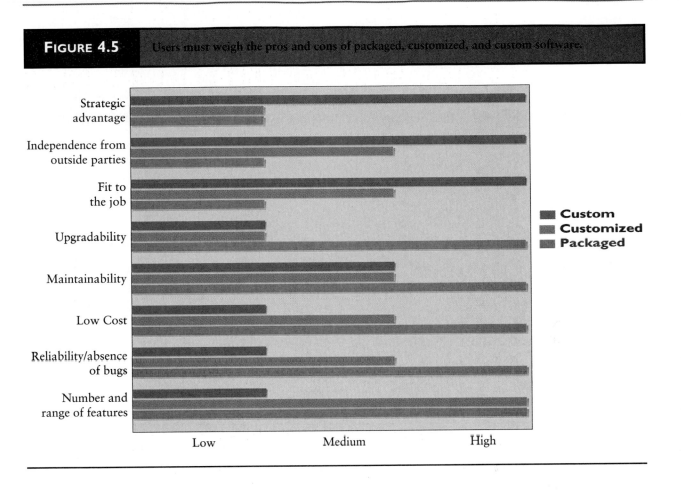

FIGURE 4.5 Users must weigh the pros and cons of packaged, customized, and custom software.

software manufacturers, World Wide Web search engines can easily find vertical software in any industry.

Packaged software offers three major advantages: low price, extensive features, and high reliability. These advantages arise from the software's use by multiple companies. In general, the more popular the software, the greater these advantages.

Packaged software often benefits from the large number of users who have tested the software in a variety of environments. This widespread use decreases the likelihood that the software will have major defects and will omit desired features. Motorola Inc.'s computer group recently migrated from a mainframe environment running custom software to an environment consisting of workstations running mostly packaged software. This migration allowed the group to reduce its budget by 40 percent while shortening application development cycles. Use of packaged software reduced the amount of time that the in-house staff needed to spend modifying software for new versions of its systems software and new hardware platforms. It also increased the group's ability to standardize on a single set of accounting and operating packages for all departments.[6]

On the negative side, packaged software can create a dependency on the software manufacturer. Once a company installs one vendor's vertical software, it will incur heavy costs in licensing, training, and work redesign if it changes to another

TABLE 4.1	Vertical products exist for an array of industries, some of which are illustrated here.

Industry	Product	Vendor
Casino management	Casino Management System (CMS)	Advanced Software Technologies Inc.
	PitTrack	Precision Resource Company
	Table Trac Inc.	Table Trac Inc.
	Excaliber/400	ZDS Information Systems
Construction	Contractor II	A-Systems Corp.
	Best Estimate	Best Estimate Software
	Caesar	Caesar Systems Inc.
	CAPS Construction Suite	Construction Application Software Inc.
Farm management	Dairyman	AGPRO Software
	Track N Field	Agricultural Data Systems
	Ranch Master	AgriSoft
	FarmTrac	Farm Works Software
School administration	ADM2000	ACE Software
	As-Admin	Aldrich Computer Services Inc.
	CLASS School Administrative Software	Campus Management Corp.
	POISE	Educational Systems Products

vendor. As a result, the vendor can charge high prices for upgrades and support. In addition, whenever business managers want a new feature, they can only ask and wait for a future software release.

Customized Software. Although most vertical software requires some degree of customization, **customized software** involves more than merely customizing it when installed. Instead, value-added resellers customize the software to a customer's specifications and add value to it.

A company may select a package and a VAR because executives have heard favorable comments about the VAR and its software from a friend or relative. Often this ad hoc approach to evaluation results in selecting software that does not meet the information needs of the purchaser. A more formal search process usually produces better results. It includes the following steps:

1. The company develops a **request for proposal (RFP)** that clearly identifies its information processing requirements and information needs. The RFP should include details of data collection and entry, the nature of all desired reports, and any other specifications.
2. The user identifies vendors and solicits bids.
3. Each vendor identifies the requirements met by its package and those requirements that need customization.
4. The user compares the responses by assessing the proposed features, costs, and vendor characteristics and selects two or three vendors for more detailed negotiation.

THE MANAGER IN ACTION

Francs, pounds, dollars, and rupees just didn't add up at W.R. Grace, in any language.

In 1994, chemical and materials company W.R. Grace & Co.'s financial services staff was using disparate systems that didn't communicate with one another or with manufacturing applications. The systems also didn't deal well with international currencies. The company, then going through consolidations and spinoffs, wanted to get away from regional management and operate globally to tie together its 20,000 employees.

"We knew we couldn't piece together global information with the montage of systems that we had," says Stephen Noone, vice president of financial services development at Grace.

Grace undertook a general review of its financial services, and learned that it scored lower than many first-tier companies on the overall cost of providing financial services. More time was spent collecting information than analyzing it, which left the company with an overload of paper and not enough answers.

Grace needed a new underlying system, so it chose SAP AG's R/3 integrated financial suite. R/3 had the most complete graphical user interface, offered good international currency and language support, and was several steps ahead of the rest of the applications market in moving to client/server, says Mary B. Akyuz, manager of software engineering at Grace's Boston IT service center.

Grace started the companywide rollout with its construction products and consealant business units in Boston. Once it began the SAP implementation, Grace [executives] decided that the sales and distribution and production and materials management units should be moved to SAP as well. On Jan.1, it migrated 600 users in these business units.

Extracted from A. Malloy, Case study: SAP falls into Grace, *Computerworld* (May 26, 1997): 79.

5. Each qualifying vendor performs an **operational capability demonstration (OCD)**, which simulates the user's application as closely as possible. This simulation allows the user to judge how rapidly the system performs under the expected processing loads, gives a better indication of the system's operation, and helps identify any necessary changes in the software and the user's operations. Although users typically pay part of the cost of an OCD, the investment results in a more informed purchase decision.

6. The user and vendor negotiate a payment schedule and agree on a test of the software's acceptability to the user.

Customizing packaged software helps a company meet more of its information requirements and may reduce its dependency on the software manufacturer to make changes: Through the VAR the customer buys influence with the manufacturer in the design of features in future releases. Because most software manufacturers who sell customizable software list many VARs who can provide support, the user does not depend on a single consultant.

Customized vertical software may suffer from a disproportionate number of software bugs. Whereas developers of packaged software spend a great deal of time and effort designing and testing their software, custom software developers cannot test their products as much because only one company uses it. Customized software also cannot readily accommodate new releases without being totally customized again. As a result, companies using customized software do not benefit from the software manufacturer's continuing development efforts. A company may spend a lot to add a feature that the manufacturer might include in its next release for a minimal upgrade fee. Riscorp, a managed care firm in Sarasota, Florida, customized its FlexiFinancial general ledger and accounts payable software, licensed from FlexiInternational, to integrate with its other operational systems. However, Riscorp has attempted to limit customization of the financial package itself so as "not to lose the future benefit of that package."[7]

Custom Software.   Organizations develop their own **custom software** from scratch, rather than use or customize packaged software for three reasons. First, no packaged software meets the required specifications, and modifying existing software is too difficult. Second, the company plans to resell the custom software at a profit. Third, custom software may provide the company with a competitive advantage by providing services for customers, increasing management's knowledge and ability to make good decisions, reducing costs, improving quality, and providing other benefits. Only custom software can provide such a competitive advantage because the competition can easily buy packaged and customized software. Merrill Lynch recognized such a competitive advantage when it planned to invest $1 billion in software (and associated hardware) to allow its financial consultants to operate with mobile computers at customer sites.[8]

Custom software is expensive to produce, costly to maintain, subject to bugs, and usually takes many years to develop. Not only does this development time delay the benefit, but it reduces the value of the software as company needs and the competitive environment change constantly. Finally, if software developers can mimic the key features of the software's design and resell it to a company's competitors, they may quickly dilute any competitive advantage the company has gained.

Mutual originally developed CNS because the available packaged software did not meet its needs and because it felt that it could achieve a competitive advantage with CNS. At the time it developed CNS, no software provided an integrated view of a customer across multiple insurance products. CNS gave Mutual agents a competitive advantage by allowing them to cross-sell products where appropriate. Conder has learned that about one-half of all companies in the insurance industry who replace their software use custom software, primarily for these same reasons. By contrast, in the health care industry, less than one-fifth use custom software.[9]

Managers who decide to develop custom software must decide whether to use internal company resources or to hire a company that specializes in software development. VARs develop customized software cost-effectively because they have substantial expertise in the base software product, but this advantage disappears for custom software because they cannot use preexisting packages.

Small organizations that lack internal resources for software development may create custom software by paying another company to do it. Boston Software Corporation and ECTA Corporation, for example, develop software for companies in the insurance industry.[10] Managers in large organizations usually must use internal IS personnel or let the IS staff decide who will develop the software. Sometimes company policy allows functional managers to seek development bids from both internal and external candidates. Grange Mutual Casualty Company, an Ohio-based insurer with annual premium sales of $500 million, has outsourced some of its development and operations to Policy Management Systems Corporation.[11]

INTEGRATED SOLUTIONS

Integrated solutions coordinate the activities of suppliers, distributors, and customers. This integration, called **supply-chain management,** requires the cooperation of companies outside of the company's own and a secure way of communicating between them. Supply chain management can reduce the costs of a company with $600 million in annual sales by as much as $42 million. Companies using supply-chain management needed only two weeks on average to increase production by 20 percent compared to several months without supply-chain management. Also, companies with supply-chain management delivered goods on time 96 percent of the time compared to 83 percent for the average company.[12] Ames, the $200 million maker of garden tools, and Ace Hardware Corporation use Manugistics supply-chain management software to keep track of and replenish Ames's products sold in Ace hardware stores.[13]

The grocery industry calls supply-chain management efficient consumer response (ECR). ECR software breaks barriers between trading partners, such as retailers and manufacturers, and between internal functions such as category management and product replenishment (see Figure 4.6). Companies such as Land O' Lakes Inc. and Kellogg Company have begun to implement integrated ECR packages to improve internal processes, gain greater efficiency in distribution, and globalize their operations.[14] Oracle and SAP have moved into the ECR market to respond to the growing demand with software derived from their manufacturing packages.

FIGURE 4.6   Components of ECR include buying and merchandising, logistics and stock management, sales and marketing, and production and distribution.

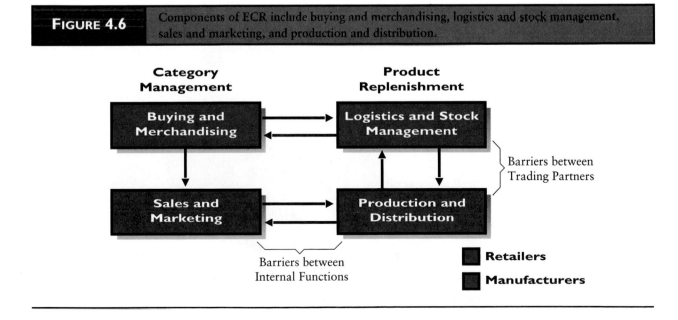

Enterprise-resource-planning (ERP) software products, such as those developed specifically for each industry by SAP, Oracle, Baan, and PeopleSoft, provide seamless support for the supply-chain, value-chain, and administrative processes of a company. They integrate diverse activities internal and external to the company, support many languages and many currencies, and help companies integrate their operations at multiple sites and business units.

Most ERP applications are customized products. The major vendors begin with an application template that is precustomized by industry (Figure 4.7 provides an industry distribution). Then, the vendors, consultants, or the company purchasing the software further customize it to meet individual company needs. Although the ERP vendors build their software to minimize the amount of customization and to simplify the customization process, most large companies spend anywhere from 100 percent to 500 percent of the cost of the software for its customization.

An integrated ERP solution lets managers analyze their operating units as a whole and make decisions from a global perspective. Integrated ERP software eliminates the need to build bridges between applications to share data. For example, sales managers can respond to a manufacturing or ordering plan that might affect the availability of a product. The Monsanto Company, Dow Chemical, and the DuPont Company, all major chemical manufacturers with global operations, have converted their business systems to ERP software products known as R/2 (mainframe based) and R/3 (client/server based), packages produced by SAP AG. The conversion allows them to support simplified business processes as well as communication and collaboration worldwide.[15] GATX Capital Corporation, a lessor of commercial aircraft,

| **FIGURE 4.7** | The electric/electronic industry and the chemical/pharmaceutical industry accounted for almost 50 percent of all ERP sales in 1995. |

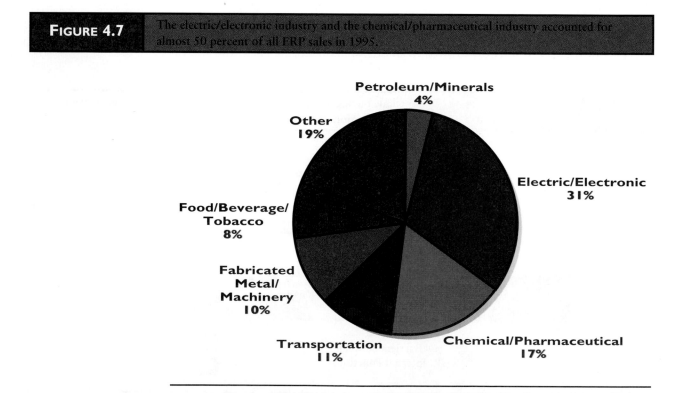

customized the R/3 version of SAP to fit its business. Now it plans to sell its customized work to its competition.[16]

ERP software often requires companies to change their processes to accommodate the software. ERP lets them introduce improved, redesigned processes because ERP software incorporates the best processes of companies in the industry. However, when a company has unique processes that give it a competitive advantage, adoption of ERP software can have negative consequences.

ERP and any integrated software may not provide as many features or provide them as well as software specifically designed for a particular application, such as inventory management. Functional managers and general managers need to choose between the best software they can find in each functional area or an integrated package that provides 80 to 90 percent of the features they need in each area. In making this decision, they need to consider the cost of customizing the software to achieve the additional 10 to 20 percent of functionality.

ERP software has not penetrated the service industries because managers are less likely to use systems that their competitors can purchase. Nevertheless, the economic advantages of customized and packaged systems and the success of ERP in manufacturing industries have accelerated the acceptance of integrated packages for a subset of functions in many service industries. Springer-Miller Systems has penetrated the hotel market with software that handles all front- and back-office functions. The software performs and integrates such tasks as maintaining guest histories, booking golf tee times and dinner reservations, preparing correspondence, maintaining reservations, and managing multiple properties in a chain.[17]

PREPARING FOR THE YEAR 2000

Modifying vertical application software to deal properly with dates in the year 2000 and beyond is a major problem worldwide. The Gartner Group, a well-respected industry forecaster, estimates the cost to be between $300 to $600 billion.[18] Other estimates run as high as $1.6 trillion.[19] According to Viasoft, a consultant involved in these conversions, a typical *Fortune* 1000 company will spend between $10 and $15 million, consume more than 14 decades of staff time, and require a peak staffing of 48 programmers.[20] Surveys have indicated that 83 percent of companies plan to spend more than 25 percent of their information systems budgets in 1998 and 1999 just to fix their applications for the year 2000.[21]

Companies can take three approaches to fixing the problem:

- *Use Automated Tools.* These tools examine each line of code, identify those that likely refer to dates, and, with some user help, alter them to deal properly with a four-digit year. Vendors and consultants for Tampa Electric, the Florida utility, estimated that it would cost the company about $1 per line to fix its 4.5 million lines code in their 6,000 mainframe programs. After completing a pilot program with automated tools, Tampa Electric estimates that it can complete the task at a substantially lower (although yet unspecified) cost using no more than seven employees over a 22-month period.[22]

- *Replace Existing Software with Year 2000 Compliant ERP Products.* Because ERP software affects every process in the company, an ERP installation in a large company may take two or three years. If managers want

INFORMATION TECHNOLOGY AND GLOBAL BUSINESS

Some horizontal application software, such as word processing software, may be loaded on almost every desktop in a company. Managing upgrades of such software is difficult for companies that have thousands of users at many locations around the world. Here's how Hewlett-Packard does the job:

It's 9 A.M. Monday in Palo Alto, California, and Hewlett-Packard Co. is primed to roll out a new company-wide word processing application. But first there are some last-minute details. Brandt Faatz, Fort Collins, Colorado-based head of HP's PC common operating environment team, calls his key players in the United States, Europe, and Asia. Together they iron out the final bugs of the rollout and post a synopsis of their discussion on the World Wide Web, alerting thousands of HP employees to the pending upgrade. By 5 P.M., the new software is loaded onto a master server in Palo Alto and from there is transmitted globally to 400 file servers, which in turn distribute the software to more than 100,000 HP desktops worldwide. By 5 P.M. Wednesday, just 48 hours later, the roll-out is complete.*

Before electronic software distribution (ESD) software became available at Whirlpool, it used to take Jim Wolf, a systems analyst, and others like him 90 minutes to install new software on each of the company's 1,000 PCs. That does not include the time necessary to send the diskettes or CDs to remote locations. Now, as with HP, the process requires some set-up time, but thereafter operates automatically and almost instantaneously.

Bill Holder of Micropath Inc. (Bellevue, Washington) estimates that "a company with 2,000 PCs can save as much as $1 million by

access to existing data, they also need to fix all date fields, convert the data into a form acceptable for loading into the ERP software, and eliminate any inconsistencies among the data stored by minimally integrated systems. Despite these difficulties, this strategy may be largely responsible for the recent popularity of ERP software.

- *Build Software That Will Intercept and Convert Dates as They Are Entered, Stored, or Output.* This strategy would first convert all data to four-digit dates. Then the existing software would run under the supervision of the date-intercepting software. The existing software would not change except where it performs calculations based on the date. This approach slows performance by adding a layer of operations and makes complex systems even more complex but minimizes the amount of effort required to perform the conversion.

Conder likely prefers to replace Mutual's existing systems in their entirety with an ERP package because he is dissatisfied with the company's current systems.

THE APPLICATION SOFTWARE LIFE CYCLE

Customized and custom software progress through a life cycle of conception, development, maturation, and decline. When managers first perceive the need for new

using electronic software distribution."[†] But what is ESD? Quite simply it is a network and systems management tool that automates the installation of software on computers connected to a network. ESD software allows managers to control exactly who gets what software and in what manner. Among the features of ESD software are the following:

- The ability to identify users or groups of users to receive the selected software
- The ability to "push" the software onto the user's system or allow the user to install the software at a more convenient time at the click of a mouse
- The ability to detect insufficient disk space to load software, to abort the loading in such a case, and to log the exception
- The ability to detect failures during a software installation and to log these errors

- The ability to detect current versions of software on systems and select the appropriate upgrade path accordingly

ESD software can be used to update vertical application software as well as horizontal software. Although such upgrades generally affect fewer systems, they may be more complicated.

SOURCE: William Brandel, Software distribution tools come of age, *Computerworld* (March 6, 1995), http://www.computerworld.com/search/AT-html/9503/ 950306SLesd2.html; and Nick Wreden, Sneaking away from the sneakernet, *Software Quarterly* 2(1) (1995): 18–24.

*Tom Field, Getting in touch with your inner Web, *CIO Magazine* (January 15, 1997), http://www.cio.com/CIO/011597_intranets_content.html.

†Quoted in Stuart Johnston, Chevron takes control—Energy company launches a broad-based plan to rein in the costs of PCs, *Information Week* (July 2, 1997), http://www.techweb.com/se/directlink.cgi?IWK19961104S0061.

software, they evaluate a variety of options for meeting their needs. If packaged software cannot meet their needs, they'll need to develop software from scratch or customize software that almost meets their needs. As their needs change, they may make minor modifications to enhance the software and improve its functionality. The software matures and at some point becomes relatively stable.

In the long run, as managers, corporate strategy, business environment, and technology change, the value of the software declines. Each manager brings a different perspective to her role and defines different information needs. The business needs also change in response to changes in corporate strategy or changes in the competitive environment. Technological advances also affect the value of software, turning a state-of-the-art, strategically positioned system into one that lags its competition. Managers should continuously evaluate their software to ensure that it meets their needs. At some point, they must again determine which software product best meets the changed organizational requirements, incorporates modern software technology, and runs on the most cost-efficient hardware available.

The application software life cycle differs from the software development life cycle, which we will address in Chapter 12. The application software life cycle describes by analogy to the human life cycle the evolution of software maturity and usage. The systems development life cycle (SDLC) prescribes an approach, as a series of steps, for developing and maintaining software.

HORIZONTAL APPLICATION SOFTWARE

Horizontal application software addresses tasks that are common to users in all or almost all industries. Managers should understand the options and help find software that best meets their needs. Typically, information systems professionals and corporate purchasing agents rather than business managers assume responsibility for selecting and buying horizontal application packages. They may purchase these packages in volume or purchase a single site-license for the entire organization. They often value a low price and good terms over the particular features offered by competing packages. Horizontal application software appeals to a mass market. Its developers and manufacturers can sell it at a relatively low price and still recover their costs. They can distribute it at low cost through retail outlets and mail-order houses.

Managers and clerical employees, for example, use generic word processing software to create documents such as letters and reports; spreadsheet software to chart trends, perform what-if analyses, and carry out repetitive calculations; and desktop publishing software to create camera-ready copy for advertisements, brochures, reports, and public-relations documents.

Horizontal application software commands a higher selling price when used on multiuser computers and servers, although the price per user, often called the price per seat, is lower than that of similar software sold for individual use. Software vendors may offer **site licenses.** These allow an organization to use a specified number of copies of the licensed software or to give a certain number of users access to a single copy of the software at a discount relative to the price of an individual license. Sometimes, in exchange for this discount, the vendor requires all contact to pass through a single representative at the organization's site and provides only a single copy of software documentation.

In evaluating a horizontal software package, buyers consider not only the quality of the software, but also the quality of the vendor or manufacturer, the quality of its documentation, and the availability of ancillary materials such as textbooks and training courses. The stability and market position of a software manufacturer affect the likelihood of continued development and support of its products and the continued availability of third-party auxiliary software and publications. The quality and responsiveness of a manufacturer's technical support staff are important, even for organizations that have excellent internal support staffs. Often only the software manufacturer can diagnose the causes of problems, find ways to work around the difficulties, and fix them if necessary. Buyers can use trade magazines and the World Wide Web as primary sources of information about a vendor's market share and support quality.

Buyers of horizontal applications software also assess a manufacturer's policies and pricing for support and upgrades. Vendors differ in the length of time for which they provide free technical support, as well as the price of technical support after this period. Some vendors offer a money-back guarantee to unhappy users of their products. Most vendors provide free access to an electronic bulletin board for sharing information about known flaws or bugs, ways of working around problems, and upgrade release notices. Other vendors provide bulletin boards for users to talk with other users about their experiences with the product. Buyers should consider the hours of the vendor's technical support, particularly if the vendor is located in a distant time zone.

ETHICAL ISSUES IN IT

Software piracy is the use of unlicensed software. Software piracy accounted for approximately $11 billion in 1996 according to the results of a study conducted by International Planning and Research. Piracy rates range from about 27 percent of software used in the United States to 99 percent in Viet Nam.*

It is illegal to copy software for personal or organizational use in most countries. In December 1996, members of the 160-country World Intellectual Property Organization signed a treaty aimed at reducing the piracy of all digital material, including software. In the United States, the illegal copying of software is a criminal offense, punishable by fine and jail. Software piracy stifles innovation by reducing or removing the financial incentive to develop new software.

Many of the largest software publishers, such as Microsoft, Novell, and Autodesk, use hot lines to catch software pirates. An employee who suspects that her company is using unauthorized copies of software can call these hot lines to report the suspected piracy. In many cases, software publishers can obtain search warrants to inspect the computers of suspected software pirates. Using this approach, Novell has reached legal settlements worth more than $1.3 million.[†]

The Business Software Alliance (BSA) and the Software Publishers Association (SPA) are two organizations that fight software piracy for their members. Small and medium-sized organizations that do not have the resources to wage court battles or even to staff hot lines can avail themselves of the piracy fighting arms of these two organizations. The BSA has filed more than 600 lawsuits on behalf of its members since its formation in 1988.[‡]

1. Is software piracy unethical? Why or why not?
2. What role should employees play in reporting software piracy?
3. Should software manufacturers hire policing organizations such as BSA and SPA? What ethical issues should they consider?

---

*Software industry lost $11B to piracy, *Computerworld Online* (May 8, 1997).
[†]Rory J. Thompson, Pirates' plunder plan plagued, *Information Week* (June 30, 1997), http://www.techweb.com/se/directlink.cgi?IWK19970630S0014.
[‡]See the Business Alliance Software Piracy Website , http://www.bsa.org/piracy/piracy.html.

Buyers in an organization that uses several different types of computer systems (for example, IBM mainframe, IBM-PC, and Macintosh) or several different types of systems software should assess whether the horizontal software can run on all systems. The organization benefits from the lack of retraining needed to use horizontal application software on different computers. In addition, the computers' hardware and systems software can be changed without affecting the users' ability to perform their work.

In this section we discuss two generic types of horizontal application software: office automation software and business function application software. Web browsers (see Chapter 7) can also be classified as horizontal software.

OFFICE AUTOMATION

Managers, clerks, and other office workers use office automation software to perform routine office tasks. The following list identifies some of the most commonly used types of office automation software and the tasks that they perform:

- *Word processing* creates text-based documents.
- *Presentation graphics* create presentations and graphical documents.
- *Spreadsheets* perform repetitive calculations and what-if analyses.
- *Database management* maintains records.
- *Electronic mail* sends messages and attachments.
- *Scheduling software* manages and coordinates appointment calendars and to-do lists.
- *Work flow software* automates the flow of documents.

In this section we briefly describe and discuss the technology associated with the different types of office automation software. We also describe integrated packages and office suites, two types of horizontal software that combine or integrate many of the functions of the individual office automation packages. In Chapter 8, we will examine the business implications of automating office work.

FIGURE 4.8   Microsoft Word for Windows produces documents like the one shown here.

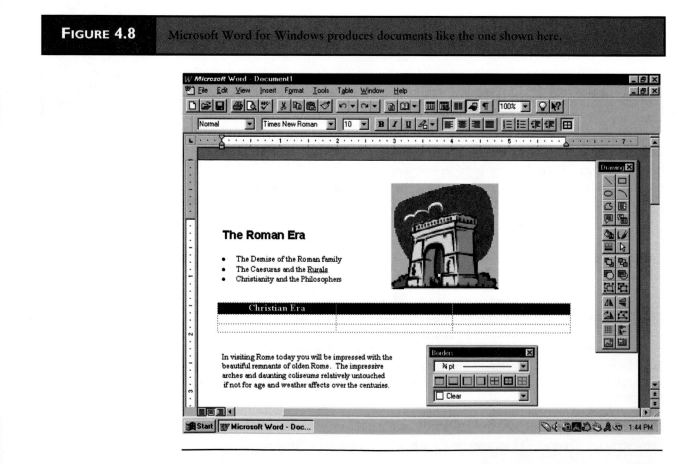

Word Processing.   Word processing software (see Figure 4.8), such as Word or WordPerfect, assists users in creating, modifying, and printing text-based documents. These documents may include graphics and other nontextual elements, although presentation graphics software and desktop publishing software work better for creating documents that are more visual than textual. Managers can evaluate whether their word processing software provides the array of functions shown in Table 4.2.

Presentation Graphics.   Presentation graphics software (see Figure 4.9), such as PowerPoint or Harvard Graphics, helps people without graphics training produce professional-looking slides, overheads, or prints to support their presentations. Managers can evaluate whether their presentation graphics software provides the features shown in Table 4.3.

TABLE 4.2	High-quality word processing software should at least include the features shown here.
Editing	• Undo changes • Replace all occurrences of one word or phrase with another • Mark a location in the text and then return to it after examining other parts of the document • Show two or more parts of the document on the screen simultaneously • Insert, move, or delete columns in a table • Perform automatic hyphenation
Formatting	• Change the size or shape (font) of characters in the text • Show text in bold, italicized, or underlined formats • Change margins, paragraph spacing, line spacing, and indentations • Create and apply styles, groups of formats that are used for parts of documents such as section headings or figure captions
Proofing	• Find and fix spelling and grammatical errors
Graphics Manipulation	• Import a figure created elsewhere • Create simple graphics, then size, crop, and rotate them • Create text that the user can manipulate graphically by shaping, stretching, or tilting it • Include sound or motion pictures within a document
Linking	• Include files created by different software by either inserting them intact (as if photographed into the text) or inserting them by reference so that the document reflects the most recent version whenever the referenced file is changed
Indexing and Referencing	• Automatically number a series, such as tables or figures • Cross reference numbered series in the text, even as some are added or deleted • Reference text by its page number
Versioning	• Compare different versions of the same document to keep track of and view changes between versions • Identify the person or persons responsible for creating and modifying the document • Identify the date created and dates modified

FIGURE 4.9 A Microsoft PowerPoint display illustrates presentation software.

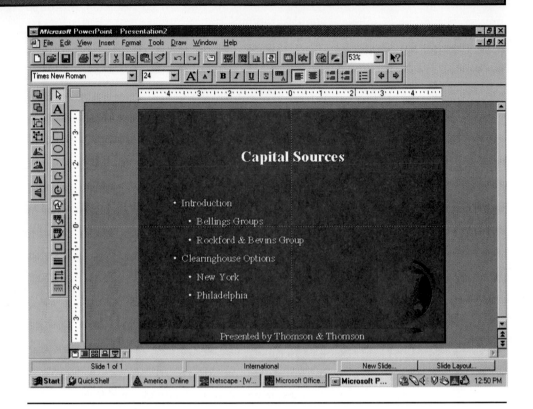

TABLE 4.3 Presentation graphics software should have the features shown here.

Choice of Chart Types	• Templates provide default designs and settings for a wide variety of charts, including bullet charts, organization charts, title pages, numeric graphs, and compound charts.
Integrated Design	• The software provides overridable automatic or recommended colors, sizes, fonts, alignment, and background, so that all the slides or charts in each presentation appear to arise from a common design
Clip Art	• Clip art is ready-made art that can be inserted into the user's presentation.
Slide Show	• Slide shows present charts directly from the computer, rather than from slides or transparencies. Users can select from a variety of visual effects between charts, such as fading (one chart slowly disappears while the next chart slowly forms), wiping (one chart moves to the right while another replaces it from the left or vice versa), and scrolling.
Multimedia Effects	• Multimedia functions allow the inclusion of sound and video clips within a slide-show presentation.

Spreadsheets.　Spreadsheet programs (see Figure 4.10), such as Excel or Lotus 1-2-3, calculate tabular information containing interdependent values and help automate the process of performing repeated calculations. Managers can use spreadsheets to track budgeted amounts, calculate pay increments, or support other analytical activities.

Three enhancements have influenced the use of spreadsheets:

- *Graphic functions* display data in a spreadsheet, such as graphs or charts, and have motivated people to use spreadsheets to visualize data even when few or no calculations are performed.
- *Basic database features* allow a user to sort data by column or row, to identify and extract rows or columns meeting a specified set of criteria, or to compute statistics such as the minimum, maximum, mean, and standard deviation of data meeting specified criteria.
- *Optimization features* allow the software to find the best combination of values for some data so as to achieve a desired result.

Database Management.　As you will learn in Chapter 5, database management software, such as FileMaker Pro or Access, allows users to store, organize,

FIGURE 4.10　A Microsoft Excel spreadsheet supports calculations, what-if, and other mathematical analyses.

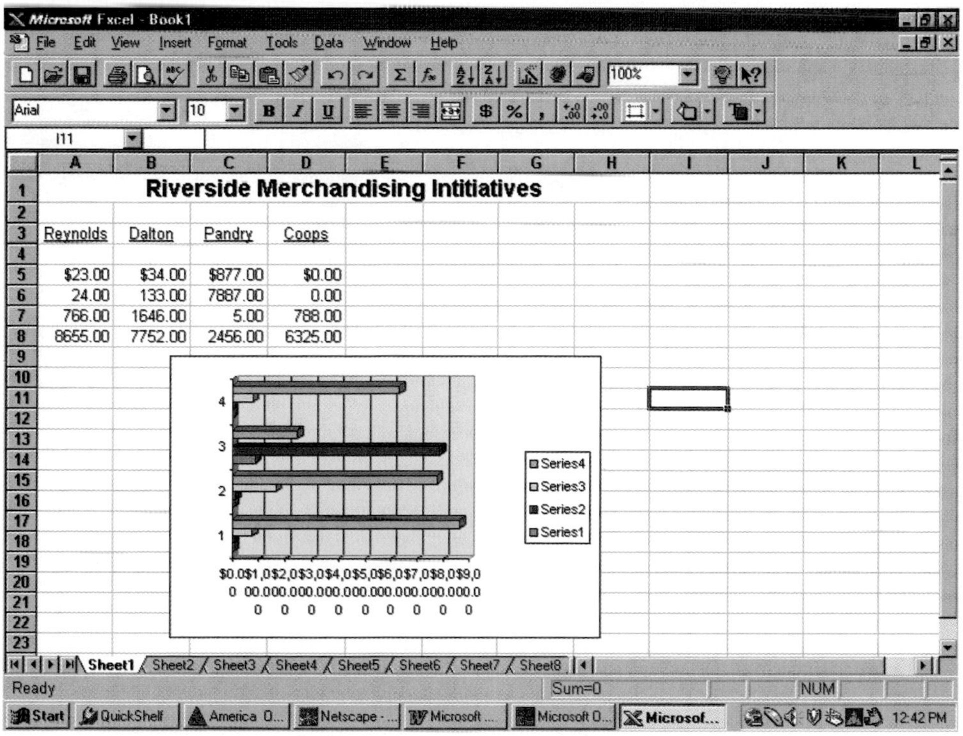

and retrieve data of any type. A database manager generates screens for data entry, cross-references data of different types (for example, which employee is the sales representative for a given customer), and retrieves data meeting a selected set of criteria and in a specified sorted order.

Electronic Mail. Businesspeople use electronic mail systems (see Figure 4.11), such as cc:Mail or Beyond Mail, in place of the postal service and internal company mail services to exchange information. Electronic mail software generally supports the ability to attach a document or another file to a message as if it were an enclosure in an envelope. Electronic mail software also generally supports the following functions, among others, which increase its value relative to physical mail:

- *Mail Handling.* Senders can schedule messages for mailing at a later time and date, request a return receipt verifying that the message was read, and mark a message as urgent or of low priority.
- *Mail Sorting.* Recipients can set up folders to organize their incoming mail.
- *Mail Screening.* Recipients can screen their messages according to its subject, sender, or even content. They can then place messages in different folders or discard them.

FIGURE 4.11 Employees can send electronic mail with Beyond Mail.

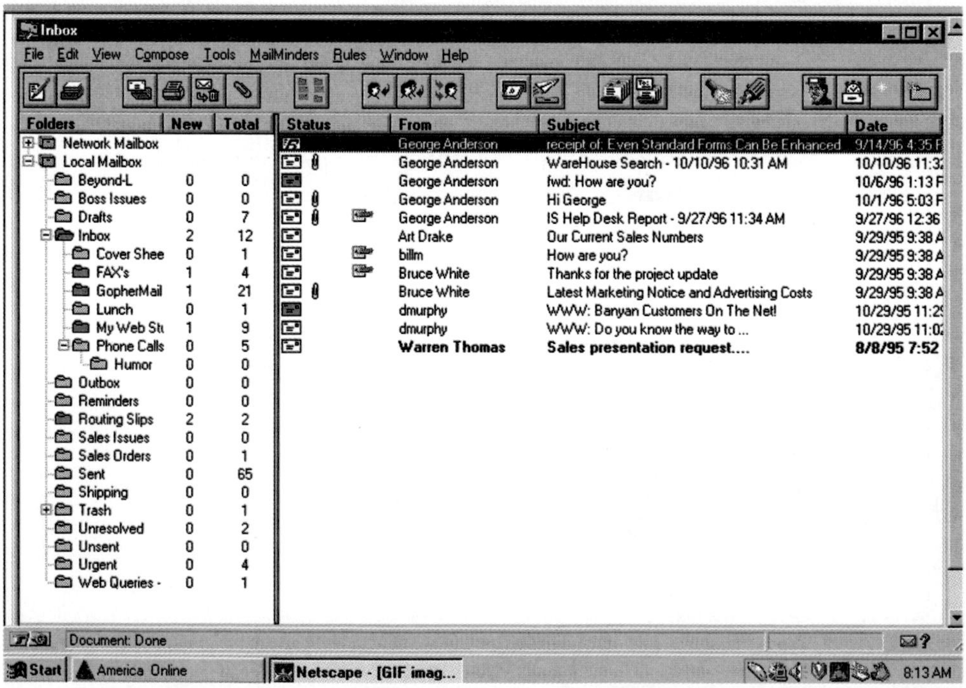

- *Mailing Lists.* Electronic mail users can set up mailing lists and then send messages to people on the list without retyping any addresses.

Scheduling Software.

Scheduling software helps automate appointment calendars and to-do lists (see Figure 4.12). This software uses a visual and audio prompt to remind users of appointments and activities they have entered. Users can schedule periodic appointments with a single entry. Scheduling software also helps people share calendars and can automatically suggest appointment dates and times for a set of networked users. It can organize to-do lists by date due, project, and other characteristics.

Work Flow Management.

Work flow management software (see Chapter 8 for a discussion of work flow management) controls the flow of electronic documents and activities between workers or groups of workers. Work flow management software can generate documents or mail in response to certain conditions, route documents, request that users add their digital signatures, notify managers of tasks done late or improperly, and select free workers from among a pool to perform certain processes. It can also help managers document and redesign their processes. In this

FIGURE 4.12   Microsoft Schedule provides a day's schedule with a keystroke.

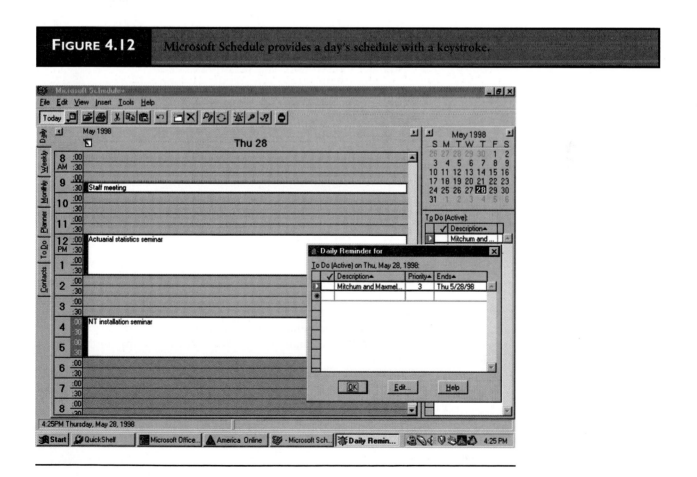

respect, work flow management software has many applications beyond office automation.

Office Suites and Integrated Office Software.

Many vendors sell several types of office automation application software in a single-package called an **office suite**, such as Microsoft Office or Ami Pro. Most office suites include word processing, spreadsheet, database, and presentation graphics software. Some may also include database management, scheduling, and electronic mail software. Vendors sell their suite products at a significant discount relative to the prices of the components they include. The components present a common look and feel to the user and can easily exchange information with one another. For example, someone working on a document in the word processor can include tables and charts created with the spreadsheet and presentation graphics software.

Office automation software is also sold as **integrated office software.** Integrated office software compresses several office automation packages into a single program. Microsoft Works, for example, consists of software for word processing, spreadsheet, database management, and scheduling. Integrated software does not make the user switch between programs to use its different functions as with a suite. Integrated software also costs less than a suite and can be so inexpensive that computer manufacturers package it for free with their hardware. However, integrated office software offers less functionality than similar software in a suite.

BUSINESS FUNCTION APPLICATIONS

Vendors sell horizontal application software to address many types of functional activities common to most industries. These activities include sales force management, human resources management, inventory management, bookkeeping, customer support, project management, and the production of marketing materials. Many small companies and some midsized firms buy packaged generic software to support these functions. As companies grow, their information needs in these areas become more specialized and less suited to horizontal software. They likely turn to vertical software that crosses functions to address many of their information needs in a more integrated and industry-specific fashion.

In this section we review project management and desktop publishing (for the development of marketing materials) as examples of horizontal software that addresses functional business needs.

Project Management.

Project management software, such as Microsoft Project, assists project managers in planning, scheduling, and monitoring the progress of projects (see Figure 4.13). Project management software performs the following functions:

- *Identification of Critical Tasks.* Critical tasks are those activities that delay the project if they are not completed on time.
- *Identification of Critical Resources.* Critical resources, including people, material, and money needed to perform tasks, delay a project if they are reduced in any way.

FIGURE 4.13 Microsoft Project creates GANTT and PERT charts for tracking project progress.

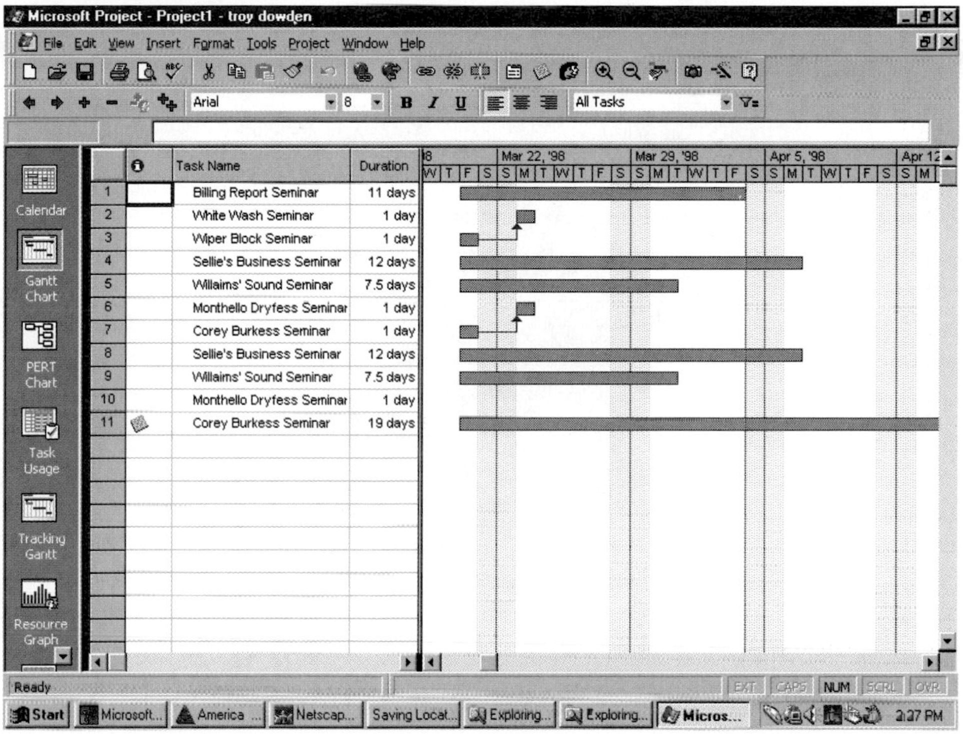

- *Assignment of Resources.* The software can help managers identify scarce resources and determine how to assign them to complete the required tasks.
- *Creation of PERT and Gantt Charts.* PERT and Gantt charts graphically show which tasks must be completed before others can be started (or sometimes finished), clarify their timing, and plot the progress of the project.
- *Creation of Task Lists.* The software can create lists of activities on a daily or weekly basis for each member of the project team and automatically send the lists by electronic mail to the team members.

Project management software for vertical applications differs from horizontal project management software in that it comes preset with typical activities for an industry. For example, software for the construction industry might ask the user to select from the different types of buildings and enter information such as the dimensions of the structures and local labor rates. Project management software for software developers might prompt the user to select from among different types of software development projects (large scale, phased, prototype, purchased system) and to enter the size of the project.

Desktop Publishing. Desktop publishing (DTP) software, such as Corel Draw, helps users lay out text and graphics in a form suitable for publication (see

FIGURE 4.14   Graphic designers can use Corel Draw.

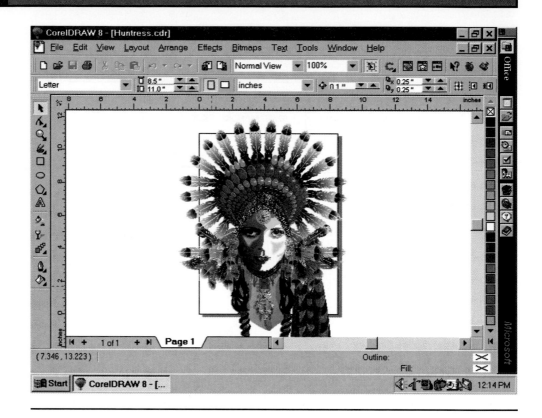

Figure 4.14). Although both word processing and desktop publishing help users to create highly presentable documents, word processors attempt to meet writers' needs, whereas desktop publishing software addresses publishers' needs. The key features of desktop publishing software include those shown in Table 4.4.

COMPUTER LANGUAGES

Although most managers rely on IS professionals to create or change software, they should know that each type of computer recognizes and responds to a different set of instructions. Computer programs organize and sequence these instructions. Programmers use computer languages, such as C, COBOL, Pascal, or Visual Basic, to create a single computer program that performs the same task on different computers. Programs written in such languages can be translated into the language of the target computer before being run. Languages also increase the efficiency of software development because programmers can use simple, understandable commands rather than instructions written in a format required by the target computer.

TABLE 4.4	Desktop publishing software should include the features shown here.

Layout	• Support the arrangement of text and graphics on the pages of a publication, including multiple columns on a page
	• Wrap text around graphics
	• Control the placement, size, style, and font of text material
	• Control flow of text across pages (as for a headline)
	• Crop pictures
	• Automatically balance columns on a page
Typographic Controls	• Justify paragraphs
	• Set size, style, and font of text
	• Deal with the space used by a letter relative to its environment (kerning)
	• Rotate text
	• Support mathematical and other symbols
	• Exert microcontrol over vertical and horizontal spacing.
Text Handling	• Compose or modify text as with a word processor
	• Cut, paste, and copy text
	• Search for and replace text
	• Check spelling
	• Generate an index, cross-references, and table of contents
	• Format tables
Graphics Manipulation	• Draw lines, rectangles, ellipses, and circles, and fill them with patterns or various shades of gray
	• Crop and resize graphics with or without distorting the aspect ratio (the relationship between the length and width of a graphics design)
	• Flip or rotate graphics, square or round corners, fill regions with colors, and blend colors from one region to another
Importing, Exporting, and Linking	• Exchange data or link objects with word processors and graphics packages

Computer languages differ in the way they are translated, their level of abstraction, whether they are procedural or nonprocedural, and whether they are command/data oriented or object oriented. Table 4.5 describes some common computer languages according to these parameters.

LANGUAGE TRANSLATION METHOD

A **language translator** translates software from the language used by software developers into a computer's language (known as **machine language**) and so lets developers use a common language for software destined for many different types of computers. Each computer translates the same software into instructions that it alone can use.

TABLE 4.5   Common computer languages differ on at least four dimensions.

Language	Primary Translation Method	Level of Abstraction	Procedural	Object Oriented
BASIC	Interpreted or compiled	Moderate	Yes	No
C	Compiled	Low-moderate	Yes	No
C++	Compiled	Low-moderate	Yes	Somewhat
COBOL	Compiled	Moderate	Yes	Somewhat*
FORTRAN	Compiled	Moderate	Yes	No
Java	Intermediate code	Moderate	Yes	Yes
Pascal	Interpreted or intermediate code	Moderate	Yes	No
Smalltalk	Interpreted	Moderate-high	Yes	Yes
SQL	Interpreted or compiled	High	No	No
Visual Basic	Interpreted or compiled	High	Yes	Yes

*Object-oriented COBOL.

Two types of language translators exist: compilers and interpreters. A **compiler,** such as one used for C, COBOL, and FORTRAN, translates a program, called **source code,** written in the developer's language into computer code called an **object module.** A linker combines object modules that perform related tasks with already-compiled object code from a library of commonly used functions to create a program called an **executable module,** or a **load module** (see Figure 4.15). A user can load the executable into a computer and run it. The computer running the executable does not need a copy of the compiler because the program has already been translated.

An **interpreter,** such as one used for BASIC and Pascal, translates language commands into computer code one instruction at a time and then executes each instruction before translating the next instruction. The user simply loads the interpreter into the computer and runs it. The interpreter treats the source code as data, reading, translating, and obeying its commands.

Interpreters have two major advantages relative to compilers. First, the developer can distribute his source code to anyone who has an interpreter. The same source code will run on any computer and in any operating system. In contrast, a developer using a compiled language must create executable modules for each type of computer and for each operating system. Second, an interpreter offers a friendly environment for the software developer. The developer can interrogate the interpreter about the state of the program, reset data values, and continue or restart the program. In contrast, every time a developer makes a change in a compiled-language program, she must recompile the program and relink it before testing and using it.

Interpretive languages also have several disadvantages. An interpreted program runs slower than a similar compiled program because translation occurs during the run. A user running an interpreted program must have a copy of the interpreter on her computer, whereas a user running a compiled program does not need a copy of

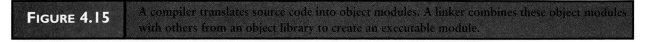

FIGURE 4.15 A compiler translates source code into object modules. A linker combines these object modules with others from an object library to create an executable module.

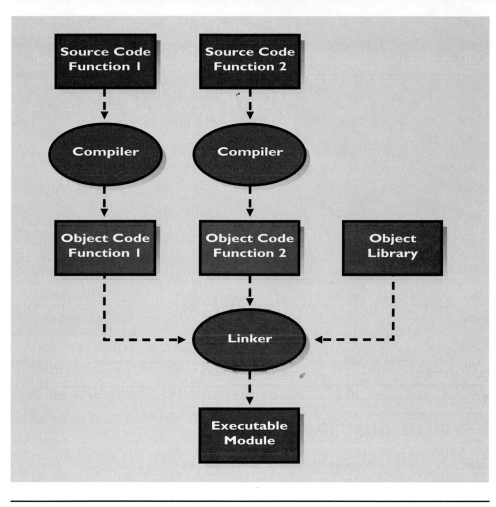

the compiler. Users of interpreted programs must have access to the source code to run the programs, so protecting interpreted software from piracy is much harder than protecting compiled software.

Some languages, such as BASIC and xBASE, exist in both interpretive and compiled forms. Developers can create their software using the interpretive form of the language and distribute their software in the compiled form, but these programs cannot run on any computer. Other languages, such as Java, compile source code into an intermediate code that preserves much of the source language in a highly compact, incomprehensible form, yet still requires an interpreter. This solution allows the program to run on any computer, provides protection from piracy, and speeds program execution, although not to the extent of a compiled language.

Computer programmers can use compiled languages, such as C, COBOL, or FORTRAN. They can use interpretive languages, such as Pascal or BASIC. They can also use languages such as xBASE that exist both in interpretive and compiled forms.

LEVEL OF ABSTRACTION

Although IS professionals rather than managers choose the language to use for a given application, managers should know that they can probably understand and use some high-level interpretive languages such as SQL sufficiently well to meet some of their information needs. Computer languages differ in the number of steps the translator has to go through to get from the user's command to computer-executable commands as well as in the amount of instruction a single command provides.

- **Second-generation languages** are relatively low level and require many steps. A single command provides very limited instruction.
- **Third-generation languages** are moderately abstract and require fewer steps. A single command includes a medium amount of instruction.
- **Fourth-generation languages (4GLs)** are relatively high level and require the smallest number of steps. A single command includes an extensive amount of instruction.

Consider the following analogy: How do you give a robot instructions to brush its teeth? If you have a sufficiently intelligent and trained robot, you might simply say, "Brush your teeth." If it has not performed this task before, you might say, "Take the toothbrush from its holder. Open the tube of toothpaste. Squeeze enough toothpaste onto the brush to cover the bristles. Turn on the cold water. Wet the toothpaste and toothbrush bristles. Brush the toothpaste onto your teeth. Rinse your mouth." If the robot has less intelligence or training, you might have to give it even more detailed instructions. It might need to know how to take the toothbrush from its holder or how to squeeze the tube.

The earlier general-use programming languages, known as assembly languages or second-generation languages, required programmers to specify in painstaking detail every step they wanted the computer to perform. Later languages, such as COBOL, FORTRAN, and Pascal, included much more powerful commands. A single command in such a third-generation language might require ten to fifty second-generation commands. Later languages, such as Progress and xBASE, operate in conjunction with database management software to convey even more meaning with each instruction. A single instruction in such a fourth-generation language often equals hundreds or even thousands of instructions written in a second-generation language. Because developers can convey a great deal of meaning with a few instructions, they can reduce development time by about 25 percent relative to that required when using languages such as COBOL.[23] Managers should insist that software developers select 4GL products that provide user-friendly interfaces for end users, support linking personal computers with corporate computers, and ease the rapid development of applications.

Low-level languages, such as 8086 Assembler or C, have two advantages over higher-level languages. First, they can provide more flexibility and speed in performing a job. Using the robot analogy, a robot instructed at the highest level to brush its teeth will likely have a fixed way of doing it, perhaps brushing the top teeth before the bottom. If you wanted the robot to brush its bottom teeth before the top ones, you might have to resort to a lower-level language. Low-level languages allow more control over how the computer handles its data and instructions for some programming tasks. Higher-level languages generally do more checking and allow for more contingencies than the same code written in a lower-level language.

Programmers can use both high- and low-level languages to develop a single software application. Where possible they use the highest level language available to maximize their productivity and reduce development time. If parts of the program run too slowly or if the higher-level language is too inflexible to accomplish some tasks, the programmers can write some code in a lower-level language. The program would compile each part of the program using its own language translator and link the compiled parts into one complete program with a software development tool called a **link-loader**.

PROCEDURAL VERSUS NONPROCEDURAL

Procedural languages, such as C, COBOL, or FORTRAN, force a software developer to give step-by-step instructions to the computer. Procedural languages allow the computer to vary its steps depending on the data supplied. Extending the robot analogy, one instruction might read, "If the tube of toothpaste is empty, get a fresh tube from the closet." The steps performed by the robot following this command depend on the state of the toothpaste tube. Software written in a procedural language also allows the computer to determine its directions based on the data it finds.

ADVANCED TECHNOLOGY

Speech recognition software is not exactly new technology. Relatively capable software to translate microphone input into text has been available since the mid-1980s. However, only recently has the technology advanced to the point where new applications are becoming widely available.

Speech recognition software can be classified according to whether or not the software requires the speaker to pause after each word and whether or not the software requires that it be trained to recognize the voice of its user. The most advanced systems operate without word-end pauses, a mode of operation called "continuous speech," and without training, also known as "speaker independent." Software products also differ by the size of their vocabulary. A trade-off may exist between vocabulary size and performance in continuous speech mode.

According to an IBM survey, users list four reasons for buying speech recognition software:

finding a convenient alternative to the keyboard; increasing productivity; making the computer easier to use; and just having fun. The primary application in the PC world is for dictation systems. People find it easier to put their rough ideas into the computer by speaking rather than typing, especially if they are working from documents on their desk. Later, they may use the keyboard to revise and edit. Dictation systems are also particularly useful on mobile computers where the keyboard is small and where users may not have access to a surface on which to type.

Wearable computers with voice-recognition systems can be made without a keyboard. The Boeing Company, for example, developed wearable computers with voice-recognition systems for airplane maintenance technicians. The technicians using such systems can record what they observe and what actions they take without having to wait until they crawl out from under an aircraft or from a tight space. This

---

Nonprocedural languages were developed after the first fourth-generation languages. The first type, such as SQL, requires the software developer to state an outcome he desires. The language processor rather than the programmer determines the instructions to give the computer to achieve this outcome. For example, a command in such a language might read, "Produce a report showing the name, address, and telephone numbers of all customers in the Northeast region owing more than $3,000." The language translator, not the software developer, decides how to achieve this output.

A second type of nonprocedural language, such as Prolog, states facts and rules. Products called **expert systems shells** use an **inference engine** to process the language statements and data supplied by users to reach conclusions, answer questions, and give advice. The developer of expert systems software does not know and generally cannot specify the order or steps that the inference engine will use to reach its conclusions.

Following is a simple example of a short program (two facts and one rule) that might be expressed in the language of an expert systems shell (see Figure 4.16).

real-time input improves their accuracy. Also, the technicians can ask the computer to display specific pages from a manual, which they can then see while they are operating on the aircraft. Voice recognition is often used in hands-busy environments, such as hospital emergency rooms or auto mechanic shops.

Another potential PC application is within an operating system. If an operating system were sufficiently enabled, other software could rely on voice input just as it does now for keyboard and mouse input, which are provided through the operating system kernel. Users could supply commands by speaking to the computer. IBM's OS/2 currently provides some voice-recognition capabilities, but they do not extend to all programs run under the operating system. The eventual goal, to have interactive conversations with the computer and have it carry out your commands, requires not just voice recognition, but artificial intelligence software that can properly interpret the commands given.

Other applications for voice recognition include computer-controlled devices. For example, IBM's Home Director software lets people control electronic devices in the home by talking to their computer. The company is modifying the software so that it accepts commands over the telephone.

Voice recognition is particularly useful for users who do not have direct access to a computer but do have access to a telephone. For example, new software should make it possible for users to access the Web over the telephone. Similar applications can bring the computer to people who are keyboard shy or who cannot use a keyboard because of physical disabilities.

SOURCES: Clare Haney, User's to PCs: Turn on the lights, *TechWire* (February 26, 1997), http://www.techweb.com/se/directlink.cgi?WIR1997022616; and Chappell Brown, Wearable computing looks good, *EE Times* (March 31, 1997), http://www.techweb.com/se/directlink.cgi?EET19970331S0084.

Fact 1: Jane is Alan's mother. Fact 2: Mary is Jane's sister. Rule 1: An aunt is the sister of one's mother or the sister of one's father. An inference engine would use this program to determine whether or not Mary is Alan's aunt. The order in which the facts and rules are processed in reaching this answer cannot be determined from the program. Expert systems and their applications are described in fuller detail in Chapter 8.

COMMAND/DATA ORIENTED VERSUS OBJECT ORIENTED

Command/data oriented programming languages, such as FORTRAN, COBOL, or Pascal, separate data storage from procedural parts of a program. The procedural parts of a program operate on the data received.

Object-oriented languages, such as C++, Java, and Smalltalk, merge procedures and data into a structure called an object. A programmer uses an object-oriented

FIGURE 4.16 In an expert system, an inference engine uses a rule base and a fact base to respond to user queries.

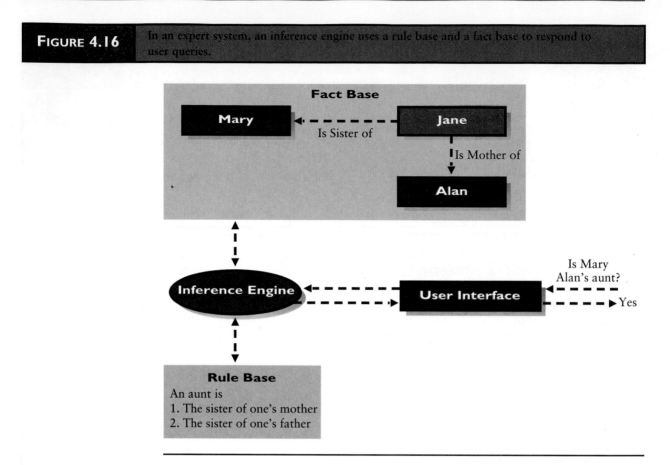

language to build objects. She then builds a program by linking such objects to one another and to objects in a prewritten object class library.

The software developer who uses an object orientation specifies the relationships among objects in two ways. First, the developer establishes a hierarchical relationship in which occurrences (called instances) of objects create object classes, and object classes may belong to other classes. For example, Helen and Paul may be objects of the object class "employee." The object class employee may be a member of the class "person," from which it inherits many of its characteristics (see Figure 4.17). Second, the software developer specifies how objects communicate with one another through messages. For example, any person object should respond in an appropriate way to the message "What is your name?" Figure 4.18 illustrates a more complex example of message communication among objects.

In an object-oriented environment, a software developer models the objects and processes in an organization that are necessary to manage its information. Using such objects, the programmer can easily and relatively quickly create a limited prototype of a program to perform almost any information processing function required by the organization. Once developers create software objects that represent the real objects in their business environment, they can use these software objects repeatedly, saving development time and cost. Norfolk Southern Railway, for example, estimated that its switch from COBOL to object-oriented development saved the company

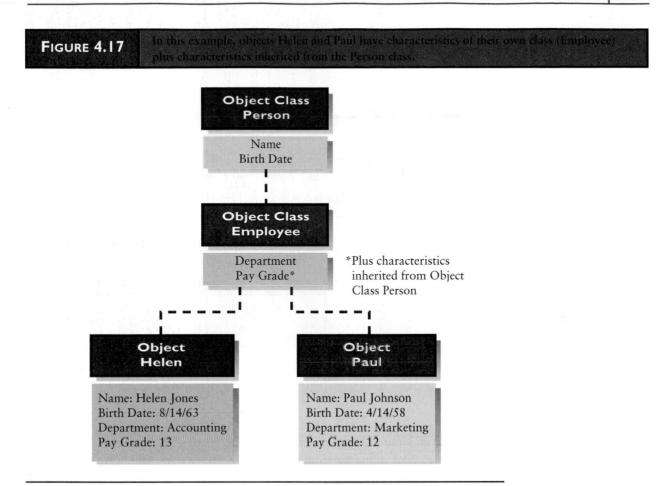

FIGURE 4.17 In this example, objects Helen and Paul have characteristics of their own class (Employee) plus characteristics inherited from the Person class.

between $20 and $30 million per year.[24] Companies can save additional time by buying ready-made software object classes from vendors to include in their own software. The managers at PepsiCo believe that the use of such classes increases the speed with which the company can develop new software, increasing its flexibility, adaptability, and market agility.[25]

SYSTEMS SOFTWARE

Systems software performs tasks to manage the devices and resources of a computer and its network.

- *Systems utilities* allow computer owners and users to perform basic maintenance and resource control functions.
- *Network and systems management software* allows computer professionals to monitor and control computer and network resources.

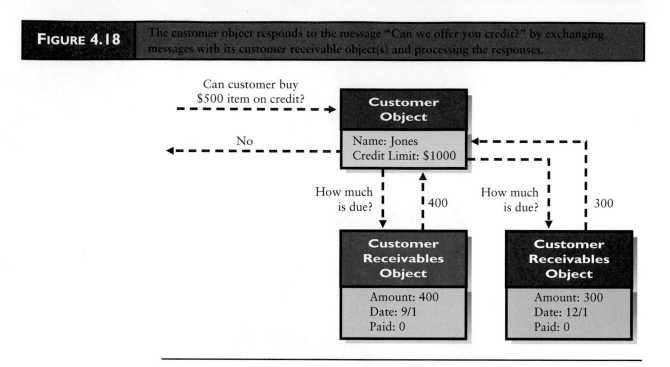

FIGURE 4.18   The customer object responds to the message "Can we offer you credit?" by exchanging messages with its customer receivable object(s) and processing the responses.

- *The operating system kernel* consists of computer programs that perform the most basic housekeeping, resource allocation, and resource monitoring functions for a computer and operates with a minimum of user input or control.

SYSTEMS UTILITIES

Systems utilities operate primarily under user control and provide basic resource management functions, such as the ability to copy or back up files, change file names, or sort data, as shown in Table 4.6. Most vendors of operating systems include many systems utilities as an integral part of their operating system software. As a result, the distinction between operating systems and systems utilities is often fuzzy. Computer scientists call the basic part of the operating system its "kernel" to distinguish it from the utilities packaged with the operating system. The kernel manages the parts and devices of the computer, and no computer can operate without it. A computer can operate without systems utilities, although users would find it extremely cumbersome.

Third-party vendors sell a variety of systems utilities to augment or improve the systems utilities included with an operating system. For example, utilities for a command-driven operating system might include programs to generate and use menus. They might also include programs that retain a history of commands that a user enters and allow the user to retrieve this history, select a past command, edit it, and then reissue it.

TABLE 4.6	Computer operating systems include a variety of systems utilities.

Utility	Description
Archiving	Allows users to remove data to a permanent storage medium, such as a floppy or optical disk. May compress or encrypt the data for improved storage capacity and security. May maintain an archive history and do incremental as well as complete archiving.
Diagnostics	Allows the user to diagnose problems with various parts of the computer, including files created and used by the operating system.
Font extenders	Provide type fonts to change the shape of characters. Some font extenders allow the user to edit, rotate, shade, and manipulate fonts in many ways.
Keyboard modifiers	Allow keys on the keyboard to be reassigned or to be assigned a series of keystrokes so that one or two keystrokes can perform the roles of many.
Menu utilities	Create and edit menus for command-based operating systems or GUIs.
Miscellaneous	Includes programs used to capture and recall screen displays, programs used to recover data that have been erased, programs that allow the user to substitute a mouse in place of arrow keys for programs that do not support a mouse, and programs used to manage several printers.
Plug and play	Reconfigures the operating system to recognize new devices when they are added to a computer.
Screen savers	Display moving designs on the screen if the computer has not been used for a period of time. May prevent others from using the computer without entering a password.
Security	Keeps unauthorized users from using a computer or accessing data. Encrypts data so that they cannot be read or profitably stolen. Checks the integrity of data and programs to make sure they have not been altered.
Viewers	Read documents created with a variety of software packages and saved in special formats.
Virus checkers	Identify and eliminate computer viruses.

NETWORK AND SYSTEMS MANAGEMENT

Network management software monitors the state of a company's network and the devices connected to it. This software can provide real-time displays of the traffic on various parts of the network relative to the network capacity, as well as reports that show patterns of usage over time. These reports allow network service management to anticipate capacity shortages and to plan for hardware upgrades in a rational manner. Network management software can also query the status of devices connected to the network, including workstations, printers, routers, switches, hubs, scanners, and any other shared equipment. The software can automatically adjust network parameters so as to avoid malfunctioning devices. For example, the software can route jobs for an out-of-service printer to a printer designated as its standby.

Systems management software monitors the state of a particular computer. Technical specialists generally run this software on key system servers such as file servers, network servers, or Internet servers. Systems management software can

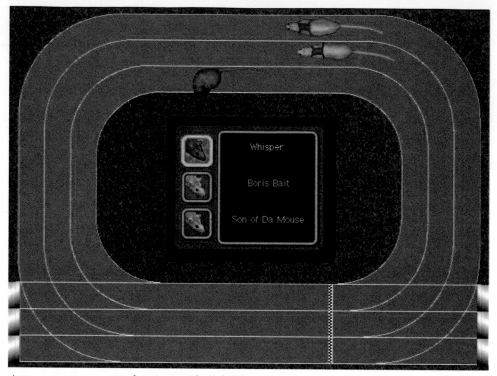

Whisper

Boris Bait

Son of Da Mouse

A screen saver, a type of systems utility, displays a moving image when the computer is not in use.

identify what programs are running, how much of the computer's resources they use, and why certain performance problems have arisen. It can alert management to impending problems and can provide periodic reports to document usage and performance. It can prioritize and schedule the running of programs that are not time critical. Systems management software can identify and remove temporary files that abnormally terminated programs have left.

THE OPERATING SYSTEM KERNEL

The kernel includes programs that start the computer when the user turns the power switch on, that find and initiate application programs the user wants to run, and that transfer the letters typed at the keyboard to the application program. The **operating system** refers to software packaged with the operating system kernel. Traditionally, it includes many utilities, some network and system management software, and even some horizontal application software. Operating systems are built in layers, much like application software. An operating system may, for example, have a memory-management layer, a process management layer on top of that, and a network management layer on top of the process management layer. Exactly where the kernel ends and the system and network management utilities begin is often unclear.

Managers can rarely select an operating system or its kernel when they buy their computers. The manufacturer selects the operating system and installs it prior

TABLE 4.7	Popular operating systems differ in their user interface, portability, and ability to deal with multiple tasks, users, and processors.

Operating System	User Interface	Portability and Openness	Multiple Tasks	Multiple Users	Multiple Processors
Windows 95	GUI	Intel only	Yes	No	No
Windows NT	GUI	Minimal	Yes	Yes	Yes
UNIX	Command*	High	Yes	Yes	Yes
Macintosh Version 7	GUI	Mac only	Yes	No	No
OS/400	Menu	IBM AS/400 only	No	Yes	No
VSE	Command*	IBM mainframe	Yes	Yes	Yes

*Add-on software is available to provide GUI interface.

to the sale. However, computer buyers can often change the operating system at a later time. Many people who bought personal computers with Microsoft's Windows 3.1 operating system later replaced it with Windows 95 or Windows NT. Some people who purchase Apple Macintosh systems prefer the Be operating system (BeOS), sold by Be, Inc.

Operating system kernels differ from one another in five primary ways: their user interface, their portability and openness, their support for multiple tasks and users, their support for multiple processors, and their system calls. Table 4.7 compares some popular operating systems along these dimensions.

User Interface.   Operating system kernels may support command-driven interfaces, menu interfaces, or graphical user interfaces.

- A **command-driven interface** requires users to direct a computer's next action by entering a command, typically by typing it at a keyboard. Although these commands are hard to learn, once learned they result in fast and accurate processing. Command driven interfaces, such as Microsoft's MS/DOS, popular in the 1980s, have disappeared from personal computer products but still exist in mainframe and midrange computer operating systems such as Digital's VMS, many versions of the popular UNIX operating system, and IBM's VM/CMS.
- A **menu-driven interface** presents a list of possible commands. The user then chooses among them by typing the first letter of the preferred command or highlighting the desired command using input devices such as a light pen or a mouse. A menu-driven interface often organizes menus hierarchically. This structure increases the time needed to select a task or application and may become excessive as the depth of the hierarchy increases to support a rich set of commands. IBM's popular AS/400 systems support a menu-driven interface.
- A **graphical user interface,** also known by its initials **GUI** and pronounced "gooey," uses both menus and icons (pictorial representations of operations or resources) to interface with a user. Apple Computer popularized the GUI interface with its operating system for the Macintosh computer in 1984. Microsoft followed with Windows for IBM-PC compatibles in 1986. Although easy to

use, a GUI requires that the computer constantly send a great deal of information to the display unit. Personal computers, which are tightly tied to their display units, handle this requirement without problems. Computers that support multiple users and multiple displays require a great deal of processing and intelligence in their display units to provide a graphical user interface.

Portability and Openness. Because the operating system kernel handles the most basic functions of a computer, it is customized for a specific type of computer hardware. The operating system for the Apple Macintosh, for example, lacks **portability**: other computers, such as those based on the Intel series of processors, cannot use it. Many users want operating systems that will work on a range of computers to ease the migration of applications between computers. A common operating system also reduces users' training needs because the same knowledge applies to an array of computers.

UNIX was designed as such a common operating system. When first introduced, UNIX was the proprietary software of AT&T, although it ran on several different types of computers. AT&T provided licenses at relatively little cost to vendors who wanted to modify it for other computers. In spite of UNIX's portability, several problems arose. Customers resisted being tied to a single software vendor in the same way they disliked being tied to a single hardware vendor. Users also found that the versions of UNIX provided by their hardware manufacturers often lacked consistency with AT&T's standard.

As a way of addressing these concerns, users called for the development of an **open operating system**. A large group of vendors would agree to the specifications but not own them. A set of tests would check for conformance to a standard. Any company could develop a version of an open operating system and make it available for any computer. Users of such operating system software could, therefore, select from a number of software vendors. The Open Software Foundation (OSF), a joint venture of several major software and hardware manufacturers, including IBM, Hewlett-Packard, and Sun Microsystems, has created several open operating systems "standards." These include a version of UNIX, a GUI for UNIX called OSF/Motif, and an environment for network operating systems called DCE (distributed computing environment).

Support for Multiple Tasks and Multiple Users. When multiple users or multiple tasks share a computer, the operating system must keep the data and commands of each task and user separate while it provides an opportunity for sharing information among them. A sales manager, for example, can run a monthly sales report at the same time that a warehouse manager checks the inventory of a particular product. The operating system allows systems administrators to establish the rules and priorities for sharing computer resources. A customer-credit request, for example, might temporarily delay completion of a sales report because the credit request, with the customer waiting, has a higher priority.

Support for Multiple Processors. Manufacturers of high-end computer hardware bundle multiple computer processors into an integrated computer system (see Chapter 3). Some operating systems can optimize the use of these processors. They might, for example, route tasks to the least-busy processor to balance the workload and reduce bottlenecks. They might even split a task into parts that can be performed in parallel by different processors to reduce the time it takes to complete the task.

System Calls.   Application software calls on the operating system kernel to request computer resources such as memory, storage, the network, or the display unit. These **system calls** vary among operating systems, making changes and upgrades difficult. Microsoft wrote the kernel for Windows 95 to honor the Windows 3.1 system calls, so software written for Windows 3.1 generally runs under Windows 95, making upgrading the applications software easier.

PACKAGING THE OPERATING SYSTEM

Operating system vendors bundle a variety of software with the kernel of the operating system. In most cases, the software packaged as an operating system includes a large number of systems utilities and some horizontal software. For example, Microsoft Windows 95 includes screen savers, electronic mail, diagnostic software, and a Web browser. Microsoft Windows NT contains sophisticated network management software. Most versions of UNIX include network management and systems management software, word-processor-like text editors, and several computer languages (C++ and awk, for example). IBM's OS/2 contains database management software.

Vendors package software with the operating system so that computer buyers can run their computers immediately upon purchase. Buyers simply take their computers out of the box, set them up, and turn them on. Vendors also package software with the operating system for competitive reasons. An operating system vendor that sells database management software can package the database management software with the operating system so that users have no reason to purchase a competing product. Microsoft recognized the wisdom of this strategy by packaging its Explorer Web browser with its Windows 95 operating system. It quickly captured a market share that it could not otherwise have achieved had it tried to sell Explorer against the Netscape browser.

NETWORK OPERATING SYSTEMS

A **network operating system** (NOS) manages and controls the joint or shared resources of a group of computers connected by a network. It provides the following services:

- *Security Services.* Security services assure that only authorized users can access the network and enforce limitations on their access privileges.
- *Directory Services.* Directory services identify the addresses of network users.
- *Device Management.* Device management services monitor and manage the devices on a network.

Many operating systems, including UNIX and Windows NT/Server, provide such services within their kernel and in their systems and network management programs. As a result, sales of network operating system software, such as Novell's Netware and Banyan's Vines, have declined dramatically in recent years.

SUMMARY

Software refers to commands that direct a computer to process information or data. Business application software performs business tasks to satisfy business needs. Software-development software helps people to create new software products. Systems software manages the computer and its network.

Business application software includes vertical and horizontal application software. Vertical application software performs tasks common to a specific industry. It includes packaged software, customized software, and custom software, which differ in the amount of customization the software allows. Horizontal application software performs generic tasks common to many types of problems and applications within and across industries. It includes office automation software and some business function applications. Office automation software includes products such as word processors, presentation graphics packages, spreadsheets, database managers, electronic mail software, scheduling software, and work flow software.

Software-development software includes computer languages and computer-aided software engineering (CASE) tools. Computer languages differ in their language translation method, their level of abstraction, whether they are procedural or nonprocedural, and whether they are command/data oriented or object oriented.

Systems software includes utilities, network and systems management software, and the operating system kernel. Systems utilities, such as menu utilities, archivers, and virus checkers, operate primarily under user control and provide basic resource management functions. Network and systems management software allows computer professionals to monitor and control computer and network resources. The operating system kernel performs the most basic housekeeping, resources allocation, and resource monitoring functions for a computer. The operating system bundles the kernel, key utilities, and other software into a software package that is sold with a computer and is necessary for the computer to operate properly. A network operating system manages and controls the shared resources of a group of computers connected by a network.

KEY TERMS

application
application software
business application software
client
command/data oriented programming
   language
command-driven interface
compiler
custom software
customized software
desktop publishing (DTP) software
enterprise-resource-planning (ERP)
   software
executable module
expert systems shell

fourth-generation language (4GL)
graphical user interface (GUI)
horizontal application software
inference engine
integrated office software
integrator
interpreter
language translator
link-loader
load module
machine language
menu-driven interface
multitier client/server model
n-tier client/server model
network management software

network operating system (NOS)
nonprocedural language
object module
object-oriented language
office suite
off-the-shelf software
open operating system
operating system
operating system kernel
operational capability demonstration
  (OCD)
package
packaged software
portability
presentation graphics software
procedural language
program

request for proposal (RFP)
second-generation language
server
site license
software
software-development software
source code
supply-chain management
system call
systems management software
systems software
systems utility
third-generation language
three-tier client/server model
two-tier client/server model
value-added reseller (VAR)
vertical application software

DISCUSSION AND REVIEW QUESTIONS

1. Define "software."
2. How does application software use the operating system kernel?
3. Compare and contrast horizontal application software and vertical application software.
4. Compare and contrast the two-tier client/server model with the three-tier client/server model.
5. What are the advantages of n-tier client/server software over three-tier client/server software?
6. Why does vertical software usually cost more than horizontal software?
7. What are the advantages and disadvantages of packaged vertical software as compared to custom or customized vertical software?
8. What is the role of a value-added reseller?
9. Why do companies sometimes outsource the development of vertical software?
10. What are the major advantages and disadvantages of integrated ERP software as compared to best-of-breed vertical software?
11. What are six types of office automation software?
12. What is the difference between an office suite and integrated office software?
13. How does a language interpreter differ from a compiler?
14. Why is software development generally quicker and easier in a high-level than in a low-level language?
15. What does an inference engine do?
16. What is the difference between an object and an object class?
17. What is the purpose of network and systems management software?
18. What are three kinds of systems utilities?
19. In what way do operating system kernels differ?
20. What is the purpose of a network operating system and why have sales of such systems declined in recent years?

IS ON THE WEB

Exercise 1: You are an intern assigned to the office manager of a medium-sized management consulting company. The company employs approximately 50 consultants and 100 staff members to support their work. Recently the vice president of administration asked the office manager to recommend new desktop software for the office. Each employee has a personal computer networked to the others in the office. Before the network, employees were allowed to select the software they desired, resulting in numerous packages being used. Use the Web to find three options for the office. Write a memo to the vice president listing the advantages and disadvantages of each.

Exercise 2: Find three examples of project management software on the Web. Compare and contrast their features. If you were the vice president of engineering in a *Fortune 500* firm, which software would you purchase? Briefly present your conclusions in a short memo.

MINICASE

CAN ERP WORK AT IKON?

Ikon Office Solutions is one of the world's leading office technology companies with fiscal 1996 revenues of $4 billion and operations in the U.S., Canada, Mexico, the United Kingdom, France, Germany, and Denmark. Ikon is pursuing a growth strategy, announced in 1996, to move from what was more than 80 individually operating copier dealers to an integrated $10 billion company by the year 2000, providing total office technology solutions ranging from copiers, digital printers, and document management services to systems integration, training, and other networking technology services. During 1996, the company rapidly expanded its service capability with an aggressive acquisition effort that has included technology services and document management companies.

Given these objectives, the company seemed to need ERP software. In 1994 it began a pilot project in the Northern California district to assess the possibility of using SAP's enterprise software applications companywide. CIO David Gadra, who joined Ikon about a month after the pilot system was turned on in July, 1996, however, decided not to roll it out. Ikon will take a $25 million write-off on the cost of the pilot.

"There were a number of factors that made us decide this project was more challenging than beneficial for us," says Gadra, a former manager of corporate information services at General Electric Co. "When we added everything up—human factors, functionality gaps, and costs incurred—we decided our environment is ill-defined for SAP." Instead, Ikon is bringing all 13 of its regional operations onto a home-grown, Unix-based proprietary application system, Gadra says.

SOURCE: Case extracted from: Ikon press release dated March 20, 1997, http://www.ikon.com/news/ppress18.htm, July 3, 1997; and Marianne Kolbasuk McGee, Ikon writes off $25m in costs on SAP pilot—Company cites bad fit with software, plus its own errors, *InformationWeek* (April 21, 1997), http://www.techweb.com/se/directlink.cgi?IWK19970421S0032.

"I don't blame the consultants or SAP," he says. "We were very short in our own systems and process expertise. We made errors on our side in estimating the amount of business change we'd have to make as part of this implementation."

CONSULTANT CLUTTER

The $25 million in project-related expenses, recorded in the fiscal second quarter ended March 31, 1997, included a write-off of some capitalized expenses. The vast majority of that total represents consulting fees; less than 10 percent went to pay for the software itself, says Robert Kearns, Ikon's senior VP of finance and chief financial officer. At any given point in the project, Ikon was paying 40 to 50 outside consultants $300 an hour, Kearns says.

Ikon budgeted $12 million to get the system running. That cost came in at $14 million, including $8 million paid to IBM for consulting, says SAP global support manager Geoffrey Yoder, who worked with Ikon. Kearns, the Ikon CFO, says the initial implementation costs actually exceeded $14 million, but he won't say by how much. The remainder of the $25 million total represents consulting fees paid since the system was turned on, plus the projected costs to dismantle it, Kearns says.

SAP's Yoder says Ikon's costs were higher than they needed to be because Ikon relied on consultants more than SAP recommends. "There was no knowledge transfer at all" from the consultants to Ikon's staff, he maintains, adding, "We don't recommend that because then you are beholden to consultants."

CIO Gadra says Ikon had great difficulty assembling an internal team of SAP experts.

Ikon's Kearns says a big reason the company decided to drop SAP was its conclusion that the software didn't sufficiently address the needs of a service company like Ikon, as opposed to manufacturers. For example, he says, SAP didn't have an adequate feature for tracking service calls. "There were just too many work-arounds that we had to do," he says.

SAP's Yoder says Ikon opted not to install a later version of its Service Management module that provided more functionality but was "still in the early phases."

"I am extremely disappointed by Ikon's announcement," says SAP America president Jeremy Coote, describing the pilot as on time and "extremely successful." Coote calls Ikon's decision to scrap the project "an example of what happens when you don't sell at the corporate level" as well as the divisional level.

Ikon's Gadra disputes the SAP executive's characterization. "This pilot was funded and supported by corporate, and initiated by corporate," Gadra says.

Irene Pulfer, VP of IS for Ikon's Northern California district, says she and her 50-member project team were also disappointed that the SAP project didn't pan out. "I really thought we were breaking all kinds of records for fast SAP implementations," she says. But she adds that the rationale for scrapping the project was reasonable.

Case Questions

Diagnosis

1. What are the information needs at Ikon?

Evaluation

2. What alternatives does Ikon have to meet these needs?

Design

3. What are the advantages of ERP software in meeting these needs?
4. What are the disadvantages of ERP software?
5. What risks did the company take in selecting SAP software for evaluation?
6. What risks will Ikon take in developing proprietary software to meet its needs?
7. What are the advantages to Ikon of developing proprietary software for its enterprise information needs?

Implementation

8. Why did Ikon cancel the SAP project?
9. How might Ikon have better used its consultants on this project?

ACTIVITY 4.1   YARMOUTH INC.

Step 1:   Read the following Yarmouth Inc. case:

The division manager, Lisa Harwood, had just told Dan Tobin, director of marketing, that the productivity of the sales staff had to increase. The statistics Harwood referred to came from a recent trade magazine. They suggested that the sales staff at Yarmouth was performing well below industry averages. Average order size per salesperson, for example, and the number of calls per day were about half those reported by other companies in the same business.

"Dan, we've got to act now or we'll never hit our profit goals for the quarter," Harwood said. "Can you get back to me tomorrow with some ideas on how we can show some fast improvement?"

Tobin had been with Yarmouth Inc. for six years. He was hired as a salesperson and last spring was promoted to director of marketing.

Yarmouth produces a line of industrial cleaning equipment including vacuum cleaners, waxers, and polishers, and maintains a staff of 142 salespeople who call on industrial accounts within a several hundred mile radius of their homes.

Tobin went home that evening concerned about his ability to make the changes that were needed. On the ride home it occurred to him that he could give the staff a pep talk but it probably would have only a short-term effect. Without close supervision, they were on their own, and any effort to manage their performance from this distance was difficult. The only hard data he had were the monthly sales reports, which he received nearly a month after the reporting period closed. The January sales data, for example, would be received at the end of February. Perhaps, he thought, he might get these data sooner. Then he could respond faster to those who weren't getting the job done.

CONSULTING THE MIS DEPARTMENT

Tobin's first stop the next morning was the MIS [Management Information Systems]department. There he told Maurice Brown, director of MIS, about his problem.

"We're not your problem," Brown said. "You are. The data coming in from the field travel at a snail's pace. Your salespeople fill out order forms and then a few days later put them in the mail. Before the sales data show up here and are

---

SOURCE: Activity 4.1 selections from *Cases in Computer Information Systems,* by Barry Shore and Jerry Ralya, copyright © 1988 by Holt, Rinehart and Winston, Inc.; reprinted by permission of the publisher.

entered by data entry clerks into the sales order entry system, the data are sometimes several weeks old. Then, after the goods are shipped it takes another few weeks for the data to be entered by data entry clerks into the sales history database. The report we send you accesses the sales history file, and until that file is updated, we can't send you your monthly reports. If the past is an indication of the future, I'm afraid the best we can do is get you a report within a month of the end of the period, unless, of course, you get your orders in here quicker."

Although Tobin was not confident that Brown could help him obtain more timely data, he went on to explain some additional information he needed to maintain closer control over the sales staff.

NEW APPLICATIONS

"Maurice, last night I sketched a few reports that would help me maintain tighter control over the sales force. These reports would let me scrutinize their efforts much more closely. And I think the information the salespeople would get from these reports would help them to schedule their time more effectively and do a better job."

Tobin showed him two reports—sales diary and sales productivity analysis.

Sales Diary

The sales diary would report the number of calls per day for each salesperson, the number of hours per day that the salesperson spent with prospects, the number of sales calls year-to-date, and the cost per call.

Sales Productivity Analysis

The order analysis report would include, for every salesperson, the cost per call, revenue per call, revenue to expense ratio, and the call to close ratio. The call to close ratio is the number of total calls made divided by the number of calls that resulted in a sale.

Tobin finished describing these reports. "Maurice," Tobin asked, "how long do you think it would take for you to begin producing these reports on a weekly basis?"

"Dan, I don't understand your logic. If I use the current sales history database to produce your reports, I might be able to get them to you a few weeks after the data are in that database, but you have just complained that a report like this would be too out-of-date to be useful."

Step 2: Prepare the case for class discussion.

Step 3: Answer each of the following questions, individually or in small groups, as directed by your instructor.

Diagnosis

1. What are the information needs of the sales staff and managers in the marketing department of Yarmouth Inc.?
2. Do they feel that these information needs are currently being met?

Evaluation

3. What software do they currently use to help meet these needs?
4. How well does this software meet their information needs?

Step 4: In small groups, with the entire class, or in written form, share your answers to the questions above. Then answer the following questions:

1. What issues did you consider in identifying the information needs of Party Planners Plus?
2. What types of software should receive the highest priority?
3. What other issues should Tanner consider in purchasing software for her company?

ACTIVITY 4.4 DEALING WITH SUSPECTED SOFTWARE PIRACY

Step 1: Read the following scenario:

You work in a company of about 600 employees. One day, while working on a project, you conclude that you need to use a small database management system. After doing some research, you decide that Microsoft Access is the product you would like to use. You call your rep at the Technical Services Department.

"John," you say, "Will you please order me a copy of Microsoft Access?"

"No problem," he replies. "We have a copy of the distribution CD on the network. Let me mail you instructions on how to install it on your computer."

"Thanks, John. I didn't realize that we had a site license."

"Well, we don't exactly. But we do have quite a few licenses, and I'm sure that not everyone is using their copy."

"In that case," you say, "I'd prefer you order me a licensed copy."

"I'm afraid we're out of budget. Really, don't worry about it. We do this all the time. I've had some misgivings about it myself, but the boss says it's okay."

Step 2: Identify your alternatives. Be sure to consider such actions as going directly to the president of the company and calling the Microsoft software piracy hot line anonymously.

Step 3: Answer each of the following questions, individually or in small groups, as directed by your instructor.

1. For each alternative, who benefits and who is harmed?
2. From the ethical principles of least harm, rights and duties, professional responsibilities, self-interest and utilitarianism, consistency, and respect, how would you evaluate each alternative?
3. What course of action would you take? Why?

RECOMMENDED READINGS

The following publications provide regular features about computer software:

Byte	*PC Week*
Computerworld	*Software Magazine*
Information Week	*Software Quarterly*

NOTES

1. This scenario is adapted from Robert L. Scheier, Face up to it, *Computerworld* (March 25, 1996):83–84.
2. Emily Kay, Serving up your order faster, *InformationWeek* (April 24, 1995): 66–73.
3. Julia King, IS revamp on track, *Computerworld* (April 10, 1995): 1, 15.
4. Charles T. Conway, Jr., *PMSC News* (December 23, 1996), http://www.pmsc.com/eire.html, June 3, 1997.
5. Interpolated from statistics and estimates in Bruce Caldwell, Insurance: Reduced risk through innovation, *InformationWeek* (September 9, 1996): 152–157.
6. Wayne Eckerson, User downsizes in an off-the-shelf way, *Network World* (July 13, 1992): 19, 21.
7. Colleen Frye, Financial$ toolsets earning interest, *Software Magazine* (January 1996): 83–89.
8. Bruce Caldwell and Katherine Bull, Merrill's $1 billion upgrade, *InformationWeek* (August 7, 1995): 14, 15.
9. Deloitte & Touche Consulting Group, *Leading Trends in Information Services* (Chicago: Deloitte & Touche LLP, 1996).
10. Boston Software Corp Homepage, http://www.bostonsoftware.com/rfram.htm, June 3, 1997. What's New, http://www.ecta.com/fintro.asp.
11. Charles T. Conway, Jr., Policy Management Systems Corporation announces business process outsourcing agreement with Grange Mutual, at http://www.pmsc.com/r15.html, June 3, 1997.
12. Study by Pittiglio Rabin Todd & McGrath, Weston, MA, cited in Tom Stein, Manufacturing systems orders from chaos, *InformationWeek* (June 23, 1997), http://www.techweb.com/se/directlink.cgi?IWK19970623S0041.
13. Tom Stein, Manufacturing systems orders from chaos, *InformationWeek* (June 23, 1997), http://www.techweb.com/se/directlink.cgi?IWK19970623S0041.
14. Joshua M. Greenbaum, Efficient consumer response: How software is remaking the consumer packaged goods industry, *Software Magazine* (June 1997): 39-48.
15. Monua Janah, Chemicals: A search for the right formula, *InformationWeek* (September 9, 1996): 92–97.
16. Randy Watson, ERP users find competitive advantages, *Computerworld* (January 19, 1998): 9.
17. Thomas Hoffman, Hot hotel system nips Jack Frost, *Computerworld* (December 18, 1995):65. Thomas Hoffman, IT to boost resort sales, *Computerworld* (October 28, 1996): 69.
18. Cited in Elizabeth U. Harding and Jack Vaughan, The sky is falling! Plan now, *Software Magazine* (January 1996): 27–28.
19. Capers Jones, quoted in John Charles, Slow Response to year 2000 problem, *IEEE Software* (May/June 1997): 114.
20. Ibid.
21. Rick Saia, Year 2000 scoreboard: Money talk, *Computerworld* (May 5, 1997): 72.
22. Craig Stedman, Utility charges to 2000, *Computerworld* (March 18, 1996): 71.
23. Robert Klepper, Third and fourth generation language productivity differences, *Communications of the ACM 38* 9 (September 1995): 69–79.
24. Elizabeth Heichler, Railway switches tracks to objects, *Computerworld* (June 26, 1995): 71.
25. Doug Bartholomew, Objects take off, *InformationWeek* (February 26, 1996): 14–16.

Chapter 5

Database Management Systems

LEARNING OBJECTIVES

After completing Chapter 5, you will be able to

1. Define database and database management system.
2. Describe eight functions for which managers use a database management system.
3. Define metadata and describe how organizations use them.
4. Describe four distribution architectures and the advantages and disadvantages of each for managers.
5. Describe the relational, object, network, and hierarchical database models and the advantages and disadvantages of each for managers.
6. List the responsibilities of a database administrator and data administrator.
7. Show how the globalization of management has affected database management in organizations.

DATABASE MANAGEMENT AT PIONEER HI-BRED INTERNATIONAL

At Pioneer Hi-Bred International Inc., Des Moines, Iowa, a database houses extensive information on the company's 550,000 commercial farming customers. The company, which sells seed, not only records a farmer's name, address, and size of operation, but also tracks the crops planted, the yield, the farmer's livestock interests, and what, when, and how much product the farmer purchased the previous year. It maintains this information in a central database that salespeople can access from the field on a laptop computer. Unlike IBM, which used a database marketing program to reduce the number of salespeople needed, Pioneer uses the database to enhance the efforts of its sales force.

"This information drives the personal selling process," explains Dennis E. Gaukel, database marketing manager. By knowing ahead of time what a farmer has purchased in the past, the salespeople can make suggestions on new products or provide comparative information on competitive products. They also can bring relevant literature to the sales presentation and immediately answer the question: "What did I order last year?"

The database also influences Pioneer's direct-mail efforts. "Before databases were available, companies had to rely on direct selling and mass media to get their message through," Gaukel says. "As a reader, listener, or viewer, the farm operator would receive everyone's message, whether he was a good prospect or not. The database helps us tailor messages both in person and through direct mail specifically to the needs and interests of a particular farmer." For example, Pioneer customers now receive customized newsletters based on their particular farming interests.[1]

To be most effective, Pioneer's employees need to know more than who their customers are and how to contact them. They need to know their customers on a

Pioneer Hi-Bred International uses database management systems to provide information on its farming customers. The systems support sales and service to its customers.

more personal basis. Database management systems can help satisfy this need. Managers and salespeople can use database management systems to perform their jobs better.

In this chapter we first answer the question "What is a database management system?" Then we investigate the uses of a database management system. Next we examine the development of databases through data design. Then we consider the technological underpinnings. Finally we look at ways of using data effectively.

WHAT IS A DATABASE MANAGEMENT SYSTEM (DBMS)?

A **database** is an organized collection of related data. The key terms here are "organized" and "related." A collection of data is not a database *per se*. Organized means that you can easily find the data you want. For example, a file cabinet, with folders sorted alphabetically, is a database; a bunch of papers stuffed into a drawer is not. A collection of data about the books you own and your friends' telephone numbers is not a database because these data do not relate to one another. Instead, they form two separate collections, or two databases. Many organizations consider all of their organized data part of a database because of their potential interrelationship.

What databases does Pioneer have? It has data about its customers and products. It also has data about prior orders, which clearly relate to both its customer and product data. It probably has a great deal of data about its suppliers. Whether these data form a database or databases depends on the extent to which they are organized in a meaningful and systematic way and the degree to which they are related.

Managers and employees often use **computerized databases,** those stored on computer-readable media such as disks, diskettes, tapes, and CD-ROMs. Computerization of data does not ensure that they form a database. For example, many companies use word processors to computerize their correspondence; however, they organize these documents in a haphazard fashion and should not consider them to be a database. Many companies keep both computerized and noncomputerized, or manual, databases. For example, Pioneer maintains a computerized customer database, but it might keep a manual employee database.

A **database management system (DBMS)** comprises programs to store, retrieve, and otherwise manage a computerized database, as well as to provide interfaces to application programs and to nonprogramming users. Today every company developing serious application software should use one or more DBMSs for its data management functions. DBMSs are a key component of almost all vertical application software.

✳ WHY USE A DATABASE MANAGEMENT SYSTEM?

Managers find DBMSs valuable because they perform the following functions:

- Storing and retrieving data
- Managing metadata
- Limiting and controlling redundant data in multiple systems
- Supporting simultaneous data sharing
- Providing transaction atomicity
- Providing authorization and security services
- Enforcing business rules
- Increasing programmer productivity

How can managers at Pioneer use DBMSs? The following sections examine their use for each of these functions.

STORING AND RETRIEVING DATA

A database management system makes it easier for managers and employees to store and retrieve data. People using a DBMS can permanently store and retrieve data without running any other programs or doing any computer programming. Users can create data-entry forms, such as the one in Figure 5.1, that automatically check the validity of entered data. Managers and other users can retrieve data sorted in a prespecified way or according to criteria that they specify at the time of retrieval. Customer assistance representatives at Mercedes-Benz, for example, can access their customer database by last name, home phone number, or vehicle identification number.[2]

A salesperson at Pioneer using Pioneer's DBMS can secure any information she wants about a customer. For example, she can make a simple query to the database to identify what a particular customer last purchased. She might also request a sales history, showing subtotals by product category. If the company has a sale on a particular product, the salesperson can identify all customers in her district that purchased that product within the past year.

Managers might require programmers to quickly modify programs that use data. Before DBMSs existed, each program stored its data in data files. Programmers typically compressed different types of data, such as dollar amounts, customer codes, or invoice numbers in different ways to minimize the amount of file storage and maximize speed of retrieval. Other programmers writing code to access the same files had to know their compression format. Many errors, especially in large, complex systems resulted. An efficient file format for one application might not be efficient for others. If programmers needed to change the file format for some data, they would have to change all programs addressing that data, often rewriting programs if the nature of the data changed. For example, if the space required for the customer zip code increased from five to nine digits, programmers likely would have had to modify any programs that accessed the customer files, whether or not they used the zip code.

Now, using a DBMS, the programmer specifies only what data to store or retrieve. The DBMS decides the data's physical organization and representation on

FIGURE 5.1 DBMSs can generate data-entry screens, such as this contact management data entry screen generated by Microsoft Access.

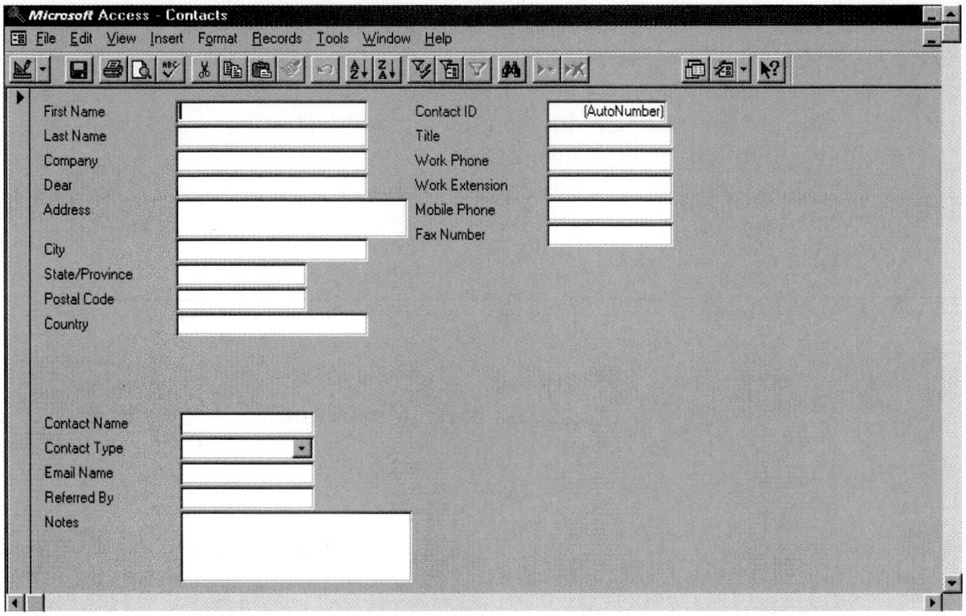

the storage medium. The database sees the **physical view** of the data but presents a **logical view** to the user and programmer. The physical view includes how the data are compressed and formatted, which data are stored near each other, and which indexes are created to simplify and speed finding data on the storage medium. The logical view organizes and presents data elements in ways that managers and other users find helpful. As a result, if an organization changes the form of its data, it usually does not have to rewrite its programs.

As the year 2000 approaches, companies are examining how their programs deal with a date that uses only two digits for the year, as discussed in Chapter 4. DBMSs help solve this limitation by allowing data administrators to increase the space for data fields to four digits and by adding 1900 to all existing two-digit dates.

MANAGING METADATA

Metadata are data about data. For example, the fact that a company's invoice numbers are six digits long, with the first digit being either a 1 or 3, is metadata. Another example of metadata is the fact that zip codes are nine digits, the last four digits are optional, leading zeroes must display, and a dash exists between the fifth and sixth digit. Also, metadata might indicate that zip codes in a report should be titled "Zip," whereas zip codes in a data entry screen should be titled "Zip Code:."

Metadata also include the logical views of data called schemas and subschemas. A **schema** represents an integrated, enterprise-wide view of how data relate to one another. For example, a schema might indicate that customers have shipping and billing addresses, and that they are billed with invoices that have invoice numbers, discount rates, and invoice lines with part numbers and extended prices.

Managers can focus employees on the elements of data that are most relevant to their work, can hide sensitive data, or can present unusual relationships among data in views called **subschemas**. For example, they might create views that eliminate the sensitive discount rate code for employees who should not see it. Workers in shipping might not see a billing address, only a shipping address for customers. Warehouse workers might see invoice lines as a pick list, with shelf locations rather than part numbers.

The **data dictionary** refers to the part of a database that holds its metadata and acts as a CASE tool for automating programming (see Chapters 4 and 12). Figure 5.2 illustrates the contents of a hypothetical data dictionary entry. Many data dictionaries also contain information about what programs, reports, and data entry screens use or refer to each data element. This information makes it relatively easy to analyze the impact of changing the characteristics of data. Data dictionaries are also available as stand-alone products that can connect to a number of databases. Top-level managers use such data dictionaries along with their DBMSs' data dictionaries to maintain a consolidated view of data across all their databases.

Why are metadata important? Metadata allow a program to know enough about an item of data that it accesses, such as an invoice number or zip code, to store and display it properly. Metadata allow a DBMS to check for data entry errors. Data managers can request metadata reports to identify changes in the database structure or to compare user needs against existing data. They can query the data dictionary to determine the creation or update date of a particular data item, find what system it came from, and determine what tools have accessed it. If a manager would like to change an element of data or access an element of data, he can see who controls access or approves changes to it.

LIMITING AND CONTROLLING REDUNDANT DATA IN MULTIPLE SYSTEMS

Companies often collect and store the same data in two or more different information systems. For example, a company that manufactures and sells office equipment might maintain information about its customers in three places: a service system that tracks customer service requests and mails service bulletins; an accounts receivable system that tracks the amount that customers owe the company; and a sales system that assists its sales agents in identifying customers who might need additional equipment. This duplication of computer storage not only wastes storage capacity, but it also wastes time and might cause inconsistencies in data entry. For example, if a customer moves to a new location, employees must reenter the customer's address in all three systems. If the customer told a sales agent about the address change, the agent might forget to inform the people in charge of the service or accounts receivable systems. The company might then have two or more inaccurate addresses for the customer.

A DBMS reduces the need to store redundant data because it easily joins information about different business components. As illustrated in Figure 5.3, Pioneer

FIGURE 5.2 A data dictionary holds metadata. This hypothetical entry shows metadata for the data item "Customer Payment Amount."

CUSTOMER-PAYMENT-AMOUNT

Attribute of: CUSTOMER PAYMENT

Data input screen:
      Prompt: Amount of payment:
      Edit(s):   >0
                   <100.000
      Type: Currency
      Display: $99,999.99

Report heading:
                   Payment
                   Amount

Aliases: CUST-PAYMENT, CHECK-AMOUNT, CPAMT

Appears in the following views: ACCTS-PAYBLE, CUST-RECRD, PAYMNT-RECRD

Appears in the following programs: ARP-84X, ARP-84Y, ARP-85Z, CUS-RECPT-PROC
                   I54X3T22, I23X4T23, P94.XX.2;2

Security level (without view): 12

Owner(s): John Marshall

Help prompt: Enter payment amount without dollar signs or commas.

Integrity:
      On creation of CUSTOMER-PAYMENT:
                   Update TOTAL-PAYMENTS=TOTAL-PAYMENTS +
CUSTOMER-PAYMENT-AMOUNT
      On update:
                   Update TOTAL-PAYMENTS = TOTAL-PAYMENTS + change

needs to store only a customer number in the data it retains about an order. If a manager requests a list of orders sorted by customer name, a DBMS would look up the customer number in the customer contact list to retrieve the detailed customer data, such as the company name, contact name, and phone number, associated with each order. In the example shown, use of a customer number saves repeating the customer name, telephone number, and conceivably other information such as the customer address in the records for orders 567891 and 567892. Similarly, a DBMS makes it easy to combine this general customer information with information unique to other systems. For example, it could combine the customer address with her unpaid invoices for accounts receivable, her previous orders for the sales agent, and her calling record for the service agent. The DBMS stores the customer information only once, reducing redundancy and eliminating the possibility of inconsistent records.

Of course, errors can occur in data entry and manipulation. One airline installed some defective software that created false passenger reservations. The airline

FIGURE 5.3	A DBMS combines information from different tables; for example, customers and their orders combine to provide the customer telephone number and the date in the same row.

Order Information

Order #	Customer #	Order Date	Order Status	Ship Date
567891	397	02/07/99	1	02/09/99
567892	221	02/07/99	2	02/09/99
etc	...	...	...	...

Customer Information

Customer #	Company Name	Contact	Phone
221	Aggrow, Inc.	Alan Smith	312-555-2189
397	Arlington Farms	Joe Hudson	617-555-3838
etc	...	...	...

Combined Information Sorted by Company

Order #	Order Date	Company Name	Phone
567892	02/07/99	Aggrow, Inc.	312-555-2189
567891	02/07/99	Arlington Farms	617-555-3838
etc	...	...	...

corrected the software problem but failed to correct the data in the database resulting in partially empty planes due to the booking errors.[3]

SUPPORTING SIMULTANEOUS DATA SHARING

Without sophisticated control procedures, errors arise when two people or programs attempt to access and update the same data at the same time. Consider the following example. John and Mary call the same national mail-order company to order two sweaters in style #1037. The clerk handling John's order determines that there is an inventory of three such sweaters. Simultaneously, the clerk handling Mary's order obtains the same information. John and Mary, both believing that the two sweaters they want are in stock, request immediate shipment. As John's clerk registers the sale, the computer completes the transaction by changing the available stock to one. At the same time, Mary's clerk registers the sale, also changing the available stock to one. Although the available stock cannot fill both orders, such processing allows the clerks and customers to think that the orders had been fulfilled.

Concurrency control describes the proper management of simultaneous data updates when multiple users or multiple tasking occurs (see Chapter 4). DBMSs

THE MANAGER IN ACTION

While selling Pepsi, one of the world's best-loved soft drinks, may seem to be an easy task—planning, targeting, and tracking those sales isn't. The soft drink business turns on a dime—targets and planned numbers are the name of the game. That means planning and forecasting must be nimble too. However, the company's planning environment wasn't keeping up. According to Roberto Waddington, Manager Financial Analysis at Pepsi-Cola International's (PCI) Latin America Division (LAD), "Our planning models were cumbersome and slow. In an effort to combine accounting, forecasting, planning, and consolidation into a single system, we linked 10–12 spreadsheets together. However, data handling became tremendously slow, the model required endless debugging, formulas were calculated differently, and the whole thing was difficult to maintain."

Waddington knew that the ideal planning platform would have to allow flexible multidimensional data management, combine powerful planning and modeling capabilities, and be easy to use. LAD worked with Andersen Consulting of Miami and Kefal Sistemas of Mexico to develop PCI's Financial Planning System Project.

The new system receives data from almost all other Pepsi systems and applications, including accounting systems, product case sales data, marketing expense data, the invoicing system, and the product pricing system. Data arrive in a myriad of data formats including ASCII files, SQL files, DBF files, AS400 files, and individual spreadsheet files.

Data from all sources are loaded into an Essbase (Arbor Systems) multidimensional model. The model itself contains 354 data elements spread across seven data dimensions—Time, Geography, Products, Packages, Legal entities, Accounts, and Categories. Analysts can now calculate sales to specific markets by product and by container (12-oz. Pepsi can, 26-oz Diet Pepsi bottle, etc.). They can simulate specific price-volume scenarios. They can assess the effect of a promotion on a given container size. And they can quickly and easily receive P&Ls, balance sheets, and reports that incorporate various pricing, marketing, and cost fluctuation assumptions.

"Multidimensional analysis brings us new ways of thinking about real-world markets and a better understanding of our business" says Waddington, "which is especially important when revenue is spread over so many elements. For example, being able to view the lowest levels of data gives the planning team lots of information that we didn't have before. And with Essbase, the necessary data is available instantly—the system is fast. This speed and flexibility enables us to better advise management about attainable targets, accurately plan market strategies, and implement specific percentage sales increases. Essbase allows us to fine tune the business objectives without a nightmare of numerical detail."

SOURCE: Extracted from Essbase in action: PepsiCola International, at http://www.arborsoft.com/essbase/datasht/pepsi.html, July 8, 1997.

employ a variety of techniques to ensure concurrency control.[4] In critical applications, such as disbursing cash or reserving inventory, a DBMS will allow only one user to update the specific data at a given time. For example, it would show both John's and Mary's clerks the inventory of three sweaters. However, when both clerks decide to reserve two of the sweaters, the computer would only allow one update to proceed. Then, before processing the second update, it would again read the inventory data and would find that the request for two sweaters exceeded the inventory of one and inform the clerk.

PROVIDING TRANSACTION ATOMICITY

Most business transactions change a database in several ways. Consider what happens, for example, when a banking customer transfers $100 from a savings to a checking account. The bank must reduce the customer's checking account balance, increase her savings account balance, and record the transaction. **Atomicity** prevents the division of a transaction. If the DBMS reduces the checking balance or increases the savings balance and the computer crashes before it changes the other balance, then the balances will be inconsistent, resulting in an unwarranted and undesired loss for the bank or the customer.

Most DBMSs provide tools to identify and correct incomplete transactions before they can cause damage.[5] For example, the DBMS can create a temporary record, known as a **log,** at the start of each transaction. It adds to the log upon each successful update and closes this record when the transaction is complete. After a system failure, the DBMS uses the log to trace the transaction process and undo all partially completed transactions. Incorporating such security into every program that processes multiple-update transactions, rather than using a DBMS, is exceedingly complex and difficult.

Software developers can use a product called a **transaction processing monitor (TP monitor)** to enforce transaction atomicity. Table 5.1 lists some basic functions

TABLE 5.1	TP monitors provide a range of functions that simplify and coordinate transaction processing on distributed systems.

Function	Benefit Provided
Enforce data integrity and atomic updates.	When transactions affect data on multiple computers, a TP monitor maintains data integrity if some computers involved in the transaction fail or the network fails.
Log transaction errors.	Error logs provide data for reports that managers use to diagnose unreliable processes and technicians use to identify network hardware or software problems.
Provide queue services that allow business applications to accept transactions faster than the database can handle them for short periods.	This feature is particularly important for Web-based transactions whose volumes cannot be reliably predicted (as opposed to local transactions limited by the number of terminals).
Provide a common language for transactions that affect different databases.	This feature allows for a common interface that databases from different vendors use to pass data among themselves.
Prioritize requests for database services.	This feature ensures reliable response times for critical applications.
Provide centralized management of distributed applications.	This feature ensures coordination among the applications.

of a TP monitor. Developers typically use TP monitors instead of the TP features of a DBMS when writing software that simultaneously updates several uncoordinated DBMSs. For example, the Regency Systems Solutions Division of Hyatt Hotels Corp. now runs centralized databases to support reservations, sales, registration, accounting, and property management on a network that serves ten reservation centers and 175 hotels. However, the hotel chain is moving to a client/server system and anticipates that a TP monitor will give the company "more flexibility, more functions, and the ability to [execute] transactions across multiple databases."[6]

PROVIDING AUTHORIZATION AND SECURITY SERVICES

Organizations must control who sees the data they collect. For example, managers often treat salary data, personnel evaluations, and financial information as confidential. In addition, managers must protect accounting information from tampering and fraud.

Most DBMSs can limit who has access to specific data.[7] A DBMS makes a prescribed subset of the database, called a **view**, available for certain classes of users or applications. For example, most users may see a view of employee data that contains job title, length of service, and name of health care insurance, but does not contain salary information. Managers can also create views for metadata. Such views, for example, might prevent certain users from knowing whether the database contains salary information.

In addition to views that hide data, most DBMSs allow views of aggregated data or joined data. For example, a manager might authorize a user to view average salary by department but not individual salary data.[8] Managers must exercise care in allowing statistical views of data. Sophisticated users can often infer detailed data by asking dividing and overlapping queries. Joined views can combine data that users often view together. For example, a manager might use a view that combines customer name with data relating to the customer's sales representative; the manager will see the name, telephone, and address of each customer's sales representative as if the DBMS stored them with the customer. Non-DBMS systems generally cannot hide data from all users because users have access to the entire record of data. DBMSs make it easier to control access to systems with hundreds of programs written by different programmers. They centralize the access control function, dramatically simplifying software development and providing additional power to a data administrator.

ENFORCING BUSINESS RULES

A DBMS enforces rules that ensure related data are logically consistent. For example, assigning a sales representative to every customer expresses a relationship between two types of data: customer and sales representative. Without a DBMS, each program that modifies information about either sales representatives or customers would have to check that the assignment of sales representative to customer occurred. For example, a program deleting a sales representative would have to check that all of his customers had first been reassigned. Deleting a sales representative and so leaving some customers without a representative breaks the assignment rule. When a DBMS modifies data, it can enforce such rules, simplifying the programs and ensuring that a programmer or program designer cannot violate business rules due to ignorance.

INCREASING PROGRAMMER PRODUCTIVITY

Because a DBMS provides many of the functions that programmers would otherwise have to develop on their own, a DBMS increases programmer productivity. A DBMS does the following:

- Simplifies dealing with concurrent updates to a database
- Handles control of access to data
- Helps write code

Most DBMS vendors use the **ODBC (Open Database Connectivity)** standard that allows programs to access their databases in a uniform way and makes moving databases from one DBMS to another easy. A number of fourth-generation languages (see Chapter 4) use DBMSs to increase programmer productivity, such as directing "for every customer in the database, do the following." The DMBS's data dictionary can automatically check errors on data entry and create default reports and data entry screens.

DEVELOPING DATABASES THROUGH DATA DESIGN

Data design is the process of identifying and formalizing the relationships among the elements of data that will form an organization's database. Managers often work with computer specialists to determine the design that best meets their business's needs. For example, must a customer have a sales representative? If so, how should the database store a customer, if at all, before the company assigns her a sales representative? How many customers can a sales representative represent? What happens to a sales representative's customers when the sales representative leaves the company? Should the database contain the same information for walk-in customers as for repetitive customers? If the customer's shipping and billing address are the same should the address be stored twice?

Decisions such as these are not simple and tend to evolve over the life of a database application. DBMSs, however, make it possible to consider an organization's data design independently of its application programs. As a result, it is often possible to change the design without a massive reprogramming effort. Nevertheless, software developers, database managers, and functional managers must understand the interrelationships that business processes require for an organization's data elements to properly reflect them in the database.

INFORMATION TECHNOLOGY AND GLOBAL BUSINESS

Striking the balance between providing core systems that offer a global view of his company and still catering to varying local needs is an issue that is always foremost for Nigel Green, Hong Kong-based information technology planning manager for DHL Worldwide Express Asia-Pacific.

"The whole ethos of our company is to think globally and act locally," he said. "While we offer global services, we are perceived as locally integrated into the community of each country, and our IT systems need to reflect that."

An example is DHL's global shipment database. Certain countries may wish to add extra shipment checkpoints to the system because of more stringent regulations. In those cases, users can input their unique checkpoint data—data other countries won't see—into the common global database.

The global database actually consists of three Informix Corp. databases held on servers in Singapore, Burlingame, Calif., and Brussels. Shipment messages are transmitted among 400-plus Hewlett-Packard Co. servers around the world. All systems are linked on DHL's worldwide network, DHLnet, built on a TCP/IP over frame-relay architecture. Operations in all 220+ countries have access to this network, which also carries corporate electronic mail and intranet traffic.

Green and his colleagues are also faced with the daunting task of encouraging all local operations to abide by a standard set of IT and business rules. These rules govern activities such as storing shipment information in the global database rather than a locally defined database or capturing and transmitting data in a timely manner.

Probably the biggest challenge for DHL's IS management lies in just trying to communicate concepts and standards around the globe, Green noted. "We are hoping that intranets and online conferencing will help in that area," he said. The company is already publishing IT standards on Web pages, "and that's making a difference."

SOURCE: Extracted from Anna Foley, DHL Worldwide Express, *Computerworld* (March 10, 1997), at http://www.computerworld.com/search/AT-html/9703/970303globSL97 glob7.html.

BASIC DATA CONCEPTS

From a logical perspective, we can consider a database to be a combination of data elements. Figure 5.4 shows how these elements form a hierarchy. At the highest level is the database itself. You might think of this as a file cabinet. Continuing the analogy, think of the database as composed of **files**, groups of data about similar things, just like the files in your file cabinet. A customer file, for example, holds all data about a company's customers.

A file contains **records**. Each record generally holds data about a person, place, or thing, concrete or abstract. For example, data about a particular customer might be a record in the customer file. Data about a particular invoice might be a record in an invoice file. Each record contains fields, data about one of the characteristics or attributes of a record. For example, a customer phone number might be a field in a customer record. An invoice number or invoice amount might be a field in an invoice

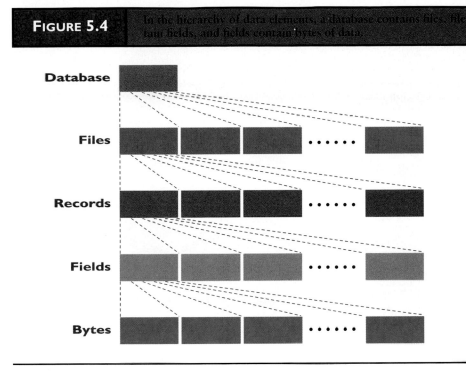

FIGURE 5.4   In the hierarchy of data elements, a database contains files, files contain records, records contain fields, and fields contain bytes of data.

record. A **field,** the lowest element of data that has meaning, contains words, bytes, and bits of data (see Chapter 3).

As we will see shortly, this hierarchical model of data is too simplistic. It ignores the relationships between elements at the same level in the hierarchy. For example, Pioneer's customer file relates to its order file: each customer has one or more orders. This model also ignores actions as opposed to attributes of data elements. For example, this model cannot indicate that a customer may do such things as order seeds or pay bills when due.

THE ENTITY-RELATIONSHIP MODEL

Although a number of models express the relationship among an organization's data elements, the entity-relationship (E/R) model is among the most widely used. The E/R model offers a pictorial way of showing the interrelationships among various types of data.[9]

Figure 5.5 illustrates a portion of an E/R model for a hypothetical wholesaler. Rectangles identify entities about which the organization collects data, corresponding to files, as shown for customers and orders. Diamonds enclose and name relationships between entities. In the figure, the *places* relationship indicates the fact that customers place orders. The lines connecting entities to the diamond represent the relationships among them and show whether the relationship is exclusive. In this example, each customer places zero to many (N) orders, but every order is placed by one (1) customer. This relationship is called one to many. Relationships can also be one to one—as when each employee has a company car and each car is assigned to one employee—or many to many—as when each order may be an order of many products and each product may appear on many orders. Ovals indicate attributes of entities and relationships. For example, in Figure 5.5, Tel# is an attribute of customer and Total Quantity is an attribute of the relationship "order_of."

FIGURE 5.5 An entity-relationship diagram illustrates how entities relate to one another and describes the attributes of all entities and relationships.

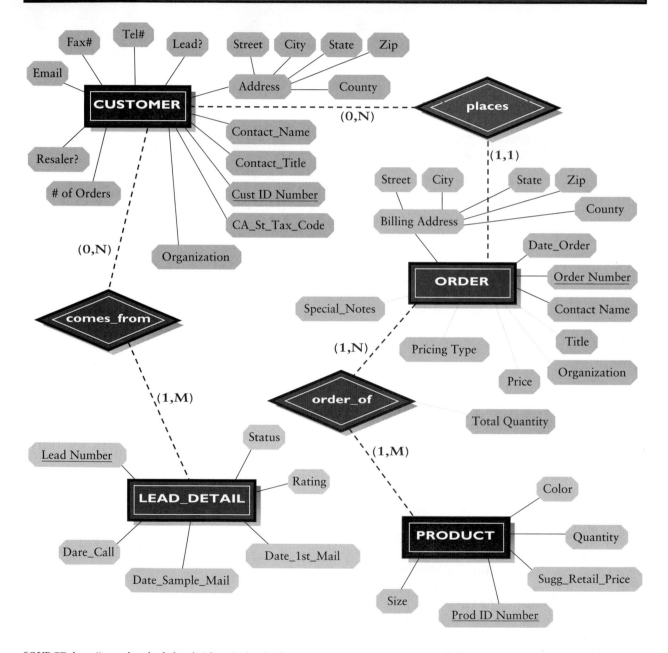

SOURCE: http://www.leor.berkely.edu/~hans/er.html. This diagram was created by Handy Halim, Trevar Oelshig, and Annie Wang for Back-a-Line, a company that makes athletic belts for back support.

✗ TECHNOLOGICAL UNDERPINNINGS

Managers who understand the fundamental ways databases can differ can generally work more effectively with computer specialists to choose the DBMS that best meets their information needs. In this section we look at two fundamental properties: the distribution architecture and the database model.

DISTRIBUTION ARCHITECTURES

Distribution architecture refers to how the organization distributes data and database processing physically among the computers in a network. Distribution architecture has important consequences for database performance and database use. Computer networks allow a DBMS running on one computer to access data stored on another computer. We will study computer networks in Chapter 6 and learn how data flow through the network. Obtaining data through the network is likely to be slower than obtaining it directly from the storage devices of the computer running the DBMS. Moving data across a network consumes network resources and network capacity needed for other tasks.

Managers and computer specialists can choose DBMSs with one of four data architectures: decentralized, centralized, client/server, and distributed. Table 5.2 identifies differences among these architectures and shows their advantages and disadvantages.

Decentralized Architecture. A **decentralized architecture** involves no data sharing; it has "islands of information." Generally, this architecture arises from users developing databases as required by individual applications, without central planning and without central control.

The absence of central planning in the decentralized architecture gives users freedom to develop applications that meet their needs and maintain control over the applications they develop. But this architecture generally prevents users from easily

TABLE 5.2	The four data architectures differ in their basic characteristics, as well as their performance and use.

		Decentralized	Centralized	Client/Server	Distributed
Defining Characteristics	Shared data	No	Yes	Yes	Yes
	Data location	Distributed	Centralized	Centralized	Distributed
	Processing location	Distributed	Centralized	Shared	Distributed
Performance and Usage Characteristics	Performance	Excellent	Network Constrained	Network Constrained	Mixed
	Ease of management	Simple	Easy	Moderate	Difficult
	Redundancy	High	Low	Low	Moderate
	Consistency	Low	High	High	High
	Scalability	High	Low	Moderate	High

combining or comparing data in various databases. It also encourages data duplication, requiring dual entry and dual storage and possibly leading to inconsistencies. Decentralized architectures often arise in companies having a decentralized management approach and in companies built through acquisition.

Centralized Architecture.

A **centralized architecture** has a single DBMS running on a single computer and maintaining data centrally. This architecture provides a consistent set of data to authorized users with limited redundancy. It is relatively easy to control and manage, at least for small databases. Having a centralized storage capability also makes it easy to consolidate corporate-wide data and determine whether a data item currently exists within the database.

With centralized processing, a single program accepts the input of many users and sends output to them accordingly. Therefore, a centralized architecture needs more concentrated processing power than a decentralized architecture, often requiring mainframes or large midrange systems. Because the competition in these markets is small relative to personal computing markets, these systems might be more expensive, even if they have less total processing power and storage.

As database size and usage grow, more powerful equipment must often replace the existing hardware to respond to greater processing and data storage needs. Hardware upgrades of mainframe systems are expensive and sometimes require software changes to support them. The integration of new with existing applications becomes more complex and time consuming as the centralized database grows.

Client/Server Architecture.

A **client/server architecture** (see Chapter 4) divides the functions of a DBMS among connected computers on a network while centralizing permanent storage for all data on a computer called the **database server.** The computers connected to the server are called its **clients.** The clients run the parts of the DBMS that process user requests and display results. The server runs the parts of the DBMS that store and retrieve data. A variety of models exist to divide the functions of the DBMS between the client and the server.[10] In three-tiered client/server systems, applications that access the database might run on servers separate from the database server and separate from the user clients.

To illustrate the application and benefits of the client/server architecture, consider an accounts receivable program running on one client and a customer service application running on another client (see Figure 5.6). At the accounts-receivable station, the data entry clerk processes a customer's check, first entering the customer ID. The accounts-receivable program sends a request to the client DBMS to determine whether the customer ID is a valid one. The client DBMS passes this request to the server DBMS, which accesses the database to determine whether the ID is valid. The server responds to the client DBMS, and the client DBMS responds to the application program, which then proceeds to accept data about the check. When the user finishes entering the payment data, the client DBMS processes and compresses the data and forwards them to the server DBMS for storage. At the customer service station, the clerk also accesses client data, such as a list of payments outstanding, through a program running on his or her computer. If the server receives two requests to update the same data at the same time, it mediates the conflict. The server may also keep a log to recover from system crashes.

The primary advantage of the client/server architecture is that it off-loads the application programs and many of the functions of the DBMS from the server. In the

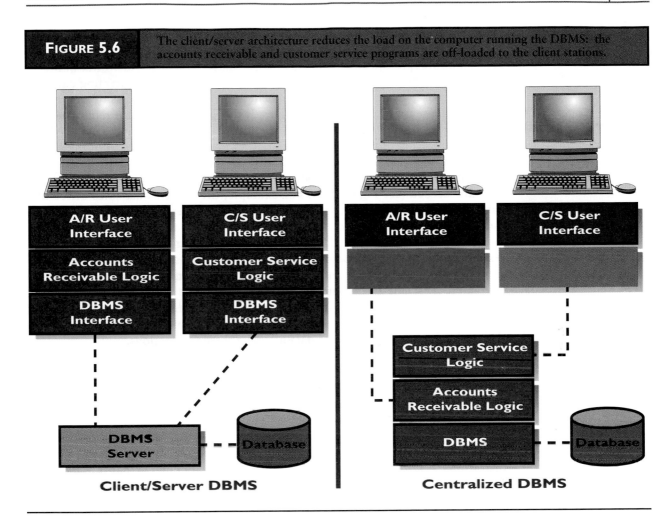

| FIGURE 5.6 | The client/server architecture reduces the load on the computer running the DBMS: the accounts receivable and customer service programs are off-loaded to the client stations. |

Client/Server DBMS

Centralized DBMS

preceding example, the accounts-receivable station operates almost autonomously, barely affected by the number of other programs running on the network. With a centralized architecture, the accounts receivable and customer service applications run on the same computer. When the company adds new applications, accounts receivable processing will slow down unless the company upgrades the computer to provide more processing power.

The client/server architecture encourages the movement of a large amount of data over the network. Because processing occurs at many client locations, and the client and server interact frequently and extensively, data must flow rapidly between server and clients for adequate DBMS performance. The client/server DBMS thereby places a heavy load on the network capacity.

Another disadvantage of the client/server architecture is difficulty controlling data. Employees with access to diskettes on client computers can remove data that the organization means to keep confidential. As a result, some organizations insist that no client computers be equipped with removable media. This, however, limits the usefulness of such computers for other functions.

centralized architecture. Local data managers can add or delete elements of data to their databases without compromising the integrity of the combined database. To support the distributed architecture, however, DBMS software must be in place or obtainable at all computers that intend to store data.

Distributed DBMSs are more complex than single-computer DBMSs for several reasons. First, the distributed DBMS must be able to determine the location of specific data. Second, it must be more sophisticated in determining the optimal way to request data. The order in which the DBMS processes a request can make a significant difference in the amount of data transmitted over the network. Finally, anticipating computer failures and prioritizing requests for data are extremely complex.[12] Sometimes it is difficult to determine whether a computer has completed an update before it or the network fails. In addition, when two requests to access the same data occur at about the same time, it is not easy to determine which request came first or what other requests are part of the same transaction if one of the requests must be blocked.

Besides the technical difficulties, organizational issues sometimes impede the acceptance of distributed DBMSs.[13] Traditionally, a single administrator or administrative office designs and controls the corporate database. DBMSs exist to reduce redundancy in data entry and processing by centralizing such control. Distributing authority and control over the data resource negates this reason for using a DBMS. Many managers believe that isolated and potentially conflicting islands of data will arise as local managers add their favorite modifications to the enterprise data model. Of course, an organization can use a distributed architecture purely for its technical advantages, such as reducing network flow and increasing response time, while refusing to relinquish control to local managers. Still, many managers view distributed architecture as the first step toward distributed control and potential loss of personal information and power.

Mixed Architectures.   In practice, mixed architectures arise frequently. A company with multiple sites might use a distributed architecture with redundant data to maximize performance. The company might use a centralized architecture at one site to consolidate processing, and it might use a client/server architecture at another site to distribute processing. Some of its managers will likely create unshared databases for their own personal use. For example, they may keep an electronic Rolodex or a list of customer contacts in a personal database. Although the company might prefer that managers share such data, in practice they may find sharing impractical or too invasive of privacy. As a result, some elements of a decentralized architecture also arise.

DATABASE MODELS

The **database model** refers to the underlying methods that a database uses for associating, storing, and retrieving related data. This model also has profound implications for performance and type of use. DBMSs do not completely eliminate an organization's concern about organizing its data. Although users and programmers need to worry less about the physical data storage, they must still pay attention to the **logical relationships** among the data. For example, a student and the courses she takes relate logically to one another. Also, a student relates to her phone number. But these two relationships differ. A student takes many courses at a given time, and the history of courses that a student takes is of interest. By contrast, a student usually has only one or two phone numbers, and old phone numbers have no interest. A phone number might be considered to be an **attribute,** or characteristic of the student, as might her hair color, height, and weight. Courses, on the other hand, exist independently of students and have attributes of their own, such as prerequisites, time of day, and professors. In addition, the relationship between a student and the courses she takes may have attributes, such as the grade received. Companies must address the relationships among their data elements to organize their data properly.

DBMSs can treat the relationships among data elements differently. Their approaches fall into a few broad categories, known as database models. In this section, we review the relational, object, network, and hierarchical database models. The first successful commercial DBMSs, based on the hierarchical model, were followed by DBMSs based on the network model, the relational model, and the object model, in that order. We begin instead with the most widely accepted model, the relational model. We cover the object model next because its use is growing most rapidly and it works best for certain applications. We cover the network model and the hierarchical model primarily because of their historical importance, although many large transaction systems continue to employ them. Table 5.3 compares the data models.

Relational Model.   The **relational model,** first proposed as a theoretical model in 1970 but not widely adopted until the late 1980s, acts as the basis for most DBMS products.

In the relational model, a **table** represents a file with rows called **tuples** and columns called **attributes.** For example, the data in Table 5.4 represent the customer file with rows, or tuples, identifying each customer's number, name, address, and credit limit. Each column presents a specific attribute for all customers: the left-most column shows all customer numbers, the right-most column shows all credit limits.

TABLE 5.3	Database models differ in standards, speed, ease of use, and target.			
	Relational	**Object**	**Network**	**Hierarchical**
Standards	Yes	Yes	Yes	No
Speed	Low	Moderate	Moderate	High
Ease of Query	High	High	Low	Low
Ease of Software Development	Moderate	High	Low	Low
Primary Target	Decision support	GUI	Transaction	Transaction
Ease of Data Distribution	Moderate	Moderate	Low	Low
Representative Products	Access	Gemstone	IMS	IDS
	DB2	Ontos		IDMS
	Oracle	Versant		
	Sybase			

database to change the telephone numbers. Deleting data, such as a sales representative's customers, can cause the loss of other important information, such as the sales representative's telephone number. The bottom of Figure 5.8 normalizes the data by breaking it into two tables, one for the customer and one for the sales representative.

Object Model. The **object model,** the most recent of the widely accepted database models, derives from object-oriented programming (see Chapter 4).[15] Recall that this type of programming views an object as an encapsulation of attributes (or data) and programs (called methods), tightly bundled and closed from the view of users and other programs. For example, a customer might be an object with attributes such as name, sales-rep, credit-limit, and invoices along with methods such as change-credit-limit and pay-invoice. Some attributes, such as invoice, may themselves be other objects. Messages, which give directions to the object, provide the only interface between the user and an object or between objects. A customer object might send its name in response to the message "tell me your name." It might change its representation of the customer's credit limit and reply with the message "done" in response to the message "change credit limit to 3000."

Object-oriented DBMSs store objects and object-class metadata. Objects may belong to an object type, normally called an object class. Figure 5.9 shows a company object class with attributes of name, phone numbers, and contact, and the method add-phone-numbers, which accepts and processes messages about additional phone numbers. All subtypes of an object, such as a customer company, retain the characteristics of their object (such as company name, phone number, contacts, and add-phone), and could have other attributes and methods, such as orders and take-order.

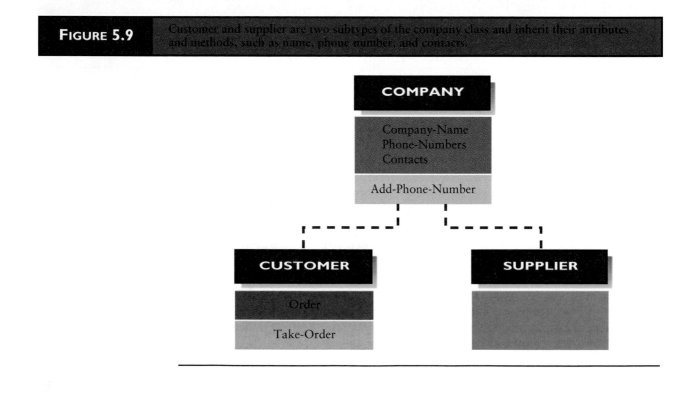

FIGURE 5.9 Customer and supplier are two subtypes of the company class and inherit their attributes and methods, such as name, phone number, and contacts.

ADVANCED TECHNOLOGY

The European Center for Particle Physics (CERN) is building the world's largest accelerator and gathering real-time data from nuclear particle physics experiments. The data and analysis database, to be deployed in 1999, is expected to be many petabytes. A petabyte is 1,000 terabytes, or one quadrillion bytes. CERN will use an object DBMS from Objectivity Inc. to store these data. The planned database is interesting from the standpoint of both its size and complexity.

The database is expected to handle the following types of data:

- Histograms
- Detector calibration and geometry
- Production control
- Event data

The event data is the main target of the database and will accumulate at the rate of at least one petabyte per year, assuming 100 days of operation per year. Data input rates will be as great as 1.6 gigabytes per second. The database will need to be expandable, up to 100 petabytes in 20 years. The DBMS will be distributed and operating in a heterogeneous environment. This means that different parts of the database will reside on different types of computers.

Database designers are investigating ways to use the metadata so that physicists can see what event collections are available, as well as how these collections were selected, and provide intuitive interfaces, such as drag and drop, to permit the user to select and refine collections of interest. Another important design initiative is to retain a history of objects, so that researchers can trace their evolution to the current version from prior versions.

SOURCES: RD45 Collaboration, RD45 project execution plan, Geneva, Switzerland, April 15, 1997, http://www.info.cern.ch/asd/cernlib/rd45/reports/rd45_pep97.htm; Jamie Shiers, *Status report of the RD45 project*, http://www.info.cern.ch/asd/cernlib/rd45/slides/1997/CHEP97.htm, March 17, 1998; and http://www.objectivity.com/Customers/scicust.html, March 17, 1998.

The object model easily integrates with object-oriented programs and readily represents complex data types such as images, sound, and objects embedded within other objects. For example, object-oriented models can easily represent organization charts and engineering drawings, which are hard to represent using the traditional data models. As multimedia becomes more predominant in computing, so too does the use of objects. Object-oriented DBMSs provide a facility to capture such objects in a database.

Current implementations of object DBMSs have evolved in two ways. First, proponents of object-oriented languages have created object DBMSs to provide permanence for objects represented in the languages that they use. Second, relational DBMS vendors have added object features to their products. This second approach has produced hybrid object-relational DBMSs, commonly known as **universal servers**. Administrators at a large state college in Hamilton, Ontario, for example, use the object features of IBM's DB2 relational database to store photographs of students in their administrative database. Previously, the school had been plagued by students cashing phony checks at the campus's bursar office. Now, officials can access the database whenever a student cashes a check to compare the student's face with the picture corresponding to the name on the check.[16]

Most universal servers, however, store objects such as pictures, signatures, or sound recordings simply as a series of bytes. Because the model does not represent object properties, users cannot find all photographs of birds in the database unless the records with those photos include captions containing the word "bird." Although standards do not yet exist for queries on true object databases, many object-oriented DBMSs use a graphical interface that pictures objects as icons on a screen. When clicked, these icons open to reveal the indicated data. Lines and arrows on the screen illustrate relationships among objects and clicking on them allows the user to move between object types. Figure 5.10 shows a more textually-based query.

The existence of standards for representing object data independent of any computer language, operating system, or hardware has increased the popularity of object DBMSs. Most software vendors have adopted the **CORBA (Common Object Request Broker Architecture)** standard; Microsoft has instead adopted **DCOM (Distributed Component Object Model)**. Most object DBMSs support both standards, simplifying their interface to object-oriented programming languages.

FIGURE 5.10 The user-interface of an object-oriented database showing a query in progress.

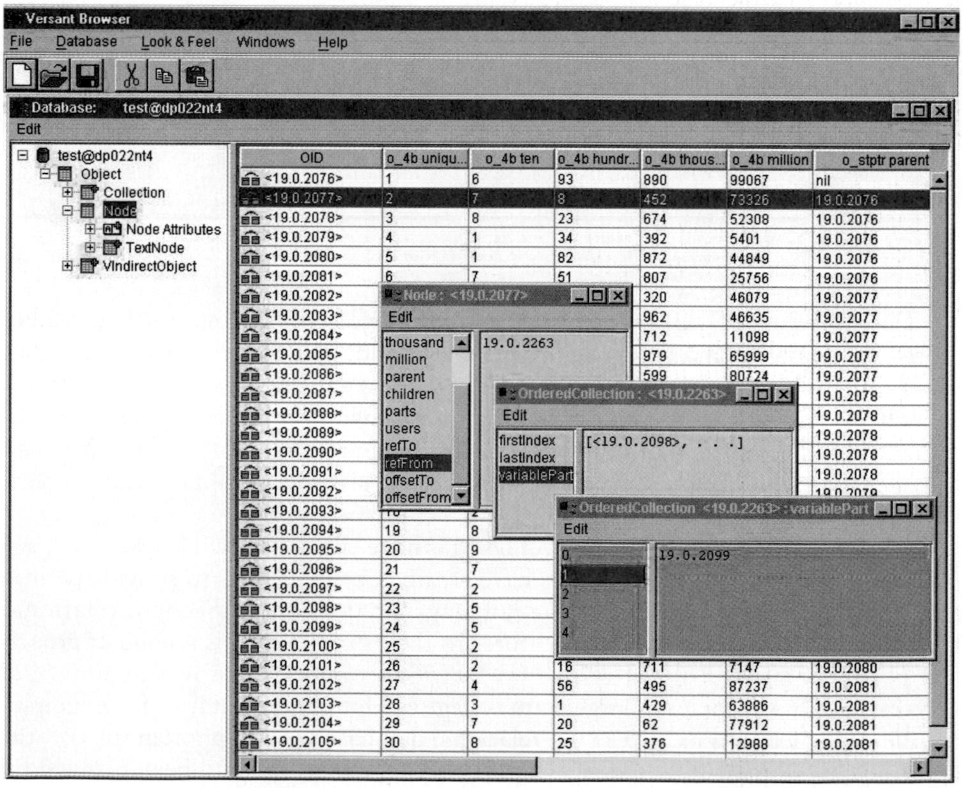

Network Model.   The **network model** builds a tighter linkage (called a **set**) between elements of data, such as between customers and sales representatives. A customer/sales-rep set implements the rule that each customer must have a sales representative. Each entry in the set includes data about a single sales rep and all of his customers. The network model does not store the sales rep identifier with the customer's data, as would the relational model. It stores the customer's data as part of the set belonging to its representative. One data element may belong to several sets. In Figure 5.11, for example, each order line is part of an order/order-line set and a product/order-line set. An item may be a member of one kind of a set and an owner of another. For example, in Figure 5.11 an order is a member of a customer/order set and an owner of an order/order-line set.

Using sets retrieves related information faster and more efficiently than with the relational model. The database administrator may specify that the DBMS store members of a set near one another so that a single access to the storage medium retrieves them all. For example, one disk access might retrieve a customer and all of its orders.

From the user perspective, sets complicate rather than simplify data access. The user cannot access data simply by its title or characteristics. Instead, she must prescribe procedures to get the data by navigating through the network of related items. How would a customer services manager determine which customers to contact about delays in processing their orders due to a product recall? First, the manager would use the order-line/product set to identify all order lines in which the defective product appeared. The order-line/order set for each line would identify the affected orders. The order/customer set would identify the affected customers. The manager or a technical support person uses a procedural language such as COBOL to search through the related items for the answer. A manager using the relational model, in contrast, would simply specify the relationships among the data requested without doing any programming. Loosely speaking, the user would ask the DBMS to obtain

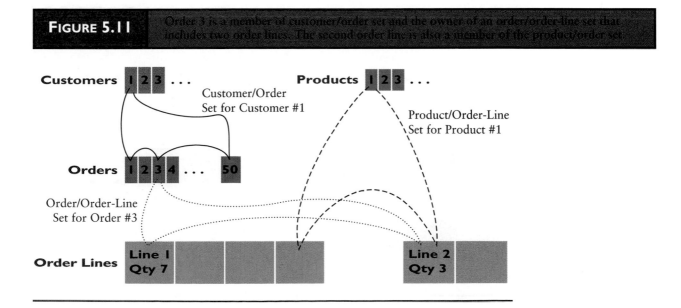

FIGURE 5.11   Order 3 is a member of customer/order set and the owner of an order/order-line set that includes two order lines. The second order line is also a member of the product/order set.

the names of all customers whose identification matched a customer identification in the order table and which order contained an order-line matching the defective part. Modern network DBMSs generally include an SQL user interface that translates SQL requests into programs that navigate the databases to extract the desired data.

Several factors explain the popularity of the relational model over the network model.

- The decreasing cost of faster computer processing makes using the relational model more cost-effective, while the programming costs required to use the network model remain high.
- The increasing availability of personal computers has caused users who are not computer professionals to insist on the ability to access data without programming.
- The relational model is more flexible than the network model. Simply adding and deleting columns changes the relationships among data; programs rarely must be changed as in the network model.

Hierarchical Model. We can view the **hierarchical model,** a precursor to the network model, as a network model with additional restrictions. The hierarchical model, also called **hierarchial,** views data as organized in a logical hierarchy. An entity may be a member of no more than one type of set: for example, customers can belong only to the sales-rep set, not to the discount-class or any other data set.

The hierarchical restriction makes it extremely difficult to represent many interrelationships among data. Consider, for example, the order line in Figure 5.12. Although order line logically deserves to be part of the order set and the product set, the hierarchical model prohibits this dual membership because it violates the hierarchical view of data. Instead, the model requires two hierarchies to represent the data, forcing the DBMS to store the order lines twice.

FIGURE 5.12 Order lines must be duplicated in the hierarchical model because they are a part of two hierarchies.

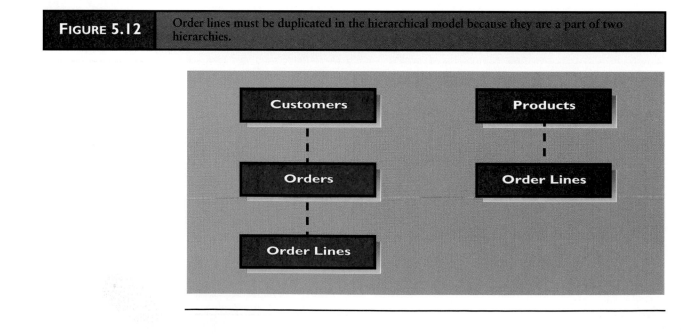

Most implementations of the hierarchical model have technical ways to loosen the hierarchical restriction somewhat, eliminating data duplication. Nevertheless, it remains cumbersome for data modelers. Although access is intrinsically faster for the hierarchical model than for the network model, current computer technology has removed this advantage.

Despite its drawbacks, the hierarchical model remains one of the most widely used models because of the large installed base of a product called IMS.[17] Developed by IBM in 1968, millions of applications have used IMS. In many cases, and particularly for transaction-based systems, the cost of reprogramming these applications outweighs the benefits of converting them to a network or relational form.

USING DATA EFFECTIVELY

A manager's effectiveness in using data depends greatly on how her organization sets up, administers, and manages its databases. In this section, we explore issues and options in organizing and managing the data resource for most effective use.

WAREHOUSING DATA

A **data warehouse** is an enterprise-wide database designed solely to support management decision making. Although a data warehouse might contain copies of some current transaction data, it mostly contains historic and summary data aggregated at various levels and along various dimensions. For example, it might contain daily, weekly, and monthly sales by store, state or province, country, and region. It might also aggregate sales by product, product group, and business unit. It might aggregate sales by type of customer as well. Omni Healthcare, a Northern California health maintenance organization, used its data warehouse as a competitive advantage. Omni put all of its provider, member, revenue, and marketing information into a data warehouse, which allowed it to analyze information about expenses, revenues, and the provider network.[18]

A **data mart** also provides summary and historical data for management decision making, but for a single department or division rather than an entire organization. Managers in a single department or division set up a data mart for their managerial needs. Bayer AG's Rubber Group uses the RUBI financial data mart to provide information to managers at all levels within the group. They can use the system's financial information to help accomplish their strategic goals.[19] Sometimes, managers create data marts by extracting data from an existing data warehouse, perhaps to provide a longer history or more levels of aggregation than the warehouse manager provides. More frequently, managers develop data marts when their company has not implemented a data warehouse.

Data marts cost less to develop and operate than data warehouses and can be built more quickly. Designers can more easily meet the needs of managers who want them without imposing on the limited time of managers who will not use them. When managers decide to build data marts rather than an integrated data warehouse, they risk creating isolated islands of information that resist being linked or reconciled. First Data Resources, a company that processes transactions for credit-card companies, experienced this problem. The company's seven departments each created their own data marts. Managers who want to obtain a consolidated view of a client's activities and status must go to seven different databases. The company plans to resolve this problem by replacing the data marts with a data warehouse capable of holding up to four terabytes of information.[20] Ryder Systems Inc., a truck leasing and logistics company, retains an enterprise view of data despite a data mart strategy. It administers its data marts centrally and imposes standards on data names, technology, and tools used to extract the data from its production databases.[21]

Data extraction is a primary concern of data warehouse managers. How often should they move data from production systems to the data warehouse? Extracting the data places an extra-heavy processing burden on the production systems. Warehouse managers must implement systems that identify inconsistencies in data extracted from different locations. Extraction of data from non-DBMS systems complicates loading the data warehouse. Fortunately, software products exist to simplify such extraction, but occasionally technical people must write programs to extract data from old transaction processing systems. United Parcel Service (UPS), despite using data scrubbing and transfer tools from Prism Solutions Inc., required eight people for nine months to import data into its new data warehouse.[22]

Business mergers are a major concern for data warehouse managers and users. Jim Wolff, director of information access at PacifiCare Health Systems Inc. after its acquisition of FHP International Corp., became responsible for merging PacifiCare's data warehouse with two FHP data warehouses. Ironically, he had just spent two years at FHP attempting to merge its warehouses following a prior acquisition. Merging incompatible warehouses causes stress both for the technical people responsible for the warehouse project and for the managers who need to access their data.[23]

Many tools, including data mining and online application processing tools, exist to help managers use the data collected in a data warehouse effectively. **Data mining** describes the process of identifying patterns in large masses of data. **Online analytical processing (OLAP)** tools aggregate, display, and analyze data to draw inferences and make decisions. We discuss these tools and their applications more thoroughly in Chapter 10.

Multidimensional database managers are among the most powerful of the OLAP tools. With a few exceptions, these products are not true DBMSs, but rather analytical software that creates views, expressed in a database or spreadsheet form, of a large relational database from multiple dimensions. Multidimensional DBMS products provide aggregation features that most other DBMSs do not provide. For example, calculating a moving average requires data sequenced by time. Relational DBMS products do not preserve a sequence in the rows of their tables, nor does SQL operate in the order of rows retrieved. Relational DBMSs also have difficulty determining what dates to aggregate for durations such as semimonthly periods.

MANAGING THE DATA RESOURCE

Managing the data resource is both a business and a technical problem. Business managers must define their data needs and data sources. Information professionals must make data easily and rapidly accessible to managers, ensure the consistency and accuracy of information collected and stored, and set standards and procedures for reacting to changes in the business information needs. Data administration describes the business role, and database administration describes the technical role. These two roles often overlap and fall to a single person in the organization. More frequently, however, a company will have one data administrator and multiple database administrators, one or more for each DBMS used.

Data Administration.

A **data administrator** ensures the integrity of the data resource. The data administrator must know what data the organization collects, where it stores the data, and how it names data items.

The data administrator performs the following duties:

- Tries to minimize the redundancy of data by keeping centralized documentation of all data elements. She may impose naming standards on the data throughout the organization and use a data dictionary to keep track of data names and uses.
- Establishes the security of data and sets up appropriate access controls. She works closely with businesspeople to set up appropriate logical views.
- Ensures that data loaded into corporate databases are clean. When Chase Manhattan Bank NA created a new customer database to track all accounts by household, it dedicated 22 people for four years to clean about 20 million records.[24]
- Helps the business establish rules regarding data formats and relationships. For example, rules establishing credit limits for customers may differ not only by type of customer but also by business units within a company, even for the same type of customer.

A data administrator should have a background in database design. Most importantly, a good data administrator needs a broad understanding of the business. Business managers ultimately determine business rules, establish data quality standards, set authorization policy, and decide other matters relating to data integrity. The data administrator needs to work well with business managers, asking them probing questions that result in proper decisions about design and process.

Database Administration.

A **database administrator (DBA)** oversees the overall performance and integrity of a DBMS on one or more databases. The DBA regularly backs up the databases and recovers them after a system crash. The DBA supervises and monitors the development of software that uses or affects the databases. He creates separate development databases for testing new software and approves the transfer of such software to a production database after completing testing. The DBA monitors and installs bug fixes and new releases from the DBMS vendor.

Most DBMS vendors include tools to monitor database performance. The DBA can address performance problems in a number of ways:

- The DBA can make procedural changes that improve performance to satisfactory levels. For example, he can restrict certain types of database activities to off-peak periods or reduce their priority so that they do not impair performance.

- The DBA can build indexes into the database to speed frequently performed queries.
- The DBA may be able to change the amount of cache storage and working memory available to the database.
- The DBA can modify the data design through denormalization. When users rejoin records after breaking them apart to reduce duplicate storage and eliminate possible inconsistencies, the database must correctly respond to their requests. Denormalization puts the records back together permanently, reducing the load on the database.

The DBA should have strong technical skills, extensive experience with the DBMS in use, and excellent communication skills. Companies such as Walt Disney World, for example, have found that DBAs who are too technical are not effective. As a result, they look for people with good interpersonal skills to fill the DBA position.[25]

GLOBAL ISSUES

Companies that operate globally often cannot find a convenient time to stop processing in order to back up their data. They may address this problem in two ways:

- Use DBMS systems that operate in parallel on two storage devices. Periodically, the DBA detaches one of the storage devices from the database application to create a backup copy. Afterward, the DBMS updates this storage device using the database log from the storage device that remained attached.
- Write all database updates to a temporary log during the backup process. The database itself remains constant during the backup. The DBMS uses both the database and the temporary log to answer queries so that the user always "sees" current versions of the data. After the backup finishes, the log brings the database up to date.

The data architecture is often more challenging for global than domestic companies. Poor data communication infrastructure in some countries makes it difficult to transfer data internationally. Some countries impose regulations on the export of data. Some companies, therefore, may prefer to keep local data at local sites using a distributed architecture.

SUMMARY

A database is an organized collection of related data. Database management systems perform numerous functions in organizations, including storing and retrieving data and metadata, limiting and controlling redundancy, supporting simultaneous data sharing, ensuring transaction atomicity, providing authorization and security services, enforcing business rules, and improving programming productivity.

Data design describes the process of identifying and formalizing the relationships among the elements of data in a database. The entity-relationship model shows these relationships pictorially.

Distribution architecture refers to the physical distribution of data and database processing among the computers in an organization. A decentralized architecture provides no data sharing. Individual application designers create databases on an ad hoc basis, without central planning or control. A centralized architecture refers to running a DBMS on a single computer. A client/server architecture divides DBMS processing among networked computers while centralizing permanent storage on a database server. The distributed architecture distributes processing and allows data to reside anywhere on the network of computers. Replication of data in this architecture improves performance.

Database models reflect the logical relationships among data in a DBMS. The relational model describes a data object by a table of rows and columns. Normalization of data ensures the effective grouping of the data elements of a database. The object model views an object as a combination of attributes and methods. Universal servers combine support for objects with a relational framework. The network model builds a tight linkage, called a set, between elements of data. The hierarchical model resembles a network model but also views data as organized logically into a hierarchy.

A data warehouse is an enterprise-wide database designed solely to support management decision making. A data mart is a database for decision support focused around an application or department. Multidimensional database products help managers view and analyze data in data warehouses and data marts from multiple perspectives.

A data administrator ensures the enterprise-wide integrity of the data resource. A database administrator focuses on the overall performance and integrity of a single DBMS on one or more databases. Both jobs require good technical and business skills. Global issues in database management include timing backups and choosing flexible data architectures.

KEY TERMS

atomicity
attribute
centralized architecture
client
client/server architecture
computerized database
concurrency control
CORBA (Common Object Request
  Broker Architecture)
data administrator
data design
data dictionary
data mart
data mining
data warehouse
database
database administrator (DBA)
database management system (DBMS)

database model
database server
DCOM (Distributed Component
  Object Model)
decentralized architecture
distributed DBMS architecture
distribution architecture
field
file
hierarchical (or hierarchial) model
log
logical relationship
logical view
metadata
multidimensional database manager
network model
normalization
object model

ODBC (Open Database Connectivity)
online analytical processing (OLAP)
physical view
record
relational model
replication
schema
set

SQL
subschema
table
transaction processing monitor (TP monitor)
tuple
universal server
view

DISCUSSION AND REVIEW QUESTIONS

1. Do data have to be computerized to form a database?
2. What are six reasons that a manager might want to use a database management system?
3. Why do DBMSs store metadata?
4. Why would a manager want a stand-alone data dictionary?
5. Why is reducing data redundancy advantageous?
6. Why is concurrency control necessary?
7. Give an example that shows why transaction atomicity should not be violated.
8. How do views enhance data security?
9. How do database management systems increase programmer productivity?
10. Compare and contrast four distribution architectures.
11. What are the advantages and disadvantages of a distributed architecture relative to a centralized architecture?
12. What are key characteristics of the four database models?
13. How does the relational database model represent data?
14. What is an example of a problem that might arise from using a data model that has not been normalized?
15. What are the advantages of the object model relative to the relational model?
16. What advantages and disadvantages do sets give the network model relative to the relational model?
17. How does a data warehouse differ from a data mart?
18. What is the role of a data administrator?
19. What is the role of a database administrator?
20. What options does a database administrator have to improve database performance?

IS ON THE WEB

Exercise 1: Visit the sites of three object-oriented database vendors. Read and summarize the white papers that compare object and relational databases.

Exercise 2: Visit an online database. How might managers use the information presented? Prepare a brief description of possible uses.

MINICASE

GTE EMPOWERS DECISION MAKERS

"I need a complete report on Hispanic households with a median income of less than $40,000 that generated more than $50 per month in telephone toll revenue during the third quarter of 1994."

That's exactly the kind of information a product manager needs to determine the viability of a new service or product offering. It's also the kind of query that might have taken GTE Corp.'s GTE Telephone Operations unit weeks to execute. Data from a variety of different sources would have to be accessed, integrated, and reconciled. And, in the end, all that work would have been done to satisfy a single request.

But no more. GTE's business managers can now get information requests answered fast because their enterprise data warehouse allows them to draw from a variety of disparate data sources. That's not only convenient, it's essential in the intensely competitive world of telecommunications services.

"If we can get data delivered to decision makers more quickly, we can beat the competition," says Perry Kosieniak, a senior application consultant.

OPERATIONS VERSUS DECISIONS

The distinction between operational and decision-making needs was a key factor in GTE's move to data warehousing. Although existing applications and infrastructure may be adequate to support day-to-day functions such as order taking and billing, they are often insufficient for strategic decision making.

"Decision making usually requires integration of data across multiple subject areas, such as customers, network usage, and billing," says Kosieniak. "It may also require the use of sources outside the existing application environment, such as zip code tables or demographic data."

There are performance issues that also distinguish the two types of data management. Operations systems such as online transaction processing tend to place a fairly consistent burden on computing resources. Online query processing, on the other hand, tends to be unpredictable, with periods of intense activity alternating with periods of minimal use.

"You don't want to suddenly submit a large query to an operational server," says Kosieniak. "Not only could you get a slow response, but you may also adversely affect the performance of your operational system." By providing two distinct infrastructures for legacy systems and decision making, GTE can tailor each environment to meet specific needs.

SOURCE: Case from GTE empowers decision makers, *Computerworld,* Special Advertising Supplement: "Shedding Light on Data Warehousing for More Informed Business Solutions" (May 1, 1995): DW18.

Down the road, however, GTE plans to use a data warehouse to supplement some of its operational applications, such as customer profiling.

Speedier decision making is not the only benefit that GTE expects to realize from its data warehouse solution. The company also expects to increase the efficiency of both information technology (IT) and the business units. On the IT side, the need for numerous staffers to service the constant stream of data requests is being significantly diminished. "With the data warehouse, you make available resources [that were] previously committed to extraction, replication, and reporting," says Susan Guess, another GTE application consultant.

By improving these processes, GTE can reduce its costs and thereby lessen the need for outside contractors. The cost reductions enable the company to offer its own services at lower rates, which is essential to maintaining its competitive position.

On the business side, staff resources can be used more efficiently. "People in the business functions utilize querying tools as well," says Guess, "and they can spend a lot of time trying to obtain the data they need." Now they can focus on their real jobs, she says, to analyze and respond to decision data, rather than struggle to access it.

The main benefit of data warehousing, though, continues to be GTE's ability to respond quickly to the need for accurate, comprehensive data. "The demand for information is continuous," says Guess. "Data warehousing will help IT satisfy that demand and be an enabling factor in the business equation."

Case Questions

Diagnosis

1. What are some of the information needs of GTE's business managers?
2. How do the decision-making needs of GTE's managers differ from their operational needs?

Evaluation

3. What problems did business managers at GTE face in obtaining information prior to the development of GTE's data warehouse?

Design

4. What benefits did GTE hope to achieve with a data warehouse?
5. Why doesn't GTE use its data warehouse to support its operational processes?
6. Where does the data come from to populate GTE's data warehouse?

Implementation

7. How do businesspeople use the data warehouse?
8. What were the benefits to the business of the data warehouse at GTE?
9. What were the benefits for the IT staff?
10. In what way does the data warehouse add to the efficiency of the IT infrastructure?

THE HUMAN RESOURCES DATABASE PROBLEM   ACTIVITY 5.1

Step 1:   Read the following scenario:

Westin Hotels & Resorts, a corporate hotel management company, is responsible for centralized payroll, benefits administration, and a variety of other human resources services. Westin's corporate payroll and human resource departments have historically relied on multiple systems. An outside service bureau processed payroll for its 4,000 salaried employees, and individual, hotel-based stand-alone computers processed the payroll for its 6,000 hourly employees. The service bureau collected general personnel data, such as performance evaluations and employment histories, for the analysis of trends across all member hotels. It also tracked data for use in government reporting for tax purposes and other regulatory requirements. The benefits department used several in-house PC databases to administer group benefits, including group medical and life insurance benefits for management and hourly, nonunion employees at all hotels. This department negotiated with local health maintenance organizations, paid insurance premiums, and acted as a central office for claim and eligibility inquiries, among other functions.

The compensation department used an in-house PC database to process statistical information, such as employee salaries, in order to analyze it for competitive purposes. The human resources department used a manual filing system to maintain and update employee personnel records. Making a single personnel change, such as a hiring, termination, salary adjustment, or position transfer, required significant negotiations among the various departments and complicated procedures to interface the various reports and information. Each department in turn would then process the information using its individual system. This resulted in very high costs, a perpetually backlogged work load, inconsistent data, and inconsistently timed data changes. The individual hotels also were dissatisfied with this approach because when they received their benefits and payroll registers, they had to spend time reviewing them and cross-referencing the two, checking that all changes were accurate and consistent.

Step 2:   Prepare the case for class discussion.

Step 3:   Answer each of the following questions, individually or in small groups, as directed by your instructor:

Diagnosis

1. What are the information needs of Westin's compensation managers?
2. What are the information needs of managers at individual Westin hotels?

Evaluation

3. What problems exist with the systems that are currently in place?

SOURCE: Activity 5.1 based on information presented in J. E. Santora, Database base integrates HR functions, *Personnel Journal* (January 1992): 92.

Design

4. What are the objectives of an improved system?
5. Offer a plan for integrating the multiple systems into a single database management system.
6. What is the appropriate architecture for such a system?
7. What database model would you recommend and why?

Implementation

8. How should the new database system be administered?

Step 4: In small groups or with the entire class, share the plans you have developed. Then answer the following questions:

1. What elements do these plans have in common?
2. How well do the plans respond to the information needs at Westin?
3. What are the strengths and weaknesses of each plan?
4. What should be the components of an effective and responsive database management system for the hotels?

ACTIVITY 5.2   USING A MICRO DBMS

Step 1: Your instructor will give you instructions for accessing a DBMS on your computer system. Then follow the directions presented below.

Step 2: Create the structure for the STUDENTS table with seven fields of the lengths shown: SID (3), last (20), first (20), middle (1), sex (1), major (3), GPA (3 with one decimal place).

Step 3: Add the data for the ten student records shown in the following table:

SID	Last	First	Middle	Sex	Major	GPA
987	Peters	Steve	K	M	Mgt	3.2
763	Parker	Charles		M		2.7
218	Pichard	Sally		F	Fin	3.6
359	Pelnick	Alan	R	M	Fin	2.4
862	Fagin	Emma		F	Mgt	2.2
748	Meglin	Susan	B	F	MIS	3.8
506	Lee	Bill		M	Fin	2.7
581	Cambrell	Ted		M	Mkt	2.8
372	Quigley	Sarah		F		3.5
126	Anderson	Robert	F	M	Acc	3.7

Step 4: Sort the records to appear in descending GPA.

Step 5: Modify the structure of the table to reflect the possibility of a student last name of 25 characters.

Step 6: Create a data entry form that limits the user to entering GPA values to be between 0.0 and 4.0.

Step 7: Create a query that finds all female students who have a GPA greater than 2.5.

Step 8: Create a printed report of the information about each student that allows the dean of students to identify only those who qualify for Latin honors (top 5 percent of their class).

PROBLEMS IN DATABASE ADMINISTRATION   ACTIVITY 5.3

Step 1: Read the following problems with administering a centralized database system. For each problem, decide what you would do, and then offer a way of preventing the situation from occurring again.

Problem 1: Since its installation the centralized database at Watson Manufacturing has had duplicate records. When customer service converted to its new system it did not want any duplicate records transferred from the centralized database to the new system. Therefore, the department personnel carefully reviewed all records, identified duplicates, and purged them from the system. Several months after this occurred, the director of market research attempted to analyze the potential customer base for a new product the company was considering. The director was distressed to find that some customer files were labeled "duplicate record" and that no further information about them existed. The director was further outraged that anyone could erase information about customers from the database.

Problem 2: Human resources (HR) is responsible for capturing and maintaining personnel data. HR quit the centralized system because of concerns over system security. However, certain personnel data, which had been maintained by HR, were also used by a number of other offices. When HR abandoned the system, it informed administrative systems that it would not pass new or changed information to other offices. Maintaining employee addresses, locating employees in emergencies, generating mailing labels, verifying employment, and countless other functions now all had to be routed through HR because data on the central system became unreliable. Management reports or analyses requiring the merging of HR data with other system data (e.g., employee workload analysis) became impossible. Multiple, alternative, and disparate personnel files began to be maintained by various offices, each for its own use. The advantages of a common database were lost, and people could not understand why administrative systems, which maintained the database, couldn't just "fix" this.

SOURCE: Activity 5.3 reprinted from P. T. Farago, J. Whitmore-First, and E. A. Kallman, Managing data standards and policies in an integrated environment, *Journal of Systems Management* (March 1992): 33.

Problem 3:   Jennifer Smith recently joined the Hartley Engine Company as its first database administrator. Hartley Engine had a sophisticated distributed database management system that encompassed all basic business functions. The system had grown from a multitude of individually designed applications to a coherent system that an external consultant had designed and implemented. Managers at Hartley were used to making their own decisions about what data would be included in the database, who would have access to the data, and what applications should be included. Making changes in the system had been as easy as writing a request for the IS department to make the adjustment. After her first month on the job, Smith discovered that the system was not working as efficiently as it should be. Managers often had to use convoluted ways to access data held in remote locations. The security for data access was ineffective, and anyone could read confidential information. No rationale existed for placing data on the corporate database as opposed to retaining it on local microcomputers. The system was overloaded, processing was slow, and it was costing the company at least three times the money that was reasonable for a firm the size of Hartley.

Step 2:   In groups of four to six students, reach a consensus about how to handle each situation.

Step 3:   In small groups, with the entire class, or in written form, as directed by your instructor, offer a set of five guidelines for developing an effective way of administering a centralized database system. How would these guidelines change if the database system were distributed?

ACTIVITY 5.4   YAHOO! PEOPLE SEARCH

Step 1:   Read the following scenario:

In April 1996, Yahoo! Inc. and Database America Companies made available on the World Wide Web a database called Yahoo! People Search, which listed the telephone numbers and addresses of 90 million people nationwide. Shortly thereafter Yahoo! and Database America received complaints from people whose telephone numbers were unlisted on the telephone company white pages. These people had assumed that their telephone numbers were unavailable and thought that their privacy had been violated. They wanted their names removed from the database.

Step 2:   Assume that you are in charge of the Yahoo! People Search project. Assume that the companies have compiled the database legally and have a substantial investment in its development. Assume also that you have sold advertising for the service based on a certain number of queries and that you will have to refund these sales if the database is not used to the extent projected.

Step 3:   Answer each of the following questions, individually or in small groups, as directed by your instructor.

1. What alternatives do you have?
2. For each alternative, who benefits and who is harmed?

3. From the ethical principles of least harm, rights and duties, professional responsibilities, self-interest and utilitarianism, consistency, and respect, how would you evaluate each alternative?
4. What course of action would you take? Why?

DBMS AT BANKERS TRUST   ACTIVITY 5.5

Step 1:   Read the following case:

Bankers Trust believes it has saved up to 50 percent of potential development time by rewriting its internally developed global risk management system using object-oriented technology rather than basing it on the relational model.

The investment bank began developing its new system, based on Object Design's Objectstore database, in March and delivered the first phase of the project in August, when it was rolled out to 25 traders in the firm's offices in London and New York. The second phase, supporting a further 25 New York traders, is due to follow by the end of the year. The software will be deployed across the organization worldwide over the next two years. Thousands of support staff are expected to use it.

Colin Savery, Bankers Trust's vice president of technology, said, "We needed a lot of flexibility because a risk management application is a complex thing. It's also a very dynamic industry, so we needed the ability to extend, change, and evolve over time, and to do it fast. Object technology is the clear paradigm to meet those requirements."

He added that if he had based the object-oriented application on a relational database, it would have taken 25 percent more programming time to code persistence into it and 25 percent extra time to test the end result. This would have added six months to the development.

But the risk involved in choosing an object database led the organization to develop its application in the C++ language rather than use an object-based fourth-generation language. "Object-oriented databases are not employed widely and we weren't in R&D mode—this is a production system," Savery explained. "We felt we had enough risk with the database, so we went for C++, which also offered better performance."

Step 2:   Prepare the case for class discussion.

Step 3:   Answer each of the following questions, individually or in small groups, as directed by your instructor:

Diagnosis

1. What are the information needs of Bankers Trust's risk managers?
2. What characteristics of the industry affect those needs?

Evaluation

3. Why did Colin Savery reject a relational database solution?

SOURCE: Activity 5.5 scenario taken from object option halves bank's rewriting time, *Computer Weekly*, Copyright © Reed Business Publishing 1996, http://www.computerweekly.co.uk/news/24_10_96/08611354460/C8.html.

Design

4. What are the advantages of an object database design?
5. What do you think are the risks of an object database design?

Implementation

6. How did Bankers Trust minimize the risks of using an object DBMS for its new systems?
7. What were the benefits of using an object-oriented DBMS?

Step 4: In small groups or with the entire class, answer the following questions:

1. Why did Bankers Trust choose an object-oriented DBMS for its new system?
2. How did that selection address Bankers Trust's information needs?
3. What steps did Bankers Trust take to minimize the risks associated with using what was for it a new technology?

RECOMMENDED READINGS

Bischoff, Joyce, and Alexander, Ted. *Data Warehouse: Practical Advice from the Experts.* Englewood Cliffs, NJ: Prentice Hall, 1997.

Bontempo, Charles J., and Saracco, Cynthia Maro. *Database Management: Principles and Products.* Englewood Cliffs, NJ: Prentice Hall, 1996.

Hernandez, Michael J. *Database Design for Mere Mortals: A Hands-On Guide to Relational Database Design.* Reading, MA: Addison-Wesley, 1997.

Kroenke, David M. *Database Processing: Fundamentals, Design, and Implementation.* Englewood Cliffs, NJ: Prentice Hall, 1997.

The following publications provide regular features about database management systems:

Database Programming & Design (http://www.dmreview.com/)
DBMS Magazine (http://www.dbmsmag.com/)
DMReview (http://www.dmreview.com/)

NOTES

1. Extracted from Shari Caudron, Right on target, *InformationWeek* (September 2, 1996): 45–50.
2. Tom Groenfeldt, The luxury-class database: Mercedes-Benz integrates its systems to aid car owners, *InformationWeek* (April 3, 1995): 100–102.
3. William M. Bulkeley, Databases are plagued by reign of error, *Wall Street Journal* (May 26, 1992): B6.
4. See P.A. Bernstein, V. Hadzilacos, and N. Goodman, *Concurrency Control and Recovery in Database Systems* (Reading, MA: Addison-Wesley, 1987). For a discussion of concurrency control in less traditional applications, see N. S. Barghouti and G. E. Kaiser, Concurrency control in advanced database applications, *ACM Computing Surveys* 23(3) (September 1991): 269–317.
5. A survey is presented in T. Haerder and A. Reuter, Principles of transaction oriented database recovery—A taxonomy, *ACM Computing Surveys* 15(4) (December 1983).

See also Bernstein et al., *Concurrecy Control and Recovery.*

6. Barbara Francett, Relational DBs rev up for high-end TP, *Software Magazine* (October 1995): 87–92.

7. For a discussion of security issues and techniques, see T. F. Lunt and E. B. Fernandez, Database security, *Sigmod Record* 19(4) (December 1990): 90–97.

8. For a full discussion, see A. Shoshani, Statistical databases: Characteristics, problems, and some solutions, *Proceedings of 8th International Conference on Very Large Data Bases,* Mexico City, Mexico, September 1982.

9. P. Chen, The entity-relationship model—Toward a unified view of data, *ACM Transactions on Database Systems* 1(1) (1976); Robert W. Blanning, An entity-relationship framework for information resource management, *Information & Management* 15(2) (September 1988): 113–119.

10. See N. Roussopoulos and A. Delis, Modern client-server DBMS Architectures, *Sigmod Record* 20(3) (September 1991): 52–61.

11. George Black, Replication takes off at Lufthansa, *Software Magazine* (September 1995): 132, 133.

12. W. Cellary, E. Gelenbe, and T. Morzy, *Concurrency Control in Distributed Database Systems* (Amsterdam: North-Holland, 1988).

13. S. R. Gordon and J. R. Gordon, Organizational hurdles to distributed database management systems (DDBMS) adoption, *Information & Management* 22 (1992): 333–345.

14. American National Standards Institute, Database Language SQL, ANSI X3.168-1992, 1992. (See International Organization for Standardization, *Database Language SQL, ISO DIS 9075:1991,* 1991.)

15. W. Kim, Object-oriented databases: Definition and research directions, *IEEE Transactions of Knowledge and Data Engineering* 2(3) (September 1990): 327–341; D. Livingston, Here come object-oriented databases!, *Systems Integration* (July 1990): 50–58.

16. T. C. Doyle, High stakes databases—New object-relational technology raises the stakes for RDBMS VARs: Here's how to make the right play, *VAR Business* (April 15, 1997), http://www.techweb.com/se/directlink.cgi?VAR19970415S0027.

17. For a detailed description, see CODASYL Systems Committee, Feature Analysis of Generalized Data Base Management Systems, *Technical Report,* May 1971. Available from the Association for Computing Machinery.

18. Tim Hoy, Omni Healthcare and business objects, *DM Review* (March 1998): 62–63.

19. Werner Schumann, Bayer AG and MIS AG financial data mart, *DM Review* (February 1998): 70–73.

20. Craig Stedman, No mart is an island: Incompatible formats can isolate data, *Computerworld* (October 7, 1997): 53.

21. Ibid.

22. Alan Radding, So far it's tactical at UPS, *Software Magazine,* Special Editorial Supplement (August 24, 1996): S18.

23. Craig Stedman, Warehouse mergers give IS headaches, *Computerworld* (May 18, 1997): 1, 16.

24. Tony Baer, Mister data clean, *Computerworld Client/Server Journal* (November 1995): 48–50.

25. Interview with Melanie Pipkin, IS project manager at Walt Disney World Co., Orlando, FL, in Melanie Menagh, DB dandies, *Computerworld* (April 21, 1997): 99.

Chapter 6

Internal Networks

LEARNING OBJECTIVES

After completing Chapter 6, you will be able to

1. Discuss three major applications of internal networks.
2. Delineate the components of the communications infrastructure.
3. Describe the six types of hardware used for data communication.
4. Describe the two basic types of telecommunications software.
5. Compare and contrast the basic types of internal networks.
6. Discuss the key issues involved in managing internal networks.
7. Discuss the difficulties of establishing and managing cross-border internal networks.

IMPROVING CUSTOMER SERVICE OPERATIONS AT AC INDUSTRIES

AC Industries (ACI) is an international manufacturer of large and small home appliances and other electrical and motorized equipment, including computers, outboard motors for boating, and video cameras. Several years ago the company organized its customer support services to provide a single point of contact for all products. If the customer service agent who answers the phone cannot answer a customer's question immediately, the agent forwards the call to a product specialist. Product specialists deal in a single area, such as refrigerators, and are responsible for all models of that product.

Cathy Cook heads the department that handles all calls originating in North America. Her staff of 150 agents uses personal computers to log and track service calls. They reference service and part manuals from CD-ROMs published by the company monthly for internal use. Each morning, the agents load service bulletins and engineering changes into their computers from a diskette using custom software that updates a change file stored on their hard drives. Cook's computer is attached to the company network, but the company tries to avoid the cost of networking operational employees unless management can justify the need. Currently, Cook uses the network only for electronic mail.

Cook feels that networking the agents' computers would greatly simplify the agents' and her work and improve the level of customer service. She believes that a network would give agents up-to-date access to service bulletins and engineering changes. Now, although changes are loaded daily, several weeks pass from the time the engineering or service department issues bulletins or changes to the time the diskettes documenting these changes are distributed.

Appliance manufacturers and other businesses use internal communication networks for electronic messaging among employees, tracking service calls, providing data for budget updates, and other operational and service functions. Increasingly they create intranets to provide information for corporate employees and customers.

Currently, Cook cannot be sure that all calls are followed appropriately. She can only request hard copies of an agent's work logs. Networking computers would let her create reports to identify all incomplete calls. She could then monitor and improve service levels and better evaluate her employees. Networking would also allow agents to order parts for customers rather than telling the customers what parts to order and then switching them to a separate order desk.

For these and many other reasons, Cook has decided to request that her agents' computers be networked in the next budget cycle. She has made an appointment with her company's networking people to determine the costs. She would like to be prepared for this meeting by understanding her options. Would the entire floor have to be specially wired? Is it possible to establish direct connections to the engineering department, located in a different city? Would the confidentiality of her electronic mail be compromised by giving her employees access to the network? How could she monitor and assure the reliability of the network once it was established?

Managers like Cook increasingly need to understand the basics of communication and computer networking. In this chapter, we first explore the business needs that drive the establishment of computer networks. Next we examine the communication industry, transmission media, communication hardware, and related software. We then investigate the technology and management of local and long-distance networks. Finally, we look at the issues involved in providing data communication in a global environment.

USES OF INTERNAL NETWORKS

Computer networks have improved corporate communications, simplified and improved business processes, and made it possible to use worldwide teams effectively on projects. Managers can now decide how to use internal networks to perform their jobs more effectively.

CORPORATE COMMUNICATIONS

Managers at most companies use electronic mail, voice mail, videoconferencing, and corporate intranets to communicate with their coworkers, supervisors, subordinates, and others.

Electronic Mail.   Companies with corporate networks have essentially replaced memos and other written correspondence with **electronic mail** (**e-mail**), which uses computers to deliver messages. E-mail has reduced telephone traffic and time wasted by employees responding to telephone calls. Employees now send messages that are not time critical by electronic mail, knowing that people can read them at their convenience. Electronic mail software (see Chapter 4) allows users to share documents, both text and multimedia, by attaching them to a mail message. Employees can send electronic mail to and receive it from addresses outside the company if its internal network is connected to the Internet (see Chapter 7) or other public networks.

Voice Mail.   Voice mail uses computers to deliver voice messages. The process works as follows. A caller dials the **voice mailbox** of the person to whom she wishes to speak. After receiving a signal to begin, the caller leaves a message. The recipient can access the message either at his telephone or remotely by dialing into the voice mailbox. Communication technology records the voice data in the appropriate location and retrieves it for replay. Most voice mail systems today do not reside on the corporate data network. New products now integrate voice mail with electronic mail and facsimile to produce a single listing of messages and allow users to route voice messages using their internal computer networks.[1] Some products even do voice to text translation, so that users can read a voice mail message before opening it with sound.

Video Conferencing.   Video conferencing (see Chapter 10) can also occur through an internal network. Bear Stearns & Co., a Wall Street financial firm, uses the company's network to bring its traders and analysts together for training and conducting business. Employees do not have to leave their desks.[2] Figure 6.1 shows a typical setup for videoconferencing on a networked personal computer.

FIGURE 6.1   A personal computer equipped with PictureTel camera and software permits users to see each other as well as shared documents in sizable windows.

Intranets.   Many companies have turned their internal networks into **intranets,** internal networks that present multimedia in a World Wide Web format. These companies use intranets to publish and share such information as internal phone books, procedure manuals, and training materials in this way. Employees use **browsers,** originally developed for viewing material on the Internet (see Chapter 7), to view material published on their company's intranet. Web publishing tools can prepare most documents for viewing by a browser.

Companies adopt a Web-based internal communications strategy because it makes more information available to more people at a lower cost. They can quickly and inexpensively set up Web servers and roll out Web applications, making access to information fast and user-friendly. They can establish Web sites on any type of computer system, removing a concern about hardware and software compatibility. Because the Web includes access to both text and multimedia, it increases the effectiveness of presenting information for employees, customers, and vendors who have access to a company's intranet. Although some managers remain wary about potential hidden costs and security problems, adopters of this technology have remained enthusiastic and have not experienced major problems.

Companies use intranets to support sales, human resources, manufacturing, and other business activities. For example, Home Box Office uses a corporate intranet to make its schedules, direct mail pieces, and other marketing materials directly available to its representatives, even before they reach potential customers. A new feature provides historical data that helps its sales reps set sales goals for their cable systems, which are tied into a corporate bonus system.[3] Marshall Industries, a $1.2 billion electronics distributor, uses intranets to get information about its products into

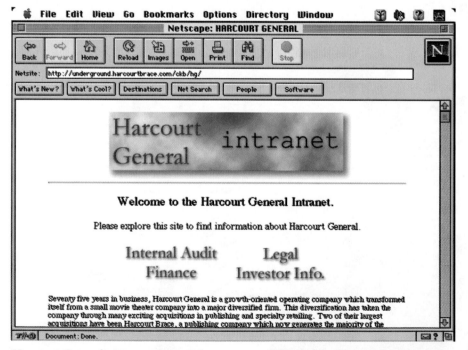

Harcourt General's Intranet lets employees access information about various departments and their activities. The Intranet presents up-to-date information in a lively and accessible manner.

the hands of employees and customers quickly. GlobalNet provides digital pictures of the company's employees, information about benefit options, and employee directors. PartnerNet gives electronics vendors access to sales volume, design registrations, and credit information. SEINet serves a Paris-based electronics-distributor partner. The company even delivers seminars directly to employees' desktops over an intranet, rather than conducting training off-site.[4]

Motorola uses an intranet for document management. Compass, Motorola's system, includes small-group collaboration and company-wide sharing of knowledge, as well as basic document storage and retrieval. The company has developed virtual communities where people can publish and discuss information with their peers, regardless of the location of their offices.[5] Mazda use the corporate intranet to post the latest vehicle service and repair information for its North American dealerships.[6] Knight-Rider, Inc., the newspaper chain, created a shared services center through which all of its newspapers buy ink and newsprint. Managers and other employees use a Web browser to send purchase requests to the home office. The company's financial software either automatically processes the order or routes it to the purchasing group for consolidation with other orders before processing.[7]

BASIC BUSINESS ACTIVITIES

A network helps managers and employees coordinate business activities throughout their company. Manufacturing might collect and use information about costs, supplies, inventory, special product changes, and quality control tests. Corporate property managers might use records about real estate owned and managed by the company. Engineering might maintain the latest specifications of company products, updates on customer complaints, and computer-aided design and manufacturing online for access throughout the company. Human resources might regularly update job descriptions, benefits, and other compensation information for the company's employees to access. Marketing and sales departments might maintain a database of customer leads that employees at sites throughout the world can access.

Computer networks help employees communicate among functional areas. When a sales clerk in the order department takes an order, for example, people in warehousing, manufacturing, billing, and shipping have access to the order so that they can act on it. Communication becomes even more important in a global environment. A company might order its raw goods in one part of the world, assemble its product in another, and sell the product elsewhere.

Talent Tree Staffing Services, for example, a $350 million Houston-based temporary employment agency, needs to match its clients' needs against the talents of its temporary labor pool. The company's 350 service specialists respond to calls in 100-plus offices nationwide. Sales representatives in the office connect through a network to any of 15 sites having access to the employee database. The network allows representatives to manage every aspect of the matchup process no matter where the customer's request originated.[8]

Chase Manhattan Bank's securities traders gain a competitive advantage by learning about news that might affect the market even a few seconds before the competition does. They rely on their network to connect their London, New York, and

ETHICAL ISSUES IN IT

An employer might monitor its employees' e-mail for many reasons. They range from legitimate concerns of illegal conduct to worrying that workers are simply wasting the company's time and money. But if you're monitoring or planning to monitor e-mail, you should consider both your reasons for such monitoring and your employees' expectations of privacy.

Generally, courts view e-mail as a tool provided to employees for work-related communications. As such, the employer has the right to access and monitor employee e-mail messages, as long as the employer does it for legitimate business purposes. These include suspicions that an employee is compromising employer or customer trade secrets; harassing another employee; uploading or downloading objectionable materials; infringing the copyrights or trademarks of another; defaming another person; or stealing from the company or another employee.

Many lawsuits have been filed on the basis of an employee's reasonable expectation of privacy under certain circumstances. For example,

employees given the right to select their own personal passwords to access their messages on a company e-mail system frequently assume that the password confers absolute privacy. Employers should inform their workers if that assumption is incorrect. Employers should create and distribute policy statements emphasizing that employees should have no expectation of privacy. The policy should alert workers to how easily they can inadvertently send an e-mail message to the wrong person.

1. Is it legal for an employer to monitor its employees' e-mail? Is it ethical?
2. What right to privacy do e-mail users have?
3. How can an employer balance an employee's right to privacy and the company's legal and ethical obligations?

SOURCE: Extracted with modification from Larry M. Zanger, E-mail expectations—Are you monitoring mail? Tell your workers, *VARBusiness* (June 1, 1997), http://www.techweb.com/se/directlink.cgi?VAR19970601S0047.

Tokyo offices. In New York, a local area network connects their 450 traders on two trading floors.[9]

Rush-Presbyterian/St. Luke's Medical Center in Chicago has 40 radiology rooms that generate 2 terabytes of data each year. An image server stores and distributes the 1,000 X-rays shot each day. Doctors rely on a network based on fiber optics to download the images as they need them in just about two seconds.[10]

As these examples show, networks keep businesses running smoothly and efficiently. The exchange of information among employees in different locations is crucial for almost all operational and transactional systems. Information exchange is also critical for managerial decision making, particularly when teams or groups are involved.

GROUP DECISION MAKING

Managers may introduce **groupware,** computer hardware and software that support a group's interactions, to help teams perform their tasks and accomplish their goals more effectively. Groupware supports information sharing among group members and so improves task coordination, the conduct of meetings, and problem solving. Some futurists believe that improvements in communication and networking technologies will fundamentally change the way people work, deriving productivity not from the individual but from the group.[11] Chapter 10 discusses groupware in more detail, focusing on the way it facilitates group decision making and group project activities.

COMMUNICATION INFRASTRUCTURE

Managers and other users need a basic understanding of data communications to make reasoned decisions about internal networks. Although many modes of communication exist, most computer networks rely on data, video, and voice communication to transfer information. **Data communication** refers to the transmittal of digitized data, that is, data represented as a series of zeros and ones. If video or voice is digitized before transmission and then undigitized upon receipt, its transmission is considered data communication rather than video or voice communication.

Data communication requires at least the following five steps, as shown in Figure 6.2.

1. The source computer generates a message.
2. A communications device at the source computer creates a signal on a transmission medium.

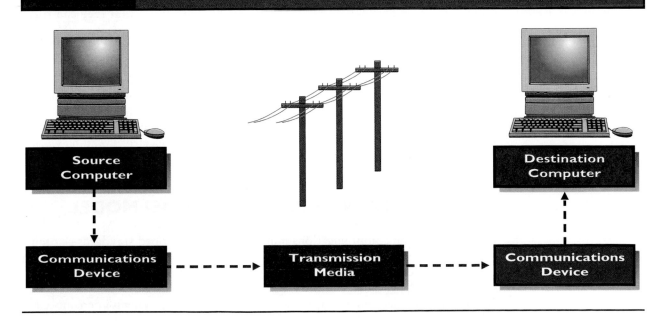

FIGURE 6.2   Communication devices help send messages from their source to their destination.

3. Transmission media transport the data from source to destination.
4. Another communications device at the destination converts the signal to computer input.
5. The destination computer processes the input data.

THE COMMUNICATION CARRIER INDUSTRY

A **communication carrier** is a government agency or private company that provides communication services and facilities to the public. Private carriers are almost always regulated to some degree and are called **common carriers.** In many countries, a postal, telephone, and telegraph company (a **PTT**), operated or owned by the government, provides communication services as a monopoly carrier.

Carrier Structure in the United States.   Regional Bell Operating Companies (RBOCs), such as Bell Atlantic and SBC, each serve a region called a LATA (local access transport area), which covers approximately one metropolitan area or a large rural or semirural district. Long-distance carriers, such as AT&T and MCI, provide service between LATAs and internationally. RBOCs and long-distance carriers jointly handle long-distance calls and share the revenue according to federal regulations. As a result of the U.S. Telecommunications Deregulation and Reform Act of 1996, long-distance carriers, RBOCs, and cable television companies can now each provide long-distance, local, and cable TV service.

Cellular Services.   Cellular technology makes telephone calls without a cabled connection to a telephone company. Instead radio antennas strategically cover an entire service region. Cellular phones transmit users' calls over radio signals to the nearest antenna. As shown in Figure 6.3, the call is passed from antenna to antenna until it reaches the telephone office, which routes it by land or satellite to other cities or countries. As a cellular phone moves out of the range of one antenna and into the range of another, computers track its movements so that they can route signals to it appropriately.

Value Added Networks.   Resellers of telephone and satellite capacity, commonly called **value-added networks** (**VANs**), purchase communication services from common carriers in bulk and resell them for a profit. They bundle the messages of many companies and people and transmit them on lines leased from common carriers. Resellers achieve scale economies that let them offer lower prices. They may also offer extra services, such as electronic mail, access to electronic databases, and electronic banking.

INDUSTRY STANDARDS AND THE OSI MODEL

The computer and communications industries have developed **standards**—specific characteristics of telecommunications media, hardware, and software—that make it possible to mix computer and communications products from different vendors. Managers such as Cathy Cook should understand their options and the implications of these choices on price and performance. The **OSI model (open systems interconnection**

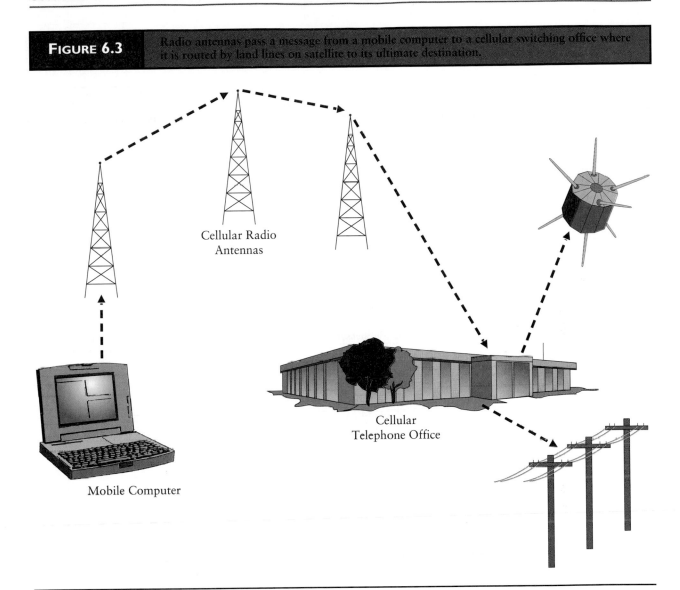

Cellular Radio
Antennas

Cellular
Telephone Office

Mobile Computer

model) provides a framework for thinking about communication standards. The International Standards Organization (ISO) created the OSI model to divide the communication process into layers, as shown in Table 6.1. This model encourages the creation of standards to address each layer independently and sets boundaries on the scope of new standards.

You will need to understand several communication concepts to understand the OSI model. A **session** refers to an ongoing connection between two computers or computer devices, established, for example, by logging into a remote computer. A session is analogous to a telephone call. The parties to the communication send **messages** back and forth. Some standards divide a message into smaller units called **blocks.** These blocks are sent sequentially: along its route from A to E, a message block might pass through devices at points B, C, and D. The path segments AB, BC, CD, and DE are called **data links.** Blocks might be divided into **packets** or **frames**

TABLE 6.1	The OSI model divides the communication process into parts and identifies the responsibilities of standards within each part.

General Description	Specific Layer	At Origin	In Route	At Destination
Application Generates messages based on the user's applications. (e.g., e-mail)	7 Application	Interface the communication with the application.		Interface the communication with the application.
	6 Presentation	Perform data compression. Format messages for transmission.		Decompress data. Prepare data for receipt by application.
Network Takes messages generated by the application level, breaks them into blocks, ensures their integrity, and reassembles them into messages; establishes and ensures the correct order of sessions.	5 Session	Establish session connection. Associate message with session. Terminate connection.	Create end-to-end circuit if required.	Establish session connection. Associate message with session. Terminate connection.
	4 Transport	Divide message into blocks. Determine end-to-end routing over subnetworks.	Implement routing.	Assemble blocks into messages. Ensure integrity of message.
Data Link Controls the physical layer by determining how and when to send signals over it; breaks messages into blocks and ensures their integrity.	3 Network	Divide block into frames. Determine routing of subnetwork.	Implement routing. Ensure integrity of block over each subnetwork.	Assemble frames into blocks.
	2 Data link	Insert packet into frame.	Ensure integrity of packet over each circuit.	
Physical Deals with transmission media and hardware necessary to create circuits and send data as signals; also deals with the connections between the hardware and the media used.	1 Physical	Type of connectors. Timing of signal.	Nature of cable.	Type of connectors.

for transmission over the data links. The packets might travel over different paths to reach their destinations. At the receiving end, packets or frames are reassembled into blocks; blocks are held until a complete message is formed; and messages are sent to the terminal or application. At each layer of the OSI model, certain services assure the integrity of messages and improve security or performance.

Industry standards allow equipment and software manufacturers to develop products that work with other equipment and software. A company might also select internal standards from the industry standards to simplify the support of the interfaces between products and the management of a company's data communications. For this reason, ACI policies may limit Cook's choices for networking the customer service agents.

TRANSMISSION MEDIA

Managers and computer professionals often select the **medium of transmission,** the carrier of a data signal between two or more computers. The most common media include twisted-pair wire, coaxial cable, fiber-optic cable, microwave signals, and infrared and radio signals. Table 6.2 highlights the most relevant characteristics of these media.

- **Twisted-pair wire** connects a telephone to its telephone jack in most homes. Because many buildings have excessive amounts of this wire that can be used

TABLE 6.2	Data communication media have different characteristics.
Twisted-Pair Wire	Least expensive Widely available Moderate capacity Easy to install
Coaxial Cable	Moderately expensive Moderate to high capacity Cumbersome and thick wires Entry into homes through cable TV
Fiber-Optic Cable	Relatively expensive Very high capacity Very high security Difficult to bend or manipulate
Microwave Signals	Expensive Requires no cabling Can use satellite Best for high volume, long distance Limited to line of sight
Infrared and Radio Signals	Low to moderate capacity Inexpensive Short distance limitation Requires no cabling Infrared limited to line of sight

for telecommunications purposes, it is inexpensive and readily available. Transmission speeds up to 10 megabits per second are normal, and high grades of twisted-pair wire can support rates of up to 100 megabits per second.

- **Coaxial cable,** used by cable television companies, brings television signals into the home. Although more bulky, more expensive, and less common in buildings than twisted-pair wire, it has a higher theoretical capacity, called bandwidth, than twisted-pair wire, and so it can transmit more data per second.
- **Fiber-optic cable,** which has the greatest capacity of the telecommunications media, carries messages on a beam of light rather than using an electrical signal. Many long-distance telephone companies use it to carry telephone calls simultaneously between major switching stations. Private companies use it to carry data within their buildings and between closely spaced buildings. Fiber-optic cable offers great security because of its low resistance to tapping and provides greater immunity to electrical interference than does electrical cable. It costs about 20 times more than the cheapest twisted-pair cable but exceeds its capacity by more than one thousand times. It also does not need **repeaters,** devices that twisted-pair and coaxial cable need to boost their signal, which weakens as it travels through the cable.
- Microwaves carry data. Relay towers, used for long-distance transmission, receive an incoming signal and retransmit it to another station within its view. Companies may buy capacity on an orbiting communications satellite that receives and retransmits their microwave signal. Microwaves effectively transmit data over long distances without using a telephone company.
- Infrared signals function only within line of sight; radio waves can penetrate walls. They carry data for short distances, such as within a building. Numerous vendors now supply wireless hardware for intercomputer communication. Although capacity varies, the high-end systems can provide nearly the same capacity as most coaxial cable systems. Cook may want to consider connecting her computers with infrared and radio, because most reside in a single large room, and all are on the same floor in her building.

TELECOMMUNICATIONS HARDWARE

Managers frequently contribute to decisions about telecommunications hardware.

- A **modem** provides an interface between a computer or terminal and the phone or cable lines of a communication carrier. Table 6.3 lists the types of modems. Standards define transmission speeds, compression technologies, and commands that direct the modem to perform such tasks as dialing a telephone number. The transmission speed and compression technology together determine how many bits can be transmitted in one second.
- An **adaptor,** also called a **network interface card (NIC),** provides a direct connection between a computer or terminal and a network (see Figure 6.4). The adaptor sends signals through connector ports to a network according to a selected standard. For example, an Ethernet adaptor provides a connector that conforms to Ethernet standards (see section on local area networks) and creates and interprets Ethernet signals and addresses.

TABLE 6.3	Numerous types of modems interface between the computer or terminal and the phone or cable lines.

Type	Characteristics
Internal	Located inside a computer; directly connects the computer's data bus and the telephone or cable line
External	Connects to the back of the computer through a serial or printer port and then to a telephone or cable line
Cable	Connects to coaxial cable
Wireless	Connects directly into cellular telephone network without the use of cables
Asynchronous	Has a data link protocol that makes this type commonly used with PCs; operates at the speed of the lowest device it communicates with
Synchronous	Has a data link protocol that makes this type commonly used with mainframes
Multiport (or multiplexor)	Combines signals from several ports or computers (usually midrange or mainframe) into a single phone line for long-distance transmission to another multiplexor that separates the signals at the receiving end

- A **hub** connects computers and sections of a network to one another. A hub forwards (without reading) every message it receives to everything connected to it. Network designers often use hubs to connect a group of computers to a network at a single point. All connections to a hub must have compatible

FIGURE 6.4	An Ethernet adaptor card for 10BaseT Ethernet has a telephone-jack-like port.

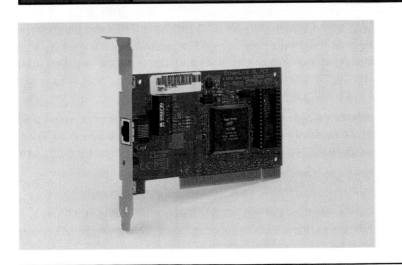

standards for sending signals over the transmission media and hardware and creating and ensuring the correct order of sessions.

- A **switch** connects two or more computers, hubs, subnetworks, or networks that have compatible standards for sending signals over transmission media and hardware and creating and ensuring the correct order of sessions. They examine the destination address of each incoming packet and forward the packet directly to the appropriate destination port without changing the packet.

- A **router** connects two or more hubs, subnetworks, or networks that have the same network protocol and passes data between networks almost simultaneously. A router may modify the packet surrounding the data it transmits but does not change the data within the packet. A router examines the address of a packet's ultimate destination and determines the best path through the network to reach that destination. It then changes the packet so that it addresses the next router on the way to the ultimate address.

- A **gateway** moves data between two networks that use different data link and network standards. It accepts data from one network, processes it into a format for another network, and then retransmits it. Some gateway products perform a specific conversion quickly, say between an SNA and an Ethernet network. Other gateway products combine software and hardware dedicated to the gateway and operate more slowly, possibly taking several hours before transferring messages between networks.

TELECOMMUNICATIONS SOFTWARE

Although managers generally do not select network operating systems and terminal emulation software, understanding their basic characteristics helps managers use them most effectively.

Network Operating Systems. A network operating system (NOS) manages and controls the joint or shared resources of a group of computers connected by a network. The NOS acts as a client/server product (see Chapter 4) in monitoring and managing the devices on a network. The client side provides the user interface to the entire network. Ideally, it makes the network and devices on the network appear as devices of the personal computer. For example, files on the network might seem to reside on disk drives attached to the computer.

As a server the NOS provides a number of key services:

- *Device management services* recognize the devices, including computers and printers, that are connected to the network. Each has an address or label by which the client software can access it and network management can control it.

- *Security services* provide entry into the network and establish a relationship between a user and a client station. The network administrator determines who has access to specific services, devices, and data on the network. Figure 6.5 shows a screen that a network administrator can use from within the Microsoft Windows NT/Server to provide these functions.

| **FIGURE 6.5** | Microsoft's NT/Server network operating system allows network managers to add or delete users and to specify their permission to access files, devices, and services. |

- *File services* provide access to shared files. Cook, for example, wants the customer service agents in her department to access equipment manuals and service documentation files created by the engineering and service departments.
- *Print services* provide central access to a common printer. Currently, each ACI agent has a small, inexpensive printer at her terminal. Once a network is installed, a single larger printer could serve the entire department.
- *Fax services* allow network users to send or receive a facsimile electronically, without having to create a hard copy. An ACI agent could simply identify the page from the service manual to be sent to a customer in the field and the customer's telephone number. The fax client software would send the page to the fax server, which would then send it to the customer.
- *Directory services* provide an enterprise-wide telephone book that identifies and connects network uses to each other and to software, such as electronic mail and groupware.

Terminal Emulation.
Terminal emulation refers to software that simulates a computer terminal on a personal computer or other workstation. As you may recall from Chapter 3, midrange and mainframe computers generally use terminals rather than monitors to provide their video output. Terminal emulation software interprets the

stream of bits produced and sent by the midrange or mainframe computer, processes them, and displays what a terminal would have displayed. The terminal emulation software also simulates the keyboard of the terminal to send the appropriate characters back to the computer. Most terminal emulation software can emulate a fairly large number of terminal types.

Software also exists to simulate the activities of one personal computer on another. Using products such as pcAnywhere, by the Symantec Corporation, one PC on a network can view the screen of another PC on the network. As with terminal emulation software, typing a keystroke or moving a mouse on the remote PC will have the same effect as on the original (host) PC. Such software, in effect, allows a user to operate another user's computer if given permission.

TYPES OF INTERNAL NETWORKS

An **internal network** connects the computers, printers, and other computing equipment in a single organization. It might connect as few as two computers in a small company or as many as tens or hundreds of thousands of computers in a large company. Internal networks may reside entirely within one building or spread over many countries. Managers frequently work with computer professionals to determine the best type of internal network for their business needs.

Many companies provide access to the Internet for their employees. Many also make their internal networks accessible to other companies through direct connection, dial-up, or the Internet.

LOCAL AREA NETWORKS

A **local area network (LAN)** connects devices in a single building or a campus of nearby buildings. The widespread acceptance of standards, the decreasing cost of hardware, and the increasing sophistication and power of network operating systems have motivated organizations to invest in LANs at a remarkable pace. Now, almost every medium and large business has networked at least some of its computers.

The success of LANs has been widely blamed for the demise of mainframe and midrange computer usage. PC monitors provide a graphics capability that mainframes and midrange computers cannot easily replicate. They have lower costs per MIPS, are easily scaleable, and usually have lower software costs. The development of LAN technology, which lets users share data, allowed PCs to compete for the first time with mainframes and minicomputers for company-wide applications. LANs can also connect PCs with larger computers for **cooperative processing**, using each type of equipment for what it does best.

Managers work with computer professionals in selecting the right standards for their organization because this choice can influence subsequent hardware and software options, some of which may fit better with their business activities. As you read about the two most popular standards—Ethernet and token ring—remember that other technologies such as AppleTalk and Arcnet also exist and may be standard in your company.

Universities use local area networks to connect their buildings. These LANs support the widespread use of electronic mail, remote data entry and retrieval, and computers in the classroom.

INFORMATION TECHNOLOGY AND GLOBAL BUSINESS

Hoechest and Schering, two of Germany's largest chemical companies, formed AgrEvo, a manufacturer of agricultural chemicals based in Berlin, by joining two of their key divisions. Unlike a typical start-up, AgrEvo had 8,000 employees, enjoyed a 9 percent share of its market, and ranked among the top five producers in its field. The new company needed to establish a global network to support the full international span of AgrEvo's activities. Specifically, AgrEvo had to begin building an infrastructure that would eventually support users in 73 countries.

AgrEvo wanted to tie the management of its network to the management of its business processes, so that managers could quickly see the impact of network failures on the business and prioritize which devices to fix. With the help of Munich-based consultant Intelligent Communications Systems, AgrEvo selected the SPECTRUM network management product from Cabletron. SPECTRUM allows users to create modules that graphically depict the relationship between business processes (such as that involved in the production and sale of an insecticide to protect a potato crop) and network devices (primarily routers, switches, and hubs). When a network device fails, an operator knows not only what device has failed, but also what business processes the faulty device affects.

Consider a business process called "Potato," which involves all of the steps involved in the production and sale of AgrEvo's Brestan, a product designed to eliminate potato fungi. If a router connecting AgrEvo Berlin to the AgrEvo facility in the U.K. went down, the network management software would indicate that the Potato Process was involved. Since Brestan is one of AgrEvo's best sellers, a network operator or business analyst would assign the highest priority to fixing this router.

The AgrEvo global network consists of several Ethernet and token ring LANs located in Berlin, the United Kingdom, the Netherlands, North America, East Asia, and France. The company has installed the SPECTRUM solution at five sites so far—Berlin, the United Kingdom, France, Spain, and Canada—and will eventually install it at all 73 AgrEvo sites.

SOURCE: Excerpted and adapted from Growth management, *Internetworking* (July 1996), http://www.cabletron.com/internetworking/1996/jul96/worldwide/growth.html, July 18, 1997. Copyright ©1995-1997 by Cabletron Systems.

Ethernet.   Every device on an Ethernet network has a unique address. To initiate communication, a device puts its data onto a bus cable (see Figure 6.6) along with the address of the intended recipient; and the intended recipient reads the data. If two devices attempt to transmit at the same time, both notice that a collision has occurred and will each wait a random amount of time and then resend the data.

The Ethernet bus is located inside a single hub device as illustrated in Figure 6.7 and shown in Figure 6.8. Connections to the device appear to form a star shape. Ethernet standards limit the maximum distance between any two Ethernet devices. As a result, Ethernet designers may need to link several hubs to complete a LAN, as illustrated in Figure 6.9. Ethernet standards exist at several levels of price and performance, as shown in Table 6.4.

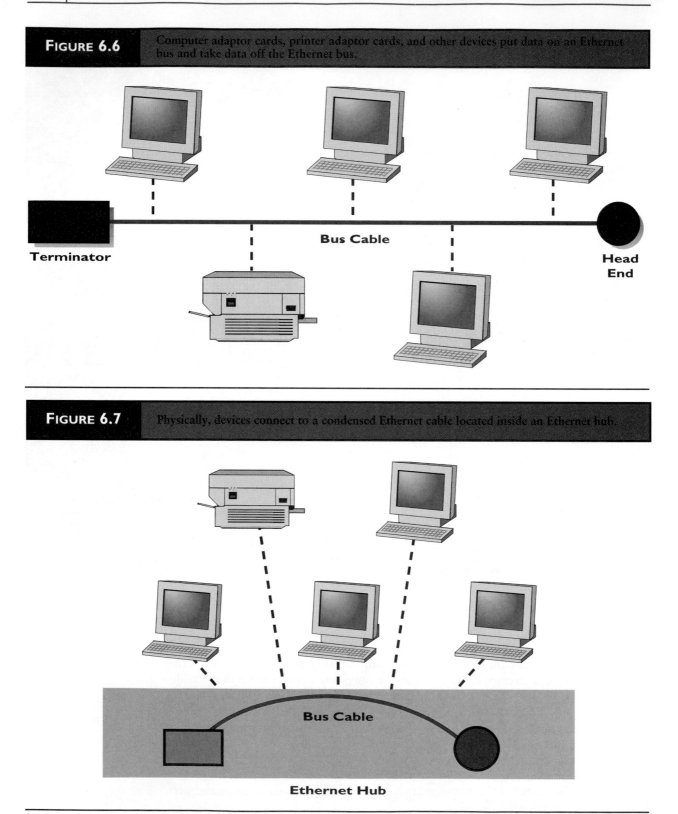

FIGURE 6.6   Computer adaptor cards, printer adaptor cards, and other devices put data on an Ethernet bus and take data off the Ethernet bus.

Terminator

Bus Cable

Head End

FIGURE 6.7   Physically, devices connect to a condensed Ethernet cable located inside an Ethernet hub.

Bus Cable

Ethernet Hub

FIGURE 6.8 3Com's SuperStack II Hub 10 provides ports to connect many Ethernet devices.

FIGURE 6.9 Ethernet hubs can be networked to provide Ethernet connections between devices that are too far apart to be connected by a single Ethernet hub.

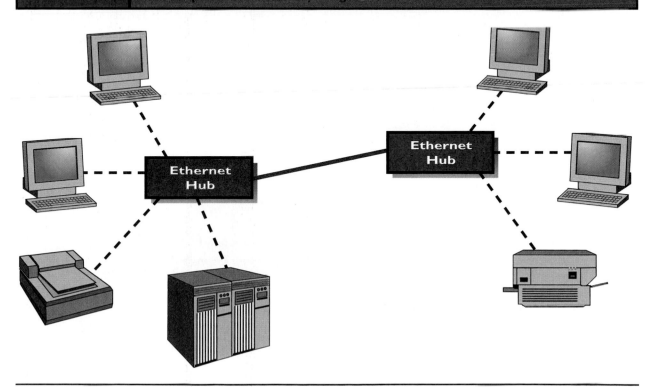

TABLE 6.4 Three main Ethernet standards vary in price and performance.

Standard	Speed	Requirements
10BaseT (Ethernet)	10 megabits per second	Standard telephone wire
Fast Ethernet	100 megabits per second	High-grade telephone cables or fiber-optic cable
Gigabit Ethernet	1 gigabit per second	Currently under development

Token Ring. A token ring network connects its devices in a unidirectional ring inside a hub, as shown in Figure 6.10. Unlike Ethernet, only one computer can directly read the output of another computer. When the network is turned on, the token monitor computer creates a message called an empty token. When a computer receives an empty token message, it will either resend the empty token or attach a message to the token and send it. Each computer in turn receives the message and passes it on until it reaches the intended recipient, which saves the message and attaches an acknowledgment to the token for the sender. Upon receiving the acknowledgment token, the sender either sends another message or creates a new empty token to pass to the next computer.

FIGURE 6.10 Circuits in a token ring connect each device to the next device. Messages are forwarded around the ring until they are received by the intended recipient.

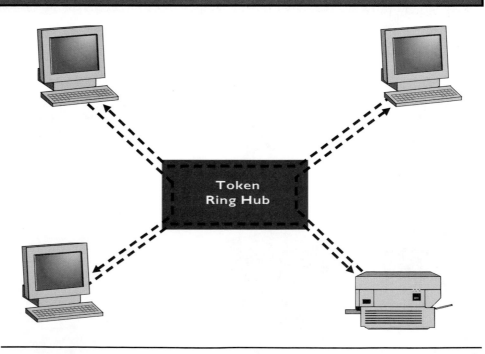

Collisions cannot occur, but wasted capacity results. Sharing capacity and computer failure also provide challenges for the operation of this type of network. Token ring hubs are generally connected to form a large network because the standard limits the distance between the devices in a token ring.

Wireless LANs.   Wireless LANs operate the same way as cabled LANs except without cabling. Each computer in a wireless Ethernet LAN will include a wireless Ethernet adaptor that communicates via radio frequencies to an Ethernet hub or router. Network designers use wireless technology when it is expensive or difficult to cable or rewire the area receiving a new or upgraded LAN or when they expect the physical layout of the area to change in unexpected ways.

The Indiana legislature uses a wireless LAN because it would have been expensive and difficult to wire the marble-floored statehouse. Legislators use notebook computers equipped with wireless adaptors to hook into the LAN. They can communicate with their staffs while in session, at committee hearings, or simply when roaming the hallways.[12]

Internetworking with LAN Backbones.   What would you do if your company had a number of independent LANs that you wanted to integrate into one network? You might create a network of networks. You can implement this solution relatively easily using routers and switches if the networks are the same type. You can connect them using gateways if they are different types. In either case, the network that connects all the others is called a **backbone.** Figure 6.11 illustrates the

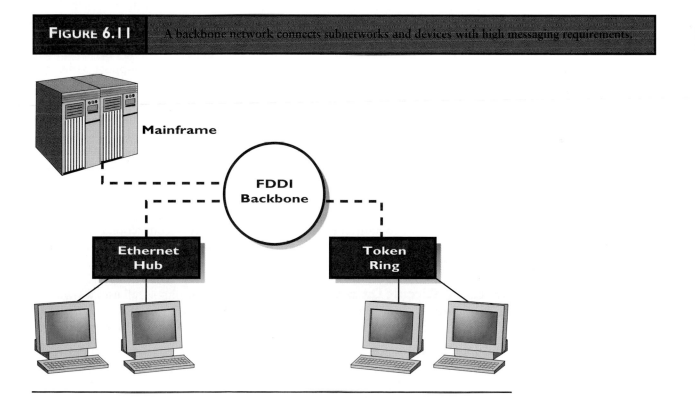

FIGURE 6.11   A backbone network connects subnetworks and devices with high messaging requirements.

Mainframe

FDDI Backbone

Ethernet Hub

Token Ring

use of a backbone to connect subnetworks into a complete LAN. **Fiber distributed data interface (FDDI)**, one of the most popular technologies for backbone networks, is a token-passing technology that uses two rings operating in opposite directions and operates at 100 megabits per second over fiber-optic cables. Audi AG, the automotive manufacturer, employs an FDDI backbone to connect the 4,300 PCs and workstations attached to its Ethernet subnetworks.[13]

Network designers typically plan the network backbone to have as much capacity as possible. This flexible planning approach allows them to expand the LAN by adding more LAN segments to the backbone. Most of the traffic will flow on the LAN segments, the original LANs, and any new ones. However, as the network grows, the backbone will experience increasing amounts of traffic.

Network Protocols.   A variety of protocols provide end-to-end transmission of messages that operate over one or more subnetworks and that can accommodate both Ethernet and token ring technologies. The **transmission control protocol/Internet protocol (TCP/IP)** originated for transmission across the Internet, but local and wide area networks also use it. Novell made **internetwork packet exchange/sequenced packet exchange (IPX/SPX)** popular by adopting it as the basis for its popular network operating system, Netware.

WIDE AREA NETWORKS

A **wide area network (WAN)** covers a larger area than a LAN. Metropolitan area networks (MANs) operate within a metropolitan region and primarily use WAN technologies. Most organizations implement wide area networks using services purchased from communication carriers. U.S. telephone carriers and telephone companies in most developed countries and many developing countries provide similar services. Table 6.5 compares various data services available to support wide area networks.

Leased Lines.   A **leased line** creates a direct connection between two numbers rather than using a switch to provide a temporary connection to one or more circuits. When you sign a contract to lease a line, the telephone company hard-wires the connection you requested. You pay for the capacity to send messages on that leased line whether or not you use it; nobody else can use it.

Leased line prices generally depend on the mileage between the points connected and the capacity of the line. A leased line costs less than paying for the same capacity on a pay-as-you-go basis. It establishes a better quality of connection between two points. In many areas of the world, telephone companies lease SONET (Synchronous Optical Network) circuits that use optical cable instead of telephone wire.

Switched Circuit Data Services.   A normal telephone call uses a **switched circuit service**—a connection made between two points for the length of a session. Telephone charges accumulate according to the number of minutes connected.

- **Integrated Services Digital Network (ISDN)** describes a set of standards for integrating voice, computer data, and video transmission on the same telephone line. First introduced in the late 1970s, only 1 million lines had been

| TABLE 6.5 | Organizations can choose from five types of wide area networks. | |

Type	Examples	Comments
Leased line	T-1, Fractional T-1 (for example, ½ and ¼ T-1), T-4, SONET OC-48	A T-1 circuit works at 1,544 kilobits per second and provides more than 24 times the capacity of a normal voice-grade telephone at less than 24 times the cost. Frational T-1 lines are slightly more expensive. T-4 lines have much larger capacity (equal to 168 T-1 lines) and cost somewhat more also. An OC-48 line provides 2,488 gigabits per second, the equivalent of more than 38,000 voice lines.
Switched circuit	ISDN, BRI, ISDN PRI, SMDS, ADSL	The speed ranges from 128 kilobits per second to 1,544 kilobits per second for the ISDN lines. ADSL lines operate much faster: 8.192 megabits per second from phone to subscriber and 1.088 megabits from subscriber to phone company.
Packet switch	X.25 frame relay, ATM	Frame relay at 8 kilobits per second and ATM are replacing X.25 service.
Cellular	CDPD	This service operates at speeds of 19.2 kilobits per second.
Cable television		This service has delivery rates between 27 and 38 megabits per second and return rates between 0.32 and 10 megabits per second.

installed in the United States by the mid 1990s.[14] In the United States and Canada the basic rate interface (BRI) standard uses existing telephone lines and the primary rate interface (PRI) standard requires a special box at the customer's site and special cabling from the customer's site to the local company office or to another line. European standards differ from the U.S. standards, and no worldwide standards exist.

- **Switched Multimegabit Data Service (SMDS)** provides a higher capacity than ISDN but at a higher cost and with limited switching. You can think of SMDS as if each company location leased a short line to the local telephone office, and the telephone company provided switching between these lines. A company with offices in ten locations would then need only ten short leased lines rather than the 45 longer ones it would otherwise need to connect each office to every other one. Originally SMDS was offered only within a single metropolitan area; now intercity SMDS is available.

- **Digital subscriber line (DSL)** provides megabit/second speed over regular copper telephone lines. **Asymmetric digital subscriber line (ADSL)** delivers data faster from the phone company to the subscriber and returns data at slower rates. Not all telephone circuits can handle DSL, and telephone companies have rolled out the service slowly. Dataquest, a technology research firm, estimates that only one million DSL lines will be installed by the year 2000.[15]

Packet Switched Services. Like switched circuit services, **packet switched services** provide a direct connection between any points on the telephone network, but the packet switched services do not necessarily provide a fixed circuit for the entire session. Packet switched services break a message into packets, route these packets at the discretion of the phone company, and reassemble them at the destination, as illustrated in Figure 6.12. The phone company or VAN can mix pieces of messages between different origins and destinations on the same long-distance line. They charge for these services by the amount of data transmitted, not by the length of a session.

The most popular packet switched technologies are X.25, frame relay, and ATM. X.25, a 20-year-old standard, has many installations worldwide. START Informatik GmbH uses an X.25-based WAN to connect to travel agencies at 16,400 locations throughout Germany. During peak hours, the WAN handles 318 transactions per second.[16]

Frame relay, which works like X.25 but faster and less expensively, has become more popular. A computer opens a session during a frame relay transmission by requesting the maximum amount of capacity it needs for the transmission. The network, if it accepts the request, creates a virtual circuit among a series of circuits and switches between the origin and destination of the transmission session. Frame relay breaks each message into variable length packets of up to 8 kilobytes and sends them sequentially through the virtual circuit. If the computer exceeds its requested transmission rate, excess packets are transmitted if capacity is available, but transmission is not guaranteed. Choice Hotels International, a franchiser of 60- to 150-room hotels, replaced leased lines with frame relay at five U.S. sites and replaced X.25 services with frame relay in six sites outside the United States. The network connects Choice's 11 busiest reservation centers and a central data center in Phoenix, Arizona.[17]

FIGURE 6.12 A packet switched network mixes packets from various messages and reassembles them at their destination.

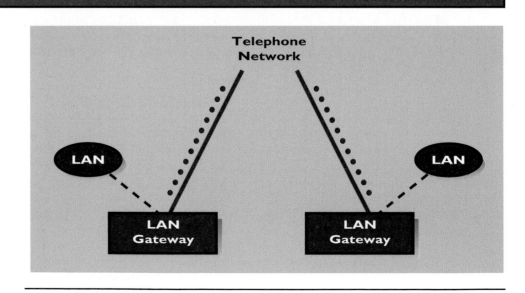

Asynchronous transfer mode (ATM) resembles frame relay except that it has a fixed packet size of 53 bytes, and the capacity responds to the demand. A fixed packet size lets switches examine routing information more easily, resulting in faster, less costly equipment. The small packet size also assures that no packet has to wait for very long, enabling the carrier to provide better guarantees about the delay between transmission and receipt. Companies can also use ATM for their LAN backbone and so can eliminate the need for a gateway between their LAN and WAN. Amoco Corporation, the oil producer and refiner, uses frame relay primarily for data communication at sites with low to medium traffic. It uses ATM for higher-speed applications that mix voice, video, and data, such as Amoco's international data communication needs.[18]

Cellular Services. Cellular services allow data transmission across the cellular telephone network at about the same speed as voice land lines. **Cellular digital packet data (CDPD)** uses a cellular carrier's spare capacity to transmit data packets. The service charges users only for traffic time. Users can remain continually connected to another phone line without incurring any additional costs. American Airlines uses CDPD technology to provide wireless access to its Sabre network for mechanics, baggage handlers, gate agents, and customer service representatives. Many of these employees use mobile computers and would not have access to American's information systems without cellular modems.[19]

ARDIS, a cellular VAN created and operated by Motorola, operates within the United States. Created before CDPD service became available, it uses its own technology and infrastructure. Sears is rolling out rugged, ARDIS-enabled mobile computers to its 14,000 plus service technicians. Sears expects the computers to improve customer service, reduce time spent on repair calls, and eliminate much of the paperwork involved with repair calls.[20]

Cable. The cable television industry has begun to leverage the capacity it has in its cable networks to deliver data communication services. After using most of its capacity for television transmission, cable still has plenty of capacity for simultaneous data transmission. Because cable companies mostly serve local areas, they work best for WANs but still need to interact with long-distance carriers to provide WAN service. They provide Internet service even more effectively than WAN service. Most cable networks use a type of cable that can only transmit in a single direction, reducing their speed and efficiency.

NETWORK MANAGEMENT

When network traffic at the Deaconess Health System in St. Louis rocketed from 10 percent of capacity to almost 70 percent in one week, Bob Bowman, the chief information officer, used network management hardware and software to identify the problem. He found that a new application to track pagers worn by staffers caused the problem.[21]

THE MANAGER IN ACTION

George Kendall, senior vice president at the St. John Medical Center, a 723-bed acute-care facility in Tulsa, Oklahoma, decided that the hospital needed an innovative approach to fulfill a vision of using technology to help provide cost-effective, high-quality health care. At the time of the decision, the hospital's departments each had their own computer systems. The programming staff had custom-programmed interfaces between many of these systems. Although the hospital had about 750 mainframe (3270) terminals and 750 personal computers, the number of PCs was growing rapidly.

The computer network hindered effective management throughout the hospital. It consisted of several token ring LANs connected to one token ring backbone running IPX protocol through Novell servers and another token ring backbone running a (mainframe-oriented) SNA protocol through gateway devices. Although this network provided some redundancy, the paths between computers became complex, making the network difficult to monitor and control. Response time became unpredictable and the network occasionally dropped PCs at random, causing major problems in entering and accessing information throughout the hospital. Also, St. John had Ethernet, DECNET, and other segments, some not connected to the main hospital network.

With the help of consultants, Kendall designed an enterprise-wide network that could reliably handle the growing traffic volumes and would be simple to run and monitor. The new architecture is based on an ATM backbone with switching hubs linking servers and LAN segments to the backbone. 10BaseT and Fast Ethernet segments covering geographic areas of the hospitals have replaced the token ring LANs. SNA traffic is being isolated to a single token ring. Fiber-optic cable was installed between the hubs.

The new network better meets the needs of the hospital's medical and nonmedical staff. They can access and share data from many sources, making information systems a strategic business tool for St. John. Soon access to reference databases, treatment protocols, medication use and interaction notes, patient educational material, and current medical journal articles will increase. Kendall plans to link St. John and its allied hospitals and research institutions through an ATM-based WAN. The network will handle large data loads such as medical images, video conferencing, training video, and voice as easily as administrative and test data.

SOURCE: Excerpted and adapted from Case Study: Network Transformation Yields Strategic Advantage for St. John Medical Center (Atlanta: Lanier Wordwide, 1996), http://www.lanier.com/st_john.html.

MANAGEMENT DEVICES

Most network devices, such as hubs, routers, switches, printers, and even servers, collect information about the data they process and about their own performance. These devices can send their data to a monitoring station when polled or when certain conditions arise. Standards, such as **simple network management protocol (SNMP),** define how these devices operate and the data they keep. When SNMP operates centrally, each device sends its information every few seconds to a central network management server, which enters it into a database for future analysis. The constant movement of SNMP information over the network reduces the capacity of the network for its primary purposes. When SNMP uses remote monitors located near or included in SNMP devices, these monitors collect information over long periods of time and retain the data in a distributed database or consolidate it into a central database in off-peak periods. Network management software, as shown in Figure 6.13, polls SNMP devices to create a picture of the network and graphs of network traffic.

A **network analyzer** plugs into a network and analyzes the traffic that passes by or through it. It displays this information in real time or produces reports for later review. Normally network managers use network analyzers when they have identified the location of a problem but do not know its cause. Network analyzers move among locations to solve different network performance problems rather than perform long-term monitoring.

FIGURE 6.13 Using Cabletron's VLAN SecureFast network management software, a network analyst examines a map of the network and identifies a trouble spot.

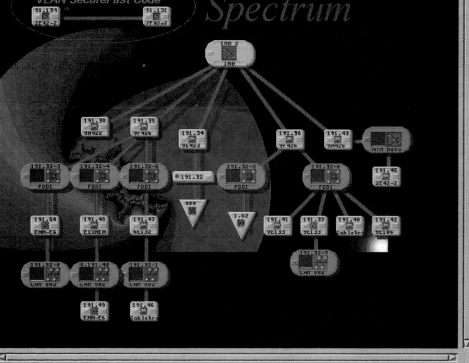

Chapter 7

The Internet and Other External Networks

LEARNING OBJECTIVES

After completing Chapter 7, you will be able to

1. Identify the three major uses of the Internet.
2. Describe how the Internet fosters electronic commerce.
3. Explain how EDI can help a company automate intercompany transactions.
4. Compare and contrast electronic mail and Internet news groups.
5. Briefly describe the development of the Internet.
6. Describe how an individual or company obtains access to the Internet.
7. Define the World Wide Web and discuss the role of HTML in presenting Web documents.
8. Identify and contrast three types of WWW search engines.
9. Help a company design a Web site that meets its objectives.
10. Critique a company's Internet or extranet security plans.

AUTOMATING BIDDING AT GE LIGHTING

John Blossom, manager of the global sourcing systems unit at GE Lighting, walked into a meeting and shook his head. "We're dying on the vine here by conducting our bidding process manually," he said. "We need to automate the process and we need to do it without a lot of expense."

GE Lighting had centralized its IT sourcing systems to better support the centralized global purchasing department for its 55-plus production plants worldwide. Conducting bids with paper and fax machines had simply become expensive, time-consuming, and nearly impossible. The global sourcing operation worked with some 100 suppliers worldwide—55 of those on a daily level. Many of the parts purchased were custom designed, based on ever-changing GE specifications, which meant that blueprints had to be located, printed, and distributed to suppliers. Some three million blueprints exist, with about 750,000 of those stored electronically.

Still, because the bidding process was done manually, blueprints had to be printed and verified manually, increasing the cost to process such bids and driving up the potential for human error. On average, the department was processing some 200 requests for quotes (RFQs) daily on custom-made parts. The process was so time

GE Lighting, headquartered here, could use the Internet to give its suppliers access to its automated bidding and purchasing systems.

Yahoo!. After clicking on *travel* on Yahoo!'s home page, you would then click on *lodging*, then *regional*, *countries*, *Spain*, and finally *Madrid*. Most hierarchical search engines also provide an indexed lookup based on words in the category or listing, not on words in the Web page itself. For example, to find hotels in Madrid, you could search in Yahoo! for "Madrid and hotel."

- **Reviewed search engines**, such as Magellan (www.mckinley.com) and Lycos's Top 5% (point.lycos.com/categories), carefully screen and review Web pages, creating links to and reviews of the sites that the reviewers find most interesting and relevant, by topic. Figure 7.6 shows reviews for links found by a Magellan search for Web pages about board games.

HyperText Markup Language.   Hypertext markup language (HTML) is the language of hypertext and hypermedia documents. It consists mostly of text surrounded by special words called **tags** that identify what type of text, images, or links they surround. For example, the tags <b> and </b> surround text to display in bold type. Table 7.3 offers a more complete list of HTML tags.

HTML is a living, evolving language whose standards undergo frequent revision.[23] In addition, Netscape and Microsoft, the developers of the two most popular browsers, have created many nonstandard tags that their browsers use to perform tasks that they otherwise could not accomplish. Although the competition

FIGURE 7.6   A Magellan search reviews links to Web pages about board games.

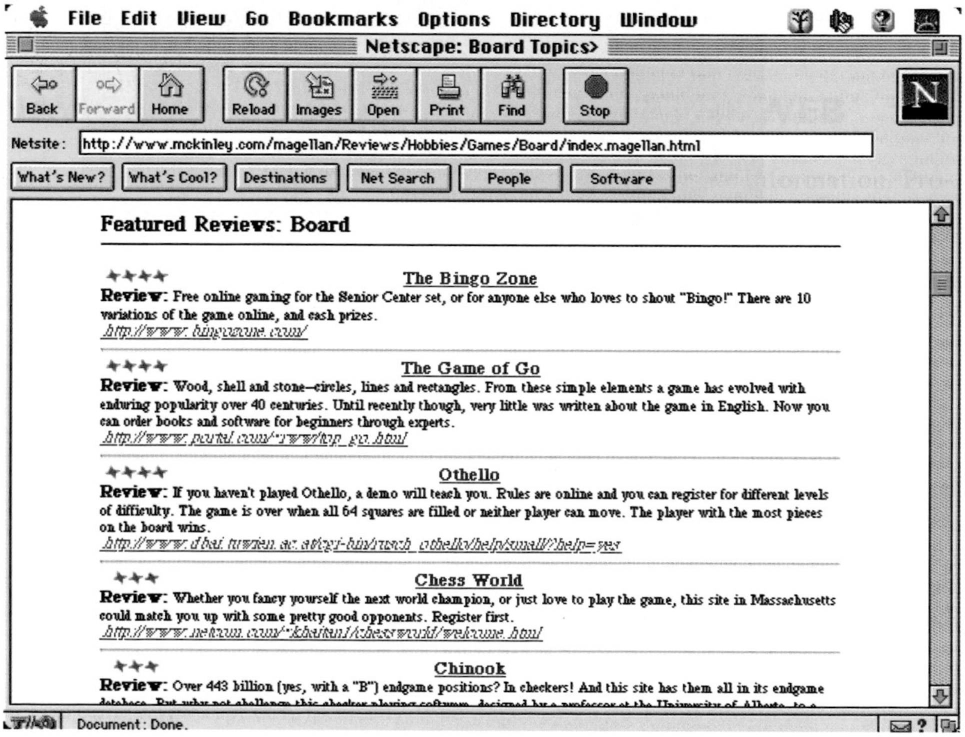

TABLE 7.3	HTML tags format the appearance and placement of text and images on a page. They also create links between documents.

Tag	Function
<html> . . . </html>	Encloses the entire document.
<head> . . . </head>	Encloses the header portion of the document.
<title> . . . </title>	Encloses the title of the document.
<body> . . . </body>	Encloses the body of the document. Can include parameters to specify the color and image of the background and the color of links and text.
<p> . . . </p>	Encloses paragraphs. Paragraph marks and white space in the html document are ignored.
<h1> . . . </h1>	Encloses header level-1 text. Similar tags for header levels 2 through 6.
<i> . . . </i>	Displays enclosed text in italics.
<b> . . . </b>	Displays enclosed text in boldface.
<ul> . . . </ul>	Enclosed text is a bulleted list.
<ol> . . . </ol>	Enclosed text is a numbered list.
<li> . . . </li>	Encloses an item in a bulleted or numbered list.
<table> . . . </table>	Encloses a table.
<tr> . . . </tr>	Encloses the rows of a table.
<td> . . . </td>	Encloses individual data items in a row of a table.
<a href="#name"> . . .</a>	Creates a name for the enclosed text so that it can be referenced by a link.
<a href="URL"> . . .</a>	Identifies the enclosed text or image as a link to the indicated URL.
<img src="URL">	Inserts a graphic image from the indicated URL.
<hr>	Inserts a horizontal line to separate parts of the document.
 	Inserts a line break.
&lt	Displays a less than sign (<).
&gt	Displays a greater than sign (>).
&amp	Displays an ampersand (&).
&eacute	Displays an *é* with an acute sign over it; can substitute other letters for the *e*.
&egrave	Displays an *è* with grave sign over it; can substitute other letters for the *e*.
&ntilde	Displays an *ñ* with a tilde over it; can substitute other letters for the *n*.
&ouml	Displays an *ö* with an umlaut over it; can substitute other letters for the *o*.

between these developers has accelerated the evolution of the language, the non-standard extensions can lure users into using tags that a different browser cannot interpret.

Java and Its Derivatives. Web documents can contain computer programs as well as text and images. **Java** is a programming language that Sun Microsystems developed to work with programs that users download from the Web, but may not know their source and hence their idiosyncracies. Java programs can perform such tasks as running an animation, providing a mortgage calculator, or formatting information nicely on a screen. Java programs cannot change or store data on your computer, introduce a virus, or harm your computer in any way. Most Web browsers now recognize Java programs and interpret them properly.

Software developers compile Java programs into an intermediate code called byte-code. When a user downloads Java byte-code from the Web, his browser starts a Java interpreter (see Chapter 4) known as a virtual machine. This virtual machine interprets the byte-code the same way on every computer and operating system, accounting for Java's popularity as a universal language.

Computer professionals can also use ECMAScript, a standard interpreted language, for programming Web pages. Netscape's JavaScript and Microsoft's JScript are the most popular implementations of ECMAScript. Despite their names, these interpreted languages resemble Java only in their common application to Web-page programming.

Helper Applications. The **extension** of a document's URL, that is, the letters after the last dot in its file name, indicates the type of document it is. For example,

- *htm* or *html* are files written in hypertext markup language,
- *gif* indicates a graphics file stored in graphics interchange format, and
- *pdf* indicates a file stored in the print definition format of Adobe, the desktop publishing vendor.

Browsers use special programs called **helper applications** or **plug-ins** that recognize and properly interpret their format to view these files. Table 7.4 identifies some of the most popular helper applications. Many of these are free on the Internet. This free distribution assures people creating files for publication on the Internet that everyone will be able to read what they publish. The programs' authors make their profit by selling software to those who want to create such files.

DESIGNING WEB SITES

Managers must consider the content and style when designing Web pages. They need to follow four rules:

- Make it useful.
- Make it interesting.
- Make it easy.
- Give users a reason to return.

Determining What to Publish. People who create a Web site must first determine their objectives. They can often get ideas for a story they want to tell by

TABLE 7.4	Many of these popular helper applications are available at no charge at the URLs indicated.

Application	Company	Function
Acrobat Reader	Adobe (www.adobe.com)	Displays Adobe desktop publishing files
KEYview	Verity (www.verity.com)	Processes more than 200 file formats, including many desktop suite documents, LOTUS Notes documents, and Adobe desktop publishing files
Quicktime	Apple (quicktime.apple.com)	Processes multimedia files in a variety of formats including digitized audio, soundtracks, 3-D animation, and virtual reality
Real Audio	Progressive Networks (www.realaudio.com)	Processes a large variety of sound files
Real Video	Progressive Networks (www.realaudio.com)	Displays a wide variety of graphics files
Shockwave	MacroMedia (www.macromedia.com)	Provides vector-based graphics in real time; provides interactive buttons for user control

examining other Web pages that represent organizations similar to theirs. Some companies provide information about their products and services. For example, Dow Chemical's product and services information page lets users look up any of more than 150 products and services by name, application, product area, or global industry.[24] Other companies use their Web pages for recruitment. The human resource information page for Oracle Corporation, the database vendor, allows visitors to check available positions, learn more about the company, learn about benefits Oracle provides to its employees, and even send a resume.[25] Many companies use their Web pages for advertisements. For example, Simware Inc., the Canadian developer of Salvo, a software product used to bridge mainframe applications to the Web, includes customer success stories, press releases, magazine articles reviewing its products, white papers, and product demos on its Web page.[26] Companies can also use Web pages for product support and other customer services.

Government agencies might use Web pages to provide information about their services or offer services directly. The United States Library of Congress helps fulfill its mission by creating access to its card catalogs.[27] The Pennsylvania Department of Motor Vehicles provides a Web page that gives all necessary information about title, registration, and drivers' licenses in Pennsylvania.[28]

Defining a Common Layout.   The pages of a Web site should have a common theme and design. Corporate sites should use recognizable trademarks to reinforce the brand image. If a company uses a standard layout for its print material, it should closely follow that layout for its Web-based material. Graphic artists can help small companies develop material that looks professional and is easy to use.

INFORMATION TECHNOLOGY AND GLOBAL BUSINESS

Xilinx Inc., a fast-growing $571 million semiconductor manufacturer in San Jose, California, uses an extranet to communicate with manufacturers in Asia and with sales contractors worldwide. Xilinx sells software to chipmakers who, in turn, design programmable logic chips to their own specifications. Customers such as Cisco Systems, Hewlett-Packard, and IBM return their designs to Xilinx, which then contracts the chip manufacturing to fabrication plants in Asia.

Three hundred representatives who work for several contracting organizations in numerous time zones worldwide handle Xilinx's sales. "We used to fax and mail all the information to them," says Sandy Sully, VP and CIO at Xilinx. "When sales reps needed a piece of information, they'd have to call us anyway because they couldn't find it."

Xilinx introduced the sales reps to communication via Web browsers. "We gave them login IDs and told them what kind of information is available and what they can do with it," Sully says.

Then Xilinx extended the extranet to its manufacturing partners in Asia. "In the past, we'd send them a change in specs by overnight mail in hopes they'd get it in time," Sully says, explaining that the time differences between California and East Asia sometimes resulted in parts being built to the wrong specifications. "Now, we send them an E-mail saying a change is being made in the spec, and they log on to the extranet to look at it."

SOURCE: Tom Davey, Extranets unlock your business, *InformationWeek* (June 9, 1997), http://www.techweb.com/se/directlink.cgi?IWK19970609S0046.

Customizing Content. Customizing the content of a Web site for each visitor and visit keeps it interesting so that visitors will return frequently. For example, customized pages can present material in the visitor's native language and according to the visitor's geographic location. Avon Products Inc. plans to customize its Web page layouts to appeal to different ethnicities. In Hispanic countries, Web pages written in Spanish will feature Hispanic models to show Avon's products.[29]

A company can register visitors to customize content. Visitors to a registration site must present some identifying information and answer questions during their first visit. Their responses affect what they will see at the site. For example, if you provide travel services, your registration screen can ask questions such as "What are your favorite destinations?" and "What airlines do you prefer to use?" When the visitor returns to your site and logs in, your Web page might present information about events and accommodations at the visitor's selected destinations or special fares available on her preferred airline. Some visitors resist registration, resenting the time and effort it requires or feeling that it invades their privacy.

Companies can also customize Web pages by using a **cookie**, a small amount of information that the Web server asks the visitor's browser to store on his computer. The cookie might, for example, indicate which Web page the visitor last examined at a site or the date of the last visit to the site. The opening page might say, "Here's what has happened since you last visited our Web site." Using a cookie requires no effort or active participation by the visitor to your site. It also provides relatively little information to usefully customize pages. Companies cannot use cookies to customize pages for visitors who choose to disable this option on their Web browsers.

Simplifying Navigation.   Navigation refers to the process of moving among Web pages to find the information you want. No matter how logically you think you have organized these pages, some people will find your organization confusing or complicated. To make your pages easier to use, you can simplify navigation by including a search engine and a detailed table of contents, known as a **site map.**

Frames, which divide a screen into parts with independently defined contents (see Figure 7.7), can also help navigation. Many designs keep an abbreviated table of contents in one frame of the screen and the current page in another frame. Users can then navigate easily by moving between the two frames.

Other Considerations.   Companies that run Web sites with thousands of documents linked together need strategies and procedures to ensure that they

FIGURE 7.7   Frames break a Web page into parts. Here the table of contents remains on the left and the selected topic shows on the right.

remove or update outdated information and add new information when appropriate. Some organizations centralize this function by giving a Web master the responsibility for managing the currency of Web documents proactively. The Web master needs to develop a database of information about who controls each Web page and its revision timetable. Organizations that decentralize the removal, updating, and addition of information rely on informal coordination among their managers and employees.

Many organizations require their legal departments to approve the content of every Web page before making it available to the public. This approval adds significant time and cost to the Web design process and may reduce an organization's ability to respond quickly to events and opportunities. Because legal approval is the safest way to avoid plac̄ the organization to litigation, industrie̜ tice essential.

USING WEB DEVELOPM

Publishing documents on the Web is eas̄ office automation suites, such as Micro̜ ument in HTML format. Users can p̄ sheets, database reports, and graphic̄ HTML may affect the format of these them exactly as they appear in their orī ucts provide a Web interface. This int̄ that creates a query. The database ā HTML format for display by any brov̄

Web page development products following:

- Templates and style sheets that create a common look among the Web pages on a site
- The ability to edit the html code underlying the Web page in a user-friendly format, even for users with little or no knowledge of the html language
- Libraries of graphics that enhance the appearance of a Web page
- Tools that organize the documents of a Web site in a logical way and automatically provide links among the documents in accordance with the organization selected
- Libraries of Java routines that can enhance the function of a Web page
- Tools to monitor the currency of Web links to external sites outside the control of the developer

Figure 7.8 shows a document being created with a popular Web page development product.

Some Web development tools create an interface between other applications and a Web site. These use a standard called the **common gateway interface (CGI)**. Although most packaged applications include a Web interface, companies that want to create a Web interface for applications that they have developed on their own rely on CGI tools.

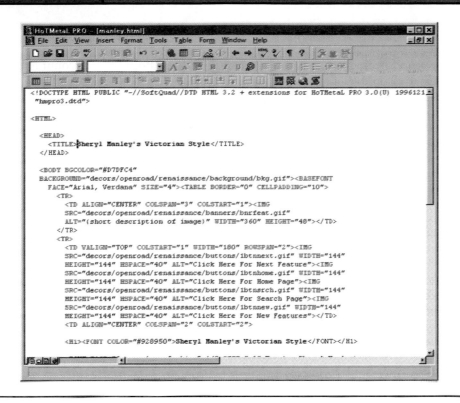

FIGURE 7.8 Using HotMetal PRO, a Web page developer, users can create tables, insert pictures and hypertext links, control the colors and fonts of text, and break the screen into frames.

ENSURING SECURITY OF INFORMATION AND ACCESS

Organizations use firewalls and security management to secure their internal networks from tampering by outsiders. They use encryption and secure protocols to hide and protect the content of messages.

Firewalls. A **firewall** acts as a blockade between an internal network and an external network such as the Internet. A person who enters an order at a store's Web site cannot get into the store's internal ordering or inventory system. Firewalls aim to protect an organization's internal network with trusted users, from unknown, external users who might have malicious motives. A firewall usually consists of screening routers and proxy servers:

- **Screening routers** filter incoming IP packets using information in their IP header, such as their IP number or protocol. These routers are inexpensive, but the small amounts of information in the IP header limit their effectiveness.
- **Proxy servers** refer to gateways between two networks for specific applications. A proxy server might require users to enter a user ID and password at

SUMMARY

The Internet is a network of networks, owned by nobody and managed by consensus. Managers and employees use the Internet for information acquisition and dissemination, electronic commerce, and communication.

The Web consists of hypermedia documents in HTML format that browser software and helper applications can read. A URL identifies each Web document and the server that is responsible for making that document available to the Web. Push technologies send documents meeting selected criteria to users who have requested them.

Electronic commerce refers to electronic transactions related to the purchase and delivery of goods and services. The WWW has popularized virtual stores, where customers can shop 24 hours a day, seven days a week. Customers can pay by credit card or use electronic cash. Extranets open internal networks to selected suppliers and customers to reduce the cost of transactions and create interorganizational linkages that can become strategically advantageous. EDI uses standard electronic documents to transact business among trading partners. Companies can exchange EDI documents over the Internet. People communicate on the Internet using electronic mail and news groups.

Every device attached to the Internet has a unique IP number as its address. Domain names identify servers on the Internet. Domain name registries maintain the relationship between domain names and IP numbers. Most people and companies connect to the Internet through an Internet service provider.

World Wide Web documents may include Java programs, which cannot change or store data on your computer or harm it in any way. Spider, hierarchical, and reviewed search engines help people find Web documents they might want. Web sites should be useful, interesting, and easy to navigate, and should offer visitors a reason to return. Frames and site maps facilitate navigation. Web designers can use registration and cookies to customize their Web sites for each user and provide new information with each visit.

Screening routers, proxy servers, and physical firewalls as well as security management policies and procedures help keep outsiders from tampering with data on internal networks connected to the Internet. Encryption and secure protocols, such as S-HTTP and SET, hide and protect the content of messages. These protocols are important to the success of electronic commerce.

KEY TERMS

browser	encryption
channel definition format (CDF)	extension
common gateway interface (CGI)	extranet
cookie	firewall
digital signature	frame
domain name	helper application
domain name server (DNS)	hierarchical search engine
electronic cash	hypermedia
electronic commerce	hypertext
electronic data interchange (EDI)	hypertext markup language (HTML)

hypertext transport protocol (HTTP)
information superhighway
Internet
Internet service provider (ISP)
IP number
Java
key certification
link
mapping software
multipurpose Internet mail extensions
   (MIME)
navigation
news group
physical firewall
plug-in
point of presence (POP)
post office protocol (POP3)
proxy server

public key encryption
push technology
review search engine
screening router
secure electronic transport (SET)
security management
site map
spider
tag
thread
universal resource locator (URL)
USENET
very high speed Backbone Network
   Service (vBNS)
virtual store
Web page
World Wide Web (WWW)

DISCUSSION AND REVIEW QUESTIONS

1. What is the Internet?
2. Compared to electronic mail, how do news groups reduce the amount of traffic over the Internet?
3. What is the World Wide Web?
4. What is the function of a browser?
5. What are push technologies, and why might companies want to use them?
6. How can consumers pay for goods and services purchased over the Internet?
7. How do extranets facilitate intercompany commerce?
8. How can companies process EDI documents if their systems do not support EDI?
9. How is it possible to process EDI transactions over the Internet?
10. How do Internet domain names and IP addresses relate?
11. How do generic and country domain names differ?
12. What is the role of an Internet service provider (ISP)?
13. How do Internet users ensure compatibility among messages sent by various electronic mail packages over the Internet?
14. What is the role of tags in the hypertext markup language (HTML)?
15. What are the key features of Java that make it attractive as a programming language for programs intended to be downloaded from an unknown source?
16. How do spider and hierarchical search engines differ?
17. What are four rules for Web design?
18. How can Web designers simplify navigation through their Web pages?
19. How can companies customize the content of their Web pages to best satisfy visitors to their site?
20. How can companies protect their internal networks from malicious activities when they are connected to the Internet?

IS ON THE WEB

Exercise 1: Visit the Web sites of two or more fast food companies. What do you think are the objectives of each site? How well do they accomplish them. In a brief report compare and contrast the sites. Comment about which site appears to be more effective.

Exercise 2: Join a USENET news group that is related to your major area of study or one of your hobbies. Read some of the messages that were recently posted to the news groups. How interesting or educational are they? Post a question to the news group. How long did it take to get a response? How many responses did you get? How helpful were they?

MINICASE

AN INTERNET STRATEGY FOR VOLKSWAGEN

Volkswagen Inc.'s Jack Shafer knows he has a potential conflict on his hands, and he's doing everything he can to avoid it. Shafer is manager of new technology at the Auburn Hills, Mich.-based subsidiary of the German car maker and is overseeing the company's efforts to sell products through its World Wide Web site. It seems like a good idea. As Shafer pointed out, the demographics of VW buyers and Web surfers are remarkably similar in age, disposable income, and technological proclivities.

But VW has a loyal dealer base that has stuck with the company through lean years in this country. And VW's fortunes here have recently begun to turn. If all of a sudden VW were to start selling products directly through its Web site, what would the dealers say? "They are afraid of the ramifications," Shafer said.

Shafer and Volkswagen face a dilemma confronting companies across all industries. As vendors hurtle into the electronic commerce age, how do they set up cybershop without competing with their existing sales channels?

In some cases, such competition is inevitable. But Shafer said VW dealers don't have to worry. The company has drawn up an electronic commerce strategy intended to work with, not against, them. The plan is simple. Every sale generated by the VW site is credited to the dealer located nearest the purchaser.

The strategy makes sense to at least one VW dealer Bob Lewis, owner of Bob Lewis Volkswagen in San Jose, Calif. "The Internet is too big, too important for VW to ignore. They should give the consumer as much information as they can

---

SOURCE: Case from Mark Halper, Volkswagen's commerce plan shouldn't bug dealers, *Computerworld* (emmerce insert, April 28, 1997): 5,6.

about their product. As long as they sell through an authorized dealer, it's not a threat to us."

In order not to alarm its dealers, VW is introducing the idea slowly, "selling" only promotional, low-margin items such as coffee mugs, caps, and T-shirts, which the company dubs "trinkets and trash." It does not include automobiles or dealers' other sacred cow, spare and replacement parts. Shafer said he does not anticipate selling these until at least 1998.

That's probably a good idea because just the mention of VW-initiated parts sales is enough to raise dealer hackles. "That absolutely would be a conflict if they started selling parts," said Mike Sullivan, owner of a Lexus, Isuzu, and Volkswagen dealership in Santa Monica, Calif., who agreed the "trinkets and trash" program was not a concern.

Shafer said he realized that although VW's plan entails crediting the dealer, that notion won't necessarily sink in right away. The company is, therefore, proceeding slowly. "We're doing this in stages so the dealers become comfortable with it and are not threatened by it," he said.

VW is approaching electronic sales so cautiously, it is not yet offering accessory items such as mud flaps, floor mats, and spoilers. These items will probably be the next VW offers online. With these sales as well, the dealer nearest the buyer will receive a normal markup on the item. The buyer will have a choice of receiving the product from VW or from the dealer. "Dealers will have an infinite return on investment because there is no investment," Shafer said.

VW is, however, encouraging its dealers to develop their own Web sites and to establish online facilities for promoting products and taking orders. It is here that Shafer is noticing resistance. "We're really dragging these people kicking and screaming onto the Internet, but that's our No. 1 goal right now," he said. "There are other people all over the Internet today trying to sell new cars, and they're presenting a formidable challenge."

The "other people" are electronic middlemen such as Irvine, California-based Auto-By-Tel. This new breed of car salesman lists new products from various car manufacturers and refers buyers to dealers that pay to be part of the middleman's service. A VW dealer who does not belong to an Auto-By-Tel-type service competes with any dealer that is a member. Thus, Shafer pointed out, it behooves any dealer to aggressively develop its own Web-based marketing and sales plans.

"The number one thing I preach is for them to learn about this new medium, to become a part of it," Shafer said. "If they don't learn the medium, they will lose sales this year."

Case Questions

Diagnosis

1. What are the information needs of automobile purchasers?
2. What are the needs of Volkswagen's dealers?
3. What are the needs of Volkswagen's corporate planners?

Evaluation

4. How are Auto-By-Tel and others affecting the automobile market?
5. Should Volkswagen and its dealers be threatened by these electronic intermediaries?

Design

6. How does Shafer plan to bring Volkswagen and its dealers into the electronic marketplace?

Implementation

7. Do you think Shafer's plan will work?
8. What criteria would you use to evaluate the eventual success of his plan?

ACTIVITY 7.1   SELLING FINANCIAL DATA ON THE WEB

Step 1:   Read the following scenario:

Giving a major financial institution a consumer-friendly face on the Internet is no easy task, as Ray Kingman has discovered. When Kingman took over management of the Thomson Consumer Products Group and its flagship Web site, MarketEdge, last December, he had his work cut out for him. "For Thomson, this is a very different kind of business," Kingman says.

The $8 billion Toronto-based financial conglomerate provides information to full service brokerages and financial institutions through divisions like FirstCall, a publisher of earnings forecasts, and Investext, which offers brokers' research reports. In the past, the company knew its customers well; the salespeople had a one-on-one relationship with their customers. Yet the MarketEdge business model couldn't be more different. On the Web, MarketEdge doesn't get to meet all the new customers that visit its home page. So it has to rely on first impressions. "With the Internet-based financial solution we're building, the packaging and presentation of the site is 50 percent of the sale. It's essentially impulse-buying."

Kingman, 40, created the infrastructure to support this new business model at MarketEdge's headquarters in Rockville, Md. He hired a team from AOL, Netscape, and other consumer software companies who understood the importance of packaging the message in a form online consumers could digest. Kingman learned the art as president of DeltaPoint, a graphics software company he founded in 1989.

Kingman says he was lucky that Thomson executives realized the significance of consumer promotions when they developed the idea for MarketEdge in early 1996 and launched the site with market quotes, stock pricing alerts, and user bulletin boards. Some areas were free and others required a subscription. At the time, discount brokerage firms, including online brokers like E-Trade, were undercutting the prices of full-service houses. The low fees charged by the discount brokers prevented the full-service houses from buying traditional Thomson services such as FirstCall and Investext, but a large market was emerging among individual investors who manage their own portfolios and do their own research, mainly online.

After a year of learning the needs of this new clientele, MarketEdge was relaunched with a much easier user interface. More expert commentaries, IPO information, small-cap investment opportunities, and a "newsroom" for investment-

SOURCE: Activity 7.1 scenario from Hilary Marsh, Selling market data, one investor at a time, *Internet World* (June 1997): 46.

related stories were added. Users can now track news and opinions that relate to their portfolio.

Kingman admits that the free offerings are not as broad as some competitors', including Dow Jones and Morningstar, but he maintains that MarketEdge has the lowest price ($7.95 per month) and offers the most content to subscribers. "The Thomson connection is professionally rich, and we don't have to charge as much as we would if we were buying information from a third party." Thomson's greatest worry is the underlying system.

Because 70 percent of the site's pages are dynamically generated, an overload on the Oracle 7 databases on Sun Sparc servers could conceivably lead to a noticeable "brownout." So far, the system has held up well, leaving Kingman free to worry about something more fickle: a new breed of investor.

Step 2: Prepare the case for class discussion.

Step 3: Answer each of the following questions, individually or in small groups, as directed by your instructor:

Diagnosis

1. What are the information needs of MarketEdge's customers?
2. What are MarketEdge's marketing needs?
3. Who are MarketEdge's competitors, and how do they compete with Market-Edge?

Evaluation

4. How did MarketEdge satisfy its marketing needs in the past?
5. How well did MarketEdge satisfy its customers in the past?
6. Why did Kingman feel that changes were necessary?

Design

7. How did MarketEdge's Internet strategy address its competitive position?
8. How did MarketEdge attempt to address the needs of its customers?

Implementation

9. Why did MarketEdge need to relaunch its Web site after a year of experimentation?
10. What possible problems exist with the current implementation?

Step 4: In small groups or with the entire class, share your answers to the questions in Step 3. Then answer the following questions:

1. What were the threats to MarketEdge's competitive position?
2. Why did Kingman feel that MarketEdge needed to develop a Web strategy?
3. What were the key components of the strategy Kingman designed?
4. What concerns does Kingman have for the current system?

ACTIVITY 7.2   AN INTERNET HUNT

Using your favorite Web search engine or engines, find the answers to the following questions. Print the Web pages that display the answers.

1. What is the most current exchange rate between the French franc and the U.S. dollar?
2. What are the latitude and longitude of Concord, California?
3. What line follows the line "The Lord is my shepherd, I shall not want," in the King James version of the Bible?
4. What is the most recent edition and copyright year of Paul Samuelson's economics textbook?
5. What is the Internet address of your congressman or congresswoman?
6. What stock had the largest gain of those on the New York Stock Exchange in yesterday's trading activity?
7. Who scored the most points ever in a professional basketball game? When did it happen, and how many points did he score?
8. What tropical storms are currently active in the Atlantic?
9. How old was Marilyn Monroe when she died?
10. What was the number one song on the country billboards last week?

ACTIVITY 7.3   CREATING YOUR OWN WEB PAGE

Step 1: Using a text editor, a word processor, or Web page authoring software, as directed by your instructor, create a Web page that contains a short biography of yourself and a link to the Web page for this textbook (your instructor will provide its URL). If you are using a word processor that does not support HTML files, use the following template and be sure to save your work as a text file with the extension htm.

Here's the template:

```
<HTML>
<HEAD>
<TITLE>My First Web Page</TITLE>
</HEAD>
<BODY>

                    YOUR HTML CODE GOES HERE

</BODY>
</HTML>
```

Step 2: Start your Web browser. Open the page you have just created. If it has errors, correct the file and view it repeatedly until you have eliminated all errors.

ACTIVITY 7.4   SPAM THREATS

Step 1: Read the following scenario:

SOURCE: Activity 7.4 scenario from Andy Patrizio, Flame Games, *Information Week* (January 13, 1997), http://www.techWeb. com/se/directlink.cgi?IWK19970113S0011.

Fearing return flame mail [very obnoxious e-mail] while hawking a hair-growth product via e-mail recently, Cyber Promotions tacked on this threat: "DON'T DO IT! If we are flamed, we will (a) FLAME YOU 1,000 times as much, and (b) e-mail 3 million people a questionable item with your return e-mail address. We want respect as much as anyone else, so if you give it, you'll receive it."

Step 2: Prepare the case for class discussion. Consider the viewpoints of the manager flooded with junk mail, and the management of Cyber Promotions.

Step 3: From the perspective of the business manager and the Cyber Promotions manager, answer each of the following questions, individually or in small groups, as directed by your instructor.

1. What alternatives do you have?
2. For each alternative, who benefits and who is harmed?
3. From the ethical principles of least harm, rights and duties, professional responsibilities, self-interest and utilitarianism, consistency, and respect, how would you evaluate each alternative?
4. What course of action would you take? Why?

EDI AT HARKNESS HARDWARE ACTIVITY 7.5

Step 1: Read the following scenario:

Harkness Hardware Company, a $60 million distributor of hardware supplies to steel companies, building contractors, and major retail outlets, stocks approximately 10,000 items of various sizes. The company publishes a catalog that lists the items, and it regularly sends sales representatives to meet with customers and identify their needs. Increasingly its customers have been complaining about the difficulty of reaching order clerks. They also say that they frequently order items that are out of stock but that could easily be replaced with other items if they were informed quickly about the problem. The executives of Harkness Hardware understand their customers' frustration because they have experienced the same problems with Harkness's suppliers.

Step 2: Assume that you are an EDI vendor. Individually or in small groups, offer a plan for converting Harkness Hardware to EDI.

Step 3: Share your plans with the entire class.

Step 4: In small groups or with the entire class, answer the following questions:

1. What are the information and operating needs of Harkness and its customers?
2. How well are the needs currently being met?
3. Does the implementation of EDI address these needs?
4. How should Harkness develop and implement an EDI strategy?

RECOMMENDED READINGS

Baker, Richard H. *Extranets: The Complete Sourcebook*. New York: Computing McGraw-Hill, 1997.

Gascoyne, Richard J., and Ozcubukcu, Koray. *Corporate Internet Planning Guide: Aligning Internet Strategy with Business Goals*. New York: Van Nostrand Reinhold, 1997.

Tittle, Ed, James, Steve, and James, Steven N., *HTML for Dummies*. 3rd ed. Edited by Tittel. Foster City, CA: IDG Books Worldwide, 1997.

Jilovec, Nahid M. *The A to Z of EDI: A Comprehensive Guide to Electronic Data Interchange*. Loveland, CO: Duke Communications, 1997.

Snyder, Joel, Sheldon, Tom, and Petru, Tim. *Internet Security—Professional Reference*. 2nd ed. Indianapolis: New Riders Publishing, 1997.

Wayner, Peter. *Digital Cash: Commerce on the Net*. 2nd ed. Boston: Ap Professional, 1997.

NOTES

1. Excerpted and adapted from Julie Bort, Internet: Big money beyond EDI: GE's bid to automate bidding, *Client/Server Computing Online* (June 1997), http://www.sentrytech.com/cs067f3.htm; see also Inside extranets: Linking business partners, *Computeworld Intranets* (June 23, 1997): 1–4, 9.

2. Eric R. Chabrow, Wall Street on the desktop, *InformationWeek* (March 11, 1996): 61–66.

3. Scott Hamilton, E-Commerce for the 21st century, *Computer* (May 1997): 44–47.

4. Sharon Machlis, GM site gets sales, mixed reviews, *Computerworld* (January 12, 1998): 41–42.

5. Ibid.; Blane Erwin, Mary Modahl, and Jesse Johnson, *The Forrester Report: Business Trade & Technology Strategies* 7 (July 1997), http://access.forrester.com/index-bin/do_userform.pl?authcheckOP&URL=/business/1997/reports/jul97btr.htm&ID=6815; Dramatic Growth of Web Commerce: From $2.6 Billion to more than $220 Billion in 2001, http://www.idcresearch.com/f/HNR/ic2001f.htm, August 8, 1997.

6. Facts & figures, *Database* (June/July 1997): 16.

7. http://www.amazon.com, About our Store, August 6, 1997.

8. http://www.uvision.com, August 6, 1997.

9. Mitch Wagner, Extranet aids in insurance sales, *Computerworld* (August 4, 1997): 47.

10. Steve Alexander, Extranet app lets clients track transactions, *Computerworld Intranets* (February 23, 1998): 11.

11. ActivMedia study cited by Tom Davey, Extranets unlock your business, *InformationWeek* (June 9, 1997), http://www.techWeb.com/se/directlink.cgi?IWK19970609S0046.

12. Tom Davey, Extranets unlock your business, *InformationWeek* (June 9, 1997), http://www.techWeb.com/se/directlink.cgi?IWK19970609S0046.

13. Julie Bort, Big money beyond EDI, *Client/Server Computing* (June 1997): 44–47.

14. The EDI Connection, Retailer EDI announcements, http://www.ediconnection.com/news05.htm, August 9, 1997, *Client/Server Computing* (June 1997): 44–47.

15. Jim Brown, Banks increase use of EDI, *Network World* (January 25, 1988): 1, 82; James Johnston, EDI implementation at PPG industries, *Journal of Systems Management* 43(2) (February 1992): 32–34.

16. Bort, Big money beyond EDI

17. Jay M. Tenenbaum, Tripatinder S. Chowdhry, and Kevin Hughes, Eco system: An Internet Commerce Architecture, *Computer* (May 1997): 48–55.

18. Richard Adhikari, EDI heads for the Net, *InformationWeek* (May 6, 1996): 59–60.

19. Jupiter Communications and Forrester Research, as reported by *Computerworld*, http://www.computerworld.com/emmerce/depts/stats.html, August 7, 1997.

20. International Data Corp., as reported by *Computerworld*, http://www.computerworld.com/emmerce/depts/stats.html, August 7, 1997.

21. Forrester Research, as reported by *Computerworld*, http://www.computerworld.com/emmerce/depts/stats.html, August 7, 1997.

22. Will new domains spark a free-for-all?, *Internet World* (February 1998): 15–16.

23. See Wayne Bremser, The big 4.0, *Internet World* (January 1998): 64–70, for discussion of changes to HTML.

24. http://www.dow.com/products/finder.html, March 22, 1998.

25. http://www.oracle.com/corporate/hr/html/index.html, March 22, 1998.

26. http://www.simware.com/salvo/, March 22, 1998.

27. http://lcweb2.loc.gov/catalog/, March 22, 1998.

28. http://idt.net/~tagman71/, July 25, 1997.

29. Kim S. Nash, Parallel worlds: Internet, *Computerworld* Supplement, 100 Best Places to Work in IS (June 1997): 32.

30. Julie Bort, Liar, liar, *Client/Server Computing* (May 1997): 40–42.

31. Shron Machlis, Internet team cracks 56-bit encryption code, *Computerworld* (June 23, 1997): 3.

32. Jon Kaplan, Unscrambling the secret of encryption, *Security Management* (February 1995): 67–70.

33. Mitch Wagner, Get SET to secure transactions, *Computerworld* (July 28, 1997): 41, 44.

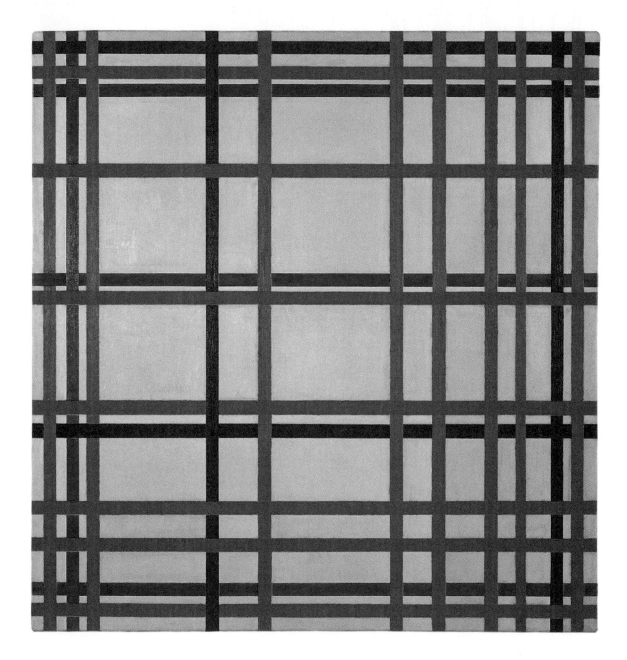

Piet Mondrian, *New York City I*. 1942. Private collection. Giraudon/Art Resource, New York.

III

DESIGNING INFORMATION SYSTEMS

Information systems use information technology to satisfy information needs. Part III investigates an array of information systems. Chapter 8 looks at automation and support systems. It discusses automation for offices, work flow, sales forces, design, factories, and education and training, as well as expert systems. Chapter 9 examines transaction processing systems. These systems collect and disseminate information associated with the day-to-day operation of organizations. Chapter 10 presents management information systems. In particular, it describes management reporting systems, decision support systems, groupware, and executive information systems. Chapter 11 considers strategic information systems. These systems help organizations obtain low-cost leadership, differentiate their products and services, create focus, support linkages, and develop information leadership.

Chapter 8

Automation and Support Systems

LEARNING OBJECTIVES

After completing Chapter 8, you will be able to

1. List the functions office automation can support.
2. Discuss the role of intelligent messaging, electronic imaging, and the virtual office in office automation.
3. Describe the process of work-flow automation.
4. Identify the use of automation for sales support and customer service.
5. Identify the major uses of computer-aided design.
6. Discuss the major features of CAD software and how they support high-quality design.
7. Show how flexible manufacturing, robotics, and automated guided vehicles can automate manufacturing.
8. Compare and contrast computer-aided manufacturing and computer-integrated manufacturing.
9. Cite the advantages and disadvantages of automating education and training.
10. Describe the components of an expert system.
11. Describe the major characteristics and use of neural networks.

AUTOMATION AT
WOODS MEMORIAL HOSPITAL

How can a hospital meet the challenge of the changing health care industry? It can deliver high-quality care at a low cost. Woods Memorial Hospital, a 72-bed hospital in the rural community of Etoway, Tennessee, has met the challenge; it has survived and even flourished.

Why has Woods Memorial thrived? The hospital has transformed itself by focusing on cost containment through automation. Led by an administrator who applied a near-military zeal to automating all of the institution's operations, Woods has shown that even organizations caught in the center of an industry's downward spiral can buck the trend.

With the help of automation, admissions went from 30-minute waits in the lobby—while nurses completed forms, typed hospital bracelets, and made requests for lab tests in triplicate—to the almost instantaneous assignment of patients to and arrival at their hospital beds. The pharmacy and therapeutics committee now employs information systems to track the use of drugs to determine if less expensive drugs will work equally well. The hospital has reduced food waste by tracking patient satisfaction with selection and portion size, as well as improving the accuracy of orders delivered. Nurses now order lab tests through an automated computer system that can also deliver results to numerous locations throughout the hospital. Patients receive completed and accurate bills on discharge.

A dramatic increase in patient revenues, from $16 million in 1991 to $28 million in 1995, and a corresponding increase in net income, from $953,327 in 1991 to $1.6 million in 1995, are indicators of the success of automation at Woods Memorial. The price of care did not change in those five years. The hospital required no new clerical staff, but instead expanded services and recruited more physicians; the hospital even paid for their medical education as an incentive for committing to a position at Woods Memorial. As Dr. Charles Cox noted, "Today we have all the technology that big urban medical centers have. So doctors can come here and not feel at a disadvantage."[1]

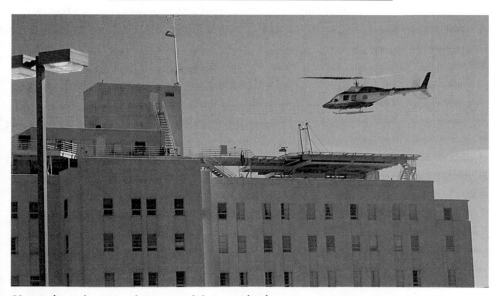

Hospitals, such as Woods Memorial, have used information systems to automate patient admissions, monitoring, and release, as well as various aspects of their medical care. Automated systems also monitor food services, laboratory services, and other operational activities.

Automation describes the use of computers to perform tasks previously performed by people. It frees workers from performing tedious, precise, or dangerous tasks, and so generally increases worker productivity and efficiency. Support systems automate tasks for knowledge workers, helping them to use their skills and improve the reliability, uniformity, and overall quality of the products and services they provide. At the same time, automation and support systems may displace low-skilled workers by decreasing the amount of available work. They may also disrupt the social environment in an organization and alienate some workers.

Automation frequently accompanies the redesign of work. Business process design in particular, which completely re-creates the flow of work in organizations completely, heavily uses automation to speed work processes and reduce the number of staff members necessary to perform them. In this chapter we investigate seven types of automated systems: office automation, work-flow automation, sales force automation, design automation, factory automation, automation of education and training, and expert systems (see Table 8.1).

OFFICE AUTOMATION

Office automation computerizes a variety of activities typically performed by office staff, such as desktop publishing, scheduling, document creation, and communication. Traditionally, most offices have used paper for maintaining and storing information. But paper is hard to share, easily lost or misplaced, and requires extensive space for storage. Automating an office eliminates these problems by using the computer as the main way of dealing with information. It improves communication and record keeping by helping workers to more effectively acquire, organize, manipulate, and exchange information. For example, the U.S. Postal Service replaced 300 paper business forms with electronic ones. It introduced new software, developed by F3 Software Corporation of Burlington, Massachusetts, that provided employees with electronic travel vouchers, expense reports, training requests, and other documents that employees completed and then sent through the agency's electronic mail system. Figure 8.1 provides an example of a single electronic form similar to one that the U.S. Postal Service might use for expense reports. The Postal Service expected that this change would save several million dollars over a three-year period, as well as reduce errors and speed work.[2]

FUNCTIONS OF OFFICE AUTOMATION

Computer systems can automate document storage, data analysis, document preparation, time management, and communication. Owens Corning eliminated all file cabinets in its new headquarters and expects to save $50 million in annual operating costs. Managers and employees now conduct all internal business electronically,[3] as shown in Figure 8.2. They use office automation systems to perform functions such as the following:

- *Document Storage.* Manual filing and retrieving paper documents wastes time and space and creates opportunities for loss of information. Computer systems

TABLE 8.1	Automation and support systems provide a variety of functions in a broad range of settings.

Type of Automation	Purpose	Examples of Uses and Features	Types of Hardware and Software
Office automation	Computerizes activities performed by office workers	Document creation Data analysis Time management Communication	Intelligent messaging Electronic imaging Virtual office
Work-flow automation	Coordinates the flow of work among knowledge workers	Document routing Process modeling Process monitoring	Document management
Sales force automation	Supports salespeople by computerizing information about leads, sales, service, and other client contact	Lead management Customer management	Sales support Customer service
Design automation	Supports the prototyping and development of engineering and architectural design	Product design Process design	Computer-aided design (CAD) Rapid prototyping
Factory automation	Automates the operation and monitoring of manufacturing equipment and machinery	Automated production line Flexible manufacturing Process control	Computer-aided manufacturing (CAM) Robots Automated guided vehicles Computer-integrated manufacturing (CIM)
Automation of education and training	Supports and leverages the work of teachers and trainers	Computer-based training (CBT) Virtual reality settings	Courseware Authorware Videoconferencing
Expert systems	Supports the knowledge worker as an expert would	Medical diagnosis Equipment repair Risk assessment Bank fraud identification	Expert systems shell Neural network Fuzzy logic software Intelligent agent

can electronically store information in a database, eliminating the filing function entirely. Staff at Woods Memorial Hospital maintain patient files on the computer, accessing them from terminals with a few keystrokes. Electronic filing typically reduces the number of clerical staff needed and speeds the retrieval of information.

- *Data Analysis.* Computers can easily summarize data for accounting, financial, human resources, and other management purposes. Spreadsheet software, for example, allows office workers to perform calculations much less expensively and more quickly than manually. It can also display the results of such calculations graphically so that managers can understand them more readily.

FIGURE 8.1   Using an electronic expense report form speeds the paper flow in an organization.

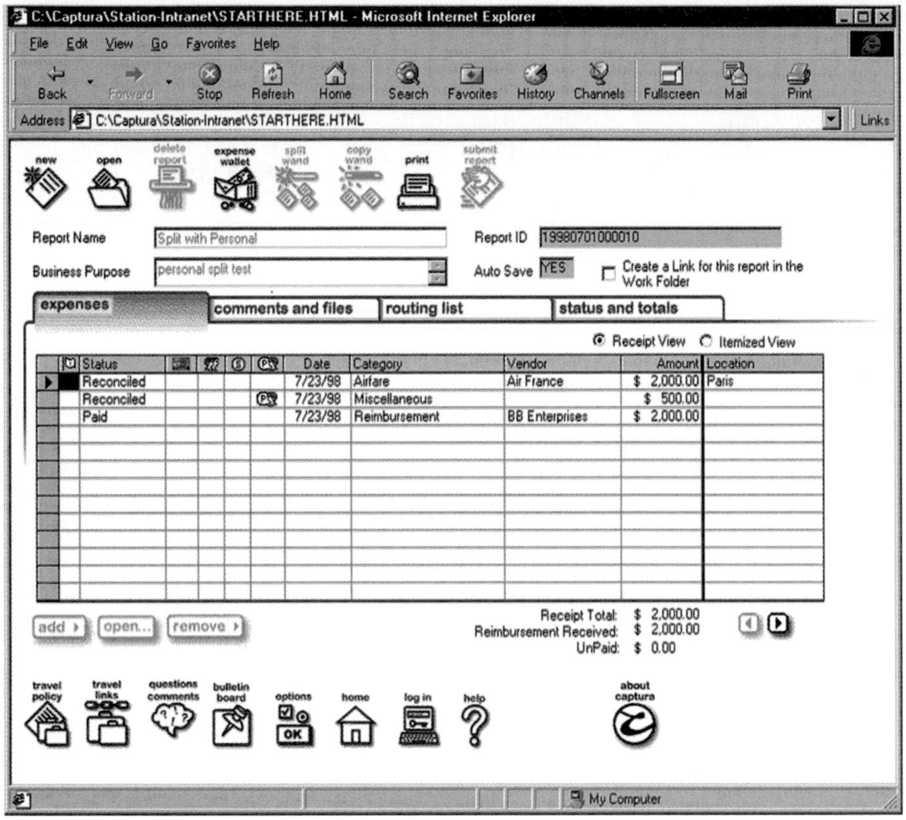

Managers at Hitchiner Manufacturing Inc., in Milford, New Hampshire, use spreadsheet software to analyze the company's financial data.[4]

- *Document Preparation.* Word processing, desktop publishing, presentation graphics, and electronic mail software have automated the process of document production at many offices. Office workers using these products can write, edit, and package almost any type of document with minimal professional assistance and without retyping or reentering information by other means.
- *Time Management.* Project management software and calendar software can automate the scheduling of appointments. Figure 8.3 illustrates the screens from such software, which can also compare calendars of meeting participants to avoid conflicts, reducing the time required to arrange meetings. Managers at TransCanada Energy Ltd. of Calgary, Alberta, used such software to improve collaboration among its units worldwide.[5]
- *Communication.* Electronic mail, voice mail, bulletin board, electronic notes, and a host of other software can ease interpersonal communication, both for information exchange and for decision making. Groupware typically includes communication software that supports group decision making, which is critical to the contemporary team-based office environment.

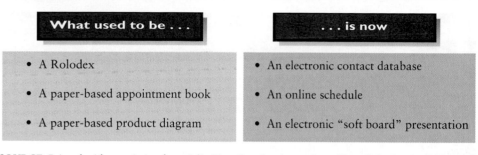

FIGURE 8.2 Owens Corning eliminated file cabinets and now conducts all internal business electronically.

What used to be . . .	. . . is now
• A Rolodex	• An electronic contact database
• A paper-based appointment book	• An online schedule
• A paper-based product diagram	• An electronic "soft board" presentation

SOURCE: Printed with permission from Julia King, People who work at (fiber)glass company shouldn't use paper, *Computerworld* (April 21, 1997): 8.

An **electronic desk** (see Figure 8.4), available with GUI operating systems, shows all office automation functions, such as electronic mail, word processing, and spreadsheets, as options on the computer screen and allows a user to easily shift between functions.

FIGURE 8.3 Calendaring software helps employees schedule meetings and other events as part of their jobs.

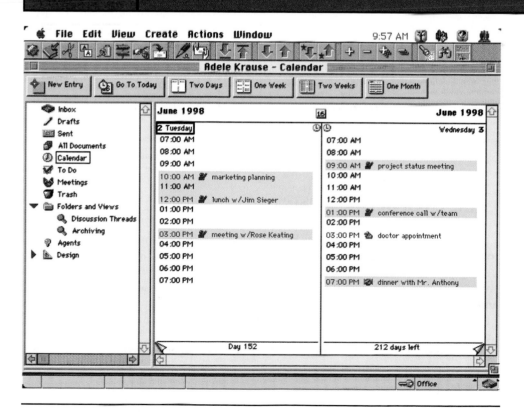

FIGURE 8.4 An electronic desk shows all office automation functions and allows the user to shift among them.

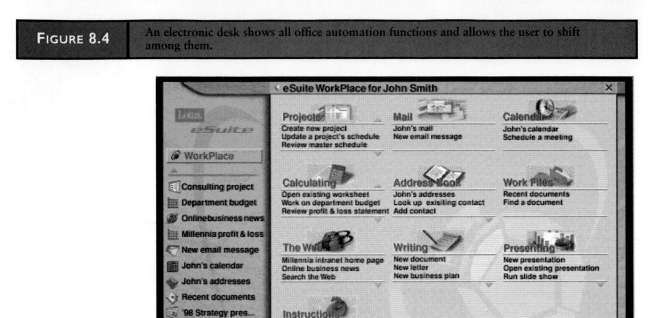

INTELLIGENT MESSAGING

Intelligent messaging refers to communications software that automates diverse communication functions. For example, Adaptive Micro Systems's SMART ALEC delivers data from alarm systems and process control systems in manufacturing plants to pagers, e-mail, voice-mail, intranet, and public address systems.[6]

ELECTRONIC IMAGING

Electronic imaging management (EIM) systems store documents, including photographs, invoices, and personnel records, on computers and then retrieve and reproduce them instantly. An EIM system uses a high-speed, high-resolution scanner to capture documents in digital form and an optical disk system to store the massive amount of data generated. It has software that compresses data to reduce the amount of storage needed to save a picture. A high-speed laser printer produces quality images as output.

EIM systems use three main methods to process paper electronically; Figure 8.5 graphically illustrates the differences: [7]

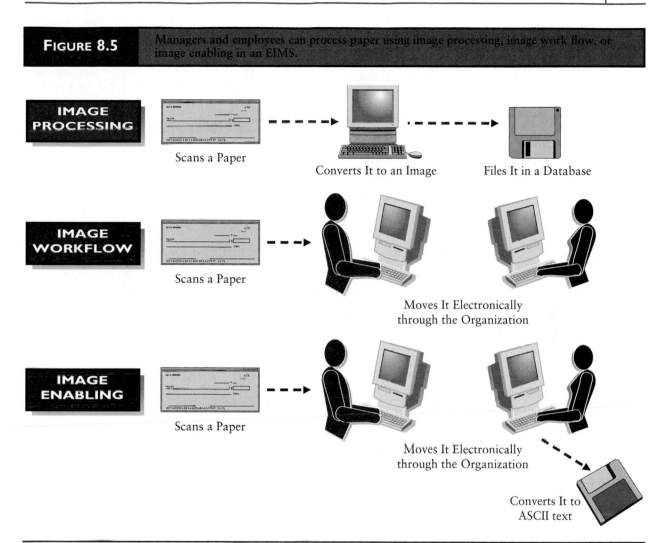

FIGURE 8.5 Managers and employees can process paper using image processing, image work flow, or image enabling in an EIMS.

IMAGE PROCESSING

Scans a Paper — Converts It to an Image — Files It in a Database

IMAGE WORKFLOW

Scans a Paper — Moves It Electronically through the Organization

IMAGE ENABLING

Scans a Paper — Moves It Electronically through the Organization — Converts It to ASCII text

- **Image processing** scans a paper, converts it into an image, and files it in a database for later use. Teachers Insurance and Annuity Association (TIAA), which provides portable retirement plans for 1.7 million American educators and their staffs, uses electronic imaging to maintain a comprehensive file for each customer. The imaging system provides fast, more personalized service at lower costs.[8]
- **Image work flow** scans the paper and then electronically moves it through the organization as employees complete work on it. Chemical Bank uses image work flow to process incoming debt securities and equities. Employees pass the incoming paper through a scanning station and then use proprietary software to continue the processing after storing the securities. This process replaced a system in which securities arrived in the mailroom and then spent time on seven different desks. The imaging system reduced errors and increased productivity by 40 percent.[9]

THE MANAGER IN ACTION

Tom Smith, president of Tom Smith Industries Inc. (TSI), a 15-year-old modeler of thermoplastic material for the automotive industry, has slowly automated the design process in his company. He didn't want to demand that his tool designers and machinists change the way they create the high-precision molds used in the company's injection machines. Instead, he has introduced design software and computer-driven metal-cutting tools gradually, letting the employees figure out how they want to use them. Right now, for example, TSI's designers and machinists use technology to create the rough cuts in the mold-making process, while they do the precision detail work by hand.

When they first introduced a computer-controlled machine tool for cutting each mold component, the toolmakers seemed only slightly interested in it. Now they have become so accustomed to using it that Smith is leading TSI in building a full-blown machining center. It will use a computer-controlled machine tool that requires almost no human intervention. This technology combined with other forms of automation have TSI running at 85 percent of its capacity. For Smith, "My biggest dilemma now is do I manage the growth, or do I slow it down?"

SOURCE: Based on Jeffrey Zygmont, "When slow and steady wins the race," *Inc. Technology* (4) (1996): 72–76.

- **Image enabling** scans the paper, electronically moves it through the organization, and then uses optical character recognition software to convert its text into searchable ASCII text. For example, First Call Research Direct includes search and retrieval capabilities for bringing research documents directly to fund managers' screens.[10]

EIM systems offer the greatest benefits to organizations that maintain extensive paper records, such as the U.S. Patent Office, the U.S. Internal Revenue Service, registries of deeds, motor vehicle registries, and insurance companies. According to a study prepared for the Association for Information and Image Management International, the top five industries that use electronic imaging are insurance, utilities, manufacturing, the federal government, and banking.[11] The clerk of the 18th Judicial Circuit Court of Illinois, for example, has kept the number of staff constant by using electronic imaging for record management.[12] Bank America Corporation uses imaging technology in its Las Vegas auto-lending center and reduced loan approval time from two hours to 20 minutes.[13]

THE VIRTUAL OFFICE

Telecommuting, where an individual works from home and typically communicates extensively with the corporate office using electronic media, has increased in popularity. American Express in New York, for example, mandates telecommuting for some employees and makes it optional for others. The company has about 600 employees who telecommute and 15,000 who work remotely in some capacity.[14] Experts estimate that about 75 percent of all information workers, encompassing more than 55 percent of the U.S. workforce, are potential telecommuters.[15] A home office offers the advantages and disadvantages shown in Table 8.2. Workers can also participate in **after-hours telecommuting,** where they perform their work on the computer at home outside of regular office hours,[16] and they can work in **satellite offices,** which are established away from the city center and near employee residences.

Companies usually set aside shared office space for employees, such as traveling salespeople and telecommuters, to use for meetings or other events. Some companies manage these office spaces as hotels. A concierge greets the employee upon check in, shows him to a suite, forwards his phone service to a phone in the suite, and enables network support for his mobile computer.

As more employees work from home or other remote sites, they require computer capabilities typically found in offices. The **virtual office** refers to the conduct of office functions in locations outside corporate buildings. Companies create virtual offices as a way of reducing real estate expenses, increasing productivity, improving customer service, and increasing profitability.

The virtual office includes portable computers, dial-in modems, cellular phones, facsimile machines, and software that automates office procedures and allows communication from remote locations. Field-based loss control specialists for Cigna Property & Casualty operate in a virtual office. They use software that solves technical loss control problems, updates the knowledge base of information, links to external databases of standards and information, and also links them to internal consultants who can locate answers to specific questions.[17] Xerox Corporation accelerated plans to give its sales representatives notebook computers and create virtual offices after the 1994 earthquake struck the Los Angeles area.[18]

TABLE 8.2	Telecommuting offers workers and organizations both advantages and disadvantages.
Advantages	Reduces time spent commuting
	Increases the ability of telecommuters to purchase less costly homes distant from city centers
	Increases the worker's personal autonomy and control
	Allows for the availability of talented employees who want to work at home
	Makes it easier for organizations to deal in foreign markets or with foreign companies outside of normal working hours
Disadvantages	Decreases face-to-face communication with others in the organization
	Causes managers to fear a loss of control over workers

WORK-FLOW AUTOMATION

Automating work flow attempts to improve customer satisfaction, daily operations, and productivity through implementing computerized control and coordination of various organizational activities. A **work-flow management system** drives, coordinates, and monitors the flow of activities that relate to administrative, production, and other business processes. **Work-flow automation** supports knowledge workers by coordinating their activities and improving the flow of information among them. Connecticut Mutual Life Insurance Company adopted work-flow technology early and implemented a "one image" strategy that eliminated paper, consolidated fragmented systems, and compressed complex work processes. The system resulted in a 30 to 60 percent savings in labor and increase in productivity.[19]

A computerized system generally includes a tool that graphically shows the work in the organization and details who does what tasks; the process cycle times and costs; the required forms, reports, and information; and the relationships of work flows in the overall system.[20] Work-flow management systems have three major components:[21]

- *Modeling* uses graphical tools to create and map processes.
- *Monitoring* assists workers with following and analyzing in-process and completed work flow.
- *Managing* provides instructions about how the work should flow, controls how these instructions are implemented, and reports what functions occurred.

Work-flow software lets people define the units of work, the steps that compose them, and the sequence of the work steps. The software identifies the conditions that determine the right work step, whether a parallel series of work steps can exist, and how long a unit of work may remain pending. Work-flow software also details which users should perform which work steps, which programs should be run at each work step, and what data the programs should use.[22] Woods Memorial Hospital, for example, might use work-flow software to plan the movement of patient records from admissions to various medical specialty areas. Many companies use work-flow software to help them manage projects. It particularly helps identify interdependencies among various project tasks.

Stop and Shop, a New England grocery chain, combined a work-flow and document imaging system (see the following section) with its accounting system. Now the company can route all invoices from a particular supplier to the same employee, as well as change the priority of work. The system also pays most invoices automatically. Using work flow in this way has not only reduced costs but also improved relationships with suppliers.[23] Figure 8.6 provides a checklist of the business value of work-flow management.

DOCUMENT MANAGEMENT

Document management, a set of services that help users keep track of stored electronic documents, has become a key component of work-flow automation. Computers can track and retrieve documents more quickly and accurately than can manual systems. Similar to Woods Memorial Hospital's movement to electronic record keeping, Boston Children's Hospital electronically records emergency room treatment as it

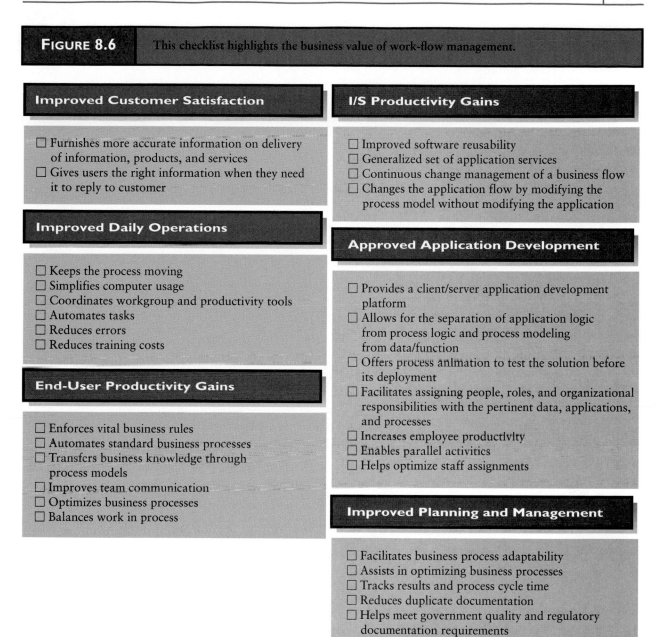

FIGURE 8.6   This checklist highlights the business value of work-flow management.

Improved Customer Satisfaction

- ☐ Furnishes more accurate information on delivery of information, products, and services
- ☐ Gives users the right information when they need it to reply to customer

Improved Daily Operations

- ☐ Keeps the process moving
- ☐ Simplifies computer usage
- ☐ Coordinates workgroup and productivity tools
- ☐ Automates tasks
- ☐ Reduces errors
- ☐ Reduces training costs

End-User Productivity Gains

- ☐ Enforces vital business rules
- ☐ Automates standard business processes
- ☐ Transfers business knowledge through process models
- ☐ Improves team communication
- ☐ Optimizes business processes
- ☐ Balances work in process

I/S Productivity Gains

- ☐ Improved software reusability
- ☐ Generalized set of application services
- ☐ Continuous change management of a business flow
- ☐ Changes the application flow by modifying the process model without modifying the application

Approved Application Development

- ☐ Provides a client/server application development platform
- ☐ Allows for the separation of application logic from process logic and process modeling from data/function
- ☐ Offers process animation to test the solution before its deployment
- ☐ Facilitates assigning people, roles, and organizational responsibilities with the pertinent data, applications, and processes
- ☐ Increases employee productivity
- ☐ Enables parallel activities
- ☐ Helps optimize staff assignments

Improved Planning and Management

- ☐ Facilitates business process adaptability
- ☐ Assists in optimizing business processes
- ☐ Tracks results and process cycle time
- ☐ Reduces duplicate documentation
- ☐ Helps meet government quality and regulatory documentation requirements

SOURCE: Reprinted with permission from Workflow Management Solutions, http://www.sybase.com, May 28, 1997.

occurs. Copies of examination results, diagnosis, and recommended treatment then immediately go to the patient's referring physician.[24]

An electronic document management system can range in complexity from a simple file tracking system to a fully integrated work-flow system that incorporates diverse functional areas.[25] Figure 8.7 shows a screen from such a system. High-quality document management systems can handle documents from a number of systems, such as

FIGURE 8.7 This screen from a document management system helps track electronic documents through a large organization.

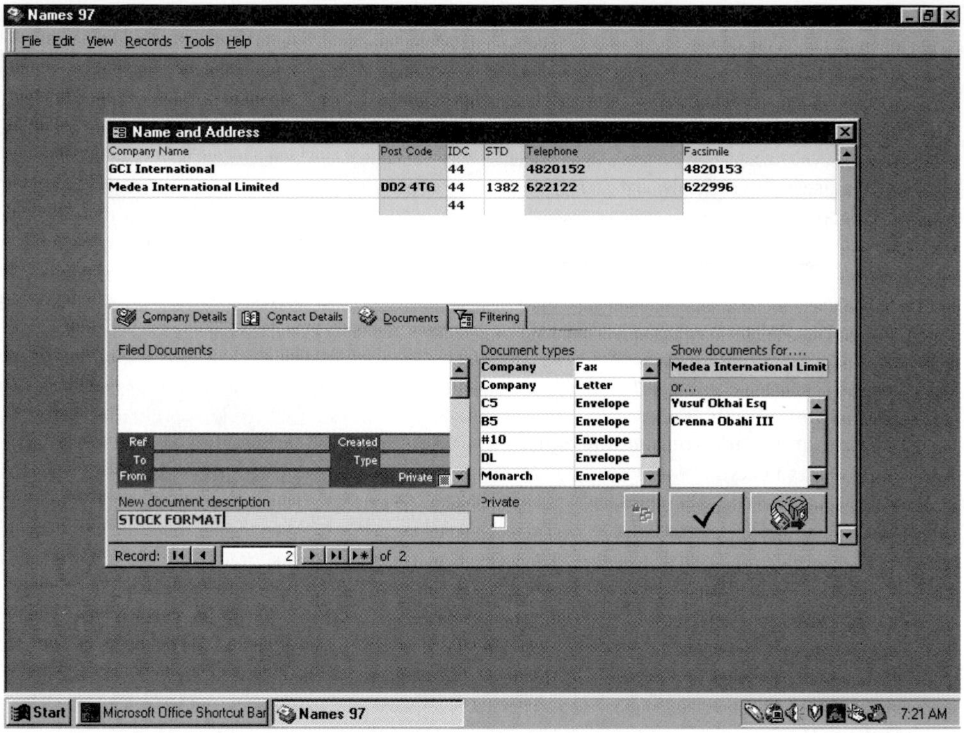

electronic imaging systems, sophisticated database systems, and publishing systems.[26] Such systems typically include three components:[27]

- *Document Creation.* Complex document management systems require advanced authoring software that integrates work from multiple sources easily.
- *Document Storage and Routing.* Companies require software that effectively organizes and accesses documents, recognizes the status of all documents, and provides sufficient security to ensure their integrity.
- *Document Retrieval and Manipulation.* Companies can publish completed documents or make them available electronically. Life insurance agents, for example, search and retrieve documents while at clients' offices.

Fireman's Fund Insurance, in partnership with Executech, a value-added reseller in Norwalk, Connecticut, has created a document management system that provides full text searches of 9 million pages of legal documents. The insurance company introduced the system to help it respond to a court-ordered requirement to locate and deliver any paperwork relating to environmental lawsuits involving the company. Company representatives scan documents in motels near their origin, and then Executech implements the rest of the scanning and management systems. Not only is this system faster than the microfilm system it replaced, but it costs only a small fraction of what the microfilm system costs to run.[28]

Document management systems can have a significant impact on the time and expense involved in processing documents. For example, the registry of deeds in Essex County, Massachusetts, used a document management system to reduce the processing of paperwork for property sales from 48 hours to five minutes.[29] Solvay Human Health, a drug manufacturer, now assembles the 120,000 pages of a federal drug-approval application in two hours rather than three weeks.[30] Hoechst, another drug manufacturer, reduced the drug application time for Dolasetron, an antinausea medicine, from 40 to 17 weeks and for Fexofenadrine, an antihistamine, from 52 to 24 weeks by replacing its manual document-gathering system with an automated one.[31]

SALES FORCE AUTOMATION

Just as many office workers and managers still rely on paper to record, exchange, and store information, many salespeople use Post-it notes, index cards, or memo pads to track sales leads. Many district or regional managers still prepare typed summary reports for distribution to their salespeople. **Sales force automation** dramatically changes this way of doing business. It replaces manual systems of tracking leads, sales, service requests, and other sales-related information with computerized systems that use sophisticated database software and laptop computers. It supports salespeople by taking care of routine activities and providing them with the information they need to close new sales and support current customers. The 800-person sales force at Yellow Freight System Inc., a Kansas trucking firm, uses automated sales software that allows them to retrieve customer information and complete administrative work on the road. In addition to using the system to solve more customer problems as they meet face-to-face with clients, the sales reps can use e-mail to easily obtain transportation plans designed for other reps' customers that might apply to their customers.[32]

SALES SUPPORT

Automating sales requires a special set of software applications. Its core includes a prospect database—a list of potential customers and key information about them. A sales automation system can sort this database by industry, company, company size, sales-call history, purchasing history, product requirements, and other characteristics. Figure 8.8 shows a screen from such a database. Word processing, electronic mail, graphics, spreadsheets, and other applications work with the prospect database to provide instantaneous summary reports.

MCI invested $75 million in an automated system that included outfitting 5,600 field sales and technical employees with laptops and links to the corporate sales and customer service database. The salespeople submit orders and can access data about the customer and the product. They even have online remote access to other employees who can answer customer questions immediately. Six months after the rollout, sales representative productivity increased by 21 percent and sales branches increased their revenue by 23 percent.[33]

FIGURE 8.8 This screen illustrates a prospect database, which includes key information about potential customers for use by salespeople.

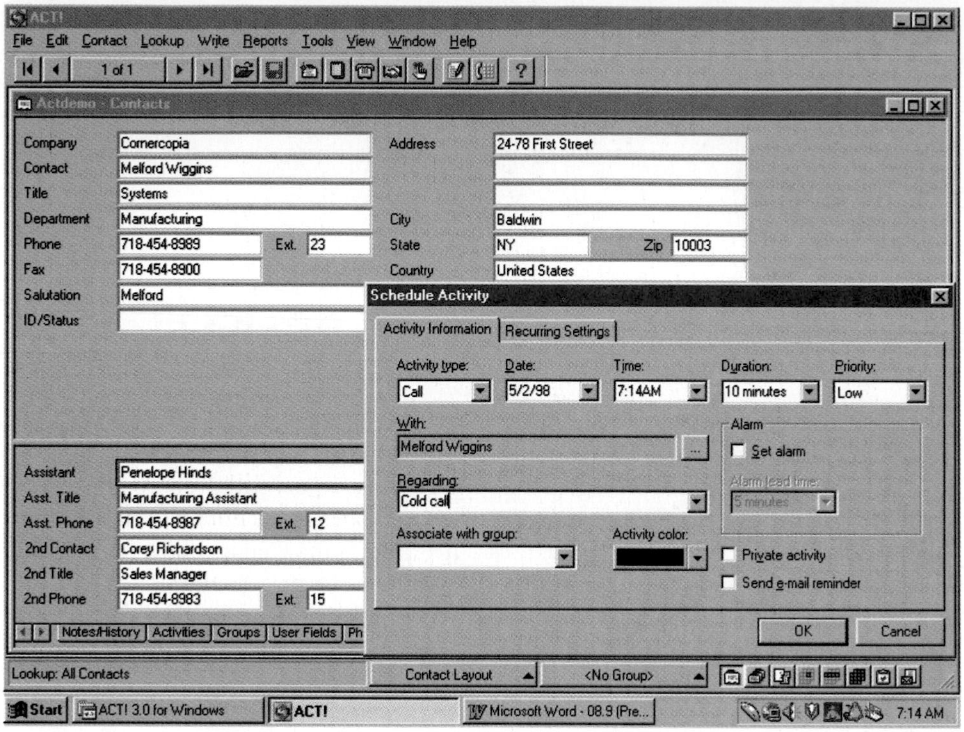

Sherlock, Pfizer Pharmaceutical's sales-automation system, combines information acquired by the company's 2,700 sales representatives about physicians' prescribing patterns and requirements of their managed-care organizations with information about the company's promotional programs. Sales representatives can then access critical information faster and so get the greatest payback from their short face-time with physicians. In one year sales rose 26 percent, in part due to Sherlock's impact.[34]

CUSTOMER SERVICE

Integrating field service into a sales force automation system can reap greater efficiency and cost savings for companies. Companies can use automation software to dispatch technicians, convey information about customers' products, and then update both product and customer information in the corporate database after their call.[35] Customer service systems generally have two components:[36]

- **Automated call directors** make sure customers' calls reach the appropriate person. These automated attendants need to have well-constructed initial menus so that callers can reach the correct person quickly.

INFORMATION TECHNOLOGY AND GLOBAL BUSINESS

The VeriFone sales rep knew his big sale of the quarter was unraveling when he left the offices of an Athens bank at 4:30 P.M. A competitor had raised doubts about whether VeriFone could deliver a new payment-service technology, one that had not been used extensively in Greece. In fact, VeriFone was the main supplier of that technology in the United States and many other countries, with more than half a million installations and many satisfied customers. But the rep didn't have any particulars about those users to be able to make a rebuttal.

He scouted out the nearest phone and hooked up his laptop to it. Then he sent an SOS e-mail to all VeriFone sales, marketing, and technical-support staff worldwide. The e-mail launched a process that would create a virtual team to gather customers' testimonials and other data to make his case while he slept.

In San Francisco an international marketing staff member who was on duty to monitor such SOS calls got the message at home when he checked his e-mail at 6:30 A.M. He organized a conference call with two other marketing staffers, one in Atlanta and one in Hong Kong, where it was 9:30 A.M. and 10:30 P.M., respectively. Together they decided how to handle the data coming in from everyone who'd received the post. A few hours later the two U.S. team members spoke on the phone again while they used the company's wide area network to fine-tune a sales presentation that the San Francisco team leader had drafted. Before leaving for the day, the leader passed the presentation on to the Hong Kong team member so he could add Asian information to the detailed account of experiences and references when he arrived at work.

The Greek sales rep awakened a few hours later. He retrieved the presentation from the network, got to the bank by 8 A.M., and showed the customer the data on his laptop. Impressed by the speedy response to get business, the customer reasoned that VeriFone would also respond as fast to keep business. He placed the order.

SOURCE: Excerpted with permission from William R. Pape, Group insurance, *Inc. Technology* (2) (1997): 29.

- Computerized databases track customer service calls, problems, and repairs. These systems should provide accurate, up-to-date information. They should also offer the capability for clerks to override data-entry fields and insert comments about customers' questions, problems, and complaints.

Siemens Nixdorf Printing Systems links a database at headquarters to a national paging service that broadcasts to its technical support engineers. The designated service engineer receives the incident number, company name, name and telephone number of the person calling, and a brief problem description and then telephones the customer to set an arrival time. After providing the required service, the engineer calls dispatch, who then updates the customer database with the incident number, time spent on the call and traveling, and parts involved. This type of automation saved engineers one-half day a week of data entry and reduced data entry positions and overtime for the company.[37]

INTEGRATED SYSTEMS

High-quality integrated systems, such as those illustrated in Figure 8.9, should provide sales representatives with a picture of the entire relationship between their company and their customer. Sterling Software of Columbus, Ohio, lets its 30 field salespeople tap into a database newly consolidated from seven smaller databases and shared by sales, customer service, accounting, and marketing departments. People from different departments can obtain different views of the same data; for example, sales representatives see information for use in sales proposals and accountants see what products are sold at what price and which customers pay their bills.[38]

The success of sales force automation ultimately rests with the salespeople's willingness to use the new system. One study suggested that 80 percent of salespeople return to their old ways of doing business unless they receive significant training in the new system.[39] The system must also include tools that salespeople want. For example, one U.S. manufacturer automated three sales functions—lead generation, telesales,

FIGURE 8.9 New client/server applications are relying on distributed databases to provide mobile sales reps with an integrated view of their relationships with customers.

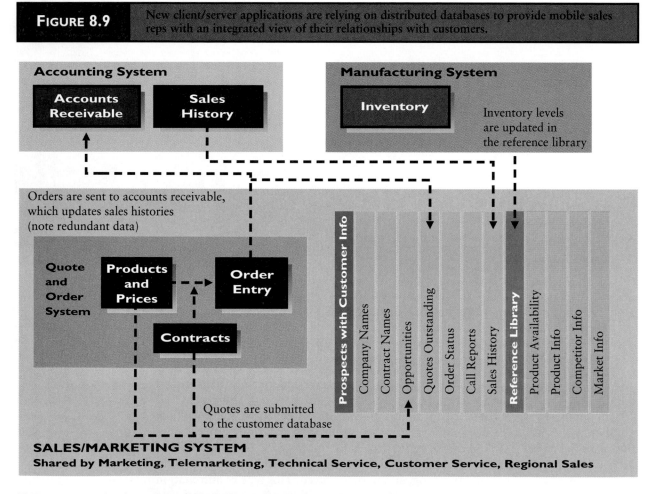

SOURCE: Reprinted with permission from Steve Alexander, Designed, sold, delivered, serviced, *Computerworld Client/Server Journal* (October 1995): 42.

and lead tracking—in response to sales force complaints that the company was technologically backward. After a $200,000 investment, with little use of the system by salespeople, management ended the project. The company executives later learned that the salespeople found their own leads, so had little use for lead generation and telesales, and that they considered lead tracking as a way of spying on them. What they had wanted instead were tools for pricing, product configuration, and credit checking.[40]

DESIGN AUTOMATION

Computers can help designers translate their mental images into physical drawings and specifications. Designers create and develop both products and processes.

- *Product design* refers to the creation of a concept and specifications for a finished good. For example, designers determine the specifications of a new videocamera or television set.
- *Process design* describes the creation and specification of equipment and procedures for manufacturing the finished goods. Designers develop the specifications for manufacturing the videocameras or televisions.

USES OF COMPUTER-AIDED DESIGN (CAD)

Computer-aided design supports both product and process design. Although computers recently have had some success in imitating human creativity,[41] they have contributed most to improving the design process by removing much of the drudgery from it. Today, for example, computers automatically transcribe the music that composers play on a piano-like keyboard input device. Computer-aided design has allowed carpet designers to create more daring designs, more easily custom-tailor orders, and manufacture them faster.[42]

Product and process designers can use computers to transcribe their ideas into engineering drawings, redraw designs from different angles, and evaluate the technical characteristics of alternative designs. Consider this. Designers use computers to make better basketballs, baseballs, and other sports equipment at Spalding Sports Worldwide. This company uses imaging software to improve its product development process. Developers create, share, discuss, and update product specifications online; they no longer send paper copies to offices around the world. The company now handles twice as many specifications and updates as it did before computerizing its design process and has reduced development time from one and one-half years to a few months.[43]

Engineers, architects, graphics designers, and others who compose their designs on a computer can view them from multiple perspectives, analyze them from an engineering perspective, edit them, document them, and output them in a format suitable for manufacturing the product. They also can save designs for subcomponents and insert them into other designs. Boeing used computers to design each part of the 777 aircraft and again used computers to fit each part into the three-dimensional puzzle of the finished aircraft before it reached the factory floor.[44]

ETHICAL ISSUES IN IT

Automation of life-critical systems often adds an element of risk. Consider these examples:

In August 1996, an airliner attempting to land in Cali, Columbia, crashed when the pilot mistakenly entered the airport code for Bogata instead of Cali into the aircraft's automated navigation system. The pilot realized the error too late to prevent the aircraft from turning around and heading into the side of a mountain.*

A flaw in a computer program controlling an automated cancer radiation treatment device killed one person and left two others deeply burned and partially paralyzed in three separate accidents in Texas and Georgia. The software defect was so subtle that the cause of the first two accidents remained a mystery until the third accident, almost a year later. †

In both cases, manufacturers had tested their equipment and software under a variety of conditions and thought that they were safe.

1. How can buyers of automation systems weigh their benefits against the risks involved? What are the ethical issues involved in automating systems that could threaten lives when they fail?
2. What steps should developers and vendors of automation systems take to minimize the risks of failure? What are the ethical issues involved in deciding how much testing is enough?

---

*Washington Post article (week of August 26, 1996), cited at http://irecall.com/vve/fiascos.htm, December 7, 1997.
†Richard Saltos, Boston Globe (June 20, 1986), p. 1, cited at http://catless.ncl.ac.uk/Risks/3.9.html, December 7, 1997.

Designers can also take their designs into the field. Members of the restaurant supplier Aramark's Design Group take laptops, projectors, and special software on-site to clients. They can change a drawing on the spot, show the client how the changes would appear, and then send the changes to the CAD department at their headquarters in Philadelphia.[45]

CAD software for networked computers allows several designers to work together on the design of complicated products. Worldwide Web communication software can support global product design by letting designers send a 3-D product model to anyone with Internet access worldwide.[46] BAA PLC, owner of Heathrow Airport, is using CAD software to replace the design paper trail with electronic drawings of its $550-million fast-track rail link to London. Contractors have instant access to the latest drawing revisions from remote design teams.[47]

Recent advances to CAD software should allow technical service people to retrieve CAD models of products, such as the wire-frame diagram shown in Figure 8.10. They can then use the CAD capabilities to see different views of the product as part of their repair instructions.[48] Consider how a CAD capability might help a technician service an MRI, X-ray, or ultrasound machine at Woods Memorial Hospital. The ability to easily obtain many views of the machine should ease troubleshooting and repair.

Computer-aided design can speed the design process by showing a true picture of the finished product. CAD can spot potential design mistakes before they occur in production. It also allows designers to focus more on the creative aspects and less on the mechanical aspects of product and process design.

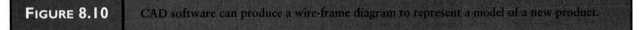

FIGURE 8.10   CAD software can produce a wire-frame diagram to represent a model of a new product.

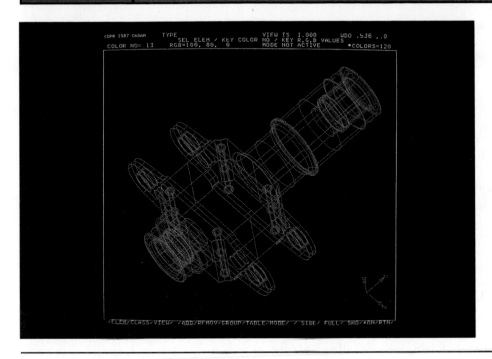

FEATURES OF CAD SOFTWARE

Computer-aided design (CAD) software automates many design processes and removes noncreative tasks associated with design. In selecting CAD software, users should consider how it handles composition, viewing, modeling, editing, documentation, output, and storage, as shown in Table 8.3. Think for a moment about designing part of an airplane. How might designers use the CAD software to make their job easier?

RAPID PROTOTYPING

Rapid prototyping refers to the conversion of an electronic computer-aided design model into a solid physical model. Imagine designing a product, pressing a key, and having a plastic, wax, metal, or ceramic model of the product produced in your office. A variety of technologies now support rapid prototyping at relatively low cost.[49] For example, a product called Sculptor, by Visual Impact, creates a physical model of a design by building it in slices. It uses one material to correspond to solid parts of the design and another material to correspond to the void or empty areas. The process ends with heating the cube; the material corresponding to the void or empty areas melts and drains away, leaving a model of the design. Alternatively, the solid part can melt away, leaving a mold for casting the product. In many cases rapid prototyping can reduce the design-to-market time by 75 percent or more.[50]

| **TABLE 8.3** | High-quality CAD design systems aid designers in composing, viewing, modeling, editing, documenting, outputting, and storing designs. |

Composition. CAD products should allow the user to scan in a hand-drawn sketch; use a pen interface to draw directly on the screen; import sketches from business graphics packages; or compose directly using a mouse, trackball, or keyboard. The software should include numerous sketching tools that support the drawing of a three-dimensional design from a single perspective, as two-dimensional slices at selected intervals, or as projections of the design from each of three dimensions.

Viewing. Users should be able to rotate an object, view it from any angle, or zoom into or from a particular point on the object. CAD products should also show the object in three dimensions as it would appear with light coming from one or more lamps placed at the user's direction, render it as a wire-frame diagram, display slices, or provide a physical model.

Modeling. Modeling allows users to determine not only how a design looks, but also how well it will perform, such as how well it stands up to heat or pressure, creates drag or noise, conducts heat, or resists fluid flowing through or around it. For example, CAD software can help design dies that stamp out parts from sheet metal. It can predict the thickness of material in different locations, as well as the distribution, wrinkles, tears, and deformation that occur after pressing.

Editing. Editing functions allow CAD users to modify a design simply and easily by moving, rotating, sizing, coloring, shading, and applying new textures to previously defined objects. CAD software also allows users to place several views of the design or parts of the design on the screen simultaneously, thereby showing the complete implications of the editing.

Documentation. Documentation consists of putting labels, measurements, and symbols on a design. Most CAD packages have standard tools that can rotate, size, and color text. CAD software can also attach nonprinting attributes—such as a part number, vendor, price, or other descriptive information—to parts or subparts of the design.

Output. CAD software generally supports a wide choice of printers and plotters that let the user zoom, position, and crop the picture during printing. Most software packages support a standard graphic storage format, such as GIF (Graphics Interchange Format) and TIFF (Tagged Image File Format), as well as the DXF (Drawing Exchange Format) and IGES (Initial Graphical Exchange Standard) used for exchanging designs between different CAD packages.

Storage. Product information managers control large volumes of engineering information; they store metadata about drawings and documents such as part numbers, date of last revision, storage location, and acceptable viewers.

SOURCES: From Paul Dvorak, FEA software shapes manufacturing's future, *Machine Design* (May 28, 1993): 102–114; and Seth B. Hunter, PIM systems manage the information morass, *Machine Design* (May 28, 1993): 114–124.

FACTORY AUTOMATION

Electronic machinery, including computers, can control, monitor, and generally support the manufacturing process of transforming raw materials into finished products. Consider this. Computers can replace humans in all steps in manufacturing ice cream, candy, food products, and an array of consumer goods. They can dramatically decrease the time required to produce an ingot-ton of steel or automobile parts. Managers can introduce computer-aided manufacturing, flexible manufacturing, robotics, automated guided vehicles, or computer-integrated manufacturing to automate manufacturing processes.

COMPUTER-AIDED MANUFACTURING (CAM)

Computer-aided manufacturing (CAM) systems partially or totally automate manufacturing. They offer advantages in reliability, control, training, quality, speed, and flexibility, as described in Table 8.4.

Managers must decide to what extent automation can replace human judgment in machine monitoring and control. Ideally, companies should use computers and humans to each perform what they do best. For example, automated systems vary in their ability to determine when to shut production lines for maintenance, evaluate which machinery or parts may cause quality problems in a finished product, and schedule the order and length of production runs of multiple products sharing production equipment. Some activities, such as the repair of some equipment, remain too complex for automation; rapid technical advances continue to address these limitations.

TABLE 8.4	Computer-aided manufacturing (CAM) systems automate production and assembly to provide advantages in reliability, control, training, quality, speed, and flexibility.

Advantage	Description
Reliability	Computers do not make as many mistakes, forget to act as expected, get sick as often, or tire.
Control	A single computer can control more machines and monitor them more frequently and precisely.
Training	Although automation requires training during start-up, workers can more easily transfer their knowledge to new computer systems.
Quality	Through its consistency and predictability, automated systems increase the quality of products.
Speed	Automated systems can produce goods more quickly by performing individual processes faster and reducing the time required for start-up.
Flexibility	Automated systems can more easily modify assembly lines and other parts of the manufacturing process to respond to changes in product and process.

Managers need to assess the feasibility, cost, and appropriateness of automation for their own operation. Although a single computer may replace several people, it can cost more to buy, operate, and maintain than the labor it replaces. System failures can also have disastrous consequences. A computer malfunction may affect many machines and reduce production for days or weeks, while a pool of operators in a manual production environment can generally compensate for the loss of a single machine operator.

FLEXIBLE MANUFACTURING

Flexible manufacturing requires that machinery potentially have multiple uses. This approach contrasts with having factories designed to produce a single product, such as one car model or one type of steel. Computers have made flexible manufacturing possible. Streparava s.p.a., an Italian company, builds machine parts for the automotive industry. They use equipment that can produce an array of parts on demand to meet performance, service, and environmental requirements.[51]

Because changes in product design generally required significant changes in manufacturing machinery and plant layout, managers had trouble responding quickly to changing customer requirements. Now, flexible manufacturing can support a rapid response to changes in customer demands.

ROBOTICS

A **robot** is a computer-controlled machine that has humanlike characteristics, such as intelligence, movement, and limbs or appendages. General Motors purchased the first commercial robot, called Unimate, in 1961. The early robots of the 1960s and 1970s were expensive and unreliable. The second generation of robots evolved in the mid-1980s and benefited from technical advances in both mechanics and electronics. Today's robots, as shown in Figure 8.11, have further gained from advances in computing technology that allow machines to perform tasks that were previously too complex for automation. The Scania Trucks plant at Oskarsham, Sweden, uses a robotic system to cut interior panels for truck cabs. Operators can customize the cabs' size, color, and special equipment.[52] In the pharmaceutical industry, robots can sample drugs for quality control during the intermediate stages of production. They also reduce the risk of contamination when compared to workers.[53]

Small, precise motors allow robots to position items more accurately than people can. Video cameras and pressure-sensitive sensors give robots sight and a sense of touch, enabling them to align one item with another. The Meta Torch system gives welding robots "sight" so they can avoid obstacles and deal with a changing welding environment.[54] Some experts believe that by the year 2025 robots will have replaced most machine operators, a job class that currently accounts for approximately eight percent of the workforce.[55]

Software allows a computer to identify and classify different types of objects, select those required for a given task, and move obstacles to the tasks. Companies use robots to monitor and control almost every type of equipment. Sony Electronics' San Diego television manufacturing division, for example, routes finished TV sets to

SOURCE: Courtesy of Ford Motor Company.

two robotic packaging stations. The use of these robots has increased production by more than 30 percent.[56]

AUTOMATED GUIDED VEHICLES (AGVS)

Automated guided vehicles (AGVs), as illustrated in Figure 8.12, are computer-controlled vehicles that move along a guidance system built into a factory or warehouse floor. Primarily used for material handling, employees can program them to retrieve parts for constructing an assembled unit. Modern AGVs can even depart from the guidance system for short distances as long as no obstacles block their paths. Frymaster, a large manufacturer of fryers for restaurants, uses AGVs to delivery inventory to the plant floor.[57] The Aluminum Company of America (Alcoa) uses AGVs to transport 28,000-pound coils from hot rolling to cold mill, slitting, cut-to-width, and packing stations.[58]

AGVs contribute to a flexible manufacturing environment. If a manufacturer mounts assembly line conveyors on AGVs, it can reconfigure its assembly lines simply by moving the AGVs. Workers and machines in such an environment then assemble the finished goods directly on the vehicles.[59]

FIGURE 8.12 Denver International Airport uses automated guided vehicles for handling baggage. Early problems in the system delayed the airport's opening.

COMPUTER-INTEGRATED MANUFACTURING (CIM)

Companies that design products that they can manufacture easily and efficiently have an advantage in the market place. Otherwise, design engineers spend a great deal of effort to produce a prototype that they cannot easily or cost-effectively manufacture.[60] Integrated systems permit design engineers to participate in the solution of manufacturing problems. These advanced computer automation systems can create a manufacturing plan from the design produced by design engineers.[61]

Computer-integrated manufacturing (CIM) refers to the coordination of CAD and CAM automation systems with each other and with information systems that relate to design and manufacturing. CIM attempts to improve business processes by sharing information across departments by automating the flow of data among design, manufacturing, and the other functional areas. It allows companies to respond more quickly to changes and threats in the environment.

Product designs benefit from a review by different functional groups: marketing people who have a customer orientation, production engineers who can anticipate manufacturing difficulties, financial planners and controllers who can pass judgment on the implications of the design for cost and financing, and senior management who can assess how well the designs reflect the company's strategic focus.

ADVANCED TECHNOLOGY

Unified messaging has the potential to change the way you work. Today, most users bounce around their electronic mail, fax, and voice systems to gather messages and information. A unified messaging system funnels all of those messages to a single, universal inbox that you can peruse with just a few clicks of the mouse or by speaking through a telephone handset.

Although vendors have talked about delivering unified messaging systems since the early 1990s, "unified messaging is not yet a broadly deployed technology, and many of the initial expectations were overstated," said Joseph Staples, senior vice president of worldwide marketing at Applied Voice Technology, Inc., of Kirkland, Washington.

The unified messaging systems have been delayed for several reasons:

- integrating several technologies is difficult;
- no standard application programming interface links voice-messaging systems to e-mail packages;
- voice-messaging system interfaces that would allow different vendors' voice-messaging systems to interoperate have evolved very slowly.

The Internet is helping to overcome these limitations. Voice-messaging vendors now view the Internet as the next infrastructure for their applications. "The Internet enables the traveling executive—the road warrior—to access messages," said Staples.

This has spurred two voice-messaging specs. One is the Electronic Messaging Association's Voice Profile for Internet Mail, which solves the problem of passing voice messages from one vendor's voice-messaging system to another's over the Net.

The second specification is the Internet Engineering Task Force's streaming audio specification, which defines how computers present voice messages to users. Applied Voice Technology's Staples said that while previous techniques delivered poor quality messages, streaming audio sounds almost as clear as a regular telephone connection.

The emergence of standards is good news for unified messaging. Unified messaging helps executives sort through information faster and more efficiently.

SOURCE: Excerpted from Technology issues have held back acceptance—Will the university inbox take off? *Communications Week* (June 23, 1997): SC32.

Production managers can better schedule their manufacturing equipment if they have access to product orders. Organizations can also integrate production schedules with inventory and purchasing systems to ensure the availability of materials for production. Because production requirements affect staffing, human resources information systems would benefit from integration with manufacturing systems.

The quality of products at Acro-Matic Plastics, a 19-machine plant in Leominster, Massachusetts, increased as a result of integrating a manufacturing monitoring system with accounting, quality, and manufacturing systems.[62] The effective implementation of CIM depends on careful planning and selection of technology that fits with both the operational and strategic needs of the company.

AUTOMATION OF EDUCATION AND TRAINING

Computers cannot yet totally replace teachers and trainers in a classroom. However, they can automate many of the functions that teachers traditionally perform, such as giving lectures, administering and grading multiple-choice examinations, showing slides or movies, and even answering student questions.

Increasingly, students have access to computers at a young age to prepare them for using computers in the educational process. An innovative program called Anytime Anywhere Learning pairs Microsoft software with Toshiba laptops for students in such diverse school systems as New York City School District No. 6 in Harlem, Snohomish School District in Washington State, and school districts in Melbourne, Australia. The program builds critical thinking skills and helps students take control of their learning process by using word processing, graphics, spreadsheet, and presentation software. "Engineers who visited one of [the] fifth grade classes were blown away by PowerPoint presentations given by young students."[63]

COMPUTER-BASED TRAINING (CBT)

Computer-based training (CBT) describes training programs that rely on the computerized presentation of materials. A study by SB Communications of Hingham, Massachusetts, suggested that most companies with more than 3,800 employees use computer-based training.[64]

CBT uses **courseware** to automate education and training. Automating education allows students to receive a customized experience at a relatively low cost. For example, computer software can mimic the role of a tutor, and training software can provide more explanation more slowly than otherwise possible. Woods Memorial might use automated training software to help educate office or technical staff. Computer software can also offer as much practice and testing as a student needs without substantially increasing the costs of training the individual. Finally, CBT can standardize the delivery of material and the assessment of outcomes across trainers: CBT exposes all students to the same material, resulting in a common set of skills and knowledge.

The Chattanooga Group, a $40 million manufacturer of rehabilitation equipment, put its 200-page manual for how to use its Kin-Com machine, a $35,000 to $50,000 machine that helps assess and exercise every muscle group, on disk using Microsoft PowerPoint. A trainer goes to a customer's clinic with the program and charges $1,500 a day. The company offers the training program, which includes interactive touch-screen technology, in Japanese, Spanish, and German. Using these and other types of CBT, the Chattanooga Group reduced its training staff from six to one and made its training profitable.[65]

Trainers use **authorware** to develop courseware, as shown in Figure 8.13.[66] Authorware software includes tools that allow developers to script text and incorporate audio, graphics, text, and animation into course materials. Recent advances have included the ability to incorporate peripheral presentation devices, such as interactive videos, CD-ROM, and other multimedia. Software for developing Web-based applications has become readily available. Authorware can also keep track of

FIGURE 8.13 Authorware supports the development of course materials used in distance education.

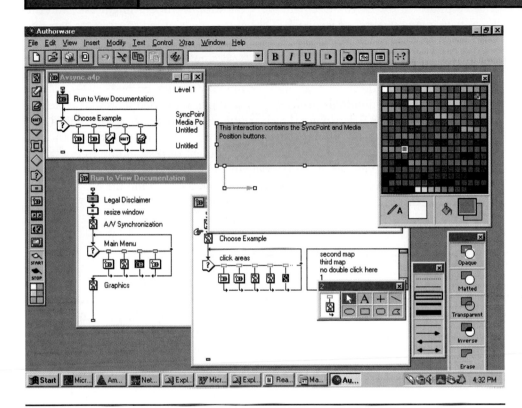

lesson parameters, such as the amount of time students spend on various questions or sections, the number of questions answered correctly, and whether students finish the course in the time allotted.[67]

Those responsible for training and development in organizations must first assess the training needs of workers and then determine whether automation of training and education meets these needs. Although companies can buy computer-based training programs, small companies often find them cost prohibitive. Professional Analysis Inc., a $16 million environmental and safety consulting firm, addressed this problem by transforming its in-house training to CBT when it hooked the personal computers in its four main offices into a wide area network. During downtime from other assignments, a staff programmer began to create and install in-house training materials. He first converted the benefits handbook to a disk using authorware that allowed him to include text, pictures, and many question-and-answer sections. He then focused on converting the quality control and OSHA training classes to CBT, creating an interactive format that allowed employees to click on terms they did not understand, and move from incorrect answers on tests to the relevant materials. Not only did CBT help the investment in the WAN pay off, but it also made training the 124 full-time and 200 part-time employees at eight offices across the country much easier.[68]

In addition to the high cost of developing software, the disadvantages of automating training include the lack of personal contact during training, the inability of computer software to anticipate every question a student might ask, and the difficulty in giving qualitative feedback. The value of developing courseware depends largely on the number of people who need training because the cost per person declines as the number of people trained increases. Sales of courseware outside the organization can help defray the expense of developing it. Some companies buy courseware from outside vendors as another way of reducing costs.

Although some individuals prefer to work alone, most people find the lack of personal contact in CBT detrimental to learning. Combining computer-based and instructor-led training can reduce such limitations. The combination can also increase qualitative feedback and alleviate the problem of responding to questions that the courseware developer did not anticipate. The most effective CBT programs combine appropriate self-pacing, interactivity between the user and the program, and use of multimedia.[69]

VIRTUAL REALITY AND CBT

A **virtual reality** environment, which allows the student to act upon and affect the computer images and other output in a realistic fashion, provides highly effective training. A student of human anatomy, for example, using a headset and gloves such as shown in Figure 8.14, can view a three-dimensional image of a brain, rotate it, zoom in and out, and even dissect it. For example, the University of Washington's Human Interface Technology Laboratory has created a virtual reality emergency room at a local hospital where medical students can get "hands on" experience in the classroom. The Laboratory for Integrated Medical Interface Technology has created a virtual reality operating room that shows the patient, equipment, and relevant data. Physicians can move and reposition the data like objects so they can confer in a natural-like setting.[70]

Trainers can also create a virtual reality environment by using a multimedia program that places an employee into real situations. At North West Water, for example, a video clip might state the following:

> You are on your first day of your new job as a customer service representative for North West Water, one of Great Britain's largest private utilities, when a worried customer calls. There are little "bits in the water," she says. So you ask what you think is a logical question: "Are they swimming?" The caller excitedly answers, "Yes, they're swimming all around." You know that little swimming things might be microorganisms, so you tell the customer the water is contaminated, warning, "Whatever you do, don't drink it!" But you neglected to ask enough questions and failed to learn that a crew working in the neighborhood had churned up "bits" of rust, dirt, and other debris.[71]

An on-screen mentor, a video clip of a real customer service representative, then explains the error and tells the trainee when he made the same mistake (or praises the trainee when he responds correctly). This experience allows trainees to make mistakes without causing damage and lets managers evaluate and correct employees' actions. It also gives trainees the competence that they will need when they assume the full responsibilities of their jobs.

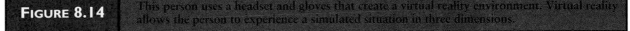

FIGURE 8.14   This person uses a headset and gloves that create a virtual reality environment. Virtual reality allows the person to experience a simulated situation in three dimensions.

Multimedia applications also speed instruction time. AMR Corporation used a multimedia system to train flight attendants to operate an electrical control panel in an emergency. Replacing a mock-up of the panel with multimedia training reduced training time from 90 to 25 minutes. Using multimedia also allowed standardization of the course materials, as well as increased coverage. Students' retention rate increased from 20 to 70 percent.[72]

Vitual reality can also help solve non-educational and organizational problems. Engineers at Searle used virtual reality to inspect a new factory they were planning to build. The engineers wore 3-D glasses and entered the virtual reality theater at the University of Illinois at Chicago. There they inspected the virtual ceiling and the virtual fluid bed drier, a major piece of equipment, of the proposed factory to determine whether the ceiling was high enough to accommodate the two pipes that sit on top of the fluid bed drier. They happily learned that the pipes would fit between the equipment and the steel girders in the ceiling.[73]

DISTANCE EDUCATION

Distance education uses data communication technology to bring educational resources to students at distant locations. These programs typically use videoconferencing, Web-based interactions, CD-ROM, electronic discussion groups, and other electronic formats to support skill acquisition and discussions. An instructor in

Milwaukee, Wisconsin, can use computers to simultaneously provide training to a company's employees in Singapore, New Zealand, and Mexico. Not only can employees seated at terminals connected to the communication system see and hear the instructor, but they can also enter questions or answers addressed to the instructor or other trainees at their terminals. An instructor in New York can take the trainees on a live tour through their manufacturing plant in Ireland guided by an employee at the Irish plant.

Interactions between the instructor and students can occur in numerous ways:[74]

- *One-Way, One Site-to-Multiple Sites.* Communication occurs in one direction and is broadcast from the teacher site to all remote student sites.
- *Two-Way, Site-to-Site.* Communication occurs simultaneously in both directions between two sites, such as from teacher site to remote student site and vice versa.
- *Partial Two-Way, Multiple Sites.* Communication occurs from the teacher site to all remote student sites. It also occurs from a single, selected student site to the teacher.
- *Two-Way, Multiple Sites.* Communication occurs simultaneously from every site to every other site. This type can also include more than one teacher.

Numerous universities, including the University of Wisconsin at Madison, Pennsylvania State University, and New York University offer distance learning programs that companies can incorporate into corporate training. The University of Alberta, for example, offers a unique Web-based program where all interactions occur on the Internet.[75]

EXPERT SYSTEMS

An **expert system (ES)** describes computer software that automates the role of an expert in a given field. The software supports workers as an expert would, helping them solve problems and make decisions (and even making decisions itself), and explaining the reasoning behind its recommendations. At Woods Memorial Hospital, for example, an expert system might help a doctor diagnose an illness with unusual symptoms by asking her a series of questions about the patient that helps pinpoint the diagnosis. Expert systems incorporate the findings of **artificial intelligence,** the branch of computer science that emulates human behavior and thought in computer hardware and software.[76]

Because expert systems can help people make decisions, many texts classify them as a tool for decision support (see Chapter 10). In practice, however, companies apply ESs most often to technical rather than managerial decision making. For example, repair technicians often use ESs to help them diagnose and solve problems with machinery. Human resources professionals might use expert systems to support staffing, training and development, and control activities. Table 8.5 lists an array of manufacturing application areas in which to use expert systems.

Expert systems may also automate training. They can provide instructions to trainees who do not know how to accomplish a particular task or solve a particular problem, and they can identify, correct, and explain errors that trainees might make

| **TABLE 8.5** | Managers can use expert systems for a variety of purposes in manufacturing alone. |

Configuration

Selection and arrangement of components of systems or facilities

Selection of quality assurance methods

Diagnosis

Computer hardware

Computer networks

Mechanical equipment

Mechanical parts

Electronic instruments

Circuits

Data exchange troubleshooting

Preventive maintenance of machines

Assembly

Robotic assembly

Visual verification of assembly techniques

Process or materials selection

Interpretation and Analysis

Interpretation of SPC data

Circuit analysis

Interpretation of diagnostic instrument output

Recommendation for disposition of rejected components and assemblies

Part master set-up

Incoming material inspection

Voice input of product faults

Identification of parts with vision systems

Automated visual inspection

Self-configuring production lines

Monitoring

Equipment

Factory monitoring/crisis management

Industrial reports

Product design for manufacturing

Open work on shop floor for dynamic reassignment of work due to down machines or material shortages

Planning

Asset and liability management

System specification and selection

Intelligent object-oriented material requirements planning

Contracts

Shop scheduling

Project management

Planning experiments

New product introduction

Computer-assisted process planning (routing and standards generation)

Object-oriented MRP

Design Systems

Object-oriented mechanical CAD

Manufacturability testing

VLSI

Circuit synthesis

Design of manufacturing facilities

Design of automated storage and retrieval systems

Process development (IDEF input and evaluation)

Software Development

Automated programming

Management

Preparation of first article delivery schedule

Return on investment planning

Intelligent policies and procedures

Education

Qualification of employees for technical jobs

Tutoring systems based on complete work (that is, the development of a test evaluation program that suggests changes for optimization to the test engineer)

SOURCE: Reprinted with permission from Dan Rasmus, AI in the '90s: Its impact on manufacturing, Part 2, *Manufacturing Systems* (January 1991):36.

FIGURE 8.18 Intelligent agents allow users to browse through complicated databases or the Internet more efficiently.

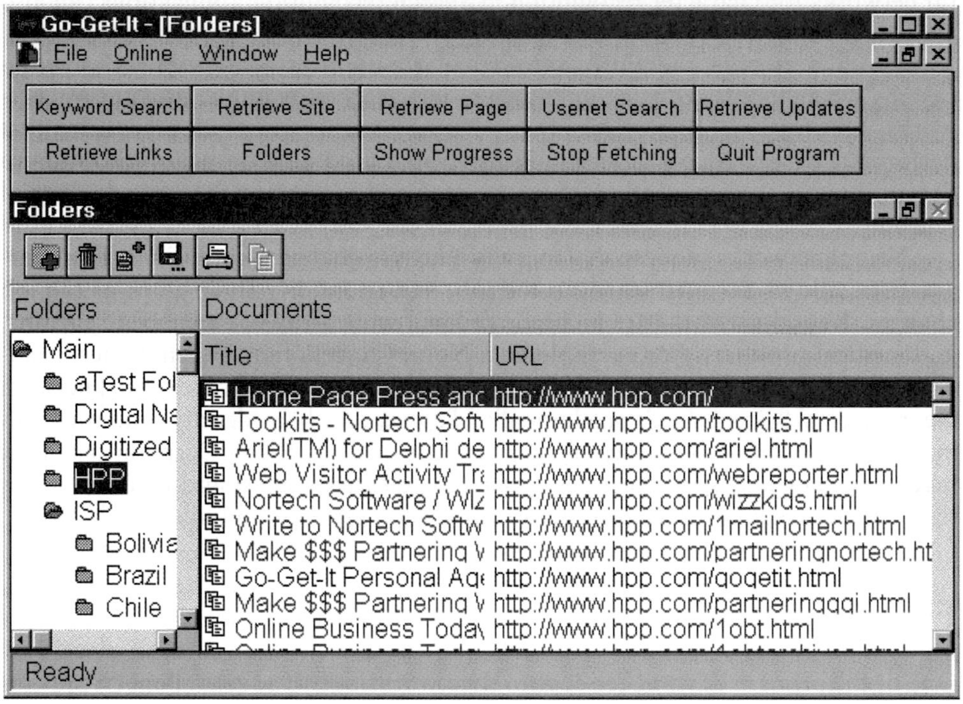

Andersen Consulting introduced Bargain Finder, an intelligent agent that lets customers compare prices at eight sources for compact disks on the Internet. Customers complete an electronic form at the BargainFinder Web site about what types of CDs they want, and the software automatically checks prices and gives the information to the user.[92] CareerSite, another Web site, uses intelligent agent technology to let users create profiles to match to job openings.[93]

Operating systems, e-mail applications, browsing software, work-flow systems, and network devices include intelligent agents. Here are some examples of how various types of software use intelligent agents:[94]

- *Systems and Network Management.* Intelligent agents can filter information about network traffic and device status and take automatic action to resolve network problems.
- *Mobile Access.* Intelligent agents can carry out user requests despite network disturbance.
- *Mail and Messaging.* These agents can help users handle e-mail more efficiently by sorting and prioritizing messages.[95]
- *Information Access and Management.* Intelligent agents can help users search, filter, categorize, prioritize, selectively disseminate, annotate, and share information and documents.
- *Collaboration.* Intelligent agents can help pinpoint information to be shared and arrange meetings by using lists or electronic agendas provided by the participants.

- *Work-Flow Management.* Intelligent agents can determine messaging requirements and then automate them.
- *Electronic Commerce.* Intelligent agents can do a user's shopping and return with recommendations for purchases. They can also represent sellers by providing product or service information and troubleshooting problems.
- *Adaptive User Interfaces.* Intelligent agents can learn user habits and help with problems; they help software become more humanlike in its interactions with people.

DEVELOPING EXPERT SYSTEMS

Given the quality and sophistication of today's ES shells, the critical and most difficult component of expert systems development is translating the knowledge of experts into the knowledge base that the shell software requires. A **knowledge engineer,** a professional trained to probe experts on how they know, understand, or suspect their diagnoses to be true, often performs this task. Advances in expert systems shells have improved their ability to obtain an expert's knowledge by directly asking the expert questions without the assistance or interference of a knowledge engineer. Recent research has found that experts can generally acquire the computer skills necessary to generate and test a knowledge base more easily and successfully than knowledge engineers can acquire knowledge about a particular problem domain.[96]

Developing an expert system, even to automate what appears to be a simple task, often takes a great deal of time. American Express, for example, required almost six months to develop a 520-rule prototype of an expert system called *Authorizer's Assistant,* which automates the authorization of credit-card purchases. The final product took more time to develop and included more than 1,000 rules. Was it worth the investment? American Express claims that Authorizer's Assistant now saves tens of millions of dollars per year and does the work of 700 authorization employees.[97] Coopers & Lybrand estimates that it spent almost $1 million on the development of *ExperTax,* an expert system to assist auditors performing corporate audits. The effort occupied more than 1,000 hours of some of Coopers & Lybrand's most expensive talent, but now this talent is available to each of its 96 offices through the *ExperTax* system.[98] Although examples like these are common, expert systems do not have to be complex to help address well-defined problems. Reportedly, most corporate expert systems use fewer than 100 rules and are built in a six-week to six-month time frame.[99]

SUMMARY

Automation describes the use of computers to perform tasks previously done by people. It increases the efficiency and reduces the cost of performing various tasks in the workplace. Besides replacing humans with machines, it redesigns the way jobs are done.

Office automation systems perform the functions of information storage, data analysis, document preparation, time management, and communication using computer hardware and software. Electronic imaging systems ease the translation of paper documents into computerized data files. The virtual office allows workers to perform office functions at remote sites, such as a client's company or home.

Work-flow automation refers to the computerized control and coordination of related activities in an organization. A work-flow management system drives, coordinates, and monitors the flow of activities in an organization that relate to administrative, production, and other business processes. Document management helps users keep track of stored electronic documents.

Sales force automation provides computerized systems for tracking sales leads, sales, service requests, and other sales-related information. Sales support includes a prospect database combined with other applications that provide instantaneous summary reports. Customer service systems include automated call directors and computerized databases to track service calls, problems, and repairs.

Computer-aided design (CAD) allows engineers, architects, graphics designers, and others to compose their product and process designs on a computer rather than on paper. Computer-aided design software includes composing, viewing, modeling, editing, documentation, storage, and output capabilities. Rapid prototyping refers to the conversion of an electronic computer-aided design model into a physical model.

Computer-aided manufacturing (CAM) automates machine monitoring and control through the use of flexible manufacturing, robotics, and automated guided vehicles. Computer-integrated manufacturing (CIM) coordinates CAM and CAD systems into an integrated information system that automates the sharing of data among departments.

Automating education and training occurs through the computer-based training materials composed of courseware developed with authorware. Students can learn in a virtual reality environment. They can also participate in distance learning, where computer and communication technology brings educational resources to students at remote locations.

Expert systems can support manufacturing, design, training, and numerous other activities. Composed of a knowledge base, an inference engine, an explanation module, and a user interface, an expert system automates the role of an expert in a given field. Neural networks are a class of self-teaching expert systems that operate by mimicking the human brain. Fuzzy logic extends the type of problems expert systems can handle to ambiguous situations. Developing expert systems can pose significant challenges to organizations.

KEY TERMS

after-hours telecommuting
artificial intelligence
authorware
automated call director
automated guided vehicle
automation
computer-aided design (CAD) software

computer-aided manufacturing (CAM)
  system
computer-based training
computer-integrated manufacturing
  (CIM)
courseware
distance education

electronic imaging management (EIM)
  system
expert system
expert systems shell software
explanation module
flexible manufacturing
fuzzy logic
image enabling
image processing
image work flow
inference engine
intelligent agent
intelligent messaging
knowledge base

knowledge engineer
neural network
rapid prototyping
robot
rule base
sales force automation
satellite office
telecommuting
user interface
virtual office
virtual reality
work-flow automation
work-flow management system

DISCUSSION AND REVIEW QUESTIONS

1. What is automation and what are its advantages?
2. What advantages do computerized systems offer over manual systems in offices?
3. What are the major functions of office automation?
4. What is an electronic desk and how do employees use it?
5. How do electronic imaging management systems work?
6. Why are companies increasing their use of the virtual office?
7. What types of work-flow automation exist in companies?
8. What does a typical document management system look like?
9. How does sales force automation change the activities of salespeople?
10. What advantages and disadvantages do integrated sales force automation systems offer?
11. What are the major uses of computer-aided design?
12. What are the important features of high-quality CAD software?
13. How does rapid prototyping improve the design and development process?
14. What advantages does computer-aided manufacturing offer?
15. How does flexible manufacturing make companies more responsive to their customers?
16. How do automated guided vehicles and robots differ?
17. How do courseware and authorware differ?
18. How can companies use distance education?
19. What are the components of an expert system?
20. How do expert systems use fuzzy logic?

IS ON THE WEB

Exercise 1: Follow the Chapter 8 Web links to vendors that produce CAD software. Visit the Web sites of four of such vendors, and examine the features of their software. Then compare and contrast their software products. In what ways are they similar? How do they differ?

Exercise 2: You can download expert systems development software as shareware or as evaluation/demo software. Follow the links for this chapter to download an expert systems development tool. Learn to use the tool. Create a small expert system to give advice on a subject about which you consider yourself an expert.

MINICASE

THRIVING ON BUREAUCRACY

We've all heard those infamous stories of the Pentagon's profligate ways—$250 for a hammer, $600 for a toilet seat. Rick Lewandowski, secretary-treasurer of MDP Construction Inc., has a few of his own.

You might think that having a spendthrift client like the U.S. military would be every small contractor's dream. But to hear Lewandowski tell it, there are plenty of nightmares, too. Even though every penny of MDP's $12 million in revenues comes from the government and the company stands to get a decent slice of the $87 million the Pentagon has earmarked for construction projects at Colorado military installations in 1997, it's a system fraught with such stifling bureaucratic inefficiency that most smaller contractors are at a decided disadvantage. Winning one of those fat government contracts, Lewandowski notes, means having to contend with a thicket of regulations and a mountain of paperwork. Even worse, he says, it means grappling with pointless and infuriating cost overruns and scheduling delays.

For Lewandowski, a self-taught computer fanatic since his own days in the military, the answer is automation: harnessing information technology (IT) to achieve efficiency and order in a business that's notorious for waste and chaos.

To appreciate the difference automation has made for Lewandowski's operations, you first have to envision the daunting trail of red tape that comes with a typical government construction contract. Take payroll, for example. On each project, Lewandowski has to file official documents showing that his company complies with the Davis-Bacon Act, which requires government contractors to pay at least the local prevailing union wage. He therefore must submit a weekly certified payroll for each of his subcontractors, which can number as many as 60 per week. The government also requires that the company file monthly equal-opportunity reports, weekly payroll tax reports, biweekly contract-progress reports, and an assortment of other standard forms.

Before a government contractor can procure the building materials for a given project, the firm must complete what is known as a submittal register, a form that lists the types and grades of the construction materials that will be used, sometimes

SOURCE: Case excerpted with permission from Christopher Caggiano, Thriving on bureaucracy, *Inc. Technology* (1) (1997): 63–66.

right down to the specs for nuts and bolts. Each item on the register—often more than 500 of them—must then be approved by as many as four different government officials. Simply clearing the register can amount to a full-time job. "You constantly have to prod them to make decisions," Lewandowski says. "Papers might sit on someone's desk for days."

Today, virtually every aspect of Lewandowski's business operation—in and out of the office—has been revamped by IT. Every piece of government-required paperwork, for example, has been scanned into MDP's network so that project supervisors equipped with laptops and modems can download any form from the company's file server. This function comes in handy when MDP has a project under way in a remote area because it enables supervisors to access necessary documents while remaining on-site. Supervisors can also gain instant access to subcontractor insurance and payroll information, serial letters, and submittal registers by logging onto MDP's databases.

Perhaps the biggest benefit MDP reaps from all this automation is the ability to coordinate logistics with improved speed and accuracy. Key to that end is a project-management program called SureTrak Project Manager, which Lewandowski uses to establish and track time lines for the myriad tasks of his construction projects. Manufactured by Primavera Systems Inc. and retailing for about $400, SureTrak is what software mavens refer to as a dynamic tool, which means that when the user makes changes in one task, the program automatically rearranges the schedules for all related tasks. Lewandowski finds that particularly helpful in critical path management—that is, identifying the tasks most important to keeping a project moving forward.

Because its graphical display function can process new information immediately, SureTrak allows Lewandowski to generate a precise time line for any job or subcontractor, revise deadlines and cost projections when modifications are requested, and produce daily progress reports.

Lewandowski and his project supervisors used to chart all those steps manually, an arduous effort when you're managing a complex construction project that can easily entail more than a thousand tasks. Now, at any point during the project, SureTrak gives them a snapshot of the big picture, dramatically improving their ability to anticipate obstacles and to compare actual progress with original goals.

Armed with SureTrak, Lewandowski no longer has to speculate about the consequences of delays or last-minute modifications. He can call up bar charts and crunch numbers to demonstrate how those alterations will affect the job overall. When MDP was building a fire station at Peterson Air Force Base in the fall of 1996, the government wanted to make a mid-project change in wall color. Using SureTrak, Lewandowski showed how that one "simple" change would add 12 weeks to the schedule. "It's not just waiting for the materials," he says. "It's all the other aspects of the job that the change delays." By clearly illustrating how even so-called minor project adjustments eat up time and money, Sure Trak's graphics capabilities can also help Lewandowski collect additional costs caused by delays, although he admits that this doesn't always work. "Often, we just do the work ahead of the dollars," he says, "but that's really dangerous."

Lewandowski says government officials have come to appreciate this streamlined efficiency—even though, at times, it's been cause for chagrin. He recalls a negotiation on one project during which government officials carped at him for not meeting project deadlines. "So I called up my submittal database," he smiles. "They had 120 submittals outstanding and didn't even know it. And they're telling me *I'm* behind schedule?"

All in all, though, Lewandowski has been pleased with his automation efforts. In fact, he plans to start a consulting business to help other construction companies do what he's done. Although computers aren't exactly unheard of in the construction industry, even in small operations, Lewandowski claims that a surprising number of companies still track everything on paper. "We already have two potential clients," he says.

The final irony: The government's inefficiency has not only made Lewandowski's current business more competitive, it has also given rise to a new business opportunity.

Case Questions

Diagnosis

1. What information needs did MDP Construction have?

Evaluation

2. How do MDP's automated systems meet these needs?
3. How well do the systems meet the Pentagon's requirements for information?

Design

4. How have MDP's systems changed since Lewandowski introduced automation?
5. What difference has automation made in MDP's operations?
6. What additional changes does Lewandowski plan?

Implementation

7. What have been the costs of automating the system?
8. Who has been responsible for automating the system?
9. How effective has the implementation process been?
10. What issues must Lewandowski address in moving to a Web-based system?

ACTIVITY 8.1   WILL AUTOMATION HELP?

Step 1:   Read each of the following cases. Then determine for each situation whether automation could improve it.

CASE 1

Fabulous Candy Company began in the owner's kitchen in 1970. The company soon opened a larger plant with ten employees who guided the manufacturing process. All candy was made by hand until the late 1970s, when the owner installed some assembly-line equipment to speed up the processing. In the 1980s, the company introduced a number of new products that sent sales skyrocketing. The company had difficulty keeping up with demand for chocolates in the original plant and soon opened several additional plants that produced more standard chocolate bars and other novelties. Company performance remained strong through most of the 1980s. Recently, some of the original employees, who had a strong sense of taste, color, and aesthetics, which was key for the chocolate production, retired. The owner of Fabulous Candy, which has become a major national candy manufacturer, feels that product quality and output are suffering.

CASE 2

Taco City is a national chain of fast-food franchises that sells Mexican-style food in the United States. Taco City recently made a public offering of stock and plans to expand from 150 outlets to 400 outlets in the next two years. Currently, individual franchise owners use a basic menu in their stores but can make any adjustments in the product they wish. For example, one store owner recently introduced a special hot sauce based on an old family recipe. The executives of Taco City believe that there may be some benefits to standardizing the product across all franchises and are considering automating purchasing, cooking, and sales.

CASE 3

Secretaries Inc. is a ten-person firm that provides secretarial and graphics design services to approximately 50 clients. A client calls Secretaries Inc. with job specifications, and the firm's office manager records the relevant information and then gives the client a price for the job. Assuming that the price is acceptable, the office manager then assigns the job to either the most qualified employee or a qualified employee with the lowest workload. Employees log in the job and then maintain a work log until it is finished. Currently, all record keeping is done manually.

CASE 4

Greybolt University, a moderate-sized private university, is experiencing significant financial problems. Increases in faculty salaries and benefits plus major capital improvements have had a tremendous impact on the university's budget. The school has introduced new technology to support classroom learning but has not used technology to increase class size or replace faculty in the classroom. The provost of Greybolt University has read extensively about the industry's experiences in automating training and is considering automating the classroom experience at Greybolt.

Step 2: For those situations in which automation would help, (1) identify the elements of the situation that should be automated, and (2) offer an approach for automating those elements.

Step 3: Individually, in small groups, or with the entire class, review your answers to step 2. Then answer the following questions:

1. What elements do the cases described in step 2 have in common?
2. What factors influence whether a system should be automated?
3. What options for automation exist?

ACTIVITY 8.2   AUTOMATING AN ATTORNEY'S OFFICE

Step 1:   Jeremy Smith and Joan Jackson have recently hired you to automate their legal office. They have a patent law practice that has grown dramatically since they received their law degrees five years ago. They have recently moved from Jeremy's house into a new office building. They have already added two paraprofessionals to their practice and plan to add two more attorneys within the next two years. Smith and Jackson know that they must have an administrative system that can support this growth.

Currently the office has one secretary/receptionist, Martha Elliot, who schedules clients, does client billings, updates their files, and generally performs the clerical and administrative functions of the office. She uses a personal computer for word processing but has not computerized any other aspects of her job. The attorneys have periodically hired temporary employees to assist Martha Elliot with the administrative work, but now they know that they must invest in automating the office. They are prepared to acquire the hardware and software necessary to support their practice as well as hire any additional staff required within reasonable limits.

Step 2:   In groups of two to four students, perform the following activities:

1. Diagnose the information needs in this practice.
2. Evaluate the current information systems.
3. Design improved systems by proposing a plan for automating the office. Be as specific as possible in proposing specific hardware and software. Design how the information will flow in the office and who will input and have access to the data. You may find it helpful to visit an attorney's office and interview the office staff to obtain a better understanding of how it functions.

Step 3:   Share your plans with the rest of the class. Compare the information needs you identified. Compare and contrast your evaluation of the existing system and design of new systems.

Step 4:   In small groups or with the entire class, answer the following questions:

1. What needs does office automation meet?
2. What types of processes should be automated?
3. What trade-offs must be made in selecting the hardware and software for automating the office?
4. What can the attorneys expect to be a reasonable cost for automating the administration of their practice?

ACTIVITY 8.3   AUTOMATING THE SALES FORCE AT RIGHT-TIME INSURANCE

Step 1:   Read the following scenario:

You have just been hired as the re gional sales manager for Right-Time Insurance. This medium-sized family company sells all types of insurance to customers in a Midwest city. The company has begun to automate some of the office procedures, but all salespeople use manual systems for getting leads, getting and providing information about products to customers, keeping track of customers' insurance needs and policies, and generally conducting and completing the sale.

You believe that it is time for the company to automate its sales and marketing activities. You know that software exists to handle most of the functions of the company, but you need to spend some time with the salespeople identifying their specific information needs.

Step 2: Individually or in small groups diagnose the information needs of the sales staff and offer a plan for automating the sales force at Right-Time Insurance.

Step 3: Share your plans with the rest of the class.

Step 4: In small groups or with the entire class, answer the following questions:

1. What types of processes should be automated?
2. What options exist for automating these processes?
3. What trade-offs would you make in selecting the hardware and software for automating the sales process?

THE AUTOMATED GUEST-HISTORY PROGRAM   ACTIVITY 8.4

Step 1: Read the following scenario:

Business traveler Chris Talioferro has just picked up luggage at the airport baggage claim area. As Chris steps out to the ground transportation stop, the hotel courtesy van is waiting to meet the flight. In the van is Talioferro's favorite caffeine-free soft drink. Arriving at the front desk, the clerk greets Chris by name and asks for a quick signature on the hotel's registration card. All relevant guest information is already on the card, including the method of payment. Just to be sure Talioferro hasn't changed plans, the clerk confirms that payment will be by Gold Card. Chris can see that his assigned room is the same as he had during his last stay at the hotel. During that visit Chris mentioned that the room's glass-topped dinette-style table was useful.

Entering the room, the bellhop turns the television to the CNN network, which the housekeeper noticed was always on when Talioferro occupied the room before. In the closet are much-needed hangers plus a personally monogrammed robe. On the table is the *International Herald Tribune,* the newspaper Chris requested during the last visit. Opening the minibar, Talioferro finds plenty of macadamia nuts (the minibar attendant noticed that five packages disappeared during Chris's last stay) and Famous Amos chocolate chip cookies. Chris also notices a bottle of 1964 Chateau Latour, a preferred wine. Finally, Chris notes a message from the concierge telling about tickets to tonight's performance at the theater.

SOURCE: Activity 8.4 scenario reprinted from Carl R. Ruthstrom and Charlene A. Dykman, *Information Systems for Managers Casebook* (St. Paul, MN: West, 1992): 67–68; adapted from Chekitan S. Dev and Bernard D. Ellis, Cornell University, Guest histories: An untapped resource, *The Cornell H.R.A. Quarterly* (August 1991): 29–37.

Step 2: Individually or in small groups, identify the components of the automated guest-history program described here.

Step 3: Write a program that incorporates three of these components into a mini guest-history program or create a computerized database to provide this information.

Step 4: Propose at least two additional components for the guest-history program.

ACTIVITY 8.5   THE TRAINING PROBLEM

Step 1: You are the director of training for a *Fortune 500* computer manufacturer. Your company conducts more than 3,000 seminars worldwide in both technical and managerial subjects. The company also sends numerous employees to courses at local colleges and universities throughout the world. Your training budget for the next year has been cut by 20 percent, although you are expected to continue the same level of training worldwide.

You know that there have been numerous advances in training that use multimedia, CD-ROM, videoconferencing, audioconferencing, and other computer-based technologies. Within the next few weeks you would like to conduct a pilot training program with one division of the company, one hundred people in each of four sites around the world who require training in a new software design approach.

Step 2: Individually or in small groups, offer a plan for this pilot training of 400 employees worldwide. Include options for automating some aspects of training to allow you to meet your budgetary constraints while maintaining your training target.

Step 3: In small groups or with the entire class, share your plans. Identify the advantages and disadvantages of each plan. Specify any additional options for automating aspects of the training.

RECOMMENDED READINGS

Boucher, Thomas O. *Computer Automation in Manufacturing: An Introduction.* London: Chapman & Hall, 1997.

Caldwell, D. G. (ed.) *Advanced Robotics & Intelligent Machines.* London: Institute of Electrical Engineers, 1996.

NOTES

1. Joshua Macht, Critical care, *Inc. Technology,* (2) (1996): 61–65.
2. Stephanie Stahl, Postal Service tries to slow paper chase, *Information Week* (August 28, 1995): 76.
3. Julia King, People who work at (fiber)glass company shouldn't use paper, *Computerworld* (April 21, 1997): 8.
4. Lisa Picarille, SmartSuite 97 offers 32-bit version of 1-2-3 application, *Computerworld* (March 3, 1997): 45, 48.
5. Robert L. Scheier, When less is better, *Computerworld* (August 18, 1997): 76.
6. Kim Secrist, Intelligent messaging system notifies plant personnel, *Control Engineering* 44 (3) (February 1997): 27–28.

7. Steve Anderson, How you can make document imaging work for your agency, *Rough Notes* 138(8) (August 1995): 26–30.

8. Bryant Duhon, Customer service—The ultimate premium, *Inform* 9(9) (October 1995): 52–53.

9. Peal Bosco, Imaging debt securities process, *Bank Systems and Technology* 32 (8) (August 1995): 29.

10. Simon Brady, High-tech organization, *Global Investor* (June 1996): 8.

11. Tony Baer, Picture worth 'n' words, *Manufacturing Systems* 14(3) (1996): 14.

12. Technology helps clerk keep lid on staff size, *American City and County* 11(13) (1996): 26.

13. Liz Moyer, Bank of America automating indirect car loans, *American Banker* (January 22, 1997): 22.

14. Kim Girard, Hold that (telephone) line, *Computerworld* (December 29, 1997/January 5, 1998): 31–32.

15. K. Burger, Offices without walls: Remote computing in the '90's, *Insurance & Technology* 17(8) (1992): 46–50.

16. This discussion of after-hours telecommuting is based on L.E. Duxbury, C.A. Higgins, and S. Mills, After-hours telecommuting and work-family conflict: A comparative analysis, *Information Systems Research* 3(2) (1992): 173–190.

17. Susana Schwartz, Intranet links loss control experts, customers, *Insurance and Technology* 21 (May 1996): 38–40.

18. Daniel Lyons, Northridge quake prompts Xerox to take care of its faults, *InfoWorld* 18 (June 3, 1996): 74.

19. Emily Leinfuss, Suppliers reposition to go with the flow, *Software Magazine* (February 1995): 69–73.

20. Workflow management solutions, http://www.sybase.com/Workflow/index.html, May 28, 1997.

21. Ibid.

22. David B. Black, Workflow, *Inform* 9 (September 1995): 56.

23. Barb Cole-Gomolski, Workflow system improves grocer's supplier ties, *Computerworld* (June 2, 1997): 53, 56.

24. Steve Alexander, Boston's Children's Hospital reduced its ER paper trail, *InfoWorld* 19 (March 10, 1997): 68.

25. Virginia A. Jones, Breaking free from traditional document management, *Office Systems* 13 (June 1996): 62–68.

26. Lynda Radosevich, Going with the flow, *Computerworld* (April 10, 1995): 87–97.

27. Ibid.

28. Martin J. Garvey, Digital discovery, *InformationWeek* (October 28, 1996): 107–108.

29. Chuck Appleby, Document witchcraft, *InformationWeek* (Janury 9, 1995): 59; Emily Kay, Order from chaos, *InformationWeek* (May 13, 1996): 65–74.

30. Kay, Order from chaos.

31. Thomas Hoffman, Document management helps medicine go down, *Computerworld* (June 10, 1996): 73.

32. Julia King, Trucking firm nets automation payback, *Computerworld* (July 17, 1995): 43.

33. Steve Alexander, Sales force automation, *Computerworld Client/Server Journal* (October 1995): 41–50; Mindy Blodgett, Virtual office prototype puts field service reps to work at 'hearth' of MCI, *Computerworld* (February 26, 1996): 73–76.

34. Jill Gambon, Sales sleuths find solutions, *InformationWeek* (July 22, 1996): 51–52.

35. Colleen Frye, Ground control to field service... Do you read me? *Client/Server Computing* (October 1995): 74–79.

36. William R. Pape, Putting customers on the line, *Inc. Technology* (1) (1997): 23–24.

37. Frye, Ground control to field service.

38. Steve Alexander, Remote users: Dialing for dollars, *Computerworld Client/Server Journal* (October 1995): 51.

39. Mike Fillon, The biggest myths about salesforce automation, *Client/Server Computing* (August 1996): 73–76.

40. Ibid.

41. See, for example, Kyle Heger, Whiz…bang…eureka! The automation of creativity, *Communication World* (November, 1991): 18–21; Patricia D. Prince, A showcase for computer art, *Personal Computing* 13 (October 1989): 132–134.

42. With CAD, carpet goes high tech, *Facilities Design and Management* 15 (October 1996): 50–52.

43. Tim Ouellette, Spalding Sports' Imaging, workflow system on tap, *Computerworld* (October 23, 1995): 57, 62.

44. Rochelle Garner, Flight crew, *Computerworld* (February 5, 1996): 66–67.

45. Road warriors: Aramark brings design company to its clients, *Nation's Restaurant News* 30 (November 18, 1996): 19.

46. Brian Kuttner and Dan Deitz, Reviewing designs in cyberspace, *Mechanical Engineering* 118 (December 1996): 56–58; Uri Klement, A global network for plant design, *Mechanical Engineering* 118 (December 1996): 52–54.

47. CAD network helps rail link *ENR* 237 (December 23, 1996): 13.

48. Sidney Hill, CAD vendoers saying "Ole!" *Manufacturing Systems* 13 (July 1995): 8.

49. See Dan Rasmus, Conceptually speaking, *Manufacturing Systems* (March 1993): 14–18, for examples of concept modeling.

50. Philip Balsmeier and Wendell J. Voisin, Rapid prototyping: State-of-the-art manufacturing, *Industrial Management* 39 (January/February 1997): 1–4.

51. Italian machine builders target lean production, *Manufacturing Engineering* 118 (January 1997): 22–24.

52. Robots on the cutting edge, *Robotics Today* 9 (Fourth Quarter 1996): 6–7.

53. Dennis Melamed, Robots on drugs, *Robotics World* 14 (Spring 1996): 21–23.

54. Sensing a better robotic weld, *Robotics Today* 9 (Fourth Quarter 1996): 6.

55. Robert K. Robinson, Ross L. Fink, and William B. Rose, Jr., *Robotics Today* 5 (Third Quarter, 1992): 5–6.

56. Robots tune in to Sony TVs packing, *Packaging Digest* 34 (January 1997): 76.

57. When it's hot, it sizzles, *Automatic ID News* 12 (September 1996): 18, 41.

58. John Schriefer, Automated coil handling to improve efficiency and quality, *Iron Age New Steel* 11 (August 1995): 60–62.

59. Guy Castleberry, *Robotics World* 10 (September 1992): 10, 12.

60. Julia King, Life in the slow lane, *Computerworld* (February 3, 1992): 67, 71.

61. Jerry R. Robertson, How to accelerate manufacturing, *Machine Design* 65 (April 9, 1993): 79–82.

62. Doug Smock, Conversion to Windows helps boost CIM systems, *Plastics World* 54 (November 1996): 41–45.

63. Neil Gross, Mindshare is a terrible thing to waste, *Business Week* (May 5, 1997): 88, 92.

64. Anne Field, Class act, *Inc. Technology* (1) (1997): 55–59.

65. Ibid.

66. Nick Rushby, The expanding market in authoring systems, Personnel Management 22(4) (1990): 89; Nico Krone, Third parties embrace windows for multimedia, *InfoWorld* 13 (February 25, 1991): S15.

67. See, for example, Gary P. Maul and David S. Spotts, A comparison of computer-based training and classroom instruction, *Industrial Engineering* 25 (February 1993): 25–27.

68. Field, Class act.

69. Bob Filipczak and Michele Picard, Put SPIMM in you CBT, *Training* 30(2) (1993): 12–14.

70. Chappell Brown, Experts' prognosis: Technology has potential as teaching, decision-making aid—Dose of VR prescribed for medical data, *Electronic Engineering Times* (August 12, 1996): 914.

71. Simson Garfinkel, AI as training tool, *Technology Review* (August/September 1995): 16–18.

72. Michael Sullivan-Trainer, Slogging to multimedia, *Computerworld* (July 24, 1995): 71–75.

73. Jane Stevens, Virtual Reality 1: Exploring the CAVE, *Technology Review* (March/April 1998): 16–17.

74. Factors that characterize a distance learning application, http://www.oit.itd.umich.edu/reports/DistanceLearn/sect2.html, May 28, 1997.

75. See University of Alberta Distance Education Web site at http://gpu.srv.ualberta.cal~tanderso/adi/deg/deframe.htm.

76. Dan Rasmus, AI in the '90s: Its impact on manufacturing, Part 1, *Manufacturing Systems* (December 1990): 30–34, discusses the relationship of artificial intelligence to robotics and expert systems.

77. Bob Francis, Help for the help desk, *Datamation* 39 (April 1993): 59–60.

78. Doug Fine, Help desk's new hat—Help desk takes on a new role, *Infoworld* (October 23, 1995), http://www.infoworld.com/cgi-bin/displayArchives.pl?dt_data43_71.htm.

79. Marialuisa Sanseverino and Fulvio Cascio, Model-based diagnosis for automotive repair, *IEEE Expert/Intelligent Systems and Their Applications* 12, 6 (November/December 1997).

80. Making brain waves, *CIO Archives* (January 15, 1996).

81. Otis Port, Computers that think are almost here, *Business Week* (July 17, 1995): 68–73.

82. Darryl K. Taft, OCR packages debut, *Computer Reseller News* (February 21, 1994): 139; E. I. Schwartz and J. B. Treece, Smart programs go to work: How applied-intelligence software makes decisions for the real world, *Business Week* (March 2, 1992): 97–105.

83. David E. Rumelhart, Bernard Widrow, and Michael A. Lehr, The basic ideas in neural networks, *Communications of the ACM* (March 1994): 87–92.

84. Gene Bylinsky, Computers that learn by doing, *Fortune* (September 6, 1993): 96–102.

85. Bernard Widrow, David E. Rumelhart, and Michael A. Lehr, Neural networks: Applications in industry, business, and science, *Communications of the ACM* (March 1994): 93–105.

86. Harlan L. Ethridge and Richard C. Brooks, Neural networks: A new technology, *CPA Journal* (March 1994): 36–39.

87. Port, Computers that think are almost here.

88. Matteo Lo Presti, Hardware vs. software routes to fuzzy, *Electronic Engineering Times* (July 29, 1996), http://www.techweb.com/se/linkthru.cgi?EET19960729S0056.

89. R. I. John and S. C. Bennett, The use of fuzzy sets for resource allocation in an advance request vehicle brokerage system: A case study, *Journal of the Operational Research Society* 48(2) (1997): 117–123.

90. Dan Richman, Let your agent handle it, *InformationWeek* (April 17, 1995): 44–56.

91. Justin Hibbard, Intelligent agents may boost broser speed, *Computerworld* (February 3, 1997): 57–58.

92. Julie Ritzer Ross, "Intelligent agent" test probes consumers' on-line shopping needs, Stores (November 1996): 47–48; Alan S. Horowitz, The next sales force, *Computerworld* (November 18, 1996): 3, 128.

93. Leslie Goff, CareerSite, *Computerworld* (November 18, 1997): 130.

94. Applications of intelligent agents, http://www.comedia.com/broadcatch/agent_thesis/h31.htm, May 28, 1997.

95. Michael Cooney, IBM agents are secret no more, *Network World* (January 13, 1997): 1, 37.

96. Marc H. Meyer and Kathleen Foley Curley, Putting expert systems technology to work, *Sloan Management Review* (Winter 1991): 21–31.

97. H. P. Newquist, It actually works!, *Computerworld* (April 18, 1994): 133, 135.

98. Ibid.

99. Harvey Newquist, Nearly everything you want to know about AI, *Computerworld* (July 29, 1991): 64–65.

Chapter 9

Transaction Processing Systems

CHAPTER OUTLINE

LEARNING OBJECTIVES

After completing Chapter 9, you will be able to

1. Offer four reasons for recording transactions.
2. Illustrate the use of a TPS to record point-of-sale transactions.
3. Cite the key components of order-entry systems.
4. Illustrate the use of reservation systems for processing transactions.
5. Give two examples of purchasing/receiving systems.
6. Show why a general accounting system is a TPS.
7. Discuss ways of capturing and processing transactions.
8. Compare and contrast batch and real-time processing.
9. Offer an approach for developing fast, reliable, and accessible systems.
10. Comment about ways to update transaction processing systems.

ORDERING FROM BEAMSCOPE CANADA INC.

You can't blame Danny Gurizzan for being a little bit delighted with his company's new computer system, especially when he considers how things used to work. "When I say it was manual, I mean manual," says Gurizzan, director of business systems development and information technology at Beamscope Canada Inc., a Richmond Hill, Ontario, electronics distributor. "When a customer called to place an order, the clerk would scribble it down, run down the hall to the credit check guys, and flip through files and folders to see if their credit was OK." The clerk would then run to see whether Beamscope actually had the item in stock and then go back to the telephone to confirm the order.

Today, when Beamscope's largest customers call to purchase PCs, printers, software, or the latest Nintendo and Sony games, they connect over the Internet and an intranet, where they can browse 250,000 square feet of shelves holding 8,500 different products in the company's two warehouses. Customers can place orders themselves, check the status of previous orders, and download product literature. If an item is temporarily out of stock, the system will suggest a substitute or put the customer on a list for back orders.

All incoming shipments are barcoded and scanned. "When a new order comes in," Gurizzan explains, "our runners go out, pick the order, send it down a conveyor belt, and shoot it before and after with the RF gun. Then the order gets dropped, boxed, and put on the truck." The system is directly tied into United Parcel Service, Inc.'s electronic shipping system.

Under the old system, phone orders were manually routed to the warehouse, where they would sit for at least a week. Plus, it was hard to know what was actually in the warehouse and where it was. Now that orders are placed electronically, they show up

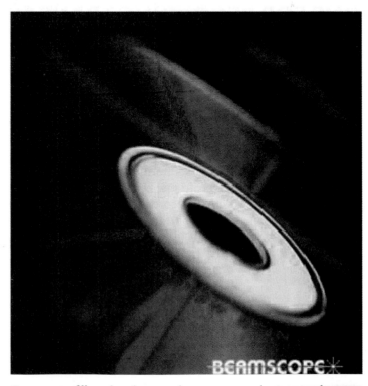

Beamscope fills orders faster and more accurately since implementing a new transaction processing system.

information to generate and mail the ticket and boarding pass. Still later, if the customer does not take the trip, another agent will use the transaction information to process a refund. Other transactions, such as aircraft and crew scheduling, must have occurred for the sale to succeed. Many different employees, each relying on the record of transactions to handle their own part of the job, perform the transactions that lead to and include the ticket sale and supply of the service.

As this example illustrates, businesses record transactions so that employees executing related activities can coordinate their work. However, even companies that have a single employee need to record transactions to track business activities over time. Consider, for example, an attorney who bills clients for the number of hours she works for them. The attorney records the time spent and the content of the work for each client so she can accurately bill her clients. When a client has questions about a bill a month or two later, the attorney can then explain her charges by telling the client precisely what work she had done and how much time she spent doing the work. In this case, recording the transaction preserves information needed to generate revenue.

INFORMATION FOR MANAGEMENT

Managers use summarized and detailed records of business to make decisions. They need to follow trends, identify problems, and verify that their decisions have the impact they expect. The warehouse manager at Beamscope might view all data about product delivery to assess whether UPS meets its delivery deadlines. The manager might also use data summaries to inform purchasing managers about inventory patterns. Seafood City, an independent supermarket chain in California, uses software called RETAIL to provide managers with accurate reports about inventory, price movements, and sales. These reports have helped them identify some inventory-loss problems. Seafood City electronically transfers data from each store to the company's main offices in West Covina, California. Analyzing these data about daily sales, inventory, prices, and store deposits gives managers better information about store performance.[2]

Decision-makers at all organizational levels use transaction data to make decisions. Chapter 10 further addresses how transaction processing systems feed data into managerial decision-making processes.

INFORMATION FOR CUSTOMERS, SUPPLIERS, AND BUSINESS PARTNERS

Transaction processing systems provide records of transactions between two companies and between a company and an individual. For example, as a customer of Beamscope, you would receive a receipt of any purchases you made. Although Beamscope may only need the internal record of the transaction made by its TPS, your physical receipt might be useful for reconciling your accounts monthly or for exchanging merchandise.

In transactions between two companies, receipts and other documents, such as purchase orders, produced by one company's TPS enable the other company to verify and record the transactions into its own TPS. For example, when Beamscope buys computers from a supplier located in another city, its purchasing agent probably sends the supplier an electronic purchase order communicating the items ordered, the expected price, the quantity, and the terms of sale. Upon receipt of the purchase order, the supplier's sales department may log the order into its TPS. When the supplier ships the order, its TPS will probably produce copies of the shipping documentation for the shipper and for Beamscope, and it will prepare an invoice for Beamscope. Beamscope's TPS needs this information to prepare for and verify the receipt of new inventory and to prepare to pay the supplier. Companies that exchange transaction data electronically using EDI (electronic data interchange) may eliminate some of these steps.

AUDIT TRAILS

Most countries have laws that require businesses to record transactions to substantiate the calculation of tax due to the government. In addition, the United States government and most state and foreign governments require every company doing business with them to verify periodically that the company charges fairly for the goods and services it sells. When government agencies audit a business, they use transaction records to trace and verify the company's reporting of its revenues and expenses.

Public corporations, those that sell stock to the public, have a fiduciary responsibility to accurately report their financial state. Most countries codify this responsibility into law and regulate it with government agencies such as the Securities and Exchange Commission in the United States. Companies in the United States must employ independent auditors to corroborate their financial reporting. These auditors rely on the company's transaction records to verify that its financial statements accurately summarize and reflect its business activities.

Companies also use audit trails internally to trace problems, as shown in Figure 9.2. For example, suppose a customer at Beamscope complains that he failed to receive an item he had ordered and paid for. Consider the trail of information the company might use to address this complaint. First the company would verify that it received the order and payment. Next the company would certify that it filled the order. Finally, the company would access the records that register the shipment of the order. The company identifies the shipping company, shipping date, and waybill number from these records. This information now allows the company to contact the shipper to verify delivery.

EXAMPLES OF TRANSACTION PROCESSING SYSTEMS

Transaction processing systems include components to collect, retrieve, and report transaction data, as well as make these data available for processing other transactions for management or strategic purposes. In this section, we examine point-of-sale systems, order-entry systems, distribution and logistics systems, purchasing/receiving systems, reservation systems, and general accounting systems. Although we discuss them as stand-alone applications, most companies include these TPS applications as components of a more comprehensive system.

| FIGURE 9.2 | Companies use audit trails to identify the sources of problems and to correct them. |

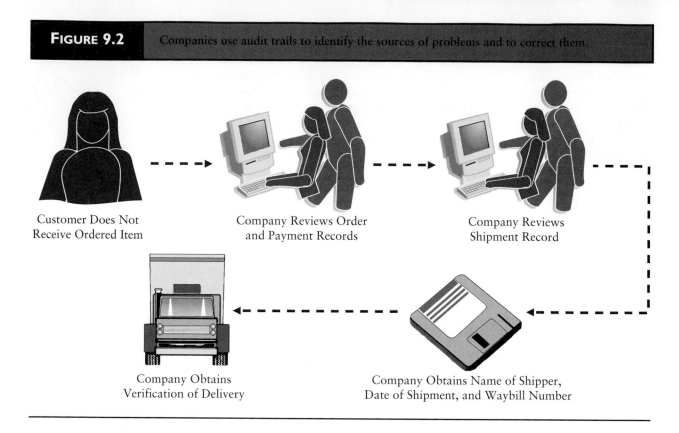

Customer Does Not
Receive Ordered Item

Company Reviews Order
and Payment Records

Company Reviews
Shipment Record

Company Obtains
Verification of Delivery

Company Obtains Name of Shipper,
Date of Shipment, and Waybill Number

POINT-OF-SALE (POS) SYSTEMS

A **point-of-sale (POS) system** records the sale of a product or service and updates company records related to the sale. Figure 9.3 shows a typical POS transaction.

A customer brings an item to the sales counter or register. The sales clerk scans the product code with a bar-code reader, manually enters the code for the product into the POS terminal, or presses the appropriate button for that product on the POS terminal. The POS system retrieves the price for the item and uses it to create a receipt for the customer and the company. The TPS records the type of item, sale price, method of payment, and often the time and date of purchase into the corporate database.

If the customer pays by check, the POS system might check with its own or an external database to verify that the person does not routinely write bad checks. In addition, it will receipt the check for processing at the bank. If the customer pays by credit card, the POS system might access a similar database to verify the customer's credit. It will process the request for payment by the credit-card company. If a customer uses a discount coupon, the TPS will store information relating to the coupon. The POS system will store key elements of the payment, such as the credit card or check number, along with the other transaction data.

The TPS may also store ancillary data, such as the zip code of the customer, which is entered by the sales clerk and subsequently used for marketing research. The POS system can track the amount of cash and checks in the register. Some systems

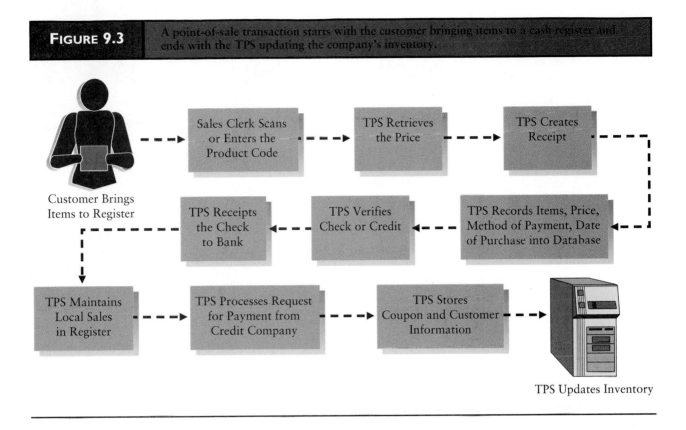

FIGURE 9.3 A point-of-sale transaction starts with the customer bringing items to a cash register and ends with the TPS updating the company's inventory.

also update inventory, either at the time of sale or in a batch process after the sales registers close. Point-of-sale systems can record service as well as sales transactions. For example, they might record service calls for appliance repairs or telephone installation. The state of Maine has designed a point-of-sale system for pharmacies to use in tracking Medicaid claims. Pharmacists, physicians, and Medicaid administrators can use an online database that stores all prescription information.[3]

Point-of-sale systems satisfy the business need to capture and supply information at the point of customer contact. They improve customer satisfaction by increasing the speed of the transaction, providing data to answer customers' questions, producing records and other receipts for the customer, and providing timely checks on transaction activities. They capture transactional and managerial information efficiently, accurately, and without delay.

Point-of-sale systems often use special input hardware to improve the speed, ease, and convenience of transacting a sale. They may include magnetic card readers to assist in processing credit-card and bank cash-card transactions and scanning devices to process bar codes attached to products and discount coupons. Wesleyan Assurance, for example, gives its agents laptops to use in its POS system, named Faith (financial advice in the home).[4]

POS terminals operate independently or are networked to a central computer. Independent terminals usually have more limited functionality because they have self-contained databases. For example, they may not contain pricing information or customer credit information. Diskettes can transfer transaction logs from independent

THE MANAGER IN ACTION

Tom Brown, vice president of purchasing at Aetna Insurance Company, needed to replace the company's antiquated procurement process, which cost the company $20 million a year. He considered his charge as reducing the costs of materials acquisitions and speeding the process for procuring goods, which currently took 50 days and 27 steps.

Brown replaced the company's financial software, which Aetna had developed in-house, with software from Walker Interactive Systems that let them obtain real-time analyses of purchasing trends. The new system lets Aetna focus on specific purchasing areas and has helped the company to limit the number of suppliers and thus reduce costs.

Implementation went fairly smoothly, even though it occurred as part of a reengineering of the purchasing department. "It was a little like blowing everything up and starting over," said Brown, "but it was done carefully and slowly with a plan and schedule that was reviewed daily. We ran the legacy and Walker systems in parallel for awhile, just in case. But from a timing standpoint, the transition worked: all of our milestones for the implementation were met."

Brown also needed to provide training for about 4,200 employees. The company trained 50 to 100 people at a time until they could use the system: "We physically sat with each one of them to make sure they understood how to use it," Brown added.

The company has saved more than $7.5 million in three years in copier-related costs alone and more than $45 million in total since introducing the new system. The new software decreased net material acquisition cost by 60 percent and reduced the time for procurement to one day and eight steps!

SOURCE: Based on Success in insurance, http://www.walker.com/walker/success/aetna.html, July 10, 1997.

POS stations located at a single site to a central computer for consolidation and batch processing to update sales and inventory databases. POS systems with stations located at several sites poll the POS terminals by telephone to collect the transaction records and provide an alternative to the real-time updating of inventory.[5] Diamond Shamrock, which operates 1,500 convenience stores, uses the Intelligent Retail Information System (Iris), which handles all in-store operations, including a point-of-sale system. The client/server system provides nightly feeders from the stores to the corporate databases by way of dial-up connections.[6]

Networked POS stations provide the benefit of centralized database management, greater storage, and increased computing power. If the central processor or the network fails, however, the failure affects all POS stations, which may significantly slow the selling process and reduce the number of sales. Installing a network may also be difficult and expensive and result in less flexibility for the organization. Wireless LANs (local area neworks) can provide a solution to this problem.[7] Pepsi Cola Allied Bottlers use Fast Access, a wireless sales order-entry system. Salespeople use handheld computers to place orders and monitor deliveries at customers' sites. They enter the amount of beverage to be shipped for the next delivery. The warehouse receives the orders and places the beverages on pallets for next-day delivery.[8]

Small companies often lack the expertise to select, purchase, install, and run a POS system. These companies can purchase services from businesses established to support their POS needs. For example, AT&T provides a service that links the POS terminals of a client company to computers at designated companies that perform the transaction processing for their clients.[9] Third-party vendors also perform credit checking.

Companies that want to run their POS systems in-house can purchase **turnkey systems** from POS vendors. Such systems include hardware and software that have been sufficiently customized for the target industry that buyers can simply plug them in and turn them on. Buyers can also select from a broad range of customized input devices, monitors, and keyboards, all of which interface with standard PCs running any of a number of customized POS vertical packages.

Wave Riding Vehicles, a retail surf shop with stores in Virginia Beach, Virginia, and Kitty Hawk, North Carolina, uses a POS that tracks specific customer purchases, assists with receipt of merchandise, and supports inventory control. To perform their last physical inventory, for example, employees scanned the merchandise, downloaded the information, and ran the reports.[10]

ORDER-ENTRY SYSTEMS

Order-entry systems record and process the taking of an order. Businesses such as pizza stores, mail-order distributors, insurance companies, newspaper advertising departments, and steel manufacturers use these systems to support prompt and rapid customer service. Order-entry systems can also capture information that helps obtain future orders from customers. Bell Atlantic, for example, introduced its Sale-Service Negotiation System to improve relationships between the customer and small-business telephone sales representatives and their customers. The system provides comprehensive information about customers, sales, and products. Bell Atlantic experienced a 30 percent increase in consumer product sales over three years, in part because of this order-entry system.[11]

An order-entry system typically functions as shown in Figure 9.4. When a customer calls to place an order, a clerk requests identifying information. For example, a customer number might appear on the merchandise catalog. Other companies use the customer's telephone number, birth date, corporate federal identification number, individual social security number, club membership number, or name. If the order-entry system determines that the company database includes the customer, the system will display additional identifying information, such as the customer's telephone number and address, for verification. The order-entry system may require the clerk to register an unregistered or incorrectly registered customer. This transaction updates the company's customer database. Occasionally order-entry systems, such as in the restaurant industry, do not require or store specific customer information.

The system next takes the order. An order-entry system should include many features of a POS system, such as identifying and recording the price and quantity of specific items purchased, as well as the method of payment. Unlike POS systems, however, order-entry systems may also require a shipping address, a billing address, and the ability to deal with back orders. Order-entry systems must verify the inventory of ordered goods so that the sales clerk can inform the customer about

FIGURE 9.4	An order-entry system records and processes the taking of an order in manufacturing or service businesses.

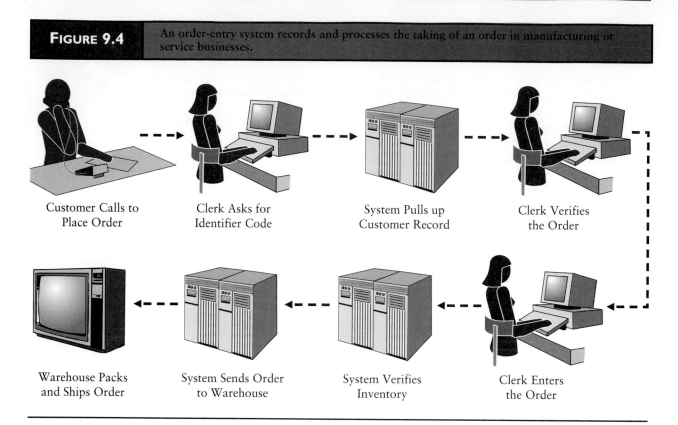

Customer Calls to Place Order   Clerk Asks for Identifier Code   System Pulls up Customer Record   Clerk Verifies the Order

Warehouse Packs and Ships Order   System Sends Order to Warehouse   System Verifies Inventory   Clerk Enters the Order

shipping delays and the system can generate orders to replenish depleted stock. Private Spring Water Company found that its order-entry system was too limited. It could not track the progress of orders after they were received. The company replaced the system with a more complete system that has since reduced order-processing time by 15 percent and saved thousands of dollars a month in rush shipping costs.[12]

Stanley Hardware uses a voice order-entry system to provide service to smaller volume and stock order customers. First the customer contacts customer service to obtain an account number and password. Then employees can dial into the system using a toll-free number. A recorded voice asks them to enter their customer number and password, which the system then verifies. Next the voice order system prompts the customer to enter the item number and quantity desired. The system repeats the information entered as confirmation. The caller then accepts or changes the information. Upon completion of the order, the system says the customer's reference number and ship date. The system can also ask customers if they wish a hard copy of the order, which they then receive by fax. The system validates all inputs, as well as information in Stanley's database.[13]

Order-entry systems differ markedly by industry and often need customization for companies within an industry. How would the data needed by a mail-order distributor, a fast-food chain, or an advertising department differ? A mail-order distributor uses a product number, which displays a product description. A fast-food chain uses a food name and size. A newspaper's advertising department accepts advertising text, its size, and date of publication. The order-entry systems must be specially designed to include the precise information needed by the businesses. For example, Brigham and Women's Hospital in Boston, like many other hospitals, now has a medical order-entry system that flags potentially dangerous prescription orders.[14]

Firearms dealers in California use a specially designed order-entry system. Previously dealers sent a record of sale by mail to the state's Department of Justice for a criminal cross-check, a process that could take as long as 20 days. Now an automated transaction processing system sends the order electronically to the Justice Department for approval, significantly reducing the time between purchase and approval. The system automatically checks 60 items on the dealer's application to the Justice Department on behalf of the customer. MCI, the computer system vendor, will track purchases and bill dealers monthly for fees owed to the Justice Department.[15]

DISTRIBUTION AND LOGISTICS SYSTEMS

Systems that move, store, and track inventory complement point-of-sale and order-entry systems. Transaction processing systems handle inventory by first monitoring its arrival in the warehouse. They can maintain a database of items catalogued by number, style, color, quantity, and other features. They then interface with POS or order-entry systems to restock supplies. Distribution systems also automatically reorder from vendors when inventory reaches unacceptably low levels. Ryder Trucking, for example, has seen major gains from inventory management. For example, Ryder designed a logistics system for Saturn Motors that schedules the arrival of parts just in time to assemble cars.[16]

But distribution systems can also experience major problems. Difficulties arise when companies hire untested vendors and introduce proprietary systems that require a lot of debugging. Particular problems can occur in warehouses where the systems need to coordinate complex equipment, such as tilting trays, conveyor belts, and lifting equipment.[17]

When Adidas, the shoe manufacturer, tried to introduce a new warehouse distribution system, it had constant problems. Adidas planned to increase capacity and productivity and reduce staff and delivery times by introducing a computerized warehouse system. The company planned to pass bar-coded items through a central tilt-tray sorter, which would next drop the shoes and apparel into chutes directed toward stocking or shipment. Wireless computers mounted on armbands and terminals mounted on trucks or at the end of conveyor lines would give workers picking instructions. The software that ran the system did not work properly. Inadequate documentation prevented the IS staff from fixing software bugs introduced by the vendor's attempt to modify the software for Adidas's Stratus computers. Furthermore, Adidas went online with the new system before the project was completed. Problems with the system resulted in major shortages of athletic equipment to retailers, reducing one retailer's sales by about 90 percent.[18]

Shipping of goods comprises a significant part of logistics and distribution systems. Transaction processing systems support the logistics of shipment delivery particularly well. VF Corporation, which distributes women's apparel such as blue jeans and lingerie, uses a computerized market-response system to help restock its shelves. In contrast to the month it can take to replenish stock of Levi's jeans, VF can stock Lee and Wranglers within three days of an order. For example, Wal-Mart sends sales data about Wrangler jeans collected on its register scanners directly to VF. If VF has the jeans in stock, it sends replacements the next day. Otherwise VF's computers automatically order them and ship them within a week. Of course, VF is not the only company with such a system. JCPenney already has its own, so that it can restock as fast as VF can.[19]

Managers see reducing the costs of shipping as having a major potential for cost savings. Computerized systems can help them identify the fastest and lowest cost shipping routes. They also can identify the best sizes and combinations of goods for shipment. For example, Trane, manufacturers of residential heating and air conditioning systems, uses software that produces a loading diagram designed to optimize the use of space for its shipment.[20] Tracking shipments also improves with these transaction processing systems.

FMC Resource Management, for example, received complaints from customers that its shipments were too large. FMC made the decision to keep a larger inventory and ship goods to customers more often. But going from 25 outbound shipments daily to 500 or 1,000 created major logistical problems. The company solved these problems by introducing an automated system that routes and tracks packages almost instantly and chooses from several overnight carriers to get the best price. Sales went from $600,000 to $16 million in about eight years.[21]

Companies can also use transaction processing systems to improve their own fleet management. Winston Flowers, a $12 million Boston-area florist, uses an order-entry and tracking system that comes with electronic maps and bar-code scanners. When a person orders flowers, the operator enters his name and address. The computer looks through a database of maps to verify the address and assign the delivery to one of 15 delivery zones. The system prints the order and a bar-code tag in the flower design area. The designer arranges and tags the flowers. A warehouse worker then checks the zone on the tag and carries the flowers to the correct loading bay. The driver scans the tag before loading the flowers, recording the time the flowers left the building and the driver. The driver then radios the dispatcher or returns to the warehouse after the delivery and updates the record. The system keeps a running record of drivers' commissions, which is about 40 percent of the delivery fee, and can total them with a single keystroke. The system can also provide routes and maps for inexperienced drivers. The company believes that the new system has paid off, particularly in improved customer service.[22]

PURCHASING/RECEIVING SYSTEMS

Purchasing/receiving systems document transactions between a company and its suppliers. Beamscope Canada likely incorporates a purchase/receiving system into its transaction processing system. Such purchasing transactions have both internal and external implications, as suggested in Figure 9.5.

When a company orders goods, it either pays for the goods at the time of the order or commits to paying for them at a later date. In either case, the order reduces the budget available for further orders of a similar type. The purchasing TPS records

| **FIGURE 9.5** | Ordering goods has numerous consequences for other parts of a purchasing system. |

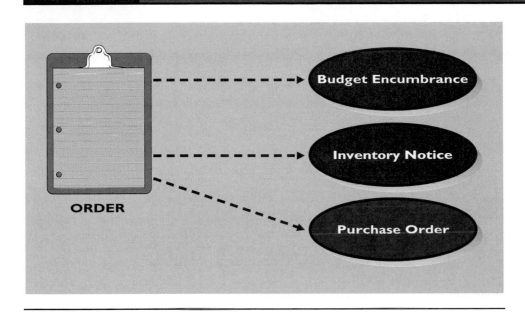

the encumbrance on the budget so that other people who use the same budget can determine whether additional funds remain.

An order may produce an inventory notice to advise clerks and managers that inventory is being replenished. This notice reduces the likelihood that other employees will place or attempt to place duplicate orders. Also, the notice allows order-entry clerks to advise customers that the items they need will shortly be in stock.

An order also produces and records a purchase order. A purchase order is a form sent to a supplier to document an order. The purchasing staff can reference the purchase order record when suppliers call with questions about the order. In some cases, the TPS may use EDI to transfer the order electronically to the supplier. An electronic copy of the EDI order sent to the supplier serves as the purchase order record.

When the supplier ships the items ordered, it may send an EDI or paper record of the shipment that usually arrives prior to the shipment itself. The TPS logs this record to alert receiving and inventory clerks and managers to the impending delivery. If the delivery does not arrive when expected, clerks can contact the shipping company to address the difficulty.

The arrival of the shipment generates additional transaction records. A record of the shipment's contents notes any discrepancy between the contents and the order. The customer can then accept or return the order. In addition, the customer may perform quality tests on the received goods. The TPS logs the results of these tests so that managers responsible for deciding what suppliers to use for future orders can base their decisions on concrete data. The TPS then updates the inventory with goods passing the quality tests. It may also generate an order return record, packing slips, and quality documentation for items not passing quality

GENERAL ACCOUNTING SYSTEMS

Every financial transaction affects the income statement and the balance sheet of the company. Fleet Capital, for example, has a general ledger system that automates key financial processes using a client/server environment. Its integrated financial database provides the company with information that supports decision making.[27] Integrated accounting systems generally include the following subsystems:

- **Payroll systems** track employee hours, wages, and other benefits; they automatically generate paychecks and records of additional benefits or payments to employees on a prescribed schedule.
- **Accounts receivable systems** track money owed to the company as payment for goods and services provided; the TPS may generate reports used for checking credit, monitoring bad debts, pursuing overdue accounts, and reducing payment lags.
- **Accounts payable systems** may generate purchase orders and produce checks for paying the organization's bills. The accounts payable system may automatically review the discounts received by the company for early payment of bills, select the optimal time for paying the bills, and automatically generate the check.

A **general accounting system** records all financial transactions and classifies them into specific accounts. Periodically, the TPS summarizes and consolidates these accounts so that managers and investors can assess the financial health of the company. Nevertheless, the TPS retains the transaction detail for some period so that auditors can verify the accuracy of the accounting system. Barrie Pace, a direct mail seller of women's clothing, replaced its accounting system with an internal, PC-based system that gives the company instant access to data and produces reports on a timely fashion. For example, managers can view the general ledger account history and then easily show supporting documents.[28]

General ledger systems often accompany other electronic systems such as those listed in Table 9.1. For example, Pet Food Warehouse uses Merchandise Management System, which includes modules for inventory management, sales tracking, and merchandise planning, in addition to the general ledger module.[29]

CHARACTERISTICS OF TRANSACTION PROCESSING SYSTEMS

Transaction processing systems capture and transcribe data. They perform these functions using either batch or real-time processing.

CAPTURING AND TRANSCRIBING DATA

As Figure 9.7 illustrates, companies can capture data in either paper or electronic form. Data captured on paper must be processed manually or converted into an electronic form to be processed by computer. Data captured electronically generally

TABLE 9.1	Integrated accounting systems often include modules, such as those shown here, to process many types of transactions that can affect the general ledger.

Software Module	Function
Bill of materials/manufacturing	Generates work orders for assembling components from their parts, creates work in process from raw goods, generates inventory from work in process
Billing	Generates account statements and bills to customers
Cash management	Maintains information about the receipt and distribution of cash
Credit-card authorization	Interfaces with order processing and accounts receivable
Fixed-asset accounting	Depreciates and amortizes fixed assets
Inventory control	Reorders stock, transfers stock among warehouses, values inventory, records shipment receipts, records picked items
Investment tracking	Records investment transactions
Order processing	Enters and processes orders, prepares pick lists, prepares packing orders, interfaces with invoicing and accounts receivable
Purchasing	Prices alternatives, creates purchase orders, tracks receipts, interfaces with accounts payable

undergo some simple verification and storage processing during data collection. Travelers Insurance Co. switched to a paperless system for processing workers' compensation cases at its 50 remote sites. Previously case managers handed unfinished cases to clerical people who lacked the information they needed to handle the claims. The new system makes it easier to track claims and resolve them. Experienced case

FIGURE 9.7	Transaction processing systems can capture and process data both manually and electronically.

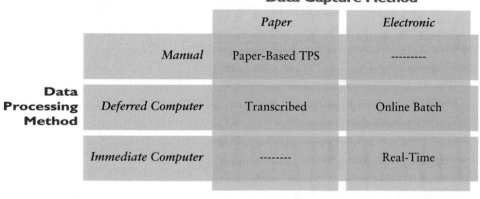

Data Capture Method

Data Processing Method		Paper	Electronic
	Manual	Paper-Based TPS	---------
	Deferred Computer	Transcribed	Online Batch
	Immediate Computer	--------	Real-Time

managers now have a clear picture of an entire case and can now handle a 100-case rather than the former 30-case workload.[30]

Paper Data. Predesigned forms, called **source documents**, capture transactions on paper and provide a secure, hardcopy record of transactions. Examples of source documents include purchase orders, sales receipts, invoices, and check registers. Employees, customers, suppliers, or other outside parties may complete source documents. Even companies that have computer-based TPS use source documents to record transactions with information that cannot easily be keyed into the system, such as a customer signature or a drawing. Increasingly, companies are eliminating paper source documents and using electronic versions instead.

Electronic Data Capture. Computers can use **online data entry** to capture transactions directly, eliminating the need for source documents. They may use predesigned forms similar to source documents that appear on a computer screen, as shown in Figure 9.8. As an employee performs a transaction, he records transaction data in the appropriate place on the screen.

FIGURE 9.8 Customers enter order information directly onto the screen, eliminating the need for paper source documents.

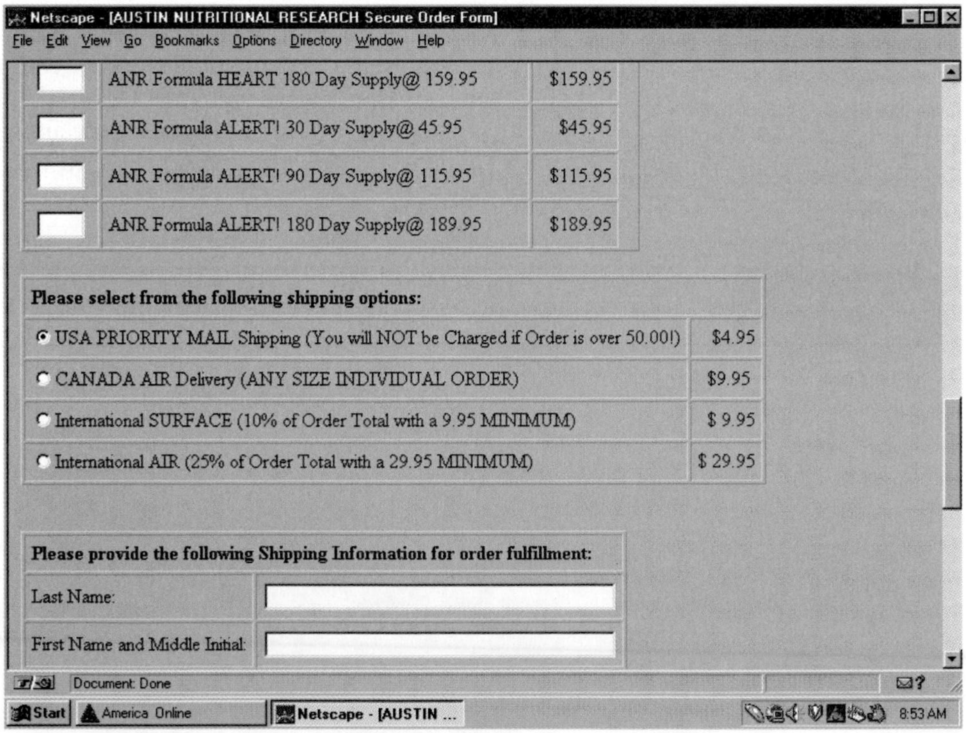

ETHICAL ISSUES IN IT

TRW Information Systems and Services provides credit information. Businesses and individuals can request credit reports for use in real estate transactions, marketing campaigns, and credit approval processes. Prior to 1991 TRW was criticized for violating the consumer's trust in the information it provided to other agencies. In response to these criticisms, TRW developed a set of Fair Information Values to guide its information collection and dissemination. The company decided that values provided a clear, workable, and flexible way of setting and following highly ethical policies and practices when handling information. The five core values are as follows:

- Partnership—TRW considers the interests of the customer and the consumer in developing products.
- Fairness—TRW acts openly about how it obtains and uses information. The company provides data only to those with a legal right to it.
- Balance—Any benefit or service must provide greater benefit than harm to the consumer.

- Education—TRW educates consumers about how it collects and uses information about them.
- Dialogue—TRW listens actively and responds openly to its consumers and critics.

The company also overhauled its credit bureau, improving its information systems to provide more accurate information to banks and other financial institutions related to loan and credit-card applications.

1. How might these values translate into ethical practice?
2. Would you expect TRW to benefit if its employees adhere to these values? Why or why not?

SOURCE: Based on D. Van Skilling, Values, ethics and data about people: A report and challenge from an information business, *Vital Speeches of the Day* (August 15, 1996): 659–662; Drew Clar, TRW sharpens data system in credit bureau it's selling, *American Banker*, August 2, 1996, 14.

Computerizing the recording of transactions offers many advantages:

- Employees can use input hardware such as bar-code scanners to reduce the amount of work and time required to record transactions, particularly when compared to employees recording transactions by hand.
- Computers can perform calculations, find prices, and automate other tasks for an employee performing a transaction.
- Computerization reduces the amount of paper to store.
- Computers minimize information loss, provide more flexible access to information, and promote data sharing among employees.
- Computers allow the summarizing of data for management planning and control.
- Computers allow the data entry person to immediately verify data and catch errors at their source.

Online data entry also has disadvantages:

- It requires a computer or a computer terminal at each location that a transaction may occur. The number of terminals used and the computer hardware and software to support their use can be expensive.
- A company that uses computers to record its transactions may experience significant problems if the computers fail. Even though they may have paper backup, business slows dramatically and often inconveniences customers.

Transcribing from Paper into Electronic Form. Organizations that capture data on paper can realize many of the benefits of online data entry by transcribing their paper records into an electronic form. **Data entry clerks** can either key or scan in data. Using source documents rather than entering transaction data directly into a computer can realize cost savings by reducing the number of terminals required to enter the data. However, the transcription process typically introduces errors, duplicates work, and increases the time between the transaction and the availability of information. The absence of advanced input devices and a computer to make calculations and perform table lookups at the time at which the transaction occurs increases the time and effort needed to process transactions.

Companies are moving away from this approach, relying more on direct entry of data by the employees who have the data. In the case of orders, for example, customers themselves are entering the data more frequently in electronic form through the use of EDI systems, Web-based ordering systems, or other electronic tie-ins to the company.

Nolato Gejde AB, a Swedish plastics manufacturer, was forced by Electrolux, one of its major customers, to switch to an EDI system for tracking product orders and shipments. Now Nolato Gejde uses EDI and bar coding together to improve quality control and warehouse shipping.[31]

Fruit of the Loom has created Web sites for its distributors to use as order-entry vehicles. Each distributor lists Fruit of the Loom's products in its online catalog. Customers can move from browsing the catalog to order placement. Fruit of the Loom's order-entry system then processes the order. The Web initiative, known as Activewear Online, has increased business for the Activewear division by $800 million and saved each distributor $10 to $20 per order in order-entry costs.[32]

BATCH VERSUS REAL-TIME PROCESSING

Companies use two substantially different methods to process transaction data.

- **Batch processing** stores electronic records or transcribed paper records in a stand-alone computer file that other parts of the company's information system cannot use or access. Periodically, typically at night, the computer processes the entire batch of records, thereby updating the company's information system.
- **Real-time processing** handles data on entry, immediately updating the information system and making the data available to all users.

Batch processing uses fewer and less costly computer resources than real-time processing. Because real-time processing handles transactions as they occur, it requires the computer to run programs for every type of active transaction simultaneously.

Salespeople can use hand-held computers to enter information about current inventory or price changes. This information then enters a transaction processing system that includes order entry, purchasing, distribution, and shipping.

When the computer operator instead batches transactions by transaction type, the computer can run one program at a time, decreasing the amount of memory the computer requires. Batching transactions also allows a company to evenly spread the load on its computers over the entire day, reducing the peaks and thereby reducing the need for processor power during peak periods.

Real-time processing, in contrast, makes transaction information immediately available. State Medicaid programs, for example, allow health care providers to tap into patient eligibility files and obtain real-time responses.[33] At Beamscope inventory information is always current. With batch processing, inventory would probably be unavailable until the next day. Real-time processing also simplifies error processing and encourages entry of only relevant data. Consider the processing of customer orders at Beamscope. The order form contains the customer's name and address. Using real-time processing, when the data entry clerk enters the name of an existing customer, the computer can retrieve the address; the clerk verifies it, making entries only upon observing an error. Using batch processing, the data entry clerk must always enter the customer address because she does not know if the file already has information about the customer. If a company uses customer codes on the order form, the real-time processing would immediately check the codes entered for accuracy. In batch processing no data checking occurs until the computer processes the batch. An error file would record errors for correction and entry in another batch. Table 9.2 summarizes the differences between batch and real-time processing.

Electronic data interchange (EDI), as described in Chapter 7, exemplifies effective real-time processing. Businesses that use EDI exchange data using a standard electronic format. They can exchange purchase orders, invoices, shipping invoices,

TABLE 9.2 Batch and real-time processing differ in their speed, cost, and reliability.

	Batch	**Real Time**
Number of Computers	Fewer computers	More computers
Computer Expense	Lower cost	Higher cost
Computer Load	Spread evenly over the day	Occurs in peaks and valleys
Information Availability	At a later time, often the next day	Immediate
Error Processing	More complex	Simpler
Data Entry	Large amounts	Reduced amounts

and checks using EDI. Although large companies have used EDI for more than a decade, its perceived high cost of implementation has hindered wider adoption. In addition, some companies, as well as their customers and vendors, continue to rely on paper for documentation. Also, companies can face challenges in integrating EDI with legacy systems. Now, Web technology is transforming EDI, making it easier to install and more attractive to companies.[34] A pilot study suggested that using the Internet instead of private lines for transmission of financial EDI could reduce the EDI bills of giant banks such as Chase Manhattan, Bank of America, and Mellon Bank by 90 percent through the elimination of data charges and reduced communication costs.[35]

ENSURING EFFECTIVE TRANSACTION PROCESSING SYSTEMS

Increasingly, organizations prefer real-time transaction processing systems over those that involve any manual recording or entry of data or batching of data processing. Regardless of their applications and functions, all real-time transaction processing systems should be fast, reliable, and accessible.

DEVELOPING FAST SYSTEMS

Employees and others who use a real-time TPS expect it to respond immediately to input. For example, Sabre, American Airline's reservation system, handles more than 5,000 transactions per second with worldwide response times of less than two seconds.[36] Lack of a rapid response delays the activity of business, possibly increasing costs or resulting in lost revenue. Developers usually consider a three-second response time acceptable.

Catalogue sales depend on transaction processing systems that are fast and reliable.

Consider this. What happens if a catalog retailer cannot tell a customer if a sweater is available? The customer may call another retailer. What happens if a box office agent cannot tell a patron if Saturday night tickets are available for the new musical theater? The patron might go out for dinner rather than wait. The inability to process transactions quickly may impact customer' behaviors, employee performance, and the organization's bottom line.

To keep management inquiries from affecting the response time of transaction processing systems, many companies prohibit the direct use of transaction data for management reporting and querying. Instead, as illustrated in Figure 9.9, management accesses such data from a data warehouse (see Chapter 5), which periodically downloads the data from the transaction processing system during off-peak periods.

ENSURING SYSTEM RELIABILITY

Because an electronic record might provide the only documentation of a transaction for companies using real-time TPS, failure of a TPS to record a transaction properly might result in lost sales, lost billings, and customer complaints, among other consequences. TPS failures include the following:

- *Incorrect Recording.* Incorrect or missing transactions leave no record of failure and can result in a company making poor decisions, losing revenue, and failing to abide by promises made to customers or suppliers.
- *Failure to Operate.* Although employees can sometimes revert to manual procedures, inoperable transaction processing systems generally cause a slowdown or stoppage of work, resulting in substantial business losses.

FIGURE 9.9 Managers can access transaction data from a data warehouse that downloads data from the transaction processing system at off-peak times to avoid slowing the TPS.

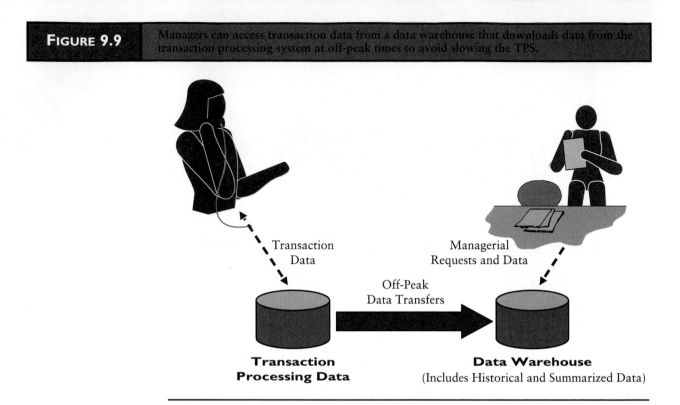

Transaction Data

Managerial Requests and Data

Off-Peak Data Transfers

Transaction Processing Data

Data Warehouse (Includes Historical and Summarized Data)

Imagine the consequences of a failure in the systems that support trading on the New York Stock Exchange. Consider the consequences for a bank whose ATM systems fail frequently. Most supermarkets need transaction processing systems that are highly reliable because scanning and price calculation upon checkout would be disabled upon a system failure. The consequences of system failure depend, of course, on the situation. Managers need to determine the degree of reliability they can tolerate and design or acquire systems that meet these needs.

Fault-Tolerant Systems. **Fault-tolerant systems,** also known as **nonstop systems,** achieve extremely high reliability by using redundant hardware components and software designed to take advantage of this redundancy. The enhanced 911 system of the New York City Police Department uses such a fault-tolerant system. The NYPD needed a system that would keep running regardless of catastrophes and disasters, such as the bombing at the World Trade Center or major power outages. The new system is the first public safety system to employ a software-drive, "three-level failover capacity." The first level handles failure from the primary server that is hooked up to each answering center. The second level uses multiple servers to create redundancy throughout the system. The third level lets each workstation take 911 calls and dispatch help without a server.[37]

Systems designed for maximum reliability use dual or triple processors, RAM, and disk storage. The amount of redundancy depends on the extent of reliability desired. Special hardware can identify component failures and then automatically shut down the failing parts. Operators can then replace malfunctioning circuit boards and other components while the redundant parts of the system continue to operate.

An **uninterruptible power supply** (UPS) provides secondary sources of power such as a battery or electric generator, along with circuitry that can recognize and react to a loss of power from the primary supply before it can affect the computer. Fault-tolerant systems generally include remote diagnostic capabilities so that vendors can troubleshoot a system in operation.

Companies that have a higher tolerance for failure may limit their failure protection to their data storage. RAID storage systems (see Chapter 3) provide various levels of redundancy and failure protection at a much lower cost than complete fault-tolerant systems.

Recoverability.   When failures occur—even in fault-tolerant systems—the TPS, along with users and computer professionals, should be able to reconstruct incorrectly logged or unlogged transactions. Because database management systems provide a variety of tools and services to help achieve these objectives, TPS developers generally build a TPS onto a database management system.

Transaction Processing Monitors.   How does a mutual fund company ensure that it credits a customer's "buy" or "sell" order to the correct account? Companies use transaction processing monitors (TP monitors, see Chapter 5) to ensure acceptable and consistent performance in processing transactions.[38] For example, GE Capital Mortgage, a seller of mortgage insurance, uses TP monitors to help link 200 users in 26 branch offices around the country and to record all sales in real time.[39] TP monitors also help manage the interaction among layers of client/server systems and can support multiple databases. Operators use the TP monitor to control the interactions between the layers or the databases to make them operate seamlessly and reliably. They help integrate various tools and eliminate bottlenecks in transaction processing.

HAVING AN ACCESSIBLE SYSTEM

Accessibility allows employees to record transactions whenever and wherever they occur. Employees who perform their transactions away from a desk may require innovative solutions and advanced communication technologies. Consider how a truck driver might record a package delivery. She could place a cellular phone call to a central computer, enter her identification code on the touch-tone pad, and then enter the waybill number of the delivered package. The employee could also enter the delivery information into a laptop or palmtop computer; when the employee returns from her round of deliveries she or another employee would then off-load the entries to the central computer.

Most companies stop their real-time TPS for an hour or more each day to back up their systems when data are not changing. Otherwise, operators could not reconstruct a system always in flux if hardware or software failure occurs.

Companies that operate globally experience the problem of keeping real-time transaction processing systems operating 24 hours a day. Real-time TPS may deal with this problem in two ways. They may partition the transaction data by area of the world, backing up independent partitions when they are inactive. Or they may keep multiple transaction logs, starting new ones when old ones are ready for backup.

PROVIDING SECURITY

Because many transaction processing systems record financial transactions, security is an important requirement. If employees could change the content of transaction records, they could easily steal from the company. Competitors or vandals could irreparably harm a company by destroying its transaction records, leaving it unable to respond to customer orders and to collect payments.

Transaction processing systems are often vulnerable to security breaches because they collect transaction information from all locations where a company does business. To exchange and consolidate such information, TPSs must rely on wide area networks, including the Internet. Chapter 7 addresses the problems of providing security in such an environment and discusses potential solutions.

DEVELOPING AND UPDATING TRANSACTION PROCESSING SYSTEMS

Transaction processing systems pose unique challenges to their developers. Although Chapter 12 explores the general issues of systems and software development, we discuss issues important to TPS in this section.

THE DEVELOPMENT, TESTING, AND PRODUCTION ENVIRONMENTS

The reliability requirements of TPSs hinder their modification because TPSs often consist of more than 100,000 lines of code that have withstood the test of long-term use. Even small changes in one line of a TPS program can produce unanticipated errors that occur rarely and remain undetected for days or weeks and cause significant damage when they occur. For this reason many companies consider their TPSs to be legacy systems, systems passed on by their developers to generations of successive support staffs, with little opportunity for change or replacement. Nevertheless, as a business changes, situations will arise that demand changes to its TPS.

How can a business ensure that its TPS remains reliable as developers change the TPS software? The most common solution creates three parallel environments:

- *Development Environment.* The **development environment** contains in-process copies of the TPS software and data for software developers to use in checking and improving their new programs. Typically, the developers correct any errors found in the development environment and then move the software to the testing environment.
- *Testing Environment.* The **testing environment** contains a copy of working software plus a complete copy of all transaction data that users test for performance. When users believe they have a sufficiently robust testing environment, they move the modified software to the production environment.
- *Production Environment.* The **production environment** contains the current software and all transaction data and emphasizes high system reliability. The

ADVANCED TECHNOLOGY

Fisher Technology Group (FTG), a leading supplier of business-to-business electronic commerce application solutions, has acquired UniKix Technologies, a high-performance transaction processing software business. The acquisition will allow FTG to build larger electronic malls with the capacity to serve more customers by buying and selling goods on the Internet or corporate intranets....

The rapid growth of traffic at FTG's electronic malls led to a search for a higher-performance transaction solution that could manage the many thousands of requests for quotes, purchase orders, and catalog update transitions that can occur in Internet-based electronic commerce....

Robert Grzyb, vice president of FTG, sees three ways that UniKix will help FTG's electronic commerce business. "First, UniKix provides the fast transaction engine needed by our large customers. Second, WebKix provides the Internet client that our customers need for Web browser access. Our customers will also be able to use Web Client for a high-end, Java-based interface. Third, and very important for FTG, UniKix provides strong capabilities for interfacing our distributed applications with customers' legacy systems. For example, FTG's solution will directly access these systems so purchasers can obtain their negotiated contract price—not the list price that customers of FTG's competitors get. This is a distinct competitive advantage."

SOURCE: Based on Internet mall developer and transaction processing vendor join to expand electronic commerce capabilities, http://www.unikix.com/pr1125.html, August 29, 1997.

system records all transactions in both the testing and production environments. Periodic tests verify the compatibility of the data in the testing and production environments and eventually signal the end of the testing environment.

DATABASE MANAGEMENT SYSTEMS AS THE HEART OF TPS

Database management systems provide a variety of services needed by a TPS:

- Simplify the storage and retrieval of data
- Control the simultaneous access and update to data by two or more users and allow data sharing
- Maintain transaction integrity when hardware or software failures terminate processing in the middle of a transaction
- Ease the development of screens to automate data entry
- Reduce the dependence of the TPS on a particular hardware environment, allowing systems to grow and evolve with major redesign

For these reasons, TPS software usually uses a DBMS to record its transactions.

SUMMARY

Transaction processing describes either the manual or computerized record keeping in a business. Transaction processing systems refer to systems that perform such collection, maintenance, and updating of business data.

Companies record transactions to provide information needed by other employees to transact business and perform their jobs, collect information that managers use in making decisions, and create audit trails for verifying corporate financial information.

Point-of-sale systems record the sale of a product and update company records related to or affected by the sale. Order-entry systems record and process the taking of an order. Distribution and logistics systems move, store, and track inventory, as well as ship finished goods. Purchasing/receiving systems document transactions between a company and its supplier. Computerized reservation systems refer to specialized order-entry systems used by companies such as airlines or automobile rental agencies. General accounting systems track the financial transactions and translate them into income statements, balance sheets, and other accounting records in an organization.

Businesses may capture transaction data using predesigned paper forms called source documents or directly in electronic form. Companies that use electronic capture can process the data with batch or real-time processing. Real-time systems must demonstrate speed, reliability, accessibility, and security.

Transaction processing systems pose special development challenges. The large amount of computer code and reliability requirements of such systems constrain their subsequent revision. Systems move through development and testing environments before their releases into a production environment. Database management systems function as the heart of TPS.

KEY TERMS

accounts payable system
accounts receivable system
audit trail
batch processing
computerized reservation system
  (CRS)
data entry clerk
development environment
fault-tolerant system
general accounting system
nonstop system
online data entry

order-entry system
payroll system
point-of-sale (POS) system
production environment
purchasing/receiving system
real-time processing
source document
testing environment
transaction
transaction processing system (TPS)
turnkey system
uninterruptible power supply (UPS)

DISCUSSION AND REVIEW QUESTIONS

1. What is a transaction processing system?
2. What is a transaction?
3. Why do companies record transactions?
4. Who uses audit trails and for what purpose?
5. What does a typical point-of-sale transaction involve?
6. What are the advantages and disadvantages of a networked POS system?
7. How does a computerized order-entry system work?
8. How does a logistics system complement a POS or order-entry system?
9. How can a transaction processing system improve the shipping of goods?
10. How do customers get access to computerized reservation systems?
11. What is the relationship between an order-entry system and a purchasing/receiving system?
12. What are the major components of a general accounting system?
13. Can an organization computerize only parts of a general accounting system?
14. What are the main methods for capturing and transcribing data in a transaction processing system?
15. What is the difference between batch and real-time processing?
16. How do companies use the Web in real-time processing?
17. What types of failures occur in TPSs?
18. How do fault-tolerant systems increase the reliability of a TPS?
19. What are some of the characteristics of fault tolerant systems?
20. What are the major steps in developing and updating a TPS?

IS ON THE WEB

Exercise 1: Locate three companies that produce point-of-sale systems, then compare and contrast their products. In what ways are they similar? How do they differ?

Exercise 2: Visit two merchants that sell products or services over the Web. Prepare an order for one or more items or services, but do not give your credit-card number. Compare and contrast the order-entry features of the Web sites you have visited.

MINICASE

CICS ENHANCES IMAGE OF LEADING U.S. CARRIER

If you are a large transportation company, handling thousands of freight shipments daily, losing a parcel can be painful—and expensive. The ability to track the whereabouts of a consignment, whatever it is and wherever it is, and deliver it to the right destination on time is crucial to success in the highly competitive transportation business.

Overnite Transportation Company, headquartered in Richmond, Virginia, USA, is the fifth-largest general freight carrier in the United States. Founded in 1935, the company handles in excess of 33,000 shipments daily and achieved revenues in 1994 of over $1 billion. Overnite is a full-service motor carrier of general commodities, providing short- and long-haul truckload and less-than-truckload (LTL) services to the public.

Nine years ago, Overnite became a wholly-owned subsidiary of Union Pacific Corporation and currently has 175 service centers operating across the US, employing 14,000 employees nationwide.

Overnite owns its entire fleet of vehicles, comprised of more than 5,000 tractors and 19,000 trailers. The company continues to make significant investments to expand and upgrade both its service centers and its operation fleet, and to develop and implement the new technologies necessary to maintain and strengthen its position as a major national carrier.

Information technology is central to the company's operations. Overnite has three data centers: one in Richmond handling all the company's imaging applications, another in St. Louis that runs a large portion of the organization's business, and systems back-up handled at a third data center in Omaha.

Overnite has an historical ability to track freight using line-of-business applications, and wanted to make this tracking process more accurate to ensure the smooth running of its business. CICS for MVS/ESA (a TP monitor) has a pivotal role in managing the millions of daily transactions involved.

Every organization has key applications that are the lifeblood of its business. CICS Application Server is industrial-strength transaction software used by leading enterprises worldwide for running mission-critical applications safely, securely, and reliably.

SOURCE: Case reprinted with permission from CICS enhances image of leading US carrier, http://www.hursley. ibm.com/cics/ overnite.html, July 10, 1997.

"We can obtain substantial savings by successfully pinpointing where freight is and ensure it is delivered to the right place, and on time. That is one of the biggest benefits of an image-based system supported by CICS."

CICS continues to evolve from the desktop to the data center. As well as supporting the latest mainframe technology, it now provides a cost-effective, low-risk way to move to multi-platform, client/server networks.

Overnite relies on IBM's CICS Application Server running on the mainframe to support its line-of-business activities. It underpins an application called EDGE to track all freight from pick-up to delivery. Currently, each shipped item has to be hand-keyed into the EDGE application under CICS. This process is prone to keying errors, so a new process is being put in place to remove such errors, called NiteTrack.

With NiteTrack in place, once a parcel is picked up, the company's delivery person uses a hand-held bar code reader to identify it, then transfers this data via wireless technology to one of the company's local service centers. Here, the data on the consignment is gathered and forwarded to the company's mainframe, where CICS manages the EDGE transaction. Around 2.5 million transactions per day are involved.

All of Overnite's customers have their own bills of lading, and, in order to be customer-responsive, the company sought to take the forms for bills of lading, delivery tickets, and all the other paperwork that comes in from customers, and put them into its line-of-business system via an imaging system.

Roger Morrison, systems programmer at Overnite, said: "IBM provided a turn-key solution using Image Plus. We use Image Plus to capture the images from field locations. We have a staff here at Richmond that can pull up the images on their monitors and key off the images into our line-of-business applications running under CICS. The information then gets transferred into our customer database electronically."

Before Image Plus was introduced into Overnite, the company's 175 service centers were doing their own bill entry. The intention was to consolidate that work so that all the bill entry could be done at the head office in Richmond.

Morrison added: "Capturing all the information using imaging technology gives us centralized access to data that would normally be found on thousands of pieces of paper flying around the organization. Previously, if someone in the company (typically in the central office or at the receiving service center) needed a particular document, a call would be made to the shipping service center, which would spend time digging up the document and faxing it to the interested party. With Image Plus, all the data is captured on-line, and anyone who needs to can just call it up on screen. This saves a lot of time and greatly reduces the headache of storing all that paper. We can discard paper documentation after 90 days, as opposed to three years of storage previously."

Substantial savings [would result] Morrison concluded: "If we lose freight, we have to pay for it. If we put the freight on the wrong truck, and it goes to the wrong part of the country, we have to ship it back to where it is supposed to go. If freight is late, customer satisfaction is affected, and there is also the cost of additional paperwork. That comes straight off the bottom line.

"We can obtain substantial savings by successfully pinpointing where freight is and ensure it is delivered to the right place, and on time. That is one of the biggest benefits of an image-based system supported by CICS."

Case Questions

Diagnosis

1. What information needs does Overnite Transportation Company have?

Evaluation

2. How does Overnite use a transaction processing system to meet these needs?

Design

3. What refinements is Overnite making to its transaction processing system?
4. How will these changes better met Overnite's needs?

Implementation

5. What implementation issues has Overnite considered?
6. What costs are associated with Overnite's system?

ACTIVITY 9.1   THE CATALOG PROBLEM

Step 1:   You run a small business that sells children's toys through a catalog distributed by mail to 10,000 families. You publish four catalogs a year. Each catalog includes about 200 items, with about 30 percent overlap in items between catalogs. Many of the items are specially crafted and require some lead time to bring into inventory. You have developed a selective customer group, and most of your customers order significant numbers of toys from you each quarter.

You use a personal computer with a Windows 98 system and off-the-shelf database software to maintain inventory and customer records. Recently, however, you have experienced significant problems with this system. The system has failed to flag out-of-stock items in time to reorder them; customer billings have lagged; and receivables have increased dramatically. Each quarter the number of items with very few sales and those with huge sales have increased, but you have not been able to explain which products sell well and which do not so that you can adjust future catalogs. You have an 800 number for telephone sales, but the number of errors in recording product numbers has increased. You believe that the system needs some adjustments.

Step 2:   Individually or in small groups, propose five changes for the existing system.

Step 3:   In small groups or with the entire class, share your list of changes. Together, compile a comprehensive list of changes and develop a plan for upgrading the systems.

ACTIVITY 9.2   SELLING "THE LIST"

Step 1:   Read the following scenario:

Sandy Jeffries, the chief operating officer of Home Products Inc., a major catalog retailer of thousands of products used in the home, has just had a brainstorm. The company has a list of more than 100,000 customers around the world. Jeffries has been looking for new sources of revenue for the company. Jeffries wants to propose to the executive board that Home Products sell its list of customers to anyone interested in using it for sales, promotion, solicitation, or other legal purposes.

Jeffries has approached Lee Montgomery, the vice president for information systems for the company, about the idea. Montgomery immediately opposes the idea, calling it unethical.

Step 2:   Your instructor will divide the class into small groups. Each group should complete the following chart:

Reasons Selling the List Is Ethical	Reasons Selling the List Is Unethical
1. _____	_____
2. _____	_____
3. _____	_____
4. _____	_____
5. _____	_____
6. _____	_____

Step 3:   Evaluate each position using basic ethical criteria.

Step 4:   Should the company sell the lists?

KIDS LIMOUSINE SERVICE   ACTIVITY 9.3

Step 1:   Read the following scenario:

John Cardy began an after-school limousine service for children in 1987 using a single van. He transported local children from school to after-school activities, lessons, friends' houses, or home. Parents paid an annual fee to enroll their child in the service plus an additional toll for each trip. During the first two years, business boomed, and Cardy bought two additional vans and hired additional drivers. During the next three years he expanded the service throughout the eastern part of the state. He bought 15 more vans and hired additional drivers. Cardy relinquished his role as a van driver and part-time manager and devoted his time to managing the business.

He soon discovered that the manual system of recording clients' requests, scheduling drivers, and billing customers was not working. Although Cardy's reputation was based on the reliability and safety of his service, he had several near misses: drivers almost failed to pick up several children from school because of scheduling mistakes. In addition, many vans crisscrossed their towns several times because Cardy did not have time to determine the best routes and schedules for them and their drivers. Bills were mailed late, and Cardy did not have time to track tardy accounts.

Cardy knew that the business could operate more effectively if he computerized the entire system. He believed that improved cash flow and the savings obtained from a more efficient scheduling of vans and drivers would offset the costs of computerization.

Step 2: Individually or in small groups, identify what transactions John Cardy and Kids Limousine Company need to record in order for Cardy to operate the business more effectively. Specifically, consider the order-entry, scheduling, and billing processes as well as any other processes you feel might generate transactions.

Step 3: Select one of the transactions you identified in step 2 and determine exactly what data items need to be recorded as the transaction takes place. Identify how the transaction you selected uses data from other transactions or creates data that is needed for efficiently processing other transactions.

Step 4: Your instructor will provide you with instructions for accessing a database management system on your computer. Using this database management system, design and implement a data entry screen and database to capture the transaction you selected in step 3. Create some hypothetical transactions and enter them into your database using the data entry screen you created.

ACTIVITY 9.4 FLIGHT INC.

Step 1: Read the following scenario:

You have recently joined the family business, an aircraft repair service that provides maintenance services for corporate aircraft. Your father began the service in 1962 at a single location. Since its founding, Flight Inc. has expanded to five sites across the United States and employs 50 technicians. The company has developed a reputation for offering impeccable, highly personalized customer service. Company representatives meet charter customers at the airport, quickly complete a service order, and then arrange for accommodations for the pilot during servicing of the aircraft. The company attempts to minimize the time the aircraft is out of service and prides itself on solving mechanical problems quickly and accurately.

Although your father has built a successful business, you know that its future success will rely on increasing its efficiency while continuing to ensure personalized service. In addition, you hope to expand the business and know that the manual system for recording customer requests, repair schedules, regular aircraft maintenance, and even customer billing is antiquated and will hinder your expansion plans.

Step 2: Individually or in small groups, design a transaction processing system for this company. Your instructor will provide you with the specifications for the system.

Step 3: Exchange your systems with a partner group. Individually or in small groups, critique your partner group's plan. Offer suggestions for improving its system.

Step 4: Revise your system based on suggestions received from your partner group. What components would an effective transaction processing system for Flight Inc. include?

TRANSACTION PROCESSING
AT ADOPTIONS INTERNATIONAL   ACTIVITY 9.3

Step 1: You have just taken the position of business manager of Adoptions International, a large adoption agency based in Nashville, Tennessee. The agency helps people who want to adopt children find adoptable children throughout the world. It also serves as the liaison to state adoption agencies in the United States.

The agency has branches in six states in the United States. It also has partner agencies in twenty other states and thirty countries that help place children with U.S. families. Agency personnel handle all of the paperwork required in the United States and abroad for the adoptions. They make travel arrangements for newly adopted children and their families. They also provide the home visitation services required for adoptive parents. They recently started an education group that schedules seminars for prospective and newly adoptive families.

Step 2: Individually or in small groups, design a transaction processing system for the adoption agency. Your instructor will provide you with the specifications for the system.

Step 3: Exchange your designs with a partner group. Individually or in small groups, critique your partner group's plan. Offer suggestions for improving its system.

Step 4: Revise your system based on suggestions received from your partner group. What components would an effective transaction processing system for Adoptions International include?

RECOMMENDED READINGS

Bernstein, Philip A., and Newcomer, Eric. *Principles of Transaction Processing*. San Francisco: Morgan Kaufmann, 1997.

Bodnar, George H., and Hopwood, William S., *Accounting Information Systems,* Prentice Hall, 1998.

Ernst, Ricardo; Kouvelis, Panos; Dornier, Philippe-Pierre; and Fender, Michel, *Global Operations and Logistics: Text and Cases,* John Wiley & Sons, 1998.

Glossman, Diane B. *Transaction Processing: Merging with the Information Superhighway*. New York: Salomon Brothers, 1994.

Pooler, Victor H., and Pooler, David J., *Purchasing and Supply Management: Creating the Vision,* Chapman & Hall, 1997.

Pradhan, Dhiraj K. *Fault-Tolerant Computer System Design*. Englewood Cliffs, NJ: Prentice Hall, 1996.

Weber, Ron, *EDP Auditing: Conceptual Foundations and Practice,* McGraw Hill, 2nd Edition, 1998.

NOTES

1. Telephone conversation with Danny Gurizzan, Director of Business Systems Development and Information Technology, March 25, 1998; Chris Staiti, Beamscope Canada, Inc., *Computerworld Client/Server Journal*, Special Issue (August 1996): 49–50.

2. Seafood City, http://www.mssretail.com/MSRetail/Main/seafood.htm, July 8, 1997.

3. Thomas Hoffman, Maine drives Medicaid reform with decision-support system, *Computerworld* (January 20, 1997): 67–68.

4. How laptops helped transform the Wesleyan, *Insurance Systems Bulletin* (July 1996): 3–4.

5. For example, Mrs. Fields Cookies operates in this fashion; see Jack Schember, Mrs. Fields' secret weapon, *Personnel Journal* 70(9) (1991): 56–58.

6. Rosemary Cafasso, Diamond Shamrock, Inc., *Computerworld Client/Server Journal Supplement* (August 1996): 26.

7. Judy Murrah, Service maximized in the wireless store, *Chain Store Age Executive* 69 (April 1993): 76.

8. Wireless unclogs Pepsi's distribution bottleneck, improves merchandising, *Systems Management* (March 1996): 22–23.

9. Bob Wallace, AT&T rolls out new transaction service, *Network World* (March 29, 1993): 25–26.

10. Spotlight—Wave Riding Vehicles, http://www.retailpro.com/spotlights/wrvspot.html, March 29, 1998.

11. Tom Field, A good connection, *CIO* (February 1, 1997): 70–74.

12. Wayne Seel, Integrated order processing helps supplier save money and keep better track of jobs, *Marketing News* (January 6, 1997): 10.

13. Application review: Order entry at Stanley Hardware, http://www.midrangecomputing.com/tradeshow/link/hardware.htm, March 29, 1998.

14. Peter Fabris, A speedy recovery, *CIO* (February 1, 1996): 34–36.

15. Kim Girard, Gun dealers get a shot in the arm, *Computerworld* (January 20, 1997): 49, 51.

16. Chabrow, Ryder has the right moves, *InformationWeek* (January 30, 1995): 44.

17. Marianne Kolbasuk McGee and Doug Bartholomew, Meltdown, *InformationWeek* (March 11, 1996): 14–15.

18. Ibid.

19. Joseph Weber, Just get it to the stores on time, *Business Week* (March 6, 1995): 66–67.

20. Tom Andel, Load plans make room for profit, *Transportation and Distribution* (March 1996): 58–62.

21. Joshua Macht, Delivering the goods, *Inc. Technology* (4) (1996): 34–41.

22. Ibid.

23. Scott Woolley, Double click for resin, *Forbes* (March 10, 1997): 132–134.

24. John P. Desmond, Targeting transport transactions, *Object Magazine* (January 1998): 14, 16.

25. Central-res operator uses Internet for WAN, *Hotel and Motel Management* (November 18, 1996): 75–76.

26. Elizabeth Heichler, Airline hacking case reveals CRS' security shortcomings, *Computerworld* (January 18, 1993): 2.

27. Holly Sraeel, Fleet Capital tackles complex general ledger reporting requirements, *Bank Systems and Technology* (September 1996): 61.

28. Linda Perri, Barrie Pace instant accounting, *Apparel Industry Magazine* (September 1996): 124–128.

29. Data feeds expansion at Pet Food Warehouse, *Chain Store Age* (November 1996): 8A–10A.

30. Ed Scannell, Travelers reduces risk of claims errors, *Computerworld* (February 13, 1995): 74.

31. When the customer is always right, *Automatic ID News* (March 1997): 30–31.

32. Clinton Wilder, Web sites a gift to distributors, *InformationWeek* (August 26, 1996): 36–37.

33. James J. Moynihan, Using EDI for eligibility reporting, *Healthcare Financial Management* (January 1997): 82–83.
34. Suruchi, Mohan, EDI's move to prime time stalled by cost perception, *Computerworld* (February 20, 1995): 91.
35. Kimberly Weisul, Heavy hitters open doors to EDI over the Internet, *Investment Dealers Digest* (November 11, 1996): 10–11.
36. Big deal, Microsoft, *Information Week* (May 5, 1997).
37. Sana Siwolop, Saving time—and lives, *Information Week* (February 12, 1996): 29–50.
38. Rich Levin, TP monitors gain importance, *Information Week* (November 18, 1996): 174–178.
39. Dan Richman, Transaction monitors: The open view, *Information Week* (September 4, 1995): 45–52.

Chapter 10

Management Information Systems

LEARNING OBJECTIVES

After completing Chapter 10, you will be able to

1. Explain how information systems support decision making and meet managers' needs for information.
2. Describe the types of information provided by three types of management reports.
3. Describe alternative schedules for producing reports.
4. Discuss the components and uses of a decision support system.
5. Explain how decision support systems can support group decision making.
6. Identify the elements and major uses of groupware.
7. Describe the typical features and uses of an executive information system.
8. Compare and contrast management reporting systems, decision support systems, groupware, and executive information systems.

MANAGEMENT INFORMATION SYSTEMS AT BETTER FURNITURE RENTALS

Sue Johnson manages Better Furniture Rentals Inc., a company that provides short-term and long-term rental of office and apartment furnishings. The company has served a large midwestern metropolitan area with six stores for more than 30 years. Johnson recently replaced her father, the founder of the company, on his retirement.

One of her first priorities is to expand the extent and sophistication of the computerized information systems that support her running of the enterprise. Most of the systems have relied on manual input of information and have provided some summary statistics. Johnson believes that she can improve the store's bottom line by more closely tracking sales, inventory, and customer service. She wants a system that can help her managers make better decisions about products to stock, sales approaches to use, and ways to deal with supplier and customer problems. She also wants a system that can support her information needs as the chief corporate executive.

What types of information systems should Sue Johnson install at Better Furniture Rentals to provide the information she needs to manage effectively? In this chapter we explore the use of management information systems to provide such information. We investigate how management reporting systems, decision support systems, groupware, and executive information systems can provide the information that Johnson needs.

Computerized information systems support businesses such as furniture rental companies by tracking sales, service, inventory, and shipping. Management information systems provide executives of such companies with easily accessible information for analyzing company performance along a variety of dimensions.

FIGURE 10.3	An exception report helps managers at Better Furniture identify potential problems or unexpected situations.

Sales Exception Report
Month Ending 3/31/99
Store #5

PRODUCT #	DESCRIPTION	CODE
773	WALNUT ENDTABLE	A,M
821	FLOOR LAMP	M

CODES:
    A: SALES OF THIS ITEM ARE AT LEAST 10% BELOW THAT OF THE AVERAGE
         STORE'S SALES AS ADJUSTED FOR TOTAL SALES VOLUME.
    M: SALES OF THIS ITEM ARE AT LEAST 5% BELOW THAT OF LAST MONTH
         AS ADJUSTED FOR TOTAL SALES VOLUME.

FIGURE 10.4	Notification systems alert managers to situations as an event occurs.

Virtual Proposal Center

Menu   Exit

Workplan Table	Notification Table	Calendar

Task #	Trigger	Target
	Complete	All
2	Start	ST
3	CompletionPastDue	JA
4	AnticipateStart	TM

Message: Proposal is now available on line.

	Task Description	User ID	Sched. Start	Duration	Sched. Compl	Predecessor #	Actual Start	Actual Comp
1	Set Up proposal	TS	05/12/1998	4	05/18/1998	2	05/13/1998	05/19/1998
2	Assemble Kickoff	ST	05/08/1998	2	05/12/1998	5	05/11/1998	05/13/1998
3	Develop Strategy	JA	05/13/1998	1	05/14/1998	3	05/14/1998	05/15/1998
4	Edit and Format	TM	05/15/1998	6	05/25/1998		05/18/1998	05/26/1998

REPORT SCHEDULES

Most organizations produce a large proportion of their reports on a scheduled basis and distribute them to a predetermined list of recipients. Management systems may also produce reports on demand or generate them in response to specified events. Firms such as Moyer Packing Company have created integrated systems, including inventory management, sales order processing, cost accounting, and distribution, that generate management reports more quickly and deliver them automatically directly to the end users.[6] Table 10.1 compares periodic, event-initiated, and on-demand reports.

Periodic Reports.   Management reporting systems produce most **periodic reports** on an occasional basis and deliver them to a specified list of employees. For example, one company produces a report of sales by region every weekend so that all senior managers receive the report on Monday morning prior to their weekly planning meeting. Each day an airline produces a report of reservations by rate class for each flight so that managers can adjust the number of seats open for special fares. Most companies produce financial statements every month or every quarter. What types of reports might Better Furniture Rentals generate daily? Weekly? Monthly? Periodic reports should provide information essential for managerial decision making and action without overloading the manager with too much detail.

Event-Initiated Reports.   MRSs may also generate **event-initiated reports** on the occurrence of a specified event, typically either a milestone or an expected problem. For example, a government contractor produces a contract status report each time the contractor completes part of its contract and each time a deadline passes without completion of the contracted work. A catalog company produces a back-order report when a customer orders a product that is out of stock and again when it replenishes the stock. A prespecified list of recipients generally receives such event-initiated reports.

On-Demand Reports.   Management reporting systems provide **on-demand reports** for authorized managers when they request specific information. In most cases the system already includes programs to generate the reports, and managers can activate them when they want. In some cases technically skilled managers use a high-level report-generating language to prepare reports in a variety of formats. Sue Johnson might want a one-time report of recent advertising expenditures, employee hires, or customer complaints.

TABLE 10.1   Managers can prepare or request reports on a periodic, event-initiated, or on-demand schedule.

Report	Frequency	Delivery	Example
Periodic	Periodically—daily, weekly, monthly	To specified list of people	Financial report
Event initiated	After occurrence of specified event	To specified list of people	Contract progress report
On demand	Upon manager's request	To specified list of people	New customer report

MANAGEMENT REPORTING SYSTEMS AND TRANSACTION PROCESSING SYSTEMS

Management reporting systems in many organizations comprise the reporting components of a transaction processing system. Sometimes MRSs combine data from two or more transaction processing systems (TPSs) to provide data that managers could not obtain from the individual systems. For example, they might combine reports about the types of defective items and reports about the sales of those items. Home Depot reduced its list of hundreds of reports to 20; these reports now go to every manager. The reports automatically generate suggested purchase orders, which individual store managers can modify.[7] Organizations such as the Centers for Disease Control and Prevention in Atlanta and Abbott Laboratories use a combination of transaction processing, database, and management reporting systems to track computer and software for regulators at the Food and Drug Administration. NationsBank built an asset-management system in-house using off-the-shelf hardware to keep track of its equipment and services.[8]

The use of both management reporting systems and transaction processing systems can strain computer resources. MRSs require significant computer resources for accessing, sorting, and otherwise manipulating data. When an MRS runs concurrently with a TPS, the requirements for computer resources may slow the TPS, resulting in unacceptable or unreliable response times for important business transactions.

Organizations have two options for dealing with this overload. First, they may run MRSs only on weekends, overnight, or at hours when transaction activity is likely to be low. Although this is an acceptable solution for most reports, it may

NationsBank uses information systems to track its assets. It chose off-the-shelf hardware rather than specially-configured hardware for its asset-management system.

not work for organizations whose transaction processing occurs all day, every day. A second solution involves downloading selected detail and summary data from a transaction processing system into a data warehouse, as described in Chapter 5. This frees the TPS from performing the time-consuming data sorts typically required by management reports and allows it to run more smoothly and with a more regular and predictable response time. The downloading also gives managers broader access to data because they cannot delete, modify, or corrupt the transaction data. A database interface allows more flexible access to data than does a typical TPS; therefore, managers can more easily generate on-demand reports.

DECISION SUPPORT SYSTEMS

Should a newer, more powerful machine replace two older pieces of equipment? Should the company sell directly to the retail market, continue to sell through distributors, or both? Should the company order parts more frequently and in smaller lots? Will lower marketing and sales expenses offset the revenue loss of a price decrease? A **decision support system (DSS)** can help managers make more effective decisions by answering complex questions such as these. Madison Paper Company uses computer software to figure the best way to load and ship its paper on trucks and trains. Madison reduced transportation costs by 6 percent by using the software. The same software helps the company determine how running one customer's order affects another order in the pipeline.[9] Such computer systems provide information required for effective planning and organizing.

Middle- and upper-level managers use DSSs to reach decisions in ambiguous and complex environments. Unlike management reporting systems, which provide managers primarily with current data to use in problem analysis, DSSs offer forecasts of future conditions. They also give managers the ability to quantitatively analyze alternative decisions. Essentially they model a complex set of circumstances. The decision maker can manipulate various parameters of the model to assess the impact of diverse conditions.

Singapore Airlines, for example, uses the integrated crew management system to handle crew scheduling. It includes two modules that automate the tracking and scheduling of flight crews. A third module tracks the location of the crew and handles disruptions in the crew pattern, such as illness, delayed flights, or other unexpected situations. The system can locate a backup to avoid understaffing a particular flight, as well as deal with the consequences of reassigning the backup person. The system can advise managers responsible for crew scheduling the best action in potentially disruptive situations.[10]

The benefits of a DSS include the following:

- Improved decision making through better understanding of the business
- An increased number of decision alternatives examined
- The ability to implement ad hoc analysis
- Faster response to expected situations
- Improved communication
- More effective teamwork

- Better control
- Time and cost savings

Mercantile Stores uses a DSS to support its promotion planning and analysis. The system stores information on the 3.5 million store cardholders in a data warehouse. It can deliver the information to individual PCs for managers to use in analyzing the best ways to attract new customers and use advertising dollars effectively.[11] The Westland Cooperative Dairy Company has significantly reduced its labor costs by using a decision support system that helps plan schedules. It generates alternative plans, assesses them, and then chooses the best one for scheduling employees.[12]

The extent to which DSSs help managers make more effective decisions depends to a large degree on the user's familiarity and expertise with the decision support tool, the user's knowledge about the problem to be solved, and the interaction of the cognitive style of the user with the DSS.[13]

COMPONENTS OF A DECISION SUPPORT SYSTEM

A full-featured decision support system consists of four major components, as shown in Figure 10.5: (1) a database, (2) a knowledge base, (3) a model base, and (4) a user interface.

A database provides access to internal or external data relevant to the decisions. Data from a database form a baseline that mathematical models use in

FIGURE 10.5 Decision support systems include a database, knowledge base, model base, and user interface.

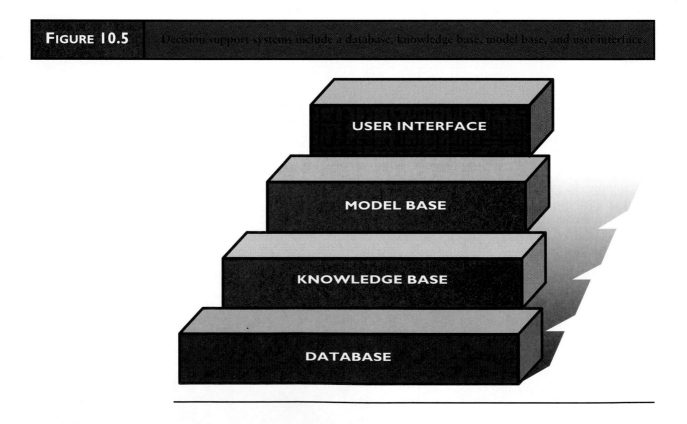

extrapolating from past to future conditions. The data can help calibrate and validate parameters of models used for forecasting. For example, in evaluating a proposed price cut, a DSS should have the capability of analyzing how past price changes have affected sales.

Intermountain Health Care in Salt Lake City built a DSS that includes a computerized patient record database that stores every drug, symptom, and medical test for each patient. The system helps physicians prescribe the best drugs. It also identifies patient drug sensitivities, specifies bacteria that likely will cause infection, and calculates how fast the body will absorb the drug. It provides the cost-effectiveness of several drugs if more than one will work. This system has essentially eliminated adverse drug reactions and saved Intermountain $1 million a year.[14]

The **knowledge base** provides information about highly complex relationships among data that a database has problems representing. It consists of rules of thumb, known as **heuristics,** that define acceptable solutions and methods for evaluating them. For example, in analyzing the impact of a price reduction, a DSS should signal if the forecasted volume of activity exceeds the volume that the projected staff can service. Such signaling would require the DSS to incorporate some rules of thumb about an appropriate ratio of staff to sales volume.

A **model base** includes an array of spreadsheets, simulation packages, forecasting tools, and statistical packages. The user can access the appropriate tools without developing a new model each time. The user should also have access to previously developed models that she may then reuse. For example, a DSS that helps managers of mutual funds decide which stocks to buy would include a variety of mathematical models that analyze various aspects of the potential purchase.

Finally, the DSS must include a sophisticated **user interface,** which allows users to control which data and models to include in their analyses. The design of user interfaces is an MIS specialty that combines information and technology concepts with the rich realms of human factors and psychology.[15] A DSS must be designed to support the greater freedom users experience in manipulating data and processing information. The flexibility of the DSS user interface contrasts with that in transaction processing systems and management reporting systems where the user is more passive, receiving the data in limited formats or entering data into carefully crafted screens or forms.

A state-of-the-art DSS should ease the assembling of data and knowledge from a variety of sources. It should support their use as inputs to previously developed models or models currently under development. Because DSSs support complex decision making and users typically analyze many alternatives and extensive data about each alternative, a quality DSS should compare, contrast, and aggregate data in a wide range of graphical and tabular formats.

USING A DECISION SUPPORT SYSTEM TO ANSWER QUESTIONS

A decision support system handles unforeseen questions by providing access to internal and external data and models to manipulate the data. It supports ad hoc queries and offers analytical capabilities. An **ad hoc query** calls on the computer system to perform the comparison and linkages among the elements of a database, combining them in unanticipated ways. Because managers are usually not computer programmers, a decision support system should provide a language for queries that managers can easily use. Eastman Kodak, for example, designed a laboratory information management system based on World Wide Web software components. Users inside the company can access chemical information from a corporate database and use the information in product development and other decision-making activities.[16]

Management reporting systems provide access to data in a predefined format. In most cases, these formats do not address unforeseen questions. Suppose, for example, a manufacturer receives a bad set of circuit boards from a supplier and has unwittingly used the boards in its own product, which the company has shipped to customers. When the manager responsible for recalling finished goods from customers discovers the problem, he could first look at receiving reports that identify the serial numbers of the bad boards. Then he could scan the manufacturing reports to identify which products had the boards with those serial numbers. The manager then could trace these products to shipping orders and then review customer detail reports for the telephone numbers and contact names of customers identified from the shipping records. The manager could avoid this laborious process if he could perform an ad hoc query on a database of product and customer information. In such a query, the manager would request the names and phone numbers of all customers that received any product that included any board that was received in a specified shipment from the supplier.

Decision support systems now use object-oriented user interfaces, as illustrated in Figure 10.6, for performing ad hoc queries. In the preceding example, the manager might perform the query as follows. Initially, a screen showing icons for suppliers, shippers, parts, and other information would appear. The manager would click on the supplier icon. A list of suppliers would appear. The manager would then click on the company that supplied the bad circuit board. Attributes of the company, such as its address and phone number, would appear, along with a number of buttons for more detailed information, such as shipments from the company. The manager would click on the shipments' button and identify the bad shipment. The list of circuit boards in the bad shipment would appear. Proceeding in this manner, the manager would cross-reference the circuit boards with the company's finished product and then with the customers receiving the product. This process would only take a few seconds. Then the manager would click on a report button, identify what information the report should include by clicking on the list of available fields, and select which field or fields should be used to sort the report. Finally, the DSS would print a copy of the report.

Managers incorporate data from external sources into a DSS. The Internet now provides easy access to a wide array of data, such as macroeconomic data about foreign countries, financial data about publicly traded companies, demographic data about potential customers, and information about patents. DSSs allow users to import the data from external sources and incorporate such data into analyses that respond to queries.

ANALYTICAL ELEMENTS OF A DECISION SUPPORT SYSTEM

A decision support system should give managers the opportunity to evaluate the impact of alternative decisions, such as whether to locate a new restaurant in a city

FIGURE 10.6 Object-oriented interfaces give the user a more intuitive query language for decision support systems.

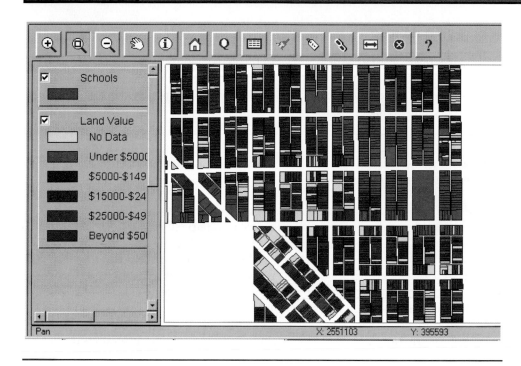

or suburban location of a large metropolitan area. Because a decision's impact will not be felt for a period of time, a DSS must include an ability to forecast the effect. In addition, the impact of decisions often depends on numerous factors outside the manager's control, such as the general economic conditions, introduction of new technology, or changing customer requirements. The DSS must provide opportunities for the manager to vary the assumptions inherent in the forecasting process to account for such factors. Ryder Dedicated Logistics, a subsidiary of Ryder, the trucking company, uses the analytical tools in its logistics management DSS to reduce clients' costs, delivery times, and inventory.[17] Such a DSS must support the manager in comparing, contrasting, summarizing, and evaluating the alternative scenarios that arise from the forecasting effort. Sue Johnson can use a DSS to help her decide whether to offer a new line of furniture or open another store.

The analytical elements of a DSS vary dramatically among organizations, depending on the industry, the sophistication of the DSS users, and the computing resources available in the organization. A manager should evaluate whether a product meets his specific needs. Table 10.2 lists an array of elements that DSS may incorporate. In this section we discuss the most common tools available in a state-of-the-art DSS: data mining, online analytical support (OLAP), simulation

TABLE 10.2	A DSS can incorporate numerous tools.		

Simulation languages	Forecasting models	Risk assessment and evaluation tools.
Optimization support	Database support	Stochastic modeling support
Statistical support	Graphical analysis tools	Multicriteria decision models
Geographical systems	Word processing integration	Capital finance models
Expert system shells	Markov process models	Pert/CPM and other project management models
Accounting modeling support	Decision tree models	

languages, goal-seeking (optimization) software, statistical packages, geographical systems, and expert systems.

Data Mining. Decision support systems can include a capability that uses artificial intelligence and relational databases to automatically discover patterns, associations, irregularities, or changes in data.[18] **Data mining** software helps firms probe more deeply into information they typically collect. For example, banks use data mining to get a better picture of their customers' accounts and help them cross-sell other bank services to them. If a bank knows when a customer makes the last payment on her car loan, it can let her know about the bank's attractive loan rates for a new car purchase.[19]

CUC International, a time-sharing firm, uses data mining techniques to identify the consumers to target with particular services. CUC has used statistical modeling techniques to predict customer behavior, such as what enticements will cause club members to renew their memberships. CUC also uses data mining techniques to give time-share resort developers profiles of likely purchasers.[20] Citibank uses data mining in its Cards Analytical Model project to predict future consumer patterns.[21]

Online Analytical Processing. Online analytical processing (OLAP) involves reading and combining large groups of diverse data, often found in a company's data warehouse.[22] Imagine entering a large store that stocks all kinds of products, but everything is disorganized so that you are not able to find anything you need within a reasonable amount of time. Companies that have large amounts of data can suffer from the same problem. OLAP helps solve it by analyzing huge quantities of data and looking for patterns, trends, and exceptions. The Land O' Lakes Dairy Cooperative in Minneapolis uses OLAP and other techniques to understand customer buying habits so it can sell more cheese and butter.[23]

OLAP gives companies the ability to combine data at multiple levels, beginning with individual products, extending to families of products, then to even larger groupings; or from one location to a region, to all national locations.[24] Some OLAP systems use intelligent agents to extract data from a data warehouse and then run calculations according to specified models. The OLAP then stores the results in a special database. OLAP works particularly well in businesses that use a lot of statistical analysis, such as stock trading and real estate investment.

Wellcome Foundation, the British drug giant, lets users perform OLAP on data coming from both inside and outside the company using the LightShip System. This system gives senior managers key data about corporate sales, prices, industry news, and exchange rates quickly at their desktops. OLAP lets them identify trends and easily analyze data to get information about how quickly sales of specific drugs changed, the percentage each drug contributed to corporate revenue, and the amount of sales in different countries.[25]

Simulation Languages. **Simulation** refers to the method of representing real processes with analytic models. Most DSSs provide several languages to assist the user in developing a simulation. Spreadsheets, the most common simulation language, provide a simple one-, two-, or occasionally multidimensional way of interrelating data using formulas. Most simulation languages, including spreadsheets, offer a way to represent random occurrences in nature or business, such as unexpected changes in the gross national product, the rate of inflation, or the unemployment rate. Some simulation languages such as SIMSCRIPT and GPSS are particularly well suited to performing random processes many times and automatically calculating and storing statistical information about the outcomes. Such languages effectively represent processes that perform operations in sequence or in a variety of sequences over a period of time, such as occur on the floor of a manufacturing shop. SIMULEX, a decision support system that does short-term rescheduling for manufacturing, uses simulation and expert systems (discussed later) to help production managers handle production disturbances. It includes a simulation that models scheduling plans and then evaluates the results of various approaches to rescheduling.[26]

Goal-Seeking Software. Simulation languages excel in analyzing the impact of a few decision choices. When the number of choices becomes large or infinite, **goal-seeking software** can quickly narrow the choices to one or a few. Goal-seeking software requires that the user specify in advance the criteria (for example, cost, speed, or revenue) for evaluating the outcomes of different decisions. After the user supplies such a formula, the software applies a variety of tools to quickly determine the best or optimal solution. A food products company could use a least-cost linear programming model to set the percentage of ingredients in soups, hot dogs, or even baked goods.

Unfortunately, most goal-seeking software products are fairly limited in the nature and form of problems they can solve. The most popular goal-seeking software includes packages for linear programming, integer programming, goal programming, quadratic programming, and unconstrained optimization.

Statistical Packages. Statistical packages assist managers in drawing inferences about the relationships among data elements. Building effective models calls for developing such relationships and having confidence that they reflect underlying processes rather than random occurrences. For example, assume that historical analyses show that an 8 percent increase in sales accompanied every 10 percent decrease in price. But, this would not describe perfectly the relationship between price and sales. Sometimes sales increased by a larger amount and sometimes by a smaller amount given the same price change, reflecting differences in economic conditions, type of product, or time of year. Statistical packages would determine the degree of confidence a manager can have in the eight/ten formula and its likelihood of applying to future price cuts or increases. The U.S. Army uses HANS, a decision support system that includes an econometric model that forecasts the availability of off-the-post rental housing for Army personnel. The Army then uses the results of the analysis to make decisions about building housing on the post or leasing housing off the post.[27]

Geographical Information Systems.

Certain decisions require the ability to examine and manipulate geographical information, such as that represented on maps, telephone directories, and other locators. Industries such as public utilities, transportation, retail marketing, and environmental management are driving a dramatic increase in the use of **geographical information systems (GISs),** which can improve customer service and cut costs.

GISs combine digital mapping with databases to allow both graphical representations and sophisticated access and storage of geographical data.[28] Most high-quality GISs can manage geographic information, do geographic analyses, and provide geographic and mapping capabilities for custom applications.[29] Figure 10.7 illustrates a map from a GIS.

The city of Scottsdale, Arizona, has a GIS that has lowered costs, improved service to citizens, and improved managerial decision making. The GIS supports

| **FIGURE 10.7** | This image, from a GIS by CDS Business Mapping (Hartford, Connecticut), shows an insurance company's exposure to claims related to coastal flooding. |

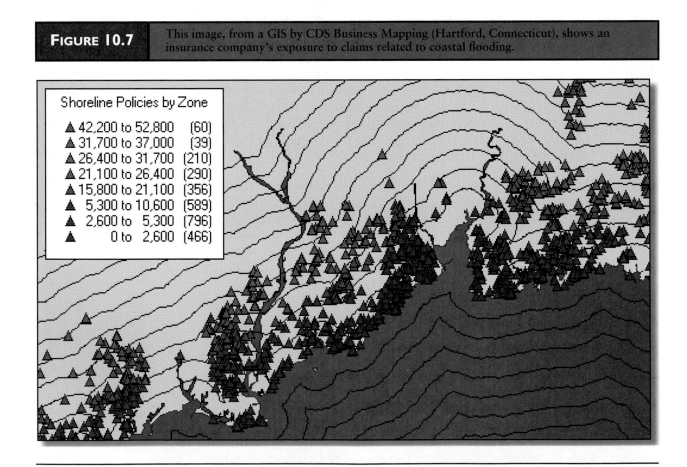

Shoreline Policies by Zone

▲ 42,200 to 52,800 (60)
▲ 31,700 to 37,000 (39)
▲ 26,400 to 31,700 (210)
▲ 21,100 to 26,400 (290)
▲ 15,800 to 21,100 (356)
▲ 5,300 to 10,600 (589)
▲ 2,600 to 5,300 (796)
▲ 0 to 2,600 (466)

resource management, land use, and public safety. It helps with zoning, code enforcement, building permits, inspections, and emergency response, among other functions. The GIS reduced the time required to process complaints about building code enforcement by 60 to 80 percent. The city also used its GIS to prove that the federal census had undercounted Scottsdale's population, resulting in a $9 million windfall in additional federal payments over five years.[30]

Douglas Kelly, media director for Black Rock Golf Corporations in Englewood, Colorado, uses mapping software to plot sales of golf clubs by city, state, and region. The software lets him see actual and projected sales by location, as well as comparative sales before and after an infomercial. Kelly can use the results to make decisions about buying television advertising time.[31]

International firms also use GISs. NESA, a Danish electric utility, uses a GIS to provide data about physical plants for transmissions and distribution, as well as transformers, switches, and service point location for its customers.[32]

Expert Systems. Expert systems, as discussed in Chapter 8, allow managers to use the collective wisdom of experts in the field to help make decisions. Sue Johnson may use expert system components of a DSS to assist with pricing, staffing, advertising, or expansion decisions. Expert systems add power to DSSs by improving analyses when data are unreliable, contradictory, or of limited validity.[33] Banc-Boston, a mortgage lending firm, uses an automated underwriting program that includes a loan scoring expert-based protocol. The company can lock in mortgage rates and issue conditional approvals in less than two hours. Countrywide Fund Corporation, a mortgage financing company in Pasadena, California, has direct links to 500 partners and can lock in interest rates and prequalify loans before home buyers look at their first house. The company takes information over the telephone and uses expert systems to quickly preapprove a loan at a guaranteed rate for 30 days, so the buyers know exactly what they can afford.[34]

DECISION SUPPORT SYSTEMS AND TRANSACTION PROCESSING SYSTEMS

A DSS usually obtains its database from an organization's TPS. Hallmark Cards, for example, feeds sales information from point-of-sale scanners in its stores into its decision support system. Managers then use the DSS to analyze sales trends and forecast demand. Hallmark has also linked its computerized inventory and distribution system to the DSS to improve product delivery.[35]

The DSS, like a management reporting system, usually requires significant computer resources that would interfere with a company's TPS if run on the same computer. As a result, information systems staff usually download DSS databases from selected and sometimes aggregated TPS data. Alternatively, companies have switched to using client/server systems that allow access to the data from multiple locations in real time. At Burlington Northern, for example, dispatchers in the operations center and employees in customer service can both access the same information but from different angles and using different interfaces.[36] Companies now look to the Internet as the backbone of both transaction processing and DSS systems.

USING A DECISION SUPPORT SYSTEM FOR GROUP DECISION MAKING

The increasing use of teams in the workplace has prompted the need for decision support systems to support cooperative decision making. A **group decision support system (GDSS)** addresses any or all of the following aspects of joint decision making: idea generation, alternative analysis, alternative evaluation, and consensus building.[37] Companies use GDSSs for tasks such as long-term planning, setting standards, redesigning processes, and setting budget priorities.

In addition to the elements found in a standard DSS, GDSSs include analytical and operational tools to improve group decision-making processes. For example, polling software allows group members to vote on alternatives, with or without anonymity. Other software implements a variety of brainstorming techniques, guiding group members to react in various ways to the ideas of other group members. GDSSs often include software to help group members identify areas of agreement and areas of disagreement. They may include software to help elicit and explain the underlying reasoning and preferences of group members as they search for common ground when making difficult decisions.

Many GDSSs require **electronic meeting rooms**. Participants work at their own computers on a U-shaped table facing a common computer at the front of the room, which can be seen by all participants, as shown in Figure 10.8. Any participant can control the common computer. Alternatively, the computer can merely assimilate the entries of the participants onto a single, large screen. This approach allows participants to contribute anonymously to the problem-solving effort. Such anonymity allows GDSSs to improve conflict management and foster group cohesiveness.[38] Groups focusing on a public screen tend to perceive all ideas as "our" ideas rather than "my" idea or "your" idea. This perspective tends to reduce the emotional ownership of ideas and allows decisions to be made with less conflict.

Duke Power, an electric utility serving the Piedmont regions of North and South Carolina, uses Ventana Corporation's GroupSystem GDSS for such activities as analyzing and addressing inventory problems and critiquing and improving work processes.[39] The Chevron Pipe Line Company estimates that using a GDSS to help make decisions on product standardization and process improvement saves the company more than $5 million per year.[40] In one study at IBM, teams using electronic meeting systems saved an average of 50 percent in labor costs and reduced elapsed project time by an average of 91 percent compared to a control group. A duplicate study produced similar results. IBM now has more than 90 electronic meeting rooms.[41]

GROUPWARE

Group decision support systems exemplify a class of software called **groupware, computer-supported cooperative work (CSCW)**, or **group support systems (GSSs)**. Groupware supports the group activities of managers and other workers. Because managers participate in groups both as supervisors and as members working on common tasks, groupware assists them in exchanging information, coordinating

FIGURE 10.8 Computer conferencing rooms can be set up in a variety of ways, one of which is shown here.

activities, and managing work flow. W.L. Gore and Associates, the maker of Gore-tex and other high-technology materials, uses a Lotus Notes database of product and customer data as a way of connecting its worldwide field sales force with its product development teams. A field engineer meeting with a customer about a new product can takes notes on his laptop. These notes then appear in the corporate database within hours and provide widely-available information about the new product's performance.[42]

Groupware provides an electronic mechanism for enhancing communication among group members and hence improving group coordination, discussions, problem solving, and meetings. Table 10.3 illustrates how groupware reduces the impact of separation among group members in time and space.

Frontier Media, which designs multimedia products for *Fortune* 500 companies, used TeamTalk to save and organize comments about the company's ongoing projects. As illustrated in Figure 10.9, the software creates a topic for each project, and users can then access the topic several times each day to give or receive updates. The company's president noted that "TeamTalk enables me to keep my finger on the pulse of what's

INFORMATION TECHNOLOGY AND GLOBAL BUSINESS

Though still struggling to modernize its economy, Poland is automating its railway system's finances in a big way.

In a $7 million deal with Computron Software, Inc. in Rutherford, N.J., the Polish State Railways System is installing Computron's client/server financial software, backed by the vendor's Computer Output OnLine (COOL) system that manages mainframe-based reports and makes them readily accessible.

Up to 7,000 of the railway's 250,000 employees will access the system, mostly from remote locations. It will be housed on 10 Digital Equipment Corp. Alpha servers throughout the country.

"Poland took a big step in joining the free market, now we have to join Europe as quickly as possible," said Mariusz Zienkowicz, deputy finance director and project manager at the railway.

Poland must meet various requirements to join the European Community by 1997, one of which is to upgrade the management of its railway system. Currently, all financial information is stored on microfiche, making research and decision making a slow and tedious affair for finance employees.

"All the information going to the management level is delivered by post and comes printed on a piece of paper," Zienkowicz said. "It is always difficult to get."

COOL will put this data online. The system's server software writes and indexes host batch reports to optical disc, replacing the traditional

PROBLEMS IN MANAGING GROUPWARE

Groupware does not solve all group performance problems. It can result in the following:

- *Inappropriate Information Sharing.* Some people will not share information despite having the technological capability. The corporate culture may also not support the sharing of information electronically. Some people share irrelevant or unnecessary information, making it difficult to stay focused. Groupware also encourages socializing, which may interfere with job performance.
- *Information Overload.* When faced with a flood of information, managers often cannot differentiate important from unimportant information. Workgroup editors that screen, edit, and consolidate messages, especially with electronic lists and notes, are one solution to the overload problem.
- *Too Many or Inappropriate Meetings.* Groupware may increase the number of meetings because it reduces the time needed to arrange them. Online meetings do not work for all types of communication. Managers need to diagnose when face-to-face contact benefits team members. They need to diagnose both the information required and the best context for delivery.

green bar reports or microfiche. The client software lets users search, select, and output the data stored on disc faster than they could with microfiche.

"There is a cost reduction with eliminating microfiche and time delays, but the advantage of the enterprise access is the immediate access to electronic reports," said Mason Grigsby, principal at Output Strategies, Inc. in San Francisco.

Because COOL stores compressed data instead of the full image of a report, users can query and download the indexed data faster, while taking up less bandwidth on the railway's own X.25 network.

Computron also will analyze how users typically use the data, and it will prepare standard queries and COOL reports so that only the page of data the customer requires will come over the lines, said Scott Grisanti, product manager for COOL and workflow at Computron.

Because COOL is independent of the financial system and shows a fast return on investment, Zienkowicz said he expects other uses for it. "It can be used in any part of the environment for the railroads," he said.

SOURCE: Reprinted with permission from Tim Ouellette, Poland's railways get COOL on finances, *Computerworld* (September 4, 1995): 48.

EXECUTIVE INFORMATION SYSTEMS

Executives require somewhat different information from middle- and lower-level managers. **Executive information systems (EISs)**, although they resemble decision support systems, respond to the particular requirements of top-level managers. Unlike DSSs, which deal with specific problems, EISs are characterized by enterprise-wide and external data. They focus less on modeling and more on assembling and displaying data, recognizing trends, determining underlying causes, and communicating knowledge.

Executives use EISs to answer specific questions or monitor performance, which requires greater efficiency in looking at information. Cooper Tire and Rubber uses the Traffic Executive Information System to help its managers make sense of data about customer calls. The executives use this information to determine the best services and promotions to offer.[57] Some executives scan information in an EIS without specific questions in mind. For them, EISs helped broaden their outlook, challenge their assumptions, and provide greater insight into their businesses.[58]

Most EISs include mainly hard information, such as financial data, sales, shipments, and other historical information. Increasingly they include soft data, such as predictions, opinions, explanations, and forecasts. Table 10.4 compares these two types of information.

| TABLE 10.4 | Executive information systems can include both hard and soft data. | |

Characteristics	Hard	Soft
Perceived accuracy	High	Depends on source
Source	Machine resident; often internal	Human; often external
Subject to interpretation	Generally accepted	Individually assessed
Timeliness	Historical	Current
Perceived value	Low	High
Availability	Regular	Ad hoc
Standardization	High	Low
Richness	Low	High
Existence	Generally known	Often known
Ownership	Generally available	Often tightly held
Lifetime	Long	Short
Communication channel	Formal	Informal

SOURCE: S. Z. Dix, A bunch of softies, *Computerworld* (October 19, 1992): 105.

External pressures, such as the increasingly competitive and dynamic environment, and internal pressures, such as a need for timely information, improved communication, and access to data, lead to the development of an EIS. Usually an organization's chief executive officer or president sponsors development of an EIS, but over time its use spreads to lower-level employees as subordinates become aware that they can access unique information available to the organizational leaders.[59] Do It All, Ltd., a British home-improvement retailer, introduced an EIS that shows senior executives how their business is performing. It reduces large amounts of information to its essentials. It also lets managers obtain specific details about a particular product, department, or customer so they can offer customers what they want.[60]

TYPICAL FEATURES OF AN EXECUTIVE INFORMATION SYSTEM

Because most executives use an executive information system without the benefit of technical intermediaries, an EIS must have a friendly user interface. In addition, an EIS must provide access to company data, electronic mail, external database and news access, work processing, spreadsheets, and automated filing.

User Interface. Most executives cannot type well and so dislike using a keyboard to request information. An EIS generally includes a graphical user interface to limit keyboard use. Most systems present numeric data in a variety of tabular and graphical formats. The user can select among the formats with a mouse or touch screen. The systems use color and graphics consistently to cue the user to the information. For example, red might highlight any number outside an expected range, and blinking red might highlight an item that requires immediate attention. Often the

ETHICAL ISSUES IN IT

A spot-check of employee electronic mail revealed this alarming message: "I'll lose my job if they find out what I sent you."

Had company secrets been transmitted over the Internet? To find out, anxious officials at the West Coast company called Computer Forensics, Inc., a Seattle firm that combs through hardware and software for evidence that some people expect to be hidden or erased.

Enter Joan Feldman, the 44-year-old president of the cybersleuth firm, rolling her hard-sided Samsonite suitcase. It's packed with portable hard drives and proprietary software tools that help her pry open computer files and backup tapes.

As it turns out, the e-mailer hadn't revealed corporate goodies. But he had sent pornography, allegedly to a minor in a chat room.

"The good news was the guy wasn't a thief. The bad news was he was a potential pedophile," Feldman said.

Feldman and her team of former Secret Service agents, retired military investigators, and hard-core geeks root around a company's information systems and look for evidence. The field is called computer forensics.

Sometimes a company hires forensics experts, but more often they are hired by opposing attorneys seeking the "smoking gun" that could lead to a courtroom victory.

1. What are the ethical implications of reading employees' electronic mail?
2. What rights do employees have in using electronic mail that is part of groupware?
3. What might be the impact on the use of groupware if employees knew that cybersleuthing was occurring?

SOURCE: Excerpted with permission from Kim S. Nash, Computer detectives uncover smoking guns, *Computerworld* (June 9, 1997): 1, 26.

screen shows the name and telephone numbers of those individuals responsible for acting on the data presented on the screen.

Most EISs also provide a drill-down capability. They first present data at their most aggregated levels. The executive can then select a line and request the detail behind it. The executive can drill down through greater and greater levels of detail or return to higher levels of aggregation as desired.

Communication with Employees.   Most EISs contain a variety of groupware features, including calendaring systems, electronic mail, electronic notes, and electronic bulletin boards. Top executives who travel frequently use a laptop and modem to access electronic mail and contact key employees, suppliers, and customers.

Scanned News Updates.   Although executives read newspapers and magazines widely to learn about events that might have an impact on their organization's operations, searching through news sources for relevant articles is time consuming and relatively unproductive. Many organizations now purchase news services that scan the media for relevant items. Executives specify in advance the types of articles they find relevant, and computerized expert systems with online access to news services and article abstracts scan for them.

Query Features. EIS vendors are adding query functions to compete with decision support systems for general management functions. In particular, new software includes the possibility of making interactive queries across the World Wide Web.[61]

Functional Support. Increasingly EISs support functional applications. For example, they may provide software that addresses corporate functions, such as sales, budgeting, and marketing. They may also include software that supports the needs of vertical industries, such as financial services, insurance, or retailing.[62]

ADVANCED TECHNOLOGY

ADEPT (Advanced Decision Environment for Process Tasks) is an intelligent agent system for the management of business processes being developed at the University of London. The ADEPT project addresses the problems involved in coordinating semi-autonomous departments of a large organization or multiple organizations by using an agent's autonomy and managing their dependencies through automated negotiation.

Company managers make informed decisions based on a combination of judgment and information from marketing, sales, research, development, manufacturing, and finance departments. Ideally, all relevant information should be brought together before judgment is exercised. However obtaining pertinent, consistent and up-to-date information across a large company is a complex and time-consuming process.

Given these characteristics, it was decided that the most natural way to view the business process is as a collection of autonomous, problem solving agents that interact when they have interdependencies. In this context, an agent can be viewed as an encapsulated problem solving entity that exhibits the following properties:

- Autonomy—Agents perform the majority of their problem solving tasks without the direct intervention of humans or other agents, and they have control over their own actions and their own internal state.
- Social ability—Agents interact, when they deem appropriate, with other artificial agents and humans in order to complete their problem solving and to help others with their activities. This requires that agents have, as a minimum, a means by which they can communicate their requirements to others and an internal mechanism for deciding what and when social interactions are appropriate (both in terms of generating requests and judging incoming requests).
- Responsiveness—Agents perceive their environment and respond in a timely fashion to changes which occur in it.
- Proactiveness—Agents do not simply act in response to their environment, they exhibit opportunistic, goal-directed behaviour and take the initiative where appropriate.

SOURCE: The Intelligent Systems Group, Queen Mary and Westfield College, University of London, http://www.elec.qmw.ac.uk/dai/ and http://www.elec.qmw.ac.uk/dai/projects/adept/index.html, December 29, 1997.

LIMITATIONS TO EXECUTIVE INFORMATION SYSTEMS

The promise of executive information systems has yet to materialize. At General Electric, for example, Jack Welch gets "a couple of reports over the PC, but most of his information comes in the form of faxed reports or by talking to people," according to a GE spokesperson. The executive team at Eastman Chemical also gets reports on company performance by hard copy.[63]

EISs have failed to deliver for several reasons:[64]

- Programs prescribed a path of inquiry, allowing users little leeway in the types of questions they could ask. New software based on artificial intelligence should reduce this limitation.
- Consolidating data from a variety of information systems into a single EIS posed technical and practical problems. Access to information on a client/server system with special EIS interfaces may solve this problem.
- Many EISs lacked intuitive appeal, making executives reluctant to tackle them. Current systems can more easily be made user-friendly.
- EISs had slow response time because data were stored in standard relational databases making complicated queries difficult. Advances in data storage should speed query time.
- Many executives preferred the status quo, choosing to rely on traditional ways of obtaining information. The arrival of new generations of executives who have used computers since childhood should eliminate this obstacle.

SUMMARY

Top-, middle-, and lower-level managers require extensive and diverse types of information to perform their jobs. Managers in a global environment need information systems that help them access and analyze current comprehensive information. They can use management reporting systems, decision support systems, group decision support systems, and executive information systems.

Management reporting systems (MRSs) include detail, summary, and exception reports. Managers can request periodic reports, reports initiated by a particular event, or reports published on demand. MRSs in many organizations comprise the reporting components of a transaction processing system.

Decision support systems (DSSs) include a database, knowledge base, model base, and user interface. DSSs can answer unforeseen questions by supporting ad hoc queries and providing analytical abilities. A DSS usually obtains its database from an organization's transaction processing system. The analytical elements of a DSS can include data mining, OLAP, simulation languages, goal-seeking software, statistical packages, geographical information systems, and expert systems. Group decision support systems help group members cooperate in decision making.

Groupware, computer-supported cooperative work, or group support systems support a group's interaction in performing a task or reaching a goal. Groupware can include group decision support systems, message systems, multiuser editors, computer conferencing, intelligent agents, and coordination systems. Organizations can face challenges of appropriate information sharing and scheduling of meetings in managing groupware.

Executive information systems (EISs) are used primarily by top-level executives to help them look at and evaluate already-analyzed information. Typical EISs include a user-friendly user interface, facilities for communicating with employees, and options for scanning news updates. EISs have not lived up to their promise because of technical and human limitations.

KEY TERMS

ad hoc query
computer-supported cooperative work (CSCW)
data mining
decision support system (DSS)
desktop conferencing
detail report
electronic bulletin board
electronic list
electronic meeting room
electronic notes
electronic polling
event-initiated report
exception report
executive information system (EIS)
geographical information system (GIS)
goal-seeking software
group decision support system (GDSS)
group support system (GSS)

groupware
heuristics
knowledge base
management information system (MIS)
management reporting system (MRS)
message system
model base
notification system
on-demand report
online analytical processing (OLAP)
periodic report
real-time conferencing
simulation
statistical report
summary report
sysop
teleconferencing
user interface

DISCUSSION AND REVIEW QUESTIONS

1. What is a management information system?
2. How do MISs help managers who function in a global environment?
3. What is a management reporting system?
4. How do detail, summary, and exception reports differ?
5. When would a manager use a notification system instead of an exception report?
6. How do periodic, event-initiated, and on-demand reports differ?
7. What is the relationship between an MRS and a transaction processing system?
8. What are the benefits of a decision support system?
9. What are the components of a DSS?
10. How do DSSs answer unforeseen and ad hoc questions?
11. What types of analytical capabilities do DSSs provide?
12. How do DSSs interface with external data?
13. What analytical elements can a DSS provide?

14. What role does data mining play in a DSS?
15. What role does OLAP play in a DSS?
16. What are the major elements of groupware?
17. What are the advantages and disadvantages of group decision support systems?
18. What three ways can managers hold conferences?
19. How do executive information systems differ from decision support systems?
20. What are the typical features of an EIS?

IS ON THE WEB

Exercise 1: Locate and visit the Web sites of three companies that produce OLAP products. Compare the OLAP products on their overall features and their applicability to a DSS in support of product pricing.

Exercise 2: Locate and visit the sites of two companies that produce videoconferencing systems. How are their systems similar? How do they differ?

MINICASE

AIRLINE MOVES UP

Stressing the value of planning, Alex Benevides, project leader for [Lotus] Notes development at British Airways Information Management Group in New York, says his Notes 4.0 upgrade began a year before Lotus released the product.

British Airways started using Notes 3.x several years ago for a sales-force automation project with about 200 mobile users. They were using Notes to keep track of their accounts, send e-mail, file meeting reports, research information, and contribute marketing intelligence.

Because the airline had good results with Notes 3.x, it wanted to put another 1,000 people on the platform and migrate the rest of the company from cc:Mail to Notes Mail. It also looked forward to Notes 4.x as the platform for developing an Internet presence, publishing brochures, and marketing and internal materials on a World Wide Web site. Success for the Notes 4.0 migration in the United States was important because the airline expects to bring Notes 4.0 to its European operations in the near future. "We're the guinea pigs for new technologies," Benevides confides.

For development, there was a big difference between Notes 4.0 and Notes 3.x. "It has a different interface for the forms and views, and menus don't always show

SOURCE: Case excerpted with permission from Peter Ruber, Early adopters urge caution, *LanTimes Online,* http://www.wcmh.com/lantimes/96jul/607a072a.html.

up where you expect to find them," he says. "But a skilled Notes 3 developer should not have too much difficulty making the jump."

British Airways brought in consultants to move critical Notes 3.x databases to Notes 4.0 and to set up and size the servers and test them out.

Despite the legwork, the airline still ran into some problems, such as unexpected mail failures when Notes Mail 4.0 users sent encrypted documents to cc:Mail users. They continually received a delivery-failure notice. That did not happen under Notes Mail 3.x. "We're hoping for a quick resolution," Benevides says, "because our policy is to encrypt all documents."

Benevides recommends that other companies begin planning far in advance of actual deployment. "But you don't want to take forever and analyze it to death," he says. "Select a group of 20 users, hook them up quickly, and let them work with it. That way you can buttonhole all the little problems and find the things that people don't understand."

Case Questions

Diagnosis

1. What information needs did British Airways have?
2. How have these needs changed over time?

Evaluation

3. How does groupware meet these needs?
4. How well did Notes 3.0 meet these needs?

Design

5. What improvements did Notes 4.0 offer?

Implementation

6. What implementation issues did British Airways face in upgrading the Notes software?

ACTIVITY 10.1 FINE JEWELRY AT HAMPSTEAD DEPARTMENT STORES

Step 1: Read the following scenario:

Carl Elkins manages the fine jewelry division of Hampstead Department Stores, a major retail chain of 19 stores in the southwest United States. Unlike managers in other departments at Hampstead, Elkins manages all employees who work in the fine jewelry departments in all of the chain's stores, a total of three buyers, five assistant buyers, and 70 salespeople across the country. Elkins has bottom-line responsibility for the fine jewelry division. He needs to have a good understanding of the sales in his departments so that he can stock and staff them appropriately.

Step 2: Individually or in small groups, as directed by your instructor, design a set of reports that provide the information Elkins needs to run the fine jewelry division. Your design should indicate what information each column of the report includes, what totals (if any) should appear, and on what schedule the report should be produced.

Step 3:   Exchange your report designs with another student or group. Compare the designs you received with your own designs. Then answer the following questions:

1. How many reports are necessary to give Elkins the information he needs?
2. Are detail, summary, or exception reports most useful for providing this information?
3. What reporting schedule is best for providing this information?
4. Would a decision support system be more appropriate than a management reporting system for providing the required information?

L&A SCALE COMPANY   ACTIVITY 10.2

L&A Scale Company manufactures digital industrial scales. The company has expanded greatly in its 20 years, going from a job shop of 5 employees with sales of $500,000 to a bona fide manufacturer with 100 employees and $30 million in annual sales.

Donald Jenner, the president, has installed an array of computer systems over the years. They mainly support the processing of transactions around ordering, shipping, and payroll. The system provides numerous management reports, but Jenner's managers find that they cannot easily get answers to questions such as the following: How have customers' buying patterns changed over time? Does offering discounts for early payments successfully reduce accounts receivable? Do piece-rate incentive systems lead to better productivity than paying workers straight salary?

Step 1:   Individually or in small groups, as directed by your instructor, write five questions that Jenner likely would want answered.

Step 2:   List the characteristics of a decision support system that would answer these questions. Be as specific as possible in identifying the type of information the system should include, the queries it should address, and the screens it should produce.

Step 3:   Share your lists with the rest of the class. What types of information can a DSS provide? What costs and benefits would be associated with developing a DSS for Jenner's managers? What issues must Jenner address in integrating a DSS with the rest of the information systems in the company?

BREACHING THE SECURITY OF THE HUMAN RESOURCES
INFORMATION SYSTEM   ACTIVITY 10.3

Step 1:   Read the following scenario:

Jennifer Blair is the director of Human Resources Management at Smithton Associates. In the past the Human Resources Information System (HRIS) was used to produce affirmative action reports in response to government requirements. She recently learned that several employees who had authority to run those reports also ran additional, unauthorized queries. She was particularly concerned because the HRIS included confidential information about the medical status of the company's employees. In fact, she discovered that one of the department managers had done an ad hoc query that had created a list of all employees who were HIV positive.

20. Linda Wilson, Digging for consumer gold in buying habits, *Computerworld* (July 21, 1997): 73, 76.

21. Martin J. Garvey, Citibank mines data, *Information Week* (October 7, 1996): 85.

22. This discussion is based on large part on Karen Spinner, Unlocking the data warehouse with OLAP, *Wall Street & Technology* (Winter 1997): 18–20.

23. Land O'Lakes butters up brokers, *Software Magazine* (December 1996): S15.

24. Sandeep Tungare, An eye on the horizon, *Manufacturing Systems* 15 (January 1997): 48–54.

25. George Black, Wellcome prescribes OLAP for decision support, *International Software Magazine* (December 1995): 94–95.

26. R. Belz and P. Mertens, Combining knowledge-based systems and simulation to solve rescheduling problems, *Decision Support Systems* 17 (May 21, 1996): 141–157.

27. G. A. Forgionne, Forecasting Army housing supply with a DSS-delivered econometric model, *Omega* 24 (October 1996): 561–576.

28. Tom Spitzer, A database perspective on GIS, Part I, *DBMS* (November 1996): 95–96.

29. Tom Spitzer, Year of the GIS, Part 2, *DBMS* (January 1997): 63–69.

30. Gary H. Anthes, City blazes own IS trail, *Computerworld* (September 16, 1996): 81, 85.

31. Tim McCollum, High-tech marketing hits the target, *Nation's Business* 85(6) (June 1997): 39–42.

32. Paul Westmose, Danish utility implements enterprise-wide GIS, *Transmission and Distribution World* 48 (September 1996): 28–33.

33. Alfs T. Berztiss, Software methodologies for decision support, *Information & Management* 18(5) (May 1990): 221–229.

34. Leslie Goff, Home swift home, *Computerworld* (March 13, 1995): 101–108.

35. Scheier, Timing is everything.

36. Julia King, IS revamp on track, *Computerworld* (April 10, 1995): 1, 15.

37. Kenneth R. MacCrimmon and Christian Wagner, The architecture of an information system for the support of alternative generation, *Journal of Management Information Systems* 8(3) (Winter 1991–92): 49–67.

38. Laku Chidambaram, Robert P. Bostrom, and Bayard E. Wynne, A longitudinal study of the impact of group decision support systems on group development, *Journal of Management Information Systems* 7(3) (1991): 7–25.

39. Ventana Corporation, GroupSystems success story, Determining the GroupSystem ROI, http://www.ventana.com/html/vc_ss2.html, December 29, 1995.

40. Ventana Corporation, GroupSystems success story, Improving business processes, http://www.ventana.com/html/vc_ss1.html, December 29, 1997.

41. Jay F. Nunamaker, Jr., Robert O. Briggs, and Daniel D. Mittleman, Electronic meeting systems: Ten years of lessons learned, *Proceedings of the 29th Annual Hawaii International Conference on Systems Science* (1996): 418–427.

42. Gary H. Anthes, Learning how to share, *Computerworld* (February 23, 1998): 75–77.

43. Colleen Frye, Groupware strikes collaborative chord, *Software Magazine* (October 1995): 94–102.

44. Elisabeth Horwitt, Remote control, *Computerworld* (June 12, 1995): 107–110.

45. Stephanie Stahl, Hire on one, get 'em all, *Information Week* (March 20, 1995): 120–124.

46. This discussion is based on C. A. Ellis, S. J. Gibbs, and G. L. Rein, Groupware: Some issues and experiences, *Communications of the ACM*, 34(1) (January 1991): 38–58.

47. Michele N. K. Collison, Taking note from Lotus, *Black Enterprise* 26(8) (March 1996): 38–40.

48. Groupware enhances teamwork at the Sports Authority, *Chain Store Age* 72 (November 1996): 73–76.

49. Amy Doan, Shell deploys Notes as its extranet, *InfoWorld* (February 10, 1997): 19.

50. Sylvia Feder, Order within chaos, *Automatic ID News* 12 (October 1996): 30–31.

51. Jay F. Nunamaker, Jr., Robert O. Briggs, Daniel D. Mittleman, Douglas R. Vogel, and Pierre A. Balthazard, Lessons from a dozen years of group support systems research: A discussion of lab and field findings, *Journal of Management Information Systems* 13 (Winter 1996/1997): 163–207.

52. Collison, Taking note from Lotus.

53. Ellis et al., Groupware.

54. Robert A. Gable, Videoconferencing perils: "Murphy was an optimist!" *Business Communications Review* 26 (October 1996): 52–54.

55. Mark R. Cutkosky, Jay M. Tenenbaum, and Jay Glicksman, Madefast: Collaborative Engineering over the Internet, *Communications of the ACM* 39 (September 1996): 78–87; see also http://www.madefast.org/mf/Overview/overview.html and http://www.madefast.org/ mf/Design-Documentation/current-state.html.

56. Horwitt, Remote control.

57. We've got your number, *Chief Executive*, CEO Brief Supplement (October 1996): 12–15.

58. Betty Vandenbosch and Sid L. Huff, Searching and scanning: How executives obtain information from executive information systems, *MIS Quarterly* 21(1) (1997): 81–105.

59. Hugh Watson, R. K. Rainer, Jr., and Chang Koh, Executive information systems: A framework for development and a survey of current practices, *MIS Quarterly* 15(1) (1991): 13–30; C. Barrow, Implementing an executive information system: Seven steps for success, *Journal of Information Systems Management* 7(2) (1990): 41–46.

60. Clive Couldwell, Just do it all, *CIO* 9 (May 1, 1996): 64–68.

61. Wayne W. Eckerson, Drilling for data, *Computerworld* (December 2, 1996).

62. Ibid.

63. Doug Bartholomew, When will EIS deliver? *Industry Week* (March 3, 1997).

64. Drawn in part from Bartholomew, When will EIS deliver?

Chapter 11

Strategic Information Systems

LEARNING OBJECTIVES

After completing Chapter 11, you will be able to

1. Describe what makes an information system strategic.
2. Discuss three purposes of strategic information systems.
3. Identify the five strategies companies use to derive a competitive advantage.
4. Illustrate how companies can use information systems to reduce costs.
5. Discuss how companies can use information systems for differentiating products, services, quality, and customer service.
6. Compare the use of information systems for identifying opportunities in existing market segments and creating new market segments.
7. Discuss the use of information systems to support customer, supplier, and logistics linkages.
8. Offer examples of infusing products with information and selling proprietary information.

STRATEGIC SYSTEMS AT PFIZER PHARMACEUTICALS

Pharmaceutical firms no longer simply make and distribute drugs. As part of the dramatically changing health care industry, they now gather and deliver health care information to their customers. Managed health care has forced them to develop new ways of doing business. "Within the pharmaceutical industry, there's an aggressive move to 'knowledge management,' or the ability to take data from a variety of sources and use it to make good strategic decisions," says Saul Kaplan, a managing partner of Andersen Consulting's pharmaceutical and medical products practice in Boston. Pharmaceutical companies now use information technology as strategic weapons to provide customers with important information and value-added services.

Pfizer, Inc. introduced sales-force automation that allowed sales representatives to provide physicians with information about a product's side effects, costs, and effectiveness. It is also exploring using the Internet to link with suppliers and other partners. It has developed a private network called VendorGate that links Pfizer's research labs to its genetic engineering contractors worldwide.[1]

How does Pfizer use information technology to enhance its strategy? What advantages does this offer? In this chapter we explore the strategic uses of information systems. Specifically, we investigate key issues in introducing strategic information systems. Then we consider the use of information systems for five purposes: (1) low-cost leadership, (2) differentiation, (3) focus, (4) linkage support, and (5) information leadership.

Pfizer and other drug manufacturers use sales-force automation to ensure that they keep stores well stocked and physicians informed about the most recent products. These companies use this and other types of automation as part of their strategic plan to provide physicians and consumers with important, current information and to support their research and development groups in creating new products.

WHAT IS A STRATEGIC INFORMATION SYSTEM?

Strategic information systems help organizations implement their long-term direction and the activities used to achieve their goals. Strategic systems can support both externally and internally focused strategic initiatives.

- Externally focused initiatives focus on systems used by customers, clients, or suppliers to create special relationships with the firm.
- Internally focused initiatives focus on systems used by the firm to reduce costs, increase profits, or improve quality.

KEY ISSUES RELATED TO STRATEGIC INFORMATION SYSTEMS

Effective systems align with organizational goals, create a sustainable competitive advantage, and support business process redesign, as shown in Figure 11.1.

ALIGNMENT

Strategic alignment refers to the fit between an organization's strategic goals and objectives and its information systems. As more organizations view information technology as a strategic weapon they have developed information systems that help them create new market opportunities and enhance relationships with customers and suppliers. For example, the information systems at Pfizer must support its strategy of providing more comprehensive medical information to physicians and patients.

Numerous surveys indicate that senior managers outside the IS function and IS executives consider the alignment of information systems with business strategy a critical priority.[2] When Pizza Hut opened an electronic storefront on the World Wide Web, it initially saw limited action. But now Pizza Hut plans to expand Internet ordering to many markets. "Our goal is to be wherever our customers are," according to Dan Cooke, vice president of MIS. In addition, Pizza Hut regularly monitors customer satisfaction. The company calls thousands of customers each week to get feedback on their experience. Employees then enter information into a customer database, which Pizza Hut uses to track the buying patterns of more than 25 million delivery customers. As shown in Figure 11.2, Pizza Hut uses this system to build customer loyalty and meet its strategic goals.[3]

SUSTAINABLE ADVANTAGE

Strategic information systems need to provide organizations with a **sustainable advantage**. They can create such an advantage in numerous ways, as summarized in Table 11.1. For example, they might try to design or introduce a technology that

FIGURE 11.1 Strategic information systems improve organizational performance through alignment, sustaining a competitive advantage, and supporting business process redesign.

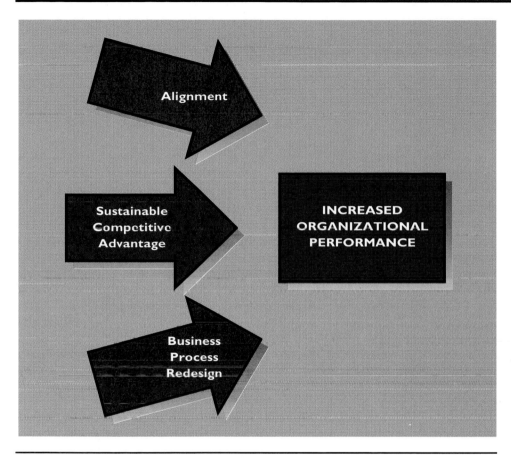

provides unique benefits that competitors cannot duplicate. Delta Airlines, for example, has rolled out six kiosks near its Atlanta, Georgia, headquarters that let customers talk in real time with airline ticketing agents using the Internet. Customers can buy and receive flight tickets, check a frequent flier account, or register for the frequent flier program.[4]

Companies might also implement a strategic system that alters industry characteristics.[5] Pfizer's VendorGate, for example, which links its research labs to its genetic engineering contractors, might foster a new model for partnerships in the industry.

Southwest Airlines uses its information systems to sustain its grasp on the "Triple Crown" of airline service awards for best on-time performance, fewest customer complaints, and fewest lost bags. The airline automated many of its flight scheduling processes as part of a project expected to deliver productivity gains 20 times as great as the investment in the new system. The Southwest Airlines Integrated Flight Tracking System (Swift) helps dispatchers route flights around bad weather, calculate how much fuel a flight requires, and will eventually provide information for flight planning, maintenance, and other functions. Swift has allowed the dispatchers to reroute passengers from canceled or delayed flights 20

Numerous companies have purchased and installed a version of the enterprise resource planning product of German systems integrator SAP AG. This software forces companies to create well-integrated business processes across functions, departments, and applications, and so ensures consistent information. Owens-Corning, for example, went global with the SAP approach. Owens-Corning expects a $43 million saving within two years after installation of the system.[12]

Too often, managers of change fail to involve information technology experts early enough in their redesign effort. Because the managers who set business requirements often lack the time and expertise to remain current about the state of the art in information technology, they may miss strategic opportunities for redesign. Similarly, information technology specialists may miss opportunities for redesign because they lack knowledge of the business processes. Creating strong partnerships between business managers and IT executives helps avoid this problem. Such partnerships can help managers look for opportunities to use information systems for strategic advantage in the areas of low-cost leadership, differentiation, focus, linkages, and information leadership.

St. Joseph's Health System, in Orange, California, involved managers, staff, and its IT vendor in standardizing a number of core systems, such as admissions, order entry, and respiratory therapy. The staff in the system's hospitals spent eight months deciding how to standardize system elements such as diagnostic procedure codes. Using these decisions, Meditech, the vendor chosen to develop the information system, could ensure accurate, synchronized movement of data among various parts of the system and in different hospitals.[13]

USING INFORMATION SYSTEMS TO OBTAIN LOW-COST LEADERSHIP

A company with a low-cost leadership strategy tries to achieve high profits by maintaining lower costs than its competitors. With prices set by the marketplace, the lowest-cost producer will have the highest contribution margins and highest unit profits in the industry. A company can return these profits to the investor to attract more capital, reinvest them in the company to foster growth and expansion, or sacrifice the profits to eliminate competition and increase market share. If Pfizer chooses this strategy, the company will rely on achieving economies of scale in marketing and purchasing to keep cost and prices low and maximize sales volume. Such economies enhance the low-cost position of the low-cost leader and extend its competitive advantage over time. Pfizer would need to determine the information it requires to support this strategy and ensure that its information systems provide it.

USING INFORMATION SYSTEMS TO REDUCE COSTS

Early users of computer systems achieved cost reductions primarily by automating highly labor-intensive processes. Today, automation is only one of a large number of ways information systems help managers reduce costs and implement a low-cost leadership strategy. The International Telecommunications Satellite Organization (Intelsat), a Washington consortium of 138 telecom providers, is testing a new computerized system to allow its members to directly view and reserve satellite space that serves television stations. TV Max lets Intelsat customers dial in and see a graphic of available satellite space. They can then submit online orders using the same system. By saving time for their members in the ordering process, Intelsat also reduces costs and lets them win business from other satellite consortia.[14]

Automation can decrease costs by reducing the amount of labor, the time required for some processes, rework, and waste. The cost of purchasing and maintaining automation equipment and the cost of the skilled labor necessary to operate automation equipment somewhat reduce its benefits.

Pfizer could potentially reengineer processes in its accounting, customer service, manufacturing, and human resources departments if it chose a low-cost leadership strategy. Evaluating the ability of existing information systems to support business process redesign would follow the diagnosis of information needs associated with such a change. Design of information systems plays a key role in this process.

Scripps Health instituted CareTracs, a method of planning and recording care that reengineered and streamlined existing delivery systems. The system manages and documents a patient's progress through an illness. The system reduced patient charges by 10 to 18 percent. It also reduced documentation time by 40 to 60 percent.[15]

Quality purchasing and manufacturing, just-in-time inventory, and flattening the organizational hierarchy can contribute to a low-cost leadership strategy.

The International Telecommunications Satellite Organization (Intelsat) reduces costs for its member stations by streamlining the process for ordering space on satellites.

QUALITY PURCHASING AND MANUFACTURING

Poor quality not only affects customers' perceptions of a company's products and services, but it also increases a company's costs. For example, a company incurs unnecessary costs when it manufactures a defective unit that it cannot sell. A failure to identify defective products before shipping may cause customers to refuse delivery or return products after quality inspections or when the product malfunctions. Such returns not only reduce revenues but also affect the reputation of the firm, which in turn influences future sales. Even unreturned defective products can significantly affect a firm's reputation and subsequent sales.

Total quality management (TQM) is a comprehensive approach to improving quality and eliminating defects. Xerox, Motorola, Teradyne, and a host of other companies dramatically improved their bottom line by emphasizing quality, continuous improvement, and customer focus. These companies use information systems to monitor quality and track improvement efforts.

Successful companies apply for the Baldrige Award, recognition given by the U.S. Department of Labor that the company had met the highest standards of TQM. Winners include Ritz Carlton Hotels, Texas Instruments, the Cadillac Division of General Motors, Granite Rock, and Dana Commercial Credit. Figure 11.4 shows that quality pays. The 16 winners between 1988 and 1995 bested the Standard & Poor's 500-stock index by 3 to 1 in terms of their return on investment. The finalists beat the index by 2 to 1.

Quality-oriented organizations also attempt to reduce cycle time. Jones Apparel Group, for example, slashed the time required to manufacture its women's clothing. Prior to reengineering and introducing new information systems, Jones had 13

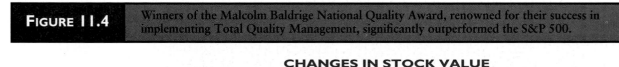

FIGURE 11.4 — Winners of the Malcolm Baldrige National Quality Award, renowned for their success in implementing Total Quality Management, significantly outperformed the S&P 500.

CHANGES IN STOCK VALUE

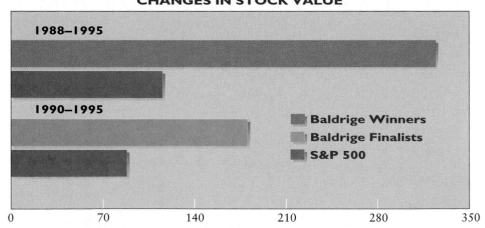

From April in the year when a company was a winner or finalist; Data: National Institute of Science & Technology.

SOURCE: Reprinted with permission from Otis Port, The Baldrige's other reward, *Business Week* (March 10, 1997): 75.

THE MANAGER IN ACTION

Few would take on the challenge that Arthur Ryan did in December 1994: to turn around the battered Goliath of the insurance industry. The Prudential Insurance Company of America was reeling under a class action suit from nearly 11 million policy holders over improper sales practices, contributing to a $900 million loss for the company that year.

Prudential's search for an outsider with a strong track record in corporate fixes ended with Ryan who, as president and COO of Chase Manhattan Bank, had shored up the financial institution's retail banking operations.

The 54-year old Ryan drew on his business expertise and 12 years in IS management at Control Data and Chase to control the damages swiftly and build a state-of-the-art network to move Prudential into the next millennium.

Prudential agreed to settle with policy holders for at least $410 million. Ryan cut Prudential's workforce from 100,000 to 83,000; streamlined business units under what he calls the "One Prudential" concept; and engineered a business model that required the information systems and business division to develop online activities jointly.

He plowed $1 billion into the insurer's IT infrastructure by installing a massive TCP/IP network and is using Web technologies to provide customers unprecedented access to information about their accounts and policies. The result is impressive: The company recorded $1 billion in net income in 1996.

Prudential has modified its business model to take advantage of the Internet and other online communication. The company has moved to what it calls "universal access," which has been made possible though the Internet and new internal networks. Universal access means making services available 24 hours a day, seven days a week. Customers are looking to do business their way, at their time and in the manner in which they choose. And it is the electronic medium that is allowing Prudential to be available virtually any time when a customer wishes to communicate with them.

SOURCE: Excerpted and edited with permission from Prudential bets future on E-Commerce, *Communications Week* (June 2, 1997): 20, 116.

---

divisions in ten countries making hundreds of styles. After instituting the Line Development Management System, which automated and streamlined the design calendar and preproduction process, as well as standardized part of the design process, Jones cut cycle time by eight weeks.[16]

JUST-IN-TIME INVENTORY AND MANUFACTURING

Excess inventory increases costs by tying up capital and increasing requirements for warehouse space. It also adds to the costs of maintaining, searching for, and retrieving inventory. Out-of-date inventory also increases costs by requiring the company to replace it. Insufficient inventory may also increase costs by forcing a company to shut down, reschedule production, or generate costly rush orders and back orders.

Just-in-time (JIT) practices provide inventory just as manufacturing requires it. For example, Polycon Industries delivers car bumpers to Ford's Oakville, Ontario, plant just-in-time for assembly, four hours after they are ordered.[17] This reduces costs by obtaining inventory precisely as needed—neither too early nor too late. It can also lower manufacturing costs because it demands better coordination between departments to sustain a low inventory. JIT requires computers and information systems to monitor complex and interrelated inventory and to plan and monitor the logistics required to replenish inventory.

Pitney Bowes' Document Services Division uses just-in-time inventory management to provide on-demand printing of documents. The company electronically stores the text of a publication on an optical disk. Then it can revise and print the exact number of copies needed in a short turnaround time. Customers can also request that Pitney Bowes publish only parts of a book, such as relevant sections of a technical manual. In this way Pitney Bowes reduces its customers' inventory and cuts both its customers' and its own storage costs.[18]

Companies that can produce goods as close to demand as possible save money in inventory, labor, and other costs. Lids, which sells sports caps, has built information systems that let the company compete by having hats available as soon after a championship sporting event as possible. Pro Player, which retails T-shirts and other sports gear, uses its information systems to notify retailers in December to place orders or visit warehouses near the football championship teams. Customers enter orders on laptops, which send them to Pro Player's computer. Pro Player then analyzes the orders and sends retailers an estimate of delivery dates.[19]

FLATTENING ORGANIZATIONAL STRUCTURES

Technology allows the flattening of organizational hierarchies and reduction in the number of managers. This outcome fits well with the movement to team-based management and more lateral communication in organizations. Pfizer, for example, could follow this trend of instituting team-based management and use information systems to distribute or replace its management functions, ultimately flattening the organizational structure.

Improvements in communication technology have also supported the management of geographically separate business units from a central corporate headquarters. Figure 11.5 illustrates the horizontal organization, one of the new flatter structures. Here information systems allow the company to organize according to business process.

USING INFORMATION SYSTEMS FOR DIFFERENTIATION

The **differentiation** strategy seeks a competitive advantage by distinguishing a company's products and services from those of its competitors. When a company and its competitors produce a product or provide a service that the market perceives as indistinguishable, such as toothpaste, shampoo, blank video tapes, or blank audio cassettes, that product or service becomes a commodity whose marginal cost determines its price. A company must differentiate its products from those of its competitors to

FIGURE 11.5   Horizontal organizations use information systems to focus on business processes rather than functions.

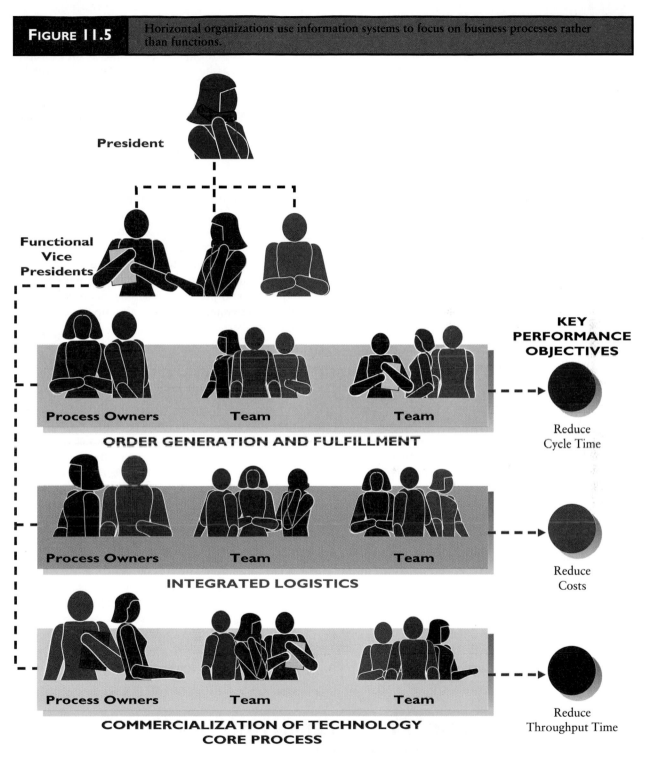

President

Functional Vice Presidents

KEY PERFORMANCE OBJECTIVES

Process Owners   Team   Team

ORDER GENERATION AND FULFILLMENT

Reduce Cycle Time

Process Owners   Team   Team

INTEGRATED LOGISTICS

Reduce Costs

Process Owners   Team   Team

COMMERCIALIZATION OF TECHNOLOGY CORE PROCESS

Reduce Throughput Time

SOURCE: Reprinted with permission from T. A. Stewart, The search for the organization of tomorrow, *Fortune* (May 18, 1992): 92–98.

increase profits or market share. The degree of differentiation determines whether or not the market will perceive a competitor's products to be substitutes for the company's products: Can Crest toothpaste substitute for Colgate toothpaste, for example? The availability of bona fide substitutes diminishes a company's latitude in setting prices and makes market share hard to retain.

Companies can differentiate on both a product's physical characteristics, such as size, shape, style, and packaging, and its nonphysical characteristics, such as quality, features, options, and embedded services. A company can also apply differentiation strategies to the way it distributes and promotes its products or services. MaryKay Cosmetics, for example, sells cosmetics "door-to-door" rather than through more traditional retail outlets. Pfizer has decided to offer high-quality medical information to distinguish itself from its competitors. Company executives must understand the information required to provide such services and then ensure that MaryKay's and Pfizer's information systems meet these information needs.

Information systems have only a limited ability to differentiate the physical characteristics of a product (except as affected by computer-aided design). They can, however, achieve a strategic advantage in addressing nonphysical attributes such as product distribution and logistics, quality, and pre- and post-sale customer service. In this section we look at how information systems can help a company differentiate on quality and customer service.

USING IS TO DIFFERENTIATE ON QUALITY

If two competitors sell a product with the same features at the same price, customers typically will choose the product that they judge to be most reliable, least likely to have defects, and most likely to perform as advertised. If two companies offer similar services of equal value at the same price, customers will typically select the one that delivers the most accurate and timely information about the services being provided. St. Luke's Episcopal Hospital in Houston uses wireless communication to meet its goals of containing costs while improving the quality of the medical care provided to patients. The hospital uses a wireless system to collect real-time information about respiratory-care services. It lets the department better match its staffing to the demand for technicians.[20]

A company can differentiate between its own and its competitors' offerings by establishing a reputation for quality. Information systems can help assure quality by monitoring the raw materials used in production, the manufacturing process, and service both before and after the sale. Information systems also help to identify and correct quality defects at the earliest possible stage. The Coca-Cola Bottling Company redesigned its warehouse loading process. The company used different techniques to load items with different velocity. The new information systems improved quality by improving load accuracy.[21]

USING IS TO DIFFERENTIATE ON CUSTOMER SERVICE

IS can help companies differentiate on customer service by improving ease of ordering, reliability of delivery, accuracy and timeliness of product support and servicing, and flexibility in response to changing customer needs.

The Coca-Cola Bottling Company attempts to differentiate its product quality by improving its warehouse loading process.

Ernst Home Centers recently introduced Direct Source, a kiosk-based ordering system, into its 95 stores in the northwestern United States. The stores sell many kitchen cabinets, doors, and windows as special orders. The customer writes the order by hand after getting the parts numbers and prices from a catalog. Then a salesperson reviews the order and sends it to the manufacturer. Ernst expects the kiosks, which include information about 45,000 items, to speed ordering by letting customers use a touch screen that automatically gives price and stock information and compiles the order.[22]

Information systems can speed a company's response to a customer's request for product maintenance through the use of product monitoring systems and computer dispatch systems. An oil company can use its IS to identify when the home heating oil reserves in an individual household drop too low—considering weather and other usage factors—and automatically send an oil truck to fill the tank.

AccuFacts Screening completely redesigned its order-taking process, replacing a paper-intensive system with a client/server system that put ordering screens on computers at customer sites. The new system allowed the company to respond three times faster in providing background information requests to its clients.[23]

INFORMATION TECHNOLOGY AND GLOBAL BUSINESS

A strong push by the Malaysian government to take the country into the digital economic era has prompted Mastercard International Inc. to include Malaysia as one of the sites for its pilot implementation of an electronic commerce system based on the Secured Electronic Transaction (SET) electronic payment protocol. In essence, the system enables a complete end-to-end electronic transaction—from the point of sale, right up to clearance by the relevant financial institutions—to take place over the insecure Internet.

Mastercard's senior vice president for electronic commerce/new ventures, Steve Mott, said the Malaysian pilot project is one of the 100 planned for various parts of the world as part of the company's initiative to establish a secured Internet-based electronic transaction system on a global scale. According to him, details on the pilot project are currently being discussed between Mastercard and potential participants—primarily member banks and service providers. "Actual implementation is expected to start in the first quarter of next year and, initially, the project would involve at least five merchants and 1,000 selected cardholders," he said in Kuala Lumpur.... He also explained that similar pilot projects are under way in Taiwan and Japan. Additional programs are also planned for Singapore, Hong Kong, Korea, and Australia.

SOURCE: Excerpted with permission from A. Shukor Rahman, Mastercard selects Malaysia as pilot site, *New Straits Times Press* (November 21, 1996).

A company can offer high-quality technical advice through the use of expert systems. An automobile repair center, for example, can use expert systems to facilitate troubleshooting and support its claim as an excellent diagnostic center. Pfizer uses information systems to inform physicians about which pharmaceuticals best meet specific medical needs.

USING INFORMATION SYSTEMS TO CREATE FOCUS

Focus seeks an advantage through attaining dominance in a focused market segment. A company may segment a market on the basis of geography, customer demographics, distribution channels, price, product characteristics, and other attributes of the customer, the product, or the product's distribution. A company can use combinations of these characteristics to further segment a market: for example, a company may choose to focus on the West Coast luxury market for a particular product.

A company choosing a focus strategy believes that it can attain a high market share more easily in a focused market than in a broad market and that this high market share provides an effective barrier to competitors. Borders Books, for example, uses its information systems to let each store find its niche in the local marketplace. An expert system helps each store's merchandise manager decide which books to order for his location.[24]

Companies often use a focus strategy in concert with a low-cost or differentiation strategy to further cement their competitive advantage.[25] For example, a regional company might not prevent market penetration by a low-cost national chain unless it can profitably offer competitive pricing.

Companies pursuing a focus strategy can use information systems effectively to identify promising market segments and create new markets. Such companies must evaluate how well their existing systems meet these strategic needs and then redesign them accordingly. For example, MillerShor Inc. uses the Internet to reach customers for the company's new line of women's silk clothing. After eight months of showcasing its products on its World Wide Web site, the company had a database of 750 customers who used e-mail to request the names of stores where they could find the company's clothing. Douglas Miller, the president, can use these data to lobby the retail stores to buy his product. Using the Web for marketing has helped increase MillerShor's revenues from $8 million to $18 million in three years.[26]

IDENTIFYING OPPORTUNITIES IN EXISTING MARKET SEGMENTS

The online availability of demographic information from the U.S. Census Bureau and private sources has made electronic searching one avenue for identifying market opportunities. Market research companies, coupon-processing companies, and mailing-list purveyors also offer sales data electronically by region, product, and buyer demographic characteristics. Geographic information systems can display such data as density of disposable income, the location of pizza parlors, and the average rental price of commercial real estate. Such indicators can help companies implement a geographically based focus strategy by identifying undeserved markets.

Tropicana Products found that its mainframe computer system did not provide good enough information about the impact of the company's promotional campaign. It often took days to obtain and analyze the information. Tropicana replaced the system with a client/server system that analyzed purchasing patterns using order and promotional data on the mainframe. Using the new analysis, Tropicana decided to replace its 12-week, one-coupon-per-day campaign with a two-week, three-time promotion. Revenues grew by 33 percent and profits increased by 20 percent.[27]

CREATING NEW MARKET SEGMENTS

Businesses can use information systems to create market segments by customizing or personalizing products and delivering products or services electronically. Charles Schwab & Company, Fidelity Investments, and others have used information technology to expand their customer base. They have introduced online trading in which customers trade stocks or mutual funds electronically from their PC. Other firms, such as Merrill Lynch, A.G. Edwards and Sons, and Prudential Securities, use Web sites to provide commentary about stocks and account information, trying to make their companies more attractive to prospective customers.[28] Pfizer Pharmaceuticals might create a new market by selling its products through a mail-order service rather than directly to pharmacies. Companies can also create market segments by altering their existing products to increase the amount of information that they contain.

The information leadership strategy discussed later in this chapter includes this aspect of a focus strategy.

Some real estate companies have used information technology to offer videos of homes for sale to prospective buyers. These companies store their videos on CD-ROM disks accessed through a friendly user interface or on the Internet. Buyers select a geographical region and price range and specify any other requirements. Software identifies homes that meet these criteria and displays outdoor pictures of those selected. Buyers can then decide which houses they want to inspect in more detail. The software allows the user to see rooms, views through windows, outdoor views from other angles, and other scenes from the selected homes. This product focuses on a segment of buyers who would rather screen houses in an office or kiosk than in person. The companies that first used these products created a new market segment. Other companies created a different new market: they sold the video display as a service (videotaping, transferring pictures to CD ROM or the Internet, and providing hardware and software) to interested real estate agents.

USING INFORMATION SYSTEMS TO SUPPORT LINKAGES

Linkage describes the strategy of forming interorganizational alliances. Although always a strategic option, for a long time the ease of shifting alliances made linkage a highly risky strategy. A competitor could woo a company's ally and achieve a competitive advantage first by breaking the alliance and second by stealing the knowledge and expertise the company had invested in the ally.

Advances in computer and telecommunications technology, however, have increased the ability of companies to link their operations more tightly to one another. New technologies have strengthened the bond between allies, making it harder and more costly to break ties, and thereby changing a risky strategic tool into a mainstream strategic practice. Diagnosing opportunities for such linkages and the information needs associated with them has become a strategic priority in many organizations.

Five forces govern industrial competition, as shown in Figure 11.6:

- The threat of new entrants
- The threat of substitute products or services
- The bargaining power of suppliers
- The bargaining power of customers
- Competition within an industry[29]

Consider, for example, the impact of the bargaining power of suppliers. If only a few suppliers manufacture a product needed by an industry (for example, memory chips needed by the computer industry), then these suppliers can exert their power by giving manufacturing or delivery priority to the customer who offers the best price. By forming tight alliances with suppliers and customers, and occasionally even with producers of substitute products or competitors, an organization hopes to lessen the impact of the other competitive forces relative to other organizations in the industry.

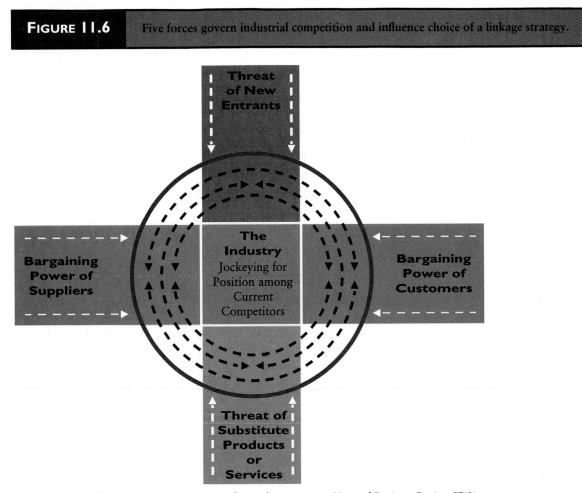

SOURCE: Michael E. Porter, How competitive forces shape strategy, *Harvard Business Review* 57(2) (March/April 1979): 137–145.

Companies can also create linkages across various parts of the value chain, a system of generic interconnected activities, such as design, engineering, manufacturing, distribution, and sales, that a company performs to add value to its products or services.[30] They can even extend the linkages to include companies in the value system, including **upstream companies**, such as suppliers, who add value to materials and services that the firm uses, and **downstream companies**, such as customers, who add value by distributing, repackaging, and reselling the product or service or incorporating it into other products, as illustrated in Figure 11.7.[31] The linkage strategy seeks to capture internally that part of the value added by upstream and downstream companies.

Recent advances in information technology, particularly in communication technology and communication standards, have eased the integration of steps in the value system.[32] **Value-adding partnerships (VAPs)** refer to the linkage of companies that view the whole value system, not just the value chain, as their compet-

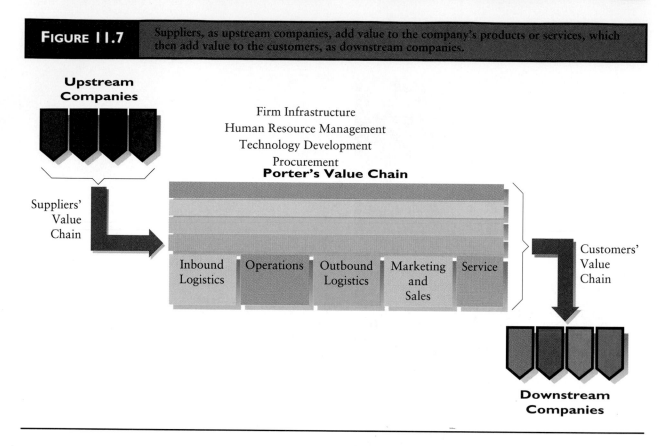

FIGURE II.7 Suppliers, as upstream companies, add value to the company's products or services, which then add value to the customers, as downstream companies.

itive unit and who share information freely with others in the value system so they can compete successfully in this environment.[33] Companies in the value system generally rely on an **interorganizational system (IOS)**—an automated information system that two or more companies share—to support their linkages.[34] In this section we explore how an IOS benefits and provides a strategic advantage for its participants.

CUSTOMER LINKAGES

A **customer-focused IOS** attempts to link a company and its customers by offering information services that mutually benefit the customer and the host. Pfizer, for example, might identify a number of major corporate customers and use an IOS to allow them to order pharmaceuticals electronically, query a database on its inventory and pricing, and use electronic mail to log complaints and suggestions and to request product specifications and service information.

Table 11.2 lists the benefits of a customer-focused IOS for both the customer and the host company. The benefits to the host company arise from increased sales, lower costs, better management information, and greater bargaining power. Sales generally increase because the IOS provides additional services and benefits to customers. Customers should find it easier and more efficient to order from the host company than

TABLE 11.2	A customer-focused IOS offers benefits to both the host company and the customer.

Benefits to the Host Company	**Benefits for the Customer**
Increases sales of products and services due to ease and efficiency of ordering and favorable display on order-entry screens	Improves service
Reduces the need for customer service agents	Provides immediate feedback on product availability
May increase profits by removing distributors	Reduces cost and paperwork involved in placing an order
Captures more precise and timely sales data	May improve price by eliminating distributor
Improves production scheduling	Improves communication for problem resolution
Reduces required inventory	May identify opportunities to obtain volume discounts
Requires cross-selling of additional products	Provides information for companies in out-of-the-way locations
Raises the cost of ordering from a different supplier	Makes product or service easier and less expensive to select, order, and account for
Provides data for evaluating marketing programs	Improves access to information about product shipment
Extends the market to customers who cannot receive conventional sales calls	
Tailors promotions, products, and services to customers' shopping habits	
Customizes sales message	
Reduces data entry and editing work	

from the company's competitors. An IOS can increase sales by displaying higher-margin products favorably on order-entry screens, cross-selling them in place of products customers may have originally intended to buy. An IOS may increase sales by removing or reducing the role of distributors; a company that sells directly to the customer can expect to receive a higher price than if it sold the same product through a distributor, even if the customer pays a lower price in a direct sale. An IOS can extend the market to distant or small customers who a conventional field sales force cannot easily reach.

IOS customer linkages lower costs in several ways. For example, an IOS reduces the need for customer service agents because customers do their own shopping. Also, an IOS reduces the data entry and editing normally associated with order entry processing. Instead, customers do their own order entry directly on the IOS system. Cost savings generally arise from better coordination of operations among production, distribution, and sales. For example, a customer IOS can capture precise and timely sales data, improving production scheduling and reducing required inventory.

The management information derived from a customer IOS can be used in other ways. An IOS provides data that enable managers to quickly and economically evaluate the effects of advertising, rebates, and other marketing programs. This knowledge allows marketing managers to increase the efficiency and reduce the cost of promotional programs. Savvy marketing managers can also observe customers'

ETHICAL ISSUES IN IT

The press is full of announcements of joint ventures and strategic alliances that facilitate the production of software products in India for the consumption of clients in the U.S. Apple Computer recently announced an investment running into tens of millions of dollars thus substantially increasing its presence in India. Tata Consulting Services and Novell have unveiled plans for a strategic alliance to develop software in India for Novell's clients. A state-of-the-art Offshore Development Center joint venture between Birla Horizons International of India and Computer Horizons Corporation of the U.S. was opened in November 1995. Novell Software Development (India) was established as a 95%–5% joint venture between Novell and its Indian partner Onward Novell with an annual budget of $20 million, about 5% of Novell's annual R&D spending. Oracle Corporation announced the setting up of a software R&D center in Bangalore, India, that will be the company's largest abroad when it reaches full operation in two years. Derek Williams, senior VP of the Asian-Pacific division of Oracle, claims that it is a combination of rich talent, government incentives, and cost-effectiveness that has prompted the company to move part of its product development and R&D from San Francisco to Bangalore.

The cost figures are compelling. For example, a Visual Basic programmer in NYC is billed to end-clients at the rate of $60 an hour or around $120,000 a year (the programmer is paid around $40,000 a year). A similarly skilled programmer in India could be hired at Rs. 10,000 a month (Rs. 120,000 or approximately $4000 a year). The mood of the organizations engaged in overseas production is summed up by the statement of one top McDonnell Douglas official (itself an organization using Indian software expertise): "We're in the business of making money. If we have to put jobs and technology in other countries, then we go ahead and do it" (*New York Times*, February 25, 1995).

1. What are the strategic purposes of the alliances described here?
2. What ethical issues do they raise?

SOURCE: Extracted from Ali Mir and Maya Yajnik, The uneven development of places: From bodyshopping to global assembly lines, http://www.solinet.org/THIRDWORLD/maya1.htm, April 8, 1998.

shopping habits and tailor promotions, products, and services to these habits. They can customize sales messages, including prices and other terms, to a buyer's previous experience with a particular product.

The bargaining power of the host company over its customers increases with an IOS because the IOS raises the cost to the customer of ordering from a different supplier. The importance of an IOS as a bargaining tool grows when products are extremely complicated to specify or order. The customer has little choice but to use a company's IOS. Switching to another purveyor would require the customer to retrain employees, modify operating procedures, and invest in new hardware or software.

A company's customers would not use its IOS unless they received benefit from its use. Generally, an IOS makes it easier and less expensive for the customer to select, order, and account for the products and services it buys. In particular, the IOS provides immediate feedback on product availability and price. It also reduces the cost and paperwork involved in placing an order. If orders do not arrive when expected, the customer can ask the IOS for the shipping date. The customer can then communicate problems in shipping, product quality, or other areas directly to the host company through the IOS.

A well-designed IOS accounts for a customer's previous orders, makes it easy for the customer to place similar orders, and allows the customer to take advantage of special offers or discounts associated with the merchandise it normally buys. An IOS can even ease a customer's operations, reducing its costs substantially.

SUPPLIER LINKAGES

A **supplier-focused IOS** attempts to forge a linkage between a company and its suppliers by providing information services that mutually benefit the suppliers and the host. A company that uses a supplier-focused IOS might allow selected suppliers to monitor its inventory and sales database and assume responsibility for keeping the inventory of identified products within specified bounds.

In most cases, the benefits to the host far outweigh the benefits to the suppliers, as shown in Table 11.3. Unlike customers responding to a customer-focused IOS, suppliers have little incentive to participate in a supplier-focused IOS other than the threat of lost business. As a result, a supplier-focused IOS works best in industries, such as the automotive industry, where many suppliers vie for the attention of a few major purchasers. Here, the purchasers can force acceptance of their IOS by virtue of their superior market power.

Wal-Mart implemented Retail Link, a decision support system that keeps vendors electronically informed about the sales of each of their items on a daily basis. The system also provides vendors with a report of 100 weeks of their products' sales history. Wal-Mart management believes that this information should allow retailers to serve individual stores better by encouraging them to select the right goods for each store. The information should also reduce prices because vendors place only products that sell into stores.[35]

TABLE 11.3	A supplier-focused IOS offers benefits to both the host company and the supplier.

Benefits to Host Company	Benefits to Supplier
Lowers inventory costs	Increases likelihood of getting orders from host
Reduces data entry and editing work by automating ordering	Improves ability to schedule production and inventory
Improves preparation for incoming goods	Reduces threat of loss of business
Lowers the cost of shopping for best price/product combination	Increases access to information about customers' sales
Encourages standardized data representation	
Improves pricing	

Whereas a supplier-focused IOS improves a company's ability to shop well for the products and services it buys, the greatest benefit of such an IOS is its ability to increase the efficiency of the company's operations. For example, an IOS might lower inventory costs by allowing just-in-time delivery. It might also improve the shipment receiving process by allowing a company to anticipate receipts and schedule its operations accordingly.

LOGISTICS LINKAGE

Logistics refers to the transport of goods and its associated activities, such as warehousing. Inbound logistics describes the transport of raw goods to a company from its suppliers. Outbound logistics refers to the transport of finished products from a company to its customers. Poor logistics results in damage or lateness of the product. Superior logistics can give a company a reputation for excellent service and reduce its inventory requirements and the inventory requirements of its suppliers and customers.

Most companies do not provide their own logistic services, relying instead on outside contractors or public carriers. Nevertheless, the importance of logistics to the relationship between supplier and customer and to the quality of product and service demands that companies pay close attention to logistics. In many cases, companies forge alliances with logistics providers to improve control over service. Wal-Mart partnered with United Parcel Service to deliver goods to customers. Customers dial Wal-Mart's site on the World Wide Web, place their order, and receive a delivery within 48 hours. Wal-Mart plans to eventually have 80,000 items that will go directly from the factory to the end customer.[36]

USING INFORMATION SYSTEMS TO DEVELOP INFORMATION LEADERSHIP

Information leadership describes the strategy of increasing the value of a product or service by infusing it with expertise and information. Most products and services incorporate some degree of information in their design and sales. A refrigerator might come with a users' manual that explains how to set the temperature, operate the appliance safely and efficiently, and obtain parts and service. The refrigerator might also process information. For example, its control systems read the temperature and humidity to decide when to turn on and off its cooling systems, operate its fans, and put the freezer through its defrost cycle. Some furniture stores include detailed information about the care of each product on special labels. Pfizer could create a competitive advantage by offering more detailed and accurate information about the specifications of its products and their performance compared to comparable products.

Advances in technology have made it possible to improve products by increasing their ability to collect and process information and use it to improve a product's functioning. Specialized computers in automobiles can sense a tire beginning to slip

ADVANCED TECHNOLOGY

Sears, Roebuck & Company is deploying speech-recognition systems to improve customer service. The systems, planned for installation at 700 stores nationwide, let callers tell a computer rather than a live operator what department they want.

Sears expects the speech-recognition systems, which can handle four calls at a time, to transfer about 120,000 calls a day. "We see this as a tremendous customer service value," says Terry McGinnis, national manager of store office policy and procedure. "Instead of the phone ringing 30 or 40 times, on the first ring it will get answered and routed."

The systems will tell customers to "speak the name of a department" and then verify with such responses as "did you say shoes?" If a customer says "no" or the system doesn't recognize a command, the customer will be immediately routed to a live operator in Golden, Colorado, or Fort Wayne, Indiana. The operator will then route the call to the customer's local-store department.

SOURCE: Excerpted and edited with permission from Mary E. Thyfault, Sears adds speech recognition—Systems will transfer calls to departments, *Information Week* (April 6, 1998), http://www.techweb.com/se/directlink.cgi?IWK 19980406S0029.

and can adjust the thrust or braking applied to the tire to keep the car from skidding. They can sense engine performance and adjust the flow of gas and air so as to react most efficiently to the operator's demands or to environmental conditions. They can measure gas usage and storage to predict and advise the driver when he or she will need to refuel. They can even sense bumps in a road and adjust the ride so quickly that the passenger does not notice them.

State Street Bank of Boston combined its expertise in processing mutual fund transactions and developing information systems. It offers a system that links the bank's and its clients' systems. Global Horizon Interchange provides investment information for pension fund and portfolio managers in an easy-to-use form. Managers at General Electric Investment Corporation, a client of State Street's, which manages $47 billion in assets, can see the impact of potential trades on their portfolio. They can view trading activity by asset type, currency, country, or other details.[37] State Street also plans to offer its corporate pension planner clients online access to summary statements about account performance.[38]

Information leadership creates additional value in one of two ways: (1) infusing an existing product with information and (2) selling information as a product in its own right. These two information strategies either use proprietary information or techniques for incorporating information in the product that are protected by copyright or patent.

INFUSING PRODUCTS WITH INFORMATION

Appropriate information adds value to almost any product or service. Information systems embedded in a product or supporting a product can provide features that customers want, differentiate the product or service, and provide competitive advantage. American Express recognized that corporate credit-card customers had to organize their expenses into categories for accounting purposes. The company provided a monthly categorized breakdown of each customer's expenses to help customers do this accounting. Diagnosing the need to provide this information to customers, which American Express could do at relatively little marginal cost, differentiated American Express's service from those of its competitors and added value that drew customers to use its card rather than others. American Express then needed to ensure that its information systems supported the provision of this information. As additional companies adopted this practice, however, American Express's competitive advantage decreased.

General Motors offered its 1997 Cadillac buyers a $1,000 option called the OnStar communications system. OnStar calls for emergency assistance when air bags inflate, notifies police upon receiving a signal from theft detection equipment, and tracks stolen vehicles. OnStar also puts a hands-free, voice-activated cellular phone in the automobile so that drivers can request routing assistance, roadside assistance, and other emergency services. Lincoln Continental introduced a similar system, but it lacked the range of features OnStar offers.[39]

SELLING PROPRIETARY INFORMATION

Some businesses own proprietary information as a by-product of their normal business activities. Grocers that use bar-code scanners have information about the products that consumers buy. The grocers can create a new business or earn additional profits from their existing businesses by selling information about consumer's purchases and preferences to market research firms or food processing companies. Vendors of durable goods such as automobiles, televisions, and audio equipment can sell the names of customers to companies that provide third-party service contracts or extended warranties.

In many cases, a company can build on its experience with processing a certain type of information to form a new business providing similar processing for others. Small banks frequently subcontract their backroom check-processing operations to a larger financial institution, creating a subsidiary business for the larger banks.

SUMMARY

Strategy refers to the long-term direction or intended activities an organization uses to achieve its goals. Companies might use low-cost leadership, differentiation, focus, linkage, and information leadership strategies to attain an advantage over their competitors. Companies face the issues of aligning strategic information systems with their strategic goals, using systems to create a sustainable advantage, and creating systems that support business process redesign.

Companies with a low-cost strategy attempt to attain high profits by maintaining lower costs than their competitors. Information systems can help these organizations reduce costs. Information systems play a particularly important role in quality efforts in purchasing and manufacturing, creating a just-in-time inventory system, and flattening the organizational structure.

A differentiation strategy seeks a competitive advantage by distinguishing a company's products and services from those of its competitors. Such companies can use information systems to help distinguish products and services on quality and customer service.

A focus strategy seeks to attain a competitive advantage through dominance in a specific market niche. Some companies use a focus strategy together with a low-cost or differentiation strategy to strengthen their competitive advantage. The role of information systems in companies that use this strategy is to monitor and analyze the marketplace, identifying new opportunities in existing markets and new market segments. The companies can also use information technology to help them deliver the product to a particular niche.

A company with a linkage strategy forms interorganizational alliances to achieve a competitive advantage. These companies can use interorganizational information systems (IOSs) to help them create customer, supplier, or logistic linkages.

Finally, organizations can use an information leadership strategy; this strategy increases the value of a product or service by infusing it with expertise and information. Information technology creates additional value by infusing an existing product with information or selling information as a product in its own right.

KEY TERMS

business process redesign
business process reengineering (BPR)
customer-focused IOS
differentiation
downstream company
focus
information leadership
interorganizational system (IOS)
just-in-time (JIT)

linkage
logistics
strategic alignment
strategic information system
supplier-focused IOS
sustainable advantage
total quality management (TQM)
upstream company
value-adding partnership (VAP)

DISCUSSION AND REVIEW QUESTIONS

1. What is a strategic information system?
2. What purposes do strategic information systems serve?
3. Why should effective strategic systems align with the organization's strategic goals?
4. How can strategic information systems give a company a sustainable competitive advantage?
5. What role does information technology play in business process redesign?
6. What role should managers play in business process redesign?
7. What five ways can companies use information systems to obtain low-cost leadership?
8. How can information systems reduce costs?

9. How would business process redesign change the work in an accounting department?
10. How does just-in-time inventory reduce costs?
11. Why are organizations flattening their structures?
12. What two approaches can companies use to implement a differentiation strategy?
13. How can companies use IS to differentiate on quality?
14. How can companies use IS to differentiate on customer service?
15. How can information systems create focus for a company?
16. How can information systems help companies identify opportunities in existing market segments?
17. How can information systems help companies identify new market segments?
18. What three types of linkage exist?
19. How do interorganizational systems create linkage?
20. How do supplier-focused and customer-focused IOSs differ and what benefits do they offer?

IS ON THE WEB

Exercise 1: Read a case study of a business process reengineering project. Write a short paper describing the strategy that the BPR effort attempted to achieve, your assessment of whether the reengineering effort succeeded or failed, and the role of information technology in that success or failure.

Exercise 2: Read a case study of an interorganizational information system (IOS). Write a short paper describing the purpose and implementation of the system. Evaluate the success of the IOS.

MINICASE

TALENT TREE STAFFING SERVICES

In order to keep up with the fast-growing temporary employment industry, Talent Tree Staffing Services knew it would have to go out on a limb. In three years, the $350 million Houston-based unit of British holding company BET PLC had already expanded to 100,000 temporary employees ranging from accountants to paralegals. But even that was not enough.

The firm's 15-year-old systems simply couldn't meet the demands of its increasingly technology-savvy clientele. "More customers are expecting Talent Tree's sys-

SOURCE: Case excerpted and edited with permission from Natalie Engler, High achievers: Talent Tree Staffing Services, *Computerworld Client/Server Journal*, Special Issue (August 1996): 34.

tems to be able to interface directly with theirs," explains Kathy Welch, vice president of information technology. They wanted to electronically exchange orders, complete employee performance evaluations, access billing information, and do management reports.

So in February 1994, Talent Tree embarked on the Market Management System (MMS), its first large-scale distributed client/server undertaking. The first step was installing EmpAct, a work order management system for the staffing services industry from Prairie Development Inc.

The off-the-shelf system was developed in Centura Software Corp.'s SQLWindows, Microsoft Corp.'s SQL Server for Windows NT, and Microsoft's Visual Basic, C, and C++ but was extensively customized by Talent Tree programmers. And while conducting the pilot, Talent Tree ported all the database tables and back-end business logic to Oracle 7 for Unix so the system could more easily integrate with its Oracle Corp.-based financial applications.

Today, the company's 350 service specialists and market management staffers in 100-plus offices nationwide use MMS to manage every aspect of the employee matchup process from "cradle to grave," says Shandace Spencer, director of the company's service delivery. The application runs in 15 remote sites, whose servers are connected by a nationwide frame-relay wide area network. Service reps connect to the hub sites via the WAN or dial-up access.

Before, reps would write down each piece of data and enter it into a Prime computer. And because of the convoluted user interface, there was no consistency in how the data was entered, so it was difficult for one rep to answer another's customer. With MMS, everything happens online and can be instantly accessed by any rep at any time.

Because the $10 million cost includes infrastructure expenditures, it is difficult to measure payback, says David Petty, director of application development and support. But the company believes it would have been crippled without MMS. "Competitors were moving ahead, and the cost of maintaining our legacy applications was growing out of control," Petty adds.

Today, Talent Tree is electronically linked to a half-dozen customers in a variety of ways. With one of its largest clients, it has completely eliminated paper time sheets and invoices by interfacing with the customer's accounting systems. Temps track their hours in the customer's time-keeping system, and every week Talent Tree extracts that information and transfers it to its own internal payroll and billing systems. Talent Tree then sends the temp a paycheck, and the customer pays Talent Tree via electronic data interchange.

Over the next year, Talent Tree plans to complete its migration to a new payroll system based on PeopleSoft Inc. software and a time and expense billing system based on Oracle. Its goal: to get off its legacy systems completely.

Case Questions

Diagnosis

1. What strategic information needs does Talent Tree Staffing Services have?
2. How have these needs changed over time?

Evaluation

3. Why did Talent Tree's systems not meet its needs?

    4. What features did the systems require to meet the company's needs?

Design

    5. What changes did Talent Tree make to its information systems?

    6. How did these changes better meet the company's needs?

Implementation

    7. What implementation issues did Talent Tree face?

    8. What factors affect the cost-effectiveness of the system?

    9. Does the new system better meet Talent Tree's need for strategic information?

ACTIVITY 11.1   STRATEGIC INFORMATION SYSTEMS FOR FITNESS INC.

Step 1:   Read the following scenario:

Jim McCarthy founded Fitness Inc. in a suburban office park as a health club for professionals who wanted high-quality, personalized service and convenience in meeting their fitness needs. The initial membership fee of $1,000 was quite steep. Monthly fees of $100 also made this club one of the more expensive to join. McCarthy's original strategy was to offer state-of-the-art equipment and services in a top-notch physical setting and bundle all services and fees into a single price. He believed that Fitness Inc. could attract a sufficiently large number of members from the workers in the office park who could afford such fees and would join only a club that pampered them.

    Club facilities included extensive weight equipment; 60 pieces of cardiovascular equipment such as treadmills, rowing machines, and stair climbers; and an Olympic-sized swimming pool. A club cafe served meals and snacks throughout the day. The club offered an initial fitness screening and regular reevaluations at no cost to the member. Aerobics and water fitness classes were offered at intervals throughout the day for no charge. Members could select a specified number of hours of personal training, nutrition counseling, and swimming instruction each month for no fee; additional services were available for a small fee.

    McCarthy projected that a club membership of 1,500 would return a minimal profit; a membership of 2,000 to 2,500 was more desirable. In the initial year, 800 members joined the club, but most of those had joined during the first six months after the club's opening. Membership had been relatively stagnant for the past six months. McCarthy wondered whether his initial vision for Fitness Inc. still made sense. He considered adjusting the type of services the club provided and trying to attract a different type of member, perhaps suburban housewives or more senior citizens. McCarthy had installed a relatively sophisticated computer system that provided detailed purchasing, accounting, and sales data. He wanted to develop a computer system that would help him reassess his strategy and develop a new one.

    McCarthy has asked you to help him analyze his existing strategy and determine which alternative strategies are available. He knows that he should be able to use his computer system to help in determining the most appropriate strategy.

Step 2: In groups of two to four students, analyze Fitness Inc.'s current strategy and identify a range of strategic alternatives Fitness Inc. might pursue. For each alternative, sketch a general plan for using information systems to support the strategy.

Step 3: Share your plans with the rest of the class. List the alternatives identified. Then identify the types of strategic information systems that would support each alternative. Cite the advantages and disadvantages of pursuing each strategy and developing the required strategic information systems.

CAN THIS JOB BE REENGINEERED?   ACTIVITY 11.2

Step 1: Read each of the following cases. Then determine for each situation whether business process reengineering could improve it.

CASE 1

At Plantland, a medium-sized retail distributor of houseplants and other gardening supplies, workers spend hours each day recording the status of thousands of plants and other items. The company buys small plants from wholesalers and grows them to the requirements of their customers in on-site greenhouses. Four times a year, the company opens late to allow the managers to hire temporary employees to validate their counts of inventory. In both their daily and quarterly inventory checking, the workers record their updated information in large ledger books, indicating changes in the size, quality, and availability of certain plants. By analyzing these records, the managers can determine how they should alter their orders.

CASE 2

At Builders' Supplies Inc., contractors place orders for lumber, hardware, and other supplies at any one of four hundred stores nationwide. These stores then individually submit the orders to the appropriate mill, plant, or warehouse to fill. Often the stores order from and bill one another to meet a customer's requirements. These processes result in a significant paper flow among the company's stores, warehouses, and suppliers.

CASE 3

The River City Library orders approximately 2,000 new books each year. Because all orders in the city originate from the city purchasing department, a librarian sends the order to the purchasing department for authorization. When the library receives the book, the librarian sends a copy of the shipping slip and invoice to the city purchasing department for payment. After the purchasing department checks that the order received by the library matches the one ordered by the department, the clerk authorizes the library to catalog the book.

Step 2: For those situations in which business process reengineering would help, offer a proposal for reengineering the job.

Step 3: In small groups or with the entire class, review your answers to step 2. Then answer the following questions:

RECOMMENDED READINGS

Avery, Christine, and Zakel, Diane. *The Quality Management Sourcebook: An International Guide to Materials and Resources.* London: Routledge, 1997.

Donovan, John J. *The Second Industrial Revolution: Reinventing Your Business on the Web.* Upper Saddle River, NJ: Prentice Hall, 1997.

Keen, Peter G. W. *The Process Edge: Creating Value Where It Counts.* Boston: Harvard Business School Press, 1997.

Neumann, Seev. *Strategic Information Systems: Competition through Information Technologies.* New York: Macmillan, 1994.

Samli, A. C. *Information-Driven Marketing Decisions: Development of Strategic Information Systems.* Westport, CT: Quorum Books, 1996.

NOTES

1. Jill Gambon, Best medicine: Data warehouses, *InformationWeek* (September 9, 1996): 180–184.

2. Yolande E. Chan and Sid L. Huff, Strategic information systems alignment, *Business Quarterly* (Autumn 1993): 51–55; Henry Pankratz, Strategic alignment: Managing for synergy, *Business Quarterly* (Winter 1991): 66–71; Roger Woolfe, The path to strategic alignment, *Information Strategy: The Executive's Journal* 9(2) (Winter 1993): 13–23.

3. Brian McWilliams, Coming back for more, *Computerworld* (February 13, 1995): 101–102, 106.

4. April Jacobs, Delta flies kiosks to land new sales, *Computerworld* (June 2, 1997): 41–44.

5. Eric K. Clemons and Michael C. Row, Sustaining IT advantage: The role of structural differences, *MIS Quarterly* 15 (September 1991): 275–292.

6. Thomas Hoffman, Airline turbocharges schedule efficiency, *Computerworld* (March 25, 1996): 1, 137.

7. Claudio Ciborra, From thinking to tinkering: The grassroots of strategic information systems, *The Information Society* 8(4) (October/December 1992): 297–309.

8. Michael R. Vitale, The growing risks of information systems success, *MIS Quarterly* 10 (December 1986): 327–334.

9. Rolls-Royce introduces electronic commerce solutions, *M2 Presswire* (March 27, 1996).

10. William J. Kettinger, James T. C. Teng, and Subashish Guha, Business process change: A study of methodologies, techniques, and tools, *MIS Quarterly* 21(1) (1997): 55–80; William J. Kettinger and V. Grover, Toward a theory of business process change, *Journal of Management Information Systems* 12(1) (1995): 9–30.

11. Julie King, On-line guide unifies automobile association, *Computerworld* (June 12, 1995): 91.

12. Anita Lienert, Getting in the pink, *Management Review* 85(5) (May 1996): 18–23.

13. Sharon Watson, Islands no more: Department systems meet the enterprise, *Computerworld* (June 1997): H8.

14. Kate Maddox, Faster satellite bookings, *InformationWeek* (June 10, 1996): 73–74.

15. Nancy Lakier, Tracking care in San Diego, *Health Systems Review* 29(5) (September/October 1996): 41–45.

16. Jeff Stiely, Keeping up with Jones, *Apparel Industry Magazine* 57(2) (February 1996): 22–30.

17. Mike Ngo and Paul Szucs, Order system keeps deliveries on track, *Canadian Plastics* 54(6) (August 1996): 12–13.

18. Feature flashes, July 7, 1997, AlJust-in-time Inventory/FeatureFlashes3.html.

19. Bob Wallace, What's more crucial, *Computerworld* (January 20, 1997): 1, 105.

20. Mary Lou Roberts, Hospital takes wireless cure, *Communications Week* (June 3, 1996): S15.

21. State-of-the-art beverage plant loading systems, *Beverage World* (August 1996): 72–75.

22. Early customer-focused technology efforts have had disappointing results, *Computerworld* (October 30, 1995): 80.

23. Paul Karon, AccuFacts gives small integrator the job of revamping data, *InfoWorld* (January 13, 1997): 65.

24. Building an image one store at a time, *Discount Store News* (June 17, 1996): 28–29.

25. G. G. Dess and P. S. Davis, Porter's (1980) generic strategies as determinants of strategic group membership and organizational performance, *Academy of Management Journal* 27 (1984): 467–488.

26. Roberta Maynard, Taking your products to the main streets, *Nation's Business* (June 1997), http://www.umi.com.

27. Willie Schatz, When data is not enough, *Computerworld Client/Server Journal* (April 1995): 25–28.

28. Stewart L. Deck, The exchanging of the guard, *Computerworld* (October 7, 1997): 105–106.

29. Michael E. Porter, How competitive forces shape strategy, *Harvard Business Review* 57(2) (March/April 1979): 137–145; Mitch Wagner, Fidelity invests in Web trading, *Computerworld* (May 19, 1997): 53–55.

30. Michael E. Porter, *Competitive Advantage* (New York: The Free Press, 1985).

31. Michael E. Porter and Victor E. Millar, How information gives you competitive advantage, *Harvard Business Review* (July/August 1985): 149–160.

32. T. W. Malone, J. Yates, and R. I. Benjamin, Electronic markets and electronic hierarchies, *Communications of the ACM* 30 (1987): 484–497.

33. R. Johnston and P. R. Lawrence, Beyond vertical integration—The rise of the value-adding partnership, *Harvard Business Review* (July/August 1988): 94–104.

34. J. I. Cash, Jr., and B. R. Konsynski, IS redraws competitive boundaries, *Harvard Business Review* (March/April 1985): 134–142.

35. Karen Schaffner, Psssst! Want to sell to Wal-Mart? *Apparel Industry Magazine* 57(8) (August 1996): 18–19.

36. Jesse Berst, How Wal-Mart will kill Mom and Pop on the Web, (December 9, 1996) http://www4.zdnet.com/anchordesk/story/story_530.html.

37. Monua Jonah, Like squeezing money from marble, *Computerworld* (August 21, 1995): 73–74.

38. Natalie Engler, State Street Bank & Trust Co., *Computerworld Client/Server Journal* (August 1996): 32.

39. Thomas Hoffman, Not your father's Cadillac, *Computerworld* (April 8, 1996): 4.

Piet Mondrian, *Broadway Boogie Woogie.* 1942–43. The Museum of Modern Art, New York. Given anonymously. Photograph © 1998 the Museum of Modern Art, New York.

IV

IMPLEMENTING INFORMATION SYSTEMS AND MANAGING THE INFORMATION

O rganizations face the ongoing challenge of designing, implementing, and maintaining information systems and delivering IS services effectively. Part IV concludes this text by examining issues associated with systems planning, development, implementation, and delivery. Chapter 12 investigates key system development concepts, including the stages of the systems development life cycle. Chapter 13 explores ways of structuring and managing the information systems function, as well as managing change in information systems and technology.

Chapter 12

Systems Planning, Development, and Implementation

LEARNING OBJECTIVES

After completing Chapter 12, you will be able to

1. Describe why systems projects succeed and fail.
2. Identify and describe the stages of the systems development life cycle.
3. Describe three pathways for the development of new systems and identify the pros and cons of each.
4. Discuss the role of data, process, and object models in the design and development of new systems.
5. Explain how CASE tools simplify and support SDLC activities.
6. Specify five ways of collecting information for a needs assessment.
7. Describe the key elements of interface design, data design, process design, object design, physical design, and test design.
8. Specify the key decisions and activities in the development stage of the systems development life cycle.
9. Cite the advantages and disadvantages of four implementation strategies.
10. Distinguish between implementation and maintenance.

DEVELOPING NEW ACCOUNTING SYSTEMS FOR GPI CORPORATION

Bob Graves, director of budgeting at GPI Corporation (GPIC), a global manufacturer of consumer goods, had just met with his boss, Greg Roberts, chief financial officer. Roberts presented Graves with a challenge that he could not refuse. "Bob," he said, "you know how I've been lobbying to replace our accounting systems. Since we've gone global, we've had a devil of a time reconciling and consolidating our books. We really need software that works better with foreign currencies and that satisfies our reporting needs and those of our subsidiaries. Also, our current system doesn't support activity-based costing. Until we can track our costs by activity, we really have no way of assessing the value of any of our processes and no way to properly control our costs. The president of the Paper Products Division and the presidents of a number of our foreign subsidiaries have backed me on this initiative, and the cabinet has finally approved a fairly substantial sum to put new systems into place. We'll be contributing a good portion of the funding from our own budget."

"Christine Harrison, our chief information officer (CIO), has warned us that modifying or replacing our accounting system is no simple task. Accounting relates to all our other systems, including operations, distribution, sales, and customer service. As you know, the Systems Group's policy is that project sponsors must not only supply funding, but they must also commit staff. In addition, they want a business manager to head the project in conjunction with a technical manager. I thought that you'd be perfect for the job if you want it, and the other cabinet members agreed. It's a high-visibility position, time limited, with an opportunity to work with the key people in all of our operating divisions. What do you think?"

Although Graves had managed a few large projects before, he had little experience with information systems. Nevertheless, he could not turn down the offer. He

Software development is a team effort. Management teams often must make decisions about and become involved in development projects.

accepted the opportunity knowing that he would need to learn a great deal about how information systems are designed and developed.

Graves's situation is becoming increasingly common. Most companies, such as GPIC, will not undertake a major systems project without the active participation of the business units funding the project. Many require a business manager to be the project leader or one of the leaders of the project. Functional and general managers should expect to participate in at least one major information systems project every year or two.

WHY SYSTEMS DEVELOPMENT PROJECTS SUCCEED AND FAIL

Graves and managers like him can learn a great deal by studying systems development successes and failures. Large-scale systems development poses a major challenge to organizations, even to those with extensive IS experience. For example, Citicorp, a sophisticated technology leader that spends an estimated $1.5 billion a year on its computer systems, was forced to abandon its MortgagePower Plus project after three years and a significant investment in time and money. The project would have approved and granted a mortgage loan in 15 minutes. In practice, mortgage brokers and real estate agents struggled to even connect to the system, and once connected they usually had to wait several hours for a reply. The system rejected loans it should have approved and approved loans it should have rejected.[1]

The London Stock Exchange spent an estimated 400 million pounds ($575 million) to develop a product called Taurus, which was supposed to be a paperless system to settle security trades within three days. The Exchange scrapped the project after six years in development and numerous delays and missed deadlines. Market participants and outside experts testing the software concluded that the project would take at least two more years, require much more funding, and would not meet many of the original specifications.[2]

Much research has addressed the question of why systems projects succeed or fail. The reasons vary from project to project, but most fall into the following five categories: riskiness of the project, definition of project scope, quality of project management, quality of process design, and adequacy of resources.

RISK

Every project involves some element of risk. Later in this chapter we will explore how to evaluate and reduce risk. Projects that depend on unproved technologies or occur in a dynamic environment are inherently risky. Time-Warner Communications (TWC), for example, invested $30 million in a customer service system

The London Stock Exchange scrapped a $575 million project to settle security trades within three days. Failures in systems development cost companies billions of dollars each year.

intended to support a new business, the company's planned entry into the local-access residential telephone business. TWC decided to develop the system to provide better services and features than its competitors could offer at a lower price. The company needed to develop the system quickly so that it would be ready when it rolled out service to the first test market, Rochester, New York. The tight time frame combined with TWC's unfamiliarity with the telephone business forced designers to select state-of-the-art technologies that would allow them to develop quickly and yet remain flexible. Unfortunately, when the system went live, it was so slow that employees had to manually record customer names and types of service ordered and then enter them into the computer. It took TWC almost two additional years, and the use of more mature software tools, to obtain satisfactory response time from its system.[3]

SCOPE

Successful projects have a clearly defined scope. One study indicated that 80 percent of IS projects go over budget and schedule because of changes in scope after estimating the project costs.[4] Without a well-defined scope, a project runs the risk of never being finished. The state of Washington abandoned a system for processing drivers' licenses and vehicle registrations after spending $40 million on the project. The project manager noted that a preliminary study underestimated the project's scope and that new laws changed some of the requirements of the system.[5]

MANAGEMENT

Projects more often succeed when experienced and effective managers run them. Project managers need to know how to plan, organize teams, assign responsibilities, set milestones and deadlines, seek and obtain resources, and resolve crises. Business managers, even those not on a project team, can affect a project's success. Managers who do not support a project can undermine or sabotage it. Top management support can help employees affected by the project to accept change. Lack of top management involvement and support can result in the development of systems that fail to anticipate the long-term needs of the organization and conflict with strategic organizational goals.[6]

PROCESS

As we will soon see, systems development is a complicated process with many alternative paths. Those familiar and experienced with the process can more readily guide development through the obstacles it might face. The process of systems development has been widely researched. Several academic and trade journals and many books and studies are devoted to it. In addition, a variety of software tools exist to guide project managers through the tasks they need to perform to maximize their chance of success. Managers, such as Graves, should familiarize themselves with these tools and with current thinking about the process before actively participating in it. Those unfamiliar with the process will make many mistakes unless they follow clear guidelines.

RESOURCES

Systems development requires time, money, and people. We will study ways to estimate the resources needed. Organizations that commit the required resources more often succeed. Those organizations that cannot or will not commit the resources necessary for success will likely encounter failure.

KEY SYSTEMS DEVELOPMENT CONCEPTS

Managers involved in developing or updating information systems should understand the systems development life cycle, development pathways, systems models, and process management.

THE SYSTEMS DEVELOPMENT LIFE CYCLE

The **systems development life cycle (SDLC)** refers to a sequence of stages in the conception, design, creation, and implementation of an information system, as shown in Figure 12.1. Our model of the SDLC consists of the following six stages:

FIGURE 12.1	The systems development life cycle describes the stages in the conception, development, and maturity of an information system.

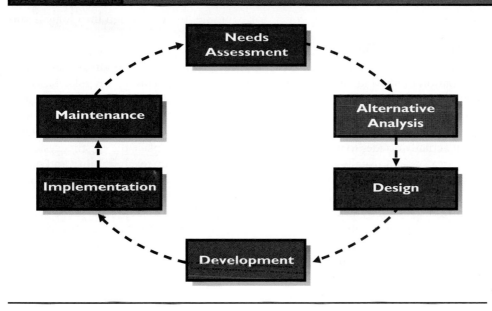

- **Needs assessment** describes a formal, integrated, and usually time-limited process of gathering data about the needs and opportunities of end users and their managers; evaluating and ranking the importance of these needs; and addressing the possibility that they cannot be satisfied by continuous improvement of existing systems.
- **Alternative analysis** considers one or more alternate designs and analyzes their advantages and disadvantages. Alternative analysis ends when developers select a preliminary design for further analysis.
- **Design** refers to the creation of detailed specifications for the proposed system. Just as a contractor would not begin to build a house without knowing the size and placement of its rooms and the location of plumbing and electrical fixtures, systems developers need to work to detailed specifications to produce desired results. If the organization plans to contract the development of the system, detailed specifications enable contractors to estimate costs and submit bids.
- **Development** refers to the creation or purchase of the hardware and software necessary to implement the design. It also includes the testing required to ensure that the system meets the design specifications.
- **Implementation** refers to deactivating the old system and activating the new one. Implementation includes converting data from the old to new system, training employees to use the system, and pilot testing or phasing in the new system.
- **Maintenance** refers to fixing errors or **bugs** in the way that the system operates. It also refers to modifying the system to provide new features or improved performance beyond that included in the design and possibly even beyond what was envisioned during needs assessment.

No uniformly accepted model of the SDLC exists. Some models combine development and implementation into a single stage. Others combine needs assessment and analysis into a single stage. Still others offer more detail, dividing each of the stages into several parts. One model, for example, divides design into logical and physical design stages.

The concept of a life cycle implies that companies replace or renew systems as they age. Business managers, such as those at GPIC, examine new opportunities, assess information needs, and address weaknesses in existing systems on a regular basis. As maintenance demands become more frequent and difficult to implement, the organization will likely want to undertake a formal needs assessment, starting the cycle anew. Needs assessment and alternative analysis might occur several times before an organization actually decides to move beyond these stages and replace the existing system.

Large systems usually require several years before they reach stability and maturity. During that time the organization may grow or shrink, move into new markets, or acquire new businesses. Technology will also change: hardware that met the initial needs may remain adequate, but failing to incorporate more recent, advanced technology into its systems may leave the organization at a competitive disadvantage. For example, a company that developed its inventory systems before barcode scanners became widely available would have less information than companies that use more recent technologies. Similarly, systems that incorporate voice-input and multimedia devices will surpass the capabilities of earlier systems that lack these technologies. Software technology also improves and becomes more efficient with time. Systems developers who maintain existing applications must use older, less efficient technology, and they cannot modify their applications to meet new demands as rapidly as competitors who use newer technology.

The decision to replace rather than modify an old system is difficult. The old system may represent an investment of many years and thousands or millions of dollars. Managers, users, and the information systems staff feel comfortable and secure in using the system; they know that despite its limitations it works. A new system poses potential risks. It should work better than the old system but may fail in unexpected ways. The organization must retrain its systems development staff in the new technologies and train end users in the new system.

Management typically has no reliable way to quantify the benefits of a new system and faces some uncertainty in estimating the system's development costs and time. The cabinet at GPIC, for example, hesitated before approving expenditures for a new system. The typical manager who faces these concerns will often try to keep current systems operating instead. As maintenance costs mount and competitors' new products display more advanced, sleeker features, managers consider replacing older systems. One rule of thumb calls for renovation rather than replacement of the existing system if the functional match between it and user requirements is at least 65 percent to 85 percent.[7]

DEVELOPMENT PATHWAYS

The SDLC implies that new systems always progress smoothly and sequentially from one stage to the next. In practice, systems do not always follow this progression. Managers and computer professionals can move through the SDLC by using the waterfall model, the spiral approach, or prototyping.

The Waterfall Model.　The **waterfall model** follows the SDLC in sequence (see Figure 12.2). Like water flowing in a waterfall, development following the waterfall model never moves backward. For example, needs assessment occurs only once. After completing each stage, the project team creates products and reports that document the results of that stage. Project sponsors approve these outputs, which become input to the next stage of the process. Because the waterfall approach requires no rework, its linear structure makes it relatively easy to manage. The project manager can set deadlines and monitor progress toward those deadlines.

At the same time, the waterfall model is highly inflexible. If, for example, user needs change during the course of the project, no formal mechanism exists for adjusting the development process. If the project manager follows the waterfall model strictly, he saves all proposed changes in a database and examines them at the conclusion of the project to see if another project should be started to meet these needs.

Using the waterfall model also means that no component of the system is delivered until near the end of the project. Often this leads to tension between users and developers, especially if deadlines slip. Sponsors wonder why they spend millions of dollars yet see no results. The final product may also surprise the sponsors. Despite the mass of documentation accompanying the waterfall model, sponsors rarely understand exactly what they have bought until the product is delivered. At that point, they cannot make changes without major costs and delays.

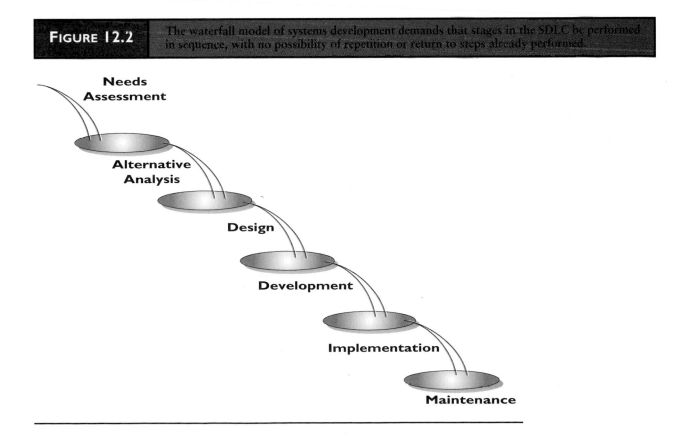

FIGURE 12.2　The waterfall model of systems development demands that stages in the SDLC be performed in sequence, with no possibility of repetition or return to steps already performed.

THE MANAGER IN ACTION

Senior managers at Capital One have unusual assistance in meeting their technology needs. They have BIOs—business information officers—who bridge the worlds of business and information technology. When a senior manager has an IS project, relating, for example, to collections, credit operations, customer service, core systems, and growth opportunities, the BIO manages it.

"BIOs have to create their own relationships with their business units, but there's no manual that tells you how to do it," according to BIO Mike D'Aiutolo at Capital One. "While the business units all expressed their desire for a single person to go to for technology issues, how that expectation is met is based on each senior vice president's personal preferences." The senior vice president in human resources, for example, wants a systems review of current projects about every six weeks. The vice president in charge of credit prefers regular meetings that focus on area strategy rather than project review.

SOURCE: Adapted from Deborah Asbrand, The BIO—An "Original Vision," *Datamation* (September 1997): 42–45.

Despite these disadvantages, GPIC will probably use the waterfall model for its accounting system. The system has an enterprise-wide scope with implications for many existing software applications in the company. Graves will want to ensure that the new system meets all users' needs and that the scope of the project does not change as development proceeds.

The Spiral Approach.   The **spiral approach** implements systems based on the concept of greatest need. As illustrated in Figure 12.3, the spiral approach delivers a system in versions. Each version goes through all the steps of the SDLC except implementation, which may apply to some versions, and maintenance, which applies only to the last version.

The "80/20 rule" drives the spiral approach: 80 percent of users' needs can be met with only 20 percent of the functions they want. Producing a basic system to satisfy 80 percent of needs then becomes simple if you can believe this rule. The first version attempts to achieve a basic system that will meet most user needs. Adding the "bells and whistles" takes the most time.

Advocates of the spiral approach often use a time-box concept to pace development. A **time box** is a set period, usually three months, within which developers must complete each version. No product specifications exist because meeting such specifications may be impossible within the time allowed. Instead, developers add features in order of priority until time runs out. Then they release the new version.

An alternative philosophy involves planning each version as much as possible at the beginning of the project. In effect, this divides the project into smaller subprojects, each more easily managed than the main project and each providing a working product as a deliverable. At the end of each project, the remaining subprojects are redefined considering user feedback.

FIGURE 12.3 The spiral model creates new systems in versions, with the most important needs being addressed first. Subsequent versions also go through many of the SDLC stages.

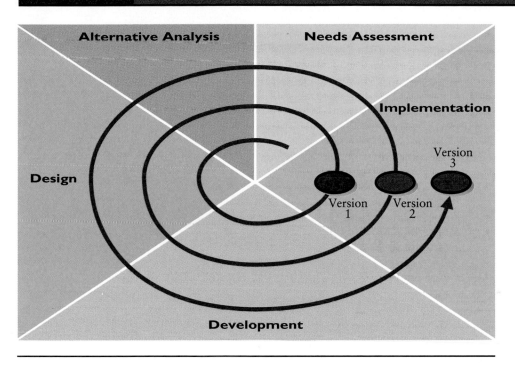

The spiral approach delivers the product rapidly. No laborious documentation of specifications occurs because users can revise the product with later versions. Users can see progress and judge how long it will take before the development system meets enough of their needs to replace the existing system.

The spiral approach also means constant rework of existing versions. Although companies can reuse some parts of old versions, they must discard and rewrite others. This rewriting generally increases the cost of the project. The product might not be usable until later versions are complete.

Prototyping. **Prototyping** describes an approach that tries to satisfy user needs by focusing on the user interface. The design and development stages, as they apply to the user interface, repeat until the user is satisfied, as illustrated in Figure 12.4. Occasionally, developers discover new user needs in the process and may need to do additional analysis.

A variation of prototyping called **joint application development (JAD)** works essentially as follows. Users meet with systems developers periodically, often every day at the start of the project. The users describe their needs during the initial meetings. Software developers use prototyping software to create a prototype of a system that appears to meet these needs before the next joint meeting. The prototype that they create might include data entry screens, reports, query screens, and other parts of the user interface, but rarely performs much processing. Developers sometimes create

FIGURE 12.4 Prototyping repeats the design, development, and occasionally analysis stages. Developing the user interface rapidly keeps data and process models current.

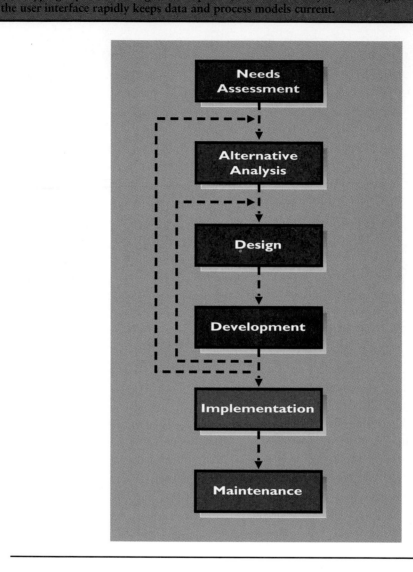

dummy data to present an illusion of a working system. At the next meeting, the developers present their prototype to the users for their review.

Discussion meetings alternate with development time for the systems developers. These ongoing discussions between users and developers allow the users to communicate their needs more accurately to the developer than would occur by building a formal specification statement during the design phase of the SDLC. As the system develops and unmet needs diminish, the frequency of meetings between users and developers decreases. Developers then spend their time more on implementation issues, optimizing the use of system resources such as storage and computing, and completing the code for processing.

INFORMATION TECHNOLOGY AND GLOBAL BUSINESS

Information systems managers developing applications for users in different countries might want to give a big thumbs-up to Tony Fernandes, author of a new book on designing international user interfaces. But then again, they might not. The thumbs-up, taken in the United States as a sign of approval, means something obscene in Australia. It's an example Fernandes uses to illustrate why pictures of hands and hand gestures are design elements best omitted when an application is to be deployed cross-culturally.

Violating taboos is one risk developers take when they ship U.S.-developed applications overseas. Expecting overseas employees to use an American-designed interface could result in higher training costs and poor productivity. "If usability and low training costs are really important, you can't get there by producing a solution for just one population in a multinational company," says Fernandes. If software is to be used internationally, design it with all users in mind from the start.

Objects and images that are familiar to Americans are often meaningless in other cultures, according to Fernandes. For example, tabbed manila folders aren't used in many European countries. Nevertheless, the visual metaphor of these common American office supplies is now ubiquitous in Windows-based applications. Lists of options are another element that can cause cross-cultural confusion. In many countries, people are accustomed to deleting items they don't want from a list and leaving untouched the items they wish to select. Yet many software applications require users to mark the items they wish to select by checking a box.

One multinational company that takes international interface design very seriously is DHL Worldwide Express. The company has three development centers—in the United States, Europe, and Asia—to address users' and customers' needs. The company tries to ease the task of localizing interfaces. So DHL designs software applications to use one common logic engine, on top of which different interfaces are layered, says Alan Boehme, director of customer access and logistics marketing. This way, developers in each locale can design interfaces using their own sets of icons, color choices, and even button styles, he says.

SOURCE: Extracted with modification from Elizabeth Heichler, When GUIs and cultures collide, *Computerworld* (September 25, 1995): 112, 113.

Prototyping offers several advantages over the waterfall approach.

- Prototyping decreases the amount of time that elapses between analysis and implementation.
- Prototyping ensures that the new system addresses user needs.
- Prototyping shows the benefits of a new system before the effort and costs become excessive.
- Prototyping exploits the skills that users have in articulating what they do not like about a system more easily than what they like about it.

Experts estimate that as many as 65 percent of very large IS projects, those with more than one million lines of code, are canceled before they are completed.[8]

ETHICAL ISSUES IN IT

Budget Rent A Car Corp. claims that Genesys Software Systems Inc. has taken it for a ride that cost the international auto rental company more than $2 million. Budget Rent A Car, in Lisle, Illinois, is suing Methuen, Massachusetts-based Genesys, claiming that Genesys failed to get its human resources software up and running and that Genesys intentionally misled Budget about the software's scalability.

Budget contends that what was meant to be a multiuser system could handle only one user at a time without freezing the whole system. Budget also alleges that transaction requests frequently failed and that workstations repeatedly froze, keeping employees from accessing information on the system.

Genesys is countersuing Budget, looking for nearly $200,000 in allegedly unpaid bills. "Budget didn't do its homework," claimed Genesys attorney Laurence Johnson. "They didn't find out if their network had enough capacity to run their software at the speed and capacity they wanted. They didn't have a network adequate to run our applications along with everything else they were running on their network."

1. Did Genesys act unethically?
2. What responsibility does the customer have to "do its homework"?

SOURCE: Extracted with modification from Sharon Gaudin, Budget Rent A Car sues software supplier, *Computerworld* (May 5, 1997): 10.

Although the cancellation rate falls as the size and complexity of the project decrease, falling to less than 10 percent overall,[9] prototyping decreases the risk of failure and cancellation.

Prototyping also has disadvantages relative to the waterfall model:

- It tends to raise the expectations of users to levels that developers cannot achieve within their budgets. When users see how rapidly developers can produce a prototype, they believe that the entire systems development effort will be equally fast and easy. Users continually ask for more features as they experiment with each prototype. Rapid prototyping hides the cost and risk of increasing the scope, because no full analysis occurs after each prototyping cycle.
- The software programs that enable software developers to quickly develop the shell of a new system and rapidly customize it to user demands currently command high prices. Although the code that many of them produce may reduce the final cost of development by more than the cost of the tool, such savings are not guaranteed.
- It delays the demonstration of system functionality. As much as one-half of the functionality may not appear until the final 10 percent of the development schedule.[10]
- The benefits of prototyping decrease if the company buys existing software rather than develops its own. If GPIC, for example, expects that off-the-shelf software exists to meet a large portion of its needs, the company will not be able to follow a prototyping approach.

Selecting a Pathway.   Table 12.1 summarizes the differences between the three pathways. The best approach for a given project depends greatly on the nature of the project and the nature of the organization. The waterfall approach works best with large, complex projects that have numerous stakeholders, affect the entire enterprise, and cannot easily be divided into subprojects. It also works well with organizations that have a formal culture and a hierarchical structure.

A spiral approach works well in more dynamic organizations that can tolerate ambiguity and need results quickly. It works well for projects that can be easily divided into subprojects and for more simple projects, especially the development of single-user systems or systems that affect a small department.

Prototyping works best for small-to-medium sized projects. It works well where the culture supports cross-functional teams. Prototyping can be combined with the spiral approach and be used for one or more of the subprojects in a spiral development.

SYSTEMS MODELING

Systems developers use data, process, and object models to understand existing systems and design new ones. These models provide a standard way of communicating about what systems do. They create a language that analysts, designers, and developers can use to communicate efficiently. Managers on systems development teams will benefit from understanding these models so they can better communicate their needs.

TABLE 12.1   Systems developers can choose from the waterfall, spiral, and prototype pathways.

Strategy	Description	Uses	Advantages	Disadvantages
Waterfall	Follows the stages of the SDLC in order	Large, complex projects with many stakeholders	• No rework • Easy to manage	• Highly inflexible • No functional interim deliveries
Spiral	Delivers a system in versions according to the 80/20 rule of greatest need	Dynamic organizations that can tolerate ambiguity and need fast results	• Rapid product delivery • Progress easy to see	• Constant rework • High costs
Prototyping	Focuses on the user interface through repetition of design and development stages	Small to medium projects in a culture that supports cross-functional teams	• Short time between analysis and implementation • System better meets needs • Avoids unnecessary costs • Lets users say what they do not want	• Raises user expectations • Cost savings not guaranteed • Delays system functionality

Products that generate computer programs directly from systems models can dramatically speed software development. Products that generate system models from existing programs can help developers understand and maintain these programs. Many products also support translation among models of the same type, for example, from one data model to another.

Data Models.   Data models describe the relationships among the elements of data that an organization uses. The entity-relationship model (see Chapter 5) is one of the most widely used data models (see Figure 12.5 for an example). The American National Standards Institute supports a different standard, the IDEF1X data model. This model resembles the entity relationship model but translates more directly to a relational database implementation. Products, such as Smart ER from Knowledge Based Systems Inc. and EasyER from Visual Systems, support both models, as well as several others.

Process Models.   Process models divide a process into its parts, show how these parts relate to one another, and indicate how the outputs of one process act

| **FIGURE 12.5** | This entity-relationship diagram shows the relationships among a publisher, its books, and their authors. |

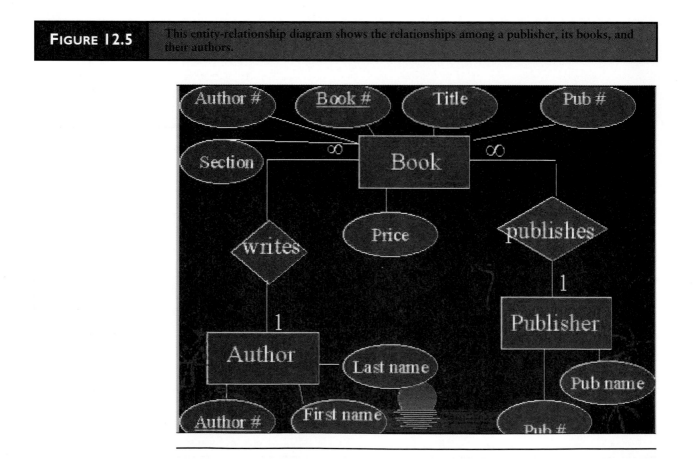

as inputs to other processes. The most popular process models include structure charts, function boxes, and data-flow diagrams (DFDs).

- **Structure charts** show the relationship among the programs and subprograms that will constitute the finished system. Figure 12.6, a structure chart for a payroll system, emphasizes the modular design of the system. Performing a given task, such as calculating net pay, requires completing all of the tasks below it (in this case calculating taxes and calculating deductions).

FIGURE 12.6   A structure chart of a payroll system divides the payroll process into three subprocesses. Subprocesses are further divided.

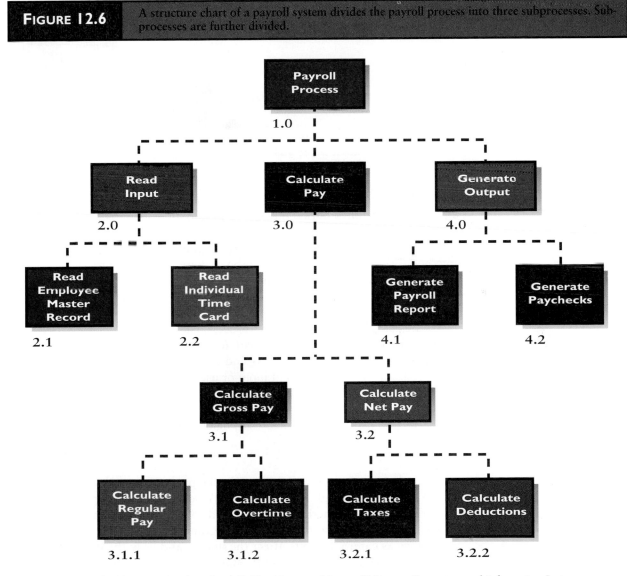

SOURCE: Reprinted with permission from Sarah E. Hutchinson and Stacey C. Sawyer, *Computers and Information Systems,* 1994–1995 ed. (Burr Ridge, IL: Irwin, 1994): 8, 21.

FIGURE 12.7   An IDEF0 function box shows how a process connects to other processes.

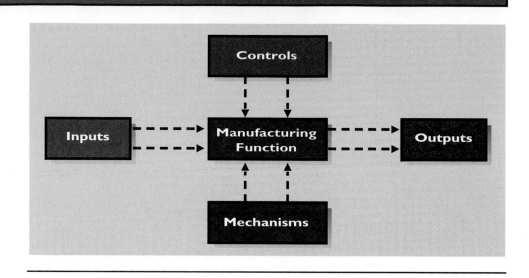

- **Function boxes,** illustrated in Figure 12.7, implement the American National Standards Institute's IDEF0 model. Each function box corresponds to a box in a structure chart. The lines between boxes show the relationships between the inputs and outputs of the procedures. Documents that support the IDEF0 methodology show a single function box, along with the division of that box into its subtasks, on each page, as illustrated in Figure 12.8.
- **Data-flow diagrams (DFDs)** model the flow of data between processes. They do not model the breakdown of processes into sub-processes or the order in which tasks are performed to accomplish a process. Figure 12.9 illustrates a data-flow diagram for a simplified payroll system. Arrows indicate data flows; open-sided rectangles represent stored data; round-edged rectangles indicate processes; and squares represent sources of input or users of output. This example shows the employee as both a source of input (time card) and a user of output (paycheck). An employee file maintains stored data about the employee's pay class, pay rate, and deductions; processes to determine gross pay and calculate net pay use these stored data.

Object Models.   Object models describe the properties of objects, their relationship to one another, and the functions they perform (see Chapter 5). Object models typically include inheritance diagrams that show how objects derive from other objects. They may also include state diagrams to show how object characteristics change as external events affect the object, and how the object responds differently to messages depending on its state. Because objects hide the characteristics of their data, programmers can readily insert objects into code. They can reuse this type of code more easily than other types, simplifying systems development.

FIGURE 12.8	The lower page shows an IDEF0 model with function boxes. The upper page provides the IDEF0 model of the parent process, allowing a view of the current process in context.

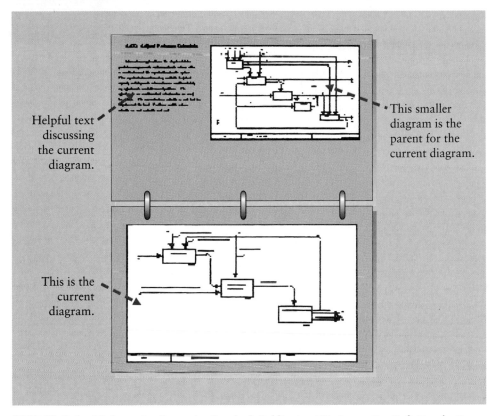

Helpful text discussing the current diagram.

This smaller diagram is the parent for the current diagram.

This is the current diagram.

SOURCE: *Federal Information Processing Standards Publication 183: Integration Definition for Function Modeling (IDEF0)* (Knowledge Based Systems Inc., and U.S. Department of Commerce National Technical Information Service, June 30, 1994), http://www.idef.com/complete_reports/idef0/html/Annex_B_Part_1.html#B.1, September 2, 1997.

PROCESS MANAGEMENT

Systems development works best if the organization can identify, institutionalize, and continually improve its practices. The Software Engineering Institute has developed and popularized a model called the Capability Maturity Model (see Figure 12.10) that managers can use to evaluate how well their organization achieves these goals and guide them in improving their systems development processes.

Process management software products can help an organization standardize and improve its systems development processes. Some of these products emphasize a particular development methodology, that is, a prescribed set of practices, tools, and even notations. Commercial packages support dozens of popular methodologies, such as Martin and Coad/Yourden. Other packages support the organization's

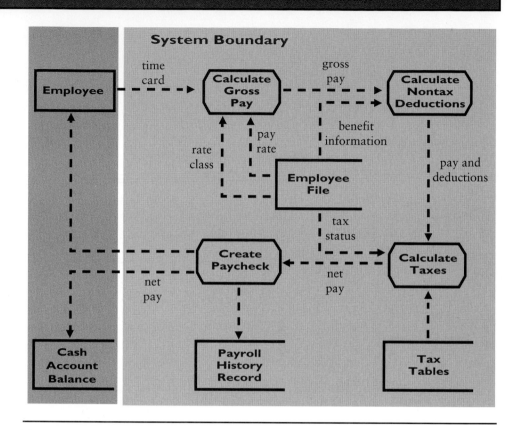

development of its own best practices. These products come with customizable process libraries, which often include several of the widely accepted methodologies as starting points.

Using process management software requires the project manager to identify the type of project, such as client-server development or package purchase, and the approach, such as waterfall or spiral (see Figure 12.11). The software then identifies the tasks in the processes associated with that type of development (see Figure 12.12). Users may export the task list into a project management package such as Microsoft Project to assign responsibilities to individuals or groups, identify tasks on the critical path, estimate time to completion, and track the percent completed.

Process management software provides templates to guide developers in the creation of intermediate products, such as designs, specifications, and other end-of-stage waterfall products. It could include tutorials to help users apply the software tools associated with their tasks. It also includes metrics that managers can use to measure and evaluate performance at a task or process level.

Organizations sometimes assign a **process manager** or **process librarian** to customize templates and tutorials to the organization's standards and collect metrics and best practices for customizing the process library. The process manager may also

| **FIGURE 12.10** | The Software Engineering Institute's Capability Maturity Model describes an organization's sophistication in regard to best practices for systems development. |

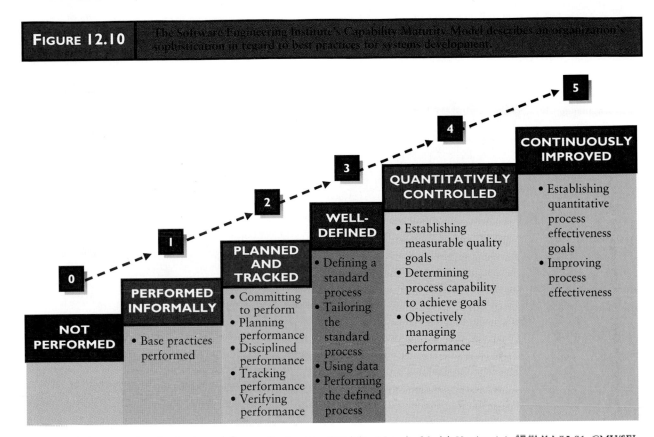

SOURCE: Software Engineering Institute, A Systems Engineering Capability Maturity Model, Version 1.1, SECMM-95-01, CMU/SEI-95-MM-003 (Software Engineering Institute, 1995): 2–28.

have training responsibilities and a mandate to educate managers, such as Graves, who are newly involved in projects and who may not be familiar with the company's systems development processes.

COMPUTER-AIDED SOFTWARE ENGINEERING (CASE)

Computer-aided software engineering (CASE) describes the use of software to automate activities performed in needs assessment, systems analysis, design, development, and maintenance. **CASE tools,** as shown in Table 12.2, refer to the software products themselves. Managers and developers might use CASE tools for a single activity or element of the SDLC, such as developing an entity-relationship diagram, or for almost all activities during the cycle. Table 12.3 shows a list of typical CASE features.

A suite of CASE tools that support and integrate the activities performed throughout the life cycle is called a **CASE toolset** or **CASE workbench.** CASE

FIGURE 12.11 The path-selection interface to the Process Manager from LBMS has an expert-system interface that selects the best process library based on the user's response to a series of questions.

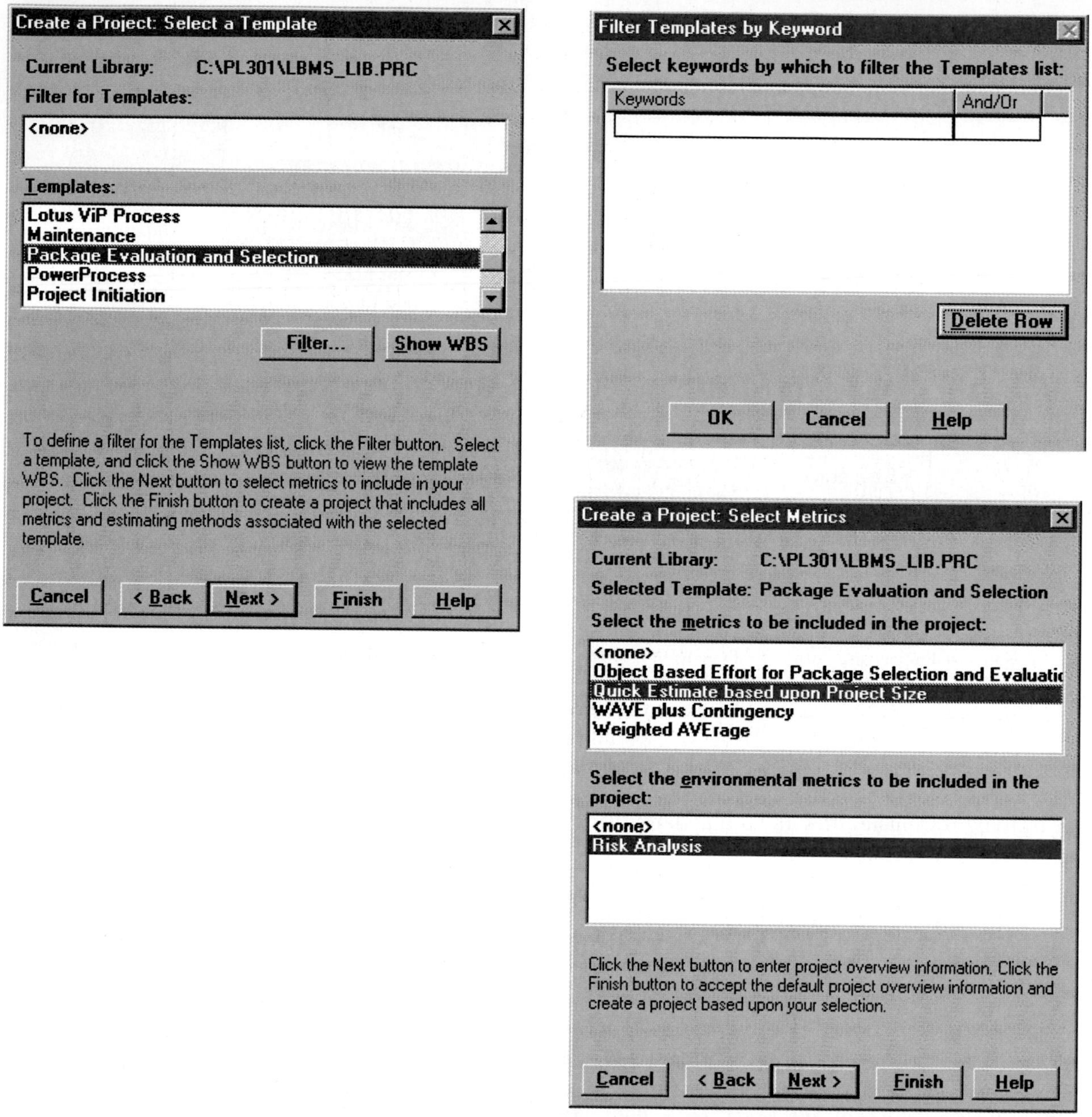

workbenches provide a consistent interface between the various CASE tools in the suite, a smooth transition for moving between tools as they follow one or more methodologies, and a common database of information about the project under development. In addition, they provide consistent and cross-referenced documentation of user needs, application processes, data flow and structure, and software design.

| FIGURE 12.12 | The LBMS process library for package selection includes some of the tasks shown here. Clicking on the + sign expands high-level processes into the tasks and subtasks. |

	WBS Co	Name	Objective	Description	Mand	Outputs
-	CS	Client/Server		The Client/Server	Yes	Client/Server
	PI	Project Initiation	To	At the start of any	Yes	Project Initiation
-	BPD	Business Process Definition	To	This stage is concerned	Yes	Business Process
+	01	Business Process Investigation	To	This step examines the	No	Business Process
+	02	Business Requirements and Opportunities	To	This step is concerned	Yes	Requirements
-	03	Business Process Redesign	To	This step is concerned	Yes	Business Process
	010	Define Business Process Improvements		Conduct an interactive	Yes	Business Process
	020	Define Workflow		Examine the process model	No	Data Flow
	030	Create Required Data Model		Determine the data entities	Yes	Data Model[<Mandatory>]
	040	Consider Buy/Build/Sourcing Options		Consider whether the	No	Problem/Requirement
	050	Consider Deployment Strategies		Determine how the new	Yes	Delivery Increment
	060	Evaluate and Define Delivery Increments		Evaluate the options for the	Yes	Delivery Increment
	070	Plan Delivery Increments		For each delivery increment	Yes	Project Plan[<Mandatory>]
	080	Define Increment Acceptance Criteria		Update the Requirements	Yes	Acceptance
	090	Establish Program Management Procedures		Identify the activities,	No	Management
	100	Review Results of Business Process Redesign		Review the results of the	Yes	Review
+	SEA	Stage End Assessment	To	An End-Stage	Yes	Stage
+	CST	Technical Architecture Definition	To	The nature of this stage	No	Stage
+	CSA	Application Definition	To	This stage is concerned	Yes	Application
-	CSE	Application Engineering	To	This stage is concerned	Yes	Client/Server
+	BID	Build Iteration Definition	To	This kernel is concerned	Yes	Build
+	02	Client/Server Partitioning and Optimization	To	This step is concerned	Yes	Physical Application
+	TD	Test Design	To	This kernel is concerned	Yes	Test
+	04	Client Build	To	This step is concerned	Yes	Database[<Optional>]¶
+	05	Server Build	To	This step is concerned	Yes	Database[<Optional>]¶
+	06	Integration and System Testing	To	This step is concerned	Yes	System
+	SEA	Stage End Assessment	To	An End-Stage	Yes	Stage

Shell Oil Company found that the documentation features of KnowledgeWare's CASE workbench allowed Shell to keep its documentation current with rapidly changing software code. In addition, completing the programs meant that preliminary documentation was complete.[11] System methodologies and CASE tools ease the development of systems that respond to users' needs in a cost-effective, timely, and technologically current fashion.

| TABLE 12.2 | Managers can choose from a variety of CASE tools. |

Product	Function	Vendor
BusinessTeam	Data and process design	Cayenne Software
ERwin	ER design	Logic Works
Imagix 4D	Reverse engineering	Imagix
Object Construction Suite	Object design and development	Genitor
PVCS	Configuration management	Intersolv
Silverrun-BPM	Process design	Silverrun Technologies
Simply Objects	Object design	Adaptive Arts
System Architect	Full suite	Popkin Software
TestWorks	Testing	Software Research
Visible Analyst	Full suite	Visible Systems

TABLE 12.3	CASE products have features, including those listed in this table, that support software development.

Common debugger
Data modeling
GUI builder
Problem tracking
Process management
Project scheduling
Rapid application development
Reverse engineering
Structured analysis and design
Technical documentation
Testing

SOURCE: http://www.qucis.queensu.ca/Software-Engineering/tools.html.

ASSESSING CURRENT SYSTEMS AND REQUIREMENTS

Needs assessment, also called **requirements analysis**, identifies the information needs of an organization. As part of this effort, analysts compare the identified needs to the specifications and performance of the current information system to determine what needs remain unmet. In later stages of the SDLC, managers evaluate the costs and benefits of developing new systems to satisfy these unmet needs.

Business managers analyze current systems and needs periodically. Some organizations have no formal review process. They have users who rarely complain or who constantly demand changes that force IS managers to conduct ad hoc reviews. Other organizations, such as GPIC, have formal systems for examining current systems and prioritizing and scheduling changes.

Documenting all the information needs of an organization presents a major challenge because these needs constantly change. Research shows that when systems developers identify needs early in the development cycle, the likelihood of development success increases and the cost of corrections in later stages of the cycle declines.[12]

COLLECTING INFORMATION FOR NEEDS ASSESSMENT

Analysts determining organizations' or users' information needs typically focus on three types of needs: outputs, inputs, and procedures.

Output Analysis. **Output analysis** describes the systematic identification of ways people in an organization use information: What type of reports do people receive? How frequently do they obtain the reports? What information do they retrieve from manual files? What information do they gain from online queries? What information would they like to obtain, and in what form?

Analysts can easily identify the formal uses of information by looking at reports and query screens that existing information systems generate and by asking employees how they use hardcopy files stored in file cabinets. Analysts can also help users compose wish lists of information that would help them perform their jobs better. Without analysts' help, end users often include on these wish lists only information they believe they can obtain. They often do not know the breadth of information that the organization can secure.

Business managers, along with IS professionals, can expand a traditional output analysis by benchmarking similar applications developed at other companies and in other industries. For example, in assessing GPIC's needs, Graves can benefit from studying the screens and reports produced by accounting programs run by computer manufacturers, chemical manufacturers, or even nonmanufacturing firms, such as real estate companies.

Input Analysis.   **Input analysis** refers to a formal cataloging and review of the information an organization collects, stores, and uses. It also includes an analysis of the data collection process. Typically, input analysis follows output analysis so that analysts can identify missing or duplicate sources of information needed to produce the desired output. Input analysis also addresses the potential input of information that an organization collects but currently does not input into its information systems. Most organizations informally collect large amounts of data, such as word-of-mouth opinions or nonstatistical projects, that do not reside on formal information systems. For example, sales agents rarely enter more than a small percentage of the data they obtain when conversing with prospective or existing customers into manual or computerized information systems. Because informal data can provide useful information, product designers, executive strategists, and marketing managers would highly value a system that captures them. Educating users to identify what information they collect can be difficult because most users lack an awareness of how they and others use and collect information.

Procedure Analysis.   **Procedure analysis** attempts to determine whether the organization collects the information it needs, uses the information it collects effectively, and has efficient processes to address the organization's information needs. Procedure analysis should examine all computerized and manual systems. Data-flow diagrams and structure charts might document existing processes and compare them with desired practices. Designers might simply compile a cross-reference between processes and data, as illustrated by the diagram in Figure 12.13, showing what data each process creates (C), reads (R), updates (U), or deletes (D).

THE ROLE OF THE SYSTEMS ANALYST

Users of information systems often cannot understand the jargon that computer professionals use, and computer professionals often do not know enough about the processes used in a specific business to understand the needs and language of its users. This communication gap may reduce the quality of a company's requirements analysis. A

| FIGURE 12.13 | This portion of a CRUD diagram shows which processes create, read, update, and delete which data in a payroll system. |

Data		Process			
		Maintain employee file	Calculate employee pay	Prepare pay by job class report	Maintain tax tables
Employee	Name	CRUD	R		
	Wage rate	CRUD	R		
	Job class	CRUD	R		
	YTD pay		U		
Tax Rates	State		R		
	Rate		R		U
Time Cards	Employee		R		
	Hours		R		
Summary Data	Hours		U	R	
	Pay		U	R	

systems analyst, a person who provides the interface between the information systems user and the information systems developer, can bridge this gap. A successful systems analyst understands the technical aspects of the system and can assess their implications for the users.[13]

Systems analysts should have strong interpersonal skills: they should listen well and ask probing questions in an unthreatening manner. The complexity of business processes often motivates systems analysts to work in a single applications area for several years to maximize their knowledge of the business specialty and its requirements. Line managers rely on such specialists to interface with IS managers. In many large organizations, systems analysts report directly to a line manager rather than an IS manager.

METHODOLOGIES AND TOOLS FOR NEEDS ASSESSMENT

Systems analysts use varied techniques and data sources to perform needs assessment. These include interviews, on-site observation, questionnaires, structured analysis, a data dictionary, and reverse engineering.[14]

Interviews. Systems analysts typically obtain information about existing systems and needs by interviewing users and their managers. Users and managers know the most about the systems they use, although they perform many activities almost subconsciously. Because users often report only standard operating practices, forgetting the exceptions that occur infrequently, analysts must ferret out these exceptions for the new system to operate effectively and efficiently. Users might resist reporting how they bypass the formal or standard systems to perform their work more efficiently. They might fear being fired or demoted if they tell what they actually do rather than what they should do. An analyst may require several interviews with the same people to verify their understanding of the processes performed, provide feedback on the use of the collected information, and build the trust necessary to reveal exceptional and nonstandard processes.

On-Site Observation.   Systems analysts can watch users doing their jobs or work alongside them.[15] This approach, called **contextual inquiry,** lacks efficiency because it can require several days or weeks to obtain information that an analyst could obtain in an hour-long interview. But it can reveal exceptional and nonstandard processes more often and more completely.

Questionnaires.   Systems analysts, such as those at GPIC, may use questionnaires to collect information when many people or geographically disbursed workers should provide information about the processes affected by the new system. Analysts may also use confidential questionnaires to obtain information about hidden processes. Questionnaires may not yield quality data because employees often fail to complete them and those that do often offer incomplete answers. Small companies have too few employees in each area to merit the use of questionnaires for data collection. Analysts prefer techniques that involve users and build a sense of ownership in the proposed system; questionnaires may fail to develop such a stake by users.

Structured Analysis.   Structured analysis uses process modeling tools to diagram existing and proposed systems so that users can understand and critique an analyst's perception of information relationships. GPIC's analysts will likely use structured analysis to share their understanding of the budgeting process with Graves. Graves will need to understand these models to ensure that budgeting processes under the new accounting system are logical and relate properly to other processes in the organization.

Data Dictionary.   A **data dictionary** refers to a database that contains descriptions of all of the computerized data items maintained by the organization (see Chapter 5). Users can access the data dictionary to validate their perceptions of the data an organization collects and uses and to identify gaps in the data they require for their business functions. Analysts may use a data dictionary to specify and clarify terms used by end users to describe their business activities. For example, when a user refers to *revenue from sales,* the analyst working with that user can refer to the data dictionary to learn whether the term means the undiscounted price of items sold, the money that changes hands at the time of the sale, or the revenue adjusted by any returns after the sale.

Reverse Engineering.   Large, entrenched systems, often called legacy systems, might consist of thousands of programs written and modified over 10 to 20 years. These programs and the processes they implement may have such complex interrelationships that no one in the organization knows exactly how they work. For example, programmers no longer employed by the organization may have made significant

COST-BENEFIT ANALYSIS

Alternative designs meet different needs and incur different costs. Consider, for example, a shipper who wishes to trace the location of a package in route without waiting for the daily transport report. One solution might locate the package within an hour, another within five minutes, and a third within seconds. Each solution meets the need with a different relative benefit and cost. A **cost-benefit analysis** weighs the benefits of meeting the needs against the projected costs in a formal, documented way.

Cost-benefit analysis techniques address the differences in the timing of costs and benefits. Most costs for a new system occur during its development and when procuring hardware. Benefits accrue over time and may decline as competitors develop similar systems. Cost-benefit analyses use economic, analytic, portfolio, or strategic methods[17] that include such techniques as discounted cash flow, internal rate of return, and payback period to translate costs and benefits accruing over time into numbers that can be compared on a current basis.

Estimating the cost of a project may be difficult at this early design stage.[18] Various techniques exist to estimate software development costs based on the number of application functions the software will provide.[19] However, knowing the number of functions is difficult even for a fully specified design. Estimates at this stage may err by 50 percent or more.

Estimating a system's benefits may be even more problematic. For example, how can a manager assess the value of responding to customers more rapidly? Although a rapid response should lead to greater sales, calculations of the impact on sales and profits may contain significant errors. Intangible benefits, such as improving morale by changing the nature of an employee's work, may be almost impossible to quantify accurately. Typical cost-justification errors include exaggerating cost savings, underestimating costs, failing to identify hidden costs, and relying on false numbers.[20]

RISK ANALYSIS

Every IS project involves risks as well as benefits. The State of California terminated the development of an automated child-support system after spending more than $100 million on the project. The system was intended to track deadbeat parents in the 58 counties in the state, but after four years it worked in only 17, and even in those experienced problems such as erasing back child-support payments from an account.[21] One systems solution may provide more benefit than another solution at the same or lower cost, but it might require the use of unproven technology or the mastery of the new technology by the IS staff. Risks exist both with technology and people. Some designs might automate a job previously done manually causing the company to lay off some staff. Although benefits accrue from reduced labor costs, risks arise from possible labor unrest or loss of morale. **Risk analysis** requires managers to identify where risks might arise and trade risk against costs and benefits.[22]

The McFarlan Risk Questionnaire (see Figure 12.15), one of the most widely accepted instruments to measure risk assessment, estimates risk as a function of project size, the intended technology, and the structure of the relationship among the project, its users, and other projects. For example, breaking a project into smaller

FIGURE 12.15	The McFarlan Risk Questionnaire is popular for assessing the risk of a systems development project. Here are selected questions from that questionnaire.

CATEGORY/QUESTION	SIZE SCORE	WEIGHT (in final score)
Size		
Total systems and programming mandays for system:		5
( )　　12 to 375	Low = 1	
( )　　376 to 1875	Med = 2	
( )　　1876 to 3750	Med = 3	
( )　　Over 3750	High = 4	
What is the estimate for the elapsed time to complete the project?		4
( )　　12 months or less	Low = 1	
( )　　13 to 24 months	Med = 2	
( )　　Over 24 months	High = 3	
To how many existing systems must the new one interface?		3
( )　　None or one	Low = 1	
( )　　Two	Med = 2	
( )　　Three or more	High = 3	
Structure		
The system is best described as:		1
( )　　Totally new	High = 3	
( )　　Replacement of existing manual system	Med = 2	
( )　　Replacement of automated system	Low = 1	
Has a joint IT/User team been established?		5
( )　　No	High = 3	
( )　　Part-time user involvement	Med = 2	
( )　　Yes, full-time user involvement	Low = 1	
Technology		
Is additional hardware required?		1
( )　　None	Low = 0	
( )　　Central processor type change	Low = 1	
( )　　Peripheral/storage changes	Low = 1	
( )　　Terminals	Med = 2	
( )　　Platform change	High = 3	
How knowledgeable is the IS team in the proposed application area?		5
( )　　Limited	High = 3	
( )　　Understands concepts but no experience	Med = 2	
( )　　Has implemented similar systems before	Low = 1	

SOURCE: Extracted from Graham McLeod and Derek Smith, *Managing Information Technology Projects* (Danvers, MA: Boyd & Fraser Publishing, 1996): 143–148.

components can reduce the risk associated with a large project size. Other risk avoidance techniques include using small teams of highly skilled and experienced professionals, minimizing the dependencies among projects, and reducing the amount of time between deliverables and review points.

DESIGNING NEW SYSTEMS

The third stage of the SDLC focuses on providing detailed specifications for the selected design. These specifications include designs of the user interface, the database, processes and procedures, and objects. In the design stage of the SDLC, designers also determine the physical characteristics of the system, such as the number, types, and locations of workstations, processing hardware, and network cabling and devices. They should also specify the procedures for testing the completed system before installation. During design, no programming occurs. Designers must provide enough information to developers to let them turn the design into software code during the development stage of the SDLC.

Some practitioners overlap the design and alternative selection stages. For example, they may select two or three alternatives for additional design, partially proceed through the design stage, and then return to the alternative selection stage to make a final decision. Rapid prototyping overlaps design and development of the user interface. Data design and development can also be iterative because unacceptable system performance might not be observable until development is nearly complete.

ELEMENTS OF DESIGN

Design elements include the user interface design, data design, and processes design. With object-oriented methods, object design is also a significant element. Physical design addresses needs of data storage, processing hardware, and networking facilities. The design stage should also include the design of acceptance testing.

Interface Design.   **Interface design** refers to the specification of the media, content, and form of input and output. Output media might include a computer screen, paper report, microfiche, or microfilm. Designers might also consider transferring some output elements directly into a spreadsheet or database on a user's personal computer. Input media might include keyboarding, scanning, or bar-code entry.

Interface design also specifies content, the elements of data that appear on an output report or screen. Designers must separate important from unnecessary information. Extraneous information clutters a screen or report making the required information more difficult to find. The designer might also provide options to obtain related information, such as clicking a button on a screen to select a more detailed report about certain aspects of the output.

On the input side, designers must determine whether users will enter data in batch or online modes, the characteristics of input screens, the nature of error checking during data entry, and the standards that apply among data entry screens. For

ADVANCED TECHNOLOGY

The brave new world of component-based development remains uncharted territory for many IS departments. The idea of creating or modifying applications by snapping together chunks of object code promises to let corporate developers respond more quickly to business needs. But many issues must be resolved before they can make that vision a reality. Potential roadblocks include major retraining issues, testing uncertainties, and the political minefield of trying to get autonomous business units to agree on corporate component standards.

"We're a long way from being ready for components," said Lander Stoddard, a divisional manager of computer resources at the Centers for Disease Control and Prevention in Atlanta. "Our central [IS] group is really just at the front end of client/server development, and asking them to swallow distributed objects is too much right now."

Component-based development herds software code into reusable modules that can automate business processes. Vying for supremacy in the component world are Java and the Object Management Group's Common Object Request Broker Architecture on one side and Microsoft Corp.'s ActiveX and Distributed Common Object Model on the other.

Lucent Technologies Inc. last month went live with an object-based customer support application and sees components as "the next logical step," said Sue Lovell, a technical staff member at the telecommunications equipment manufacturer in Murray Hill, New Jersey. "We all know we have to get there, but it's going to take a lot of retraining to get us up to speed compared with what we're used to," she said. "This is so different."

Getting different parts of the company to standardize on a common component architecture also could be "a big challenge," Lovell said. But component proponents view that as a key element to ensuring that code modules can be used in a mix of applications.

A major aerospace company spent much of the past year trying to piece together a single architectural framework for components before throwing up its hands and settling for a less complex strategy of making sure that different approaches can interoperate. "We're a very large organization, and trying to get a common set of practices in place is hard," said a technology manager at the company, who asked not to be identified. "You get into the religious wars of Microsoft against the rest of the world."

SOURCE: Extracted with modification from Craig Stedman, Component-based developers face many issues, *Computerworld* (July 28, 1997), http://cwlive.cw.com:8080/home/print9497.nsf/All/SL30tut.

example, they might decide that the F1 function key on the keyboard should always request help about the function that the data entry clerk performs and the F2 key or a mouse click on a scroll button will display a list of options.

During interface design, designers determine the form of output—the way information is presented. They determine whether data should appear in tabular form or graphically. Designing the display of tabular data includes determining the layout, the amount of white space, page margins, page length, the frequency of breaks, and the location of subtotals in the data, among other features. Designing graphical displays involves deciding these issues as well as the graphical form to use (pie, bar, or line chart) and options for switching among forms. Form also considers the choice of color. Some systems give every color a different meaning: for example, red may always show data outside the usual range or identify items that demand user attention.

Data Design.   **Data design** refers to creating the model of data supporting the system. Data models that analysts used to describe the existing system now model the planned system. Database specialists help data users and managers formalize relationships among data elements to create a logical design. Ultimately, the data users and managers, such as Graves at GPIC, are responsible for the design's accuracy.

Database specialists generate a physical design to structure the data for ease and speed of retrieval, to keep storage requirements as low as possible, and to promote data integrity (see Chapter 5). They also specify the database model (hierarchical, network, relational, or object-oriented) to use. The database model constrains the physical data design and forms the basis for the way the designers view and process the data. Designers may also select the database management system (DBMS) vendor at this time, although this selection more typically occurs in the development stage. Data designers work with the organization's data administrator to coordinate the storage and use of data that independently designed information systems might share.

Process Design.   **Process design** refers to the design of both the computational and logical processes underlying the system. The calculation of pay for hourly employees illustrates a computational process. Process designers for a payroll system identify the procedure for calculating the payroll of the employees who receive overtime pay. Users and business managers most familiar with the business processes form the core part of the process design team.

The removal of an item from inventory illustrates a logical process. The system should check whether an item has fallen below a prespecified level. When the stock of certain types of items reaches the prespecified level, the system should alert affected managers by producing a report, sending an electronic mail message, or even initiating an EDI transaction to automatically reorder the item. This example demonstrates the computer taking one or more procedural steps in response to a transaction. Process designers must specify the precise steps the system should take in response to any transaction that might occur. They must also specify what steps the computer must take to process inputs and outputs. Although IS specialists may generate the computer code, business managers such as Graves generally write the process specifications.

Object Design.   **Object design** refers to the generation of an object model. Object-oriented programming techniques translate the object model almost directly into software code. The object design identifies and isolates the characteristics and behavior of objects for programming, testing, and then assembly into a working system.

Object-oriented development requires that a software object represent a business object. The object can be used and reused, not only in the project for which it was designed, but in future projects. If this objective is to be achieved, the software object must model the characteristics and behaviors of the business model as completely as possible.

Physical Design.   **Physical design** refers to decisions about the hardware used to deliver the system. Physical design usually follows data and process designs because they determine the required amount of data storage, the volume of transaction processing, the amount of data communication activity, and the complexity of processing. Designers use such information to determine whether existing hardware will accommodate the new system or whether the organization must procure new hardware. For example, designers who recommend new hardware purchases should determine whether centralized or decentralized development and delivery of the system should occur. Although analysts might address these issues during the alternative selection phase of the SDLC, they cannot develop accurate estimates of cost and response time until they have complete data and process designs. Costs and response time that fall outside the ranges forecast during alternative analysis might call for revisiting the second stage of the SDLC.

Test Design.   **Test design** refers to the creation of tests that ensure the proper operation of developed systems. Test design includes the generation of a sample data set and a series of processes, transactions, or activities that simulate the eventual use of the system. The test design also specifies acceptable performance criteria. Test design becomes particularly important for purchased systems because it affects whether to pay the supplier.

DESIGN SPECIFICATION

Design specification refers to means for communicating the design to the programmers who will implement it. Prototyping most readily communicates the interface design. The tools available to design input and output screens, sample reports, and GUI interfaces ease the prototyping of these interfaces and consequently their design. Common interface standards can be specified in hard copy as an interface standard guide. A data dictionary or an entity-relationship diagram can also communicate the data design. In addition, CASE software helps designers perform data design, as well as store and print the result.

DEVELOPING NEW SYSTEMS

The development stage includes development or purchase of software, potentially procurement of hardware, and testing of the new system. IS professionals assemble a working system that meets the specifications formulated in the design stage. Users test the new system during the development phase, but will not use it until the implementation stage of the SDLC. Unless development is by prototype, IS professionals work more independently of end users and their managers than at any other stage of the SDLC.

THE DEVELOP-OR-PURCHASE DECISION

The choice to develop or purchase a new system is one of the most difficult decisions that senior information systems managers and other top executives must make.

Medium to large organizations usually find that packaged vertical application software will not entirely satisfy their complex information needs. The requirement of organizations such as GPIC to interface the new system to several other systems may preclude their buying packaged software unless they can customize it to provide the interfaces they need.

A company's ability to modify purchased software depends on the vendor's licensing agreements. Some prohibit any modification of the software except by the vendor itself. Some authorize value-added resellers (VARs) to modify their software. Some provide all or portions of their computer code to the purchasing company so that its staff can modify the software.

Companies that do not have the resources and skills to develop their own software but need functionality not provided by packaged products may hire another company to develop software for them. Meritor Savings Bank of Philadelphia chose this approach. The company decided to outsource all of its systems development and maintenance. Working with Electronic Data Systems as its systems integrator, the bank saved almost $9 million in two years.[23] Even large companies such as AT&T, Citicorp, General Electric, and Caterpillar employ companies in countries such as India, where a large pool of inexpensive programming talent exists, to decrease their development costs.[24]

The Virginia Department of Taxation faced a develop-or-purchase decision in its overhaul of the commonwealth's tax-processing systems. The scope of the project included 1,500 programs, 40 databases, and 25 application systems, affecting 1,800 users. The system design established deadlines for the installation of major software components every three to six months over a nine-year period. Despite having a staff of only six people, the director of IS at the department strongly supported in-house development because the department would need to maintain the system to respond quickly to changes in the tax law. Although this decision required her to increase the IS staff to 45 people, including the full-time assignment of six managers from user areas, the IS department delivered the system on time and saved the commonwealth an estimated $80 million.[25]

DEVELOPMENT TOOLS

A variety of products, including screen, report, and code generators, exist to simplify and speed the development of information systems. **Rapid application development (RAD)** describes the use of such tools, in conjunction with rapid prototyping, to speed the ultimate development of new systems.

- **Screen generators** create and edit a screen and generate programs for screen-based data entry or queries (see Figure 12.16). For example, the designer lays out the text and data portion using standard text and drawing tools and specifies where the data will appear or be entered.
- **Report generators** help examine design options, lay out reports using standard text and drawing tools, test the report, and generate a computer program to create it. For example, they identify the placement of headings and determine what triggers breaks or subtotals. They identify the sources of data for columns, specify the order for sorting rows, and identify what criteria will determine the display of rows.

| FIGURE 12.16 | Microsoft Access's screen generator simplifies design of a data entry screen. |

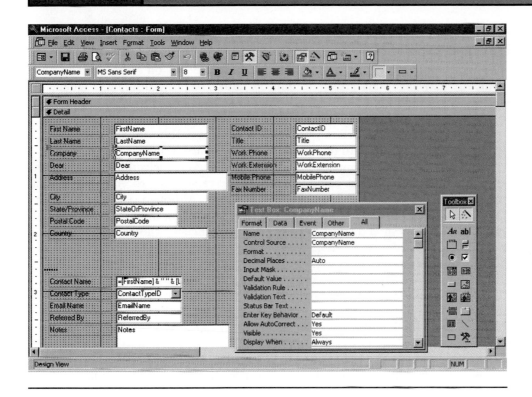

- **Code generators** create complete and working programs based on designer specifications. This code derives directly from data, process, or object models that the developers have created. It uses the outputs of screen and report generators as input.

SELECTING AND PROCURING HARDWARE

The design stage of the SDLC requires many hardware decisions, particularly those related to selecting input and output devices and deciding whether to use centralized, distributed, or decentralized equipment. The development stage includes some hardware decisions, such as evaluating and selecting alternative vendors for equipment purchases. IS professionals might decide during the design stage, for example, to use laser printers to provide certain system outputs. During the development stage, the IS professionals would evaluate the laser printer products of several vendors, seek bids from manufacturers and distributors, and select, order, and install the equipment to use in testing the system in its real-life environment.

If the company chooses to buy rather than develop its software, it may deal with software manufacturers who sell **turn-key solutions.** Organizations that purchase a turn-key system can plug it in and turn it on (presumably with a key), and it will run. The software will already be loaded onto the computer, and the vendor optimizes the hardware/software combination for the buyer's needs.

SELECTING AN APPROPRIATE LANGUAGE

The choice of languages for systems development depends on several factors. The company may have standards that limit the choice of programming language. At small companies, even without formal standards, staff expertise is often limited to at most one or two languages. The DBMS selected may restrict the languages to a small number that it supports. Customization of third-party software may require a language that interfaces with that used by the third-party vendor.

Chapter 4 discusses some common issues in language selection, including the choice of interpretive versus compiled, procedural versus nonprocedural, and command/data-oriented versus object-oriented language. Although selecting computer languages for software development is a technical decision in most organizations, business managers should address the impact that language choice has on their job performance, including their ability, for example, to make changes or to have IS professionals make changes in a timely fashion.

Standard Oil rebuilt its systems for ship scheduling and operations, known as its marine operating system (MOS), with essentially the same functionality as the system it replaced, but written in a fourth-generation language (4GL) instead of a combination of COBOL and a 4GL. The language change enabled users to modify the software without support, to achieve better ad hoc reporting, and to reduce the delay between their request for changes and their implementation by IS professionals. After five months, the change reportedly saved the company 6,000 employee hours.[26]

TESTING

Testing describes the process of ensuring that the system works as designed. A testing plan, typically created in the design stage of the SDLC, states precisely how users will recognize whether a delivered system meets their needs and expectations.

Levels of Testing.   The development phase of the SDLC includes the following four levels of testing to ensure quality:

- **Unit testing** refers to testing each small component of the system to guarantee its proper operations.
- **Component testing** examines the interaction of a series of programs within the system that likely will be used in concert, such as those that process a transaction.
- **Integration testing** addresses the interaction between large, independently developed components of the new system that were internally checked at the unit and component testing levels.
- **System testing,** also known as **alpha testing,** refers to testing the entire system under realistic conditions.

System Testing.   In the first stage of system testing, **performance testing,** developers identify and correct problems that might cause a system to slow down or fail when stressed with too many users or too much data. To simulate a realistic level of activity in a laboratory, developers use software load-testing products. These products can generate transactions from a transaction profile, provide statistical data about the speed with which the system responds, and compare outputs and final values of data elements to expected outcomes. Aetna Life & Casualty Company uses a product called SQL-Inspector to isolate performance bottlenecks. Despite the assistance of such a product, Aetna consultant Lindy Mayfield estimates that more than three-quarters of the work in finding and eliminating bottlenecks is still manual.[27]

The second stage of system testing, **usability testing,** compares the developed system to users' expectations and needs. Users ideally test the system in a **usability lab,** a place where developers can observe and record their reactions to the system for later analysis. A typical usability lab costs from $60,000 to $200,000 and includes two rooms connected by a one-way mirror, as shown in Figure 12.17. Video cameras record and store users' reactions to the system. Computer equipment, including software to log the user's keystrokes, tests the application. An audio system allows users to communicate with application developers and usability professionals. Professionals look for the time required to complete specific tasks, the types of errors made, the ways errors are corrected, whether errors are repeated, the speed of learning, the frustrations users experience, and so on. Organizations too small to have their own usability labs can hire the services of a usability consultant and use the consultant's labs to test its software.[28]

FIGURE 12.17 Developers observe users testing a new system in a usability lab. This diagram illustrates the layout of a typical usability lab.

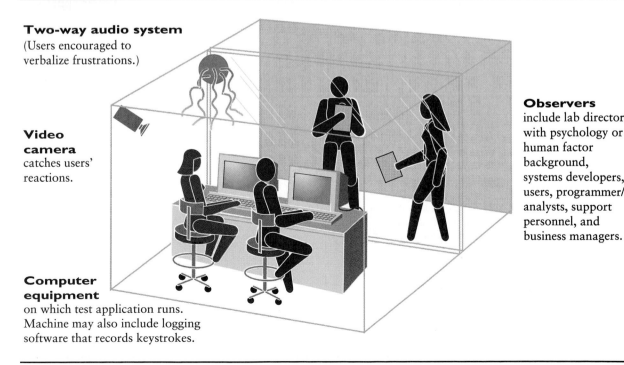

Two-way audio system
(Users encouraged to verbalize frustrations.)

Video camera catches users' reactions.

Computer equipment on which test application runs. Machine may also include logging software that records keystrokes.

Observers include lab director with psychology or human factor background, systems developers, users, programmer/analysts, support personnel, and business managers.

IMPLEMENTING NEW SYSTEMS

Moving the new system into the production environment follows obtaining satisfactory testing results. IS professionals or other organizational members must manage the transition from the old system to the new system. Graves likely will manage such a transition at GPIC; alternatively he can hire a consultant or assign an employee to oversee the transition and implementation. Organizations use a variety of strategies to move new systems into the production environment. They simultaneously act to reduce the risk of incurring serious business problems during transition and implementation.

STRATEGIES FOR IMPLEMENTATION

Companies generally use some combination of four implementation strategies, as summarized in Table 12.4. The proper strategy or combination of strategies for a given organization depends on the project, the amount of risk the organization can tolerate, the budget, characteristics of the target users, and the culture of the organization.

Direct Cutover.   The **direct cutover strategy** describes the replacement of the old with the new system overnight, over a weekend, or over some other period of time when the company does not operate. Theoretically, a direct cutover from one system to another can occur almost instantaneously. A direct cutover requires that the new system have the data that it needs to run. Transferring data from the old to the new system poses one of the major challenges of the direct cutover approach.

TABLE 12.4   The four implementation strategies differ in their riskiness and cost.

Strategy	Description	Time Required	Cost	Risk
Direct cutover	Replaces old system with new system overnight	Minimal	Low	High
Pilot implementation	Uses the new system in one or more parts of the organization and later in the entire company	Moderate	Moderate	Moderate
Phased implementation	Introduces components of the new system one at a time	High	Moderate to high	Low
Parallel implementation	Uses both the old and new systems simultaneously for a period of time	High	High	Low

Programmers should write utility programs during the development stage to transfer data from the old system to the new. They should test these programs well in advance of implementation to ensure that they work properly. The cutover period, when neither system is in use, involves the automatic transfer of data from the old to the new system. Performing such a data transfer on a large system and confirming the data transfer usually take many hours but can generally be completed over a weekend.

Companies that operate continuously experience difficulties in using the cutover approach. One or two days before implementation, data transfer from a backup copy of the old system to the new system occurs. Then transaction logs from the old system are fed into the new system. The new system should process these transaction logs as fast or faster than the old system originally processed the transactions. When the new system has processed these logs, the almost instantaneous switch of processing from the old to the new system can occur. An alternative approach keeps old files online and accesses them as needed.[29] This approach requires development of extra code that will not be used after the cutover is complete.

The direct cutover approach has the lowest cost but the highest risks of the implementation strategies. Organizations such as GPIC might use this approach if they willingly trade reduced cost for high risk. Having the new system maintain a transaction log that can update the old system and return it to action if necessary can reduce this risk. Using such a backup does not eliminate the risk completely because improper processing might not appear until it has affected business transactions in a way that harms the business. For example, if the new system fails to generate invoices for specific products or services, the company might not notice this defect until its cash flow deteriorates.

The direct cutover strategy may also result in employees lacking sufficient training to use the new system properly. Although employees receive training in the new system before the cutover date, no employee will have used the system for an extended period and no one can act as an expert to assist users who have trouble with the new system. In addition, their dissatisfaction may not surface immediately. Experiencing difficulty in retrieving information for customers may affect the business only after longer-term use of the system. Returning to the old system then may be difficult or impossible.

Pilot Implementation.

A **pilot implementation strategy**, often called **beta testing**, requires one or more segments of the company to use the new system before the entire company uses it. For example, the Los Angeles office of a company with 20 regional offices might beta test the system. Such a pilot implementation reduces risk by limiting exposure to a small fraction of the business. This limited implementation does not eliminate risk because even a few costly mistakes in a small branch of an organization can harm its performance. Even if a new system works properly in one part of the organization, it may not function properly when the entire organization uses it. The increased load on the system, for example, can slow response time to an unacceptable level.

Implementing a pilot system increases the cost of a changeover. Particular difficulties arise in dealing with transactions that cross the boundary between the old and new systems. For example, what happens to an order placed in Los Angeles using the new system for a customer in New York using the old system? What happens if the Los Angeles office wants to serve its customer by pulling from New York's inventory?

Systems developers must address questions such as these before implementation by building often expensive programs that allow the old system to access the new system's data and vice versa.

Phased Implementation. A **phased implementation strategy** introduces components of the new system one at a time. For example, the organization implements the accounts payable portion of an accounting system before the rest of the system. GPIC could easily introduce its new system using this strategy. It reduces risk by limiting exposure to the new system. Users can slowly become accustomed to the new system. The cost of building interfaces to deal with transactions that cross the boundary between the new and old systems becomes a problem, particularly as the number of phases increases. Practitioners can reduce the cost of the phased strategy by combining it with parallel implementation.

Parallel Implementation. A **parallel implementation strategy** refers to the use of both the new and the old system for a period of time. The parallel implementation essentially eliminates the risk of failure because ongoing comparisons of the results of the two systems identify inaccuracies. Parallel implementation remains infeasible where employees lack the time to use both systems or when the cost in employee time of using two systems becomes excessive. GPIC could use this approach, although it may require too much employee time.

MANAGING RISK IN INTRODUCING SYSTEMS

Employing quality measures throughout previous stages of the SDLC and paying particular attention to training can reduce the major risks of implementation. To achieve quality, users and their managers must involve themselves in system design from the outset, demand that designs meet their needs, and ensure that they have a forum to communicate their expertise regarding the processes they perform. Quality also requires a rigorous testing program that detects errors of design or development early thereby preventing a defective system from reaching the implementation stage.

Training ensures that employees have the proper skills to make the new system work. Even the best system can fail if employees cannot use it properly and efficiently. Training should occur both before and after implementation. Preimplementation training prepares employees to use the features they need and deal with exceptional conditions. Postimplementation training focuses on using the system efficiently.

MAINTAINING AND REVIEWING SYSTEMS

Maintenance refers to fixing software that does not operate properly and adding features to systems in response to new user demands. A **postimplementation review** evaluates how well the system meets user needs, sets priorities for new development, and determines when to redo a needs assessment. Maintenance and postimplementation activities typically occupy between 80 percent and 90 percent of the time of IS professionals.[30]

MAINTENANCE

Maintenance describes a continuous-improvement activity that initially consists of fixing bugs in the system and ensuring that the system continues to operate as implemented. Bugs almost always exist and may even appear after a system has operated for several years because testers cannot foresee all possible contingencies that might arise in using the system. Recently developed automated testing software has successfully reduced the number of bugs.[31]

Users also tend to discover new needs after they have used a system for several months. These needs may arise from changes in the nature of the business or environment. For example, the company may develop a new product that has sales data or post-sales data needs that differ from those for other products. Or, a competitor may launch a new program, such as a frequent-buyer discount program or extended warranty program, that the company must emulate but that requires data not captured by the existing system, reports not currently generated, or even new operating procedures. Ensuring that the information system responds to such needs generally does not require a complete redesign or rebuilding of the system.

Once users assimilate the process improvements supported by the new system, they begin to realize that they expressed too few wishes in the needs-analysis phase. They now propose changes to make the system more usable; allow managers to make better, faster, and more informed decisions; or improve the work flow of employees using the system. These users together with IS professionals must evaluate each change on the basis of its costs and benefits. Those judged worthwhile will require redesign and reprogramming as part of maintaining the system.

What distinguishes the activities that take place in the maintenance phase of the SDLC from those in the needs assessment phase? The activities in the maintenance phase resemble those of the needs assessment phase, but maintenance is less rigorous, more informal, less comprehensive, and more reactive. Whereas needs assessment addresses the possibility of completely redesigning and rebuilding existing information systems, maintenance implies continuous improvement to these systems.

Modifying a system without introducing new bugs poses a significant challenge. Any changes in complex systems likely have side effects. Following the SDLC should minimize and document the interactions among different parts of the system, thereby reducing the likelihood and scope of side effects. Maintenance remains problematic because some interactions are unavoidable and documentation may not always be complete. As more maintenance is done on a system, the likelihood of new bugs increases and the accuracy of the system's documentation decreases.

Business managers should know that political pressures face the IS staff during the maintenance phase. Because IS managers view end users as their customers, they often find refusing their requests difficult. Limits on IS resources mean that accepting too many projects puts too few resources on each, resulting in delivery delays, an overworked and demoralized staff, and poor product quality. Forming steering

risk analysis	test design
screen generator	testing
spiral approach	time box
structure chart	turn-key solution
structured analysis	unit testing
system testing	usability lab
systems analyst	usability testing
systems development life cycle (SDLC)	waterfall model

DISCUSSION AND REVIEW QUESTIONS

1. Why do systems projects sometimes fail?
2. What are the six stages of the systems development life cycle?
3. How does maintenance differ from needs assessment?
4. Compare and contrast the waterfall and spiral approaches to the implementation of the SDLC.
5. What are the advantages of rapid prototyping relative to the waterfall approach?
6. Why do managers and systems developers use models to describe an organization's data, processes, and objects?
7. What are two types of data models?
8. What are three types of process models?
9. How might managers use the Capability Maturity Model to improve systems development in their company?
10. What three types of needs do analysts focus on during the needs assessment stage of the SDLC?
11. How can managers assess and reduce the risk of new systems development?
12. What are the key elements of interface design, data design, process design, object design, physical design, and test design?
13. How do content and form design complement each other in interface design?
14. What choices do managers have in the develop-or-purchase decision?
15. What five tools support systems development?
16. What are four types of testing and how do they differ?
17. How is usability testing done?
18. What are the advantages and disadvantages of the four implementation strategies?
19. Why do bugs often exist even after testing?
20. Why should managers perform a postimplementation review?

IS ON THE WEB

Exercise 1: Download a demonstration CASE tool from the Web. Learn how to use it. Briefly present an application of it.

Exercise 2: Go to the Web site of two consulting firms that provide systems development assistance. What types of services do they offer? In a short report, compare and contrast the two firms.

MINICASE

OBJECT-ORIENTED DEVELOPMENT AT COLUMBIA GAS

When Keith Hardin became the IS director for Columbia Gas Systems—one of the largest integrated natural gas systems in the country—he had a major task ahead of him. In April 1995 he had to quickly develop a billing system that could handle the continuing changes required by the industry deregulation enacted the year before. What he ended up producing was the Gas Transportation System (GTS), a client-server billing and support system that supports 10,000 of Columbia's customers.

He knew that the COBOL systems that supported Columbia's current work couldn't be modified quickly enough and he would have to start from scratch. Though COBOL could have been used to develop the new system, possibly even hitting the deadlines required, it was not up to the fast maintenance and modification requirements the industry was forcing the company into, so Hardin knew he had to go a different way. Previous experience with object-oriented programming (OOP) made him realize that it would provide what he needed.

He quickly began object training for a custom-picked team of employees who were fast learners, only one of which had previous object experience. He supplemented this group with an existing consultant, and began intense object training.

To augment the team he had gathered, Hardin also brought in a Smalltalk expert from IBM, as Columbia had chosen to use IBM's VisualAge Smalltalk development system. This contractor served as a walking manual and was able to look over shoulders and immediately answer questions, keeping things rolling at a very fast pace. This consultant also played a significant role in laying out the framework for the project, allowing for a good foundation and ensuring that classes interrelated well. A further pleasant benefit was the consultant's direct knowledge of specific people on the Smalltalk team at IBM. Because of this, he was able to get quick fixes to the few critical bugs found in the development tools, in a very timely fashion.

FAST, ITERATIVE DEVELOPMENT

Iterative development was a key aspect of the GTS development. Hardin and his team jumped right into the project without any design document or other heavy analysis. Although this may scare many, Hardin points out that "analysis paralysis" makes many similar projects unsuccessful. So much time is spent analyzing the needed features that nothing gets produced. Things were moving so fast for the company at this time that Hardin was convinced that "If we had taken six

SOURCE: Case extracted with modification from R. Bradley Andrews, A Smalltalk Success Story, *Object Magazine* (May 1997): 47–49.

months to design the system, it would have been out of date before we even started coding."

This does not mean the team had no preparation. On the contrary, because most of the team members, including Hardin, had already been working for the company for some time, they had a good feel for the user community and their needs. They added to this experience with further investigation into the precise business needs, but maintained their focus on producing a product, not producing an analysis.

A few miscues did occur during the process, but because prototypes were continually brought before their target audience, they quickly found these and ironed them out before they became serious problems. This process also allowed many of the more mundane fixes to be carried out at the same time. Frequently, they would make instant changes to the system while the end users looked on, something that would not have been possible with a traditional compiled environment. It also allowed them to quickly explore alternatives and possible changes until the right match was found.

Hardin was especially pleased with the ability to throw out entire objects and redraft them from scratch. Over the short six months of the project, Hardin estimates they rewrote half the objects in the system. But this didn't have the negative impact it would have had in the past. "As long as the object kept the same interface, we were able to immediately plug in the redesigned object in a seamless fashion." Because of the significant design work done on the object interface, only one of the many interfaces needed redesign during the project.

The project began in early June and the first operational product was available by the end of August. A month later they had a working product that covered the entire process. By December they had ironed out all the bugs and the GTS was placed into full production.

A BIT MORE ABOUT THE GTS

The GTS tracks and bills all customers who receive transportation gas through one of Columbia's five local gas distribution companies. It is far more flexible and robust than the system that preceded it. End users can easily input, report, and maintain all the customer transportation contracts with minimal training. It is so simple to use that it didn't have a written manual for the first three months it was in production. Columbia also uses the GTS to manage the unique needs of customers who work together in groups for purchasing, banking, or billing. It automatically tracks any changes in the amount of stored gas each customer has in the Columbia system, generating bills at the end of each month.

Originally, the GTS used OS/2 Warp, but it has since switched to mostly Windows 95 workstations and Windows NT servers, though some OS/2 Warp servers remain. All these are connected with a DB/2 database and pass through a VTAM gateway to DB2/MVS. The Smalltalk code is portable and converted to Windows in about four weeks. Most of this time was needed to convert OS/2-specific interface features, not the core program logic.

A BIG RISK?

Many people would question Hardin's decision to let such a mission-critical element be his company's first foray into object technology. Though the results in this case turned out well, success cannot always be guaranteed, or at least that is what they argue. Hardin defends the decision and makes two strong points in its favor: "First, we got all the equipment and other support we needed because it was such a crucial element. Second, our success provided much more recognition than we would have received if we had the same success on only a small test project."

Although this may seem like living on the edge, Hardin finds object technology up to the task, especially a pure environment like Smalltalk. His team was able to quickly gain the object experience needed and then put it to work, producing very spectacular results.

FURTHER GTS DEVELOPMENTS

Development didn't stop on the GTS once it was put into production. It had to be continually updated to meet constantly changing business requirements. Extensive modifications were done to the GTS during 1996. In addition, significant portions of the system migrated to the mainframe to give a needed speed boost.

Hardin estimates that 30 to 40 percent of the original system is still in use today. More than ten new decision support systems were also developed during 1996. The object base was so extensive that some of these systems required as few as three additional objects, an outstanding level of code reuse.

Case Questions

Diagnosis

1. What were the information needs at Columbia Gas?

Evaluation

2. How well were those needs being met?

Design

3. What factors contributed to Hardin's decision to proceed with object-oriented programming?
4. Was the GTS an appropriate project for Columbia Gas's first foray into OOP?

Implementation

5. What pathway did Hardin use for the systems development? How successful was it? Why?
6. How did Hardin reduce the risks associated with the project?
7. How did Hardin measure the success of the project?
8. Using the Capability Maturity Model, how would you assess Columbia's systems development maturity?
9. Do you think that the processes put in place by Hardin will outlast his tenure as IS director?

ACTIVITY 12.1 A CRISIS AT THE DEPARTMENT OF MOTOR VEHICLES

Step 1: Read the following case:

"Why can't we go back to our old system? At least we know it works! Maybe it can get us out of this mess." Bill Maloney, the state's attorney general, was on the phone with Mark Bridger. Bridger, the director of the Department of Motor Vehicles (DMV), was doing his best to cope with a crisis that was becoming worse by the hour.

Two months earlier, the state began using a new data processing system designed to streamline operations at the DMV. Although the cutover—direct conversion—to the new system was without incident, problems began to mount soon after the system was placed in operation.

Now the system was unable to cope with the workload. More than a million drivers had been unable to register their cars. To make the situation even worse, many of those who registered their cars after the system went into operation were incorrectly listed in the database as operating unregistered vehicles. And renewal notices—issued automatically by the new computer system—had been sent to the wrong drivers. In fact, so many drivers had been forced to drive without a registration that the attorney general, Bill Maloney, had ordered the state police to cease citing drivers for this offense. No one, it seemed, had been spared. Even some of the vehicles operated by public works departments and local police forces throughout the state were registered to the wrong municipalities!

When the system was first conceived, a little over three years ago, the DMV expressed a need for a more up-to-date information-processing system than the ten-year-old system it was using. The DMV especially needed a system with a strong DBMS, to have more flexibility in accessing data and in making changes in the application software. Its current system used a conventional file-management approach.

In addition to performing all of the routine record-keeping functions such as maintaining automobile registration data, the DMV wanted the new system to automatically notify the state's five million drivers of license and registration renewals. It also wanted the system to be capable of allowing updates of the state's rating surcharge database to be made on a daily basis. This surcharge database keeps track of violation points against individual drivers and is used to penalize bad drivers by making them pay higher insurance rates. Under the old system, this database was updated periodically, but it was not unusual—due to inefficient update procedures—for the driver's record to be updated as much as three or four months after the conviction took place.

When the idea for a new computer system was originally suggested to the governor, he agreed that an effort such as this was long overdue. But he was not pleased to hear that it would take five years to develop and bring the project into full operation. It is alleged that he then asked DMV director Bridger to find a consulting firm to develop the system in two years so that the completed system would be finished in time to be used during his reelection campaign as an example of his administration's accomplishments.

SOURCE: Activity 12.1 extracted from Barry Shore and Jerry Ralya, DMV, *Cases in Computer Information Systems* (Holt, Rinehart and Winston, 1988): 100–103.

Shortly thereafter, Bridger met with the information services division of Driscol and Russell, one of the country's leading public accounting firms. After studying the project's objectives, the manager of this division, Mike Price, suggested that the only way it could be completed in two years would be to use a fourth-generation language.

"We will still use a structured approach and build the system in modules," explained Price, "but the 4GL will save us a lot of time in programming, debugging, and testing the project."

Bridger was impressed with Price's confidence in his firm's ability to deliver the needed software and, above all, to deliver it on time. Within three months a $6.5 million contract was signed with Driscol and Russell.

The software development process went smoothly for the DMV. The senior systems analyst for Driscol and Russell spent six weeks at the DMV, during which time he learned about the current system and the characteristics of the new one. Once the systems analysis was complete and a preliminary plan approved, Driscol and Russell had few interactions with the DMV. According to the senior systems analyst at Driscol and Russell, the DMV preferred it this way, as the DMV was already overburdened with day-to-day problems.

The system was delivered right on schedule, and during the first few weeks, as the workload on the new system increased, it seemed to perform well. But as more and more new tasks were added to the system, the operators began to report an increase in response time. When the system was finally in full operation, the response time became intolerable. At best, response times were in the five-to-eight second range and frequently took as long as one to two minutes. The original contract specified that response times were to be no longer than three to five seconds.

An increase in response time, however, was just the tip of the iceberg. First, it was not possible to process all of the jobs on the new system. Even an increase to a 24-hour operation was insufficient to update the database. Within a few months, the backlog grew to such proportions that 1.4 million automobile registrations had not been processed. Meanwhile, when police stopped cars that did not have valid registrations, the drivers were arrested. As the protest from drivers began to mount, the attorney general's office stepped in and ordered the police to stop making arrests for invalid registrations.

Then an even more dramatic problem surfaced. It slowly became apparent that the database was contaminated with bad data, that the automobile registrations listed the wrong owners.

Step 2:   Prepare the case for class discussion.

Step 3:   Answer each of the following questions, individually or in small groups, as directed by your instructor.

Diagnosis

1. What information needs did the DMV have?

Evaluation

2. How well did the old system meet these needs?

Currently, the company sends out registration material to human resources departments and many individual managers and former program participants listing the available courses and the times that they are offered. Students register for courses by filling out and returning registration forms. The forms are processed by the registration department and posted to the registration system in the evening. Students may check the status of their registration by touch-tone phone. Although the registration department updates the availability of courses daily, students still need to check to make sure that they were not closed out of courses that they had registered for.

The company executive team has sponsored a project to reengineer the registration process so that student registration will be paper free and will require no human assistance. The impetus for this project includes a need to reduce the cost of running the registration department and to respond to competitive pressure by making registration easier and more pleasant.

A start-up team consisting of Benson's operations manager, registration department head, two registration department employees, two IS department employees, and a member of Benson's quality office have met a few times and have established the following parameters for the project prior to setting up a project team:

- Students will be able to register by telephone or World Wide Web. If they or their companies have paid in advance, this registration will be effective immediately. Otherwise, the registration will be provisional pending receipt of payment (by check or purchase order) and will remain in effect for one week.
- A project team will be formed shortly consisting of the current start-up team, a software developer, and possibly several employees from Benson's corporate clients.
- The current registration system, which is built on proprietary software using a proprietary database, will be replaced rather than modified. Although functional, it is considered too inflexible to change and too costly to maintain. Benson does not have the staff or resources to develop this system from scratch. It will have to be purchased. The system will have to interface with the existing accounting system, which maintains student and corporate account information. It will also have to interface with the facility and trainer scheduling system.
- Other interfaces may be identified by the project team. The system will have to check for time conflicts. Other system requirements and information needs will be identified by the project team. A budget of $50,000 has been allocated for the preliminary analysis and design.

The company has standardized on the Banyan Vines Network Operating System (although some Novell Netware subnets exist), Windows NT servers, Windows 95 desktop systems, BeyondMail mail and work-flow management tools, Microsoft SQL-Server for enterprise database management, and Visual Basic for GUI development.

Step 2: Your instructor will show you how to use a CASE tool available within your college environment. If no such tool is available, your instructor will direct you to download a demonstration copy of such a tool from the World Wide Web.

Step 3: Using the CASE tool, develop an entity relationship diagram, a DFD, a structure chart, an IDEF1X model, a function box model, or an object model, as directed by your instructor, of the data, processes, or objects suggested by this case.

THE HINDENBERG GAS COMPANY   ACTIVITY 12.4

Step 1:   Read the following scenario:

You are Pete Bogg, the IS manager of the Hindenberg Gas Company, a regional utility providing service to more than 10 million locations. As with many large monopolies, your company suffers from a reputation for poor customer service and weak community relations. One of the things that contributed to this in the past was an ancient billing system. Because of it, customer bills were usually late, wrong, or missing. There is little information available to customer-service representatives about current bills and no history information whatsoever.

   The good news is that your department is funded to replace the system for the billing department, and everyone is very excited. The bad news is that everyone wants something very different from the project. Capp deFumes, your systems and programming manager, sees the opportunity to expand his department with many of the group technicians taking the long-awaited step into a supervisory role. The users have a long list of traditional detailed requirements and, having waited for years, are not prepared to accept any compromises. The very influential vice president of public relations, Shirley U. Jest, and the president, Dick Tator, want something very soon to put the groundswell of customer complaints and attendant nonpayment into remission. They feel that it could even be temporary; as long as it is quick, it does not have to be perfect. The vice president of finance, Amanda B. Reconwith (the likely next president, but not directly in charge of billing), on the other hand, believes that a high-technology, sophisticated state-of-the-art system is the way to go. Not only would it generate positive customer relations and favorable press, but it would last for a long time. Everyone knows based on experience that this system will have to last for a long time.

   You must decide which development pathway to use. You know that a decision on direction needs to be made and the project started.

Step 2:   Individually or in small groups, outline three plans for developing the new system, one using each of the following approaches: waterfall, spiral, and prototyping.

Step 3:   Share your plans. Then assess the risks associated with each of the development approaches? How prepared is the company to assume these risks? Overall, which approach do you favor? Why?

SOURCE: Activity 12.4 scenario excerpted from Robert K. Wysocki and James Young, Situation 10-1: The Hindenberg Gas Company, *Information Systems: Management Practices in Action* (John Wiley & Sons, 1990): 70, 71.

SYSTEMS ANALYST HIRING AT VAILTON COLLEGE   ACTIVITY 12.5

Step 1:   Your instructor will divide you into five groups; one group will represent the Registration Redesign Committee (RRC) at Vailton College, and the others will represent competing systems analyst candidates.

Step 2: Read the following scenario:

Vailton College is a small but well-respected business school located in the southeastern United States. Six years ago, the college computerized its class registration process. Nevertheless, much of the process remains manual and cumbersome. Students have complained, year after year, about waiting in line to register, having to reregister after being closed out of their selected classes, and having to make frequent trips to the registrar's office during the drop-add period. Faculty have complained about the length of time it takes before they receive final class rosters.

The computer system also allows students to register for classes for which they do not have the necessary prerequisites. Although students are supposed to have their registration plans approved by their faculty advisor in advance of registration, and faculty are supposed to check prerequisites, this process has not eliminated the problem and other similar ones associated with students not completing their requirements.

The president of the college has commissioned a committee of faculty members, staff from the registrars office, and staff from the information systems division (the technical group that runs the college's computer systems) to redesign the registration process and the information systems that support it. The committee has developed a broad outline of a new telephone-based registration system and must now design the information systems to support it. Their current task is to hire a systems analyst to coordinate the project. After an initial screening, the committee has narrowed the search to the following four candidates:

- *Gene/Jean Smith:* A 54-year-old systems manager who was recently laid off from Digital Equipment Corporation (DEC) when the division he/she worked for was closed. Smith's background includes more than 30 years of systems development work at DEC, exclusively in the DEC environment. Smith has dealt with many different DEC products, customers, and their needs. Although Smith has not been at Vailton previously, he/she is thoroughly familiar with Vailton's current DEC computer equipment.
- *Bobbie/Bobby Jones:* A 23-year-old Vailton graduate with a recent MBA, an undergraduate major in MIS at Vailton, and limited work experience. Jones is currently self-employed as an IS consultant, but she/he is looking for more permanent employment in a small company. Having gone through the registration process at Vailton, Jones is familiar with it and agrees strongly with the need to revise it.
- *Pat McDonald:* A 32-year-old former employee of Pacific Bell who has relocated near Vailton. At Pacific Bell, McDonald worked in the customer relations department and has experience dealing with customers and using computer systems. He/she enrolled in the part-time MBA program at Vailton upon returning to the area and was one of the people affected by problems with the current registration system. McDonald has some wonderful ideas for improving the system.
- *Terry Wilson:* A 38-year-old programmer for the Shawton Bank, the largest bank in the state. She/he learned how to program at Georgia Tech in the late 1970s and has been a very reliable, well-liked, easy-to-get-along-with employee of Shawton ever since. The bank has recently undergone some restructuring and appears headed for further restructuring if the recession runs its course; Wilson is looking for a more stable environment. Her/his programming skills

are excellent in four languages: FORTRAN, COBOL, BASIC, and C. She/he feels that a college community would permit further enhancement of her/his skills and provide a valuable opportunity for additional education.

Step 3: If your group is assigned the role of one of the candidates, select one of your group members to represent your candidate in an interview. Prepare a short presentation for your candidate to explain why he or she is the best person for the job. Also anticipate the questions that the committee will ask and prepare your candidate to answer them in the most favorable light. If your group is assigned the role of the RRC, prepare a job description for the systems analyst and a set of questions to ask each candidate.

Step 4: The instructor will call each team's representative to present its case. Members of the RRC will sit at the front of the class and ask the prepared questions and any additional questions they may have after each candidate has presented his or her case. Please be advised that it is illegal to ask candidates about their personal lives and families.

Step 5: The RRC will discuss the merits of the candidates in open executive session. The RRC will then vote on the four candidates.

Step 6: With the entire class, answer the following questions:

1. What are the most desirable attributes of a candidate for the job of systems analyst?
2. In selecting an analyst for a project, which is more important, familiarity with the business process or familiarity with the role of systems analyst? What are the pros and cons of each?
3. Did the RRC use appropriate criteria in selecting the candidate?

RECOMMENDED READINGS

Andriole, Stephen J. *Managing Systems Requirements: Methods, Tools, and Cases.* New York: McGraw Hill Text, 1996.

Bourne, Kelly C. *Testing Client/Server Systems.* New York: Computing McGraw-Hill, McGraw-Hill Series on Client/Server Computing, 1997.

Flynn, Donal J., and Diaz, Olivia Fragoso. *Information Modelling: An International Perspective.* London: Prentice Hall, 1996.

Sommerville, Ian, and Sawyer, Pete. *Requirements Engineering: A Good Practice Guide.* New York: John Wiley & Sons, 1997.

Whitten, Jeffrey L., Bentley, Lonnie D., and Dittman, Kevin C. *Systems Analysis and Design Methods.* 4th ed. Chicago: Irwin, 1997.

NOTES

1. When machines screw up, *Forbes* (June 7, 1993): 110–111.
2. When the bull turned, *The Economist* (March 20, 1993): 81–82; What is a stock exchange for? *The Economist* (March 13, 1993): 93.

3. Emily Kay and Larry Marion, Failed phone venture shows how not to build software, *Computerworld* (May 5, 1997): 12.

4. Gary H. Anthes, No more creeps, *Computerworld* (May 2, 1994): 107,108. Source attributed to a *Computerworld*/First Market Research Corporation study.

5. Jeff Angus with Bob Violino, State scraps IS project, *InformationWeek* (March 24, 1997): 24.

6. W. J. Doll, Avenues for top management involvement in successful MIS development, *MIS Quarterly* (Spring 1985): 17–35; M. L. Markus, Power, politics, and MIS implementation, *Communications of the ACM* 26 (June 1983):430–444; K. B. White and R. Leifer, Information systems development success: Perspectives from project team participants, *MIS Quarterly* (1986): 214–223; Robert A. Rademacher, Critical factors for systems success, *Journal of Systems Management* 40 (June 1989): 15–17.

7. Connie McCandless, Systems renovation, *Computerworld* (December 2, 1987): 19–20.

8. Capers Jones, Sick software, *Computerworld* (December 13, 1993): 115–116.

9. Susan Nykamp and Joseph Maglitta, Software speeder-uppers, *Computerworld* (August 26, 1991): 51,53; original data attributed to CSC Index Inc.

10. John G. Voltmer, Selling management on the prototyping approach, *Journal of Systems Management* 40(7) (July 1989): 24–25.

11. David Baum, Publishing tools easing chore of documentation development, *Client/Server Computing* (January 1994): 58–65.

12. See, for example, M. Telem, Information requirements specification I: Brainstorming collective decision-making approach, *Information Processing and Management* (1988): 549–557.

13. Kenneth T. Fougere, The future role of the systems analyst as a change agent, *Journal of Systems Management* 42(11) (November 1991): 6–9.

14. For a more complete list and description, see Terry A. Byrd, Kathy L. Cossick, and Robert W. Zmud, A synthesis of research on requirements analysis and knowledge acquisition techniques, *MIS Quarterly* (March 1992): 117–138.

15. See K. Holtzblatt and S. Jones, Contextual inquiry: A participatory technique for system design, *Participatory Design: Principles and Practice*, A. Namioka and D. Schuler, eds. (Hillsdale, NJ: Erlbaum, 1993).

16. McCandless, Systems renovation.

17. A sampling of justification methods, *Computerworld* (November 11, 1991): 85.

18. Michiel Van Genuchten and Hans Koolen, On the use of software cost models, *Information & Management* 21 (August 1991): 37–44.

19. See, for example, Capers Jones, *Applied Software Measurement* (New York: McGraw-Hill, 1991).

20. Tom Koulopoulos, Getting technology you want and need, *Computerworld* (November 11, 1991): 83–84.

21. Patrick Thibodeau, California dumps $100M deadbeat dad tracking plan, *Computeworld* (December 1, 1997): 2.

22. See, for example, the entire issue of the *IEEE Software Magazine* (May/June 1997).

23. Katie Crane, Meritor opens the integration door, *Computerworld* (February 4, 1991): 57, 64.

24. Jaikumar Vijayan, Look out, here comes India, *Computerworld* (February 26, 1996): 100–104.

25. Gary H. Anthes, Triumph over a taxing project, *Computerworld* (November 4, 1991): 65, 69.

26. Jan Snyders, Make it quick, make it easy, *Infosystems* (February 1988): 36–45.

27. Mary Brandel, Of bugs, tests and successful projects, *Computerworld Client/Server Journal* (February 1996): 26–29.

28. Alice Laplante, Put to the test, *Computerworld* (July 27, 1992): 75–80.

29. Merle P. Martin, The day-one systems changeover tactic, *Journal of Systems Management* 40 (October 1989): 12–14.

30. Nykamp and Maglitta, Software speeder-uppers.

31. James Daly, Bug-free code: The competitive edge, *Computerworld* (February 17, 1992): 55.

32. John F. Barlow, Group decision making in computer project justification, *Journal of Systems Management* 42 (June 1991): 13–16, 37.

33. Nykamp and Maglitta, Software speeder-uppers.

34. For postmortem analysis methodologies, see Tarek K. Abdel-Hamid and Stuart E. Madnick, The elusive silver lining: How we fail to learn from software development failures, *Sloan Management Review* (Fall 1990): 39–48; Ben Pitman, A systems analysis approach to reviewing completed projects, *Journal of Systems Management* 42 (December 1991): 6–9, 37; and John M. Nicholas, Successful project management: A force-field analysis, *Journal of Systems Management* 40 (January 1989): 24–30, 36.

35. Ralph M. Stair, Jr., Using application redesign to maintain continuity and profitability, *Journal of Systems Management* 42(8) (August 1991): 32–35.

Chapter 13

Managing the Delivery of Information Services

LEARNING OBJECTIVES

After completing Chapter 13, you will be able to

1. Describe three ways of organizing the information systems function.
2. Discuss the advantages and disadvantages of outsourcing.
3. Discuss the advantages and disadvantages of setting standards for investments in information technology and systems.
4. Compare and contrast the concepts of an unallocated cost center, an allocated cost center, and a profit center.
5. Discuss the roles and positions of employees who provide information services.
6. Describe two organizations and two modes of operation of the help desk.
7. Offer an approach for managing change in IS.
8. Describe two ways that IS managers can align IS and business priorities.
9. Discuss why companies develop an information technology architecture.
10. Offer strategies for keeping technical staff current.

THE INFORMATION ARCHITECTURE AT BOSE CORPORATION

Joel Martin, manager of information resources at Bose Corporation, has the task of designing an information architecture for the company. Bose, founded in 1964, has established itself as the developer of some of the world's premier sound systems. The privately held firm boasts annual world sales of more than $500 million.

Three years ago, management decided to structure Bose's information technology (IT) organization into six distinct groups to align them with their internal constituents in three functional areas (engineering, manufacturing, and direct marketing) and two geographies (Europe and Japan). The sixth group is the central, or corporate, IT group. Combined, the groups consist of about 60 people, and each group operates independently of the others. Bose doesn't have a chief information officer.

The important thing, according to Martin, "is that in every initiative the information systems and services groups undertake, the key requirement is to support the company's growth." What that charter means is that resources from across the company have been available to support the new initiative that Martin was hired to spearhead, namely to establish an IT architecture and data warehouse infrastructure based on client/server and open systems. "For my group, the key metric for success is for people to have the information they need when they need it in a form they can use," he said.

Martin credits his counterparts in the other IT groups and predecessors with doing much of the work to set up the infrastructure for information delivery. "We are past the point of greatest stress for the infrastructure," he said. "There are so

Bose uses sophisticated information systems to support the development of products such as the one shown here. The IT organization is organized into groups that support engineering, manufacturing, and marketing, as well as the geographical locations of Europe and Japan. Bose also has a corporate IT group that provides specialized IT services to the other IT groups.

many tools available, and the WAN is in place. Now we can focus on packaging and delivering data and information to our users."[1]

Organizations, such as Bose, periodically evaluate their information technology **infrastructure**—their investment in hardware, software, systems, and people—to ensure that it takes advantage of new technological developments and responds efficiently to the organization's information needs and changing competitive position. They might develop an **architecture**—a plan or framework to shape the future of their technical infrastructure. They might also revisit the **organizational structure** of their information delivery system. This structure defines reporting responsibilities and identifies who manages and controls key resources.

In this chapter, we focus on managing the information systems function. We start by examining decisions that shape and constrain systems management at the enterprise level, such as those related to organization and control. We then investigate issues associated with the day-to-day operations of information systems delivery. Finally, we explore how to plan for and manage change.

STRUCTURING THE INFORMATION SYSTEMS FUNCTION

Bose sought to align its information system (IS) services with its business by creating autonomous technical groups that report directly to the business units.

LOCATING CONTROL AND RESOURCES

Organizing the IS function involves deciding how much control to centralize in a corporate IS staff and how much to distribute throughout the organization. Some organizations have structures where a corporate IS department performs all IS activities, as shown in Figure 13.1. Amoco Corporation, for example, centralized IS along with other services such as legal, purchasing, materials management, and human resources primarily to achieve economies of scale and eliminate duplication. Amoco's shared services organization had achieved $400 million in annual savings by 1997.[2]

Other organizations, such as Bose, place most IS activity under the control of separate business units and have only a few employees in a corporate IS department, as shown in Figure 13.2. Xerox Corporation created a similar structure with divisional information officers (DIOs) who report directly to the presidents of their respective divisions and secondarily (dotted line) to the corporate chief information officer (CIO). The CIO sets the technology vision for the company, coordinates the activities of the DIOs, and runs the corporate IS function. The DIOs find the best solutions to satisfy the IS needs of their divisions and spread the corporate vision. They also ensure the consideration of business unit strategies in the overall planning for the company's infrastructure.[3]

FIGURE 13.1 Some organizations centralize their IS functions into a single corporate group.

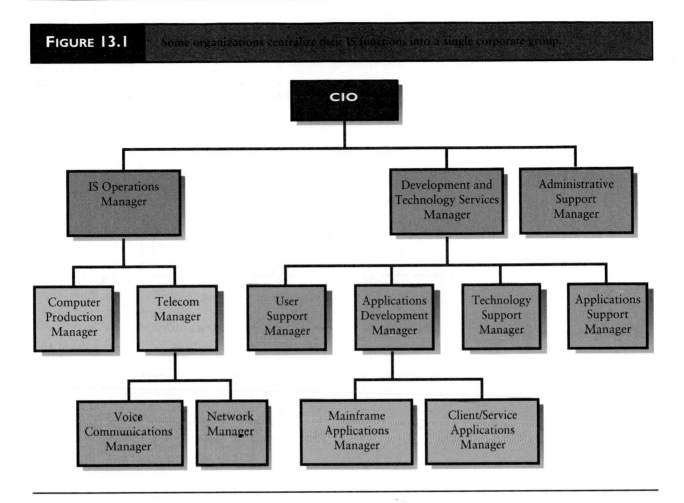

The trend toward client/server computing has eased the movement of information systems functions into the business units. Jonathan Vaughan, vice president of applied technologies at the Chase Manhattan Bank NA, attributes some of the success for Chase's client/server migration to Chase's structure. Each business area sets its own priorities, pays for its own information systems, and uses its own software developers. The corporate technology group coordinates the technology and sets priorities for projects that span business areas.[4]

Many companies adopt a mixed structure, with decentralized application development and centralized operations, as shown in Figure 13.3. The National Association of Securities Dealers (NASD), the parent to the NASDAQ Stock Exchange, recently relocated servers from its 14 district offices to its data center in Rockville, Maryland, where the information systems staff manages them centrally. Hewitt Associates, a human resources consulting firm based in Lincolnshire, Illinois, keeps its servers distributed but manages them centrally. The centralization of operations allows technical managers to oversee security, maintenance, and backup, and to take advantage of scale economies in storage. Business units, frustrated over the complexity and cost of server management, often request such centralization. However, they retain control of the development of their own applications.[5] Engelhard

FIGURE 13.2 Some organizations decentralize their IS staff to separate business units.

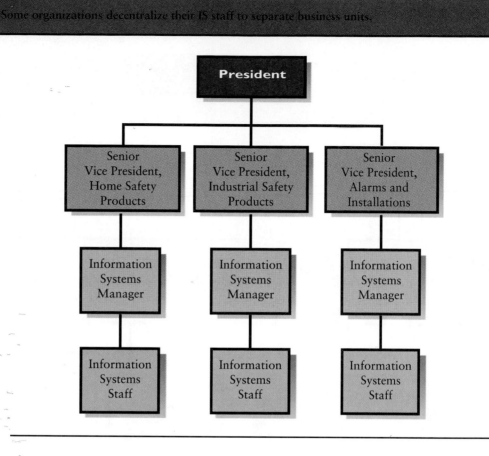

Corporation, a provider of environmental technology, changed its centralized structure. Now a corporate IT group sets standards for core technologies, and individual business units have IT groups that choose or develop software that follows corporate standards but meets the needs of the individual units.[6]

OUTSOURCING

Outsourcing, hiring an outside organization to perform services such as information processing and applications development, can reduce or eliminate a company's information infrastructure. Bose, for example, by outsourcing the processing of accounting and payroll might reduce the staff it needs to support these functions and might free some computer processing resources. Outsourcing moves both capital and human investments to a company that specializes in the outsourced service. The outsourcing company hopes to obtain better service at the same price or similar service at a lower price. The service provider leverages its expertise and investments over many companies to provide economies of scale that an individual company could not obtain. The U.S. Chamber of Commerce, for example, has outsourced all aspects of its information technology and systems in a 10-year, $75

FIGURE 13.3	Some organizations have a hybrid structure with operations centralized and applications decentralized.

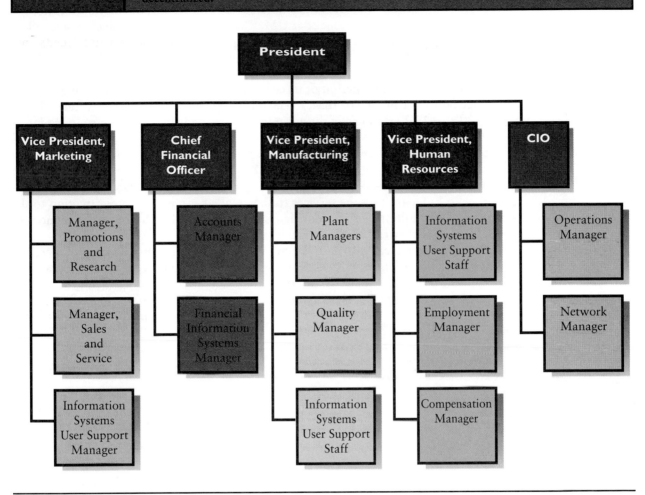

million contract with Cap Gemini America. This decision meant eliminating the Chamber's 60-person IS department.[7]

Companies often consider outsourcing their mainframe operations after moving many of their applications to a PC network. As their mainframe becomes underutilized, they can achieve savings by outsourcing mainframe operations to companies that use their mainframes more fully and efficiently.

Before 1989, few large companies considered it viable to outsource significant portions of their information services. They viewed information systems and technology as strategic resources and their information as too important and confidential to entrust to others. In 1989, Eastman Kodak stunned the business world by selling its mainframes to IBM and hiring IBM to process its data for the next ten years.[8] Although experts disagree about whether Kodak made a wise decision or a terrible mistake, its deal with IBM legitimized the outsourcing of information services. Outsourcing has since become a popular alternative to the internalization of the information infrastructure. Experts predict the outsourcing market to exceed $121 billion by the year 2000.[9]

Table 13.1 displays a sample of recent outsourcing contracts to indicate their size and scope. The $40 billion deal between General Motors (GM) and Electronic Data Systems (EDS) is by far the largest and covers almost all information technology development and management at GM. The scope and size of the contract reflect GM's size and, until recently, its ownership of EDS. The Chevron and AlliedSignal deals cover only the management of desktop computers. Of the 100 largest deals, most contracted out the management of their entire IS operation and infrastructure. All but one covered a period of three to ten years. About two-thirds involved just three outsource providers: IBM, EDS, and Computer Sciences Corporation (CSC).[10]

Table 13.2 lists some of the advantages and disadvantages of outsourcing information services and technology. Questions exist about whether outsourcing reduces costs. Outsourcing at least makes costs more explicit, leading to better decisions about where to spend company money. For example, the CIO at Kodak noted that users considered the costs of implementing systems before outsourcing "Just Kodabucks." Outsourcing the services to IBM made people pay closer attention to the costs.[11] In addition, service providers such as IBM and EDS can realize economies of scale that they can share with their customers.

Outsourcing can also ease staffing and other resource problems encountered in software development efforts. Consider a company that needs to develop a large application rapidly. Such an organization often cannot add staff simply for that effort because it would have excess staff at the end of the project. Instead, the company can contract out a fixed quantity of software development concentrated into

TABLE 13.1 These outsourcing contracts range from 3 to 25 years and $33 million to $40 billion. Experts forecast the total market to exceed $121 billion by the year 2000.

Outsourcer	Contractor	Years	Amount (in dollars)
General Motors	EDS	10	40 billion
Swiss Bank	Perot Systems	25	6 billion
DuPont	CSC and Andersen Consulting	10	4 billion
Commonwealth Bank of Australia	EDS	10	4 billion
McDonnell Douglas	IBM	10	3 billion
BellSouth Telecom	EDS	10	3 billion
Textron	AT&T	10	1 billion
State of South Australia	EDS	9	600 million
British Steel	Cap Gemini	9	400 million
Chevron	Vanstar and Hewlett-Packard	3	200 million
AlliedSignal	Entex	N/A	80 million
Curtice-Burns Foods	Software & Computer Technology	10	50 million
Coventry City Council	Siemens Business Services	N/A	34 million
Dow Chemical	Digital	3	33 million

THE MANAGER IN ACTION

Three years ago, senior managers in each of McGraw-Hill's forty independent business units held three-day planning sessions to draw up an IS road map for the company. According to CIO John Kerin, the groups unanimously concluded that the company lacked four things: technology leadership, corporate technology standards, shared services such as e-mail, and enterprise-wide sharing of information.

One result of the meetings was the creation of a corporate IS infrastructure that is now beginning to link the company's information silos via a worldwide network and corporate IS standards. At the time of the meetings, McGraw-Hill had 185 independent LANs, each with one of 13 different e-mail systems and each with its own employee directory. Since then, it has linked the LANs into a TCP/IP WAN, distributed 10,000 Internet/intranet browsers, set up a central online employee directory, and standardized an e-mail package.

Kerin says building the infrastructure was just the first phase—the tactical work needed to get McGraw-Hill ready for the twenty-first century. The next job is to address strategic matters, especially technology leadership. "My number one objective for the next three to five years is to develop a cadre of business-oriented IS executives," he says.

This summer, Kerin will kick off a management development program for the company's forty IS vice presidents. The program will focus on business skills such as planning, feasibility studies, cost-benefit analyses, and risk assessments.

SOURCE: Gary H. Anthes, A new page (Sidebar: From the CIO), http://cwlive.cw.com:8080/home/online9697. nsf/All/970623anthes.

TABLE 13.2 Outsourcing provides advantages and disadvantages. Some attributes of outsourcing, such as its cost, fall into both categories because of the variability of technology costs over time.

Advantages	Disadvantages
Could reduce cost	Could increase cost
Reduces cost of fluctuations in size of systems development staff	Locks company to a provider
Takes advantage of scale economies in hardware where they exist	Reduces cost
Makes cost/service trade-offs explicit; improves decisions	Removes knowledge of processes from the company
Allows more rapid and timely development	Decreases ability to use information technology strategically
Consolidates operations	
Frees management to focus on business	
Offers improved reliability and stability	
Provides opportunity to learn from the contractor	

chunks or spread over a long period. The service provider can more easily move its staff from one company's project to another's. This flexibility applies to all IS resources, not just staffing.

Outsourcing creates a major disadvantage by locking the outsourcing company into a long-term contract. A company may have difficulty firing a provider that misses deadlines, develops poor-quality programs, delivers insufficient processing capacity, or generally acts unresponsively. Although the contract may specify performance penalties and divorce clauses, an unsatisfied outsourcer may have to sue its service provider to terminate the contract. Long-term contracts also do not necessarily reflect rapid changes in the cost of technology, which may penalize either party. A recent survey indicates that 70 percent of outsourcers expect to restructure their outsourcing and 15 percent will terminate their contracts before they expire.[12]

Outsourcing also requires organizations to relinquish control in an area of potential strategic advantage. Although a company directs its contractor, it loses expertise in IT and may experience difficulty reclaiming the outsourced functions. For this reason organizations generally outsource only selected functions. Figure 13.4 shows the distribution of spending on outsourcing.

Even within a particular function, outsourcing need not be exhaustive. For example, a contract for PC maintenance may cover only IBM compatibles and exclude Macintosh computers. Similarly, organizations may limit outsourcing of systems development to major projects and handle minor projects in-house. Successful

| **FIGURE 13.4** | The data center dominates the spending on information technology outsourcing; however outsourcing for network and desktop management is growing most rapidly. |

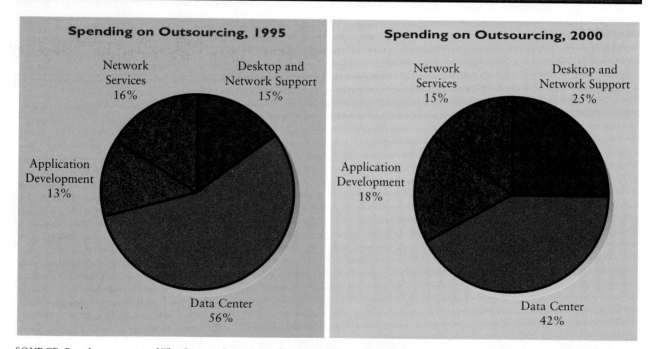

SOURCE: Based on a report of The Gartner Group's conference on IT services and outsourcing, cited in John T. Mulqueen, Industry trend toward outsourcing continues to grow strong, *Communications Week* (April 29, 1996): 75.

Many companies outsource the information systems services to companies such as EDS. For example, General Motors had a ten-year $40 billion contract and the Commonwealth Bank of Australia had a ten-year $3 billion contract with EDS.

outsourcing occurs when companies can divide the IS activities into meaningful segments for outsourcing, identify appropriate segments to outsource based on sound business analysis, and treat the outsource provider as a partner. A company should consider outsourcing if it cannot easily create a competitive advantage with its information technology processing operations, can accept interrupted information technology service, can retain critical technical competencies for future use, or has limited information technology capabilities. [13]

SELECTING AND ENFORCING STANDARDS

A **standard** refers to rules governing the types of investments an organization may make in information technology and systems. Standards strive to impose organization-wide control over IT decisions without directing those decisions. Standards can be set broadly or strictly and can apply to some or all types of products and services.

Table 13.3 identifies some types of products for which a company might set standards. Many companies, for example, standardize on IBM-compatible equipment for personal computers. An employee who wants to use an Apple Macintosh may have difficulty obtaining one in such an environment. Depending upon how

TABLE 13.3	Companies can set standards for a variety of products at the vendor level, at the product type level, or at levels of compatibility.

Computers

Specific configurations (for example, Compaq with 2-GB disk or 16 MB of memory)

Specific vendors (such as Compaq)

Level of compatibility (for example, compatible with IBM/PC)

Communications Equipment

Network interface cards

Network protocol compatibility

LAN media

Router and hub models

Compatibility (such as SQL or Corba)

Office Automation Software

Office suites

Work processors

Spreadsheets

Personal DBMS

Presentation graphics

Network operating systems

Virus checkers

Software Development Tools

Languages

CASE products

Methodologies

Database Management Software

Specific vendors (such as Oracle)

Type (for example, relational or object)

Systems Software

Operating systems

Other

Browsers

ERP software (for example, SAP)

Electronic mail

rigorously the standard is enforced, the company may do one of the following: prohibit the employee from using a Macintosh at work, allow the employee to use one if he pays for it, purchase one for the employee with the understanding that he will receive no support in dealing with hardware or software problems, or refuse to connect the Macintosh to the office computer network. Hardware and software manufacturers often standardize on ISO 9000, a set of five related quality management standards that ensure complete documentation and rigorous business practices in manufacturing.[14]

Table 13.4 identifies some benefits and drawbacks of standardization policies. Many of the benefits illustrate how standards can help reduce costs, sometimes substantially. For example, standardization can reduce costs by minimizing the duplication of software development. If each division of a company develops its own inventory system, the company will probably spend much more money in

TABLE 13.4	Companies should consider the benefits and drawbacks of standardization in deciding the nature and degree of their policies on standards.

Benefits	**Drawbacks**
Increases the quality of developed software	Reduces flexibility in applications
Reduces number of specially built interfaces	Stifles innovation and creativity
Minimizes duplication of software development	Interferes with other requirements of applications
Increases integration of systems for improved efficiency	Reduces ability to go with the lowest cost solution in each case
Increases ability to exchange data among systems	Requires more review and consensus for software/hardware selection-
Achieves economies of scale in purchasing and maintenance	Increases frequency of revision and upgrade installation
Improves negotiating position for better pricing	Decreases users' comfort about opportunities to meet their direct needs
Promotes and facilitates coherent mission and strategy	Increases cost of purchasing due to reduced supplier options
Reduces training costs and time	Increases impact of any major changes
Reduces outside projects with runaway costs	Decreases ability to make major changes
Increases flexibility in use of IS personal	Consumes political goodwill
Reduces the cost and increases the quality of support	Increases impact of poor decisions
Reduces application development time and cost	Impedes the acquisition of new technology
Lifts burden of project research from the user	

SOURCE: Steven R. Gordon, Standardization of information systems and technology at multinational companies, *Journal of Global Information Management* (Summer 1996): 6.

development than if the company standardized on a single inventory system that could handle the needs of all divisions. Other examples of cost saving include economies of scale in purchasing and improving the company's negotiating position for better pricing. A company that buys 1,000 PCs can expect to pay less if it orders them from a single supplier than if it buys 100 of ten different kinds of computers from ten or more suppliers.

Many of the benefits shown in Table 13.4 relate to efficiency rather than cost. For example, standards improve managerial and operating efficiency by increasing the integration of systems and easing the interchange of information among systems. A work team that writes a proposal under tight time constraints will fare better if each staff member prepares her component of the proposal with the same word processor. Standardizing on a word processor guarantees that the company's staff can easily integrate the parts of the proposal into one document. The absence of such integration would prevent cross-referencing, and changes to one part of the document, such as deleting a figure, would require reworking other parts of the document to achieve a coherent product. First Union National Bank of North Carolina, the ninth largest bank in the United States in 1994, standardized, for example, on Lotus Development's SmartSuite, not only to improve integration, but also to reduce support costs and gain the efficiencies of working with a single vendor.[15]

INFORMATION TECHNOLOGY AND GLOBAL BUSINESS

Striking the balance between providing core systems that offer a global view of his company and still catering to varying local needs is a priority issue for Nigel Green, Hong Kong-based information technology planning manager for DHL Worldwide Express Asia-Pacific. "The whole ethos of our company is to think globally and act locally," he said.

"While we offer global services, we are perceived as locally integrated into the community of each country, and our IT systems need to reflect that." If, for instance, Japanese customs requires more shipment information than most countries do, DHL provides it. If Japanese customers want to see Japanese characters on-screen, then that's what they get. DHL tackles the problem by adopting what Green termed a "deep fat" applications infrastructure. "We provide core applications services, accessible to all, which sit on top of a messaging and communications infrastructure," he said.

The core services include customer shipment, transit time, and billing details. They comprise the global part of the model. To cater to local needs, however, DHL has also defined standards allowing developers in individual countries to develop their own applications and link them to the core services using common application programming interfaces, even enabling them to modify their view of the core systems with local-language facilities. "The idea is that everything is built centrally but has as many hooks as possible for linking in local systems," Green said. "And the core services are highly parameterized, making the business rules easy to tune for different environments." This parameterization is achieved by designing both a flexible back-end environment and a presentation layer, Green explained. "All parameters aren't necessarily included in the first version of a service. We often add more, following feedback from the various countries."

An example is DHL's global shipment database. Certain countries may wish to add extra shipment checkpoints to the system because of more stringent regulations. In those cases, users can input their unique checkpoint data—data other countries won't see—into the common global database.

Green and his colleagues are also faced with the daunting task of encouraging all local operations to follow a standard set of IT and business rules. These rules govern activities such as storing shipment information in the global database rather than a locally defined database or capturing and transmitting data in a timely manner. "All we can do is make those rules as attractive as possible so that they have something to offer everybody," Green said. For instance, countries are given a ready-made interface so data can be uploaded to the common database in ASCII text. Also, DHL publishes an internal report analyzing timeliness of data submissions, "so noncompliance becomes very visible, creating a sense of healthy competition," he said.

Probably the biggest challenge for DHL's IS management lies in just trying to communicate concepts and standards around the globe, Green noted. "We are hoping that intranets and online conferencing will help in that area," he said. The company is already publishing IT standards on Web pages, "and that's making a difference."

SOURCE: Excerpted and modified from Anna Foley, DHL worldwide express, *Computerworld* 31(10) (March 10, 1997): S13.

Standards can increase efficiency by increasing flexibility in the use of IS personnel. If a company standardizes on a single database management system, its managers can assign programmers to different projects as needed. Managers in a less standardized environment could only assign programmers who knew about the DBMS that the project uses. Most organizations also find that they must provide some control over the variety of computers that their employees purchase. Otherwise they cannot effectively achieve a critical mass of experience to provide the know-how and support that users need.

Standardization also increases managerial effectiveness. Managers who can easily obtain data related to their decisions more likely refer to the data and make more informed decisions than managers who find access to the data difficult. Standards, particularly in the user interface, database management systems, and data dictionary systems, increase the likelihood that managers can find the data they want quickly and easily.

Standards do not automatically increase the ease of systems integration and data exchange. For example, in the 1970s and 1980s exchanging information among a variety of personal computers and minicomputers was easier than exchanging information among different types of IBM computers. Companies that standardized on IBM had difficulty exchanging data among their mainframes, minicomputers, and PCs because these products used incompatible operating systems and supported different database managers. These companies might instead have standardized on a DBMS such as Oracle that ran on mainframes, minicomputers, and personal computers, and easily exchanged information among its databases on different systems.

Standardization may conflict with the objective of letting business needs determine systems development and acquisition priorities. In particular, standards reduce a company's flexibility in selecting its application software and decrease users' comfort about whether new systems can meet their needs. For example, one type of computer might work best for accounting applications whereas a different type might work best for laboratory applications. One inventory system might function better for discrete items, such as chairs, that exist in whole quantities, whereas another might function better for continuous items, such as chemicals, that can be stored in any volume. Most organizations respond to the inflexibility of standards by specifying a standard that includes different alternatives. For example, a company may specify one type of computer for its personal computer needs, a second for business applications, a third for network servers, a fourth for scientific or laboratory work, and a fifth for computers on its manufacturing floor. A company should also review its standards frequently so that it can respond to its changing needs in a dynamic business environment.

Standardization can also require a significant organizational effort to support its implementation. IS executives and other top managers must acknowledge that employees resent having limited choices. An employee who uses a Macintosh at home, for example, might resent having to learn to use a different computer at work, especially one he does not like as well. The political significance of standardization increases when it affects a division or business unit. Managers of a subsidiary may object to changing its inventory system for the sake of standardization when its employees have the training to use the existing system and it works perfectly well. In particular, the managers may object if the standard system does not provide features of the old system they used and valued.

The Tribune Company, a Chicago-based conglomerate, consists of 28 business units that include newspapers, radio and television stations, and the Chicago Cubs baseball team. The Tribune's business units operate independently, and many have their own IS staff. For reasons of efficiency, however, the Tribune has centralized equipment procurement and maintenance and standardized certain business applications such as general ledger, accounts payable, and credit and billing. The Tribune handles the resistance of subsidiaries by justifying each standardized application with a cost-benefit analysis done at the subsidiary's site. It includes users and IS staff of the subsidiary on the project team and encourages line managers at the subsidiary to talk with their peers at other subsidiaries that have gone through the change.[16]

The organizational cost of standards includes the time and effort required to establish and review them. Setting a standard that affects the entire organization involves gathering input from many people to properly assess the impact of the standard. High-level managers with a stake in the outcome should and usually will lobby extensively for their choice. Standard setting thus uses time that they might better spend on more pressing business issues.

Ironically, standards may increase costs if poor decisions result. For example, many companies that standardized on Digital Equipment Corporation's DEC-Mate personal computer in the early 1980s discarded their entire investment in PCs when the IBM PC and compatibles became the industry standard. While software vendors produced numerous products for the compatibles, users of the DEC-Mate had little or no choice of word-processing, spreadsheets, and other productivity software. Eventually, even Digital abandoned its PC product. Similar stories abound for terminal equipment, network products, and software.

Standards may also increase costs by requiring more frequent updates of hardware and software. Companies that require a common configuration for their personal computers for easier maintenance and exchange must upgrade all computers when one user needs more capability. Similarly, many organizations require that all workstations use the same version of word processing software. When one or two people need the features of a new release, the organization must purchase the new release for everyone. If the company lacked or did not enforce standards it would pay to upgrade only for those demanding the new release. These users, however, cannot easily share their documents with others using the older software.

ACCOUNTING FOR INFORMATION TECHNOLOGY COSTS

How an organization accounts for its information systems has implications for both the acquisition and application of information technology and information systems resources and the structure of the IS function. A company such as Bose must determine whether its corporate information systems department should exist as (1) an unallocated cost center, (2) an allocated cost center, or (3) a profit center. Table 13.5 summarizes the advantages and disadvantages of these options.

Unallocated Cost Center. End users and their managers who view information services and technology as a free resource from an information systems department establish an **unallocated cost center**. This setup considers all costs of

TABLE 13.5	Companies can account for IT costs in three ways. Each has advantages and disadvantages.

Allocation Method	Description	Advantages	Disadvantages
Unallocated cost center	All IS costs are considered an organizational expense	Experiments with technology can occur. Users can request the development of new systems. IS can develop systems regardless of economic benefit.	Costs can get out of control. IS professionals cannot easily allocate their budgets among conflicting requests.
Allocated cost center	IS department allocates costs to departments that use its services.	Users request only beneficial services. It works well in an organization where changes are made regularly to all internal customers.	IS can have problems determining allocation of costs. Friction among user departments and between them and IS can occur. IS has no reason to operate efficiently.
Profit center	IS charges internal and external users the same and attempts to get both kinds of business.	Users can choose who will perform their IT services. IS department has incentives to operate efficiently.	Outsourcing may become more common. Fees may be higher than with other methods.

operating the IS department and related IS services as an organizational expense, rather than attributing costs to particular budgets. Bose, for example, might charge all IS costs to the central IS department rather than charge them separately to manufacturing or marketing budgets. Viewing the IS department as an unallocated cost center benefits organizations just developing their information architecture because it encourages users to experiment with and learn about the technology and subsequently build the infrastructure. It also encourages users to request the development of new systems.

The unallocated cost center approach allows the development of systems without regard to their economic return. As a result, the costs of information technology can quickly rise out of control. Companies then tighten their budgets for systems development and resource acquisition to control costs. Because no economic basis for choosing any particular budget level exists, financial officers usually determine the budget for information systems and technology as a percentage of sales according to the experience of similar companies in similar markets. This measure fails to reflect the company's current status, whether it needs to build its infrastructure to catch its competition or coast and wait for its competition to catch it. This approach can stifle creative and strategic uses of information technology that would yield significant benefits because the other company does not have such uses for comparison.

The unallocated cost center approach also does not give information systems professionals a way of allocating a fixed budget among conflicting requests for resources. When the IS staff or other executives decide not to fund or to delay certain projects, the user community may become angry at the lack of response and long

ETHICAL ISSUES IN IT

I spoke recently with a friend who works for a large corporation that just fired more than 100 programmers. What heinous crime did they commit? Did they surreptitiously make changes in the payroll system to double their salaries? Did they change their boss' payroll deduction for the United Way to a very generous 100 percent? No, nothing that drastic caused their dismissals. These people were guilty of being good at what they did. They were programmers for the company's mainframe applications.

It seems that the management of this company suddenly realized that it needed to have programmers for applications running on its new distributed systems, and these mainframe programmers didn't have the required skills. The solution? Bring in a new group of programmers from the outside.

Now, this was not a company that just decided last week to make the shift to distributed computing. This organization had been traveling down the path for several years. Did the company make any effort to retrain these programmers for the emerging world of distributed computing? Did IS management show any desire to retain the years of knowledge about the company and its processes?

I would be willing to place a healthy bet that this company has a list of "core values,"

and that it hypocritically includes on this list an item that says: "We value our employees." If it values them so much, why hasn't the company made any effort over the last few years to retrain these employees? Let's make this a multiple-choice test. The company didn't retrain them because: (1) It didn't know that applications on distributed systems require programmers; (2) It thought that "a programmer is a programmer," and if you can program one computer, you can program them all; (3) Training costs money, and it preferred to see that money used for more important things like executive bonuses, company cars and other perks; (4) It knew that distributed computing was coming and would force changes, but that was always in the distant future.

1. What obligation does a company have to keep its employees employed?
2. Should the company have retrained the programmers?
3. Did the company act unethically in firing the programmers?

SOURCE: Case extracted from Rick Sturm, Mainframe programmers suffer in the new world of distributed systems, *ComputerWeek* (March 10, 1997), http://www.techweb.com/se/directlink.cgi?CWK19970310S0055.

lead times for their projects. The information systems department then becomes an antagonist rather than a partner in systems development. Having IS staff determine the cost of requested services and the user department identify and quantify the expected benefits of its request can alleviate some problems with an unallocated cost center. This approach helps the IS department determine those projects likely to have the greatest net benefit and justify its decisions to end users.

Allocated Cost Center.   As an **allocated cost center,** the IS department allocates and charges its costs to the departments that use its services. Bose, for example, could allocate the costs of IS usage to its engineering, manufacturing, and marketing departments. Unlike the unallocated cost center approach, the allocated cost center approach avoids the use of and request for services that do not provide an ample benefit. This approach works particularly well in environments where departments charge other services to their internal customers. Such chargeback systems should clearly specify their objectives and emphasize simplicity, equity, minimal overhead, and consistency.[17]

Using the allocated cost center can create problems in determining the appropriate allocation. Ideally, the cost center should charge user departments for resources in proportion to the costs and usage of those resources. The charges levied should fully reimburse the cost center for its expenses. Calculating costs in this way uses information about technical factors such as units of computer use, internal memory use, input-output use, and data storage requirements, which users may find unintelligible and which likely change between periods. For example, the per-unit charge for computer time is low in a period of high usage, whereas the per-unit charge must be higher in a period of low usage to recover the fixed costs of owning and running the computer system. This variation in charges motivates additional usage during the peak periods of the year.

The average cost in the allocated cost center approach does not reflect the marginal cost—the economic way of allocating resources. For example, a company that upgrades its equipment for a new application distributes the cost of the new equipment among all applications. The purchasers of the application see their own unit costs. They do not experience changes in unit costs for other applications which, although likely to be small, when added together might have made the application uneconomical. In addition, other users see fluctuations in their costs without any changes in their activity. This strange costing behavior can lead to friction among user departments and between user departments and IS.

Finally, an allocated cost center has no reason to operate efficiently. Because it receives reimbursement for all costs, it has no incentive to keep these costs low. If some users attempt to bypass high charges by outsourcing, the cost center simply charges each of the remaining users more. This leads to overinvestment in IS and IT resources and results in dissatisfied users.

Profit Center.   An IS department that operates as a **profit center** becomes an internal option to the outsourcing of IS services. It bids for the work of internal users, charges internal users what it would charge external users, and often actively seeks external users. Kimberly-Clark actually created a wholly owned subsidiary, Kimberly-Clark Computer Services, and made its IS department a separate business venture. The company began by selling a software engineering tool that helps companies convert their current systems to a different IBM systems architecture.[18]

Internal users do not have to use the services of their IS department. IS is part of an operating unit's budget and its managers purchase the services they need. The company may limit the fees the profit center can charge internal users to make purchasing services internally more attractive. This type of pricing avoids monopoly prices for those projects that share data with other applications and for which the users have no other choice of IS supplier.

The profit center approach provides the IS department incentives to operate efficiently. It motivates users to request only economically viable services. But it may encourage outsourcing because internal prices and service likely resemble those of outsource providers. Also, because the profit center attempts to earn a return on its investments, it generally charges users more than it would as an unallocated cost center or allocated cost center (assuming that such centers operated with equal efficiency). These higher costs tend to discourage the use of information systems and technology for solving business problems.

MANAGING THE INFORMATION SYSTEMS FUNCTION

Many activities contribute to delivering information services efficiently and effectively. In this section we focus on the people who do the IS work, their interactions with the service recipients, and the tasks involved in monitoring and improving the process of service delivery.

STAFFING THE TECHNICAL FUNCTIONS

Having good people in well-defined positions is critical for providing an effective information systems organization. The human infrastructure supporting information services includes a broad array of jobs.

Most IS positions require good communication and problem-solving skills. Some also require strong management skills. Technical skills, although usually necessary, generally have a lower priority. Applicants for an entry IS position should be computer literate and should know how to program in at least one computer language or have experience with GUI software development tools. Although some companies look for experience with certain equipment, computer languages, or software development tools when hiring, others will train applicants on their equipment and the software that they use on the job. One recruitment firm that analyzed the background of the IS professionals it represented determined that 36 percent majored in liberal arts subjects such as history or literature and had no intention of pursuing a technological career when they had entered college.[19]

The positions described here, and shown relative to their usual skill and pay in Figure 13.5, present a sample of the positions found in many organizations.

Chief Information Officer (CIO).

An organization's **chief information officer (CIO)** manages its information-related resources and activities. The CIO might also be called manager, director, or vice president of data processing, information services, or management information systems. The CIO usually reports to the chief financial officer, the chief operating officer, or the president of the company. Organizations that do not have a full-time CIO generally delegate the CIO functions and responsibilities to the chief financial officer. Companies with multiple business units often employ CIOs within each unit to direct the technological services of that unit. The CIO should have the following qualities and abilities:

- Be a leader
- Have a vision for the IS architecture
- Possess the managerial savvy and political clout to implement that vision
- Act as the technology adviser for major organizational restructuring and reengineering

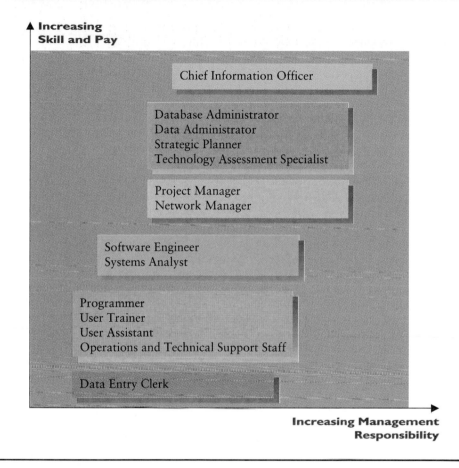

- Educate upper management about the application and value of information technology for securing a strategic advantage
- Secure the financial resources to appropriately shape the infrastructure

Most chief information officers have significant technical experience. As information technology becomes more strategic, however, management and business experience become increasingly important. For example, Kraft General Foods appointed to the job of CIO a planning executive who later became president of Boston Chicken (later renamed Boston Market).[20]

Strategic Planner and Technology Assessment Specialist.

Most large companies have at least one full-time employee who monitors advances in information technology, educates the key managers about these advances, and plans how the company can take advantage of these advances. Often these specialists, frequently called **chief technology officers (CTOs)**, have a staff and budget to pilot new technologies on real or hypothetical applications. Large organizations might have separate jobs in specific areas of technical specialty, such as communications, expert systems, and object-oriented technology. Such specialists tend to be highly technical, although those that supervise a staff and have long-term planning responsibilities should have both a technical and managerial education.

Data Administrator and Database Administrator.

The **data administrator** and **database administrator** organize, manage, and guarantee the integrity of an organization's data. Most organizations combine the data and database administrator position into a single job. Otherwise, the data administrator does the following:

- Maintains the data dictionary
- Assists project managers in defining and coordinating data needs associated with their projects
- Develops an enterprise-wide data mode
- Sets and implements company policies regarding data security and data access
- Specifies data integrity rules

The database administrator has more technical responsibilities:

- Sets and fine-tunes database parameters that affect performance
- Performs database backups
- Manages database recovery upon system crashes
- Installs DBMS updates and software tools

Network Administrator.

The **network administrator** oversees the corporate network, including both LANs and WANs. This responsibility includes not only operations and maintenance, but also planning and the supervision of a network support staff. Because of the dire consequences of network failure, network administrators with proven track records command salaries well above those of most other technical managers. Some organizations expand the role of network manager to communication manager, giving that person the responsibility for voice and data networks.

Project Manager.

A **project manager** directs a software development project and ensures that the project meets user requirements within a specified budget and time frame. He has significant supervisory responsibilities for technical and personnel decisions and therefore typically has both technical expertise and strong management skills. Project managers may have prior experience as analysts or programmers. Alternatively, project managers act as business specialists who report to line managers rather than or in addition to IS managers. The project manager position may be temporary, lasting only for the duration of a project. In some organizations, however, project managers have permanent positions, moving from project to project or supervising several projects at once.

Applications Development Manager.

Some companies have a person who monitors and coordinates the development of all software applications. This job holder helps enforce software standards. She may advise managers and computer professionals about the outsourcing of development projects, the selection of software, and the sharing of applications throughout the company. This position is particularly useful when decentralized development occurs.

These people belong to a project team that is developing a new accounting system. The project manager coordinates the work of the team members and makes sure the project is completed on time and within its budget.

Systems Analysis and Software Engineering.

Systems analyst refers to a technical position associated with all aspects of the systems development life cycle (see Chapter 12), except programming, and focuses most directly on needs analysis. Companies often recruit systems analysts from the graduating class of four-year colleges, especially those offering degrees in business or information systems. They sometimes require analysts to show proficiency in one or more programming languages. Many combine the analyst and programmer positions into a single job. Others focus more on the links with business and call the job holder a business analyst. As the power of computer-aided software engineering (CASE) increases, more companies train their systems analysts to use CASE tools. They often call analysts with CASE skills **software engineers**. Some systems analysts and software engineers who work on one application or in one application area for several years acquire expertise in that application through the process of designing and implementing software. Because of their expertise, they may join the line function where they may assume project management responsibilities.

Programmer.

Programmer describes a highly technical position associated with the production of custom software. Companies expect applicants for this position to have a two-year or four-year college degree with a computer-related major or a certificate from a technical training school and working knowledge of at least one programming language. Programmers need not have a business education or background.

User Trainer and User Assistant. Employees who train users of computer hardware and software and help users diagnose and solve problems with their equipment and software require both technical and interpersonal skills. Some companies hire full-time trainers, although many organizations prefer to use consultants as trainers or send their employees to intensive off-site training courses. Almost all medium to large companies employ people who only assist end users of information technology. These employees often work from a help desk, discussed later in this chapter.

Operations and Technical Support Staff. Operations and technical support personnel install, maintain, and operate the computers and communications equipment. In a mainframe environment, these employees usually perform such tasks as mounting tapes and disk packs, changing the paper and print element in the printers, running periodic system backup, restarting jobs after a system failure, and installing upgrades and new releases of software. In a client/server environment, the operations and technical support staff retains responsibility for backup and recovery, refilling paper and toner in laser printers, and installing software upgrades. They may also perform some hardware upgrades, such as installing new network cards in users' computers, increasing the amount of RAM or disk in users' workstations, and configuring or reconfiguring communication equipment such as routers.

Although operations and technical support employees must have a general technical background, typically they still require in-house or outside training shortly after hiring because they lack extensive experience with the specific hardware or communications equipment their employer uses. In addition, they must receive additional training as the IT infrastructure changes.

Data Entry. **Data entry clerks** hold a relatively low-skilled, low-paid position in the IS hierarchy and work for companies that process large numbers of paper transactions. An insurance company, for example, often employs data entry clerks to process its customers' paper claims. Organizations that use online data input generally do not have data entry positions. Department stores or fast food companies may use employees trained for another function, such as sales, to perform data entry as part of their jobs.

INTERACTING WITH INFORMATION TECHNOLOGY USERS

End user describes a consumer of IS services. She uses a computer for tasks such as word processing, electronic mail, statistical analysis, and report generation. End users at Bose include electrical and acoustical engineers, designers, speaker assemblers, packagers, warehouse workers, marketing managers, and sales people, among others.

As end users become more computer literate, they increasingly perform their own systems development. Although they are not officially part of the human IS infrastructure, end users contribute to building the technical infrastructure through the development of systems and the creation and storage of data. The distinction between users in IS and IS in the user community often becomes fuzzy.[21] Increasingly, such users play a more formal role in systems development by serving on development task forces, participating in rapid prototyping efforts, or engaging in sophisticated needs assessments. IS staff can support end users informally or by using a help desk.

The Help Desk. The **help desk** refers to the IS staff and associated systems that help end users solve immediate problems with their equipment or software. The staff of the help desk addresses problems as diverse as how to turn on the computer, replace the cartridge in a laser printer, handle an exception in an otherwise routine data-entry application, and produce a customized report from the corporate database. In some organizations, the user training staff also reports to the help desk. In small organizations, typically one or two individuals recognized for their technical expertise informally perform the function of the help desk.

The organization of the help desk varies. Many large companies maintain several specialized help desks scattered geographically or organized by expertise. A centralized help desk can reduce costs by achieving economies of scale and improve service by creating a single point of contact. Lockheed Martin Enterprise Information Systems, the information systems unit of Lockheed Martin Corporation, consolidated 13 help desks across the United States to create the Multiplatform Action Response System (MARS). The company expected MARS to save $7 million over five years by reducing staff, saving office space, and eliminating redundant computer systems.[22]

Help desks operate in different ways. Some companies use help desk operators with extensive expertise in the company's hardware and software who, with the help of expert systems, can handle most problems independently. Other companies ask help desk operators only to identify the problem and route it to an appropriate

The help desk, staffed by a team of support specialists, receives calls from managers and employees who have problems with the computer hardware or software they use in their jobs. For example, this help desk staff member might answer a call from a secretary who cannot access her electronic mail.

technical person or function in the company. This approach distributes the help desk function throughout the organization. Still other companies outsource help desk services. For example, Electronic Data Systems Corp. handles all of the help desk operations for Continental Airlines.[23]

A help desk can identify system flaws or user training needs by monitoring problems and tabulating the speed of their solution. Recently, many help desks have focused extensively on their role as problem logger rather than problem solver. This change in role typically results in end-user dissatisfaction because it motivates end users to solve their own problems rather than use the help desk. For example, users at the Air Force Materiel Command who found that their computers displayed "no availability" for parts that actually were in the warehouse did not call the help desk to report the problem because the help desk would log their problem but not solve it.[24] The type and quality of services provided, users' expectations about the information center, the technological environment in which the information center functions, and the organization's commitment to the information center influence its success.[25] In addition, the information center must have a competent staff and deliver effective end-user training.[26]

MEASURING AND IMPROVING PERFORMANCE

Managers can track the performance of information services over time and benchmark them against other companies. They can hire an outside consultant to perform the benchmarking study or conduct it themselves. A leading engineering firm hired Fuld & Company to evaluate a top competitor's use of information technology.[27] Fuld & Company collected an inventory of the competitor's hardware, software, and technology tools. It also assessed its IS organization and culture. The consultants identified areas of superiority in their client's and the competitor's systems. The client could then develop an appropriate strategy for changing and improving its information systems.

Table 13.6 identifies measures that managers can use to evaluate the quality of their information services. Tracking such measures can help information systems managers identify and repair weaknesses in their operations and processes.

Service level agreements (SLAs) help business managers trade off cost against the level of service they want from their technology support staff. An SLA specifies in detail a guaranteed level of performance on a variety of dimensions. These include the following:

- *Service objectives*—a statement of the objectives of the agreement.
- *Parties*—the department, customers, vendors involved.
- *Points of contact*—the persons who serve as the liaisons to the parties involved.
- *Responsibilities*—the specific responsibilities of each job holder involved in providing service.
- *Performance measures*—the metrics that reflect whether the objectives have been accomplished, including ongoing milestones or performance expectations and responses.
- *Escalation guidelines*—the procedures for changing the contract or expediting various processes.
- *Renegotiation*—the provisions for renegotiating the service level agreement.[28]

TABLE 13.6	A variety of measures can assess information service quality.

Customer Satisfaction

Overall satisfaction of users/managers with information services

User satisfaction with contacts within the IS organization

User satisfaction with response to problems

Manager satisfaction with cost and speed of development

Operations

Availability (percentage of time)

Mean time between failure

CPU usage (percentage of capacity)

Disk usage (percentage of capacity)

Average MIPS

Number of jobs handled

Quality Assurance

Defects found per 1,000 lines of code

Percentage of erroneous keystrokes on data entry

Financial

IT expense as a percentage of revenue

IT investment as a percentage of assets

Total system cost

Average cost per job

Average cost per input screen

Average cost per report produced

Staffing

Percentage of professional staff with college degree

Payroll as a percentage of the IS budget

Percentage of staff with advanced degrees

Systems Development

Projects completed in period

Average function points per employee per period

Lines of code per employee per period

Fraction of projects due on time and on budget

Technology

Percentage of IS expense in R&D

Percentage of employees with a workstation

Training

Courses taken per IS employee per year

Average courses taken per IS employee

Average IS courses taken per non-IS employee

Communications

Percentage of cost for telecommunications

LAN contention in peak periods

WAN cost per packet, per byte, and per message

Help Desk

Percentage of problems solved by first contact

Average time to problem solution

Number of problems handled per FTE

Number of problems handled

SOURCE: Steven R. Gordon, Benchmarking the Information Systems Function (Babson College, Center for Information Management Studies, Working Paper Series, 94-08: 1994).

Within a particular category, an SLA can also specify different service levels depending on how critical the task is. For example, it might require a 15-minute response to some conditions and a 24-hour response to others. It also specifies penalties if information services cannot provide the guaranteed level of service. Figure 13.6 shows an excerpt from one of IBM's hardware service level agreements.

SLAs work particularly well when information services operate as a profit center. Information service managers then have the greatest incentive to provide good service and business managers have the option of obtaining similar service from outsource contractors. Many organizations also use SLAs to guarantee adequate service levels from their outsourcers.

MANAGING CHANGE

Business change and technology change constantly affect information systems. Managing such change is one of the CIO's chief responsibilities. In this section, we start by exploring how technology managers assess changing business priorities and align their plans with these priorities. We then examine the role of the information technology architecture, the blueprint for changing the infrastructure to reflect new technology and new business needs. Finally, we address the need to develop the staff, the human infrastructure, who must also change in order to implement change.

ALIGNING WITH THE BUSINESS

Surveys of IS managers show that aligning IS and corporate goals is always a top priority.[29] Companies can achieve such alignment by giving each business unit control over its IS function. Each unit would have a CIO and an information systems staff, an alternative we examined in the context of the structure of the IS function. Even with this structure, architectural and other needs cross business unit boundaries, so IS managers need a way to coordinate IS and enterprise-wide plans and strategies. Steering committees of top business managers help to attain this goal.

Steering Committees.   An IS steering committee includes top business managers, selected users, IS managers, and technical specialists who provide direction and vision about the use and development of the IS infrastructure. Such a steering committee increases the likelihood that IS investments and activities align with organizational goals and increases the participation and buy-in of key managers in the development of the IS architecture. A steering committee, however, may have limitations:

- It may take too long to make decisions.
- Meetings may take valuable time of high-level managers.
- Arguments in committee may divide rather than unify the approach toward IS.
- Committee participants may lack the expertise to help make good decisions.

Steering committees work best when IS helps accomplish organizational goals and the organizational culture supports a participative management style.[30] IS managers in

FIGURE 13.6 This service level agreement shows the response rate a customer can expect from IBM.

Hardware Service Level Agreement

Response Times

General Agreement:
Response time is defined as:
From the time the Customer places the call with IBM to the time the Service Representative arrives on-site. It is obviously preferable that the CSR is on-site as soon as possible, however in a number of instances response may be classified as when the CSR contacts you telephonically, he may be able to diagnose the call remotely and if necessary he can order spares before he arrives on site.

Within a radius of 80km from a Branch Office, (see list in Branch Offices section) CSR will respond to calls on:

1.　 **SERVERS:**

　　❑ 80% within 1 hour
　　❑ 100% within 2 hours

2.　 **WORKSTATIONS/PRINTERS:** (For those machines that qualify for repairs to be done on site)

　　❑ 60% within 2 hours
　　❑ 80% within 3 hours
　　❑ 100% within 6 hours

Equipment installed outside the 80km radius will have the following response times:

　　1. 80 – 150 km Add 2 hours to above
　　2. 150 – 250 km Add 4 hours to above
　　3. Over 250 kms Add 8 hours to above

Deferred calls will not be included in the response time targets.

NOTE:
The above refers to our general agreement for Warranty and Maintenance Agreement machines.

Various other Service Level Agreements (SLA's) can be requested to meet your business needs through a Special Bid agreement. Special Bid agreements also cater for reduced response and MTTR times, extended warranty, conversion from carry-in to on-site service, extended hours, to name a few.

The above times refer to IBM core hours which are 8:00 to 17:00 Monday to Friday.

Particularly with reference to Workstations and Printers, the above is for machines that qualify for repairs to be done on-site.

Calls worked through to completion.

SOURCE: "Hardware Level Service Agreement," IBM Global Services, http://bigfoot.isgaix.co.za/services/as_4.htm, December 12, 1997.

ADVANCED TECHNOLOGY

Faster than you can line up and order a Chicken Fajita Wrap Supreme, Taco Bell Corp.'s 1,000 corporate-level users can now solve some of their support problems using an intranet. With last week's rollout of ServiceSoft Corp.'s Web Advisor knowledge base on its intranet, Taco Bell's IT group expects to significantly reduce the number of calls to its help desk. The new setup enables PC users above the restaurant level to consult the intranet site for help on problems with packaged software or with proprietary Taco Bell applications.

"The idea was to empower the knowledge worker," said Snorri Ogata, director of Taco Bell's Information Technology Group, in Irvine, Calif. In July, Ogata and his staff began looking for a way to leverage the intranet to eliminate some of the 4,000 to 6,000 calls the help desk received every month. With a migration to Windows 95 recently completed, the number of support calls was growing. Being able to extend the capabilities of the help desk so that users can help themselves on their own time is a great benefit.

Now, Web Advisor gives users self-service by walking them through a series of questions to clarify their problems and suggesting specific remedies. For a problem with an off-the-shelf application such as Microsoft Corp.'s Word, the interactive system depends on logic provided by the Knowledge-Pak desktop suite from ServiceSoft, of Needham, Mass. When the snag involves a homegrown Taco Bell application, the logic is based on a knowledge base built using ServiceSoft's Knowledge Builder tool. If the problem doesn't yield to a quick fix, Web Advisor offers features that enable Taco Bell users to pass it directly to the central help desk along with an activity log.

The team has been anxiously monitoring the hit rates on the freshly minted pages. Ogata is very pleased with the amount of traffic—a few hundred hits daily—that was generated in the first two business days after deployment. He expects this number to increase as word gets out via e-mail about the new application.

The trend of deploying help desk functions on an intranet is not necessarily an indicator that fewer companies will outsource their help desk needs, according to Patrick Bultema, president of Bultema Co., a consulting company in Monument, Colo. However, Bultema said, using knowledge base help desk products will slowly change the character of the help desk from being a cost center to a repository of corporate intellectual assets.

SOURCE: Extracted with modification from Taco Bell cooks up self-service support, *PC Week* (December 16, 1996), http://www.servicesoft.com/cpcpcw3.html-ssi.

less participative cultures may resent a committee that infringes on their managerial prerogatives.

The organization and composition of a steering committee influences its effectiveness. The committee should include current and potential user managers with some exposure to information technology. Many practitioners believe that having a user manager chair the committee improves alignment by reducing the likelihood of IS people dictating the agenda. Companies in which IS has strategic value (see Chapter 11) should include top-level managers, such as the executive vice president, president, or CEO, on the committee. Companies for which IS plays a less strategic role might include only middle-level managers if top-level managers feel that the committee requires too much time.

DEVELOPING AN INFORMATION TECHNOLOGY ARCHITECTURE

Information technology architecture describes an enterprise-wide, long-term structural plan for investing in and organizing information technology. The architecture for an advertising firm with 30 employees, for example, might involve networked PCs, each loaded with word processing, presentation, and electronic mail software, with the long-term addition of groupware and some computer-aided design software. Bose, whose information systems infrastructure relies on a centralized Hewlett-Packard mainframe with packaged and custom software, has planned an architecture based on distributed client/server systems using open standards.

The architecture determines the types of equipment the organization should acquire, the types of software it should use, and the telecommunications technology it should buy. Decisions about the architecture also involve decisions about standardization, right-sizing, and global performance. The architecture may specify both the current and future state for the infrastructure, as well as a transition plan for reaching the desired state.

Not all organizations develop an information technology architecture. Many companies instead make their investment decisions on a project-by-project basis, as Bose initially did. Although an architecture increases the likelihood that an organization will make coordinated decisions that reflect its long-term strategy, developing an architecture takes time, effort, and money. Because an architecture has diffuse and long-term benefits, organizations often cannot find anyone to sponsor its development. Unless top management acts as a sponsor, a company likely will remain without an architecture.

An architecture may reduce an organization's flexibility to respond to technological change. Once an organization implements architectural plans and purchases the technology that the architecture prescribes, technology managers and others resist investing in nonconforming technology. Such resistance may be counterproductive in periods of rapid technological change. Some companies with an architecture retain flexibility by seeking less rigid technologies and formalizing a structured approach for trying, evaluating, and eventually adopting appropriate technological advances.

Global Issues.   Companies that operate internationally have unique problems in designing an architecture and building a coordinated infrastructure. Standardization and networking have eased global differences in some organizations, although they may impede the local sensitivity companies should retain in meeting global needs.[31] Federal Express developed a five-year worldwide IS plan in the late 1980s that described projected hardware, software, communications, and applications. Marriott viewed standardization and support as the pillars of its global IS strategy.[32]

Language poses the most obvious barrier to coordinating the software infrastructure. Software tools exist to help developers simultaneously create software to be run in multiple languages. These tools work by separating textual screen prompts and textual report headings from the rest of the software, allowing for easier customization. Difficulties still remain because some languages are much more compact than others. Programmers may have to lay out screens differently, adjust report columns, and change the display of dates and currency for each country. Displaying and printing characters for languages such as Japanese, Chinese, Korean, and Arabic may require special hardware.

Global architecture must consider the international support hardware and software vendors provide. Companies may have difficulty standardizing on either hardware or software if vendors do not support the product selected in all countries in which the company does business. Some companies provide multiple standards to deal with this problem so that each foreign office can find local support for at least one standard. Other companies select standards only from products that receive support worldwide. Accepting multiple standards increases the cost of support and integration. Limiting selection of products reduces a company's flexibility in meeting its needs and generally increases the cost of its investments.

The laws and regulations of foreign countries may also confound a company's attempt to implement a consistent architecture. Countries differ in their laws regarding accounting practices, documentation of business transactions, and reporting requirements. Although some vendors provide packaged software that deals with the laws in many countries, such software is expensive and requires frequent updates. Most companies either customize their systems for the countries in which they do business or allow the organization in each country to make its own IS decisions. Some countries even insist that companies purchase all or a percentage of IT investments from local companies.

The organization of a global company affects whether it can implement a global architecture. Centrally organized companies, typically domestic companies doing international business, usually have the easiest job of designing and controlling the infrastructure. Such organizations have a central IS department that can make and implement plans. Most companies organized along geographical lines, even if not centrally controlled, often rely on a central IS staff to coordinate their infrastructure. Individual geographical divisions rarely have the critical mass for developing their own IS planning expertise. Global companies organized along product lines more likely will establish their own IS planning capabilities.[33] This capability typically exists because different product divisions have very different business needs. Also, such organizations often evolve from mergers between companies that had already developed their own IS capability. Coordinating the infrastructure in such an environment poses political challenges unless strong business needs can overcome the parochial perspectives of local managers.

Client/Server versus Mainframe Architecture.

The hardware architecture specifies the type of computers and communication equipment an organization will use. Today's architects choose among mainframes, networks of personal computers, stand-alone workstations, network computers, and combinations of these options. The absence of economies of scale and the ability to link dissimilar hardware into workable systems make choosing an IT architecture complex.

New companies and those with minimal IT investments can choose from an array of computer technologies. Large companies, in contrast, may have mainframe systems that are legacies from a time when personal computer networks were not available. These companies must make decisions for both new IS development and their legacy systems.

Downsizing refers to the decision to replace mainframe systems with client/server systems. Spalding Sports Worldwide downsized from a mainframe with thousands of terminals to an architecture having dedicated servers and thousands of PC clients; the company writes applications for desktop computers that use corporate data.[34] Sometimes the mainframe continues to play a role in the downsizing effort. For example, instead of upgrading a mainframe to meet requirements for additional capacity, a company may implement a client/server architecture to off-load some of the mainframe's processing to connected PCs.

Table 13.7 lists some of the advantages and disadvantages of downsizing. Initially, many companies achieved tremendous savings in hardware and software by unplugging their costly mainframes. But mainframe prices have declined significantly and the hidden costs of client/server systems have become more apparent. The costs of network and end-user support and training can exceed those for mainframe systems. Converting legacy systems to the downsized environment also may have a significant cost. Finally, end users may waste time developing their own little programs and assisting others in using PC software on downsized systems: one study suggests that this time adds between $6,000 and $15,000 for each PC.[35] Another study indicates that mainframes cost less than one-third as much as PC LANs per user and less than one-tenth as much as PC LANs per transaction.[36]

PC users, used to a GUI environment, exert a primary force for downsizing: they demand a GUI environment for all applications. Graphics processing requires too much memory per workstation for efficient implementation on mainframe systems, and few GUI tools for the mainframe environment exist. These limitations often force systems developers to choose a client/server architecture to meet user demands. The reliability of the network then becomes paramount. As more organizations move to client/server systems, however, nothing works without the network. Because users have little control over its operation, frustration increases dramatically when the network is down.

Although the mainframe can remain a central part of the architecture, with PCs providing only the GUI processing, many organizations, such as Global Marine, a $350-million oil and gas company, have seized the opportunity to eliminate the mainframe entirely.[37] Many organizations retain their mainframes as servers and

---

TABLE 13.7	Downsizing from a mainframe to a client/server architecture has advantages and disadvantages.

Benefits	Drawbacks
May lower hardware and software costs	May increase hardware and software costs
Eases GUI development	Increases user support costs
Increases end-user involvement and empowerment	Increases costs and complexity of providing security
Creates a more scaleable environment	May need to retain IS staff and end users
Improves utilization of PC investment	Incurs cost of legacy system replacement
Eases integration with PC office automation tools	Makes performance management more difficult
Widens availability of object-oriented tools	Increases likelihood of multiple platforms

archivists to handle high-volume transaction processing and to avoid having to reprogram existing systems, even as managers downsize other applications.

Downsizing also offers an increased ability to use object-oriented languages and databases for development. Object-oriented software first became widely available on PC systems, in large part because of its synergy with the graphics user environment. However, many companies now see object orientation as a means to reduce maintenance and increase software development productivity.[38] Because object-oriented tools are available mostly in the PC environment, systems developers who want to use object-oriented technology find a client/server architecture advantageous.

Some organizations move to a client/server architecture to better utilize their personal computers. If employees must have personal computers for office automation applications, using them as a terminal to the mainframe wastes their power. Instead, they can perform much of the computing, relieving the mainframe to perform other processing or allowing the company to reduce its mainframe investment.

Downsizing increases the complexity of managing information security. For example, viruses can infect client PCs, the network, or the server. Failure of the network or server can result in a loss of activities or transactions on client computers making restoration of data integrity more complex. System backups and recovery after failures is more manageable in a centralized architecture. Finally, system administrators cannot easily monitor the security precautions users take for data they store only on their own systems.

Performance problems in the client/server environment are also more common and more difficult to deal with than in the mainframe environment. Performance problems may arise from inadequate server capacity, inadequate network capacity, or underpowered PC servers. Such situations make the sizing of systems difficult. Rapid application prototyping, more common in client/server applications than on mainframe applications, compounds the difficulty of system sizing. For example, developers may successfully test an application with a few screens and a few users but find that the application does not provide the appropriate response time when 200 or more users are entering data and doing database searches.[39] Database updates cause particularly heavy traffic flow if coordination is required among different clients accessing the same database. Experts estimate that the overhead required to coordinate transaction processing increases network traffic by as much as 40 percent.[40]

The cost of retraining or replacing developers, end users, and the IS support staff may create a major hurdle in moving to a client/server architecture. IS developers not only must learn to use different products but must think differently. Experienced programmers may find moving from a traditional to an object-oriented language or from a procedural to a nonprocedural language more difficult than new programmers. Developers who formerly wrote batch-based code must now respond to meet the needs of users in a GUI environment.

The advantages of downsizing appear to outweigh the disadvantages for an increasing number of applications. The marketplace clearly reflects the movement from mainframe computing. In 1991, only 14 percent of *Fortune* 500 companies said that the number of terminals connecting people to their IBM mainframes was decreasing.[41] In 1993, 45 percent of IS executives had no client/server plans or were unsure about them.[42] By 1995, only 10 percent of companies remained uncommitted to any client/server applications.[43] As industry gains experience with client/server architectures, the trend toward downsizing likely will accelerate.

Companies that migrate to a client/server environment generally pursue one of the following four strategies:

1. They convert all existing systems as rapidly as possible.
2. They pilot a few systems, taking a wait-and-see approach to determine if further conversion is necessary.
3. They do no conversion, but phase in the client/server architecture for all new development.
4. They phase in old systems by first converting to a GUI interface and then converting to a client/server environment as necessary.[44]

The first strategy is the fastest and most risky, and the last is the slowest and least risky. In addition to reducing risks, the slower strategies also give users time to adjust to the client/server architecture and developers time to acquire and perfect their skills and tools for dealing with client/server development.

But business users or senior executives can demand more rapid change. For example, at Motorola's computer group, top management, in a drive to cut costs, instructed IS managers to reduce the cost of management information systems from 3.7 percent of sales to 1 percent of sales. Their mainframes cost $60,000 per month to maintain and program and they became too expensive to retain under the cost-reduction mandate. In two years, the IS staff converted the mainframe applications to run on a client/server network and removed the mainframes, reducing MIS costs to 1.2 percent of sales.[45] In contrast, Spiegel Inc. moved more deliberately, beginning with a client/server manufacturing application that 50 people in one department used for decision support and inquiry only. For its second project, Spiegel plans an application for up to 400 people that collects information and taps into the mainframe database.[46]

DEVELOPING STAFF

To deal with changing technology, IS managers need a concrete human resources strategy for hiring, developing, and compensating staff. Replacing staff involves hiring new employees while moving existing employees to other positions or laying them off. Most companies prefer to maintain their investment in human capital and ensure morale by keeping staff current. This strategy requires effective training programs and a culture that values and rewards development.

U.S. companies spent $7.1 billion in 1996 on IS-related education.[47] Yet according to Leilani Allen, who teaches 2,000 people per year at Tenex Consulting, "Eighty [dollars] of every $100 of IS training is a complete waste. Somebody decides to learn object orientation. Then the project they were going to work on gets delayed. In three months anything that person learned is gone. So we retrain."[48]

To maximize the effectiveness of technical training, experts suggest the following:[49]

- *Do just-in-time training.* Plan training sessions so that trainees can immediately use their new skills in an assigned project.

- *Use computer-based training to teach technical subjects or provide refresher courses.* Use teacher-led classes for concept training and developing soft skills, such as project management.
- *Include training in procurement contracts.* Vendor training is often the most effective for "train-the-trainer" education.
- *Train on company time.* Training on company time sends the message that the company cares for its employees and expects them to keep current, not as an option but as a responsibility of the job.
- *Use help desk trainers.* Train your help desk staff to provide just-in-time training as they solve users' problems.

SUMMARY

Organizing the IS function involves deciding how much control to centralize in a corporate IS staff and how much to distribute throughout the organization. Some organizations create structures where a corporate IS department provides all IS activities to simplify control and security and reduce costs. Others place most IS activity under the control of separate business units to increase responsiveness to business needs. Outsourcing gives responsibility for operations and development to a contractor.

The IS function can operate as an unallocated cost center, an allocated cost center, or a profit center. Managers may set standards that improve the efficiency of and flexibility of IS personnel, create opportunities to exercise power in purchasing, and improve coordination among applications. Standards may constrain an organization's ability to meet the needs of its end users and may stifle creativity and innovation.

The human infrastructure includes the IS jobs individuals hold. These include the positions of CIO, CTO, strategic planner, data and database administrator, network administrator, project manager, systems analyst, software engineer, programmer, user trainer, user assistant, operations and technical support staff, and data entry clerk. These positions require a combination of technical, managerial, and interpersonal skills for successful job performance. End-user computing focuses on the consumers of the IS services. Increasingly, end users contribute to systems development. Most organizations establish a help desk to help end users solve their information systems problems.

Information systems managers can track the performance of information services over time and benchmark them against other companies. Business managers can use service level agreements to guarantee adequate levels of information services.

IS managers manage change by aligning their priorities with business needs, developing an architecture, and training staff. Steering committees can help assure the alignment of IS and business priorities. An architecture lays out the plans for changing the information technology and systems infrastructure. Global organizations need to consider differences among country laws, accounting practices, and communication infrastructure in developing an architecture. Migration from mainframe to client/server systems is a prominent component of the current architecture of many companies. Training staff ensures that an organization's employees can accommodate change.

KEY TERMS

allocated cost center
architecture
chief information officer (CIO)
chief technology officer (CTO)
data administrator
data entry clerk
database administrator
downsizing
end user
help desk
infrastructure

network administrator
organizational structure
outsourcing
profit center
programmer
project manager
service level agreement (SLA)
software engineer
standard
systems analyst
unallocated cost center

DISCUSSION AND REVIEW QUESTIONS

1. What are the advantages of a distributed structure where each business unit controls its own information services?
2. How might a manager use outsourcing to ease problems encountered in staffing software development?
3. Why might managers outsource only selected information services?
4. Why do information service managers impose technology standards on the organization?
5. What are some disadvantages of standard setting?
6. On what technologies might information service managers apply standards?
7. What is the advantage of an unallocated cost center for companies with primitive information systems?
8. What problems are associated with unallocated cost centers?
9. What problems arise in distributing the costs of an allocated cost center?
10. What is the primary advantage of operating information services as a profit center?
11. How do a data administrator and a database administrator differ?
12. How do a programmer and a software engineer differ?
13. Why might a company centralize its help desk?
14. Why might business managers seek service level agreements from their information service providers?
15. How do IS managers align IS and business priorities?
16. Why do companies develop an information technology architecture?
17. What issues must managers consider in developing an IS architecture for a global company that they do not need to consider for a domestic company?
18. What are the advantages of downsizing a mainframe architecture to a client/server architecture?
19. What strategies do managers use to migrate to a client/server environment?
20. What rules should companies follow to train technical staff efficiently and effectively?

IS ON THE WEB

Exercise 1: Find three service level agreements on the Web. Compare and contrast them. What elements do they share? What elements are unique? What elements are missing from the agreements? Prepare a brief report that summarizes your findings.

Exercise 2: Visit the Web site of an outsourcer shown in Table 13.1. Prepare a brief summary of the types of projects it undertakes.

MINICASE

INFRASTRUCTURE MANAGEMENT AT USAA

"The hardest decisions are infrastructure decisions," says Donald R. Walker, a retired U.S. Air Force brigadier general and senior vice president and CIO at United Services Automobile Association (USAA) in San Antonio. "In and of themselves, there's no return on investment. There isn't an ROI until you get a business application that uses the infrastructure."

Yet infrastructure is the piece of the technology pyramid managers can least afford to avoid. If it doesn't work right, everything that rides on top of it—utilities, applications, mission-critical databases, integrated telecommunications functions—is doomed as well.

Walker has a healthy respect for wires and plugs. He and his information services group preside over a massive infrastructure that each day processes 350,000 phone calls and 16 million computer transactions for USAA, an insurance and diversified financial services association. USAA's technology structure encompasses 7,600 dumb terminals attached to IBM 9021 and 9672 mainframes for access to proprietary insurance and banking applications, customer profiles, myriad actuarial and product databases, and about 153 million documents—more than 1 billion pages—stored in the company's document imaging system. USAA's investment in LANs is significant: Roughly 18,000 PCs, running either OS/2 or Microsoft NT, are attached to token-ring networks. The company's automated call distribution system, the world's largest, incorporates 23,000 telephone lines and 8,000 AT&T trunk lines.

Yet the most important aspects of infrastructure management may not be wires or workstations but simply the wisdom to anticipate far-off problems and the willingness to tackle a tough sell head-on. Walker has had his fair share of both antici-

SOURCE: Case extracted from Tracy Mayor, Infrastructure management—Insured stability, *CIO Magazine* (August 1, 1997), http://www.cio.com/CIO/080197_management_content.html.

pating and selling in the past few years: USAA's information services group is now in the middle of a massive effort to upgrade the company's entire infrastructure to the tune of $105 million.

THE BEST-LAID PLANS

The reason for the expensive, ambitious upgrade harks back to a fundamental business tenet that's been in place at USAA since the early 1970s: Technology plays a critical and measurable role in the company's survival. USAA, the country's fourth-largest insurer of homes and fifth-largest insurer of private automobiles, caters to about 3 million customers, primarily members of the U.S. military and their dependents. But unlike traditional insurers, which maintain local agents in thousands of markets, USAA conducts its business entirely by telephone, fax, and direct mail.

"The agent has a knock on the door. Our knock is electronic," says Reggie Williams, vice president of network services and the man in charge of USAA's telephone systems, LANs and WANs, and data security. "Our marriage of computers and telecommunications has to be able to compete with that neighborly knock."

The company's multiyear Information Highway program calls for a complete rewiring of USAA's home office (which is three-fifths of a mile long) and four regional offices. Simultaneously, the desktop modernization project will put 12,000 new high-end Pentium PCs on the desktop this year, with approximately 20,000 machines slated to be installed by the end of 1999. A related Microsoft transition project calls for switching from OS/2 to Microsoft Windows NT on all desktop machines and Windows 95 on laptops.

GOAL TENDING

From the beginning, IS's goals for the new infrastructure were twofold: to provide a higher degree of responsiveness—or as the staff's rallying cry says, to provide "information where and when you need it"—and to reduce the total cost of ownership on the computing systems in general. Not only were the mainframe applications unable to provide the increasingly sophisticated analysis required by USAA businesses, Walker says, but the systems were becoming ever more expensive simply to maintain, thanks to 25 years of "spaghetti code" and undocumented changes to programs and systems.

Then, too, there is the simple matter of speed. With intranet, Internet and electronic messaging usage increasing exponentially each year, the networks were having trouble handling the traffic they already had, never mind expanding for the future.

It's one thing to propose a new architecture, as IS first did at a USAA strategic planning conference in 1995, and quite another to win $105 million in funding. CIO Walker had to sell the project not only to upper management—CEO Gen. Robert T. Herres himself signs off on IT expenditures, even approving personally the switch from OS/2 to NT—but to the managers of USAA's five lines of business who would be asked to foot the bill for the new infrastructure because IS expenditures are recovered 100 percent through chargeback.

"When you try to get the infrastructure funded, you hear, 'Well, what's the return on investment?' And of course there isn't one per se. It's almost a case of selling it by negatives," says Walker. You tell them that the train crash is going to occur a year from now, two years from now." By documenting the increasing cost of ownership, Walker was able to provide concrete numbers that expenses would increase even as the system failed to meet new business objectives.

"Changing from the old legacy to the new client/server environment, we're asking IS guys to give us a whole new world," acknowledges George McCall, senior vice president of the business development program at USAA Property and Casualty (P&C), the USAA unit responsible for the lion's share of demands for integrated client/server systems.

Confusion about costly upgrades is kept to a minimum by a CEO-mandated decision-making structure that requires executive council members to sign off on major projects at the concept definition, concept validation, full-scale development, and implementation stages as well as at other key milestones. The system ensures that the management team is on board not just at the beginning of a large project but all throughout its lifetime.

Even as Williams was overseeing the installation of state-of-the-art cabling for Ethernet networks, he had to address performance problems that couldn't wait until new switches came online. McCall and some other line-of-business managers were experiencing unacceptable network failures caused by overloaded token-ring networks.

"A couple of things were really putting a burden on our current network," Williams says. "The PC rollout had 12,000-plus PCs coming down the pike, plus there were Internet and intranet demands, plus [a new release of USAA's proprietary claims software]. Those things require greater bandwidth, and that would be fine if we had our Information Highway up. But Information Highway is due December 1998, and we still need to do business between now and then."

Williams's solution: "microsegment" the rings of the current token ring network so that no more than 50 users are on a given ring. That way, sudden increases in traffic occur less often, and if a network does go down, far fewer employees are knocked off-line at the same time.

Even as they ensure that USAA's infrastructure meets current demands, the USAA IS team remains firmly focused on the future. A bulletin board outside Williams' office displays paper bricks that represent the paving of the new Information Highway network, and each day, a few more bricks are put in place. By design, it's the only way the average USAA worker has of knowing the project is progressing at all. "Every night, things change in this building . . . and every morning nobody knows it happened," says Williams.

He's perfectly happy his efforts are invisible to the rank and file. "Listen, when exciting things start to happen during the day in the network business, it's never good news," Williams says. "When it comes to the new network, I want to be the most boring person at USAA."

Case Questions

Diagnosis

1. What are the information needs at USAA?

Evaluation

2. How well does the existing infrastructure support these needs?

Design

3. What components of the infrastructure does Walker intend to change?
4. What improvements does Walker expect to see after the change?

Implementation

5. Why did Walker think it would be hard to get the infrastructure project funded?
6. How did Walker "sell" the project?
7. What implementation problems did USAA face?
8. How did Williams solve them?
9. How should Walker evaluate the success of the infrastructure project?

MISSING AN ARCHITECTURE AT THE FAA   ACTIVITY 13.1

Step 1:   Read the following scenario:

Information technology management failures are seriously undermining the $20 billion effort to modernize the nation's air traffic control systems, charged a recently released report from the General Accounting Office. The GAO report blasts the Federal Aviation Administration for failing to develop a complete technical blueprint, or architecture, for systems to work together. And the report calls for a single entity at the FAA, such as a chief information officer, to force all FAA teams to use the same playbook.

Among the problems the GAO identified are the following:

- Seven of ten air traffic control systems modernization development teams are working without a technical architecture. Of the three that are cooperating, two specify C and C++ as acceptable programming languages, and the other accepts Ada.
- One team's architecture specifies the Ethernet Protocol, and another specifies the incompatible Fiber Distributed Data Interface.
- Software applications associated with 54 air traffic control systems were written in 53 programming languages, requiring more training and support software for programming staff.

Chastened FAA officials agreed they need a complete architecture and said they have an informal system in place to provide one.

But the GAO countered that such informal management is "neither sufficient nor working well." The GAO defined technical architecture as a plan for defining all the required information technology and telecommunications standards and critical systems characteristics for software, communications, data management, security and performance. The lack of an agency-wide architecture means the "FAA permits and perpetuates" inconsistency and incompatibilities, according to the report. The result is that "future [air traffic control] system development and maintenance will

SOURCE: Activity 13.1 scenario extracted with modification from Matt Hamblen, FAA's IT management slammed: Agency criticized for IT failures that hinder systems modernization, *Computerworld* (February 10, 1997): 14.

continue to be more difficult and costly than it need be, and system performance will continue to be suboptimal," the report concluded.

"Implementing a technical architecture should happen before the agency replaces its 30-year-old host computer system in 1999," Rona B. Stillman, the General Accounting Offices' Chief Scientist for Computers, said. The GAO report makes clear that creating a technical architecture poses a management challenge for an agency with decentralized power. The "FAA has a culture like most large agency cultures that is averse to change and has entrenched autonomous organizations that tend not to respond to challenge," Stillman said.

Federal systems consultant Warren H. Suss said the FAA's regionalized management style means it has a "difficult environment" to manage. "The FAA certainly could use stronger central direction to ride herd over the regions to ensure technological consistency," said Suss.

Step 2:   Prepare the case for class discussion.

Step 3:   Answer each of the following questions, individually or in small groups, as directed by your instructor:

Diagnosis

1. What do the FAA's IT managers need to know to plan the modernization of the nation's air traffic control systems efficiently and effectively?

Evaluation

2. How well does the existing documentation meet these needs?
3. Why has the GAO criticized the FAA's processes?

Design

4. How would an architecture satisfy the needs of the teams managing the modernization?

Implementation

5. Why is developing a formal architecture difficult for the FAA and organizations like it?
6. What should the head of the FAA do now?

Step 4:   In small groups or with the entire class, share your answers to the questions in step 3. Then answer the following questions:

1. What information do the teams designing the air traffic control system modernization need?
2. How well does the existing documentation meet these needs?
3. How would an architecture satisfy the needs of the teams managing the modernization?
4. What should the head of the FAA do now?

END-USER QUIZ ACTIVITY 13.2

Step 1: Complete the following quiz. Interpret each statement as a stand-alone situation; there is no relationship among the various scenarios. Answer each question according to this scale: I sympathize

with the user.
with IS.
with both.
with neither.

Then indicate the major problem that exists in each situation.

SCENARIO 1

User manager: Our charge-back expenses are astronomical. Sky-high salaries on the IS side don't help the situation.

IS manager: I'm sorry you feel that way, but our salaries are market driven. We pay the salaries we have to pay to attract good people—as your department does. We should sit down and discuss your charge-back expenses. They are based on the time that our people and hardware devote to your priorities.

SCENARIO 2

User manager: System development time is always quite a bit more than you estimate. Why? Why can't we ever get a system on time? What are we doing wrong?

IS manager: It's simple—you are constantly changing requirements. The system we are developing today is not the same as the system we began developing last month. You have to be more careful at the front end in gathering systems requirements. The more time you spend gathering requirements for the system, the less time it will take to code, test, and maintain the system.

SCENARIO 3

User manager: Instead of waiting for the new system, we've purchased a personal computer package and are going ahead with implementation plans. The package meets our needs perfectly. We won't have to bother you at all.

IS manager: That's fine with us as long as you don't need any help from us.

SCENARIO 4

User manager: The CEO tells me IS will not approve the purchase of any equipment other than IBM's. What is the reason for this? We want to buy Hewlett-Packard printers because they are much quieter than IBM's.

SOURCE: Activity 13.2 excerpted from Dennis Vanvick, Getting to know U(sers), *Computerworld* (January 27, 1992): 103–104, 107.

IS manager: In the interest of uniformity and standardization, we want all the computer equipment in the company to come from one vendor. The uniformity simplifies billing, maintenance, and support. Besides, IBM is the largest computer company in the world. IBM is a "safe" purchase.

SCENARIO 5

User manager: We need your staff to perform a small modification to the open purchase order inquiry display.

IS manager: It's going to take a long time. The programmer who wrote that particular program left the company, and no one else understands it very well.

Step 2: Your instructor will provide directions for scoring your responses.

Step 3: In small groups or with the class as a whole, answer the following questions:

1. What issue does each scenario describe?
2. Which party presents a better analysis and perspective on the situation?
3. What actions would improve the situation described?

ACTIVITY 13.3   UDDERLY DELICIOUS DAIRY COMPANY

Step 1: Read the following scenario:

You are Carry dePail, the IS manager for the Udderly Delicious Dairy Company, a producer and marketer of dairy products. You report to the president of Udderly Delicious along with the vice presidents of marketing and sales, product development, manufacturing, distribution, finance, and personnel. That is, until this morning. In a surprise announcement, the president shared his intentions to reorganize the company along product lines. Marketing and sales, product development, distribution, and manufacturing will be divided into four integrated groups, each focusing on one of the major product categories:

1. Whole Milk Products Group
2. Milk Solids Products Group
3. Frozen Milk Dessert and Confection Products Group
4. Milk By-products Group

The current vice presidents of the functional line units will be assigned to head one each of the new product groups. The president solicits everyone's ideas on how best to implement and support it. After a spirited discussion of mainstream issues, the issue of support comes up. The president emphasizes that IS, personnel, and finance will continue to report to him but asks each support executive how they intend to react organizationally to the new structure. Personnel says that they would probably not change but continue to provide central services with the same structure.

SOURCE: Activity 13.3 case from Robert K. Wysocki and James Young, Situation 11-2: Udderly delicious dairy company, in *Information Systems: Management Practices in Action* (New York: John Wiley & Sons, 1990): 81–82.

Finance on the other hand says that they would probably divide their analysis and transaction processing groups into four similar units so that their support people could specialize in serving one product group. When you are asked, you admit that you are undecided. The president asks you to sleep on it and give him a preliminary indication in a day or so.

Currently, you have a mainframe computer that is managed by a single operations department and supported by a small technical support department. Your systems and programming department is organized by function, with a separate group supporting each of the old organizational units. The systems they build and maintain are capable of distinguishing among product groups now so the systems can support the new organization. However, you know that requests for conflicting modifications to existing systems, especially marketing systems, are inevitable. You frankly do not know how to proceed. In critical functions, you know you do not have enough good people to assign one to each product group. Moreover, you know that with four groups making uncoordinated changes to the applications, the systems will tend to become unstable. Yet the president has made it clear that good IS service to each product group is extremely important, Currently, vice presidents are used to having a team that is highly knowledgeable about and dedicated to their systems. You are not sure you can provide both.

Step 2:   Prepare the case for class discussion.

Step 3:   Answer each of the following questions, individually or in small groups, as directed by your instructor:

Diagnosis

1. What are the IS needs of Udderly's functional managers?
2. What are your needs and the needs of your staff?

Evaluation

3. How could the current organization still support the new structure?

Design

4. What are the advantages and disadvantages of organizing IS by product line?
5. What other organizations are possible?

Implementation

6. What structure would you recommend? Why?

Step 4:   In small groups or with the entire class, share your answers to the questions in step 3. Then answer the following questions:

1. What are the IS needs of Udderly's functional managers?
2. How could the current organization still support the new structure?
3. What are the advantages and disadvantages of organizing IS by product line?
4. What structure would you recommend? Why?

ACTIVITY 13.4 LEAD, FOLLOW, OR GET OUT OF MY WAY

Step 1: Read the following scenario:

"I know this isn't what we agreed to," said Eric Cottington, VP of marketing programs at Miarhpe Services Corp.

"But we just can't wait any longer." As he looked across his desk at Polly Wood, information technology (IT) director, he could sense her frustration. But Miarhpe's competition had stepped up its promotional activity and was beginning to eat into the company's market share. "Our systems just aren't responsive enough," Cottington said. "We are hearing that the competition is able to match its customer's purchase records with the promotional programs they offer and effectively guarantee that the customer will always get the best price."

"I know, I know," Wood said, feeling sympathetic and slightly overwhelmed at the same time. "But you, the other members of the management team, and everybody else involved in the planning process agreed to the timetable we set. I don't have the staff or the budget to help you as much as I think you'll need to be helped through this process."

"I'm sorry, but I can't accept that," Cottington said. "I'll hire the people I need from the outside if I have to, but this change is going to happen. We have to get your support when it comes time to tying back into the old systems. I expect your full cooperation," he emphasized.

Wood pointed out that the combination of systems, software, and staff support Cottington would need would take his initiative into the class of projects requiring formal financial approval.

"Taken as a whole, yes. But I can get the project going without hitting the cut-off point where those controls kick in," Cottington said. "We'll do it in phases and still stay within the rules," he added.

That did not make Wood happy. She knew Cottington had the authority to proceed on a pilot basis, but she was concerned that he and his staff would quickly get in over their heads. If the IT department had to come in and "clean up," she knew there would be problems.

Wood left Cottington's office and returned to her desk, where she sent an e-mail message to Miarhpe's CFO, Doug Brockway. She outlined the situation with Cottington and requested some help in putting together a proposal to allow for an adjustment to her budget.

After sending the e-mail, Wood reviewed her situation. Roughly half of her department's budget was currently tied up in fees paid to Miarhpe's parent company. Another 15 percent was devoted to communications expenses, 10 percent to hardware, and the balance to people-related costs. There was no formal allocation for brand new development projects beyond what was in the timetable.

Step 2: Prepare the case for class discussion.

Step 3: Answer each of the following questions, individually or in small groups, as directed by your instructor:

SOURCE: Activity 13.4 case from Damian Rinaldi, Lead, follow, or get out of my way, *Client/Server Computing* (May 1994): 35–38.

Diagnosis

1. What are Cottington's needs?
2. Are Cottington's needs reasonable?

Evaluation

3. How well has the IT met Cottington's needs?
4. Why does Wood feel that she cannot meet Cottington's needs?
5. How well is IS aligned with the business at Miarhpe?

Design

6. What alternatives does Wood have now?
7. How might you redesign Miarhpe's planning process to give Wood more flexibility in the future?

Implementation

8. What should Wood do now?

Step 4: In small groups or with the entire class, share your answers to the questions in step 3. Then answer the following questions:

1. What are Cottington's needs?
2. Why does Wood feel that she cannot meet Cottington's needs?
3. What alternatives does Wood have now?
4. What should Wood do now?

PUBLIC SECTOR OUTSOURCING ACTIVITY 13.5

Step 1: Read the following scenario:

Westchester County (N.Y.) Executive Andrew O'Rourke awarded a seven-year information technology outsourcing contract to IBM in January 1997. Most of the county's 100-plus IS employees were offered jobs with IBM. But some weren't, and some chose to fight the move.

After the employees' union filed a legal complaint, a New York state judge ruled that O'Rourke lacked the authority to create or eliminate jobs in the county government. The judge said the county's charter grants that authority only to the county Board of Legislators.

Step 2: Prepare the case for class discussion. Consider the viewpoints of IBM, the county, employees who welcomed the move, and employees who brought the suit.

Step 3: From the perspective of each of the parties in the dispute, answer each of the following questions, individually or in small groups, as directed by your instructor.

SOURCE: Activity 13.5 scenario from Thomas Hoffman, County, IBM settle outsourcing: N.Y. officials reach compromise on pact, *Computerworld* (August 18,1997): 3.

1. What alternatives now exist? What compromises might you propose?
2. For each alternative, who benefits and who is harmed?
3. From the ethical principles of least harm, rights and duties, professional responsibilities, self-interest and utilitarianism, consistency, and respect, how would you evaluate each alternative?
4. What course of action would you take? Why?

RECOMMENDED READINGS

Applegate, Lynda M., McFarlan, F. Warren, and McKenney, James L. *Corporate Information Systems Management: Text and Cases.* 4th ed. Chicago: Irwin, 1996.

De Looff, L. A. *Information Systems Outsourcing Decision Making: A Managerial Approach.* Hershey, PA: Idea Group Publishing, Series in Information Technology Management: 1997.

McKeen, James D., and Smith, Heather A. *Management Challenges in ISS: Successful Strategies and Appropriate Action.* New York: John Wiley & Sons, Wiley Series in Information Systems, 1996.

Szewczak, Edward, and Khosrowpour, Mehdi (eds.).*The Human Side of Information Technology Management.* Hershey, PA: Idea Group Publishing, Series in Managing the Human Side of Information Technology, 1997.

Thomas, Andrew H., and Steele, Robert M. *The Virtual Help Desk: Strategic Management Center.* Scottsdale, AZ: International Thomson Computer Press, 1996.

NOTES

1. Excerpted with modification from Damion V. Rinaldi, Collaboration and cooperation catalyze client/server transformation at Bose Corporation, *Client/Server Computing* (February 1995): 30–32.
2. Rebecca Hirschfield, Shared services save big money, *Datamation* (September 1996), http://www.datamation.com/PlugIn/issues/1996/sept/09hr.html.
3. John G. Sifonis and Beverly Goldberg, Strategic management—Changing role of the CIO—As technology becomes central to business, the CIO becomes the key mover in the ranks of upper management, *InformationWeek* (March 24, 1997), http://www.techweb.com/se/directlink.cgi?IWK19970324S0043.
4. Candee Wilde, Chase overhauls credit-card business; reaps $4.7M in savings, $29.9M in revenue in five years: Distributed systems earn extra credit, *Computerworld Client/Server Journal,* Special Issue (June 1995): 16–17.
5. Tim Ouellette, Homecoming: Distributed servers return to the data center as IS seeks to centralize control and security, *Computerworld* (August 11, 1997): 1, 24.
6. Rosemarry Cafasso, Application development, *Software Magazine* (January 1998): 32–36.
7. Bob Wallace and Julia King, Raredeal: Self-funded outsourcing, *Computerworld* (February 23, 1998): 1, 14.
8. David Kirkpatrick, Why not farm out your computing? *Fortune* (September 23, 1991): 103–112.
9. International Data Corporation, *1996 Worldwide Outsourcing Markets and Trends* (May 1997), cited in Global outsourcing market to exceed $121 billion by 2000, http://www.idcresearch.com/gom.htm, September 2, 1997.
10. Ibid.

11. Kirkpatrick, Why not farm out your computing?

12. Gartner Group Executive Vice President Len Bergstrom as cited in Robert L. Scheier, Businesses outsourcing more, but less thrilled with results, *Computerworld OnLine* (July 21, 1997), http://cwlive.cw.com:8080/home/print9497.nsf/All/SL29gartr.

13. Paul Clermont, Outsourcing without guilt, *Computerworld* (September 9, 1991): 67–68.

14. Gary H. Anthes, ISO standard attracts U.S. interest, *Computerworld* (April 26, 1993): 109.

15. Richard A. Danca, One bank's approach to IT: Standard—But not stodgy, *Client/Server Computing* (August 1994): 34–36, 95.

16. Sheryl Kay, Tribune strives to balance independence and efficiency, *Computerworld* (December 10, 1990): 91.

17. Daniel Sommer, Information centers debate billing for services, *InfoWorld* (January 11, 1988): 38.

18. Bob Francis, Kimberly-Clark sees profits in IS, *Datamation* (May 15, 1990): 53–54.

19. Emily Leinfuss, Remember English Lit 101? *Computerworld* (June 15, 1992): 104.

20. Anne Stuart, The CIO role: The new IS role models, *CIO Magazine* (May 15, 1995).

21. Carol Hildebrand, FirstLine blurs IS and users, *Computerworld* (May 31, 1993): 74.

22. Thomas Hoffman, As Lockheed Martin slashes help desk personnel, it must ask: Will customers go ballistic? *Computerworld* (May 6, 1996): 85.

23. Bob Francis, Downsize the help desk, *Datamation* (February 15, 1992): 49–51.

24. Elisabeth Horwitt, Basic instinct: Air Force Materiel Command puts the "user" into user support—one logical step at a time, *Computerworld* (January 11, 1993): 75, 77.

25. Simha R. Magal and Dennis D. Strouble, A users' perspective of the critical success factors applicable to information center, *Information Resources Management Journal* (Spring 1991): 22–34.

26. Robert L. Leitheiser and James C. Wetherbe, A comparison of perceptions about information center success, *Information & Management* 21(1) (August 1991): 7–17.

27. Fuld & Company Inc. Research and Analysis, The Research Casebook, Case 1, http://www.ful.com/case1.html, December 12, 1997.

28. These are drawn from the CES Service Level Agreement, Draft October 23, 1996, http://www.his.ucsf.edu/(gjf/stddsktp.html.

29. See, for example, CDC survey of 340 IS managers cited in Bruce Caldwell, We are the business, *InformationWeek* (October 28, 1996): 36–49.

30. Harish C. Bahl and Mohammad Dadashzadeh, A framework for improving effectiveness of MIS steering committees, *Information Resources Management Journal* (Summer 1992): 33–44.

31. Thomas Hoffman, Here and there, *Computerworld* (April 12, 1993): 81–82.

32. Linda Runyan, Global IS strategies, *Datamation* (December 1, 1989): 71–78.

33. Steven R. Gordon, Standardization of information systems and technology at multinational companies, *Journal of Global Information Management* (Summer 1993): 5–14.

34. Rosemary Cafasso, Spalding tees up client/server, *Computerworld* (March 22, 1993): 51.

35. Mitch Betts, The bite of hidden costs, *Computerworld* (July 26, 1993): 66.

36. IDC study cited in Barbara DePompa, Mainframes: Rising for the ashes, *InformationWeek* (May 27, 1996): 44–50.

37. Dan Richman, Glass wall shattered as big iron shuttered, *Computerworld* (December 4, 1995): 8.

38. Mitch Kramer, Developers find gains outweigh OO learning curve, *Software Magazine* (November 1993): 23–33; Mitch Kramer, Large app development a job for OO A&D tools, *Software Magazine* (January 1994): 39–49.

39. Joe Panepinto, Client/server breakdown, *Computerworld* (October 4, 1993): 107–111.

40. James A. Hepler, Network jam, *Computerworld* (April 26, 1993): 89–90.

41. Peter Nulty, When to murder your mainframe, *Fortune* (November 1, 1993): 109–120.

42. Joe Panepinto, Client/Server breakdown. Source: An Interactive Data Corporation 1993 survey of 858 information systems executives.

43. Sentry Market Research, as cited in Michael Bucken, Textron stays on client/server course, *Software Magazine* (March 1996): 40–44.

44. Adapted from Jean S. Bozman, Approaching migration, *Computerworld* (March 22, 1993): 51–52.

45. Peter Nulty, When to murder your mainframe.

46. Johanna Ambrosio, Walk, don't run, with it, *Computerworld* (March 15, 1993): 65.

47. IDC survey, cited in Joseph Maglitta, Train in vain, *Computerworld* (August 25, 1997): 81.

48. Joseph Maglitta, Train in vain, *Computerworld* (August 25, 1997): 81.

49. Based on Joseph Maglitta, Train in vain: Training tips, *Computerworld* (August 25, 1997): 81.

A

Accounts payable system. A transaction processing system that monitors accounts payable; it may generate purchase orders and produce checks for paying the organization's bills.

Accounts receivable system. A transaction processing system that tracks money owed to the company as payment for goods and services provided; the TPS may generate reports used for checking credit, monitoring bad debts, pursuing overdue accounts, and reducing payment lags.

Active data entry. Actions taken by a user to enter data into a computer.

Ad hoc query. A request that has not been programmed for information from a database, generally one made by a nonprogramming user who is using a user-friendly language.

Adaptor. Also known as a controller, it resides inside the computer and converts commands and data from the data bus into signals that peripheral devices can use.

ADSL (Asymmetric Digital Subscriber Line). Delivers data faster from the phone company to the subscriber and returns data at slower rates.

Alliance. An official working partnership with another organization.

Allocated cost center. An accounting scheme in which the IS department allocates and charges its costs to the departments that use its services.

Alpha testing. Also known as system testing, testing the entire system under realistic conditions.

Alternative analysis. Considers one or more alternate designs and analyzes their advantages and disadvantages.

Application. A software product.

Application software. Satisfies specific user needs, including data management, business functions, and the interface between the user and the software.

Architecture. The long-term structural plan for investing in and organizing information technology; it acts as the blueprint for the technology portion of an organization's information systems infrastructure.

Artificial intelligence. The branch of computer science that emulates human behavior and thought in computer hardware and software.

ASCII. A code used by most microcomputers to represent characters.

ATM (Asynchronous Transfer Mode). A data communication protocol that resembles frame relay except that it has a fixed packet size of 53 bytes, and the capacity responds to the demand.

Atomicity. The property of a transaction that prevents its division into parts.

Attribute. A characteristic of an entity, such as a phone number, hair color, height, or weight of the entity "person"; a column of a relation in the relational model.

Audit trail. A permanent record of transactions that auditors use to verify corporate information reported by a company.

Authorware. Software used to develop courseware; it includes tools that allow developers to script text and incorporate audio, graphics, text, and animation into course materials.

Automated call director. Software that makes sure customers' calls reach the appropriate person.

Automated guided vehicle (AGV). Computer-controlled vehicle that moves along a guidance system built into a factory or warehouse floor.

Automation. The use of computers to perform tasks previously performed by people.

B

Backbone. A network that connects other networks.

Bandwidth. Theoretical capacity to transmit data.

Bar code reader. A device for reading input formatted as bar codes.

Batch processing. A mode of processing that stores electronic records or transcribed paper records in a stand-alone computer file that other parts of the company's information system cannot use or access.

Beta testing. Also known as pilot implementation strategy, requires one or more segments of the company to use a new system before the entire company uses it.

Billing system. Part of an accounts receivable transaction processing system that generates account statements and bills for customers.

Bit. The smallest amount of data that can be stored; holds a zero or a one.

Block. A portion of a message that has been divided into pieces for routing across a communication network.

Browser. Software used to load documents from the Internet.

Bug. An error in the way that a system operates.

Business-level strategy. Strategy that matches the strengths and weaknesses of each business unit or product line to the external environment to determine how each unit can best compete for customers.

Business application software. Software that performs business tasks to satisfy business needs.

Business process redesign. An integrated approach to changing the way that business processes are performed that incorporates continuous improvement, worker empowerment, and business process reengineering.

Business process reengineering (BPR). A process redesign that involves discontinuous rather than incremental change and the breaking of traditional notions of how an organization accomplishes its work, generally taking maximum advantage of information technology.

Byte. One byte equals eight bits. Most manufacturers measure storage capacity in bytes.

C

Cache memory. A small amount of primary storage that is faster than the rest of the primary storage in a computer.

Cartridge disks. Similar to removable hard disks. The disk is sealed in a cartridge reducing the possibility of contamination due to dust and allowing the read/write head to approach the disk surface more closely.

CASE tool. Software that helps automate the software development process.

CASE toolset. Also called a CASE workbench, it is a suite of CASE tools that support and integrate the activities performed throughout the software development life cycle.

CASE workbench. Also called a CASE toolset, it is a suite of CASE tools that support and integrate the activities performed throughout the software development life cycle.

Cash management system. A system that processes transactions related to the receipt and distribution of cash.

CDPD (Cellular Digital Packet Data). A data communication standard that uses a cellular carrier's spare capacity to transmit data packets.

Centralized architecture. A design that centralizes the data and operations of a database management system on a single computer.

Channel Definition Format (CDF). A standard proposed by Microsoft that would allow users to turn any web page into a push channel on servers supporting the standard.

Chief Information Officer (CIO). Person who manages the information-related resources and activities of an organization.

Chief Technology Officer (CTO). Specialist who frequently has a staff and budget to pilot new technologies on real or hypothetical applications.

Client. In a client/server architecture, a computer, typically dedicated to a single user, that relies on other computers called servers to perform special services, such as database services or printer services.

Client/server architecture. Design that divides processing between clients and servers; design that divides DBMS processing among networked computers while centralizing permanent storage on a database server.

Coaxial cable. Transmission medium used by cable television companies to bring television signals into the home.

Code generator. Software that creates complete and working programs based on designer specifications.

Command-driven interface. A user interface that requires users to direct a computer's next action by entering a command, typically by typing it at a keyboard.

Command/data oriented programming language. A computer language, such as FORTRAN, COBOL, and Pascal, that separates data storage from procedural parts of a program.

Common carrier. Private carrier that sells communication services to the public.

Common Gateway Interface (CGI). Standard used by some web development tools to create an interface between a web site and other applications.

Communication carrier. A government agency or private company that provides communication services and facilities to the public.

Compiler. Software that translates a program's source code into object modules.

Component testing. Testing that examines the interaction of a series of programs within the system that likely will be used in concert, such as those that process a transaction.

Computer-aided design (CAD). System that allows engineers, architects, graphics designers, and others to compose their product and process designs on a computer rather than paper.

Computer-aided manufacturing (CAM). System that automates machine monitoring and control through the use of flexible manufacturing, robotics, and automated guided vehicles.

Computer Aided Software Engineering (CASE). The use of software to automate activities performed in needs assessment, systems analysis, design, development, and maintenance.

Computer-based training (CBT). Training programs that rely on computerized presentation of materials.

Computer-integrated manufacturing (CIM). The coordination of CAD and CAM automation systems with each other and with information systems that relate to design and manufacturing.

Computer-supported cooperative work (CSCW). Also known as group support system (GSS) and groupware, information technology that facilitates the sharing or communication of information among members of a group and helps the group to perform common tasks and to accomplish its goals, including such products as electronic mail, electronic notes, bulletin board systems, and electronic meeting systems.

Computerized databases. Databases stored on computer-readable media such as disks, diskettes, tapes, or CD-ROM.

Computerized reservation system. Specialized order entry system used by companies such as airlines or automobile rental agencies.

Concurrency control. The proper management of simultaneous data updates when multiple users or multiple tasking occurs.

Contextual inquiry. A way of collecting information about how users perform their work by watching them working or working alongside them.

Controller. Also known as an adaptor, a device that resides inside the computer and converts commands and data from the data bus into signals that peripheral devices can use.

Cookie. A small amount of information that a web server asks a visitor's browser to store on his computer.

Cooperative processing. The use of local area networks to connect PCs with larger computers so that each type of equipment can be used for what it does best.

CORBA (Common Object Request Broker Architecture). Standard for representing object data independent of computer language, operating system, and hardware.

Corporate-level strategy. Strategy that addresses which lines of business a company should pursue.

Cost/benefit analysis. Analysis that weighs the benefit of meeting needs against projected costs in a formal, documented way.

Cost leadership. A strategy that seeks to achieve competitive advantage by allowing a business unit, by keeping its costs low, to make more profit than its competitors at the same price.

Courseware. Software used in computer-based training.

Cross-functional team. Also known as an interdisciplinary team, team that includes employees from several functional areas in the company.

Custom software. Software developed from scratch by organizations.

Customer-focused IOS. Links a company and its customers by offering information services that mutually benefit the customer and the host.

Customized software. Software modified to a customer's specifications.

D

Data. Raw facts whose uses and application are undefined.

Data administrator. A person whose responsibility is to ensure the integrity of the data resource. The data administrator must know what data the organization collects, where it stores the data, and how it names data items.

Data bus. The electrical connection between various parts of the computer that manages the flow of data between the processing hardware and the rest of the computer.

Data communication. The transmittal of digitized data, that is, data represented as a series of zeros and ones.

Data communication technology. Company networks, the Internet, and other technology for the transmittal of digitized data.

Data design. The process of identifying and formalizing the relationships among the elements of data in a database.

Data dictionary. The part of a database that holds its metadata and acts as a CASE tool for automating programming.

Data entry clerk. A relatively low-skill, low-paying job position with the responsibility of entering data into a computerized system.

Data-flow diagram (DFD). A diagram that graphically illustrates the creation and use of data by system processes and provides a complete picture of the relationship between inputs and outputs.

Data link. Connection or channel between two points in a communication network.

Data mart. Provides summary and historical data for management decision making for a single department or division.

Data mining. The process of identifying patterns in large masses of data.

Data warehouse. An enterprise-wide database designed solely to support management decision making.

Database. An organized collection of related data.

Database administrator. A person with responsibilities that focus on the overall performance and integrity of a single DBMS on one or more databases.

Database management system (DBMS). Software comprising programs to store, retrieve, and otherwise manage a computerized database and provide interfaces to application programs and to non-programming users, as well as provide a host of other data creation, manipulation, and security features.

Database model. The underlying methods that a database uses for associating, storing, and retrieving related data.

Database server. In a client/server architecture, a computer that stores data and runs the software to access its data in response to requests from client computers.

DCOM (Distributed Component Object Model). Standard for representing object data independent of computer language, operating system, and hardware.

Decentralized architecture. A design in which databases are developed on an ad-hoc basis as required by individual applications, without central planning and without central control.

Decision support system (DSS). System that assists managers in evaluating the impact of alternative decisions and making the best possible choice.

Density. The number of dots an output device produces per inch horizontally and vertically.

Design. The creation of detailed specifications for a proposed system.

Design specification. The means for communicating a system's design to the programmers who will implement it.

Desktop conferencing. A method of conferencing featuring the use of sophisticated workstations incorporating a video camera connected over a network or high-capacity conference line that transmits text, graphics, voice, and video.

Desktop publishing software (DTP). Software that helps users lay out text and graphics in a form suitable for publication.

Detail report. Provides managers information useful in overseeing the day-to-day operations of a department or working group.

Development. The creation or purchase of the hardware and software necessary to implement a system's design. It also includes the testing required to ensure that the system meets the design specifications.

Development environment. An environment where software development takes place, including software and data for software developers to use in checking and improving their new programs.

Differentiation. Strategy that seeks to distinguish the products and services of a business unit from those of its competitors through unique design, features, quality, or other factors.

Digital signal processor (DSP). Processor that converts an electronic wave signal, such one arising from sound or other sensory inputs, to a stream of digital bits and vice versa.

Digital signature. Encrypted code attached to a message that verifies the identity of the sender.

Digital Subscriber Line (DSL). Service that provides megabit/second speed over regular copper telephone lines.

Digital video camera. Camera that produces a digital representation of a picture that a computer can store and process.

Direct cut-over strategy. The replacement of an old with a new system overnight, over a weekend, or over some other period of time when the company does not operate.

Diskette. A random access magnetic medium consisting of a circle of mylar or similar material coated with a magnetic film and protected with a cardboard or hard plastic cover.

Distance education. Use of data communication technology to bring educational resources to students at distant locations.

Distributed architecture. Design that distributes both data and processing to many locations.

Distribution architecture. Plan that specifies how data and database processing are physically distributed among the computers in an organization.

Docking station. Special port on desktop computers that can transfer data between mobile and desktop units.

Domain name. A name that uniquely identifies a server on the Internet.

Domain Name Server (DNS). Server that looks up the IP address of a domain name for Internet users.

Downsizing. The decision to replace mainframe systems with client/server systems.

Downstream company. A company such as a customer, distributor, or repackager that adds values to a product or service offered by another company.

E

EBCDIC. A code to represent characters used by IBM for its mainframes and minicomputers; some other mainframe manufacturers also use EBCDIC.

Electronic bulletin board. A system for electronic conversation and messaging controlled by a central manager that uses a central repository to store messages.

Electronic cash. A secure method of payment for Internet transactions that preserves the anonymity of the buyer.

Electronic commerce. Electronic transactions related to the purchase and delivery of goods and services.

Electronic Data Interchange (EDI). The exchange of data (usually transactions) between two business organizations using a standard electronic format.

Electronic imaging management (EIM) system. A system that stores documents, including photographs, invoices, and personnel records, on

computers and then retrieves and reproduces them instantly.

Electronic list. A feature of some electronic mail systems that allows people interested in a particular topic to share electronic mail.

Electronic mail. A message sent electronically between two users on a computer system or on networked computers; also the software that supports the sending of electronic mail.

Electronic market system. Component of an interorganizational information system that provides information about industry players to increase competition and efficiency in vertical markets, reducing a seller's power and creating lower prices for buyers.

Electronic meeting room. Room in which participants work at their own computers on a U-shaped table facing a common computer at the front of the room, which can be seen by all participants.

Electronic notes. Software that organizes electronic messages by topic or group and provides support for sending and reading such messages.

Encryption. Use of a code to change (encode or encrypt) a message, making it unreadable.

End user. A consumer of information systems and services.

Enterprise-resource-planning (ERP) software. Software that provides seamless support for the supply-chain, value-chain, and administrative processes of a company

Event-initiated report. A report that is designed to alert managers to potential problems.

Exception report. Report that alerts managers to potential problems by showing only data that fall outside an accepted or expected range.

Executable module. A program created by a linker combining object modules that perform related tasks with already-compiled object code from a library of commonly-used functions. Also called a load module.

Executive information system (EIS). System that allows executives easy access to their favorite reports, lets them focus on interesting items in more detail, and scans news-wire and other information services for items of greatest interest to the executive.

Expert system (ES). Computer software that automates the role of an expert in a given field.

Expert systems shell. Off-the-shelf expert systems software that provides all the components of an expert system except the knowledge base.

Explanation module. The part of an expert system that tells the user how the inference engine applied the rules and facts to reach its conclusion.

Extension. (of a document's URL) The letters after the last dot in its file name; the extension indicates the type of document it is.

Extranet. An internal network that a company opens to selected suppliers and customers to reduce the cost of transactions and create inter-organizational linkages that can become strategically advantageous.

F

Fault-tolerant system. Also known as nonstop system, achieves extremely high reliability by using redundant hardware components and software designed to take advantage of this redundancy.

Fiber Distributed Data Interface (FDDI). A token-passing technology that uses two rings operating in opposite directions and operates at 100 megabits/second over fiber optic cables.

Fiber optic cable. Transmission medium that carries messages on a beam of light rather than using an electrical signal.

Field. Data about one of the characteristics or attributes of a record; it is the lowest element of data that has meaning.

File. A group or collection of data about similar things.

File server. Computer that provides programs and data to other computers through a network.

Firewall. Hardware or software that acts as a blockade between an internal network and an external network such as the Internet.

Flash memory. An electro-magnetic storage device that stores data onto computer chips in a non-volatile fashion.

Flexible manufacturing. Philosophy of manufacturing that requires that machinery to potentially have multiple uses.

Focus. Strategy that achieves competitive advantage by concentrating the organization's resources on a single market segment, allowing it to become a big player in a small market rather than a small player in a big market.

Fourth generation language (4GL). High-level language in which each statement performs steps that would require many statements in a lower-level language.

Frame. In data communication, a group of data transmitted together. In a web page, a rectangular part or area of the page.

Frame relay. Communication protocol that breaks each message into variable length packets of up to 8 kilobytes and sends them sequentially through a virtual circuit.

Function box. System design tool that shows how one process connects to other processes.

Functional strategy. Direction for individual departments to perform their tasks so as to accomplish organizational objectives.

Fuzzy logic. The reasoning of an expert system that includes rules to deal with ambiguities, rather than only "either/or" choices.

G

Gateway. System that moves data between two networks that use different data link and network standards.

General accounting system. System that tracks financial transactions and translates them into income statements, balance sheets, and other accounting records.

Geographical information system (GIS). Software with the ability to examine and manipulate geographical information, along with associated databases containing geographical information.

Goal-seeking software. Software that applies a variety of tools to quickly determine the best or optimal solution after users specify the criteria for evaluating the outcomes of different decisions.

Graphical user interface (GUI). Software that uses both menus and icons, pictorial representations of operations or resources, to interface with a user.

Graphics processor. Processor that rapidly manipulate images — rotates them, zooms in and out, presents appropriate views of three-dimensional objects, colors regions, and detects and draws edges.

Graphics scanner. Device that inputs pictures and other graphics into a computer after first converting them into a numeric format that the computer can process.

Group decision support system (GDSS). Software that supports group decision making.

Group support system (GSS). Also known as computer-supported cooperative work (CSCW) and groupware, information technology that facilitates the sharing or communication of information among members of a group and helps the group to perform common tasks and to accomplish its goals, including such products as electronic mail, electronic notes, bulletin board systems, and electronic meeting systems.

Groupware. Also known as computer-supported cooperative work (CSCW) and group support system (GSS), information technology that facilitates the sharing or communication of information among members of a group and helps the group to perform common tasks and to accomplish its goals, including such products as electronic mail, electronic notes, bulletin board systems, and electronic meeting systems.

H

Hand-held computer. Also known as a palmtop computer, a computer that typically weighs about a pound but may be as small as a credit card.

Hard disk. The most common type of fixed media storage device. It consists of magnetic-coated metal platters arranged on a spindle, encased in a vacuum chamber, and packaged with a motor, electronics, and magnetic sensors.

Hardcopy. Output on a medium such as paper that can be removed from the computer.

Hardware. The physical equipment used to process information.

Help desk. The IS staff and associated systems that help end users solve immediate problems with their equipment or software.

Helper application. Also called a plug-in, software needed by browsers to recognize and properly interpret the format of special programs and to view their files.

Heuristics. Rules-of-thumb that define acceptable solutions and methods for evaluating them.

Hierarchical model. Also called hierarchial, views data as organized in a logical hierarchy.

Horizontal application software. Software that performs generic tasks common to many types of problems and applications within and across industries.

Hub. Device that connects computers and sections of a network to one another.

Hypermedia. Document that includes graphics, sound, and links to other documents.

Hypertext. A text document that includes pointers, called links, to other text documents.

HyperText Markup Language (HTML). The language of hypertext and hypermedia documents.

HyperText Transport Protocol (HTTP). Standard protocol for exchanging web documents.

I

Image compressor. Processor that compresses and decompresses digital images by recognizing similarities among its parts and among sequential frames of a moving image.

Image enabling. A method of electronic image management where scanned paper electronically moves through the organization, and optical character recognition software converts its text into searchable ASCII text.

Image processing. A method of electronic image management where a scanned image is filed in a database for later use.

Image workflow. A method of electronic image management where scanned documents electronically move through an organization as employees complete work on it.

Implementation. Deactivating an old information system and activating a new one.

Inference engine. The component of an expert systems shell that processes the knowledge base supplied by users to reach conclusions, answer questions, and give advice.

Information. Processed data — data that have been organized and interpreted, and possibly formatted, filtered, analyzed, and summarized.

Information leadership. The strategy of increasing the value of a product or service by infusing it with expertise and information.

Information system. The combination of information technology, data, procedures for processing data, and people who collect and use the data. Information systems also include automation systems, which perform tasks that had been done manually; transaction processing systems, which process and record business activities; management systems, which supply information to managers; and strategic systems, which support the implementation of organizational theory.

Information technology (IT). Computer hardware, software, database management systems, and communication systems.

Infrastructure. An organization's investment in hardware, software, systems, and people.

Input analysis. A formal cataloguing and review of the information an organization collects, stores, and uses.

Input hardware. Device that captures raw data and eases the interaction between the user and the computer.

Instruction counter. Also known as an instruction register, a special hardware device which contains the address of a location in the computer's memory that holds the instruction a computer needs to start its operation.

Instruction register. Also known as an instruction counter, a special hardware device which contains the address of a location in the computer's memory that holds the instruction a computer needs to start its operation.

Integrated office software. Software that includes several office automation packages in a single program.

Integration testing. Testing that addresses the interaction between large, independently developed components of the new system that were internally checked at the unit and component testing levels.

Integrator. Company that packages hardware and software to meet a customer's specification.

Intelligent agent. Sophisticated software that can make decisions on its own based on what it knows about the user.

Intelligent messaging. Communications software that automates diverse communication functions.

Interactive dialogue. Input to a computer directing its action.

Interface design. The specification of the media, content, and form of input and output.

Internal network. Network that connects the computers, printers, and other computing equipment in a single organization.

Internet. Often referred to as the information superhighway, an international network of computer networks.

Internet Service Provider (ISP). A company that sells access to the Internet; it owns a large block of IP numbers for reassignment and has a high-capacity telephone connection to the Internet backbone.

Interorganizational system (IOS). An automated information system that two or more companies share.

Interpreter. Software that translates language commands into computer code one instruction at a time and then executes each instruction before translating the next instruction.

Intranet. Internal network that relies on hypermedia to make information available and browsers to access the media.

IP number. Unique address for every device attached to the Internet; this address consists of two parts (a network number and a device number.

IPX/SPX (Internetwork Packet Exchange/Sequenced Packet Exchange). Network operating system made popular by Novell which adopted it as the basis for its popular network operating system, Netware.

ISDN (Integrated Services Digital Network). A set of standards for integrating voice, computer data, and video transmission on the same telephone line.

J

Java. Programming language that Sun Microsystems developed to work with programs that users download from the Web, but may not know their source and hence their idiosyncrasies.

Joint application development (JAD). A variation of prototyping.

Joint venture. Agreement among two or more companies to jointly develop or market specific products or services.

Joystick. An input device popular for computer games where the user controls the location of a cursor by pushing a stick in the direction of the desired movement and releases the stick to stop movement.

Jukebox. A device that automates the switching of optical disks into and out of a single drive.

Just-in-time inventory (JIT). The practice of obtaining inventory precisely as needed, neither too early nor too late.

K

Key certification. A process similar to credit verification that uses a trusted party to exchange encryption keys for data communication.

Keyboard. An input device like a typewriter keyboard that consists of a plastic or metal housing containing keys that when pressed send a signal to the computer.

Knowledge. An understanding or model about people, objects, or events, derived from information about them.

Knowledge base. A database of facts and rules that an expert system uses in its reasoning.

Knowledge engineer. A professional trained to probe experts on how they know, understand, or suspect their diagnoses to be true.

Knowledge management. The management of the vast stores of knowledge and information in a company.

L

Language translator. Software that translates computer code from the language used by software developers into a computer's language (known as machine language); it lets developers use a common language for software destined for many different types of computers.

Laptop computer. A computer that weighs under 10 pounds and folds into a unit the size of a small briefcase or smaller.

Laser-servo diskette. Data storage device that looks and operates like a 1.44 MB diskette, except the tracks separating the locations on the drive are much closer to one another and are tracked by a laser, allowing capacities greater than 100 MB.

Leased line. A direct communication connection between two points that bypasses the telephone switch.

Legacy systems. Large, entrenched systems, consisting of thousands of programs written and modified over ten to twenty years that cannot be changed because of their complexity or lack of documentation.

Light pen. An input device consisting of a stylus that transmits a narrow light beam to a transparent sensor overlaying the surface of a computer screen.

Link loader. Software that links object modules into one complete program.

Links. Pointers to other documents in a hypertext or hypermedia document.

Linkage. The strategy of obtaining a competitive advantage by establishing special, exclusive relationships with customers, suppliers, and competitors.

Load module. Also called an executable module , a program created by a linker combining object modules that perform related tasks with already-compiled object code from a library of commonly-used functions.

Local area network (LAN). A network that connects devices in a single building or a campus of nearby buildings.

Log. A record of transactions processed by a DBMS and used to trace and recover transactions after a computer hardware or systems failure.

Logical relationship. Relationship among elements of a database due to the meaning of the data or to business rules that constrain the data.

Logical view. A view of data based on a data model that is independent of the way in which the data are physically stored.

Logistics. The transport of goods and its associated activities, such as warehousing.

M

Machine language. The language of zeros and ones that instruct a computer's processor.

Mainframe. A computer designed and marketed to handle the largest processing tasks of an organization, typically costing at least several hundred thousand dollars and usually requiring a separate, air-conditioned room and a staff of trained professionals to support its use.

Maintenance. Fixing software that does not operate properly and adding features to systems in response to new user demands.

Management. The process of achieving organizational goals by planning, organizing, leading, and controlling organizational resources.

Management system. A system that supplies the information managers need to perform their jobs better and communicate more effectively.

Management reporting system (MRS). A system that helps managers monitor the operations and resources of an organization and the environment in which the organization operates.

Mapping software. Software to translate an application's output into EDI documents and translate EDI documents received into input compatible with a company's software.

Medium of transmission. The carrier of a data signal between two or more computers.

Menu-driven interface. Operating system software that presents a list of possible commands for the user to select.

Message. A communication between objects in an object-oriented program or database; also the medium in an object-oriented language through which objects communicate with one another.

Message system. System that enhances group work by improving communication among group members.

Metadata. Data about data.

Microcomputer. A category of small computers which includes personal computers (PCs) as well as small processors specialized for other tasks.

MIME (Multipurpose Internet Mail Extensions). A standard that specifies how to attach non-text files, such as graphics, spreadsheets, and sound files, to electronic mail messages.

Model base. The analytic part of a decision support system that includes tools such as spreadsheets, simulation packages, forecasting tools, and statistical packages.

Modem. Device that provides an interface between a computer or terminal and the phone or cable lines of a communication carrier.

Modular structure. An organizational structure that breaks an organization into key processes and lets individual sub-contractors perform these key processes.

Mouse. The most popular pointing device for desktop computers; it is operated by the user by placing his hand on it and rolling it across a table top or other surface.

Multi-dimensional database manager. Analytical software that creates views, expressed in a database or spreadsheet form, of a large relational database from multiple dimensions.

Multi-tier client/server. Also known as the n-tier client/server model, it divides application software into multiple components, each of which can call on the others to perform services for it.

Multi-user editor. Software that allows multiple users to access and modify a common document.

N

Navigation. The process of moving among web pages to find the information you want.

N-tier client/server. Also known as the multi-tier client/server model, it divides application software into multiple components, each of which can call on the others to perform services for it.

Needs assessment. A formal, integrated, and usually time-limited process of gathering data about the needs and opportunities of end users and their managers; evaluating and ranking the importance of these needs; and addressing the possibility that they cannot be satisfied by continuous improvement of existing systems.

Network administrator. Person responsible for the oversight of the corporate network, including both LANs and WANs.

Network analyzer. Device that plugs into a network and analyzes the traffic that passes by or through it.

Network interface card (NIC). Also called an adaptor, provides a direct connection between a computer or terminal and a network.

Network management software. Software that monitors the state of a company's network and the devices connected to it.

Network model. A DBMS model that builds a tight linkage, called a set, between elements of data.

Network operating system (NOS). Software that manages and controls the joint or shared resources of a group of computers connected by a network.

News group. The facility to store messages in and retrieve them from a central location for users interested in a common topic; also the users of such a facility.

Non-procedural language. Computer language such as SQL and many expert system shells that can operate without step-by-step instructions.

Nonstop systems. Also known as fault-tolerant systems, systems that achieve extremely high reliability by using redundant hardware components and software designed to take advantage of this redundancy.

Normalization. The process of grouping data elements into tables in a way that simplifies retrieval, reduces data entry and storage, and minimizes the likelihood of data inconsistencies.

Notebook computer. Thin, lightweight laptop that folds into a unit the size of a notebook and generally weighs under 7 pounds.

Notification system. System that triggers output on a computer terminal or monitor in response to specific events.

O

Object design. The generation of an object model.

Object model. A data model derived from object-oriented programming that encapsulates data and methods and organizes objects into object classes, among which there can be a hierarchical relationship.

Object module. Computer code to perform a particular task after it has been translated by a compiler; these may be linked together into an executable module.

Object oriented language. Merges procedures and data into a structure called an object. Examples of object oriented languages include C++, Java, and Smalltalk.

Office suite. Several types of office automation application software in a single-package, such as Microsoft Office or Ami Pro. Most office suites include word processing, spreadsheet, database, and presentation graphics software. Some may also include database management, scheduling, and electronic mail software.

On-demand report. Any report that a management reporting system provides for authorized users upon request.

On-line analytical processing (OLAP). Tools that aggregate, display, and analyze data to draw inferences and make decisions.

On-line data entry. Data entry process in which computers capture transactions directly, eliminating the need for source documents.

Open Database Connectivity (ODBC). A standard that allows programs to access their databases in a uniform way and makes moving databases from one DBMS to another easy.

Open operating system. An operating system that adheres to industry standards, whose specifications are not owned by one vendor, and for which a set of tests that check for conformance to the standard is available.

Operating system. The operating system kernel and other software packaged with it including systems utilities, network and systems management software, and some application software.

Operating system kernel. Software that performs the most basic housekeeping, resource allocation, and resource monitoring functions for a computer with a minimum of input or control by the user.

Operational capability demonstration (OCD). A simulation performed before software development that allows users to judge how rapidly a system will perform under the expected processing loads and illustrates various features of the system to be developed.

Opportunity. An external or environmental factor that might help an organization to meet its strategic goals.

Order entry system. Records and processes the taking of an order.

Organizational structure. A structure that defines reporting responsibilities in an organization and identifies who manages and controls key resources.

OSI model (Open Systems Interconnection Model). Divides the communication process into layers within which compatible standards can be set.

Output analysis. The systematic identification of ways people in an organization use information.

Outsourcing. Hiring an outside organization to perform services such as information processing and applications development.

P

Package. A software product.

Packaged software. Also known as off-the-shelf software, uncustomized software packages, which exist for a wide range of applications and industries. Managers and other users can purchase a large variety of uncustomized vertical software products for all types of computers through retail outlets or directly from software developers.

Packet. A division of data used by communication software; for example, many data communication software packages send data in a packet having a fixed number bytes.

Packet switched service. Provides a direct connection between any points on the telephone network but does not necessarily provide a fixed circuit for the entire session.

Palmtop computer. Also known as a hand-held computer, it typically weighs about a pound but may be as small as a credit card.

Parallel implementation strategy. The use of both a new and old system for a period of time.

Passive data entry. The computer obtains information without the active participation of a user.

Payroll system. A system that tracks employee hours, wages, and other benefits; automatically generates paychecks and records of additional benefits or payments to employees on a prescribed schedule.

Performance testing. The first stage of system testing in which developers identify and correct problems that might cause a system to slow down or fail when stressed with too many users or too much data.

Periodic report. A report that a management reporting system produces on a periodic basis for delivery to a pre-specified list of employees.

Peripheral device. Device attached to a computer, such as a keyboard, video unit, printer, and scanner, that collects, displays, communicates, or stores data.

Permanent team. A team that works together for long periods of time, generally at least one year, on a repetitive set of tasks.

Personal computer (PC). A computer designed and marketed to be used by an individual or a small number of people and to be owned and managed by an individual.

Phased implementation strategy. An approach to the implementation of new systems that introduces the components of a new system one at a time.

Physical design. Decisions about the hardware used to deliver a system.

Physical firewall. A firewall that physically separates a company's external interface from the rest of its network.

Physical view. View of data that includes how they are compressed and formatted, which data are stored near each other, and which indexes exist to simplify and speed finding data on its storage medium.

Pilot implementation strategy. Often called beta testing, requires one or more segments of the company to use a new system before the entire company uses it.

Pixel. A dot on the computer screen.

Plotter. An output device that operates by moving a pen or pens over paper, much the way a person writes.

Plug-in. Also called a helper application, software needed by browsers to recognize and properly interpret the format of special programs and to view their files.

Point of Presence (POP). A location where the ISP has a bank of modems that connect to the ISP's Internet connection.

Point-of-sale system (POS). System that records the sale of a product or service and updates company records related to the sale.

Port. A socket usually located at the back of a computer through which the monitor, keyboard, and other input and output devices are connected via cables to interface cards inside the computer.

Portability. The ability of software to be used by different types of computers.

Post implementation review. Process that evaluates how well a new system meets user needs, sets priorities for new development, and determines when to redo a needs assessment.

Post Office Protocol (POP3). A standard that lets different mail programs exchange messages without difficulty.

Power supply. A device that regulates the voltage and amperage supplied to other components within the computer.

Presentation graphics software. Software that allows users with little graphics training to produce professional-looking slides, overheads, or prints to support their presentations.

Primary storage. Electrical device or devices that store data, resides on the bus, and is directly accessible to the processor.

Printer. Output device that produces text and graphics on paper without using a pen.

Procedural language. A computer language, such as C, COBOL, and FORTRAN, that requires the software developer to give step by step instructions to the computer.

Process design. The design of both the computational and logical processes underlying a system.

Process librarian. Also called a process manager, a person assigned by an organization to customize templates and tutorials to the organization's standards and collect metrics and best practices for customizing the process library.

Process manager. Also called a process librarian, a person assigned by an organization to customize templates and tutorials to the organization's standards and collect metrics and best practices for customizing the process library.

Processing hardware. Computer chips and other devices that manipulate information according to instructions encoded into software.

Production environment. An environment that contains the current software and all transaction data and emphasizes high system reliability.

Profit center. An organization of an IS department in which the department bids for the work of internal users, charges internal users what it would charge external users, and often actively seeks external users.

Program. Instructions that command a computer to perform a desired task.

Programmer. A person who writes computer programs.

Project manager. A person responsible for one or more systems development projects. Project managers typically supervise teams of workers who together must accomplish a specific goal.

Prospect database. A list of potential customers with key information to allow sorting by industry, company, company size, sales call history, purchasing history, product requirements, or other characteristics.

Prototyping. A systems development approach that tries to satisfy user needs by focusing on the user interface.

Proxy server. A gateway that provides security for specific applications that obtain input from outside the company.

PTT (Postal, Telephone, and Telegraph company). In many countries a PTT, operated or owned by the government, provides communication services as a monopoly carrier.

Public key encryption. Technique used by most private Internet messaging to provide security; it requires two codes—one secret code called a private key and another that is not secret called a public key.

Purchasing/receiving system. System that documents transactions between a company and its supplier.

Push technology. Technology that allows a company to send its web pages periodically to users who have given it permission to do so.

R

Random access memory (RAM). Volatile primary storage.

Rapid application development (RAD). The use of tools, in conjunction with rapid prototyping, to speed the ultimate development of new systems.

Rapid prototyping. The conversion of an electronic computer-aided design model into a solid physical model. Also the development of software prototypes using rapid application development, for the purpose of verifying system specifications.

Read-only memory (ROM). Non-volatile primary storage; ROM holds the instructions that a computer uses when it is first turned on.

Reader of formatted input. Input device that reads text specially formatted for the device in use. Examples include bar code readers, mark sense readers, and magnetic ink character readers.

Real-time conferencing. Meeting in which information is exchanged electronically. Participants do not have to be at the same location.

Real-time processing. Protocol in which data are processed on entry, immediately updating the information system and making the data available to all users.

Record. Entry in a file containing one example or instance of the type of data the file contains. Each record generally holds data about a person, place, or thing, concrete or abstract.

Redundant arrays of inexpensive disks (RAID). Device that uses a large number of relatively small hard disks in a single unit.

Reengineering. Rethinking, reinventing, and redesigning one or more of an organization's business systems, such as accounts receivable, purchasing, or product development, and its related jobs.

Relational model. A database model that provides for logical connections among files (known as tables) by including identifying data from one table in another table.

Repeater. Device that twisted-pair and coaxial cable need to boost their signals which weaken as they travels through the cable.

Replication. A feature of distributed DBMS in which the DBMS changes the data at all locations if a user or application changes the redundant data at one location.

Report generator. Software that automates the creation of programs that produce reports.

Request for Proposal (RFP). A document that identifies the information processing requirements and information needs of an organization and requests software developers to submit bids for software development responding to these needs.

Requirements analysis. Also called needs assessment, identifies the information needs of an organization.

Resolution. The quality of computer output.

Resource. An input to the production of outputs.

Reverse engineering. The process of analyzing the software that comprises a legacy system.

Risk analysis. The process of identifying where risks might arise and analyzing the tradeoff of risk against costs and benefits.

Robot. A computer-controlled machine that has human-like characteristics, such as intelligence, movement, and limbs or appendages.

Robotic output device. A device that physically moves in response to signals from a computer.

Router. A device that connects two or more hubs, sub-networks, or networks that have the same network protocol and passes data between networks almost simultaneously.

Rule base. The component of an expert system that expresses rules that are rarely changed.

S

Sales force automation. System that provides computerized systems for tracking sales leads, sales, service requests, and other sales-related information.

Screen generator. Software that creates and edits a screen and generates programs for screen-based data entry or queries.

Screening routers. Devices that filter incoming IP packets using information in their IP header, such as their IP number or protocol.

Second generation language. A relatively low-level language that requires many commands to perform simple tasks.

Secondary storage. Data storage, usually magnetic or optical, from which data must first be transferred into primary storage before they can be accessed by the processor.

Security management. Policies and procedures that reduce the likelihood of a security breach and increase the likelihood of detecting security breaches that occur.

Self-managed team. A team having members who share responsibility for managing the work group without an officially appointed leader.

Server. In a client/server architecture, a computer dedicated to performing special services for client computers on the network.

Service level agreement (SLA). An agreement between information technology providers and users that specifies in detail a guaranteed level of performance on a variety of dimensions.

Session. An ongoing connection between two computers or computer devices, established, for example, by logging into a remote computer.

SET (Secure Electronic Transport). Protocol for credit card payments over the Internet. SET is a three-way protocol that involves not only the buyer and seller, but also a certification agent.

Set. In the network model, the combinations of owners and members in a one-to-many relationship.

Simulation. The process of representing real processes with analytic models.

Site license. A legal document that allows an organization to use a specified number of copies of a specific software product or to give a certain number of users access to a single copy of the software.

Site map. The detailed table of contents on a web page.

Situational analysis. The process of collecting and analyzing information about a company's strengths, weaknesses, opportunities, and threats.

SMDS (Switched Multimegabit Data Service). Data communication service that provides a higher capacity than ISDN but at a higher cost and with limited switching.

SNMP (Simple Network Management Protocol). A protocol that defines how management devices operate and the data they keep.

Softcopy. Output on an unmovable medium, such as a computer screen.

Software. Instructions that command a computer to perform a desired task.

Software-development software. Software that helps people create new software. It includes computer programming languages and Computer Aided Software Engineering (CASE) tools that automate and provide ongoing technical support to software development.

Software engineer. Analyst with CASE skills.

Sound card. A controller that produces an electrical signal that drives one or more speakers.

Source code. A program written in the developer's computer language.

Source document. Pre-designed form that captures transactions on paper and provides a secure, hardcopy record of transactions.

Spiral approach. A software development approach that delivers a new system in versions. Each version goes through all the steps of the SDLC except implementation, which may apply to some versions, and maintenance, which applies only to the last version.

SQL. An easy-to-use nonprocedural language that has been adopted as a standard for the relational model.

Standard. Rules governing the types of investments an organization may make in information technology and systems. Also industry-wide agreements about characteristics of specific hardware, software, or telecommunications devices and protocols.

Statistical report. Also known as a summary report, a report that shows totals, averages, maximums, minimums, or other statistical data aggregated over time, personnel, products, or some other quantity.

Strategic alignment. The fit between an organization's strategic goals and objectives and its information systems.

Strategic information system. A system designed to help an organization implement and achieve its strategic goals. It often extends information systems beyond organizational borders, seeking to make customers, suppliers, and distributors that are strategic partners part of the information system.

Strategy. The long-term direction or intended set of activities for an organization to attain its goals.

Strength. An internal characteristic of an organization that enhances its ability to compete.

Structure chart. A diagram that shows the relationship among the programs and subprograms that will comprise the finished system.

Structured analysis. An analysis technique that uses process modeling tools to diagram existing and proposed systems so that users can understand and critique an analyst's perception of information relationships.

Subnotebook computer. Ultralight computer, typically weighing between 2 and 4 pounds.

Summary report. Also known as a statistical report, a report that shows totals, averages, maximums, minimums, or other statistical data aggregated over time, personnel, products, or some other quantity.

Supplier-focused IOS. A system that forges a linkage between a company and its suppliers by providing information services that mutually benefit the suppliers and the host.

Supply-chain management. An integrated solution that coordinates the activities of suppliers, distributors, and customers.

Sustainable advantage. A strategic advantage that an organization can maintain over an extended period despite competitors' attempts to erode it.

Switch. Device that connects two or more computers, hubs, sub-networks, or networks that have compatible standards for sending signals over transmission media and hardware and creating and ensuring the correct order of sessions.

Switched circuit service. A connection made between two points for the length of a session.

Sysop. The manager of a bulletin board who controls the topics of conversation on the board.

System call. An application software request to the operating system kernel to obtain computer resources such as memory, storage, the network, or the display unit.

System testing. Also known as alpha testing, testing an entire system under realistic conditions.

Systems analyst. A person who provides the interface between the information systems user and the information systems developer.

Systems development life cycle (SDLC). A sequence of stages in the conception, design, creation and implementation of information systems.

Systems management software. Software that monitors the state of a particular computer.

Systems software. Software that manages the computer and its network.

Systems utility. Program that operates primarily under user control and provides basic resource management functions, such as the ability to copy files or sort data.

T

Table. The relational model's representation of a file with rows called tuples and columns called attributes.

Tag. In HTML, words around text that identify what type of text, images, or links they surround.

Tape. Data storage medium on which information is recorded onto the magnetic coating of a thin mylar tape.

TCP/IP (Transmission Control Protocol/Internet Protocol). Protocol for data communication that originated for transmission across the Internet but is now widely used by local and wide area networks.

Temporary team. A team formed for short, pre-specified amounts of time to complete a unique set of tasks or projects.

Terminal emulation. Software that simulates a computer terminal on a personal computer or other workstation.

Test design. The creation of tests that ensure the proper operation of developed systems.

Testing environment. A computing environment similar to the production environment in which software developers can themselves test or have users test new or modified software that is ready to be moved into the production environment.

Thread. A series of messages that respond to an original message or to a response to that message.

Threat. An external or environmental factor that might hinder an organization from meeting its strategic goals.

Three-tier client/server model. A client/server model that includes a user interface, business logic, and data management layers.

Third generation language. Moderately abstract language which requires fewer steps than a second generation language but more than a fourth-generation language.

Time box. A fixed period, usually three months, within which developers must complete each version of software developed under the spiral approach.

Total quality management (TQM). A management philosophy that attempts to achieve zero defects, emphasizes responding to customers' needs, gives workers more responsibility for making decisions, fosters continuous improvement in both an organization's product and the processes for creating it, and uses statistical control techniques to improve its products and processes.

Touch pad. A pressure sensitive input device placed on a keyboard; it is popular for mobile computers.

Touch screen. A transparent surface overlaying a computer screen. When someone touches it with a finger or a stylus, it sends a signal to the computer indicating the point of contact.

Trackball. An input pointing device differs from a mouse in that the user rotates rather than moves it; it is popular for mobile computing.

Traditionally-managed team. A team having an individual designated as the official leader or manager.

Transaction. A unit of business activity, such as purchasing a product, making a banking deposit, or reserving an airline seat.

Transaction processing monitor (TP monitor). Software that enforces transaction atomicity and provides other generic transaction processing services.

Transaction processing system (TPS). An information system that records and processes an organization's routine business activities.

Tuple. In the relational DBMS model, a row in a table.

Turn-key solution. Hardware and software bundled for sale as a single product.

Twisted-pair wire. Connects a telephone to its telephone jack in most homes.

Two-tier client/server model. A client/server model that assigns the responsibility for handling all data storage and management requests to the server.

U

Unallocated cost center. A way of accounting for information services that considers all costs of operating the IS department and related IS services as an organizational expense, rather than attributing costs to particular budgets.

Uninterruptible power supply (UPS). Provides secondary sources of power such as a battery or electric generator, along with circuitry that can recognize and react to a loss of power from the primary supply before it can affect the computer.

Unit testing. Testing each small component of a system to guarantee its proper operations.

Universal Resource Locator (URL). A combination of the type and name of the server responsible for a Web-based document and the file name of the document itself.

Universal server. Common name for hybrid object-relational DBMSs.

Upstream company. A company, such as a supplier, who adds value to a product or service before the company has added its value.

Usability lab. A place where developers can observe and record users reactions to a new system.

Usability testing. The second stage of systems testing in which the developed system is compared to users' expectations and needs.

USENET. A world-wide, hierarchical system of more than 10,000 news groups.

V

Value-added network (VAN). A reseller of telephone and/or satellite transmission capacity.

Value-adding partnership (VAP). The linkage of companies that view the whole value system, not just the value chain, as their competitive unit and who share information freely with others in the value system so they can compete successfully in this environment.

Value-added reseller (VAR). A software manufacturer's representative authorized to customize its software.

Vertical application software. Software that performs tasks common to a specific industry and often has some or extensive options for customization.

Very high speed Backbone Network Service (vBNS). Developed by MCI, a network backbone operates at 155.52 megabits/second in 1997 and eventually at 2.5 gigabits/second.

Video adaptor. A circuit board inside a computer that supports its monitor.

Video conferencing. Holding a meeting in which information is exchanged electronically.

View. A subset of the database that can be made available to certain classes of users or to certain applications.

Virtual office. The conduct of office functions in locations outside corporate buildings.

Virtual organization. A modular structure tied together by computer technology.

Virtual reality. An environment which allows the user to act upon and affect computer images and other output in a realistic fashion.

Virus. A program that inserts a copy of itself into other programs.

Visit. Browsing through a Web document.

Voice mail. Use of computers to deliver voice messages.

Voice mailbox. Storage for voice mail messages.

Voice processor. Device that translates sound-wave inputs into sound-groups called phonemes and then into written words.

W

Waterfall model. An approach to systems development that follows the SDLC in sequence.

Weakness. An internal characteristic of an organization that impedes its ability to compete. Having costs above the industry average typifies a weakness.

Web page. A document on the World Wide Web.

Wide area network (WAN). A network that covers a larger area than a LAN.

Workflow automation. The computerized control and coordination of related activities in an organization.

Workflow management system. System that drives, coordinates, and monitors the flow of activities in an organization that relate to administrative, production, and other business processes.

Workstation. Powerful single-user computers used for engineering and for executive support. Also used at times to mean any desktop computer.

World Wide Web (the Web, WWW). A massive collection of documents available to the public over the Internet.

Wisdom. The ability to use knowledge for a purpose.